Fifth
Edition

A FRAMEWORK FOR HUMAN RESOURCE MANAGEMENT

Gary Dessler

Florida International University

PEARSON

Prentice
Hall

Pearson Education International

Acquisitions Editor: Jennifer M. Collins
Editorial Director: Sally Yagan
Editor in Chief: David Parker
Product Development Manager: Ashley Santora
Assistant Editor: Kristen Varina
Marketing Manager: Nikki Jones
Marketing Assistant: Ian Gold
Permissions Project Manager: Charles Morris
Senior Managing Editor: Judy Leale
Associate Managing Editor: Suzanne DeWorken
Production Project Manager: Kelly Warsak
Senior Operations Specialist: Arnold Vila

Operations Specialist: Carol O'Rourke
Associate Director Central Design: Jayne Conte
Cover Designer: Suzanne Behnke
Cover Illustration: Getty Images, Inc.
Manager, Cover Visual Research & Permissions:
    Karen Sanatar
Composition: Integra Software Services
Full-Service Project Management: Jennifer Welsch/
    BookMasters, Inc.
Printer/Binder: R.R.D. Harrisonburg
Cover Printer: R.R.D. Harrisonburg
Typeface: 10/12 Times

Credits and acknowledgments borrowed from other sources and reproduced, with permission, in this textbook appear on appropriate pages within text.

If you purchased this book within the United States or Canada you should be aware that it has been wrongfully imported without the approval of the Publisher or the Author.

Pearson Education Ltd., London
Pearson Education Singapore, Pte. Ltd.
Pearson Education Canada, Ltd.
Pearson Education–Japan
Pearson Education Australia PTY, Limited

Pearson Education North Asia Ltd., Hong Kong
Pearson Educación de Mexico, S.A. de C.V.
Pearson Education Malaysia, Pte. Ltd.
Pearson Education Upper Saddle River,
    New Jersey

10 9 8 7 6 5 4 3 2 1
ISBN-13: 978-0-13-713598-1
ISBN-10:   0-13-713598-X

To my mother

Brief Contents

Contents

SECTION 2: TRAINING, DEVELOPMENT, AND COMPENSATION

SECTION 3: MANAGING EMPLOYEE RELATIONS

Preface

A Framework for Human Resource Management provides students and practicing managers with a concise but thorough review of essential human resource management concepts and techniques in a highly readable and understandable form. Most of the books in this market (including my *Human Resource Management,* 11th edition) contain 14–18 chapters and 450–800 large-trim-size pages. At about 390 small-trim pages and 10 chapters plus Module A, *Framework* distills the essential HR material large books typically contain, but without repetition, extensive reviews of research findings, or in-depth discussions. Adopters are using this book in many ways—as the textbook in introductory human resource management courses, in conjunction with exercises in applied human resource management courses, with complementary textbooks in courses that blend several topics (such as HR and organizational behavior), in specialized courses (such as "HR for Entrepreneurial Companies"), and by practicing human resource and line managers who want to update their HR skills.

WHAT'S NEW IN THE 5TH EDITION

Given its gratifying acceptance and the reviewers' comments, *Framework 5*'s basic themes, approach, and outline are basically the same as edition 4's. All managers have personnel responsibilities, so I again aimed this book at all students of management, not just those who are or will be human resource managers. The book's basic idea—to provide a concise but thorough review of HR concepts and techniques—is the same. I kept the same table of contents and basically the same topic coverage. Each chapter again touches on, with examples, how managers use strategic human resource management and technology. Adopters can again order a Human Resource Certification Institute guide.

However, I have made several important changes. I *updated* the HR practices, methods, topics, data, examples, figures/tables, relevant legal and HR findings, and notes in all chapters. In addition to the end-of-chapter case incidents we've always had for this book, I've added *five all-new comprehensive cases* at the end. These provide readers with a means for applying what they've learned about human resource management by solving realistic and multi-faceted management problems. We again offer 10 video vignettes for adopters to use, but for this edition I added *written summaries and questions for each video scenario,* available at the book's Web site and in the instructor's manual.

INSTRUCTOR'S RESOURCE CENTER

At **www.prenhall.com/irc**, instructors can access a variety of print, digital, and presentation resources available with this text in downloadable format. Registration is simple and gives you immediate access to new titles and new editions. As a registered faculty member, you can download resource files and receive immediate access and instructions for installing course management content on your campus server. If you ever need assistance, our dedicated technical support team is ready to help with the media supplements that accompany this text. Visit **www.247.prenhall.com** for answers to frequently asked questions and toll-free user support phone numbers.

The following supplements are available to adopting instructors (for detailed descriptions, please visit **www.prenhall.com/irc**):

- **Instructor's Resource Center (IRC) online** — ISBN: 0-13-604156-6
- **Printed Instructor's Manual with Test Item File** — ISBN: 0-13-604155-8
- **TestGen Test Generating Software** — Available at the IRC Online.
- **Videos on DVD** — ISBN: 0-13-604159-0

CourseSmart TEXTBOOKS ONLINE

CourseSmart Textbooks Online is an exciting new choice for students looking to save money. As an alternative to purchasing the print textbook, students can subscribe to the same content online and save up to 50% off the suggested list price of the print text. With a CourseSmart textbook, students can search the text, make notes online, print out reading assignments that incorporate lecture notes, and bookmark important passages for later review. For more information, or to subscribe to the CourseSmart eTextbook, visit www.coursesmart.com.

ACKNOWLEDGMENTS

No book ever reaches the light of day without the dedicated efforts of many people, and *Framework* is no exception. I am grateful to past and present reviewers:

Mark Barnard, Edgewood College
Kathleen Barnes, East Stroudsburg University
Gerald Baumgardner, Penn College
Jerry Bennett, Western Kentucky University
Stephen Betts, William Paterson University
Genie Black, Arkansas Tech University
David Lawrence Blum, Moraine Park Technical College
Michael Bochenek, Elmhurst College
Henry Bohleke, Owens Community College
Patricia Buhler, Goldey-Beacom College
Jackie Bull, Immaculata University

Melissa Cardon, Pace University
Martin Carrigan, The University of Findlay
Yvonne Chandler, Seattle Community Colleges
Charlie Cook, University of West Alabama
Roger Dean, Washington and Lee University
Karen Dielmann, Lebanon Valley College and Elizabethtown College
Michael Dutch, Greensboro College
William Ferris, Western New England College
John Fielding, Mount Wachusett Community College
Michael Frew, Oklahoma City University
Alyce Giltner, Shawnee Community College
Armand Giroux, Mitchell College
Caren Goldberg, American University
John Gronholt, Modesto Junior College
Janet Henquinet, Metropolitan State University, St. Paul, MN
William Hodson, Indiana University
Peter Hughes, Cambridge College, Lawrence, MA
John Kachurick, College Misericordia
Dennis Kimble, Central Michigan University
Cheryl Macon, Butler County Community College
Patricia Morrow, Middlesex Community College
Kay Nicols, Texas State University-San Marcos
Jacquelyn Palmer, Wright State University
Rich Patterson, Western Kentucky University
Larry Phillips, Indiana University South Bend
Tracy Porter, Cleveland State University
Chris Osuanah, J. Sargeant Reynolds Community College and University
    of Phoenix
David Radosevich, Montclair State University
Carlton R. Raines, Lehigh Carbon Community College
Dr. Michael J. Renahan, College of Saint Elizabeth
Fritz Scherz, Morrisville State College
Biagio Sciacca, Penn State University
Dan Scotti, Providence College
Robert W. (Bill) Service, Samford University
John Shaw, Mississippi State University
Walter Siganga, Southern Illinois University Edwardsville
Marjorie Smith, Mountain State University
Chester Spell, Rutgers University
Jerry Stevens, Texas Tech University
Susan Stewart, University of Puget Sound
Michele Summers, Purdue University
Vicki Talor, Shippensburg University
Jeff Walls, Indiana Institute of Technology
Carol Williams, Pearl River Community College
Angela Willson, Yuba College

I am grateful to the professors, students, managers, and Prentice Hall sales associates who have helped make this a top-selling book, not only in English but also in several languages, including Chinese.

At Prentice Hall, I appreciate the efforts of all the professionals on the fifth edition team, including David Parker, editor in chief; Jennifer M. Collins, acquisitions editor; Judy Leale, senior managing editor; Kelly Warsak, production editor; Jen Welsch, senior project director (BookMasters, Inc.); and Kristen Varina, assistant editor.

At home, I appreciate all my wife Claudia's support, and my son Derek's support, assistance, and practical suggestions.

1

MANAGING HUMAN RESOURCES TODAY

- What Is Human Resource Management?
- The Changing Environment and Duties of HR Management
- The Strategic Role of Human Resource Management
- The Human Resource Manager Today
- The Plan of This Book

When you finish studying this chapter, you should be able to:

■ Answer *the question "What is human resource management?"*

■ Discuss *the components of the changing environment of human resource management.*

■ Describe *the nature of strategic planning.*

■ Give *examples of human resource management's role as a strategic partner.*

INTRODUCTION

Several years ago, Shanghai's Portman Hotel was good but not exceptional. Employee and guest satisfaction ratings averaged 70% to 80%. Finances were average.[1] When it took over the hotel recently, the Ritz-Carlton company and the hotel's new general manager Mark DeCocinis set out to make the Portman a premier property. Their strategy for doing so was to dramatically improve customer service. Mr. DeCocinis knew the hotel's employees were crucial to such efforts: "We're a service business, and service comes only from people." The question was, "What could he and his managers do to foster that kind of employee service?"

WHAT IS HUMAN RESOURCE MANAGEMENT?

Human resource management refers to the practices and policies you need to carry out the personnel aspects of your management job, specifically, acquiring, training, appraising, rewarding, and providing a safe, ethical, and fair environment for your company's employees. These practices and policies include, for instance:

>   Conducting job analyses (determining the nature of each employee's job)
>   Planning labor needs and recruiting job candidates
>   Selecting job candidates
>   Orienting and training new employees
>   Appraising performance
>   Managing wages and salaries (how to compensate employees)
>   Providing incentives and benefits
>   Communicating (interviewing, counseling, disciplining)
>   Training and developing current employees
>   Building employee commitment

And what a manager should know about:

>   Equal opportunity, ethics, and affirmative action
>   Employee health and safety and ethical treatment
>   Grievances and labor relations

Why Is HR Management Important to All Managers?

Why are these concepts and techniques important to all managers? Perhaps it's easier to answer this by listing some of the personnel mistakes you don't want to make while managing. For example, you don't want

>   To have your employees not performing at peak capacity
>   To hire the wrong person for the job
>   To experience high turnover
>   To find employees not doing their best
>   To have your company taken to court because of your discriminatory actions
>   To have your company cited under federal occupational safety laws for unsafe practices
>   To allow a lack of training to undermine your department's effectiveness
>   To commit any unfair labor practices

Why Study this Book?

Carefully studying this book can help you avoid mistakes like these. More important, it can help ensure that you get results—through people. Remember that you could do everything else right as a manager—lay brilliant plans, draw clear organization charts, set up modern assembly lines, and use sophisticated accounting controls—but still fail, for instance, by hiring the wrong people or by not motivating subordinates.

On the other hand, many managers—from presidents to generals to supervisors—have been successful even without adequate plans, organizations, or controls. They were successful because they had the knack for hiring the right people for the right jobs and motivating, appraising, and developing them. Remember as you read this book that getting results is the bottom line of managing and that, as a manager, you will have to get these results through people. That fact hasn't changed from the dawn of management. As one company president summed it up:

> For many years it has been said that capital is the bottleneck for a developing industry. I don't think this any longer holds true. I think it's the workforce and the company's inability to recruit and maintain a good workforce that does constitute the bottleneck for production. I don't know of any major project backed by good ideas, vigor, and enthusiasm that has been stopped by a shortage of cash. I do know of industries whose growth has been partly stopped or hampered because they can't maintain an efficient and enthusiastic labor force, and I think this will hold true even more in the future.[2]

Line and Staff Aspects of HRM

All managers are, in a sense, human resource managers, because they all get involved in activities such as recruiting, interviewing, selecting, and training. Yet, most firms also have a separate human resource department with its own human resource manager. How do the duties of this departmental HR manager and his or her staff relate to line managers' human resource duties? Let's answer this question by starting with short definitions of line versus staff authority.

Line Versus Staff Authority

Authority is the right to make decisions, to direct the work of others, and to give orders. In management, we usually distinguish between line authority and staff authority. **Line managers** are authorized to give orders. **Staff managers** are authorized to assist and advise line managers in accomplishing their goals.

In popular usage, managers associate line managers with managing functions (like sales or production) that the company needs to exist. Staff managers generally run departments that are advisory or supportive, like purchasing, human resource management, and quality control. This distinction makes sense as long as the "staff" department is, in fact, advisory. However, strictly speaking, it is not the name of the department the manager is in charge of that determines if the manager is line or staff. It is the nature of the manager's authority. The line manager can issue orders. The staff manager can advise.

Human resource managers are staff managers. They assist and advise line managers in areas like recruiting, hiring, and compensation. However, we'll see that line managers still have human resource duties.

From Line to Staff

Managers may move from line to staff positions (and back) over the course of their careers. For example, line managers in areas like production and sales may well make career stopovers as staff human resource managers (another good reason for all managers to know something about HR). A survey by the Center for Effective Organizations at the University of Southern California found that about one fourth of large U.S. businesses appointed managers with no human resources experience as their top human resource executives. Employers assumed that these people may find it easier to give the firm's human resource management efforts a more strategic emphasis, and might sometimes be better equipped to integrate the firm's human resources efforts with the rest of the business.[3]

Line-Staff HR Cooperation

HR and line managers share responsibility for most human resource activities. For example, human resource and line managers in about two thirds of the firms in one survey shared responsibility for skills training.[4] (Thus, the supervisor might describe what training she thinks the new employee needs, HR might design the training, and the supervisor might then ensure that the training is having the desired effect.)

Line Managers' Human Resource Management Responsibilities

In any case, all supervisors spend much of their time on HR/personnel-type tasks. Indeed, the direct handling of people always has been an integral part of every line manager's responsibility, from president down to the first-line supervisor.

For example, one company outlines its line supervisors' responsibilities for effective human resource management under the following general headings:

1. Placing the right person in the right job
2. Starting new employees in the organization (orientation)
3. Training employees for jobs that are new to them
4. Improving the job performance of each person
5. Gaining cooperation and developing smooth working relationships
6. Interpreting the company's policies and procedures
7. Controlling labor costs
8. Developing the abilities of each person
9. Creating and maintaining departmental morale
10. Protecting employees' health and physical conditions

In small organizations, line managers may carry out all these personnel duties unassisted. But as the organization grows, line managers need the assistance, specialized knowledge, and advice of a separate human resource staff.

Organizing the Human Resource Department's Responsibilities

The human resource department provides this specialized assistance. The organization chart in Figure 1.1 shows the human resource management jobs you might find in a large company. Typical positions include compensation and benefits manager, employment and recruiting supervisor, training specialist, and employee relations executive. Examples of job duties include:

Recruiters: Maintain contact within the community and perhaps travel extensively to search for qualified job applicants.

Equal employment opportunity (EEO) representatives or affirmative action coordinators: Investigate and resolve EEO grievances, examine organizational practices for potential violations, and compile and submit EEO reports.

Job analysts: Collect and examine detailed information about job duties to prepare job descriptions.

FIGURE 1.1 HR Organization Chart for a Large Organization

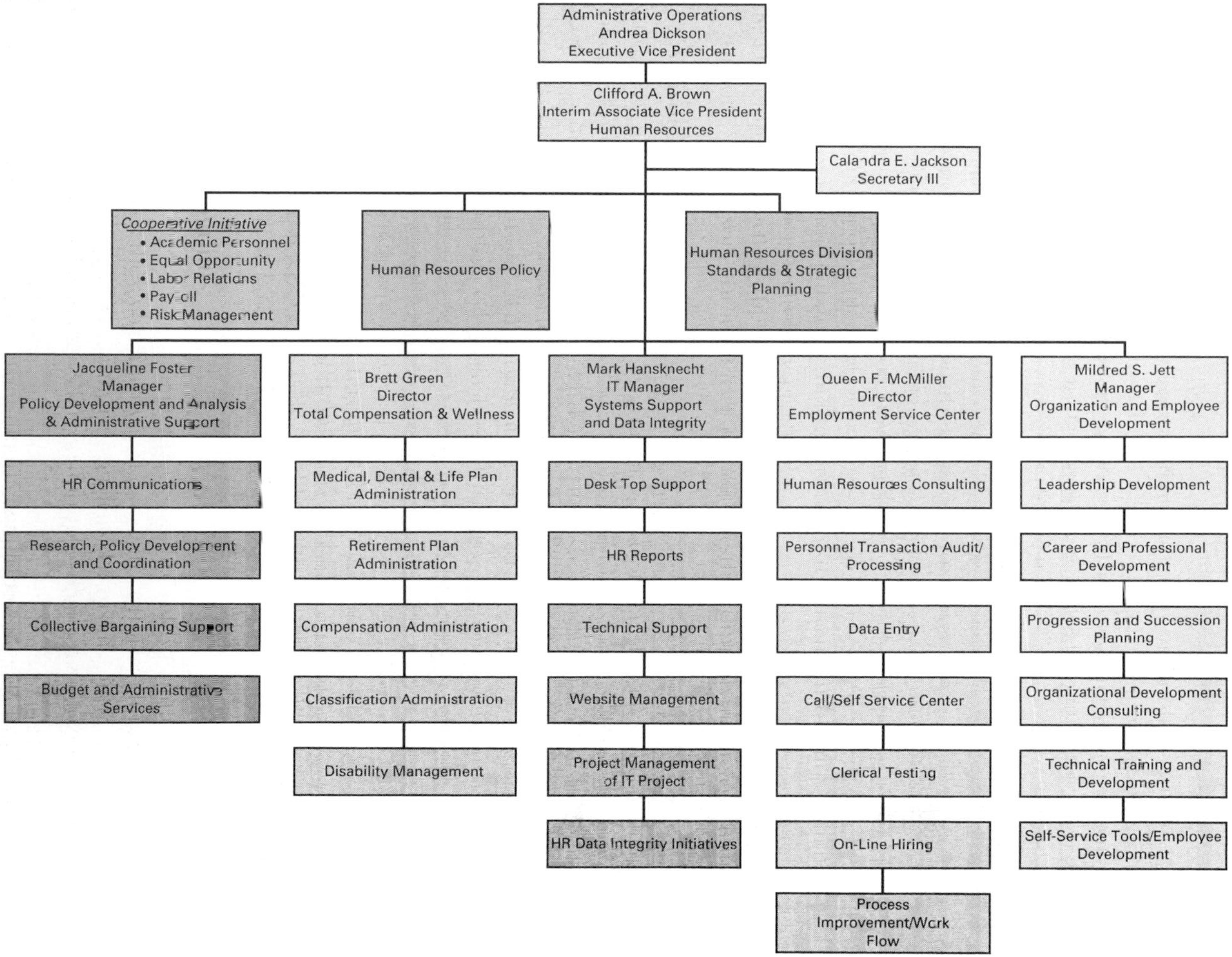

Administrative Operations
Andrea Dickson
Executive Vice President

Clifford A. Brown
Interim Associate Vice President
Human Resources

Calandra E. Jackson
Secretary III

Human Resources Division
Standards & Strategic
Planning

Human Resources Policy

Cooperative Initiative
• Academic Personnel
• Equal Opportunity
• Labor Relations
• Payroll
• Risk Management

Jacqueline Foster
Manager
Policy Development and Analysis
& Administrative Support

HR Communications

Research, Policy Development
and Coordination

Collective Bargaining Support

Budget and Administrative
Services

Brett Green
Director
Total Compensation & Wellness

Medical, Dental & Life Plan
Administration

Retirement Plan
Administration

Compensation Administration

Classification Administration

Disability Management

Mark Hansknecht
IT Manager
Systems Support
and Data Integrity

Desk Top Support

HR Reports

Technical Support

Website Management

Project Management
of IT Project

HR Data Integrity Initiatives

Queen F. McMiller
Director
Employment Service Center

Human Resources Consulting

Personnel Transaction Audit/
Processing

Data Entry

Call/Self Service Center

Clerical Testing

On-Line Hiring

Process
Improvement/Work
Flow

Mildred S. Jett
Manager
Organization and Employee
Development

Leadership Development

Career and Professional
Development

Progression and Succession
Planning

Organizational Development
Consulting

Technical Training and
Development

Self-Service Tools/Employee
Development

Source: www.hr.wayne.edu/orgcharts.php/hrdorgchart.pdf, accessed May 6, 2007.

5

> **Compensation managers:** Develop compensation plans and handle the employee benefits program.
> **Training specialists:** Plan, organize, and direct training activities.
> **Labor relations specialists:** Advise management on all aspects of union–management relations.

HR in Small Businesses

Human resource management in small firms is not just a shrunken version of human resource management in large ones. Employers usually have about one HR professional per 100 employees. Small firms (say, those with less than 100 employees) generally don't have the critical mass required for a full-time human resource manager. Their human resource management therefore tends to be "ad hoc and informal." For example, concludes one survey, small firms tend to use "unimaginative" recruiting practices like relying on newspaper ads, walk-ins, and word-of-mouth and to do little or no formal training.[5] However, that certainly does not need to be the case. Techniques like those in this book can go far toward boosting the "HR IQ" of the small business owner or manager.

The New Human Resources Organization

Employers are beginning to reorganize their human resource management functions in more innovative ways. For example, Randy MacDonald, IBM's senior vice president of human resources says the typical human resource management organization chart unduly isolates the HR functions into "silos" such as recruitment, training, and employee relations. Using this silo approach means there's no one team of human resource specialists focusing on particular groups of employees, or on individual employees' needs.

MacDonald reorganized IBM's human resources function. IBM segmented its 330,000 employees into three sets of "customers," executive and technical employees, managers, and rank and file. Separate cross functional human resource management teams (consisting of recruitment, training, and compensation specialists, for instance) now focus on serving the needs of each employee segment. This means cross functional HR teams, working together, can seamlessly ensure that the employees in each segment get the talent, learning and compensation they require to support IBM's strategy.[6]

THE CHANGING ENVIRONMENT AND DUTIES OF HR MANAGEMENT

Human Resource Management's Changing Role

IBM's new human resource organization reflects the fact that employers' human resource priorities and duties have evolved with changing times. In the early 1900s, "personnel" first took over hiring and firing from supervisors, ran the payroll department, and administered benefit plans. As technology in areas like testing and interviewing began to emerge, the personnel department began to play an expanded role in employee selection, training, and promotion.[7]

Union legislation in the 1930s meant more emphasis on protecting the firm in its interaction with unions. The discrimination legislation of the 1960s and '70s meant large potential lawsuits and penalties to employers, and thus an expansion of HR's "protector" role.

Today, those reading this book know that business is much more competitive than it's been in the past. The result is that employers like Ritz-Carleton increasingly rely on their employees' motivation and performance to provide them with a competitive edge. The metamorphosis of *personnel* into *human resource management* reflects the fact that in today's business environment, highly trained and committed employees, not machines, are often a firm's main real sustainable competitive advantage.

Important Trends

Let's sum up some of the trends that are prompting companies and their human resource managers to increasingly focus on competitiveness and performance.

Globalization

Globalization refers to the tendency of firms to extend their sales, ownership, and/or manufacturing to new markets abroad. Examples are all around us. Toyota produces the Camry in Kentucky, while Dell produces and sells PCs in China. Free trade areas— agreements that reduce tariffs and barriers among trading partners—further encourage international trade. NAFTA (the North American Free Trade Area) and the EU (European Union) are examples. More globalization means more competition, and more competition means more pressure to be "world-class"—to lower costs, to make employees more productive, and to do things better and less expensively. As at the Shanghai Portman Hotel, this pressures employers and their HR teams to institute practices that get the best from their employees.

Technological Advances

Technology is changing the nature of almost everything businesses do. For example, the Spanish retailer Zara doesn't need the expensive inventories that burden competitors like The Gap. Zara operates its own Internet-based worldwide distribution network, linked to the checkout registers at its stores around the world. When its headquarters in Spain sees a garment "flying" out of a store, Zara's computerized manufacturing system dyes the required fabric, cuts and manufactures the item, and speeds it to that store within days. Human resource managers similarly face the challenge of using technology to improve their own operations.

The Nature of Work

Technology is also changing the nature of work. Even factory jobs are more technologically demanding. In plants throughout the world, knowledge-intensive high tech manufacturing jobs are replacing traditional factory jobs. Skilled machinist Chad Toulouse illustrates the modern blue-collar worker. After an 18-week training course, this former college student now works as a team leader in a plant where about 40% of the machines are automated. In older plants, machinists would manually control machines that cut chunks of metal into things like engine parts. Today, Chad and his team spend much of their time typing commands into computerized machines that create precision parts for products including water pumps.[8] Technology-based employees like these need new skills and training to excel at these more complex jobs.

Service Jobs

Technology is not the only trend driving this change from "brawn to brains." Today over two thirds of the U.S. workforce is employed in producing and delivering services, not products. Between 2004 and 2014, almost all the new 19 million new jobs added in the U.S. will be in services, not in goods-producing industries.[9]

Outsourcing

The search for greater efficiencies is prompting employers to export more jobs abroad. For example, Merrill Lynch said it was planning on having some of its security analysis work done in India. Figure 1.2 summarizes the situation. It shows that between 2005 and 2015, about 3 million U.S. jobs, ranging from office support and computer jobs to management, sales, and even legal jobs, will likely move offshore.[10] Employers are even outsourcing human resource work. For example, several years ago BP Oil outsourced to Hewitt Associates its payroll, relocation, severance and benefits administration functions.[11]

Human Capital

For employers, this all means a growing need for "knowledge workers" and human capital. *Human capital* refers to the knowledge, education, training, skills, and expertise of a firm's workers.[12] Said one management guru, "the center of gravity in employment is moving fast from manual and clerical workers to knowledge workers, who resist the command-and-control model that business took from the military 100 years ago."[13] Managers need new world-class human resource management systems and skills, to select, train, and motivate these employees and to get them to work more like committed partners.

Example

This places a big premium on having effective human resource practices.

Here's an example. One bank installed special software that made it easier for customer service representatives to handle customers' inquiries. Seeking to capitalize on the new software, the bank upgraded the customer service representatives' jobs. The

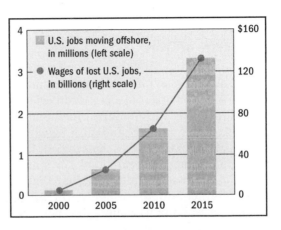

FIGURE 1.2   Employment Exodus: Projected Loss of Jobs and Wages

Source: Michael Shroeder, "States Fight Exodus of Jobs," *Wall Street Journal,* June 3, 2003, p. 84. Copyright © 2003 Dow Jones & Co., Inc. Reprinted by permission of Dow Jones & Co., Inc. in the format Textbook via Copyright Clearance Center.

bank gave them new training, taught them how to sell more of the bank's services, gave them more authority to make decisions, and raised their wages. Here, the new computer system dramatically improved profitability.

A second bank installed a similar system, but did not change the workers' jobs. Here, the system helped the service reps handle a few more calls. But this bank saw none of the big performance gains the first bank had gotten by turning its reps into motivated, highly trained sales people.[14] The moral is that today's employers need more effective human resource management selection, training, pay, and employee fairness practices than did their predecessors, if they are to capitalize on all the new technology.[15]

Demographic and Workforce Trends

At the same time, workforce demographic trends are making finding and hiring good employees more challenging. Labor force growth is not expected to keep pace with job growth, with an estimated shortfall of about 14 million college educated workers by 2020.[16] One study of 35 large global companies' senior human resource managers said "talent management"—in particular, the acquisition, development and retention of talent—ranked as their top concern.[17]

Most notably, the labor force is getting older. As the baby boomers born between 1946 and 1960 start leaving the labor force in the next few years, employers will face what one study calls a "severe" labor shortage, and will have to "rethink attitudes toward older workers and re-examine a range of established practices, from retirement rules to employee benefits."[18]

Overall, the U.S. workforce's demographics are becoming older and more multi-ethnic.[19] In the years 2004–2014, the white labor force will grow by 7%, as compared with blacks (17%), Asians (32%), and other (30%). The labor force participation rate of women, having increased from about 40% 50 years ago to about 60% today, will remain at about 60% through 2014. As the baby-boom generation ages, the number of people in the labor force age 55 to 64 will increase by about 7 million through 2014. The Hispanic and Latino labor force will increase by about 33%.[20]

There has also been a shift to nontraditional workers. Nontraditional workers include those who hold multiple jobs, or who are "contingent" or part-time workers, or people working in alternative work arrangements (such as a mother–daughter team sharing one flight attendant job at JetBlue airlines). Today, almost 10% of American workers—13 million people—fit this nontraditional workforce category. Of these, about 8 million are independent contractors who work on specific projects and move on once the projects are done.

"Generation Y"

Some experts note that the incoming crop of younger workers may have different work-related values than did their predecessors. Based on one study, for example, current employees are more likely to be work-centric (to focus more on work than on family with respect to career decisions), while younger workers tend to be more family-centric and dual-centric (balancing family and work life). Younger workers also generally don't agree that it's "better for women to stay home" than to work, and younger fathers tend to spend more time with their children on workdays.[21]

Fortune Magazine says that the "Generation Y" employees now joining the workforce will bring challenges and huge strengths. It says they may be "the most high maintenance workforce in the history of the world." But, as the first generation brought up from childhood using e-mail, their capacity for using information technology will also make them the most high-performing, because of the information they have in their heads and at their fingertips, Referring to them as "the most praised generation" the *Wall Street Journal* explains how Lands' End and Bank of America are teaching their managers to compliment these new employees with prize packages and public appreciation.[22]

Retirees

In a recent survey, human resource professionals said the aging workforce is the number one demographic trend impacting employers. Employers are dealing with this in various ways. One survey found that 41% of surveyed employers are bringing retirees back into the workforce; 34% are conducting studies to determine projected retirement rates in the organization; and 31% are offering employment options designed to attract and retain semi-retired workers.[23] Many employers make retirees an important part of their talent management strategies.[24]

THE STRATEGIC ROLE OF HUMAN RESOURCE MANAGEMENT

We saw that human resource management's priorities and responsibilities have evolved over the years, as employers' needs changed. Human resource managers' main responsibility is to institute policies and practices that produce the employee competencies and behaviors the company needs to achieve its strategic goals. A **strategy** is the company's plan for how it will match its internal strengths and weaknesses with external opportunities and threats in order to maintain a competitive advantage. Let's look at an example.

Strategy and HR Example

As in many firms today, Albertson's Markets faced competitive pressures from firms like Wal-Mart and from food stores from abroad. Albertson's top management therefore relied on the firm's human resource managers to be partners in helping the firm achieve its strategic goals.

Among other things, reducing personnel-related costs and improving Albertson's performance meant hiring employees who had a customer-focused approach, as well as reducing turnover, improving retention, and eliminating time-consuming manual processes and procedures for store managers.

Working with its information technology department, Albertson's human resource management team chose a computer system from Unicru of Portland, Oregon (www.unicru.com). The system collects and analyzes the information entered by applicants online and at kiosks. It ranks applicants based on the extent to which they exhibit the customer-focused traits that predict success in retail jobs, helps track candidates throughout the screening process, and does other things, such as track reasons for departure once applicants are hired. Human resource managers were able to present a compelling business case to illustrate the new system's return on investment. Working as a partner in Albertson's strategy design and implementation process, the HR team thus contributed in a significant way to achieving Albertson's strategic goals.[25]

Two Strategic Human Resource Challenges

Two things characterize the strategic challenges human resource managers face today. One (as at Albertson's) is the fact that most firms' strategies stress building performance. This means that human resource management's priorities increasingly focus on *boosting competitiveness, reducing costs, and improving employee performance.*

Second, (because of its expanding role in improving performance), human resource managers must also be more involved in *both formulating and implementing* company strategy. Traditionally, the president and his or her staff might decide to enter new markets, drop product lines, or embark on a 5-year cost-cutting plan. Then the president would more or less entrust the personnel implications of that plan (hiring or firing new workers, hiring outplacement firms for those fired, and so on) to his or her human resource managers.

Today, that's not enough. In formulating its strategy, top management at firms like Albertson's needs the input of the managers charged with hiring, training, and compensating the firm's employees. Human resource managers therefore need to understand strategic planning.

Basics of Strategic Planning

Managers engage in three levels of strategic planning (see Figure 1.3).[26]

Corporate Strategy

At the top, company-wide level, many firms consist of several businesses. For instance, PepsiCo includes Frito-Lay North America, PepsiCo Beverages North America, PepsiCo International, and Quaker Oats North America. PepsiCo therefore needs a

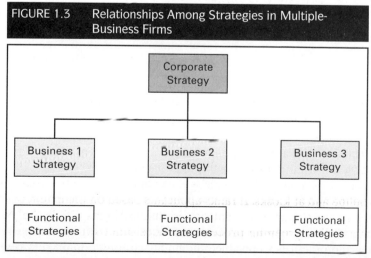

FIGURE 1.3   Relationships Among Strategies in Multiple-Business Firms

Source: Gary Dessler, Ph.D.

corporate-level strategy. A company's **corporate-level strategy** identifies the portfolio of businesses that, in total, comprise the company, and the ways in which these businesses relate to each other. For example, a *diversification* strategy implies that the firm will expand by adding new products. A *vertical integration* strategy means the firm expands by, perhaps, producing its own raw materials, or selling its products direct. *Consolidation*—reducing the company's size—and *geographic expansion*—for instance, taking the business abroad—are some other corporate strategy possibilities.

Competitive Strategy

At the next level down, each of these businesses (such as Pizza Hut) needs a *business-level/competitive strategy.* A **competitive strategy** identifies how to build and strengthen the business's long-term competitive position in the marketplace. It identifies, for instance, how Pizza Hut will compete with Papa John's or how Wal-Mart will compete with Target. Companies try to achieve competitive advantages for each business they are in. We can define **competitive advantage** as any factors that allow an organization to differentiate its product or service from those of its competitors to increase market share.[27]

Managers use several competitive strategies to achieve competitive advantage. One, *cost leadership*, means the enterprise aims to become the low-cost leader in an industry. Wal-Mart is a typical industry cost leader: It maintains its competitive advantage in part through its satellite-based distribution system.

In a *differentiation* competitive strategy, a firm seeks to be unique in its industry along dimensions that are widely valued by buyers.[28] Thus, Volvo stresses the safety of its cars, and Papa John's Pizza stresses fresh ingredients. Like Mercedes Benz, firms can usually charge a premium price if they successfully differentiate their products from their competitors. Still other firms choose to compete as *focusers*. They carve out a market niche (as for Ferrari) and compete by providing a product or service their customers can get in no other way.

Functional Strategy

Finally, each individual business has departments, such as manufacturing, sales, and human resource management. **Functional strategies** identify the basic courses of action that each of the business's departments will pursue in order to help the business attain its competitive goals. The firm's functional strategies should make sense in terms of its business/competitive strategy. Albertson's human resource management team using technology to support Albertson's low-cost competitive strategy exemplifies this.

HR and Competitive Advantage

In order to compete effectively, a company must have one or more competitive advantages, "factors that allow an organization to differentiate its product or service from those of its competitors to increase market share."

Today, most companies (such as Ford and Toyota) have access to the same technologies, so technology itself is rarely enough to set a company apart. It's usually the employees and the management system that make the difference. As at the Shanghai Portman Hotel, companies today therefore rely on their human resource management policies and practices to produce the highly committed and service-oriented employees that they need.

Strategic Human Resource Management

Because human resource management plays a bigger role in planning and achieving a firm's success than it has in the past, top managers expect their human resource managers to apply their special expertise and be strategic partners in developing and executing the firm's strategic plan. **Strategic human resource management** means formulating and executing HR systems—HR policies and practices—that produce the employee competencies and behaviors the company needs to achieve its strategic aims.[29] The term *HR strategies* refers to the specific human resource courses of action the company pursues to achieve its aims. Thus, Albertson's strategic aims include lowering costs and being customer-focused. Its human resource strategy thus includes using a special Web-based system to efficiently hire customer-focused employees. Figure 1.4 summarizes the relationship between HR strategy and the company's strategic plans and results. The human resource manager has roles in both formulating and executing the company's strategic plan.

HR's Role in Formulating Strategy

Formulating a strategic plan involves identifying, analyzing, and balancing the firm's *external opportunities and threats* and its *internal strengths and weaknesses*.

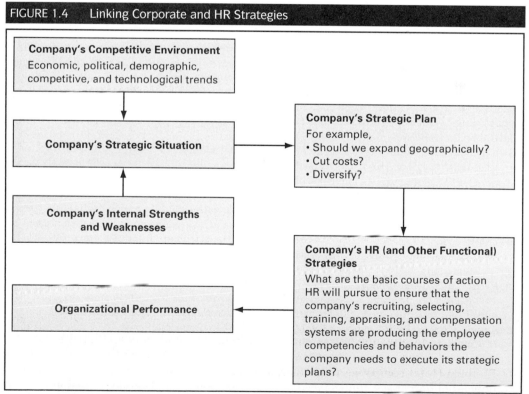

FIGURE 1.4 Linking Corporate and HR Strategies

Source: © 2008 Gary Dessler, Ph.D.

The resulting strategic plans should exploit the firm's strengths and opportunities and minimize or neutralize its threats and weaknesses.

The human resource team can play several roles here. For example, it's in a good position to supply competitive intelligence, such as details regarding competitors' incentive plans, and information about pending legislation such as labor laws. It is also in the best position to advise about the company's internal human strengths and weaknesses. For example, in the process of automating its factories, farm equipment manufacturer John Deere developed a workforce that was exceptionally talented in factory automation. This led Deere to establish a new-technology division to offer automation services to other companies.

HR's Role in Executing Strategy

As at Albertson's, human resource managers also help their firm execute their strategies. A study illustrates this. It found that mergers or acquisitions in which the human resource teams had been involved (for instance in providing advice regarding employee attitudes, and helping plan and lead the integration of the compensation and benefits plans) were more likely to successful.[30]

To illustrate human resource management's strategic role, we'll start each chapter with a vignette describing a company's strategic challenge, and then show in a brief "Strategy and HR" section in the chapter how it used human resource management to meet that challenge.

Strategy and HR

For example, to improve the Shanghai's Portman Hotel's customer service, new general manager Mark DeCocinis introduced the Ritz-Carlton management company's human resource system. He knew its practices would produce the high-quality service behaviors The Shanghai Portman required. For example, DeCocinis and his managers personally interviewed each job candidate. They delved deeply into each candidate's values, selecting only employees who cared for and respected others: "our selection focuses on talent and personal values because these are things that can't be taught. . . . it's about caring for and respecting others." Their efforts paid off. In the past few years, the Portman Ritz-Carlton was named the "best employer in Asia," "overall best business hotel in Asia," and "best business hotel in China." Profits soared. Effective human resource management helped turn the Portman Ritz-Carlton into a premier hotel.

The High-Performance Work System

As part of their strategic duties, human resource managers today most often focus on creating what they call *high-performance work system*s. A **high-performance work system** is an integrated set of human resource management policies and practices that together produce superior employee performance.

The basic aim here is to install human resource systems—in recruiting, screening, training, appraisal, and compensation, for instance—so that the company generates more job applicants, screens candidates more effectively, provides more and better training, links pay more explicitly to performance, and provides a safer work environment. In this way the human resource team can make a measurable contribution to the company's bottom line.

Example

One study looked at 17 manufacturing plants, some of which used high-performance type human resource practices. Those with the "super" HR practices also had the best performances in terms of higher profits, lower operating costs, and lower turnover. In terms of specific human resource practices, the high-performing plants paid more, with median wages of $16 per hour compared with $13 per hour for all plants studied; trained more, with about 83% of the super plants offering more than 20 hours of training per year, compared with only 32% for plants overall; used more sophisticated recruitment and hiring practices, for instance, in terms of using tests and validated interviews; used more self-managing work teams[31]; and had a higher percentage of employees receiving regular performance appraisals.[32]

Measuring HR Performance

In today's performance-based environment, employers expect their human resource management teams to provide measurable evidence of their effectiveness. For example, "How much will that new testing program save us in reduced employee turnover?" "How much more productive will our employees be if we institute that new training program?" And, "How productive is our human resource team, in terms of HR staff per employee, compared to our competitors?"

IBM's Randall MacDonald needed $100 million from IBM to reorganize its HR operations, and he emphasized human resource metrics in requesting those funds. He told top management, "I'm going to deliver talent to you that's skilled and on time and ready to be deployed. I will be able to measure the skills, tell you what skills we have, what [skills] we don't have [and] then show you how to fill the gaps or enhance our training."[33]

Sample Metrics

To make claims like these, human resource managers such as MacDonald need access to the performance measures (or "metrics"), as well as to comparable, benchmark-able figures from similar firms. For example, median HR expenses as a proportion of companies' total operating costs average about 0.8%. There tends to be between 0.9 and 1.0 human resource staff persons per 100 employees (the ratio tends to be lower in retailing and distribution firms, and higher in public, state organizations).[34] Employers can request customized benchmark comparisons (for training hours, and tests administered, for instance) from services such as the Society for Human Resource Management's Human Capital Benchmarking Service, and its database of over 1,500 organizations.[35]

The HR Scorecard

Managers at firms like IBM ultimately judge the human resource function based on whether it creates value for the company, where *value creation* means contributing in a measurable way to achieving the company's strategic goals. HR creates value by engaging in activities that produce the employee behaviors the company needs to achieve these strategic goals.

Managers often use an *HR Scorecard* process to measure the human resource function's effectiveness in producing these employee behaviors and thus in achieving the company's strategic goals. The *HR Scorecard* is a concise measurement system, often presented in a desktop window showing the relevant measures and relationships.

It shows the quantitative standards, or "metrics," the firm uses to measure HR activities, and to measure the employee behaviors resulting from these activities, and to measure the strategically relevant organizational outcomes of those employee behaviors. In so doing, it highlights, in a concise but comprehensive way, the causal link between the HR activities, the emergent employee behaviors, and the resulting firmwide strategic outcomes and performance.

THE HUMAN RESOURCE MANAGER TODAY

In addition to performance improvement and HR strategy, three other issues—technology, ethics, and professional certification—concern today's human resource managers. We'll look briefly at each.

HR and Technology

Faced with having to add about 15,000 employees in 51 countries, Dell's talent acquisition group knew they needed a more metrics-based process for attracting and acquiring employees. At the time, Dell had no centralized procedure for monitoring global recruiting. Managers outside the United States compiled their monthly hiring statistics on spreadsheets and sent these to Dell's Austin, Texas headquarters.

Dell contracted with a vendor to install a Web-based applicant tracking system. This system automated the process of recruiting employees and of managing their applications and progress through the hiring process. The vendor then worked with Dell to develop customized recruiting metrics. These included, for instance, hiring managers' evaluations of the candidates. Dell can therefore now correlate candidate performance with sources of applicants. They can therefore focus their recruiting on the more productive recruitment sources.[36]

How Human Resource Managers Use Technology

Technology applications like those in Figure 1.5 play an important role in human resource management. Technology improves HR functioning in four main ways: *self-service, call centers, productivity improvement*, and *outsourcing*.[37] Dell again provides good examples of several of these applications. For example, Dell employees use the firm's intranet-based HR applications to *self-service* many of their own HR transactions, such as updating personal information and changing benefits allocations. Technology also enabled Dell to create a *centralized call center*. HR specialists answer questions from all Dell's far-flung employees, reducing the need for multiple HR centers at each Dell location.

More firms are installing Internet- and computer-based systems for improving human resource function *productivity*. For example, International Paper Corporation finished installing its "Viking" human resource information system (HRIS) several years ago. In terms of efficiency, the system's goal was to achieve an HR staff-to-employee ratio of 1 to 150, and a cost per employee of $800 for delivering HR services.[38]

Finally, technology also makes it easier to *outsource* human resource activities to specialist service providers, by enabling service providers to have real-time Internet-based access to the employer's HR database. For instance, several years ago, BP outsourced its benefits management activities to Hewitt Associates.

FIGURE 1.5	Some Ways HR Managers Use Technology

Technology	How Used by HR
Application Service Providers (ASPs)	ASPs host and manage services (such as for processing employment applications), for the employer from their own remote computers
Web portals	Employers use these, for instance, to enable employees to manage their own benefits and update their personal information
Streaming PC video	Used, for instance, to facilitate distance training
The mobile Web and wireless net access	Used to facilitate employees' access to the company's Web-based HR activities
Personal digital assistants	For example, some firms provide incoming managers with preloaded personal digital assistants. These contain information the new managers need to better adjust to their new jobs, such as key contact information and digital images of the manager's new employees
Monitoring software	Used to track employees' Internet and e-mail activities or performance
Integrated human resource information systems (HRIS)	Used to integrate the employer's separate HR systems, for instance by automatically updating employee's qualifications list when he or she completes a training program.
Electronic signatures	Employers can use these legally valid e-signatures to expeditiously obtain applicant and employee signatures
The Web	Managers make extensive use of the Web, as for doing salary surveys

Sources: Adapted from Samuel Greengard, "10 HR Technology Trends for 2001," *Workforce, HR Trends and Tools for Business Results* 80, no. 1 (January 2001): 20–22; Jim Meade, "Analytical Tools Give Meaning to Data," *HR Magazine* 46, no. 11 (November 2001): 97 ff; Connie Winkler, "Quality Check," *HR Magazine* (May 2007): 93–98.

Improving Productivity through HRIS

HR Portals provide employees with a single access point or "gateway" via their company's intranet to human resource-related information.[39] They let employees, managers, and executives interactively access and modify certain of that information. They thereby streamline human resource management processes and enable human resource managers to focus more on strategic issues.

NCR installed an HR portal they called *HR eXpress*. It is organized into three information areas: benefits and compensation, training and career growth, and NCR values and human resource policies.[40] NCR also added a Forms Center to the site's title bar. HR eXpress gives NCR employees a shortcut to all the information they need to manage HR Tasks, such as those relating to company benefits and updating their personal information. The Forms Center gives them quick access to any HR forms they need.

Studies generally indicate Internet-based applications like these ("e-HR") lead to reductions in human resource staff, faster processes, and lower HR function costs.[41]

Managing Ethics

Ethics refers to the standards someone uses to decide what his or her conduct should be. Ethical decisions always involve *morality*, matters of serious consequence to society's well-being, such as murder, lying, and stealing. Newspaper headlines regarding ethical lapses such as questionably-timed stock option grants at various firms seem to never end. Given that some firms, such as the accounting firm Arthur Andersen, were literally put out of business by ethical lapses, one has to wonder what the managers were thinking.

Congress passed the Sarbanes-Oxley Act in 2003. To help ensure that managers take their ethics responsibilities seriously, Sarbanes-Oxley (SOX) is intended to curb erroneous corporate financial reporting. Among other things, Sarbanes-Oxley requires CEOs and CFOs to certify their companies' periodic financial reports, prohibits personal loans to executive officers and directors, and requires CEOs and CFOs to reimburse their firms for bonuses and stock option profits if corporate financial statements subsequently require restating.[42] SOX does not just involve the firm's CEO and CFO. For example, every publicly listed company now needs a code of ethics, more often than not promulgated by human resources.

The human resource manager's responsibilities for ethics don't end with Sarbanes-Oxley. One survey found that six of the ten most serious ethical issues—workplace safety, security of employee records, employee theft, affirmative action, comparable work, and employee privacy rights—were human resource management related.[43] We will explain ethics in human resource management more fully in Chapter 8.

HR Certification

As the human resource manager's tasks grow more complex, human resource management is becoming more professionalized. Over 60,000 HR professionals have already passed one or both of the Society for Human Resource Management's (SHRM) HR professional certification exams. SHRM's Human Resource Certification Institute offers these exams. Two levels of exams test the professional's knowledge of all aspects of human resource management, including management practices, staffing, development, compensation, labor relations, and health and safety. Those who successfully complete all requirements earn the SPHR (senior professional in HR), or PHR (professional in HR) certificate. The Human Resource Certification Institute recently began implementing state certifications, offering credential testing for California's human resource professionals in 2007.[44] Managers can take an online HRCI assessment exam at www.HRCI.org (or by calling 866-898-HRCI).

THE PLAN OF THIS BOOK

The Integrated Nature of HR Management Activities

This section presents a brief overview of the chapters to come; but do not think of these as independent, unrelated chapters and topics. Instead, each interacts with and affects the others, and all should fit with the employer's strategic plan. Figure 1.6 summarizes this idea. For example, how you test and interview job candidates (Chapter 4) and train and appraise job incumbents (Chapters 5 and 6) depends on the job's specific duties and responsibilities (Chapter 3). How good a job you are doing selecting (Chapter 4) and training (Chapter 5) employees will affect how safely they do their jobs (Chapter 10). An employee's performance and thus his or her appraisal (Chapter 6) depends on not only the person's motivation but also how well you identified the job's duties (Chapter 3), and screened and trained the employee (Chapters 4 and 5). And, as we've seen, each of your HR policies in each area—for instance, how you recruit, select, train, appraise, and compensate employees—should make sense in terms of the company's strategic plan.

The following is an outline of the chapters to come:

Chapter 2: Managing Equal Opportunity and Diversity. What you'll need to know about equal opportunity laws as they relate to human resource management activities such as interviewing, selecting employees, and evaluating performance appraisals

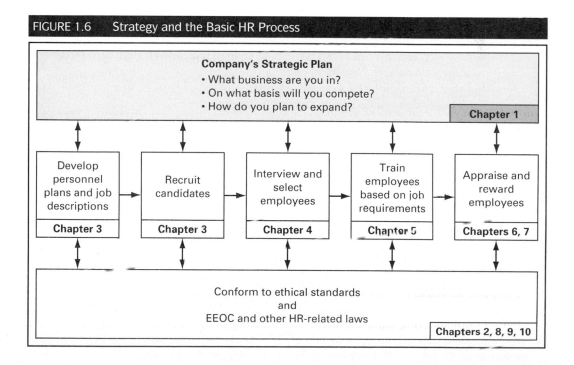

FIGURE 1.6   Strategy and the Basic HR Process

Company's Strategic Plan
- What business are you in?
- On what basis will you compete?
- How do you plan to expand?

Chapter 1

Develop personnel plans and job descriptions	Recruit candidates	Interview and select employees	Train employees based on job requirements	Appraise and reward employees
Chapter 3	**Chapter 3**	**Chapter 4**	**Chapter 5**	**Chapters 6, 7**

Conform to ethical standards
and
EEOC and other HR-related laws

Chapters 2, 8, 9, 10

Part I: Recruiting and Placing Employees

Chapter 3: Personnel Planning and Recruiting. How to analyze a job and how to determine the job's requirements, specific duties, and responsibilities, as well as what sorts of people need to be hired and how to recruit them

Chapter 4: Testing and Selecting Employees. Techniques such as testing that you can use to ensure that you're hiring the right people

Chapter 5: Training and Developing Employees. Providing the training and development necessary to ensure that your employees have the knowledge and skills required to accomplish their tasks

Part II: Appraising and Compensating Employees

Chapter 6: Performance Management and Appraisal. Techniques for managing and appraising performance

Chapter 7: Compensating Employees. How to develop equitable pay plans, including incentives and benefits, for your employees

Part III: Employee Rights and Safety

Chapter 8: Ethics and Fair Treatment in Human Resource Management. Ensuring ethical and fair treatment through discipline, grievance, and career management processes

Chapter 9: Managing Labor Relations and Collective Bargaining. Concepts and techniques concerning the relations between unions and management, including the union-organizing campaign; negotiating and agreeing on a collective bargaining agreement between unions and management; and managing the agreement

Chapter 10: Protecting Safety and Health. The causes of accidents, how to make the workplace safe, and laws governing your responsibilities in regard to employee safety and health

Module A: Managing HR Globally. Applying human resource management policies and practices in a global environment

Review

Summary

1. Staffing, personnel management, or human resource management includes activities such as recruiting, selecting, training, compensating, appraising, and developing.

2. HR management is a part of every line manager's responsibilities. These HR responsibilities include placing the right person in the right job and then orienting, training, and compensating the person to improve his or her job performance.

3. The human resource manager and his or her department provide various staff services to line management; for example, the HR manager or department assists in the hiring, training, evaluating, rewarding, promoting, and disciplining of employees at all levels.

4. Changes in the environment of human resource management are requiring HR to play a more strategic role in organizations. These changes include growing workforce diversity, rapid technological change, globalization, and changes in the nature of work, such as the movement toward a service

society and a growing emphasis on education and human capital.

5. One consequence of changes in the work environment is that HR management must be involved in both the formulation and the implementation of a company's strategies, given the need for the firm to use its employees as a competitive advantage.

6. We defined strategic human resource management as "formulating and executing HR systems—HR policies and practices—that produce the employee competencies and behaviors the company needs to achieve its strategic aims." HR is a strategic partner in that HR management works with other top managers to formulate the company's strategy as well as to execute it.

Key Terms

- human resource management
- authority
- line manager
- staff manager
- strategy
- corporate-level strategy
- competitive strategy
- competitive advantage
- functional strategy
- strategic human resource management
- high-performance work system
- ethics

Discussion Questions and Exercises

1. Explain what HR management is and how it relates to line management.
2. Give several examples of how HR management concepts and techniques can be of use to all managers.
3. Compare the work of line and staff managers. Give examples of each.
4. Working individually or in groups, develop a list showing how trends such as workforce diversity, technological trends, globalization, and changes in the nature of work have affected the college or university you are now attending or the organization for which you work.
5. Working individually or in groups, develop several examples showing how the new HR management practices mentioned in this chapter (using technology, for instance) have or have not been implemented to some extent in the college or university you are now attending or in the organization for which you work.
6. Working individually or in groups, interview an HR manager. Based on that interview, write a short presentation regarding HR's role today in building a more responsive organization.
7. Why is it important for a company to make its human resources into a competitive advantage? How can HR contribute to doing so?
8. What is meant by strategic human resource management, and what exactly is HR's role in the strategic planning process?

APPLICATION EXERCISES

Case Incident   *Jack Nelson's Problem*

As a new member of the board of directors for a local bank, Jack Nelson was being introduced to all the employees in the home office. When he was introduced to Ruth Johnson, he was curious about her work and asked her what her machine did. Johnson replied that she really did not know what the machine was called or what it did. She explained that she had been working there for only two months. She did, however, know precisely how to operate the machine. According to her supervisor, she was an excellent employee.

At one of the branch offices, the supervisor in charge spoke to Nelson confidentially, telling him that "something was wrong," but she didn't know what. For one thing, she explained, employee turnover was too high, and no sooner had one employee been put on the job than another one resigned. With customers to see and loans to be made, she explained, she had little time to work with the new employees as they came and went.

All branch supervisors hired their own employees without communication with the home office or other branches. When an opening developed, the supervisor tried to find a suitable employee to replace the worker who had quit.

After touring the 22 branches and finding similar problems in many of them, Nelson wondered what the home office should do or what action he should take. The banking firm was generally regarded as a well-run institution that had grown from 27 to 191 employees during the past eight years. The more he thought about the matter, the more puzzled Nelson became. He couldn't quite put his finger on the problem, and he didn't know whether to report his findings to the president. ■

QUESTIONS

1. What do you think is causing some of the problems in the bank's home office and branches?
2. Do you think setting up an HR unit in the main office would help?
3. What specific functions should an HR unit carry out? What HR functions would then be carried out by supervisors and other line managers?

Source: From *Supervision in Action,* 4/e, by Claude S. George © 1985. Adapted by permission of Prentice Hall, Inc., Upper Saddle River, NJ.

Continuing Case

LearnInMotion.com: Introduction

The main theme of this book is that HR management—activities like recruiting, selecting, training, and rewarding employees—is not just the job of some central HR group, but rather one in which every manager must engage. Perhaps nowhere is this more apparent than in the typical small service business. Here the owner–manager usually has no personnel staff to rely on. However, the success of his or her enterprise (not

to mention his or her family's peace of mind) often depends largely on the effectiveness with which workers are recruited, hired, trained, evaluated, and rewarded.

To help illustrate and emphasize the frontline manager's HR role, throughout this book we will use a continuing ("running") case, based on an actual small business in the northeastern United States. Each segment will illustrate how the case's main players—owner–managers Jennifer Mendez and Mel Hudson—confront and solve personnel problems each day by applying the concepts and techniques presented in that particular chapter. The names of the company and principals have been changed, as have a few of the details, but the company, people, dates, and HR and other problems are otherwise real. Here's some background information you'll need to answer questions that arise in subsequent chapters.

LearnInMotion.com: A Profile.   Jennifer and Mel graduated from State University as business majors in June 1999, and got the idea for LearnInMotion.com as a result of a project they worked on together their last semester in their entrepreneurship class. The professor had divided the students into two- or three-person teams, and given them the assignment "create a business plan for a dot-com company."

The idea the two came up with was LearnInMotion.com. The basic idea of the Web site was to list a vast array of Web-based, DVD-based, or textbook-based business-related continuing-education-type courses for "free agent learners"—in other words, for working people who wanted to take a course in business from the comfort of their own homes. The idea was that users could come to the Web site to find and then take a course in one of several ways. Some courses could be completed interactively on the Web via the site; others were in a form that was downloadable directly to the user's computer; others (which were either textbook or DVD-based) could be ordered and delivered (in several major metropolitan areas) by independent contractor delivery people using bicycles or motorized scooters. Their business mission was "to provide work-related learning when, where, and how you need it."

Based on their research, they knew the market for work-related learning like this was booming. The $63-billion U.S. corporate training market was (and is) growing at 10% annually, for instance, with no firm controlling more than 2%. In 1999, when they created their plan, 76 million adult U.S. learners participated in at least one education activity. Over 100,000 U.S. training and consulting firms offered seminars, courses, and other forms of training. They estimated that worldwide markets were at least two or three times the U.S. market.

At the same time, professional development activities like these were increasingly Internet-based. Thirteen percent of training was delivered via the Internet when they did their class project in 1999, and projections were for the e-learning/distance learning market to grow over 90% annually for the following three years. Tens of thousands of on- and off-line training firms, universities, associations, and other content providers were trying to reach their target customers via the Internet. Jennifer and Mel understandably thought they were in the right place at the right time. And perhaps they were.

Their business plan contained about 25 pages, including financial projection tables, and covered the usual array of topics: company summary; management; market trends and opportunities; competition; marketing plan; financial plan; and appendices. The one-page executive summary contained a synopsis of the plan and covered "the business," "the market," "strategies," "competition," "value proposition," "the revenue drivers," "the management," and "financials and funding." Most of this is self-descriptive. Revenue drivers referred to how the company would generate revenues (in this case, online banner ads and sponsorships, content providers' listing fees, and fees for courses actually taken). Financials and funding included basic financial projections as well as likely "exit strategies," which in this case included the possibility of a public offering, a merger with related sites, or sale of the site, perhaps to one of the superportals that were aggregating specialized sites as part of their strategies. They got an A for the business plan, an A for the course, and a standing ovation from the businesspeople the professor had invited to help evaluate the presentations.

When the two graduated in June 1999, it looked like the Internet boom would go on forever. Even then, in the pre-myspace years, it was not unusual for entrepreneurs still in their teens to create and sell Web sites. Some were selling their Web sites for literally hundreds of millions of dollars. Jennifer's father had some unused loft space in the SoHo area of New York, so with about $45,000 of accumulated savings, Jennifer and Mel incorporated and were in business. They retained the services of an independent contractor programmer and hired two people—a Web designer to create the graphics for the site (which would then be programmed by the programmer) and a content manager whose job was basically to keypunch information onto the site as it came in from content providers. By the end of 1999, they also completed upgrading their business plan into a form they could show to prospective venture capitalists. They sent the first version to three New York area venture capitalists. Then they waited.

And then they waited some more. They never heard back from the first three venture capitalists, so they sent their plan to five more. By now it was March 2000, and a dramatic event occurred: The values of most Internet and Internet-related sites dropped precipitously on the stock market. In some cases, entrepreneurs who had been worth $1 billion in February 1999 were worth $20 million or less by April. "Well, $20 million isn't bad," Mel said, so they pressed on. By day they called customers to get people to place ads on their site, to get content providers to list their available courses, and to get someone—anyone—to deliver textbook- and CD–ROM-based courses, as needed, in the New York area.

By May 2000, they had about 300 content providers offering courses and content through LearnInMotion.com. In the summer, they got their first serious nibble from a venture capital firm. They negotiated with this company through much of the summer, came to terms in the early fall, and closed the deal—getting just over $1 million in venture funding—in November 2000.

After a stunning total of $75,000 in legal fees (they had to pay both their firm's and the venture capital firm's lawyers to navigate the voluminous disclosure documents and agreements), they had just over $900,000 to spend. The funding, according to the business plan, was to go toward accomplishing five main goals: redesigning and expanding the Web site; hiring about seven more employees; moving to larger office space; designing and implementing a personal information manager (PIM)/calendar (users and content providers could use the calendar to interactively keep track of their personal and business schedules); and, last but not least, driving up sales. LearnInMotion.com was off and running. ∎

QUESTIONS AND ASSIGNMENTS

1. Would a company like this with just a few employees and independent contractors have any HR tasks to address? What do you think those might be?
2. Based on your review of the online catalogs of firms such as Office Max, Staples, and HRNext.com, what basic HR systems would you recommend to Jennifer and Mel?

EXPERIENTIAL EXERCISE

Helping "The Donald"

Purpose: The purpose of this exercise is to provide practice in identifying and applying the basic concepts of human resource management by illustrating how managers use these techniques in their day-to-day jobs.

Required Understanding: Be thoroughly familiar with the material in this chapter, and with at least several episodes of *The Apprentice*, the TV show in which developer Donald Trump starred.

How to Set Up the Exercise/Instructions:

1. Divide the class into teams of three to four students.
2. Read this: As you know by watching "The Donald" as he organizes his business teams for *The Apprentice*, human resource management plays an important role in what Donald Trump and the participants on his separate teams need to do to be successful. For

example, Donald Trump needs to be able to appraise each of the participants. And, for their part, the leaders of each of his teams need to be able to staff his or her teams with the right participants and then provide the sorts of training, incentives, and evaluations that help their companies succeed and that therefore make the participants themselves (and especially the team leaders) look like "winners" to Mr. Trump.

3. Watch several of these shows (or reruns of the shows), and then meet with your team and answer the following questions:

a. What specific HR functions (recruiting, interviewing, and so on) can you identify Donald Trump using on this show? Make sure to give specific examples based on the show.

b. What specific HR functions (recruiting, selecting, training, and so on) can you identify one or more of the team leaders using to help manage their teams on the show? Again, please give specific answers.

c. Provide a specific example of how HR functions (such as recruiting, selection, interviewing, compensating, appraising, and so on) contributed to one of the participants coming across as particularly successful to Mr. Trump. Can you provide examples of how one or more of these functions contributed to Mr. Trump telling a participant "You're fired"?

d. Present your team's conclusions to the class. ◾

Endnotes

1. Arthur Yeung, "Setting Up for Success: How the Portman Ritz-Carlton Hotel Gets the Best from Its People," *Human Resource Management* 45, no. 2 (Summer 2006): 67–75.

2. Quoted in Fred K. Foulkes, "The Expanding Role of the Personnel Function," *Harvard Business Review* (March/April 1975): 71–84. See also Warren Wilhelm, "HR Can Make the U.S. a Global Leader," *Personnel Journal* (May 1993): 280.

3. Steve Bates, "No Experience Necessary? Many Companies Are Putting Non-HR Executives in Charge of HR with Mixed Results," *HR Magazine* 46, no. 11 (November 2001): 34–41.

4. "Human Resource Activities, Budgets & Staffs, 1999–2000," *BNA Bulletin to Management* 51, no. 25 (June 29, 2000): S1–S6.

5. Susan Mayson and Rowena Barrett, "The 'Science' and 'Practice' of HR in Small Firms," *Human Resource Management Review* 16: 447–455.

6. Robert Grossman, "IBM's HR Takes a Risk," *HR Management* (April 2007): 54–59.

7. "Immigrants in the Workforce," *BNA Bulletin to Management Datagraph* (August 15, 1996): 260–261. See also Shari Caudron et al., "80 People, Events and Trends that Shaped HR," *Workforce* (January 2002): 26–56.

8. Timothy Appel, "Better Off a Blue-Collar," *Wall Street Journal* (July 1, 2003): B-1.

9. See "Charting the Projections: 2004–2014," *Occupational Outlook Quarterly*, Winter 2005–2006.

10. Michael Schroeder, "States Fight Exodus of Jobs," *Wall Street Journal* (June 3, 2003): 84. See also, Monica Belcourt, "Outsourcing— the Benefits and the Risks," *Human Resource Management Review* 16, 2006, pp. 69–279.

11. Jessica Marquez, "Hewitt–HP Split May Signal End of 'Lift and Shift' Deals," *Workforce Management* (December 11, 2006): 3–4.

12. Richard Crawford, *In the Era of Human Capital* (New York: Harper Business, 1991), p. 26.

13. Peter Drucker, "The Coming of the New Organization," *Harvard Business Review* (January–February 1988): 45. See also, James Combs et al., "How Much Do High-Performance Work Practices Matter? A Meta-Analysis of Their Effects on Organizational Performance," *Personal Psychology* 59, 2006, pp. 501–528.

14. www.knowledge.wharton.upe.edu, "Human Resources Wharton," accessed January 8, 2006.

15. See for example, Anthea Zacharatos et al., "High-Performance Work Systems and

Occupational Safety," *Journal of Applied Psychology* 90, no. 1 (2005): 77–93.

16. Tony Carneval, "The Coming Labor and Skills Shortage," *Training & Development* (January 2005): 39.

17. "Talent Management Leads in Top HR Concerns," *Compensation & Benefits Review* (May/June 2007): 12.

18. See Diane Piktialis and Hal Morgan, "The Aging of the U.S. Workforce and Its Implications for Employers," *Compensation and Benefits Review* (January/February 2003): 57.

19. "Charting the Projections: 2004–2014," *Occupational Outlook Quarterly* (Winter 2005–2006): 48–50.

20. Michael Horrigan, "Introduction to the Projections," *Occupational Outlook Quarterly* (Winter 2003–2004): 5.

21. Eva Kaplan-Leiserson, "The Changing Workforce," *Training and Development* (February 2005): 10–11.

22. Nadira Hira, "You Raised Them, Now Manage Them," *Fortune* (May 28, 2007): 155, 10, p. 38; Katheryn Tyler, "The Tethered Degeneration," *HR Magazine* (May 2007): 41–46; Jeffrey Zaslow, "The Most Praised Generation Goes to Work," *Wall Street Journal* (April 20, 2007): W1, W7.

23. Jennifer Schramm, "Exploring the Future of Work: Workplace Visions," *Society for Human Resource Management,* no. 2 (2005): 6.

24. "Talent Management Leads in Top HR Concerns," *Compensation & Benefits Review* (May/June 2007): 12.

25. "Automation Improves Retailer's Hiring Efficiency and Quality," *HR Focus* 82, no. 2 (February 2005): 3.

26. Patrick Gunnigle and Sara Moore, "Linking Business Strategy and Human Resource Management: Issues and Implications," *Personnel Review* 23, no. 1 (1994): 63–84; Gary Dessler, Human Resource Management (Upper Saddle River, NJ: Prentice Hall, 2008): p. 77–97.

27. Gunnigle and Moore, "Linking Business Strategy," 64.

28. Michael Porter, *Competitive Strategy* (New York: The Free Press, 1980), p. 14.

29. Gary Dessler, *Human Resource Management* (Upper Saddle River, NJ: Prentice Hall, 2008): p. 86.

30. Jeffrey Schmidt, "The Correct Spelling of M&A Begins with HR," *HR Magazine* 46, no. 6 (June 2001): 102–108. See also Wendy Boswell, "Aligning Employees with the Organization's Strategic Objectives: Out of Line of Sight, Out of Mind." *International Journal of Human Resource Management* 17, no. 9, September 2006, pp. 1014–1041.

31. "Super Human Resources Practices Result in Better Overall Performance, Report Says," *BNA Bulletin to Management* (August 26, 2004): 273–274.

32. See, for example, George Benson, et al., "High Involvement Work Practices and Analysts' Forecasts of Corporate Earnings," *Human Resource Management*, 45, no. 4 (Winter 2006): 519–537.

33. Robert Grossman, "IBM's HR Takes a Risk," *HR Management* (April 2007): 54–59.

34. Chris Brewster, et al., "What Determines the Size of the HR Function? A Cross National Analysis," *Human Resource Management* 45, no. 1 (Spring 2006): 3–21.

35. Contact the Society for Human Resource Management, 703.535.6366.

36. Connie Winkler, "Quality Check," *HR Magazine* (May 2007): 93–98.

37. "The Future of HR," *Workplace Visions* 6 (Society for Human Resource Management, 2001): 3–4.

38. Bill Roberts, "Process First, Technology Second," *HR Magazine* (June 2002): 40–46.

39. Chris Pickering, "A Look through the Portal," *Software Magazine* 21, no. 1 (February 2001): 18–19.

40. Jill Elswick, "How NCR Corp. Undertook an Intranet Makeover to Improve Access to HR Information," *Employee Benefits News* (January 1, 2001), item 01008001.

41. Stefan Strohmeier, "Research in e HRM: Review and Implications," *Human Resource Management Review* 17 (2007):19–37.

42. Jonathan Seggal, "The Joy of Cooking," *HR Magazine* (November 2002): 52–58.

43. Kevin Wooten, "Ethical Dilemmas in Human Resource Management," *Human Resource Management Review* 11 (2001): 161.

44. "The Human Resource Certification Institute (HRCI) Announces the California Certification", www.hrci.org/HRCI_Files/_Items/HRCI-MR-TAB2-951/Docs/At_A_Glance.pdf, accessed December 28, 2007.

2 | MANAGING EQUAL OPPORTUNITY AND DIVERSITY

- Selected Equal Employment Opportunity Laws
- Defenses Against Discrimination Allegations
- Illustrative Discriminatory Employment Practices
- The EEOC Enforcement Process
- Diversity Management and Affirmative Action Programs

When you finish studying this chapter, you should be able to:

■ Summarize *the basic equal employment opportunity laws regarding age, race, sex, national origin, religion, and handicap discrimination.*

■ Explain *the basic defenses against discrimination allegations.*

■ Present *a summary of what employers can and cannot do with respect to illegal recruitment, selection, and promotion and layoff practices.*

■ Explain *the Equal Employment Opportunity Commission enforcement process.*

INTRODUCTION

In a suit apparently prompted by its new "Eradicating Racism from Employment" campaign, the U.S. Equal Employment Opportunity Commission (EEOC) recently claimed that Walgreens discriminated against managers and pharmacists. It said Walgreens used race to determine who to assign to low-performing stores in African-American communities.[1]

SELECTED EQUAL EMPLOYMENT OPPORTUNITY LAWS

Hardly a day goes by without reports of equal-opportunity-related lawsuits at work. One survey of 300 corporate general counsels found that employment lawsuits like these were their biggest litigation fears.[2] Performing day-to-day supervisory tasks like hiring or transferring employees without understanding equal employment laws is fraught with peril. Let us start at the beginning.

Background

Legislation barring discrimination against minorities in the United States is nothing new. For example, the Fifth Amendment to the U.S. Constitution (ratified in 1791) states that "no person shall . . . be deprived of life, liberty, or property, without due process of the law."[3] Other laws as well as various court decisions made discrimination against minorities illegal by the early 1900s, at least in theory.[4] But as a practical matter, Congress and various presidents were reluctant to take dramatic action on equal employment issues until the early 1960s. At that point, "they were finally prompted to act primarily as a result of civil unrest among the minorities and women" who eventually became protected by the new equal rights legislation and the agencies created to implement and enforce it.[5]

Equal Pay Act of 1963

The **Equal Pay Act of 1963** (amended in 1972) was one of the first new laws passed. It made it unlawful to discriminate in pay on the basis of sex when jobs involve equal work—equivalent skills, effort, and responsibility—and are performed under similar working conditions. However, differences in pay do not violate the act if the difference is based on a seniority system, a merit system, a system that measures earnings by quantity or quality of production, or a differential based on any factor other than sex.

Title VII of the 1964 Civil Rights Act

What the Law Says

Title VII of the 1964 Civil Rights Act was another of these new laws. Title VII (amended by the 1972 Equal Employment Opportunity Act) says an employer cannot discriminate based on race, color, religion, sex, or national origin. Specifically, it states that it shall be an unlawful employment practice for an employer:[6]

1. *To fail or refuse to hire or to discharge an individual or otherwise to discriminate against any individual* with respect to his or her compensation, terms, conditions, or privileges of employment, because of such individual's race, color, religion, sex, or national origin.
2. *To limit, segregate, or classify his or her employees or applicants for employment* in any way that would deprive or tend to deprive any individual of employment opportunities or otherwise adversely affect his or her status as an employee, because of such individual's race, color, religion, sex, or national origin.

The **Equal Employment Opportunity Commission (EEOC)** was instituted by Title VII. It consists of five members, appointed by the president with the advice and consent of the senate. Each member of the EEOC serves a term of 5 years. The EEOC of course has a staff of thousands to assist it in administering the Civil Rights law in employment settings.

Establishing the EEOC greatly enhanced the federal government's ability to enforce equal employment opportunity laws. The EEOC receives and investigates job discrimination complaints from aggrieved individuals. When it finds reasonable cause that the charges are justified, it attempts (through conciliation) to reach an agreement eliminating all aspects of the discrimination. If this conciliation fails, the EEOC has the power to go directly to court to enforce the law. Under the Equal Employment Opportunity Act of 1972, discrimination charges may be filed by the EEOC on behalf of an aggrieved individual, as well as by the individuals themselves. We explain this procedure in more detail later in this chapter.

Executive Orders

Under executive orders that U.S. presidents issued years ago, most employers who do business with the U.S. government have an obligation beyond that imposed by Title VII to refrain from employment discrimination. Executive Orders 11246 and 11375 don't just ban discrimination; they require that contractors take **affirmative action** to ensure equal employment opportunity (we explain affirmative action later in this chapter). These orders also established the **Office of Federal Contract Compliance Programs (OFCCP),** which is responsible for ensuring the compliance of federal contracts.

Age Discrimination in Employment Act of 1967

The **Age Discrimination in Employment Act (ADEA) of 1967,** as amended, makes it unlawful to discriminate against employees or applicants for employment who are 40 years of age or older, effectively ending most mandatory retirement.[7]

Vocational Rehabilitation Act of 1973

The **Vocational Rehabilitation Act of 1973** requires employers with federal contracts over $2,500 to take affirmative action for the employment of handicapped persons. The act does not require that an unqualified person be hired. It does require that an employer take steps to accommodate a handicapped worker unless doing so imposes an undue hardship on the employer.

Pregnancy Discrimination Act of 1978

Congress passed the **Pregnancy Discrimination Act (PDA)** in 1978 as an amendment to Title VII. The act broadened the definition of sex discrimination to encompass pregnancy, childbirth, or related medical conditions. It prohibits using these for discrimination in hiring, promotion, suspension or discharge, or any other term or condition of employment. Basically, the act says that if an employer offers its employees disability coverage, then pregnancy and childbirth must be treated like any other disability and must be included in the plan as a covered condition.

Pregnancy claims to the EEOC rose about 39% in recent years, while plaintiff victories rose 66%.[8] Progressive human resource thinking notwithstanding, one firm, an auto dealership, recently fired an employee after she told them she was pregnant. The reason? Allegedly "in case I ended up throwing up or cramping in one of their vehicles. They said pregnant women do that sometimes, and I could cause an accident . . ."[9]

Federal Agency Guidelines

The federal agencies charged with ensuring compliance with the aforementioned laws and executive orders issue their own implementing guidelines. The overall purpose of these **federal agency guidelines** is to specify the procedures these agencies recommend employers follow in complying with the equal opportunity laws.

Uniform Guidelines on Employee Selection Procedures

The EEOC, Civil Service Commission, Department of Labor, and Department of Justice have approved detailed, uniform guidelines for employers.[10] These guidelines superceded earlier ones developed by the EEOC alone. They set forth "highly recommended" guidelines regarding matters such as employee relations, record keeping, pre-employment inquiries, and affirmative action programs. The OFCCP has its own *Manual of Guidelines*. The American Psychological Association has published its own (non-legally binding) *Standards for Educational and Psychological Testing*.

Historically, these guidelines have fleshed out the procedures to use in complying with equal employment laws. For example, recall that the ADEA prohibited employers from discriminating against persons over 40 years old because of age. Subsequent EEOC guidelines stated that it was unlawful to discriminate in hiring (or in any way) by giving preference because of age to individuals within the 40-plus age bracket. Thus, if two people apply for the same job, and one is 45 and the other is 55, you may not lawfully turn down the 55-year-old candidate because of his or her age and expect to defend yourself by saying that you hired someone over 40.[11] (Hiring, say, a 53-year-old may be defensible, however.)

Sexual Harassment

Harassment on the basis of sex—sexual harassment—is a violation of Title VII when such conduct has the purpose or effect of substantially interfering with a person's work performance or creating an intimidating, hostile, or offensive work environment. The EEOC's guidelines further assert that employers have a duty to maintain workplaces free of sexual harassment and intimidation. The Civil Rights Act of 1991 added teeth to this by permitting victims of intentional discrimination, including sexual harassment, to have jury trials and to collect compensatory damages for pain and suffering and punitive damages in cases in which the employer acted with "malice or reckless indifference" to the individual's rights.[12]

Sexual harassment laws do not just cover harassment of women by men. They also cover those occasions when women harass men, as well as same-sex harassment. The U.S. Supreme Court held (in *ONCALE*. v. *Sundowner Offshore Services Inc.*) that "same-sex discrimination consisting of same-sex sexual harassment is actionable under Title VII." It said that same-sex subordinates, coworkers, or superiors are liable under the theory that they create a hostile work environment for the employee.[13]

The **Federal Violence Against Women Act of 1994** provides another avenue that women can use to seek relief for violent sexual harassment. It provides that a person "who commits a crime of violence motivated by gender and thus deprives another of her rights shall be liable to the party injured."

The EEOC guidelines define **sexual harassment** as unwelcome sexual advances, requests for sexual favors, and other verbal or physical conduct of a sexual nature that takes place under any of the following conditions:

1. Submission is either explicitly or implicitly a term or condition of an individual's employment.
2. Submission to or rejection of such conduct is the basis for employment decisions affecting such individual.
3. Such conduct has the purpose or effect of unreasonably interfering with an individual's work performance or creating an intimidating, hostile, or offensive work environment.

Proving Sexual Harassment

There are three main ways an employee can prove sexual harassment.

Quid Pro Quo

The most direct way is to prove that rejecting a supervisor's advances adversely affected what the EEOC calls a "tangible employment action" such as hiring, firing, promotion, demotion, undesirable assignment, benefits, compensation, and/or work assignment. Thus in one case the employee showed that continued job success and advancement were dependent on her agreeing to her supervisor's sexual demands.

Hostile Environment Created by Supervisors

It is not always necessary to show that the harassment had tangible consequences such as a demotion or termination. For example, in one case, the court found that a male supervisor's sexual harassment had substantially affected a female employee's emotional and psychological ability to the point that she felt she had to quit her job. Even though no direct threats or promises were made in exchange for sexual advances, the fact that the advances interfered with the woman's performance and created an offensive work environment were enough to prove that sexual harassment had occurred.

Distinguishing between harassment and flirting can be tricky. The courts do not interpret as sexual harassment any sexual relationships that arise during the course of employment but that do not have a substantial effect on that employment. In one decision, for instance, the U.S. Supreme Court held that sexual harassment law doesn't cover ordinary "intersexual flirtation." In his ruling, Justice Scalia said courts must carefully distinguish between "simple teasing" and truly abusive behavior.[14]

Hostile Environment Created by Coworkers or Nonemployees

Advances do not have to be made by the person's supervisor to qualify as sexual harassment: An employee's coworkers or customers can cause the employer to be held responsible for sexual harassment. In one case, the court held that a sexually provocative uniform that the employer required led to lewd comments by customers toward the employee. When she complained that she would no longer wear the uniform, she was fired. Because the employer could not show that there was a job-related necessity for requiring such a uniform and because the uniform was required only for female employees, the court ruled that the employer, in effect, was responsible for the sexually harassing behavior. Such abhorrent client behavior is more likely when the clients are in positions of power, and when they have less reason to think they'll be penalized.[15]

Court Decisions

The U.S. Supreme Court used the *Meritor Savings Bank, FSB* v. *Vinson* case to broadly endorse the EEOC's guidelines on sexual harassment. Two more recent U.S. Supreme Court decisions further clarified the law on sexual harassment.

In the first, *Burlington Industries* v. *Ellerth*, the employee accused her supervisor of *quid pro quo* harassment. She said her boss propositioned and threatened her with demotion if she did not respond. The threats were not carried out, and she was in fact promoted. In the second case, *Faragher* v. *City of Boca Raton,* the employee accused the employer of condoning a hostile work environment: She said she quit her lifeguard job after repeated taunts from other lifeguards. The Court ruled in favor of the employees in both cases.

The Court's decisions in these cases have several important implications for employers.

First, the decisions make it clear that in a *quid pro quo* case it is *not* necessary for the employee to have suffered tangible job action (such as being demoted) to win the case.

Second, the decisions spell out an important defense against harassment suits. The Court said that an employer could defend itself against sexual harassment liability by showing two things. First, it had to show "that the employer exercised care to prevent and correct promptly any sexually harassing behavior." Second, the employer had to demonstrate that the plaintiff "unreasonably failed to take advantage of any preventive or corrective opportunities provided by the employer." The Supreme Court specifically said that the employee's failing to use formal organizational reporting systems would satisfy the second component.

Sensible employers promptly took steps to show that they did take "reasonable care." For example, they promulgated strong harassment policies, trained managers and employees regarding their responsibilities for complying with these policies, instituted reporting processes, investigated charges promptly, and then took corrective actions promptly, as required.[16]

Causes

Sexual harassment is more likely to occur under certain circumstances. The most important factor is a permissive social climate, one where employees conclude there's a risk to victims for complaining, that complaints won't be taken seriously, and that there's a lack of sanctions against offenders.[17] Minority women are particularly at risk. One study found "women experienced more sexual harassment than men, minorities experienced more ethnic harassment than whites, and minority women experienced more harassment overall than majority men, minority men, and majority women."[18]

Most people probably assume that sexual motives drive sexual harassment, but that's not always so. Studies suggest that *gender harassment* is a common form of sexual harassment. **Gender harassment** is "a form of hostile environment harassment that appears to be motivated by hostility toward individuals who violate gender ideals." In one case, for instance, her bosses told a high-performing female accountant to "walk more femininely [and] dress more femininely."[19]

Adding to the causes is the unfortunate fact that most sexual harassment victims don't sue or complain. Instead, either due to fear of losing one's job or a sense that complaining is futile, they quit or try to avoid their harassers. "The few women who do formally complain do so only after encountering frequent, severe sexual harassment; at that point, considerable damage may have already occurred."[20] The harassers themselves sometimes don't even realize that their abominable behavior is harassing or offending others. Sexual harassment training and policies can reduce these problems.

Several psychological and practical considerations complicate the problem. For example, women and men don't view harassment-related facts in the same way. "Women perceive a broader range of socio-sexual behaviors as harassing," particularly when those behaviors involve "hostile work environment harassment, derogatory attitudes toward women, dating pressure, or physical sexual contact."[21] So, what is harassment to a woman may be misperceived as innocent behavior by a man.

What the Manager/Employer Should Do

Given this, employers should do two things: They should take steps (such as issuing a strong policy statement) to ensure harassment does not take place. Second, once being apprised of such a situation, they should take immediate corrective action, even if the offending party is a nonemployee, once they know (or should know) of harassing conduct.[22] (See the *HR in Practice* box for specific steps.) The aims are to reduce or eliminate instances of sexual harassment and to minimize the employer's liability should such claims arise.

Note however that taking what courts call "reasonable" steps to prevent harassment may not be enough. This is because a sexual harassment compliance procedure may be reasonable in the legal sense, but not so reasonable to the employees who must use it. In one study, researchers surveyed about 6,000 employees in the U.S. military. Their findings made it clear that reporting incidents of harassment often triggered retaliation and could harm the victim "in terms of lower job satisfaction and greater psychological distress." Under such conditions, it's no wonder that for many of these employees, the most "reasonable" thing to do was nothing, and to avoid reporting. Managers who take preventing sexual harassment seriously therefore must ensure that the organization's climate (including management's real willingness to eradicate harassment), and not just its written rules and procedures, supports employees who feel harassed.[23]

What the Employee Can Do

An employee who believes he or she was sexually harassed can also take several steps to address the problem. Prior to taking action, the employee should understand how courts define sexual harassment. For example, "hostile environment" sexual harassment generally means that the discriminatory intimidation, insults, and ridicule that permeated the workplace were sufficiently severe or pervasive to alter the conditions of employment. Courts in these cases look at several things. These include whether the discriminatory conduct is frequent or severe; whether it is

WHAT EMPLOYERS SHOULD DO TO MINIMIZE LIABILITY IN SEXUAL HARASSMENT CLAIMS

1. Take all complaints about harassment seriously.

2. Issue a strong policy statement condemning such behavior. The EEOC's standards state that an effective antiharassment policy should contain a clear explanation of the prohibited conduct; assurance of protection against retaliation for employees who make complaints or provide information related to such complaints; a clearly described complaint process that provides confidentiality and accessible avenues of complaint as well as prompt, thorough, and impartial investigations; and clear assurance that the employer will take immediate and appropriate corrective action where harassment has occurred.[24]

3. Inform all employees about the policy prohibiting sexual harassment and of their rights under the policy.

4. Develop and implement a complaint procedure.

5. Establish a management response system that includes an immediate reaction and investigation by senior management. The likelihood of employer liability is lessened considerably when the employer's response is "adequate" and "reasonably calculated to prevent future harassment."[25]

6. Commence management training sessions with supervisors and managers, so as to increase their awareness of the issues. Then, as with all training, make sure the sexual harassment training is having the desired effect. In one study, trainees were actually *less* (not more) likely than were other groups to perceive an action as sexual harassment, less willing to report sexual harassment, and more likely to blame the victim. The program had focused too heavily on harassment's legal aspects, and not enough on its ethical and moral implications.[26]

7. Discipline managers and employees involved in sexual harassment.

8. Keep thorough records of complaints, investigations, and actions taken.

9. Conduct exit interviews that uncover any complaints and that acknowledge by signature the reasons for leaving.

10. Re-publish the sexual harassment policy periodically (see Figure 2.1).

11. Encourage upward communication through periodic written attitude surveys, hotlines, and other feedback procedures to discover employees' feelings concerning any evidence of sexual harassment.[27]

FIGURE 2.1   What to Cover in a Sexual Harassment Policy

The EEOC says the antiharassment policy should contain a clear explanation of the prohibited conduct; assurance of protection against retaliation for employees who make complaints or provide information related to such complaints; a clearly described complaint process that provides confidentiality and accessible avenues of complaint as well as prompt, thorough, and impartial investigations; and clear assurance that the employer will take immediate and appropriate corrective action where harassment has occurred.

Source: www.eeoc.gov/types/sexual_harrasment.html, accessed May 6, 2007.

physically threatening or humiliating, or a mere offensive utterance; and whether it unreasonably interferes with an employee's work performance. They also look at whether an employee welcomed the conduct, or instead immediately made it clear that the conduct was unwelcome, undesirable, or offensive. The steps an employee can take include:

1. File a verbal contemporaneous complaint or protest with the harasser and the harasser's boss stating that the unwanted overtures should cease because the conduct is unwelcome.
2. Write a letter to the accused. This may be a polite, low-key letter that does three things: provides a detailed statement of the facts as the writer sees them, describes his or her feelings and what damage the writer thinks has been done, and states that he or she would like to request that the future relationship be on a purely professional basis. Deliver this letter in person, with a witness if necessary.
3. If the unwelcome conduct does not cease, file verbal and written reports regarding the unwelcome conduct and unsuccessful efforts to get it to stop with the harasser's manager and/or the human resource director.
4. If the letters and appeals to the employer do not suffice, the accuser should turn to the local office of the EEOC to file the necessary claim.
5. If the harassment is of a serious nature, the employee can also consult an attorney about suing the harasser for assault and battery, intentional infliction of emotional distress, and injunctive relief and to recover compensatory and punitive damages.

Selected Court Decisions Regarding Equal Employment Opportunity (EEO)

Several early court decisions helped to form the interpretive foundation for EEO laws such as those involving sexual harassment. We summarize some important decisions in this section.

Griggs v. Duke Power Company

Griggs v. Duke Power Company (1971) was a landmark case because the Supreme Court used it to define unfair discrimination. In this case, a suit was brought against the Duke Power Company on behalf of Willie Griggs, an applicant for a job as a coal handler. The company required its coal handlers to be high-school graduates. Griggs claimed that this requirement was illegally discriminatory because it wasn't related to success on the job and because it resulted in more blacks than whites being rejected for these jobs.

Griggs won the case. The decision of the Court was unanimous, and in his written opinion, Chief Justice Burger laid out three crucial guidelines affecting equal employment legislation. First, the court ruled that discrimination on the part of the employer need not be overt; in other words, the employer does not have to be shown to have intentionally discriminated against the employee or applicant—it need only be shown that discrimination took place. Second, the court held that an employment practice (in this case requiring the high-school diploma) must be shown to be *job related* if it has an unequal impact on members of a **protected class.** In the words of Justice Burger:

> The act proscribes not only overt discrimination but also practices that are fair in form, but discriminatory in operation. The touchstone is business necessity. If an employment practice which operates to exclude Negroes cannot be shown to be related to job performance the practice is prohibited.[28]

Third, Burger's opinion clearly placed the burden of proof on the employer to show that the hiring practice is job related. Thus, the *employer* must show that the employment practice (in this case, requiring a high-school diploma) is needed to perform the job satisfactorily if it has a disparate impact on (unintentionally discriminates against) members of a protected class.

Albemarle Paper Company v. Moody

In the *Griggs* case, the Supreme Court decided that a screening tool (such as a test) had to be job related or valid—that is, performance on the test must be related to performance on the job. The 1975 *Albemarle* case is important because it helped to clarify what the employer had to do to prove that the test or other screening tools are related to or predict performance on the job. For example, the Court ruled that before using a test to screen job candidates, the performance standards for the job in question should be clear and unambiguous, so the employer can identify which employees were performing better than others (and thus whether the screening tools were effective).

In arriving at its decision, the Court also cited the EEOC guidelines concerning acceptable selection procedures and made these guidelines the "law of the land."[29]

The Civil Rights Act of 1991

Subsequent Supreme Court rulings in the 1980s actually had the effect of limiting the protection of women and minority groups under equal employment laws; this prompted congress to pass a new Civil Rights Act. The first President George Bush signed the **Civil Rights Act of 1991 (CRA 1991)** into law in November 1991. The effect of CRA 1991 was to roll back the clock to where it stood before the 1980s decisions, and in some respects to place even more responsibility on employers.

First, CRA 1991 addressed the issue of *burden of proof.* Today, after CRA 1991, the process of filing and responding to a discrimination charge goes something like this. The plaintiff (say, a rejected applicant) demonstrates that an employment practice (such as a test) has a disparate (or "adverse") impact on a particular group. (**Disparate impact** "means that an employer engages in an employment practice or policy that has a greater adverse impact [effect] on the members of a protected group under Title VII than on other employees, regardless of intent."[30]) Requiring a college degree for a job would have an adverse impact on some minority groups, for instance. Disparate impact claims do not require proof of discriminatory intent. Instead, the plaintiff must show two things. First, he or she must show that a significant disparity exists between the proportion of (say) women in the available labor pool and the proportion hired. Second, he or she must show that an apparently neutral employment practice, such as word-of-mouth advertising or a requirement that the job holder "be able to lift 100 pounds," is causing the disparity.[31]

Then, once the plaintiff shows such disparate impact, the *employer* has the *burden of proving* that the challenged practice is job related for the position in question. For example, the employer has to show that lifting 100 pounds is actually required for the position in question, and that the business could not run efficiently without the requirement—that it is a business necessity.

CRA 1991 also makes it easier to sue for *money damages*. It provides that an employee who is claiming *intentional discrimination* (which is called **disparate treatment**) can ask for both compensatory damages and punitive damages, if he or she can show the employer engaged in discrimination "with malice or reckless indifference to the federally protected rights of an aggrieved individual." (See also the *Global Issues in HR* box.)

Finally, CRA 1991 also states:

> An unlawful employment practice is established when the complaining party demonstrates that race, color, religion, sex, or national origin was a motivating factor for any employment practice, even though other factors also motivated the practice.[32]

In other words, an employer generally can't avoid liability by proving it would have taken the same action—such as terminating someone—even without the discriminatory motive. If there is any such motive, the practice may be unlawful.

The Americans with Disabilities Act

What Is the ADA?

The **Americans with Disabilities Act (ADA)** of 1990 prohibits employment discrimination against qualified disabled individuals.[33] It aims to reduce or eliminate serious problems of discrimination against disabled individuals. And, it requires that employers make "reasonable accommodations" for physical or mental limitations, unless doing so imposes an "undue hardship" on the business.

The Act's pivotal terms are important in understanding its impact. They provide that "impairment" includes any physiological disorder or condition, cosmetic disfigurement, or anatomical loss affecting one or more of several body systems, or any mental or psychological disorder.[34] However, the act doesn't list specific disabilities. Instead, the EEOC's implementing regulations provide that an individual is disabled if he or she has a physical or mental impairment that substantially limits one or more major life activities. On the other hand, the act does set forth certain conditions that are not to be regarded as disabilities, including homosexuality, bisexuality, voyeurism, compulsive gambling, pyromania, and certain disorders resulting from the person's currently using illegal drugs.[35]

Simply being disabled does not qualify someone for a job, of course. Instead, the act prohibits discrimination against qualified individuals—those who, with (or without) a reasonable accommodation, can carry out the essential functions of the job. This means that the individual must have the requisite skills, educational background, and

APPLYING EQUAL EMPLOYMENT LAW IN A GLOBAL SETTING

Globalization complicates the task of complying with equal employment laws. For example, Dell recently announced big additions to its workforce in India. Are U.S. citizens working for Dell abroad covered by U.S. equal opportunity laws? Are non-U.S. citizens covered? Are non-U.S. citizens working for Dell in the U.S. covered? In practice, the answers depend on U.S. laws, international treaties, and the laws of the countries in which the U.S. firms are doing

business. For example, the Civil Rights Act of 1991 specifically covers U.S. employees of U.S. firms working abroad. But in practice, the laws of the country in which the U.S. citizen is working may take precedence. Similarly, one expert argued that U.S. courts are "little help in overseas investigations, because few foreign nations cooperate with the intrusive enforcement of U.S. civil law."[36] Table 2.1 provides guidelines for when U.S. equal employment law applies.[37]

TABLE 2.1	Guidelines That Specify When U.S. Employment Discrimination Laws (Title VII, ADEA, ADA) Apply to International Employers
No.	*Guidelines*
1.	U.S. employment discrimination laws apply to jobs located inside the United States when the employer is a U.S. entity and the employee is authorized to work in the United States.
2.	U.S. employment discrimination laws apply to jobs located inside the United States when the employer is a U.S. entity and the employee is *not* a U.S. citizen but is legally authorized to work in the United States. Depending on the jurisdiction, U.S. laws may apply to workers who are *not* authorized to work in the United States, although the remedies they receive may be limited.
3.	U.S. employment discrimination laws *do not* apply to jobs located inside the United States when the employer is a foreign entity exempted by a treaty, even though the employee is authorized to work in the United States.
4.	U.S. employment discrimination laws apply to jobs located inside the United States when the employer is a foreign entity *not* exempted by a treaty and the employee is authorized to work in the United States.
5.	U.S. employment discrimination laws *do not* apply to jobs located outside the United States when the employer is a foreign entity, even though the employee is a U.S. citizen.
6.	U.S. employment discrimination laws *do not* apply to jobs located outside the United States even if the employer is a U.S. entity, if the employees are foreign citizens.
7.	U.S. employment discrimination laws apply to jobs located outside the United States when the employer is a U.S. entity and the employee is a U.S. citizen, if compliance with U.S. laws would *not* violate foreign laws.
8.	U.S. employment discrimination laws *do not* apply to jobs located outside the United States when the employer is a U.S. entity and the employee is a U.S. citizen, if compliance with U.S. laws would violate foreign laws.

Source: Richard Posthuma et al., "Applying U.S. Employment Discrimination Laws to International Employees: Advice for Scientists and Practitioners," *Personnel Psychology*, 2006 (59) p. 710. Reprinted by permission of Wiley Blackwell.

experience to do the essential functions of the position. A job function is essential when, for instance, it is the reason the position exists, or because the function is so highly specialized that the person doing the job is hired for his or her expertise or ability to perform that particular function.[38]

Reasonable Accommodation

If the individual can't perform the job as currently structured, the employer is required to make a reasonable accommodation, unless doing so would present an undue hardship. *Reasonable accommodation* might include re-designing the job, modifying work schedules, or modifying or acquiring equipment or other devices to assist the person in performing the job. Court cases illustrate what "reasonable accommodation" means. For example, a Wal-Mart door greeter was diagnosed with and treated for back problems. When she returned to work she asked her employer if she could sit on a stool while on duty. The employer rejected her request, contending that standing was an essential part of the greeter's job. She sued, but the federal district court agreed with the employer that the door greeters must act in an "aggressively hospitable manner," which can't be done sitting on a stool.[39]

The ADA in Practice

By most measures, workplace disabilities are on the rise, and employers need to accommodate increasing numbers of heavier and disabled employees.[40] It's thus not surprising that ADA complaints continue to flood the courts.

However, employers prevailed in about 96% of federal circuit court ADA decisions in one recent year. A main reason is that employees are failing to show that they are disabled and qualified to do the job.[41] The employee has to establish that he or she has a disability that fits under the ADA's definition. Doing so is more complicated than proving that one is a particular age, race, or gender. The types of disabilities alleged in ADA charges have been somewhat surprising. Mental disabilities now account for the greatest number of claims brought under the ADA.[42] Furthermore, the ADA does protect employees with intellectual disabilities, including those with IQs below 70–75.[43]

A U.S. Supreme Court decision typifies what plaintiffs face. An assembly-line worker sued Toyota, arguing that carpal tunnel syndrome and tendonitis prevented her from doing her job (*Toyota Motor Manufacturing of Kentucky, Inc.* v. *Williams*). The U.S. Supreme Court ruled that the ADA covers carpal tunnel syndrome and tendonitis if her impairments affect not only her job performance but her daily living activities too. Here, the employee admitted that she could perform personal tasks and chores such as washing her face, brushing her teeth, tending her flower garden, and fixing breakfast and doing laundry. The court said the disability must be central to the employee's daily living (not just job) to qualify under the ADA. The court will therefore look at each case (for instance, of carpal tunnel syndrome) individually.[44]

Many other judgments similarly denied the plaintiff's claim. A federal judge held that Home Depot did not violate the ADA by barring a totally deaf worker from receiving training to operate a forklift. The firm's policies prohibit those who can't hear store associates' warnings from holding such positions.[45] On the other hand, one

U.S. Circuit Court of Appeals held that punctuality was not an essential job function for a laboratory assistant who was habitually tardy. (The court decided he could perform the job's 7 1/2 hours of data entry even if he arrived late.[46]) And, Wal-Mart had to reinstate hearing-impaired workers and pay a $750,000 fine for discrimination under the ADA.[47]

Legal Obligations

The ADA imposes numerous legal obligations on employers. These include (but are not limited to) the following:

- Employers may not make preemployment inquiries about a person's disability, although employers may ask questions about the person's ability to perform specific job functions. The timing and nature of any offer are important. The central issue is this: In the event the hiring employer rescinds an offer after the medical exam, the applicant must be able to identify the specific reason for the rejection. For example, in one case, the courts found that American Airlines had violated the ADA by not making a "real" offer to three candidates before requiring them to take their medical exams, because American still hadn't checked their background references. In this case, the medical exams showed the candidates had HIV and American rescinded their offers, thus violating the ADA.[48]
- Employers should review job application forms, interview procedures, and job descriptions for potentially discriminatory items, and identify the essential functions of the jobs in question.
- Employers must make a reasonable accommodation, unless doing so would result in undue hardship.

Implications for Managers

The manager should also keep several practical implications in mind when dealing with ADA-related matters.[49] First, courts will tend to define "disabilities" quite *narrowly*. Employers may therefore require that the employee provide documentation of the disorder and assess what effect that disorder has on the employee's job performance. Employers should also ask questions such as: Does the employee have a disability that substantially limits a major life activity? Is the employee qualified to do the job? Can the employee perform the essential functions of the job? Can any reasonable accommodation be provided without creating an undue hardship on the employer?[50]

Second, it's clear from these decisions that employers generally "do not need to allow *misconduct or erratic performance* (including absences and tardiness), even if that behavior is linked to the disability."[51]

Third, the employer does not have to *create a new job* for the disabled worker nor reassign that person to a light-duty position for an indefinite period, unless such a position exists.[52]

Fourth, one expert advises, "*don't treat employees* as if they are disabled." If they can control their conditions (for instance, through medication), they usually won't be considered disabled. However, if they are treated as disabled by their employers (for instance, with respect to the jobs they're assigned), they'll normally be "regarded as" disabled and protected under the ADA.[53]

Improving Productivity through HRIS: Accommodating Disabled Employees

Technological innovations make it easier today for employers to accommodate disabled employees. For example, many employees with mobility impairments benefit from voice recognition software that allows them to input information into their computers and interactively communicate (for instance, via e-mail) without touching a keyboard. Others use alternative input devices (such as sticks held in the mouth) to strike keyboard keys. Special typing aids including word prediction software suggest words based on context and on just one or two letters typed.[54] The new Firefox Web browser incorporates special IBM software that enables people to use the keyboard arrows rather than the mouse to access pull-down menus, aiding some disabled people.[55]

Employees with hearing and/or speech impairments benefit from the teletypewriter, which lets people communicate by typing and reading messages on a keyboard connected to a telephone line. Real-time translation captioning enables them to participate in lectures and meetings. Vibrating text pagers let them know when messages arrive. Employees with vision impairments benefit from add-on computer devices that, among other things, allow adjustments in font size, display color, and screen magnification for specific portions of the computer screen. Voice recognition software transcription devices transcribe and speak out the written word for the employee. Special word processor software provides spoken instructions to aid the employee. Arizona had IBM Global Services create a disability-friendly Web site, "Arizona@YourService," to help link prospective employees and others to various agencies.[56]

State and Local Equal Employment Opportunity Laws

In addition to the federal laws, all states and many local governments also prohibit employment discrimination.

In most cases, the effect of the state and local laws is to further restrict employers regarding their treatment of job applicants and employees. In many cases, they cover employers that are not covered by federal legislation (such as those with fewer than 15 employees). Similarly, some local governments extend the protection of age discrimination laws to young people as well as to those over 40. For instance, it would be illegal to advertise for "mature" applicants because that might discourage some teenagers from applying.

State and local equal employment opportunity agencies (often called *human resources commissions, commissions on human relations,* or *fair employment commissions*) also play a role in the equal employment compliance process. When the EEOC receives a discrimination charge, it usually defers it for a limited time to the state and local agencies that have comparable jurisdiction. Then, if satisfactory remedies are not achieved, the charges are referred back to the EEOC for resolution.

Summary

Table 2.2 summarizes these and selected other equal employment opportunity legislation, executive orders, and agency guidelines.

TABLE 2.2	Summary of Important Equal Employment Opportunity Actions
Action	**What It Does**
Title VII of 1964 Civil Rights Act, as amended	Bars discrimination because of race, color, religion, sex, or national origin; instituted EEOC
Executive orders	Prohibit employment discrimination by employers with federal contracts of more than $10,000 (and their subcontractors); established office of federal compliance; require affirmative action programs
Federal agency guidelines	Indicate policy covering discrimination based on sex, national origin, and religion, as well as on employee selection procedures; for example, require validation of tests
Supreme Court decisions: *Griggs* v. *Duke Power Company, Albemarle Paper Company* v. *Moody*	Ruled that job requirements must be related to job success; that discrimination need not be overt to be proved; that the burden of proof is on the employer to prove the qualification is valid
Equal Pay Act of 1963	Requires equal pay for men and women for performing similar work
Age Discrimination in Employment Act of 1967	Prohibits discriminating against a person 40 or over in any area of employment because of age
State and local laws	Often cover organizations too small to be covered by federal laws
Vocational Rehabilitation Act of 1973	Requires affirmative action to employ and promote qualified handicapped persons and prohibits discrimination against handicapped persons
Pregnancy Discrimination Act of 1978	Prohibits discrimination in employment against pregnant women, or related conditions
Vietnam Era Veterans' Readjustment Assistance Act of 1974	Requires affirmative action in employment for veterans of the Vietnam War era
Wards Cove v. *Atonio,* and *Patterson* v. *McLean Credit Union*	Made it more difficult to prove a case of unlawful discrimination against an employer
Martin v. *Wilks*	Allowed consent degrees to be attacked and could have had a chilling effect on certain affirmative action programs
Americans with Disabilities Act of 1990	Strengthens the need for most employers to make reasonable accommodations for disabled employees at work; prohibits discrimination
Civil Rights Act of 1991	Reverses *Wards Cove, Patterson,* and *Martin* decisions; places burden of proof back on employer and permits compensatory and punitive money damages for discrimination

DEFENSES AGAINST DISCRIMINATION ALLEGATIONS

What Is Adverse Impact?

To understand how employers defend themselves against employment discrimination claims, we should first briefly review some basic legal theory.

Adverse impact plays a central role in discriminatory practice allegations. Under the Civil Rights Act of 1991, a person who believes he or she has been unintentionally discriminated against need only establish a prima facie case of discrimination; this means showing that the employer's selection procedures had an adverse impact on a protected minority group. *Adverse impact* "refers to the total employment process that results in a significantly higher percentage of a protected group in the candidate population being rejected for employment, placement, or promotion."[57] "Employers may not institute an employment practice that causes a disparate impact on a particular class of people unless they can show that the practice is job related and necessary."[58]

What does this mean? If a minority or other protected group applicant for the job feels he or she has been discriminated against, the applicant need only show that the selection procedures resulted in an adverse impact on his or her minority group. (There are several ways to do this, for example, by showing that 80% of the white applicants passed the test, but only 20% of the black applicants passed; if this is the case, a black applicant has a prima facie case proving adverse impact.) Then, once the employee has proved his or her point, the burden of proof shifts to the employer. It becomes the employer's task to prove that its test, application blank, interview, or the like is a valid predictor of performance on the job, and that it was applied fairly and equitably to both minorities and non-minorities.

(By the way, don't be lulled into thinking that such cases are ancient history. For example, a U.S. Appeals Court recently upheld a $3.4 million jury verdict against Dial Corp. Dial allegedly rejected 52 women for entry-level jobs at a meat processing plant because they failed strength tests, although strength was not a job requirement).[59]

Discrimination law distinguishes between disparate *treatment* and disparate *impact*. *Disparate treatment* means intentional discrimination. It ". . . requires no more than a finding that women (or protected minority group members) were intentionally treated differently . . . because of their gender (or minority status)." *Disparate impact* claims do not require proof of discriminatory intent. Instead, the plaintiff must show that there is a significant disparity between the proportion of (say) women in the available labor pool and the proportion hired, and that there's an apparently neutral employment practice (such as word-of-mouth advertising) causing the disparity.[60] Proving that there was a business necessity for the practice is usually the defense for disparate impact claims.

Bringing a Case of Discrimination: Summary

Assume that an employer turns down a member of a protected group for a job based on a test score (or some other employment practice, such as interview questions or application blank responses). Further assume that the person believes that he or she was discriminated against due to being in a protected class and decides to sue the employer.

All he or she has to do is show (to the court's satisfaction) that the employer's test had an adverse impact on members of his or her minority group. Then, the burden of proof shifts to the employer, which then has the burden of defending itself against the charges of discrimination.

There are then two defenses that the employer can use: the **bona fide occupational qualification (BFOQ)** defense and the business necessity defense. Either can be used to justify an employment practice that has been shown to have an adverse impact on the members of a minority group. (A third defense is that the decision was made on the basis of legitimate nondiscriminatory reasons, such as poor performance, having nothing to do with the alleged prohibited discrimination.)

Bona Fide Occupational Qualification

One approach an employer can use to defend against charges of discrimination is to claim that the employment practice is a bona fide occupational qualification for performing the job. Specifically, Title VII provides that

> it should not be an unlawful employment practice for an employer to hire an employee . . . on the basis of religion, sex, or national origin in those certain instances where religion, sex, or national origin is a bona fide occupational qualification reasonably necessary to the normal operation of that particular business or enterprise.

For example, an employer can use age as a BFOQ to defend itself against a disparate treatment (intentional discrimination) charge when federal requirements impose a compulsory age limit, such as when the Federal Aviation Agency sets a ceiling of age 65 for pilots. Actors required for youthful or elderly roles or persons used to advertise or promote the sales of products designed for youthful or elderly consumers suggest other instances when age may be a BFOQ, although the courts set the bar high: The reason for the discrimination must go to the essence of the business.

Yet Supreme Court decisions such as *Western Airlines, Inc.* v. *Criswell* seem to be narrowing BFOQ exceptions under ADEA. Here the Court held that the airline could not impose a mandatory retirement age (of 60) for flight engineers, even though they could for pilots. The BFOQ defense is not explicitly allowed for race or color.

Business Necessity

The **business necessity** defense requires showing that there is an overriding business purpose for the discriminatory practice and that the practice is therefore acceptable.

It's not easy to prove that a practice is a business necessity. The Supreme Court has made it clear that business necessity does not encompass such matters as avoiding inconvenience, or expense. The Second Circuit Court of Appeals held that *business necessity* means an "irresistible demand" and that to be retained the practice "must not only directly foster safety and efficiency," but also be essential to these goals.[61]

Thus, it is not easy to prove that a practice is required for business necessity. For example, an employer cannot generally discharge employees whose wages have been garnished merely because garnishment (requiring the employer to divert part of the person's wages to pay his or her debts) creates an inconvenience for the employer. On the other hand, many employers have used this defense successfully. Thus, in *Spurlock v. United Airlines,* a minority candidate sued United Airlines, stating that its requirements that a pilot candidate have 500 flight hours and a college degree were unfairly discriminatory. The Court agreed that these requirements did have an adverse impact on members of the person's minority group. However, the Court held that in light of the cost of the training program and the tremendous human and economic risks involved in hiring unqualified candidates, the selection standards were required by business necessity and were job related.[62]

Attempts by employers to show that their selection tests or other screening practices are valid represent one example of the business necessity defense. Where such validity can be established, the courts have often supported the use of the test or other practice as a business necessity. Used in this context, the word *validity* means the degree to which the test or other employment practice is related to or predicts performance on the job. We discuss validation in Chapter 4.

ILLUSTRATIVE DISCRIMINATORY EMPLOYMENT PRACTICES

A Note on What You Can and Cannot Do

In this section, we present several illustrations of what managers can and cannot do under equal employment laws. But before proceeding, keep in mind that most federal laws, such as Title VII, do not expressly ban preemployment questions about an applicant's race, color, religion, sex, age, or national origin. Similarly:

> With the exception of personnel policies calling for outright discrimination against the members of some protected group, it is not really the intrinsic nature of an employer's personnel policies or practices that the courts object to. Instead, it is the result of applying a policy or practice in a particular way or in a particular context that leads to an adverse impact on some protected group.[63]

For example, it is not illegal to ask a job candidate about her marital status (although at first glance such a question might seem discriminatory). You can ask such a question as long as you can show either that you do not discriminate or that the practice can be defended as a BFOQ or business necessity.

In other words, illustrative inquiries and practices such as those summarized on the next few pages are not illegal per se. But, in practice, there are two good reasons to avoid such questionable practices. First, although federal law may not bar such questions, many state and local laws do. Second, the EEOC has said that it disapproves of such practices as asking women their marital status or applicants their age. Employers who use such practices thus increase their chances of having to defend themselves against charges of discriminatory employment practices.

Recruitment

Word of Mouth

You cannot rely on word-of-mouth dissemination of information about job opportunities when your workforce is all (or substantially all) white or all members of some other class such as all female, all Hispanic, and so on. Doing so might reduce the likelihood that others will become aware of the jobs and thus apply for them.

Misleading Information

It is unlawful to give false or misleading information to members of any group or to fail to advise them of work opportunities and the procedures for obtaining them.

Help Wanted Ads

"Help wanted—male" and "Help wanted—female" advertising classifieds are violations of laws forbidding sex discrimination in employment unless sex is a BFOQ for the job advertised.[64] Also, you cannot advertise in any way that suggests that applicants are being discriminated against because of their age. For example, you cannot advertise for a "young" man or woman.

Selection Standards

Educational Requirements

An educational requirement may be held illegal when (1) it can be shown that minority groups are less likely to possess the educational qualifications (such as a high school diploma), and (2) such qualifications are also not job related. Unnecessary prerequisites (such as requiring a high school diploma where one is not required to perform the job) reportedly remains a problem today.[65]

Tests

According to former Chief Justice Burger:

> Nothing in the [Title VII] act precludes the use of testing or measuring procedures; obviously they are useful. What Congress has forbidden is giving these devices and mechanisms controlling force unless they are demonstrating a *reasonable measure of job performance.*

Tests that disproportionately screen out minorities or women and are not job related are deemed unlawful by the courts. But remember that a test or other selection standard that screens out a disproportionate number of minorities or women is not *by itself* sufficient to prove that the test *unfairly* discriminates. It must also be shown that the test's or other screening device's/results are not job related.

Preference to Relatives

You cannot give preference to relatives of your current employees with respect to employment opportunities if your current employees are substantially nonminority.

Height, Weight, and Physical Characteristics

Maximum weight rules for employees don't usually trigger adverse legal rulings. Few applicants or employees can demonstrate weight-based disability (in other words, that they are 100% above their ideal weight and there is a physiological or psychological cause for their obesity). Few are thus entitled to reasonable accommodations under the ADA. However, some minority groups have a higher incidence of obesity, so employers must ensure that their weight rules aren't adversely impacting those groups.

Managers still must be vigilant against stigmatizing obese people. Studies leave little doubt that obese individuals are less likely to be hired, less likely to receive promotions, more likely to get less desirable sales assignments, and more likely to receive poor customer service as customers, for instance.[66]

Health Questions

Under the ADA, "employers are generally prohibited from asking questions about applicants' medical history or requiring preemployment physical examinations." However, such questions and exams can be used once the job offer has been extended to determine that the applicant can safely perform the job.[67]

Arrest Records

You cannot ask about or use a person's arrest record to disqualify him or her automatically for a position because there is always a presumption of innocence until proof of guilt. In addition, arrest records in general have not been shown valid for predicting job performance, and a higher percentage of minorities than nonminorities have been arrested.

Application Forms

Employment applications generally shouldn't contain questions pertaining, for instance, to applicants' disabilities, workers' compensation history, age, arrest record, marital status, or U.S. citizenship. Personal information required for legitimate tax or benefit reasons (such as who to contact in case of emergency) are best collected after the person has been hired.[68] Note that while equal employment laws discourage employers from asking for such information, no such laws prohibit the applicants from providing such information. One study examined 107 resumes from Australian managerial applicants. It found that many provided this sort of information, such as regarding marital status, ethnicity, age, and gender.[69]

Sample Discriminatory Promotion, Transfer, and Layoff Procedures

Fair employment laws protect not just job applicants but current employees as well.[70] Therefore, any employment practices regarding pay, promotion, termination, discipline, or benefits that (1) are applied differently to different classes of persons (2) have the effect of adversely affecting members of a protected group and (3) cannot be shown to be required as a BFOQ or business necessity may be held to be illegally discriminatory. For example, the EEOC issued an enforcement guidance making it clear that employers may not discriminate against employees in connection with their benefits plans.[71]

Uniforms

When it comes to discriminatory uniforms and suggestive attire, courts have frequently sided with the employee. For example, requiring female employees (such as waitresses) to wear sexually suggestive attire as a condition of employment has also been ruled as violating Title VII in many cases.[72]

THE EEOC ENFORCEMENT PROCESS

Processing a Charge

File Claim

The process begins with someone filing a claim. Under CRA 1991, the discrimination claim must be filed within 300 days (when there is a similar state law) or 180 days (where there is no similar state law) after the alleged incident took place (two years for the Equal Pay Act). The filing must be in writing and under oath, by (or on behalf of) either the aggrieved person or by a member of the EEOC who has reasonable cause to believe that a violation occurred. In practice the EEOC typically defers a person's charge to the relevant state or local regulatory agency; if the latter waives jurisdiction or cannot obtain a satisfactory solution to the charge, they refer it back to the EEOC.

After a charge has been filed (or the state or local deferral period has ended), the EEOC has 10 days to serve notice of the charge on the employer. The EEOC then investigates the charge to determine whether there is reasonable cause to believe it is true; it is expected to make this determination within 120 days. If no reasonable cause is found, the EEOC must dismiss the charge, in which case the person who filed the charge has 90 days to file a suit on his or her own behalf. If reasonable cause for the charge is found, the EEOC must attempt to conciliate. If this conciliation is not satisfactory, the EEOC may bring a civil suit in a federal district court or issue a notice of right to sue to the person who filed the charge. Figure 2.2 summarizes important questions an employer should ask after receiving notice from the EEOC of a bias complaint.

The Equal Employment Opportunity Commission voted unanimously in 2006 to direct the agency to increase emphasis on bigger cases—ones that reflect a pattern or practice of alleged discrimination.[73]

Voluntary Mediation

The EEOC refers about 10% of its charges to a voluntary mediation mechanism. If the plaintiff agrees to mediation, the employer is asked to participate. A mediation session usually lasts up to 4 hours. If no agreement is reached or one of the parties rejects participation, the charge is then processed through the EEOC's usual mechanisms.

Faced with an offer to mediate, three responses are generally possible: Agree to mediate the charge, make a settlement offer without participating in mediation, or prepare a "position statement" for the EEOC. If the employer does not mediate or make an offer, the position statement is required. It should include information relating to the company's business and the charging party's position, a description of any rules or policies and procedures that are applicable, and the chronology of the offense that led to the adverse action.[74]

The EEOC is expanding its mediation program. For example, it signed more than 18 nationwide agreements and 300 local agreements for mediation with participating employers. Under this program, the EEOC refers all eligible discrimination charges filed against these employers to the commission's mediation unit, rather than to the usual charge processing system.[75]

FIGURE 2.2	Questions to Ask When an Employer Receives Notice that EEOC Has Filed a Bias Claim

1. Exactly what is the charge and is your company covered by the relevant statutes? (For example, Title VII and the American with Disabilities Act generally apply only to employees with 15 or more employees; the Age Discrimination in Employment Act applies to employers with 20 or more employees; but the Equal Pay Act applies to virtually all employers with one or more employees.) Did the employee file his or her charge on time, and was it processed in a timely manner by the EEOC?
2. What protected group does the employee belong to? Is the EEOC claiming disparate impact or disparate treatment?
3. Are there any obvious bases upon which you can challenge and/or rebut the claim? For example, would the employer have taken the action if the person did not belong to a protected group? Does the person's personnel file support the action taken by the employer?
4. If it is a sexual harassment claim, are there offensive comments, calendars, posters, screensavers, and so on, on display in the company?
5. In terms of the practicality of defending your company against this claim, who are the supervisors who actually took the allegedly discriminatory actions and how effective will they be as potential witnesses? Have you received an opinion from legal counsel regarding the chances of prevailing? Even if you do prevail, what do you estimate will be the out-of-pocket costs of taking the charge through the judicial process? Would you be better off settling the case, and what are the prospects of doing so in a way that will satisfy all parties?

Sources: Fair Employment Practices Summary of Latest Developments, January 7, 1983, p. 3, Bureau of National Affairs, Inc. (800-372-1033); Kenneth Sovereign, *Personnel Law* (Upper Saddle River, NJ: Prentice Hall, 1999), pp. 36–37; "EEOC Investigations—What an Employer Should Know," Equal Employment Opportunity Commission (www.eeoc.gov/employmers/investigations.html), accessed May 6, 2007.

How to Respond to Employment Discrimination Charges

There are several things to keep in mind when confronted by a charge of illegal employment discrimination; some of the more important can be summarized as follows:

1. Be methodical. Is the charge signed and dated and notarized by the person who filed it? Was it filed within the time allowed? Does the charge name the proper employer? Is it filed against a company that is subject to federal antidiscrimination statutes (for instance, only companies with 15 or more employees are subject to Title VII and the ADA)? Company records and persons with first-hand knowledge of the facts then should be scoured.[76]
2. Remember that EEOC investigators are not judges and aren't empowered to act as courts. They cannot make findings of discrimination on their own but can merely make recommendations. If the EEOC eventually determines that an employer may be in violation of a law, its only recourse is to file a suit or issue a notice of right to sue to the person who filed the charge.
3. Some experts advise meeting with the employee who made the complaint to determine all relevant issues. For example, ask: *What happened? Who was*

involved? When did the incident take place? Was the employee's ability to work affected? Were there any witnesses? Then prepare a written statement summarizing the complaints, facts, dates, and issues involved and request that the employee sign and date this.[77]

4. Give the EEOC a position statement based on your own investigation of the matter. Say something like, "Our company has a policy against discrimination and we would not discriminate in the manner outlined in the complaint." Support your case with some statistical analysis of the workforce, copies of any documents that support your position, and an explanation of any legitimate business justification for the actions you took.

5. Ensure that there is information in the EEOC's file demonstrating lack of merit of the charge. Often the best way to do that is not by answering the EEOC's questionnaire but by providing a detailed statement (as in no. 4) describing the firm's defense in its most persuasive light.

6. Limit the information supplied as narrowly as possible to only those issues raised in the charge itself. For example, if the charge only alleges sex discrimination, do not invite further scrutiny by responding to the EEOC's request for a breakdown of employees by age and sex.

7. Seek as much information as possible about the charging party's claim in order to ensure that you understand the claim and its ramifications.

8. Prepare for the EEOC's *fact-finding conferences.* These are supposed to be informal meetings held early in the investigatory process aimed at determining whether there is a basis for negotiation. However, the EEOC's emphasis is often on settlement. Its investigators therefore use the conferences to find weak spots in each party's position. Therefore, thoroughly prepare witnesses who are going to testify, especially supervisors.

9. Finally, keep in mind that preventing such claims is usually better than having to deal with them. Racism's causes are many and complex. However, studies support the commonsense observation that when people with implicit racist attitudes work in companies where there's a climate supporting racism, there is a significantly higher likelihood of racial discrimination.[78]

Strategy and HR

In September 2007 Walgreens agreed to settle the discrimination suit the EEOC had brought against it on behalf of some of Walgreens' African-American employees. In announcing the settlement, Walgreens' CEO said, in part, "Our company was built on principles of fairness and equality, and we do not tolerate discrimination in any aspect of employment . . ." His comments were in keeping with the Walgreens mission statement, which (according to the firm's official site, www.walgreens.com) says,

WALGREENS MISSION STATEMENT
We will treat each other with respect and dignity and do the same for all we serve.
We will offer employees of all backgrounds a place to build careers.
We will provide the most convenient access to healthcare services and consumer goods in America.
We will earn the trust of our customers and build shareholder value.

DIVERSITY MANAGEMENT AND AFFIRMATIVE ACTION PROGRAMS

To some extent demographic changes and globalization are rendering moot the goals of equitable and fair treatment driving equal employment legislation. Employers, in other words, have little choice but to willingly push for more diversity. Today, as we've seen, white males no longer dominate the labor force, and women and minorities will represent the lion's share of labor force growth over the foreseeable future. Furthermore, globalization requires employers to hire minority members with the cultural and language skills to deal with customers abroad. A survey of 113 MBA job seekers concluded that women and ethnic minorities considered diversity management to be important when accepting job offers.[79] In summary, companies are increasingly striving for racial, ethnic, and sexual workforce balance, "not because of legal imperatives, but as a matter of enlightened economic self-interest."[80]

In general, race, sex, culture, national origin, handicap, age, and religion comprise the demographic building blocks of diversity at work and what people often think of when asked what employers mean by *diversity*.[81]

Managing Diversity

Managing diversity means maximizing diversity's potential advantages while minimizing the potential barriers—such as prejudices and bias—that can undermine the functioning of a diverse workforce. In practice, diversity management involves both compulsory and voluntary management actions. We've seen that there are many legally mandated actions employers must take to minimize employment discrimination.

However, while such compulsory actions can reduce the more blatant diversity barriers, blending a diverse workforce into a close-knit and thriving community isn't easy. For example, one study, in a large British retailer, found that diversity prescriptions like "recognize and respond to individual differences" conflicted with the supervisor's inclination to avoid unequal treatment.[82] Diversity management therefore requires a multi-pronged approach.

One diversity expert concluded that five sets of voluntary organizational activities are at the heart of any diversity management program. We can summarize these as follows:

Provide strong leadership. Companies with exemplary reputations in managing diversity typically have CEOs who champion the cause of diversity. Leadership means, for instance, becoming a role model for the behaviors required for the change.

Assess the situation. One study found that the most common tools for measuring a company's diversity include equal employment hiring and retention metrics, employee attitude surveys, management and employee evaluations, and focus groups.[83]

Provide diversity training and education. The most common starting point for a diversity management effort is usually some type of employee education program.

Change culture and management systems. Combine education programs with other concrete steps aimed at changing the organization's culture and management systems. For example, change the performance appraisal procedure to appraise supervisors based partly on their success in reducing intergroup conflicts.

Evaluate the diversity management program. For example, do employee attitude surveys now indicate any improvement in employees' attitudes toward diversity?

Boosting Workforce Diversity

Employers use various means to increase workforce diversity. Many companies, such as Baxter Healthcare Corporation, start by adopting strong company policies advocating the benefits of a culturally, racially, and sexually diverse workforce: "Baxter International believes that a multi-cultural employee population is essential to the company's leadership in healthcare around the world." Baxter then publicizes this philosophy throughout the company.

Next, Baxter takes concrete steps to foster diversity at work. These steps include evaluating diversity program efforts, recruiting minority members to the board of directors, and interacting with representative minority groups and networks. Diversity training is another concrete activity. It aims at sensitizing all employees about the need to value differences, build self-esteem, and generally create a more smoothly functioning and hospitable environment for the firm's diverse workforce.

Strategy and HR

Workforce diversity makes strategic sense. Consider IBM's diversity programs. With strong top-management support, IBM created several minority task forces focusing on groups such as women and Native Americans. One effect of these teams has been internal: In the 10 or so years since forming them, IBM has boosted the number of U.S.-born ethnic minority executives by almost 2½ times.[84]

However, the firm's diversity program also had profound effects on IBM's strategy of expanding its markets and business results. For example, the task forces have been active in identifying and expanding IBM's multicultural markets. One task force decided to focus on expanding IBM's market among multicultural and women-owned businesses. They did this in part by providing "much-needed sales and service support to small and midsize businesses, a niche well populated with minority and female buyers."[85] As a direct result, this market grew from $10 million to more than $300 million in revenue in just 3 years.

Equal Employment Opportunity Versus Affirmative Action

Equal employment opportunity aims to ensure that anyone, regardless of race, color, disability, sex, religion, national origin, or age, has an equal chance for a job based on his or her qualifications. *Affirmative action* goes beyond equal employment opportunity by requiring the employer to make an extra effort to hire and promote those in a protected group. Affirmative action thus includes specific actions (in recruitment, hiring, promotions, and compensation) to eliminate the present effects of past discrimination.

Steps in an Affirmative Action Program

According to the EEOC, in an affirmative action program the employer ideally takes eight steps:

1. Issues a written equal employment policy indicating that it is an equal employment opportunity employer, as well as a statement indicating the employer's commitment to affirmative action.
2. Appoints a top official with responsibility and authority to direct and implement the program.
3. Publicizes the equal employment policy and affirmative action commitment.
4. Surveys present minority and female employment to determine locations where affirmative action programs are especially desirable.[86]
5. Develops goals and timetables to improve utilization of minorities, males, and females in each area where utilization has been identified.
6. Develops and implements specific programs to achieve these goals. Here, review the entire human resource management system (including recruitment, selection, promotion, compensation, and disciplining) to identify barriers to equal employment opportunity and to make needed changes.
7. Establishes an internal audit and reporting system to monitor and evaluate progress in each aspect of the program.
8. Develops support for the affirmative action program, both inside the company (among supervisors, for instance) and outside the company in the community.[87]

Affirmative Action Today

Affirmative action is still a significant workplace issue today. The incidence of major court-mandated programs is down. However, many employers must still engage in voluntary programs. For example, Executive Order 11246 (issued in 1965) requires federal contractors to take affirmative action to improve employment opportunities for women and racial minorities. It covers about 26 million workers—about 22% of the U.S. workforce.

Avoiding an employee backlash to affirmative action programs is important. A review of 35 years of research suggests several steps employers can take to increase employee support. Current employees need to see that the program is fair. *Transparent selection procedures* help in this regard. *Communication* is also crucial. Make clear that the program doesn't involve preferential selection standards. Provide details on the qualifications of all new hires (both minority and non-minority). *Justifications* for the program should emphasize redressing past discrimination and the practical value of diversity, not under-representation.[88]

Voluntary Programs

Some employers try to better manage diversity through voluntary affirmative action programs. This means they voluntarily make an extra effort to hire and promote those in protected (such as female or minority) groups. This is in contrast to the involuntary affirmative action programs courts have imposed on some employers since enactment of the 1964 Civil Rights Act.

In implementing voluntary programs, the employer should ensure that its program does not conflict with the Civil Rights Act of 1991, which two experts say may ". . . bar employers from giving any consideration whatsoever to an individual's status as a racial or ethnic minority or as a woman when making an employment decision."[89] This does not seem to be much of a problem, as long as employers emphasize the external recruitment and internal development of better qualified minority and female employees "while basing employment decisions on legitimate criteria."[90]

Improving Productivity through HRIS

The HR manager who wants to assess the efficiency and effectiveness of his or her company's EEOC and diversity efforts has numerous measures or metrics from which to choose. These might include, for example, the number of EEOC claims per year, the cost of HR-related litigation, percentage of minority/women promotions, and various measures for analyzing the survival and loss rate among new diverse employee groups.

Even for a company with just several hundred employees, keeping track of metrics like these is expensive. The HR manager may therefore want to rely on various computerized solutions. One package called *Measuring Diversity Results* provides several diversity-related software options aimed at boosting accuracy of the information at the manager's disposal and reducing the costs of collecting and compiling it. Among other things, this vendor's diversity management packages let the manager more easily calculate the cost-per-diversity hire, a workforce profile index, the numeric impact of voluntary turnover among diverse employee groups, and such things as direct and indirect replacement cost per hire.

Review

Summary

1. Legislation barring discrimination is not new. For example, the Fifth Amendment to the U.S. Constitution (ratified in 1791) states that no person shall be deprived of life, liberty, or property without due process of law.

2. Legislation barring employment discrimination includes Title VII of the 1964 Civil Rights Act (as amended), which bars discrimination because of race, color, religion, sex, or national origin; various executive orders; federal guidelines (covering procedures for validating employee selection tools, etc.); the Equal Pay Act of 1963; and the Age Discrimination in Employment Act of 1967. In addition, various Court decisions (such as *Griggs* v. *Duke Power Company*) and state and local laws bar various aspects of discrimination.

3. The EEOC was created by Title VII of the Civil Rights Act. It is empowered to try conciliating discrimination complaints, but if this fails, the EEOC has the power to go directly to court to enforce the law.

4. The Civil Rights Act of 1991 had the effect of revising several Supreme Court equal employment decisions and "rolling back the clock." For example, it placed the burden of proof back on employers and held that a nondiscriminatory reason was insufficient to let an employer avoid liability for an action that also had a discriminatory motive.

5. The Americans with Disabilities Act prohibits employment discrimination against the disabled. Specifically, qualified persons cannot be discriminated against if the firm can make reasonable accommodations without undue hardship on the business.

6. A person who believes he or she has been discriminated against by a personnel procedure or decision must prove either that he or she was subjected to unlawful disparate treatment (intentional discrimination) or that the procedure in question has a disparate impact (unintentional discrimination) on members of his or her protected class. Once a prima facie case of disparate treatment is established, an employer must produce evidence that its decision was based on legitimate reasons (such as BFOQ). If the employer does that, the person claiming discrimination must prove that the employer's reasons are only a pretext for letting the company discriminate. Once a prima facie

case of disparate impact has been established, the employer must produce evidence that the allegedly discriminatory practice or procedure is job related and is based on a substantial business reason.

7. An employer should avoid various specific discriminatory human resource management practices:
   a. *In recruitment.* An employer usually should not rely on word-of-mouth advertising or give false or misleading information to minority group members. Also (usually), an employer should not specify the desired sex in advertising or in any way suggest that applicants might be discriminated against.
   b. *In selection.* An employer should avoid using any educational or other requirements where (1) it can be shown that minority-group members are less likely to possess the qualification and (2) such requirement is also not job related. Tests that disproportionately screen out minorities and women and that are not job related are deemed unlawful. Remember that you can use various tests and standards, but you must prove that they are job related or show that they are not used to discriminate against protected groups.

8. In practice, a person's charge to the EEOC is often first referred to a local agency. When the EEOC finds reasonable cause to believe that discrimination occurred, it has 30 days to try to work out a conciliation. Important points for the employer to remember include (1) EEOC investigators can only make recommendations, (2) you cannot be compelled to submit documents without a court order, and (3) you may limit the information you do submit. Also, make sure you clearly document your position (as the employer).

9. An employer can use three basic defenses in the event of a discriminatory practice allegation. One is *business necessity.* Attempts to show that tests or other selection standards are valid is one example of this defense. *Bona fide occupational qualification* is the second defense. This is applied when, for example, religion, national origin, or sex is a bona fide requirement of the job (such as for actors or actresses). A third is that the decision was made on the basis of legitimate nondiscriminatory reasons (such as poor performance) having nothing to do with the prohibited discrimination alleged.

10. Eight steps in an affirmative action program (based on suggestions from the EEOC) are (1) issue a written equal employment policy, (2) appoint a top official, (3) publicize the policy, (4) survey present minority and female employment, (5) develop goals and timetables, (6) develop and implement specific programs to achieve goals, (7) establish an internal audit and reporting system, and (8) develop support of in-house and community programs.

11. Recruitment is one of the first activities to which EEOC laws and procedures are applied. We turn to this in the following chapter.

Key Terms

- Equal Pay Act of 1963
- Title VII of the 1964 Civil Rights Act
- Equal Employment Opportunity Commission (EEOC)
- affirmative action
- Office of Federal Contract Compliance Programs (OFCCP)
- Age Discrimination in Employment Act (ADEA) of 1967
- Vocational Rehabilitation Act of 1973
- Pregnancy Discrimination Act (PDA)
- federal agency guidelines
- Federal Violence Against Women Act of 1994
- sexual harassment
- gender harassment
- *Griggs* v. *Duke Power Company*
- protected class
- *Albemarle Paper Company* v. *Moody*
- Civil Rights Act of 1991 (CRA 1991)
- disparate impact
- disparate treatment
- Americans with Disabilities Act (ADA)
- adverse impact
- bona fide occupational qualification (BFOQ)
- business necessity

Discussion Questions and Exercises

1. What is Title VII? What does it state?
2. What important precedents were set by the *Griggs* v. *Duke Power Company* case? The *Albemarle* v. *Moody* case?
3. What is adverse impact? How can it be proven?
4. Assume that you are a supervisor on an assembly line; you are responsible for hiring subordinates, supervising them, and recommending them for promotion. Compile a list of discriminatory management practices that you should avoid.
5. Explain the defenses and exceptions to discriminatory practice allegations.
6. What is the difference between affirmative action and equal employment opportunity?
7. Explain how you would set up an affirmative action program.

APPLICATION EXERCISES

Case Incident   *A Case of Racial Discrimination?*

John Peters was a 44-year-old cardiologist on the staff of a teaching hospital in a large city in the southeastern United States. Happily married with two teenage children, he had served with distinction for many years at this same hospital, and in fact served his residency there after graduating from Columbia University's medical school.

Alana Anderson was an attractive African-American registered nurse on the staff at the same hospital with Peters. Unmarried and without children, she lived in a hospital-owned apartment on the hospital grounds and diligently devoted almost all her time to her work at the hospital or to taking additional coursework to further improve her already excellent nursing skills.

The hospital's chief administrator, Gary Chapman, took enormous pride in what he called the extraordinary professionalism of the doctors, nurses, and other staff members at his hospital. Although he took a number of rudimentary steps to guard against blatant violations of equal employment opportunity laws, he believed that most of the professionals on his staff were so highly trained and committed to the highest professional standards that "they would always do the right thing," as he put it.

Chapman was therefore upset to receive a phone call from Peters, informing him that Anderson had (in Peters's eyes) "developed an unwholesome personal attraction" to him and was bombarding the doctor with Valentine's Day cards, affectionate personal notes, and phone calls—often to the doctor's home. Concerned about hospital decorum and the possibility that Peters was being sexually harassed, Chapman met privately with Anderson, explained that Peters was very uncomfortable with the personal attention she was showing to him, and asked that she please not continue to exhibit her show of affection for the doctor.

Chapman assumed that the matter was over. Several weeks later, when Anderson resigned her position at the hospital, Chapman didn't think much of it. He was therefore shocked and dismayed to receive a registered letter from a local attorney, informing him that both the hospital and Peters and Chapman personally were being sued by Anderson for racial discrimination. Her claim was that Chapman, in their private meeting, had told her, "We don't think it's right for people of different races to pursue each other romantically at this hospital." According to the lawyer, his preliminary research had unearthed several other alleged incidents at the hospital that apparently supported the idea that racial discrimination at the hospital was widespread. ■

QUESTIONS

1. What do you think of the way Chapman handled the accusations from Peters and his conversation with Anderson? How would you have handled them?
2. Do you think Peters had the basis for a sexual harassment claim against Anderson? Why or why not?
3. What would you do now if you were Chapman to avoid further incidents of this type?

Continuing Case

LearnInMotion.com: A Question of Discrimination

One of the problems LearnInMotion's Jennifer and Mel faced concerned the inadequacies of the firm's current personnel management practices and procedures. The previous year had been a swirl of activity—creating and testing the business model, launching the site, writing and rewriting the business plan, and finally getting venture funding. And, it would be accurate to say that in all that time, they put absolutely no time into employee manuals, personnel policies, or HR-related matters. Even the 25-page business plan was of no help in this regard. The plan provided considerable detail regarding budgetary projections, competition, market growth, and business strategy. However, it was silent when it came to HR, except for containing short bios of the current employees, and projections of the types of positions that would have to be staffed in the first two years.

Almost from the beginning, it was apparent to both of them that they were "out of our depth" (as Mel put it) when it came to the letter and spirit of equal employment opportunity laws. Having both been through business school, they were familiar with the general requirements, such as not asking applicants their ages. However, those general guidelines weren't always easy to translate into practice during the actual applicant interviews. Two incidents particularly concerned them. One of the applicants for a sales position was in his 50s, which made him about twice as old as any other applicant. While Mel didn't mean to be discriminatory, he found himself asking this candidate questions such as "Do you think you'll be able to get up to speed selling an Internet product?" and "You know, we'll be working very long hours here; are you up to that?"—questions that he did not ask of other, younger candidates. There was also a problem with a candidate for the other position (content manager). This person had been incarcerated for a substance abuse problem several years before. Mel asked him several questions about this, as well as whether he was now "clean" or "under any sort of treatment." Jennifer thought questions like these were probably OK, but she wasn't sure.

There was also a disturbing incident in the office. There were already two content management employees, Ruth and Dan, whose job was to actually place the courses and other educational content on the Web site. Dan, along with Alex the Web surfer, occasionally used vulgarity—for instance, when referring to the problems the firm was having getting the computer supplier to come to the office and repair a chronic problem with the firm's server. Mel's attitude was that "boys will be boys." However, Jennifer saw Ruth cringe several times when "the boys" were having one of these exchanges, and felt strongly that this behavior had to stop. However, she was not sure language like this constituted "a hostile environment" under the law, although she did feel that at a minimum it was uncivil. The two owners decided it was time to institute and implement some HR policies that would ensure that their company and its employees adhere to the letter and the spirit of the equal employment opportunity laws. Now they want you, their management consultants, to help them actually do it. Here's what they want you to do for them. ■

QUESTIONS AND ASSIGNMENTS

1. Our company is in New York City. We now have only about five employees, and are only planning on hiring about three or four more. Is our company in fact even covered by equal rights legislation? (Hint: Does the government's Web site provide any clues?)
2. Were we within our legal rights to ask the possibly age-related and substance-abuse-related questions? Why or why not?
3. Did Dan and Alex create a hostile environment for Ruth? Why or why not? How should we have handled this matter?
4. What have we been doing wrong up to now with respect to EEO-related matters, and how do you suggest we rectify the situation in the future?

EXPERIENTIAL EXERCISE

Too Informal?

Dan Jones had run his textile plant in a midsize southern town for many years without a whiff of trouble with the EEOC. He did not take formal steps to avoid making EEO-type mistakes; just the opposite. In fact, a professor from a local college had once told him to be more careful about how applicants were recruited and screened and employees were treated. However, Jones's philosophy was "If it ain't broke, don't fix it," and because he'd never had any complaints, he assumed that his screening process wasn't "broke."

For many years Jones had no problems. If he needed a new employee, he simply asked his current employees (most of whom were Hispanic) if they had any friends who were looking for jobs. Sometimes, he would also ask the local state employment office to list the open jobs and send over some candidates. He then had his sewing supervisor and plant manager (both also Hispanic) interview the applicants. No tests or other background checks were carried out, in part, said Jones, because "most of these applicants are friends and relatives of my current employees, and they wouldn't send me any lemons."

Now Jones is being served with a formal notice from the county's Equal Rights Commission. It seems that of the 20 or so non-Hispanic applicants sent to Jones's firm last year from the state employment office, none had received a job offer. In fact, Jones's supervisor had not even returned the follow-up card to the employment office to verify that each applicant had shown up and been interviewed. Jones was starting to wonder if his HR process was too informal.

Purpose: The purpose of this exercise is to provide practice in analyzing and applying knowledge of equal opportunity legislation to a realistic problem.

Required Understanding: Be thoroughly familiar with the material presented in this chapter. In addition, read "Too Informal?" the case on which this experiential exercise is based.

How to Set up the Exercise/Instructions:

1. Divide the class into groups of four or five students.
2. Each group should develop answers to the following:
   a. How could the EEOC prove *adverse impact?*
   b. Cite specific discriminatory personnel practices at Dan Jones's company.
   c. How could Jones's company defend itself against the allegations of discriminatory practice?
3. If time permits, a spokesperson from each group can present his or her group's findings. Would it make sense for this company to try to defend itself against the discrimination allegations? ■

Endnotes

1. Mark Schoef, "Walgreens Suit Reflects EEOC's Latest Strategies," *Workforce Management* (March 26, 2007): 8
2. Betsy Morris, "How Corporate America Is Betraying Women," *Fortune* (January 10, 2005): 64–70.
3. Note that private employers are not bound by the U.S. Constitution.
4. Based on or quoted from *Principles of Employment Discrimination Law, International Association of Official Human Rights Agencies,* Washington, D.C. See also Bruce Feldacker, *Labor Guide to Labor Law* (Upper Saddle River, NJ: Prentice Hall, 2000); and www.eeoc. gov Web site. Employment discrimination law is a changing field, and the appropriateness of the rules, guidelines, and conclusions in this chapter and book may also be affected by factors unique to the employer's operation. They should be reviewed by the employer's attorney before implementation.
5. James Higgins, "A Manager's Guide to the Equal Employment Opportunity Laws," *Personnel Journal* 55, no. 8 (August 1976): 406.

6. The Equal Employment Opportunity Act of 1972, Subcommittee on Labor or the Committee of Labor and Public Welfare, United States Senate, March 1972, p. 3. In general, it is not discrimination, but unfair discrimination against a person merely because of that person's race, age, sex, national origin, or religion that is forbidden by federal statutes. In the federal government's *Uniform Employee Selection Guidelines,* unfair discrimination is defined as follows: "unfairness is demonstrated through a showing that members of a particular interest group perform better or poorer on the job than their scores on the selection procedure (test, etc.) would indicate through comparison with how members of the other groups performed." For a discussion of the meaning of fairness, see James Ledvinka, "The Statistical Definition of Fairness in the Federal Selection Guidelines and Its Implications for Minority Employment," *Personnel Psychology* 32 (August 1979): 551–562. In summary, a selection device (such as a test) may discriminate—for example, between low performers and high performers. However, unfair discrimination—discrimination that is based solely on the person's race, age, sex, national origin, or religion—is illegal.

7. Note that the U.S. Supreme Court (in *General Dynamics Land Systems Inc.* v. *Cline, 2004*) held that the ADEA does *not* protect younger workers from being treated worse than older ones. "High Court: ADEA Does Not Protect Younger Workers Treated Worse than Their Elders," *BNA Bulletin to Management* 55, no. 10 (March 4, 2004): 73–80.

8. John Kohl, Milton Mayfield, and Jacqueline Mayfield, "Recent Trends in Pregnancy Discrimination Law," *Business Horizons* 48, no. 5 (September 2005): 442–429.

9. Nancy Woodward, "Pregnancy Discrimination Grows," *HR Magazine* (July 2005): 79.

10. Thomas Dhanens, "Implications of the New EEOC Guidelines," *Personnel* 56 (September/October): 32–39.

11. 29 CFR 1625.2(a), quoted in Paul Greenlaw and John Kohl, "Age Discrimination and Employment Guidelines," *Personnel Journal* 61, no. 3 (March 1982): 224–228. See also www.uniformguidelines.com/uniformguidelines.html, accessed November 23, 2007.

12. Larry Drake and Rachel Moskowitz, "Your Rights in the Workplace," *Occupational Outlook Quarterly* (Summer 1997): 19–20.

13. Richard Wiener et al., "The Fit and Implementation of Sexual Harassment Law to Workplace Evaluations," *Journal of Applied Psychology* 87, no. 4 (2002): 747–764.

14. Edward Felsenthal, "Justice's Ruling Further Defines Sexual Harassment," *Wall Street Journal* (March 5, 1998): B1, B5. Similarly, a series of compliments and "requests for a hug" were not sufficient to rise to the level of sexual harassment in one case involving a female supervisor and her female subordinate. ("Compliments, Request for Hug Were Not Harassment by Female Supervisor, Court Says," *Human Resources Report, BNA* [November 20, 2003]: 1193).

15. Hilary Gettman and Michele Gelfand, "When the Customer Shouldn't Be King: Antecedents and Consequences of Sexual Harassment by Clients and Customers," *Journal of Applied Psychology* 92, no. 3, (2007): 757–770.

16. See Mindy D. Bergman et al., "The (Un)reasonableness of Reporting: Antecedents and Consequences of Reporting Sexual Harassment," *Journal of Applied Psychology* 87, no. 2 (2002): 230–242; see also W. Kirk Turner and Christopher Thrutchley, "Employment Law and Practices Training: No Longer the Exception—It's the Rule," *Society for Human Resource Management Legal Report* (July–August 2002): 1–2.

17. Chelsea Willness, et al., "A Meta-Analysis of the Antecedents and Consequences of Workplace Sexual Harassment," *Personnel Psychology* 60, no. 60 (2007): 127–162.

18. Jennifer Berdahl and Celia Moore, "Workplace Harassment: Double Jeopardy for Minority Women," *Journal of Applied Psychology*, 2006, 91, no. 2 (2006): 426–436

19. Jennifer Berdahl, "The Sexual Harassment of Uppity Women," *Journal of Applied Psychology* 92, no. 2 (2007): 425–437.

20. Lilia Cortina and S. Arzu Wasti, "Profile to Coping: Response to Sexual Harassment across Persons, Organizations, and Cultures," *Journal of Applied Psychology* 90, no. 1 (2005): 182–192.

21. Maria Rotundo et al., "A Meta-Analytic Review of Gender Differences in Perceptions

of Sexual Harassment," *Journal of Applied Psychology* 86, no. 5 (2001): 914–922. See also Nathan Bowling and Terry Beehr, "Workplace Harassment from the Victim's Perspective: A Theoretical Model and Meta Analysis," *Journal of Applied Psychology* 91, no. 5, (2006): 998–1012.

22. See the discussion in "Examining Unwelcome Conduct in Sexual Harassment Claim," *BNA Fair Employment Practices* (October 19, 1995): 124. See also Molly Bowers et al., "Just Cause in the Arbitration of Sexual Harassment Cases," *Dispute Resolution Journal* 55, no. 4 (November 2000): 40–55.

23. Mindy D. Bergman et al., op cit., p. 237.

24. "New EEOC Guidance Explains Standards of Liability for Harassment by Supervisors," *BNA Fair Employment Practices* (June 24, 1999): 75.

25. "Adequate Response Bars Liability," *BNA Fair Employment Practices* (June 26, 1997): 74.

26. Shereen Bingham and Lisa Scherer, "The Unexpected Effects of a Sexual Education Program," *Journal of Applied Behavioral Science* 37, no. 2 (June 2001): 125–153.

27. Federick L. Sullivan, "Sexual Harassment: The Supreme Court Ruling," *Personnel* 65, no. 12 (December 1986): 42–44. See also Gillian Flynn, "A Pioneer Program Nurtures a Harassment Free Workplace," *Workforce* (October 1997): 38–43; and for the EEOC's statement, see www.eeoc.gov, accessed November 11, 2007.

28. *Griggs* v. *Duke Power Company,* 3FEP cases 175.

29. IOFEP cases 1181.

30. Bruce Feldacker, *Labor Guide to Labor Law* (Upper Saddle River, NJ: Prentice Hall, 2000), p. 513.

31. "The Eleventh Circuit Explains Disparate Impact, Disparate Treatment," *BNA Fair Employment Practices* (August 17, 2000): 102. See also Kenneth York, "Disparate Results in Adverse Impact Tests: The 4/5ths Rule and the Chi Square Test," *Public Personnel Management* 31, no. 2 (Summer 2002): 253–262.

32. Commerce Clearing House, "House and Senate Pass Civil Rights Compromise by Wide Margin," *Ideas and Trends in Personnel* (November 13, 1991): 182.

33. Elliot H. Shaller and Dean Rosen, "A Guide to the EEOC's Final Regulations on the Americans with Disabilities Act," *Employee Relations* 17, no. 3 (Winter 1991–1992): 405–420. See also Brenda Sunoo, "Accommodating Workers with Disabilities," *Workforce* 80, no. 2 (February 2001): 86–93.

34. Elliot H. Shaller and Dean Rosen, "A Guide to the EEOC's Final Regulations on the Americans with Disabilities Act," *Employee Relations* 17, no. 3 (Winter 1991–1992): 408. The ADEA does not just protect against intentional discrimination (disparate treatment). Under the Supreme Court's *Smith* v. *Jackson, Miss* decision, it also covers employer practices that seem neutral but which actually bear more heavily on older workers (disparate impact). "Employees Need Not Show Intentional Bias to Bring Claims under ADEA, High Court Says, *BNA Bulletin to Management* 56 no. 14 (April 5, 2005): 105.

35. Ibid., 409.

36. Ibid., 265. See also Miller Brownstein, "Inquiry Free, but Money for Me: Whether the Civil Rights Act of 1991 Permits Punitive Damages in the Absence of Compensatory Damages," *Boston University Law Review* 84, no. 4 (October 2004): 1049–1076.

37. "Expansion of Employment Laws Abroad Impacts U.S. Employers," *BNA Bulletin to Management* (April 11, 2006): 119; Richard Posthuma, Mark Roehling, and Michael Campion, "Applying U.S. Employment Discrimination Laws to International Employers: Advice for Scientists and Practitioners," *Personnel Psychology* 59 (2006): 2705–2739.

38. See, for example, Paul Starkman, "The ADA's 'Essential Job Function' Requirements: Just How Essential Does an Essential Job Function Have to Be?" *Employee Relations Law Journal* 26, no. 4 (Spring 2001). 43–102.

39. "No Sitting for Store Greeter," *BNA Fair Employment Practices* (December 14, 1995): 150.

40. M. P. McQueen, "Workplace Disabilities Are on the Rise," *Wall Street Journal* (May 1, 2007): A1.

41. "Odds Against Getting Even Longer in ADA Cases," *BNA Bulletin to Management* (August 20, 2000): 229; "Determining

Employers' Responsibilities Under ADA," *BNA Fair Employment Practices* (May 16, 1996): 57.

42. James McDonald, Jr., "The Americans with Difficult Personalities Act," *Employee Relations Law Journal* 25, no. 4 (Spring 2000): 93–107.

43. "EEOC Guidance on Dealing with Intellectual Disabilities," *Workforce Management* (March 2005): 16.

44. "Supreme Court Says Manual Task Limitation Needs Both Daily Living, Workplace Impact," *BNA Fair Employment Practices* (January 17, 2002): 8.

45. "Home Depot Did Not Violate ADA by Barring Deaf Worker from a Forklift Training Program," *BNA Human Resources Report* (November 10, 2003): 1192.

46. "Differing Views: Punctuality as Essential Job Function," *BNA Fair Employment Practices* (April 27, 2000): 56.

47. www.eeoc.gov/press/5-10-01-b.html accessed January 8, 2008.

48. "Airline Erred in Giving Test Before Making Formal Offer," *BNA Bulletin to Management* (March 15, 2005): 86.

49. Lee, "Implications of ADA Litigation for Employers," pp. 35–50.

50. "Determining Employers' Responsibilities Under ADA," 57.

51. Lee, "Implications of ADA Litigation for Employers," pp. 35–50.

52. Ibid, pp. 35–50.

53. Timothy Bland, "The Supreme Court Focuses on the ADA," *HR Magazine* (September 1999): 42–46. See also James Hall and Diane Hatch, "Supreme Court Decisions Require ADA Revision," *Workforce* (August 1999): 60–66.

54. Joe Mullich, "Hiring Without Limits," *Workforce Management* (June 2004): 52–58.

55. Chris Reiter, "New Technology Aims to Improve Internet Access for the Impaired," *Wall Street Journal* (September 22, 2005): 4–6.

56. IOFEP cases 1181. See also Joe Mullich, "Hiring Without Limits," *Workforce Management* (June 2004): 52–58.

57. John Klinefelter and James Thompkins, "Adverse Impact in Employment Selection," *Public Personnel Management* (May/June 1976): 199–204.

58. John Moran, *Employment Law* (Upper Saddle River, NJ: Prentice Hall, 1997), p. 168. A recent study found that using the 4/5ths rule often resulted in false-positive ratings of adverse impact, and that incorporating tests of statistical significance could improve the accuracy of applying the 4/5ths rule. See Philip Roth, Philip Bobko, and Fred Switzer, "Modeling the Behavior of the 4/5ths Rule for Determining Adverse Impact: Reasons for Caution," *Journal of Applied Psychology* 91, no. 3 (2006): 507–522.

59. "Eighth Circuit OKs $3.4 Million EEOC Verdict Relating to Pre-Hire Strength Testing Rules," *BNA Bulletin to Management*, (November 28, 2006): 377.

60. "Eleventh Circuit Explains Disparate Impact, Disparate Treatment," 102.

61. *U.S.* v. *Bethlehem Steel Company*, 3FEP cases 589.

62. *Spurlock* v. *United Airlines*, 5FEP cases 17.

63. Ledvinka and Gatewood, "EEO Issues with Preemployment Inquiries," 22–26.

64. Anderson and Levin-Epstein, *Primer of Equal Opportunity*, 28.

65. "Many Well-Intentioned HR Policies Hold Legal Headaches, Consultant Says," *BNA Bulletin to Management* (February 17, 2000): 47.

66. Jenessa Shapiro, et al., "Expectations of Obese Trainees: How Stigmatized Trainee Characteristics Influence Training Effectiveness," *Journal of Applied Psychology*, 92, no. 1 (2007): 239–249. See also Lisa Finkelstein et al., "Bias Against Overweight Job Applicants: Further Explanations of When and Why," *Human Resource Management* 46, no. 2 (Summer 2007): 203–222.

67. "American Airlines, Worldwide Flight Sued by EEOC over Questioning of Applicants," *BNA Fair Employment Practices* (October 12, 2000): 125.

68. Richard Connors, "Law at Work," lawatwork.com/news/applicat.html.

69. Lynn Bennington and Ruth Wein, "Aiding and Abetting Employer Discrimination: The Job Applicant's Role," *Employee Responsibilities and Rights* 14, no. 1 (March 2002): 3–16.

70. This is based on Anderson and Levin-Epstein, *Primer of Equal Opportunity*, 93–97.

71. "EEOC Issues New Enforcement Guidance on Discrimination in Employee Benefits," *BNA Fair Employment Practices* (October 12, 2000): 123.

72. Matthew Miklaue, "Sorting Out a Claim of Bias," *Workforce* 80, no. 6 (June 2001): 102–103.

73. "EEOC Turning Attention to Broader Cases," *Workforce Management* (April 24, 2006): 6; "EEOC's Focus on Systemic Cases Increases Need for Preventing Bias," BNA *Human Resources Report* (May 22, 2006): 533.

74. Timothy Bland, "Sealed Without a Kiss," *HR Magazine* (October 2000): 85–92.

75. "EEOC Has 18 Nationwide, 300 Local Accords with Employers to Mediate Job Bias Claims Charges," *BNA Human Resources Report* (October 13, 2003): H-081.

76. Bland, "Sealed Without a Kiss," 85–92.

77. "Conducting Effective Investigations of Employee Bias Complaints," *BNA Fair Employment Practices* (July 13, 1995): 81.

78. Jonathan Zeigert and Paul Hangies, "Employment Discrimination: The Role of Implicit Attitudes, Motivation, and a Climate for Racial Bias," *Journal of Applied Psychology* 90, no. 3 (2005): 553–562.

79. Eddy Ng and Ronald Burke, "Person–Organization Fit and the War for Talent: Does Diversity Management Make a Difference?" *International Journal of Human Resource Management* 16, no. 7 (July 2005): 1195–1210.

80. James Coil, III, and Charles Rice, "Managing Work-Force Diversity in the 90s: The Impact of the Civil Rights Act of 1991," *Employee Relations Law Journal* 18, no. 4 (Spring 1993): 547–565. See also Stephanie Mehta, "What Minority Employees Really Want," *Fortune* (July 10, 2000): 81–188. See also "Diversity Is Used as Business Advantage by Three Fourths of Companies, Survey Says," *BNA Bulletin to Management* (November 7, 2006): 355.

81. Michael Carrell and Everett Mann, "Defining Work Force Diversity in Public Sector Organizations," *Public Personnel Management* 24, no. 1 (Spring 1995): 99–111. See also Richard Koonce, "Redefining Diversity," *Training and Development Journal* (December 2001): 22–33.

82. Carly Foster and Lynette Harris, "Easy To Say, Difficult To Do: Diversity Management in Retail," *Human Resource Management Journal* 15, no. 3 (2005): 4–17.

83. Patricia Digh, "Creating a New Balance Sheet: The Need for Better Diversity Metrics," *Mosaics*, Society for Human Resource Management (September/ October 1999): 1. For diversity management steps see Taylor Cox, Jr., "Cultural Diversity in Organizations: Theory, Research and Practice" (San Francisco: Berrett-Koehler, 1993), p. 236; see also Richard Bucher, "Diversity Consciousness" (Upper Saddle River NJ, 2004), pp. 109–137.

84. David Thomas, "Diversity as Strategy," *Harvard Business Review* (September 2004): 98–104; See also J. T. Childs Jr., "Managing Global Diversity at IBM: A Global HR Topic that Has Arrived," *Human Resource Management* 44, no. 1 (Spring 2005): 73–77.

85. Thomas, op. cit., 99.

86. Frank Jossi, "Reporting Race," *HR Magazine* (September 2000): 87–94.

87. U.S. Equal Employment Opportunity Commission, *Affirmative Action and Equal Employment* (Washington, D.C.: January 1974). See also David Kravitz and Steven Klineberg, "Reactions to Two Versions of Affirmative-Action Among Whites, Blacks, and Hispanics," *Journal of Applied Psychology* 85, no. 4 (2000): 597–611.

88. David Harrison et al., "Understanding Attitudes Toward Affirmative Action Programs in Employment: Summary and Meta-Analysis of 35 Years of Research," *Journal of Applied Psychology* 91, no. 5 (2006): pp. 1031–1036.

89. Coil and Rice, "Managing Work-Force Diversity in the 1990s," 548.

90. Ibid., 562–563.

3 PERSONNEL PLANNING AND RECRUITING

- What Is Job Analysis?
- The Recruitment and Selection Process
- Workforce Planning and Forecasting
- Recruiting Job Candidates
- Developing and Using Application Forms

When you finish studying this chapter, you should be able to:

- Describe *the basic methods of collecting job analysis information.*
- Conduct *a job analysis.*
- Explain *the process of forecasting personnel requirements.*
- Compare *eight methods for recruiting job candidates.*
- Explain *how to use application forms to predict job performance.*

INTRODUCTION

With 110 restaurants open, and adding 20 new ones per year, The Cheesecake Factory must attract and hire 24,000 people per year. For Ed Eynon, the firm's senior vice president for human resources, that means casting a wide net when it comes to recruiting—"You don't find all the people you need from one source," he says. Having the right recruiting sources is crucial to The Cheesecake Factory's success.[1]

WHAT IS JOB ANALYSIS?

Job Analysis Defined

Organizations consist of jobs that have to be staffed. **Job analysis** is the procedure through which you determine the duties of these jobs and the characteristics of the people who should be hired for them. The analysis produces information on the job's activities and requirements. This information is then used for developing **job descriptions** (what the job entails) and **job specifications** (what kind of people to hire for the job).[2]

A supervisor or HR specialist normally does the job analysis, perhaps using a questionnaire like the one in the chapter Appendix (Figure A3.3, pp. 111–112). The information collected typically includes information on the work activities performed (such as cleaning, selling, teaching, or painting) and information about such matters as physical working conditions and work schedule. The results of one study suggest that job analysis data reported by job incumbents display the lowest reliability or consistency, while those collected by job analysts are usually more reliable.[3]

Job analysis information is the basis for several human resource management activities. For example, information regarding the job's duties may be the basis for creating training programs, and information about the human traits required to do the job are used to decide what sort of people to recruit and hire. Job analysis therefore plays a central role in HR management. The U.S. Federal Agencies' Uniform Guidelines on Employee Selection "stipulate that job analysis is a crucial step in validating all major personnel activities."[4]

Job Analysis and Equal Employment Opportunity (EEO)

Job analysis therefore plays a central role in equal employment compliance. We discussed EEO issues in Chapter 2. Employers must be able to show that their screening tools and appraisals are related to performance on the job in question. To do this, of course, the manager must know what the job entails—which in turn requires a competent job analysis.

Methods of Collecting Job Analysis Information

In practice, employers usually collect job analysis data from several job incumbents, using questionnaires and interviews. They then average data from these employees from different departments to determine how much time a typical employee (say, a sales assistant) spends on each of several specific tasks (such as interviewing). However, do not assume that the way someone with a particular job title spends his or her time is necessarily the same from department to department.

Traditionally, job analysis might take several days to interview five or six sample employees and their managers, and to try to explain the process and the reason for the analysis.

Today, the same process might take 3 or 4 hours.[5] The steps might include: (1) Greet participants and conduct very brief introductions; (2) briefly explain the job analysis process and the participants' roles in this process; (3) spend about 15 minutes determining the scope of the job you're about to analyze, by getting agreement on the job's basic summary; (4) identify the job's broad functional or duty areas, such as "administrative" and "supervisory"; (5) identify tasks within each duty area, using a flip chart or collaboration software; and, finally (6) print the task list and get the group to sign off on it.

Managers use various techniques to do a job analysis (in other words, to collect information on the duties, responsibilities, and activities of the job). Some of the more popular techniques are as follows.

Interviews

Job analysis interviews may involve interviewing job incumbents or one or more supervisors who are thoroughly knowledgeable about the job. Typical interview questions might include: "What is the job being performed?" "What are the major duties of your position?" "What exactly do you do?" "What activities do you participate in?"

Interviews are probably the most widely used method for determining a job's duties and responsibilities, and their wide use reflects their advantages. Most important, interviewing lets workers report activities and behavior that might not otherwise surface. For example, a skilled interviewer could unearth important activities that occur only occasionally, or informal communication (between, say, a production supervisor and the sales manager) that would not be obvious from the organization chart.

Interviewing's major problem is distortion of information, whether due to outright falsification or honest misunderstandings. A job analysis is often used as a prelude to changing a job's pay rate. Employees, therefore, sometimes view them as efficiency evaluations that may affect their pay, and so exaggerate some responsibilities and minimize others. Obtaining valid information can be a slow process.

For example, in one experiment the researchers listed duties either as simple task statements ("record phone messages and other routine information") or as ability statements ("ability to record phone messages and other routine information").[6] Respondents were much more likely to include the ability-based versions of the statements. There may be a tendency for people to inflate their job's importance when abilities are involved, so as to impress others.[7]

Questionnaires

Employees can also be asked to fill out questionnaires to describe their job-related duties and responsibilities. Here it is important to decide how structured the questionnaire should be and what questions to include.

Some questionnaires are very structured checklists. Each employee is presented with an inventory of perhaps hundreds of specific duties or tasks (such as "change and splice wire"). Each must indicate whether he or she performs each task and, if so, how much time is normally spent on each. At the other extreme, the questionnaire can be open-ended and simply ask the employee to "describe the major duties of your job."

In practice, the best questionnaire often falls between these two extremes. As illustrated in Figure A3.3 (see Appendix, pp. 111–112), a typical job analysis questionnaire might have several open-ended questions (such as "Is the incumbent performing duties he/she considers unnecessary?") as well as structured questions (concerning, for instance, previous experience required).

Observation

Direct observation is especially useful when jobs consist mainly of observable physical activity. Jobs such as janitor, assembly-line worker, and accounting clerk are examples. On the other hand, observation is usually not appropriate when the job entails a lot of unmeasurable mental activity (lawyer, design engineer). Nor is it useful if the employee engages in important activities that might occur only occasionally, such as a nurse who handles emergencies.

Participant Diary/Logs

Another approach is to ask workers to keep a diary/log or list of what they do during the day. For every activity the employee engages in, he or she records the activity (along with the time) in a log. This can produce a very complete picture of the job, especially when supplemented with subsequent interviews with the worker and his or her supervisor. Some employees may try to exaggerate some activities and underplay others. However, the detailed, chronological nature of the log tends to mediate against this. Some employees may compile their logs by periodically dictating what they're doing into a handheld dictating machine.

Using the Internet

Most of these job analysis methods suffer from one or more of several problems. For example, face-to-face interviews and observations can be time-consuming. Collecting the information from internationally dispersed employees is challenging.[8]

Internet-based job analysis is an obvious solution.[9] The human resource department distributes standardized job analysis questionnaires to dispersed employees via their company intranets, with instructions to complete the forms and return them by a particular date.

Other Job Analysis Methods

You may encounter several other job analysis methods, most notably those in the chapter Appendix.

Writing Job Descriptions

The job analysis should provide the basis for writing a job description. A job description is a written statement of *what* the jobholder does, *how* he or she does it, and under *what conditions* the job is performed. The manager in turn uses this information to write a job specification that lists the knowledge, abilities, and skills needed to perform the job satisfactorily. Figure 3.1 presents a typical job description. As is usual, it contains several types of information.

Job Identification

As in Figure 3.1, the job identification section contains the job title, which specifies the title of the job, such as marketing manager, sales manager, or inventory control clerk.

Job Summary

The job summary should describe the general nature of the job, listing only its major functions or activities.

Relationships

A relationships statement may show the jobholder's relationships with others inside and outside the organization, and might look like this for a human resource manager:

Reports to: Vice-president of employee relations

Supervises: Human resource clerk, test administrator, labor relations director, and one secretary

Works with: All department managers and executive management

Outside the company: Employment agencies, executive recruiting firms, union representatives, state and federal employment offices, and various vendors

---

FIGURE 3.1   Sample Job Description, Pearson Education

JOB TITLE: Telesales Representative	JOB CODE: 100001
RECOMMENDED SALARY GRADE:	EXEMPT/NONEXEMPT STATUS: Nonexempt
JOB FAMILY: Sales	EEOC: Sales Workers
DIVISION: Higher Education	REPORTS TO: District Sales Manager
DEPARTMENT: In-House Sales	LOCATION: Boston
	DATE: April 2007

SUMMARY (Write a brief summary of job.)

The person in this position is responsible for selling college textbooks, software, and multimedia products to professors, via incoming and outgoing telephone calls, and to carry out selling strategies to meet sales goals in assigned territories of smaller colleges and universities. In addition, the individual in this position will be responsible for generating a designated amount of editorial leads and communicating to the publishing groups product feedback and market trends observed in the assigned territory.

SCOPE AND IMPACT OF JOB

Dollar responsibilities (budget and/or revenue)

The person in this position is responsible for generating approximately $2 million in revenue, for meeting operating expense budget of approximately $4000, and a sampling budget of approximately 10,000 units.

Supervisory responsibilities (direct and indirect)

None

Other

REQUIRED KNOWLEDGE AND EXPERIENCE (Knowledge and experience necessary to do job)

Related work experience

Prior sales or publishing experience preferred. One year of company experience in a customer service or marketing function with broad knowledge of company products and services is desirable.

Formal education or equivalent

Bachelor's degree with strong academic performance or work equivalent experience.

Skills

Must have strong organizational and persuasive skills. Must have excellent verbal and written communications skills and must be PC proficient.

Other

Limited travel required (approx 5%)

PRIMARY RESPONSIBILITIES (List in order of importance and list amount of time spent on task.)

Driving Sales (60%)
- Achieve quantitative sales goal for assigned territory of smaller colleges and universities.
- Determine sales priorities and strategies for territory and develop a plan for implementing those strategies.
- Conduct 15-20 professor interviews per day during the academic sales year that accomplishes those priorities.
- Conduct product presentations (including texts, software, and Web site); effectively articulate author's central vision of key titles; conduct sales interviews using the PSS model; conduct walk-through of books and technology.
- Employ telephone selling techniques and strategies.
- Sample products to appropriate faculty, making strategic use of assigned sampling budgets.
- Close class test adoptions for first edition products.
- Negotiate custom publishing and special packaging agreements within company guidelines.
- Initiate and conduct in-person faculty presentations and selling trips as appropriate to maximize sales with the strategic use of travel budget. Also use internal resources to support the territory sales goals.
- Plan and execute in-territory special selling events and book-fairs.
- Develop and implement in-territory promotional campaigns and targeted email campaigns.

Publishing (editorial/marketing) 25%
- Report, track, and sign editorial projects.
- Gather and communicate significant market feedback and information to publishing groups.

Territory Management 15%
- Track and report all pending and closed business in assigned database.
- Maintain records of customer sales interviews and adoption situations in assigned database.
- Manage operating budget strategically.
- Submit territory itineraries, sales plans, and sales forecasts as assigned.
- Provide superior customer service and maintain professional bookstore relations in assigned territory.

Decision-Making Responsibilities for This Position:
Determine the strategic use of assigned sampling budget to most effectively generate sales revenue to exceed sales goals.
Determine the priority of customer and account contacts to achieve maximum sales potential.
Determine where in-person presentations and special selling events would be most effective to generate most sales.

Submitted By: Jim Smith, District Sales Manager	Date: April 10, 2007
Approval:	Date:
Human Resources:	Date:
Corporate Compensation:	Date:

Source: Courtesy of HR Department, Pearson Education.

Responsibilities and Duties

This section is the heart of the job description and presents a detailed list of the job's responsibilities and duties. Here, list and describe in several sentences each of the job's major duties. For instance, you might further define the duty "selects, trains, and develops subordinate personnel" as follows: "develops spirit of cooperation and understanding," "ensures that work group members receive specialized training as necessary," and "directs training involving teaching, demonstrating, and/or advising."

Human resource managers once used the Department of Labor's *Dictionary of Occupational Titles* to find and itemize the job's duties and responsibilities. As an example of the information managers could glean from it, the *Dictionary of Occupational Titles* lists a human resource manager's specific duties and responsibilities, including "plans and carries out policies relating to all phases of personnel activity," "recruits, interviews, and selects employees to fill vacant positions," and "conducts wage survey within labor market to determine competitive wage rate."

Today, the U.S. Department of Labor's *Occupational Information Network*, or O*NET (and its Standard Occupational Classification, as in Figure 3.2) have largely replaced the *Dictionary of Occupational Titles*. Built-in software allows users to see the most important characteristics of an occupation, as well as the training, experience, and education and knowledge that are required to do the job well.[10]

Authority

This section defines the limits of the jobholder's authority. For example, the jobholder might have authority to approve purchase requests up to $5,000, grant time off or leaves of absence, discipline department personnel, recommend salary increases, and interview and hire new employees.[11]

Standards of Performance

Some job descriptions also contain a standards-of-performance section. This states the standards the employee is expected to achieve in each of the job description's main duties and responsibilities.

FIGURE 3.2	Marketing Manager Description from Standard Occupational Classification

U.S. Department of Labor
Bureau of Labor Statistics
Standard Occupational Classification

www.bls.gov | Advanced Search | A-Z Index

BLS Home | Programs & Surveys | Get Detailed Statistics | Glossary | What's New | Find It! In DOL

11-2021 Marketing Managers

Determine the demand for products and services offered by a firm and its competitors and identify potential customers. Develop pricing strategies with the goal of maximizing the firm's profits or share of the market while ensuring the firm's customers are satisfied. Oversee product development or monitor trends that indicate the need for new products and services.

Source: www.bls.gov/soc/soc_a2c1.htm, accessed May 10, 2007.

Working Conditions and Physical Environment

The job description also lists the general working conditions involved in the job. These might include noise level, hazardous conditions, heat, and other conditions.

Using the Internet

Most employers probably still write their own job descriptions, but more are turning to the Internet. One site, www.jobdescription.com, illustrates why. The process is simple. Search by alphabetical title, key word, category, or industry to find the desired job title. This leads you to a generic job description for that title—say, "computers & EDP systems sales representative." You can then use the wizard to customize the generic description for this position. For example, you can add specific information about your organization, such as job title, job codes, department, and preparation date. And you can indicate whether the job has supervisory abilities, and choose from a number of possible desirable competencies and experience levels.[12] Others use O*NET (please see the chapter appendix) to craft job descriptions.

Writing Job Descriptions that Comply with the ADA

As explained in Chapter 2, the Americans with Disabilities Act (ADA) does not require employers to have job descriptions. However, most ADA lawsuits revolve around the question: What are the essential functions of the job? Essential job functions are those job duties that employees must be able to perform, with or without reasonable accommodation.[13] Without a job description listing these functions, it is difficult to convince a court that the functions are essential.[14] The corollary is that the essential functions can't just be listed on the description, but should also be listed as "essential."[15]

Writing Job Specifications

The job specification starts with the job description and then answers the question, What human traits and experience are required to do this job well? It shows what kind of person to recruit and for what qualities that person should be tested. The job specification may be a separate section on the job description (as at the end of the first page of Figure 3.1) or a separate document entirely.

Writing job specifications for trained employees is relatively straightforward. For example, suppose you want to fill a position for a trained bookkeeper (or trained counselor or programmer). In cases like these, your job specifications might focus mostly on traits such as length of previous service, quality of relevant training, and previous job performance. Thus, it's usually not too difficult to determine the human requirements for placing already trained people on a job.

But the problems are more complex when you're filling jobs with untrained people. Here you must specify qualities such as physical traits, personality, interests, or sensory skills that imply some potential for performing the job or for having the ability to be trained for the job. For example, suppose the job requires detailed manipulation on a circuit board assembly line. You might want to ensure that the person scores high on a test of finger dexterity. Your goal, in other words, is to identify those personal traits—or human requirements—that predict which candidate would do well on the job and which would not. Identifying these human requirements for a job is accomplished either through a subjective, judgmental approach or through statistical analysis.

Common sense needs to be applied when compiling a list of the job's human requirements. Certainly job-specific human traits such as manual dexterity and education are important. However, it's important not to ignore the fact that there are also work behaviors (such as industriousness, thoroughness, good attendance, and honesty) that seem to apply to almost any job, but might not normally be unearthed through a job analysis.[16]

Job Analysis in a "Jobless" World

A job is a set of closely related activities carried out for pay, but over the past few years, the concept of job has been changing quite dramatically. Job descriptions tend to be less structured and restrictive.

"De-jobbing" reflects the fact that most workplaces need to be more flexible today. Globalized competition means more pressure for performance. Firms are therefore instituting high-performance workplace policies and practices. These include management systems (such as "just-in-time production methods") based on flexible, multiskilled job assignments, and on teamwork and participative decision making. In turn, flexible jobs and teamwork assume that job assignments may change frequently. Changes like these have blurred the meaning of *job* as a set of well-defined and clearly delineated responsibilities. Employers want and need employees to define their jobs more broadly and flexibly. The bottom line is that the trend is toward newer ways to analyze and describe jobs. One of these is Competency-Based Job Analysis.

Competency-Based Job Analysis

What Are Competencies?

We can define *competencies* as demonstrable characteristics of the person that enable performance. Job competencies are always observable and measurable behaviors comprising part of a job (we'll look at examples in a moment). We can say that *competency-based job analysis* means describing the job in terms of measurable, observable, behavioral competencies (knowledge, skills, and/or behaviors) that an employee doing that job must exhibit to do the job well. This contrasts with the traditional way of describing the job in terms of job duties and responsibilities.[17]

Traditional job analysis focuses on "what" a job is in terms of job duties and responsibilities. *Competency analysis* focuses more on "how" the worker meets the job's objectives or actually accomplishes the work.[18] Traditional job analysis is more job focused. Competency-based analysis is more worker focused—specifically, what must he or she be competent to do?

An Example

In practice, competency-based analysis often comes down to identifying the basic skills an employee needs to do the job. For example, at British Petroleum's (BP's) exploration division, the need for more efficient, faster acting, flatter organizations and empowered employees inspired management to replace job descriptions with matrices listing skills and skill levels. Senior managers wanted to shift employees' attention from a job description "that's-not-my-job" mentality to one that would motivate them to obtain the new skills they needed to accomplish their broader flexible responsibilities.

The solution was a skills matrix like that in Figure 3.3. They created skills matrices for various jobs within two groups of employees: those on a management track and those whose aims lay elsewhere (such as to stay in engineering). HR prepared a matrix for each job or job family (such as drilling managers). As in Figure 3.3, the matrix listed (1) the basic skills needed for that job (such as technical expertise) and (2) the minimum level of each skill required for that job or job family. The emphasis is no longer on specific job duties. Instead, the focus is on developing the new skills needed for the employees' broader, empowered, and often relatively undefined responsibilities.

The skills matrix method prompted other HR changes in this division. For example, the firm instituted a new skills-based pay plan that awards raises based on skills improvement. Performance appraisals now focus more on skills employees acquired. And training emphasizes developing broad skills like leadership and planning—skills applicable across a wide range of responsibilities and jobs.

FIGURE 3.3   The Skills Matrix for One Job at BP

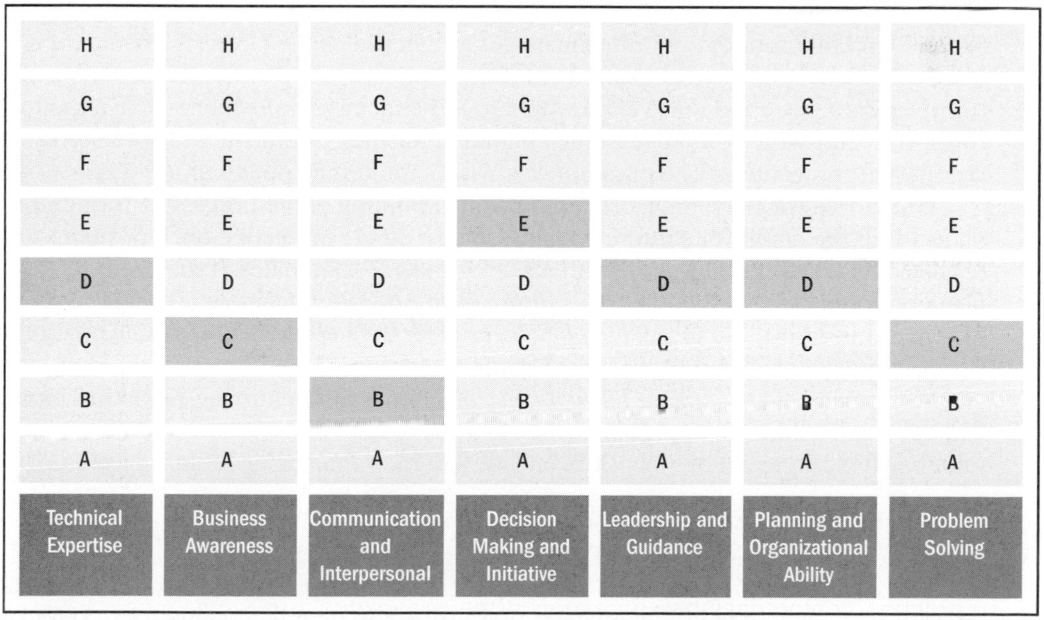

Note: The shaded boxes (D, C, B, E, D, D, C) indicate the minimum level of skill required for the job.

THE RECRUITMENT AND SELECTION PROCESS

Employers use job analysis and job descriptions for several things—for example, as the basis for developing training programs or for determining how much to pay for various jobs. But the most familiar use for job descriptions is for deciding what types of people to recruit and then select for the company's jobs.

This *recruiting and selecting process* is a series of steps, as follows:

1. Do workforce planning and forecasting to determine the positions to be filled.
2. Build a pool of candidates for these jobs by recruiting internal or external candidates.
3. Have the applicants fill out application forms and perhaps undergo an initial screening interview.
4. Utilize various selection techniques such as tests, background investigations, and physical exams to identify viable job candidates.
5. Send one or more viable job candidates to the supervisor responsible for the job.
6. Have the candidate(s) go through one or more selection interviews with the supervisor and other relevant parties for the purpose of finally determining to which candidate(s) an offer should be made.

Workforce planning and recruiting (steps 1 through 3) are the subjects of the remainder of this chapter. Chapter 4 then focuses on employee selection techniques including tests, background checks, and physical exams (steps 4 through 6).

WORKFORCE PLANNING AND FORECASTING

When Dan Hilbert became staffing manager at Valero Energy Corp., the company was not doing any employment planning. After analyzing the firm's demographic and turnover data, he found that Valero would soon be facing employment gaps in their oil refineries that were four to six times higher than they could fill with their present recruitment procedures. The question was, what should they do about it?[19]

Workforce (or personnel, or employment) **planning** is the process of formulating plans to fill the employer's future openings, based on (1) projecting open positions and (2) deciding whether to fill these with inside or outside candidates. It therefore refers to planning to fill any or all of the firm's future positions, from maintenance clerk to CEO. However, most firms use *succession planning* to refer to the process of planning how to fill the company's most important top executive positions. Today, employers often also emphasize talent management. *Talent management* involves identifying, recruiting, hiring, and developing high-potential employees. One survey of CEOs of the largest companies said they typically spent between 20% and 40% of their time on talent management.[20]

Strategy and Workforce Planning

Personnel planning is (or should be) an integral part of a firm's strategic planning processes. For example, when JDS Uniphase decided to expand its Melbourne, Florida, operations, it expanded its employment there from 140 people to almost 750. The firm needed to make fairly specific plans showing how many of what sorts of people to hire, and where these new employees should come from.

Personnel planning cannot be unduly mechanical. The heart of personnel planning involves predicting the skills and competencies the employer will need to execute its strategy. Personnel planning therefore can't just involve extrapolating the past. Instead, it must be a communicative and collaborative process. At IBM and Hewlett-Packard, for instance, human resource executives routinely discuss with their firm's finance and other executives the personnel ramifications of their company's strategic plans, for instance in terms of the employee capabilities the firms will need to achieve their goals.[21]

Inside or Outside Candidates?

One big question is always whether to fill projected openings with current employees or by recruiting from outside.

Each option produces its own set of HR plans. Current employees may require training, development, and coaching before they're ready to fill new jobs—and, thus, development plans. Going outside requires deciding what recruiting sources to use, and what the availability will be. For example, unemployment rates of less than 4% in much of the U.S. in 2007 signaled, to many human resource managers, that they'd have to ramp up their recruitment efforts to successfully fill their open positions.[22]

How does the manager decide how many employees he or she needs over the next few years? If you're planning for employment requirements, you'll need to forecast three things: personnel needs, the supply of inside candidates, and the supply of outside candidates. We'll start with personnel needs.

How to Forecast Personnel Needs

The traditional personnel planning methods involve using simple tools like **ratio analysis** or **trend analysis** to estimate staffing needs based on sales projections and historical sales to personnel relationships. Knowing your product's or service's expected demand is paramount. The usual process is therefore to forecast revenues first. Then estimate the size of the staff required to achieve this volume, for instance, by using historical ratios. In addition to expected demand, staffing needs may reflect:

1. Projected turnover (as a result of resignations or terminations)
2. Quality and skills of your employees (in relation to what you see as the changing needs of your organization)
3. Strategic decisions to upgrade the quality of products or services or enter into new markets
4. Technological and other changes resulting in increased productivity
5. The financial resources available to your department

Trend Analysis

While some firms use sophisticated computerized personnel forecasting tools, there are several simple ways for a manager to estimate future personnel needs. Trend analysis involves studying your firm's employment levels over the past 5 years or so to predict future needs. Thus, you might compute the number of employees in your firm at the end of each of the past 5 years, or perhaps the number in each subgroup (such as salespeople, production people, secretarial, and administrative) at the end of each of those years. The purpose is to identify employment trends you think might continue into the future.

Ratio Analysis

Another approach, ratio analysis, means making forecasts based on the ratio between some causal factor (such as sales volume) and the number of employees required (for instance, number of salespeople). For example, suppose you find that a salesperson traditionally generates $500,000 in sales. Then, if the sales revenue-to-salespeople ratio remains the same, you would require six new salespeople next year (each of whom produces an extra $500,000 in sales) to produce, say, the desired extra $3 million in sales.

Scatter Plots

The **scatter plot** is another method. It shows graphically how two variables (such as a measure of business activity and your firm's staffing levels) are related. If they are, then if you can forecast the level of business activity, you should also be able to estimate your personnel requirements.

For example, assume a 500-bed hospital expects to expand to 1,200 beds over the next 5 years. The director of nursing and the human resource director want to forecast the requirement for registered nurses. The human resource director decides to determine the relationship between size of hospital (in terms of number of beds) and number of nurses required. She calls several hospitals of various sizes and gets the following figures:

Size of Hospital (Number of Beds)	Number of Registered Nurses
200	240
300	260
400	470
500	500
600	620
700	660
800	820
900	860

Figure 3.4 shows the hospital size (in beds) on the horizontal axis. The number of nurses is on the vertical axis. If the two factors are related, then the points will tend to fall along a straight line, as they do here. If you carefully draw in a line to minimize the distances between the line and each one of the plotted points, you will be able to estimate (forecast) the number of nurses needed for each given hospital size. Thus, for a 1,200-bed hospital, the human resource director would assume she needs about 1,210 nurses.[23]

Managerial judgment always plays a role in employment planning. It's rare that any historical trend will continue unchanged. Important factors that may influence your forecast include, for instance, decisions to upgrade the quality of products or services or enter into new markets, technological and administrative changes resulting in increased productivity, and the financial resources you plan to have available.

Forecasting the Supply of Inside Candidates

The preceding forecast provides only half the staffing equation, by answering the question, How many employees will we need? Next, the manager has to try to assess the projected *supply* of both internal and external candidates.

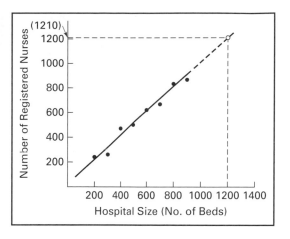

FIGURE 3.4   Determining the Relationship Between Hospital Size and Number of Nurses

Note: After fitting the line, you can extrapolate—project—how many employees you'll need, given your projected volume.

A qualifications inventory can facilitate forecasting the supply of internal candidates. **Qualifications inventories** contain summary data such as each current employee's performance record, educational background, and promotability, compiled either manually or in a computerized system. **Personnel replacement charts** (see Figure 3.5) show the present performance and promotability for each potential replacement for important positions. As an alternative, you can develop a *position replacement card* for each position, showing possible replacements as well as present performance, promotion potential, and training required by each possible candidate.

Computerized Information Systems

Employers can't maintain qualifications inventories on hundreds or thousands of employees manually. Many firms computerize this information, and there are a number of packaged systems available for accomplishing this task.

Typically, employees fill out a Web–based survey in which they describe their background and experience. The system also maintains records of performance appraisals. When a manager needs a qualified person to fill a position, he or she describes the position (for instance, in terms of the education and skills it entails) and then enters this information into the computer. After scanning its bank of possible candidates, the program presents the manager with a listing of qualified candidates.

Succession Planning

Forecasting the availability of inside candidates is particularly important in succession planning. In a nutshell, succession planning refers to the plans a company makes to fill its most important executive positions. In practice, the process often involves a fairly complicated and integrated series of steps. For example, potential successors for top management might be routed through the top jobs at several key divisions as well as overseas, and might then be sent through the Harvard Business School's Advanced Management Program. As a result, a more comprehensive definition of *succession*

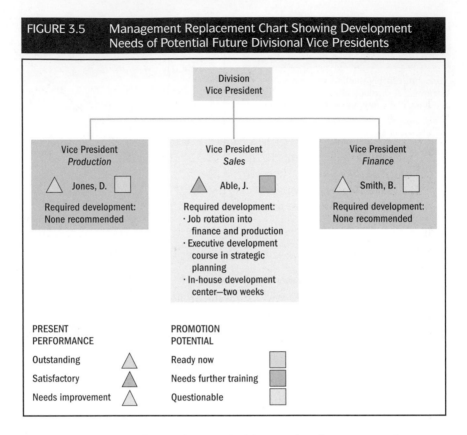

FIGURE 3.5   Management Replacement Chart Showing Development Needs of Potential Future Divisional Vice Presidents

planning is "the process of ensuring a suitable supply of successors for current and future key jobs arising from business strategy, so that the careers of individuals can be planned and managed to optimize the organization's needs and the individuals' aspirations."[24] Succession planning includes these activities:

- Analysis of the demand for managers and professionals by company level, function, and skill
- Audit of existing executives and projection of likely future supply from internal and external sources
- Planning of individual career paths based on objective estimates of future needs and drawing on performance appraisals and assessments of potential
- Career counseling in the context of a realistic understanding of the future needs of the firm, and of the individual
- Accelerated promotions, with development targeted against the future needs of the business
- Performance-related training and development to prepare individuals for future roles
- Planned strategic recruitment, not only to fill short-term needs but also to provide people to develop to meet future needs[25]

Improving Productivity Through HRIS: Succession Planning Systems

More companies are relying on software to facilitate the succession planning process. For example, when Larry Kern became president of Dole Food Co. Inc. several years ago, each of its separate operating companies handled most of their own HR activities and succession planning. Kern's strategy involved improving financial performance by reducing redundancies and centralizing certain activities, including succession planning.[26] Technology helped Dole do this. Dole decided to use special software from Pilat NAI. Pilat NAI runs the software and keeps all the data on its own servers for a monthly fee.

The Pilat succession planning system is easy for Dole's managers to use. They get access to the program via the Web using a password. They fill out online resumes for themselves, including career interests, and note special considerations such as geographic restrictions. The managers also assess themselves on four competencies. When the manager completes his or her succession planning input, the program automatically notifies the manager's boss. The latter then assesses his or her subordinate and indicates whether the person should be promoted. The person's manager also assesses his or her overall potential. This assessment, plus the online resumes, then goes automatically to the division head and the divisional HR director. Dole's senior vice-president for HR for North America then uses the information to create a career development plan for each manager, including seminars and other programs.[27]

Forecasting the Supply of Outside Candidates

If there will not be enough qualified inside candidates to fill anticipated openings, employers focus next on projecting supplies of outside candidates—those not currently employed by your organization. This may require forecasting general economic conditions, local market conditions, and occupational market conditions.

The first step is to forecast general economic conditions and, for instance, the expected prevailing rate of unemployment. Usually, the lower the rate of unemployment, the lower the labor supply and the more difficult it is to recruit personnel. Look for economic projections online, for example, from the U.S. Congressional Budget Office (CBO), www.cbo.gov/showdoc.cfm?index=1824&sequence=0; the Bureau of Labor Statistics (BLS), www.bls.gov/news.release/ecpro.toc.htm; and from private sources such as economists and the Bank of America, www.bankofamerica.com/newsroom/press/press.cfm?PressID=press.20040312.02.htm.

Local labor market conditions are also important. For example, the growth of computer and semiconductor firms recently prompted low unemployment in cities like Seattle, quite aside from general economic conditions in the country.

Finally, you may want to forecast the availability of potential job candidates in specific occupations for which you will be recruiting. Recently, for instance, there has been an undersupply of registered nurses nationally. Sources such as *Occupational Outlook Quarterly* from the U.S. Labor Department can be useful here.

RECRUITING JOB CANDIDATES

Once authorized to fill a position, the next step is to develop an applicant pool, either from internal or external sources. Recruiting is important because the more applicants you have, the more selective you can be in your hiring. With baby boomers now retiring and fewer teenagers entering the labor pool, recruitment will be a challenge in the years ahead. By several estimates, the shortage of workers will grow from almost nothing today to about 20 million workers by 2020. At that point, the U.S. labor force may only be able to fill about 90% of the available jobs.[28]

The Complex Job of Recruiting Employees

Recruiting does not just involve placing ads or calling employment agencies. For one thing, we just saw that your recruitment efforts should make sense in terms of your company's strategic plans. As with JDS Uniphase, filling a large number of anticipated openings implies that you've carefully thought through when and how you will do your recruiting—the sources you will use, for instance.

Second, we'll see that some recruiting methods are superior to others, depending on who you're recruiting and what your resources are.

Third, the success you have with your recruiting depends on many non-recruitment issues and policies. For example, deciding to pay a 10% higher salary and better benefits than most firms in your locale should, other things equal, help you build a bigger applicant pool faster.[29]

Then there are the numerous legal considerations. For example, with the EEOC's new focus on systemic, widespread discrimination, employers need to review their recruitment practices. For example, the EEOC's compliance manual makes it clear that with a non-diverse workforce, the EEOC may well view relying on word-of-mouth referrals as a barrier to equal employment opportunity.[30] A combination of factors is also making it more difficult to hire workers from abroad. Security concerns and rising resistance from Congress is making it more difficult to obtain the coveted work visas permitting work in the U.S.[31] The *HR in Practice* box provides another factor to consider.

Recruiting Effectiveness

Given all this, it's important to assess how effectively the employer is spending its recruiting dollars. Is it more cost effective to advertise for applicants on the Web or in Sunday's paper? Should we use this employment agency or that one? One survey found that only about 44% of the 279 firms surveyed make formal attempts to evaluate the outcomes of their recruitment efforts.[32] This inattention flies in the face of common sense.

HR IN PRACTICE

THE HIRING MANAGER'S OBLIGATIONS

The hiring manager needs to be careful not to interfere with the applicant's obligations to his or her current employer. In general, even without a written contract, courts generally hold that employees have a duty of loyalty to their current employers during their employment.[33] For example, they are generally expected to maintain the confidentiality of confidential employer information such as customer lists. In general, the hiring manager has both an ethical and legal obligation to respect the prospective employee's duty of loyalty. To the extent that the hiring manager participates in any breach of that loyalty—for instance, inquiring about customers' buying patterns or about new products under development—the hiring manager may share in the liability for the breach. One way to handle this problem is to make it clear at the outset that you expect applicants to honor their duty of loyalty to their current employers.[34]

Internal Sources of Candidates

Although *recruiting* may bring to mind employment agencies and classified ads, filling open jobs with current employees (internal recruiting) is often an employer's best bet. To be effective, this approach requires using job posting, personnel records, and skill banks.[35] **Job posting** means "posting the open job—on company bulletin boards and/or on the Web—and listing its attributes, such as qualifications, supervisor, working schedule, and pay rate" (as in Figure 3.6). Some union contracts require such postings to ensure that union members get first choice of better positions. Yet posting is also good practice in nonunion firms, if it facilitates the transfer and promotion of qualified inside candidates. Personnel records are also useful here. An examination of personnel records (including qualifications inventories) may reveal persons who have potential for further training or those who already have the right background for the open jobs in question.

Recruiting via the Internet

Internal candidates may not be sufficient to fill your recruiting needs. In that case, the manager turns to outside sources, often starting with placing ads on the Internet.

Most firms recruit via the Internet. Many use their company Web sites. GE's home page (www.ge.com) includes a link to www.gepowercareers.com. It not only provides useful information about working for GE but also includes numerous useful job-seeker aids, such as separate category buttons titled "experienced professionals" and "military officer." The accounting firm Deloitte & Touche Tohmatsu recently created a global recruitment site, thus eliminating the need to maintain 35 separate local recruiting Web sites.[36] Others of course post positions on Internet job boards such as Careerbuilder.com and Monster.com, or on the sites of professional associations (such as the American Institute of Chemical Engineers), or the sites of their local newspapers.

New sites are capitalizing on the popularity of social networking to provide recruiting assistance. For example, users register by supplying their name, location, and the kind of work they do on sites like Monster networking and LinkIn.com. These sites facilitate developing personal relationships for networking, hiring, and employee referrals.[37] Figure 3.7 lists some top online recruiting job sites.

Advantages and Disadvantages

Internet recruiting's wide use reflects its advantages. Newspapers may charge employers up to several thousand dollars for print ads, while job listings on one's own Web site are essentially free. Newspaper ads might have a life span of perhaps 10 days, whereas the Internet ad may attract applications for 30 days or more. Internet recruiting can also be fast, since responses to electronic job listings may start coming in at once.

Some firms have been phenomenally successful generating applications through Web-based recruiting. Yet some employers cite just such a flood of responses as a possible downside of Internet recruiting. The problem is that the relative ease of responding to Internet ads encourages unqualified job seekers to apply; furthermore, the nature of the Internet is that applications may arrive from geographic areas that are unrealistically far away. On the whole, though, more applicants are usually better than fewer, and more companies are using special software to scan, digitize, and process applicant résumés automatically.[38]

FIGURE 3.6   Job Posting Form for Hard Copy or Web Submissions

JOB POSTING FORM

Please complete all applicable areas and return via e-mail (JobForm@bigCo.com) or FAX (123-456-7890)

Date Posted _____

Reply no later than _____

Type of Employment   Summer _____   Part-Time _____   Full-Time _____

Job Title of Open Position _____

Employer _____ Department _____

Location Address _____

Web Site _____

Pay Scale _____ Shifts/Hours _____ # of Vacancies _____

Brief Job Description _____
_____
_____
_____
_____
_____
_____

Qualifications: Required Skills and Abilities _____
_____
_____
_____
_____
_____
_____

Desired Skills and Abilities _____
_____
_____
_____
_____
_____
_____

How to Apply: By FAX or e-mail as above, no later than _____ . Please ensure HR has updated copy of your résumé. Selections will be made by _____ .

FIGURE 3.7	Some Top Career and Job Search Job Boards

America's Job Bank—Almost a million job leads in their database. Job-seekers can search for jobs or post your resumes. Free.

BilingualCareer.com—Bilingual job-seekers (English and at least one other language) can search job listings, post resume, and find job interviewing and resume preparation advice.

CareerBuilder—Claims to have the largest assortment of job listings on the Net—a combination of help wanted ads of the nation's leading newspapers and job listings from the Web sites of leading employers.

Career.com—Lots of job opportunities, searchable by company, location, and discipline. Also lists jobs for new college graduates.

College Recruiter—Jobs for college students, grads and recent graduates. Entry level work and career opportunities. Part-time and full-time. A great resource for job-seekers.

Futurestep—An executive recruiting service from Korn/Ferry International that focuses on filling mid-level positions in professional services, information technology, human resources, accounting, sales and marketing, public relations, production, engineering, and planning across all industries.

Job.com—Where job-seekers can post your resume and search thousands of jobs by industry, city, state, job title, and keywords. Job listings show posted date. Free to job-seekers.

JobBank USA—Specializes in providing employment and resume information services to job candidates, employers, and recruitment firms. One of the largest employment Web sites.

Jobcentral—A national employment network formed by an alliance between two nonprofit associations to provide job seekers in all industries and occupations, entry-level to chief executive officer.

Monster.com—One of the oldest job sites on the Web, with several hundred thousand jobs worldwide. Also includes career advice and relocation services for job-seekers.

Quintcareers—Now starting its 12th year of operations, and with more than 3,500 pages of free college, career, and job-search content to empower your success in life.

TrueCareers—Find job listings, company research, and other career information (articles, advice, etc.). Search for jobs (by keywords, location, salary, employers), post resume, and use a job search agent.

Yahoo! HotJobs—Candidates create a personalized career management page called *MyHotJobs*, which provides the tools needed for an easy, simple and confidential job search.

Source: Adapted from www.quintcareers.com/top_50_sites.html, accessed January 18, 2008.

E-recruiting also has some potential legal pitfalls. For example, if fewer minorities use the Internet, then automated online application gathering and screening might mean the employer inadvertently excludes higher numbers of minority applicants. Furthermore, to prove that they've complied with EEOC laws, employers need to track applicants' race, sex, and ethnic group. But, the Internet makes it so easy to submit résumés that many applicants are unsolicited and not aimed at specific jobs. Are these "applicants" for EEOC purposes? Probably not. The EEOC says that an "applicant" must meet three conditions: he or she must express interest in employment; the employer must have taken steps to fill a specific job; and the individual must have followed the employer's standard application procedure.[39]

User-Friendly Sites

Some estimate employers have only about four minutes "before online applicants will turn their attention elsewhere."[40] Making the employer's Web site user-friendly for prospective job applicants can help boost the number of online recruits. There are several ways to do this. Make it easy to get from the homepage to the career section in just one or two clicks; keep any pre-employment screening questions simple; allow job seekers to apply online and via fax or e-mail if they prefer; and include a tool that lets visitors register and receive notices about new jobs to their e-mail.[41]

Applicant Tracking Services

More firms also install *applicant tracking systems* to support their on- and off-line recruiting efforts. Well-known applicant tracking systems (such as recruitsoft.com and Itrack-IT solutions) help employers keep track of their applicants. They also help the employers perform searches (such as by skill or college degree) and to match candidates with positions. Systems like these also help employers compile reports, such as "EEO applicant summary" and "applicants by reject reason."[42] While many employers use their own Web sites and software to attract and process applications, others farm out that work to application service providers (ASPs), who process the applicants who go to your site, using their own systems. Others let job boards like careerbuilder.com, hire.com, and monster.com post their open jobs and compile the online applications.

Advertising as a Source of Candidates

To use help wanted ads successfully, you need to address two issues: the media and the ad's construction. The selection of the best medium (be it your local paper, the Web, the *Wall Street Journal,* or a technical journal) depends on the type of positions for which you're recruiting. Your local newspaper (or the Web) is usually the best source of blue-collar help, clerical employees, and lower level administrative employees. For specialized employees or professionals, you can advertise in trade and professional journals such as the *American Psychologist, Sales Management, Chemical Engineering,* and *American Banker.* One drawback to print advertising is that there may be a month or more between insertion of the ad and publication of the journal, for instance. Yet ads remain good sources, and ads such as Figure 3.8 continue to appear.

Help wanted ads in papers such as the *Wall Street Journal* can be good sources of middle- or senior-management personnel. For instance, the *Wall Street Journal* has several regional editions so that you can target the entire country or the appropriate geographic area for coverage. Other employers, as we'll see, turn to the Internet for faster turnaround.

Employment Agencies as a Source of Candidates

There are three basic types of employment agencies: (1) those operated by federal, state, or local governments; (2) those associated with nonprofit organizations; and (3) privately owned agencies.

Public, state employment service agencies exist in every state. They are aided and coordinated by the U.S. Department of Labor. The latter also maintains a nationwide computerized job bank to which state employment offices are connected. Public agencies are a major source of blue-collar and often white-collar workers.

These agencies' usefulness is on the rise. Beyond just filling jobs, counselors will visit an employer's work site, review the employer's job requirements, and even assist

FIGURE 3.8   Help Wanted Ad that Draws Attention

Are You Our Next Key Player?

PLANT CONTROLLER   Northern New Jersey

Are you looking to make an impact? Can you be a strategic business partner and team player, versus a classic, "bean counter"? Our client, a growing **Northern New Jersey** manufacturer with two locations, needs a high-energy, self-initiating, technically competent Plant Controller. Your organizational skills and strong understanding of general, cost, and manufacturing accounting are a must. We are not looking for a delegator, this is a hands-on position. If you have a positive can-do attitude and have what it takes to drive our accounting function, read on

Responsibilities and Qualifications:

- Monthly closings, management reporting, product costing, and annual budget.
- Accurate inventory valuations, year-end physical inventory, and internal controls.
- 4-year Accounting degree, with 5–8 years experience in a manufacturing environment.
- Must be proficient in Microsoft Excel and have general computer skills and aptitude.
- Must be analytical and technically competent, with the leadership ability to influence people, situations, and circumstances.

If you have what it takes to be our next key player, tell us in your cover letter, *"Beyond the beans, what is the role of a Plant Controller?"* Only cover letters addressing that question will be considered. Please indicate your general salary requirements in your cover letter and email or fax your resume and cover letter to:

Rich Frigon
Giombetti Associates
2 Allen Street, P.O. Box 720
Hampden, MA 01036
Email: rfrigon@giombettiassoc.com
Fax: (413) 566-2009

GIOMBETTI ASSOCIATES
INSTITUTE OF LEADERSHIP

Source: The New York Times, May 13, 2007, Business p. 18.

the employer in writing job descriptions. And most states are turning their local state employment service agencies into "one-stop" shops. Under a single roof, employers and job seekers can access an array of services such as recruitment services, employee training programs, and access to local and national labor market information.

Other employment agencies are associated with *nonprofit organizations*. For example, most professional and technical societies have units that help their members find jobs. Similarly, many public welfare agencies try to place people who are in special categories, such as those who are physically disabled or who are war veterans.

Private employment agencies are important sources of clerical, white-collar, and managerial personnel. Such agencies charge a fee for each applicant they place. These fees are usually set by state law and are posted in their offices. The trend is toward "fee-paid jobs," in which the employer pays the fees.

Some specific reasons you might want to turn to an agency include the following:

- Your firm does not have its own human resource department and is not geared to do recruiting and screening.
- Your firm has found it difficult in the past to generate a pool of qualified applicants.

- A particular opening must be filled quickly.
- There is a perceived need to attract a greater number of minority or female applicants.
- The recruitment effort is aimed at reaching individuals who are currently employed and who might feel more comfortable dealing with employment agencies than with competing companies.

On the other hand, employment agencies are no panacea. For example, the employment agency's screening may let unqualified applicants go directly to the supervisors responsible for the hiring, who may in turn naïvely hire them.

Temporary Workers

Many employers supplement their permanent employee base by hiring contingent or temporary workers, often through temporary help agencies. Also called *part-time* or *just-in-time* workers, the *contingent workforce* is big and growing and is broadly defined as "workers who don't have permanent jobs."[43]

Staffing with contingent workers owes its popularity to several things. First, corporate downsizing seems to be driving up the number of temporary workers firms employ (to replace the permanent workers they lay off). Second, employers have always used "temps" to fill in for the days or weeks that permanent employees were out sick or on vacation. Today's desire for ever-higher productivity also contributes to temp workers' growing popularity. For one thing, you pay temp workers only for hours worked, not for the hours that some non-temp workers may spend sitting around. Contingent workers often aren't paid benefits, which is another saving for the employer. Temp workers also let employers readily expand and contract with changes in demand. Many firms also use temporary hiring to give prospective employees a trial run before hiring them as regular employees.[44]

Employers can hire temp workers either through direct hires or through temporary staff agencies. Direct hiring involves simply hiring workers and placing them on the job. The employer usually pays these people directly, as it does all its employees, but classifies them separately from regular employees.[45] The employer generally classifies these workers as casual, seasonal, or temporary employees, and often awards few if any benefits (such as pension benefits).

If hired through agencies, the agency usually pays the employees' salaries and (any) benefits. For instance, Nike Inc. recently signed a multimillion dollar deal with Kelly Services to manage Nike's contingent workforce (temporary hires).[46] Several years ago, federal agents rounded up about 250 illegal "contract" workers in 60 Wal-Mart stores. The case underscores the need for employers to understand the status and source of the contract employees who work on their premises under the auspices of outside contingent staffing firms that are handling activities like security, food service, or, as in Wal-Mart's case, after-hours store cleaning.[47]

The contingent workforce is no longer limited to clerical or maintenance staff. Each year, upwards of 100,000 people find temporary work in engineering, science, or management support occupations.

Alternative Staffing

Temporary employees are examples of alternative staffing—basically, the use of non-traditional recruitment sources. The use of alternate staffing sources is widespread and growing. About 1 of 10 U.S. employees is employed in some type of alternative work arrangement. Other alternative staffing arrangements include "in-house temporary employees" (people employed directly by the company, but on an explicit short-term basis) and "contract technical employees" (highly skilled workers like engineers, who are supplied for long-term projects under contract from an outside technical services firm).

Executive Recruiters as a Source of Candidates

Executive recruiters (also called *headhunters*) are special employment agencies retained by employers to seek out top-management talent for their clients. They fill jobs in the $80,000 and up category, although $120,000 is often the lower limit. The percentage of your firm's positions filled by these services might be small. However, these jobs include the most crucial executive and technical positions. For top executive positions, headhunters may be your *only* source. The employer pays their fees.

Two trends—technology and specialization—are changing the executive search business. Top firms once took months to complete a big search. Much of that time went into shuffling chores between headhunters and the researchers who develop the initial "long list" of candidates. This approach takes too long in today's fast-moving environment. Most of these firms now have Internet-linked databases, the aim of which is to create a list of potential candidates at the push of a button.

Pros and Cons

Headhunters are useful. They have many contacts and are especially adept at contacting qualified candidates who are employed and not actively looking to change jobs. They can also keep your firm's name confidential until late into the search process. The recruiter can save top management time by doing the preliminary work of advertising for the position and screening what could turn out to be hundreds of applicants. The recruiter's fee might actually be insignificant compared to the cost of the executive time saved.

But there are pitfalls. As an employer, you must explain completely what sort of candidate is required and why. Some recruiters may be more interested in persuading you to hire a candidate than in finding one who will do the best job. Sometimes, what clients say or think they want is not really what they need. Therefore, be prepared for some in-depth dissecting of your request. Also make sure to meet the person who will be handling your search, nail down exactly what the charges will be, and make sure the recruiter checks candidates' references and that you double-check selected references yourself.

Candidates' Caveats

As a job candidate, keep several things in mind when dealing with executive search firms. Some of these firms may present an unpromising candidate to a client simply to make their other one or two proposed candidates look better. Some eager clients may also jump the gun, checking your references and undermining your present position prematurely. Finally, do not confuse executive search firms with the many executive assistance firms that help out-of-work executives find jobs. The latter charge the job seekers handsome fees to assist with things like résumé preparation and interview skills. They rarely actually reach out to prospective employers to find their clients jobs.

College Recruiting and Interns as a Source of Candidates

Many promotable candidates originally get hired through college recruiting. Such recruiting is thus an important source of management trainees, as well as of professional and technical employees.

There are two main problems with on-campus recruiting. First, it is relatively expensive and time consuming for the recruiters. Schedules must be set well in advance, company brochures printed, records of interviews kept, and much recruiting time spent on campus. Second, recruiters themselves are sometimes ineffective. Some recruiters are unprepared, show little interest in candidates, and act superior. Others don't effectively screen their student candidates.

Campus recruiters should have two goals. The main goal is screening, which means determining whether a candidate is worthy of further consideration. Exactly which traits you look for depend on your specific recruiting needs. However, the checklist presented in Figure 3.9 is typical. Traits to assess include motivation, communication skills, education, appearance, and attitude.

Although the main goal is to find and screen good candidates, the other aim is to attract them to your firm. A sincere and informal attitude, respect for the applicant, and prompt follow-up letters can help you to sell the employer to the interviewee.

Job seekers should know that recruiters are usually coy when it comes to revealing the full amount they're willing to pay. For example, one researcher found that 9 out of 10 recruiters say they do not reveal, during hiring interviews, the full amount they're willing to pay to hire good employees for the job. Thus, there's often more flexibility at the top than applicants may realize.[48]

Internships

Many college students get their jobs through college internships, a recruiting approach that has grown dramatically in recent years.

Internships can be win-win situations for both students and employers. For students, an internship may mean being able to hone business skills, check out potential employers, and learn more about their likes (and dislikes) when it comes to choosing careers. Employers can use the interns to make useful contributions while they're being evaluated as possible full-time employees. One survey found that employers offer jobs to over 70% of their interns.[49]

Partnering with a college or university's career center can be useful. It provides recruiters with relatively quick and easy access to a good source of applicants. And, it can provide useful feedback to recruiters regarding things like labor market conditions and the effectiveness of one's on- and off-line recruiting ads.[50] The Shell Group of companies recently reduced the list of schools its recruiters visit to 26, using factors such as quality of academic program, number of students enrolled, and diversity of the student body.[51]

Referrals and Walk-Ins as a Source of Candidates

With *employee referrals* campaigns, the firm posts announcements of openings and requests for referrals on its Intranet and bulletin boards. It may offer prizes for referrals that culminate in hirings.

Employee referral programs have their pros and cons. Current employees can and usually do provide accurate information about the job applicants they are referring,

FIGURE 3.9   Candidate Evaluation Form for On/Off Campus Use

Candidate Evaluation Form

Interviewer _____   Date _____
Candidate
Name _____   Position _____

Scoring

Candidate evaluation forms are to be completed by the interviewer to rank the candidate's overall qualifications for the position to which they have applied. Under each heading the interviewer should give the candidate a numerical rating and write specific job-related comments in the space provided. The numerical rating system is based on the following.

| 5 - | 4 - Above | 3 - | 2 - | 1 - |
| Exceptional | Average | Average | Satisfactory | Unsatisfactory |

Educational Background - Does the candidate have the appropriate educational qualifications or training for this position?

Rating: 1   2   3   4   5

Comments:

Prior Work Experience - Has the candidate acquired similar skills or qualifications through past work experiences?

Rating: 1   2   3   4   5

Comments:

Technical Qualifications/Experience - Does the candidate have the technical skills necessary for this position?

Rating: 1   2   3   4   5

Comments:

Verbal Communication - How were the candidate's communication skills during the interview (i.e. body language, answers to questions)?

Rating: 1   2   3   4   5

Comments:

Candidate Enthusiasm - How much interest did the candidate show in the position and the company?

Rating: 1   2   3   4   5

Comments:

Knowledge of Company - Did the candidate research the company prior to the interview?

Rating: 1   2   3   4   5

Comments:

(*Continued*)

Teambuilding/Interpersonal Skills - Did the candidate demonstrate, through their answers, good teambuilding/Interpersonal skills?

Rating: 1   2   3   4   5

Comments:

Initiative - Did the candidate demonstrate, through their answers, a high degree of initiative?

Rating: 1   2   3   4   5

Comments:

Time Management - Did the candidate demonstrate, through their answers, good time management skills?

Rating: 1   2   3   4   5

Comments:

Customer Service - Did the candidate demonstrate, through their answers, a high level of customer service skills/abilities?

Rating: 1   2   3   4   5

Comments:

Salary Expectations - What were the candidate's salary expectations? Were they within the range for the position?

Rating: 1   2   3   4   5

Comments:

Overall Impression and Recommendation - Final comments and recommendations for proceeding with the candidate.

Rating: 1   2   3   4   5

Comments:

Source: Society for Human Resource Management (SHRM). www.shrm.org/hrtools/forms_published/2CMS_002131.asp, accessed August 9, 2007.

because they're putting their reputations on the line by recommending them. The new employees may also come with a more realistic picture of what working in the firm is really like after speaking with their friends who are currently employed there. Referral programs may also result in higher quality candidates, insofar as employees are reluctant to refer less qualified candidates. But the success of the campaign depends a lot on your employees' morale. And the campaign can backfire if an employee's referral is rejected and the employee becomes dissatisfied. Using referrals exclusively may also turn out to be discriminatory if most of your current employees (and their referrals) are male or white.

Employee referral programs are popular. Employee referrals have been the source of almost half of all hires at AmeriCredit since the firm kicked off its "you've got friends, we want to meet them" employee referrals program. Employees making a referral receive $1,000 awards, with the payments spread over a year. As the head of recruiting says, "Quality people know quality people. If you give employees the opportunity to make referrals, they automatically suggest high-caliber people because they are stakeholders. . . ."[52]

Walk-Ins

Particularly for hourly workers, *walk-ins*—direct applications made at your office—are a major source of applicants, and you can even encourage them by posting "for hire" signs on your property. Treat all walk-ins courteously and diplomatically, out of both common decency and to support your firm's community reputation. Many employers thus give every walk-in a brief interview with someone in the HR office, even if it is only to get information on the applicant in case a position should open in the future. Good business practice also requires answering all letters of inquiry from applicants promptly and courteously.

Don't underestimate the importance of employee referrals or in-house job postings. One review of recruitment sources concluded, for instance, that "referrals by current personnel, in-house job postings, and the rehiring of former employees are the most effective [recruiting] sources. Walk-ins have been slightly less effective, and the least effective sources are newspaper ads, school placement services, and employment agencies (government/private)."[53]

Customers as Candidates

The Container Store uses a successful variant of the employee referrals campaign. They train their employees to recruit new employees from among the firm's customers. For example, if an employee sees that a customer seems interested in the Container Store, the employee might say, "If you love shopping here, you'd love working here."[54]

Telecommuters

Hiring telecommuters is another option. For example, JetBlue Airways uses at-home agents who are JetBlue employees to handle its reservation needs. These "crewmembers" all live in the Salt Lake City area, and work out of their homes. They use JetBlue-applied computers and technology, and receive JetBlue training.[55]

Strategy and HR

To support its fast-growth strategy, The Cheesecake Factory uses four recruiting sources: employee referrals, promotions of current employees, search firms, and online job postings. The firm's head of HR, Ed Eynon, says the Web has become "our No. 1 source of recruitment, with between 30% and 35% of our new managers coming through it." The company also does not just post short print-type help wanted ads on the Web. For most jobs it includes the entire job description. This helps provide potential applicants with a realistic picture of the job, and helps to screen out people who see that the job is not for them. The server's description on CareerBuilder.com includes a 765-word list of duties, for instance.[56]

Recruiting a More Diverse Workforce

As noted earlier, the composition of the U.S. workforce is changing dramatically. More and more potential employees will be minorities and women. This means taking special steps to recruit older workers, minorities, and women.

We'll see that many factors contribute to successful minority/female recruiting. For example, flexible hours make it easier to attract and keep single parents. Overall, the important thing is to take the steps that "say" this is a good place for diverse employees to work. Projecting the right message might include using minority-targeted media outlets, highly diverse ads, emphasizing inclusiveness in policy statements, and using minority and female recruiters.[57]

Older Workers as a Source of Candidates

Employers are looking to older workers as a source of recruits, for several reasons. Because of buyouts and early retirements, many workers retired early and are ready to reenter the job market. Furthermore, the number of annual retirees is rising as the baby boom generation retires, and employers are having difficulty replacing them with younger workers. A survey by the American Association of Retired Persons concluded that about 80% of the baby boomers expect to work after retirement.[58]

Recruiting and attracting older workers involves any or all of the sources described earlier (advertising, employment agencies, and so forth), but with one big difference. Recruiting and attracting older workers generally requires a comprehensive effort before the recruiting begins, in part because older workers may have some special preferences.[59] The effort's aim is to make the company an attractive place in which the older worker can work. For example:

- *Develop flexible work options.* At Wrigley Company, workers over 65 can progressively shorten their work schedules; another company uses "minishifts" to accommodate those interested in working less than full time.[60]
- *Create or redesign suitable jobs.* At Xerox, unionized hourly workers over 55 with 15 years of service and those over 50 with 20 years of service can bid on jobs at lower stress and lower pay levels if they so desire.
- *Offer flexible benefit plans.* Older employees often put more emphasis on longer vacations or on continued accrual of pension credits than do younger workers.

The most effective ads for attracting older workers emphasize schedule flexibility and accentuate the firm's equal opportunity employment statement.[61]

Recruiting Single Parents

About two-thirds of all single parents are in the workforce, and this group thus represents an important source of candidates.

Formulating an intelligent program for attracting single parents should begin with understanding the problems that they can encounter in balancing work and family life. In one survey, working single parents (the majority are single mothers) stated that their work responsibilities interfered significantly with their family life. They described as a no-win situation the challenge of having to do a good job at work and being a good parent, and many expressed disappointment at feeling like failures in both endeavors.

The respondents generally viewed themselves as having "less support, less personal time, more stress and greater difficulty balancing job and home life" than other working parents.[62] However, most were hesitant to dwell on their single-parent status at work for fear that such a disclosure would affect their jobs adversely.[63]

Given such concerns, the first step in attracting (and keeping) single parents is to make the workplace as user friendly for single parents as practical. Organizing regular, ongoing support groups and other forums at which single parents can share their concerns is a good way to provide the support that may be otherwise lacking. Furthermore, although many firms have instituted programs aimed at becoming more family friendly, they may not be extensive enough, particularly for single parents. For example, *flextime* programs provide employees some flexibility (such as 1-hour windows at the beginning or end of the day) around which to build their workdays. The problem is that "for some single mothers, this flexibility can help, but it may not be sufficient to really make a difference in their ability to juggle work and family schedules."[64] In addition to providing increased flexibility, employers should train their supervisors:

> Very often, the relationships which the single mother has with her supervisor and co-workers is a significant factor influencing whether the single-parent employee perceives the work environment to be supportive.[65]

Recruiting Minorities and Women

The same prescriptions that apply to recruiting single parents apply to recruiting minorities and women. In other words, employers have to formulate comprehensive plans for attracting minorities and women, plans that may include reevaluating personnel policies, developing flexible work options, redesigning jobs, and offering flexible benefit plans.

An employer can do many specific things to become more attractive to minorities. To the extent that many minority applicants may not meet the educational or experience standards for a job, many companies (such as Aetna Life & Casualty) offer remedial training in basic arithmetic and writing. Online diversity data banks or minority-focused recruiting publications are another option. Checking with your own minority employees can also be useful. In one study, about 32% of job seekers of Hispanic origin cited "check with friends or relatives" as a strategy when looking for jobs.[66] The *Global Issues* box provides an additional perspective.

Sometimes the easiest way to recruit women and minorities is to make sure that they don't quit in the first place. For example, the accounting firm KPMG works hard to make sure that female employees who take maternity leave will want to return. When an expectant mother tells HR that she's going to take maternity leave, the company sends her a basket containing a description of its parental leave benefits as well as a baby bottle, a rattle, and a tiny T-shirt that says, "My mom works at KPMG."[67]

Welfare-to-Work

Employers are also implementing various "welfare-to-work" programs for attracting and assimilating as new employees former welfare recipients.

The key to welfare-to-work programs' success seems to be the employer's pretraining assimilation and socialization program, during which participants receive counseling and basic skills training spread over several weeks.[68] For example, Marriott hired 600 welfare recipients under its Pathways to Independence program. The heart

THE GLOBAL TALENT SEARCH

As companies expand across national borders, they must increasingly tap overseas recruiting sources. For example, Gillette International has an international graduate training program aimed at identifying and developing foreign nationals. Gillette subsidiaries overseas hire outstanding business students from top local universities. These foreign nationals are then trained for 6 months at the Gillette facility in their home countries.

However, you don't have to be a multinational to have to recruit abroad. Desperate for qualified nurses, many hospitals (such as Sinai and Northwest hospitals in the Baltimore, Maryland, area) are recruiting in countries like the Philippines, India, and China.[69]

Furthermore, when employers hire "global" employees, they're not just hiring employees who will be sent to work abroad. HR professionals recognize today that with business increasingly being multinational, "every employee needs to have a certain level of global awareness."[70]

As a result, many employers want their recruiters to look for evidence of global awareness early in the interview process. For example, at the U.S. headquarters of Tetra PAK, Inc., the personnel manager reportedly looks for expatriate potential every time she makes a hire: "We don't often go out and search for someone to go abroad next year . . . but when we recruit, we always look for candidates who have global potential. We're interested in people who eventually could relocate internationally and handle that adjustment well."[71] International experience (including internships and considerable travel abroad) as well as language proficiency are two of the things employers such as these often look for.

of the program is a 6-week preemployment training program. This teaches work and life skills and is designed to rebuild workers' self-esteem and instill positive attitudes about work.[72] On the other hand, other companies report difficulty in hiring and assimilating people off welfare, in part because they sometimes lack basic work skills such as reporting for work on time, working in teams, and "taking orders without losing their temper."[73]

The Disabled

The EEOC estimates that nearly 70% of the disabled are jobless, but it certainly doesn't have to be that way.[74] In Germany, for instance, customers visiting Volkswagen's Wolfsburg plant are met by receptionist Mr. Janz. If they don't check the sign on his counter, they might assume he's ignoring them. In fact, Mr. Janz is blind, and the sign tells visitors to speak directly to him so he knows they are there.[75] Volkswagen recruited Mr. Janz because the company has a policy of integrating people with disabilities into its workforce. Similarly, thousands of employers in the United States and elsewhere have found that disabled employees provide an excellent and largely untapped source of competent, efficient labor for jobs ranging from information technology to creative advertising to receptionist. As noted earlier, many public welfare agencies place people who are in special categories, such as those who are physically disabled.

DEVELOPING AND USING APPLICATION FORMS

Purpose of Application Forms

Once you have a pool of applicants, the selection process can begin, and for most employers the application form is the first step in this process. (Some firms first require a brief, prescreening interview.) The **application form** is a good way to quickly collect verifiable and therefore fairly accurate historical data from the candidate. It usually includes information about such areas as education, prior work history, and hobbies.

A filled-in form provides at least four types of information. First are data on substantive matters, such as Does the applicant have the education and experience to do the job? Second, you can draw some conclusions about the applicant's career progress. Third, you can draw tentative conclusions regarding the applicant's stability based on previous work record. (However, be careful not to assume that an unusual number of job changes necessarily reflects on the applicant's stability; for example, the person's two most recent employers may have had to lay off large numbers of employees.) Fourth, it provides information you can use to check references and to assess the veracity of the applicant's answers.

In practice, most organizations need several application forms. For technical and managerial personnel, for example, the form may require detailed answers to questions concerning such areas as the applicant's education. The form for hourly factory workers might focus on such areas as the tools and equipment the applicant has used.

Equal Opportunity and Application Forms

Employers should carefully review their application forms to ensure that they comply with equal employment laws. Questions concerning race, religion, age, sex, or national origin are generally not illegal per se under federal laws, but are illegal under certain state laws. However, the EEOC views them with disfavor. If the applicant shows that a disproportionate number of protected group applicants gets screened out, then the burden of proof will be on the employer to prove that the potentially discriminatory items are both related to success or failure on the job and not unfairly discriminatory. Perhaps due to their proliferation, online application forms may be particularly susceptible to illegal or inadvisable questions. One survey of 41 Internet-based applications found that over 97% contained at least one inadvisable question. There were an average of just over four inappropriate questions per form. Questions regarding the applicant's past salary, age, and driver's license information led the list.[76]

Figure 3.10 presents the approach one employer—the FBI—uses to collect application form information. The Employment History section requests detailed information on each prior employer, including job title, duties, name of supervisor, and whether the employment was involuntarily terminated. Also note that in signing the application, the applicant certifies his or her understanding of several things: that

FIGURE 3.10   Employment Application

FEDERAL BUREAU OF INVESTIGATION

Preliminary Application for
Special Agent Position
(Please Type or Print in Black Ink)

Date: _____

FIELD OFFICE USE ONLY
Right Thumb Print

Div: _____   Program: _____

I. PERSONAL HISTORY

Name in Full   (Last, First, Middle)

List College Degree(s) Already Received or Pursuing, Major, School, and Month/Year:

Marital Status: ☐ Single   ☐ Engaged   ☐ Married   ☐ Separated   ☐ Legally Separated   ☐ Widowed   ☐ Divorced

Birth Date (Month, Day, Year)
Birth Place:

Social Security Number: (Optional)

Do you understand FBI employment requires availability for assignment anywhere in the U.S.?

Current Address

Home Phone _____

| Street | Apt. No. | Area Code | Number |

Work Phone _____

| City | State | Zip Code | Area Code | Number |

Are you: CPA ☐ Yes ☐ No   Licensed Driver ☐ Yes ☐ No   U. S. Citizen ☐ Yes ☐ No

Have you served on active duty in the U. S. Military? ☐ Yes ☐ No If yes, indicate branch of service and dates (month/year) of active duty. Include military school attendance (month/year):

How did you learn or become interested in FBI employment as a Special Agent?

Have you previously applied for FBI employment? ☐ Yes ☐ No
If yes, location and date:

Do you have a foreign language background? ☐ Yes ☐ No   List proficiency for each language on reverse side.

Have you ever been arrested for any crime (include major traffic violations such as Driving Under the Influence or While Intoxicated, etc.)? ☐ Yes ☐ No If so, list all such matters on a continuation sheet, even if not formally charged, or no court appearance or found not guilty, or matter settled by payment of fine or forfeiture of collateral. Include date, place, charge, disposition, details, and police agency on reverse side.

II. EMPLOYMENT HISTORY

Identify your most recent three years FULL-TIME work experience, after high school (excluding summer, part-time and temporary employment).

From Month/Year	To Month/Year	Title of Position and Description of Work	# of hrs. Per week	Name/Location of Employer

III. PERSONAL DECLARATIONS

Persons with a disability who require an accommodation to complete the application process are required to notify the FBI of their need for the accommodation.

Have you used marijuana during the last three years or more than 15 times? ☐ Yes ☐ No

Have you used any illegal drug(s) or combination of illegal drugs, other than marijuana, more than 5 times or during the last 10 years? ☐ Yes ☐ No

All information provided by applicants concerning their drug history will be subject to verification by a preemployment polygraph examination.

Do you understand all prospective FBI employees will be required to submit to an urinalysis for drug abuse prior to employment? ☐ Yes ☐ No

Please do not write below this line.

I am aware that willfully withholding information or making false statements on this application constitutes a violation of Section 1001. Title 18, U.S. Code and if appointed, will be the basis for dismissal from the Federal Bureau of Investigation. I agree to these conditions and I hereby certify that all statements made by me on this application are true and complete, to the best of my knowledge.

_____
Signature of applicant as usually written (**Do Not Use Nickname**)

falsified statements may be cause for dismissal; that investigation of credit, employment, and driving records is authorized; that a medical examination may be required; that drug screening tests may be required; and that employment is for no definite period of time.

Mandatory Dispute Resolution

Although the EEOC is generally opposed to the idea, more employers are requiring applicants to sign mandatory alternative dispute resolution forms as part of the application process. For example, the employment application package for Circuit City requires applicants to agree to arbitrate certain legal disputes related to their application for employment or employment with the company.

While mandatory arbitration is on the rise, it is also under attack.[77] Courts, federal agencies, and even arbitrators are concerned that binding arbitration strips away too many employees' rights (*voluntary* arbitration is not under attack).[78] Mandatory arbitration can also inhibit recruiting. In one study, making employment arbitration mandatory had a significantly negative impact on the attractiveness to the subjects of the company as a place to work.[79]

After You Receive the Application

After you receive the application, the job of screening the applicants begins, and we turn to selection and screening in Chapter 4. Before turning to selection, however, it is useful to re-emphasize the importance of treating applicants courteously.

Courtesy

Unfortunately, some employers develop expensive recruiting programs and then drop the ball by treating candidates discourteously. A survey by Monster.com illustrates this. What interviewer behaviors most annoyed job seekers? Seventy percent of job seekers listed, "Acting as if there is no time to talk to me." Fifty-seven percent listed "withholding information about position." About half listed "turning interview into cross examination" and "showing up late."[80]

Video Résumés

More candidates are submitting video résumés, a practice replete with benefits and threats. About half of responding employers in one survey thought video résumés might give employers a better feel for the candidate's professional demeanor, presentation skills, and job experience. The problem is that a video résumé makes it more likely rejected candidates may claim discrimination.[81]

Staying in Touch

Similarly, recruiting is expensive, so some employers maintain contact with candidates who, while not hirable today, may be of interest to the employer tomorrow. Some employers use "candidate relationship management" systems for this. Similar to the customer relationship management systems companies use to decide which customer should receive which coupon offers, **candidate relationship management** systems aim to nurture relationships with prospective candidates. They do this by periodically informing past candidates about potentially interesting job openings, and by collecting data on each candidate's evolving skills.[82]

Review

Summary

1. Developing an organization structure results in jobs that have to be staffed. Job analysis is the procedure through which you find out (1) what the job entails and (2) what kinds of people should be hired for the job. It involves six steps: (1) Determine the use of the job analysis information, (2) collect background information, (3) select the positions to be analyzed, (4) collect job analysis data, (5) review information with participants, and (6) develop a job description and job specification.

2. The job description should portray the work of the position so well that the duties are clear without reference to other job descriptions. Always ask yourself: Will the new employee understand the job if he or she reads the job description?

3. The job specification supplements the job description to answer the question, What human traits and experience are necessary to do this job well? It tells what kind of person to recruit and for what qualities that person should be tested. Job specifications are usually based on the educated guesses of managers; however, a more accurate statistical approach to developing job specifications can also be used.

4. De-jobbing is a product of the rapid changes taking place in business today. As firms try to speed decision making by taking steps such as flattening their chains of command, individual jobs are becoming broader and much less specialized. Increasingly, firms don't want employees to feel limited by a specific set of responsibilities such as those listed in a job description. As a result, more employers are deemphasizing detailed job descriptions, often substituting brief job summaries, perhaps combined with summaries of the competencies or skills required for the position.

5. Developing personnel plans requires three forecasts: one for personnel requirements, one for the supply of outside candidates, and one for the supply of inside candidates. To predict the need for personnel, first project the demand for the product or service. Next project the volume of production required to meet these estimates. Finally, relate personnel needs to these production estimates.

6. Once personnel needs are projected, the next step is to build up a pool of qualified applicants. We discussed several sources of candidates, including internal sources (or promotion from within), advertising, employment agencies, executive recruiters, college recruiting, the Internet, and referrals and walk-ins. Remember that it is unlawful to discriminate against any individual with respect to employment because of race, color, religion, sex, national origin, or age (unless these are bona fide occupational qualifications).

7. Once you have a pool of applicants, the work of selecting the best can begin. We turn to employee selection in the following chapter.

Key Terms

- job analysis
- job description
- job specification
- workforce planning
- ratio analysis
- trend analysis
- scatter plot
- qualifications inventories
- personnel replacement charts
- job posting
- application form
- candidate relationship management

Discussion Questions and Exercises

1. What items are typically included in a job description? What items are not shown?
2. What is job analysis? How can you make use of the information it provides?
3. We discussed several methods for collecting job analysis data. Compare these methods, explain what each is useful for, and list the pros and cons of each.
4. Explain how you would conduct a job analysis.

5. Working individually or in groups, obtain copies of job descriptions for clerical positions at the college or university you attend or the firm where you work. What types of information do they contain? Do they give you enough information to explain what the job involves and how to do it? How would you improve the descriptions?

6. Compare five sources of job candidates.

7. What types of information can an application form provide?

8. Working individually or in groups, bring to class several classified and display ads from this Sunday's help wanted ads. Analyze the effectiveness of these ads.

9. Working individually or in groups, obtain a recent copy of the *Monthly Labor Review* or *Occupational Outlook Quarterly,* both published by the U.S. Bureau of Labor Statistics. Based on information in either of these publications, develop a forecast for the next 5 years of occupational market conditions for various occupations, such as accountant, nurse, and engineer.

10. Working individually or in groups, visit your local office of your state employment agency. Come back to class prepared to discuss the following questions: What types of jobs seemed to be available through this agency, predominantly? To what extent do you think this particular agency would be a good source of professional, technical, and/or managerial applicants? What sort of paperwork are applicants to the state agency required to complete before their applications are processed by the agency? What other opinions did you form about the state agency?

11. Working individually or in groups, review help wanted ads placed over the past few Sundays by local employment agencies. Do some employment agencies seem to specialize in some types of jobs? If you were an HR manager seeking a relationship with an employment agency for each of the following types of jobs, which local agencies would you turn to first, based on their help wanted ad history: engineers, secretaries, data-processing clerks, accountants, and factory workers?

APPLICATION EXERCISES

Case Incident   *A Tight Labor Market for Cleaners*

While most of the publicity about "tight" labor markets usually revolves around systems engineers, nurses, and chemical engineers, some of the tightest markets are often found in some surprising places. For example, if you were to ask Mary Carter, the head of her family's six-store chain of dry-cleaning stores, what the main problem was in running their firm, the answer would be quick and short: hiring good people. The typical dry-cleaning store is heavily dependent on hiring good managers, cleaner-spotters, and pressers. Employees generally have no more than a high-school education (many have less), and the market is very competitive. Over a typical weekend, literally dozens of want ads for cleaner-spotters or pressers can be found in area newspapers. These people are generally paid about $8 an hour, and they change jobs frequently.

Why so much difficulty finding good help? The work is hot and uncomfortable; the hours are often long; the pay is often the same or less than the typical applicant could earn working in an air-conditioned environment, and the fringe benefits are usually nonexistent, unless you count getting your clothes cleaned for free.

Complicating the problem is the fact that Mary and other cleaners are usually faced with the continuing task of recruiting and hiring qualified workers out of a pool of individuals who are almost nomadic in their propensity to move around. The turnover in her stores and the stores of many of their competitors is often 400% per year. The problem, Mary says, is maddening: "On the one hand, the quality of our service depends on the skills of the cleaner-spotters, pressers, and counter staff. People come to us for our ability to return their clothes to them spotless and crisply pressed. On the other hand, profit margins are thin and we've got to keep our stores running, so I'm happy just to be able to round up enough live applicants to be able to keep my stores fully manned." ■

QUESTIONS

1. Provide a detailed list of recommendations concerning how Mary should go about increasing the number of acceptable job applicants, so that her company need no longer hire just about anyone who walks in the door. Specifically, your recommendations should include:

   Completely worded classified ads
   Recommendations concerning any other recruiting strategies you would suggest she use

2. What practical suggestions could you make that might help reduce turnover and make the stores an attractive place in which to work, thereby reducing recruiting problems?

Continuing Case

LearnInMotion.com: Who Do We Have to Hire?

As the excitement surrounding the move into their new offices wound down, the two principal owners of LearnInMotion.com, Mel and Jennifer, turned to the task of hiring new employees. In their business plan they'd specified several basic aims for the venture capital funds they'd just received, and hiring a team topped the list. They knew their other goals—boosting sales and expanding the Web site, for instance—would be unreachable without the right team.

They were just about to place their ads when Mel asked a question that brought them to a stop: "What kind of people do we want to hire?" It seemed they hadn't really considered this. They knew the answer in general terms, of course. For example, they knew they needed at least two salespeople, plus a programmer, a Web designer, and several content management people to transform the incoming material into content they could post on their site. But it was obvious that job titles alone really didn't provide enough guidance. For example, if they couldn't specify the exact duties of these positions, how could they decide whether they needed experienced employees? How could they decide exactly what sorts of experiences and skills they had to look for in their candidates if they didn't know exactly what these candidates would have to do? They wouldn't even know what questions to ask.

And that wasn't all. For example, there were obviously other tasks to do, and these weren't necessarily included in the sorts of things that salespeople, programmers, Web designers, or content management people typically do. Who was going to answer the phones? (Jennifer and Mel had originally assumed they'd put in one of those fancy automated call directory and voice-mail systems until they found out it would cost close to $10,000.) As a practical matter, they knew they had to have someone answering the phones and directing callers to the proper extension. Who was going to keep track of the monthly expenses and compile them for the accountants, who'd then produce monthly reports for the venture capitalist? Would the salespeople generate their own leads? Or would LearnInMotion.com have to hire Web surfers to search and find the names of people for the sales

staff to call or e-mail? What would happen when the company had to purchase supplies, such as fax paper or computer disks? Would the owners have to do this themselves, or should they have someone in-house do it for them? The list, it seemed, went on and on.

It was obvious, in other words, that the owners had to get their managerial act together and draw up the sorts of documents they'd read about as business majors—job descriptions, job specifications, and so forth. The trouble is, it all seemed a lot easier when they read the textbook. Now they want you, their management consultants, to help them actually do it. Here's what they want you to do for them. ■

QUESTIONS AND ASSIGNMENTS

1. Draw up a set of job descriptions for each of the positions in the case: salesperson, Web designer, programmer, and content manager. You may use whatever sources you want, but preferably search the Internet and relevant Web sites, since you want job descriptions and lists of duties that apply specifically to dot-com firms.

2. Next, using sources similar to those in Question 1 (and whatever other sources you can think of), draw up specifications for each of these jobs, including things such as desirable work habits, skills, education, and experience.

3. Next, keeping in mind that this company is on a tight budget, write a short proposal explaining how it should accomplish the other activities it needs done, such as answering the phones, compiling sales leads, producing monthly reports, and purchasing supplies.

EXPERIENTIAL EXERCISE

The Nursing Shortage

As of March 2004, the U.S. economy was improving in many respects, but unemployment was still disappointingly high, and employers were still obviously holding back on their hiring. However,

while many people were unemployed, that was not the case with nurse professionals. Virtually every hospital was aggressively recruiting nurses. Many were turning to foreign-trained nurses, for example, by recruiting nurses in the Philippines. Experts expected nurses to be in very short supply for years to come.

Purpose: The purpose of this exercise is to give you experience creating a recruitment program.

Required Understanding: You should be thoroughly familiar with the contents of this chapter, and with the nurse recruitment program of a hospital such as Lenox Hill Hospital in New York (see www.lenoxhillhospital.org/nursing/index.jsp, and www.lenoxhillhospital.org/careers/joblist.jsp).

How to Set Up the Exercise/Instructions: Set up groups of four to five students for this exercise. The groups should work separately and should not converse with each other. Each group should address the following tasks:

1. Based on information available on the hospital's Web site, create a hard-copy ad for the hospital to place in the Sunday edition of *The New York Times*. Which (geographic) editions of the *Times* would you use and why?
2. Analyze and critique the hospital's current online nurses' ad. How would you improve on it?
3. Prepare in outline form a complete nurses' recruiting program for this hospital, including all recruiting sources your group would use. ■

Endnotes

1. "Help Wanted—And Found," *Fortune* (October 2, 2006): 40.
2. Frederick Morgenson and Michael Campion, "Accuracy in Job Analysis: Toward an Inference Based Model," *Journal of Organizational Behavior* 21, no. 7 (November 2000): 819–827. See also Frederick Morgeson and Stephen Humphrey, "The Work Design Questionnaire (WDQ): Developing and Validating a Comprehensive Measure for Assessing Job Design and the Nature of Work," *Journal of Applied Psychology* 91, no. 6 (2006): 1321–1339.
3. Erik Dirdorff and Mark Wilson, "A Meta Analysis of Job Analysis Reliability," *Journal of Applied Psychology* 88, no. 4 (2003): 635–646.
4. The quote is from James Clifford, "Manage Work Better to Better Manage Human Resources: A Comparative Study of Two Approaches to Job Analysis," *Public Personnel Management* (Spring 1996): 89–102.
5. Darin Hartley, "Job Analysis at the Speed of Reality," *Training and Development* (September 2004): 20–22.
6. Frederick Morgeson et al., "Self Presentation Processes in Job Analysis: A Field Experiment Investigating Inflation in Abilities, Tasks, and Competencies," *Journal of Applied Psychology* 89, no. 4 (November 4, 2004): 674–686.
7. Morgeson, op. cit., 674.
8. Roni Reiter-Palmon et al., "Development of an O*Net Web Based Job Analysis and Its Implementation in the U.S. Navy: Lessons Learned," *Human Resource Management Review* 16 (2006): 294–309.
9. Ibid., 294.
10. Matthew Mariani, "Replaced with a Database: O*NET Replaces the *Dictionary of Occupational Titles*," *Occupational Outlook Quarterly* (Spring 1999): 3–9.
11. Ibid., 18.
12. Gary Dessler, *Human Resource Management*, 9th ed. (Upper Saddle River, NJ: Prentice Hall, 2002), pp. 64–76.
13. Michael Esposito, "There's More to Writing Job Descriptions than Complying with the ADA," *Employee Relations Today* (Autumn 1992): 279.
14. Deborah Kearney, *Reasonable Accommodations: Job Descriptions in the Age of ADA, OSHA, and Workers Comp* (New York: Van Nostrand Reinhold, 1994), p. 9.
15. Ibid.
16. Steven Hunt, "Generic Work Behavior: An Investigation into the Dimensions of Entry-Level, Hourly Job Performance," *Personnel Psychology* 49 (1996): 51–83.

17. Jeffrey Shippmann et al., "The Practice of Competency Modeling," *Personnel Psychology* 53, no. 3 (2000): 703.
18. Ibid.
19. Carolyn Hirschman, "Putting Forecasting in Focus," *HR Magazine* (March 2007): 44–49.
20. Michael Laff, "Talent Management: From Hire to Retire," *Training & Development* (November 2006): 42–48.
21. "More Companies Turn to Workforce Planning to Boost Productivity and Efficiency," the Conference Board, press release/news, August 7, 2006; Carolyn Hirschman, "Putting Forecasting in Focus," *HR Magazine* (March 2007): 44–49.
22. "Demands of Tight Labor Market Will Test HR in 2007," *BNA Bulletin to Management* (January 23, 2007): 31.
23. Based on an idea in Elmer H. Burack and Robert D. Smith, *Personnel Management: A Human Resource Systems Approach* (St. Paul, MN: West, 1997), pp. 134–135.
24. This is a modification of a definition found in Peter Wallum, "A Broader View of Succession Planning," *Personnel Management* (September 1993): 45. See also Michelle Harrison et al., "Effective Succession Planning," *Training & Development* (October 2006): 22–23.
25. Ibid., 43–44. See also "Succession Planning: A Never-Ending Process That Must Mesh with Talent Management," *HR Focus* 84, no. 5 (May 2007): 8.
26. Bill Roberts, "Matching Talent with Tasks," *HR Magazine* (November 2002): 91–96.
27. Ibid.
28. Tony Carnevale, "The Coming Labor and Skills Shortage," *Training and Development* (January 2005): 36–41. "Report Says More Companies Focus on Workforce Planning to Heighten Productivity," *Training & Development* (October 2006): 10–12.
29. Tom Porter, "Effective Techniques to Attract, Hire, and Retain 'Top Notch' Employees for Your Company," *San Diego Business Journal* 21, no. 13 (March 27, 2000): B36.
30. Jonathan Segal, "Land Executives, Not Lawsuits," *HR Magazine* (October 2006): 123–130.
31. Susan Ladika, "Unwelcome Changes," *HR Magazine* (February 2005): 83–90.
32. Kevin Carlson et al., "Recruitment Evaluation: The Case for Assessing the Quality of Applicants Attracted," *Personnel Psychology* 55 (2002): 461–490. For a recent survey of recruiting source effectiveness, see, "The 2007 Recruiting Metrics and Performance Benchmark Report, 2nd ed.," Staffing.org, Inc., 2007.
33. Arthur R. Pell, *Recruiting and Selecting Personnel* (New York: Regents, 1969), pp. 10–12.
34. Jonathan Segal, "Strings Attached," *HR Magazine* (February 2005): 119–123.
35. Op. cit., 120.
36. Jessica Marquez, "A Global Recruiting Site Helps Far-Flung Managers at the Professional Services Company Acquire the Talent They Need—And Saves One Half-Million Dollars a Year," *Workforce Management* (March 13, 2006): 22.
37. Jennifer Berkshire, "Social Network Recruiting," *HR Magazine* (April 2005): 95–98. See also Karen Donovan, "Law Firms Go a Bit Hollywood to Recruit the YouTube Generation," *New York Times* (September 28, 2007).
38. Laura Romei, "Human Resource Management Systems Keep Computers Humming," *Managing Office Technology* (November 1994): 45.
39. "EEOC Issues Much Delayed Definition of 'Applicant,'" *HR Magazine* (April 2004): 29; Valerie Hoffman and Greg Davis, "OFCCP's Internet Applicant Definition Requires Overhaul of Recruitment and Hiring Policies," legal report, the Society for Human Resource Management (January/February 2006): 2.
40. Dawn Onley, "Improving Your Online Application Process," *HR Magazine* 50, no. 10 (October 2005): 109.
41. Martha Frase-Blunt, "Make a Good First Impression," *HR Magazine* (April 2004): 81–86. See also "Corporate Recruiting Web Sites Luring Workers, but Could Be Improved, Experts Say," *BNA Bulletin to Management* (March 14, 2006): 81–82.
42. Jim Meade, "Where Did They Go?" *HR Magazine* (September 2000): 81–84.
43. Allison Thompson, "The Contingent Work Force," *Occupational Outlook Quarterly* (Spring 1995): 45.

44. John Zappe, "Temp-to-Hire Is Becoming a Full-Time Practice at Firms," *Work Force Management* (June 2005): 82–86.

45. Robert Bogner Jr. and Elizabeth Salasko, "Beware the Legal Risks of Hiring Temps," *Workforce* (October 2002): 50–57.

46. Fay Hansen, "A Permanent Strategy for Temporary Hires," *Workforce Management* (February 26, 2007): 27.

47. Carolyn Hirschman, "Are Your Contractors Legal?" *HR Magazine* (March 2004): 59–63.

48. "In Negotiating Game, Most Recruiters Hold Back, Knowing Few Candidates Hold Out for Better Offer," *BNA Bulletin to Management* (2000): 291.

49. "Internships Growing in Popularity among Companies Seeking Fresh Talent and Ideas," *BNA Bulletin to Management* (March 20, 2007): 89–90.

50. Lisa Munniksma, "Career Matchmakers," *HR Magazine* (February 2005): 93–96.

51. Joel Mullich, "Finding the Schools that Yield the Best Job Applicant ROI," *Workforce Management* (March 2004): 67–68.

52. Michelle Martinez, "The Headhunter Within," *HR Magazine* (August 2001): 48–56.

53. Zottoli and John Wanous, "Recruitment Source Research: Current Status and Future Directions," *Human Resource Management Review* 10 (November 4, 2000): 353–382.

54. Jennifer Taylor Arnold, "Customers as Employees," *HR Magazine* (April 2007): 77–82.

55. Martha Frase-Blunt, "Call Centers Come Home," *HR Magazine* (January 2007): 85–90.

56. "Help Wanted—And Found," *Fortune* (October 2, 2006): 40.

57. Derek Avery and Patrick McKay, "Target Practice: An Organizational Impression Management Approach to Attracting Minority and Female Job Applicants," *Personnel Psychology* 59 (2006): 157–189, 177.

58. Dayton Fandray, "Gray Matters," *Workforce* (July 2000): 28.

59. "Older Workers Valued but Hard to Find, Employers Say," *BNA Bulletin to Management* (April 30, 1998): 129–134.

60. Robert Goddard, "How to Harness America's Gray Power," *Personnel Journal,* May 1987, p23.

61. Gary Adams and Barbara Rau, "Attracting Retirees to Apply: Desired Organizational Characteristics of Bridge Employment," *Journal of Organizational Behavior* 26, no. 6 (September 2005): 649–660.

62. Judith Casey and Marci Pitt-Catsouphes, "Employed Single Mothers: Balancing Job and Home Life," *Employee Assistance Quarterly* 9, no. 3/4 (1994): 37–53.

63. Ibid., 45.

64. Ibid., 48.

65. Ibid.

66. This compares with 21.5% for black job seekers and 23.9% for white job seekers. Michelle Harrison Ports, "Trends in Job Search Methods, 1990–92," *Monthly Labor Review* (October 1993): 64.

67. Allison Wellner, "Welcoming Back Mom," *HR Magazine* (June 2004): 77–78.

68. Herbert Greenberg, "A Hidden Source of Talent," *HR Magazine* (March 1997): 88–91.

69. Scott Graham, "Hospitals Recruiting Overseas," *Baltimore Business Journal* (June 1, 2001): 1.

70. Jennifer Laabs, "Recruiting in the Global Village," *Workforce* (Spring 1998): 30–33.

71. Ibid. See also Helen Deresky, *International Management* (Upper Saddle River, NJ: 2008): 354–355.

72. "Welfare-to-Work: No Easy Chore," *BNA Bulletin to Management* (February 13, 1997): 56.

73. Ibid.

74. Linda Moore, "Firms Need to Improve Recruitment, Hiring of Disabled Workers, EEO Chief Says," *Knight Ridder/Business News* (November 2003): Item 03309094. See also "Recruiting Disabled More than Good Deed, Experts Say," *BNA Bulletin to Management* (February 27, 2007): 71.

75. Richard Donkin, "Making Space for a Wheelchair Worker," *Financial Times* (November 13, 2003): 9.

76. J. Craig Wallace et al., "Applying for Jobs Online: Examining the Legality of Internet-Based Application Forms," *Public Personnel Management* 20, no. 4 (Winter 2000): 497–504.

77. De'Ann Weimer and Stephanie Anderson Forest, "Forced into Arbitration? Not Anymore," *Business Week* (March 16, 1998): 66, 68.

78. *Ryan's Family Steakhouse Inc.* v. *Floss,* "Supreme Court Let Stand Decision Finding Prehire Arbitration Agreements

Unenforceable," *BNA Bulletin to Management* (January 11, 2001): 11.

79. Douglas Mahoney et al., "The Effects of Mandatory Employment Arbitration Systems on Applicants' Attraction to Organizations," *Human Resource Management* 44, no. 4 (Winter 2005): 449–470.

80. Scott Erker, "What Does Your Hiring Process Say About You?" *Training & Development* (May 2007): 67–70.

81. Kathy Gurchiek, "Video Resumes Spark Curiosity, Questions," *HR Magazine* (May 2007): 28–30, and "Video Resumes Can Illuminate Applicants Abilities, but Pose Discrimination Concerns," *BNA Bulletin to Management* (May 29, 2007): 169–170.

82. Martha Frase, "Stocking Your Talent Pool," *HR Magazine* (April 2007): 67–74.

Appendix

ENRICHMENT TOPICS IN JOB ANALYSIS

Additional Job Analysis Methods

Job Analysis Record Sheet

You may encounter several other job analysis methods. For example, the U.S. Civil Service Commission has a standardized procedure for comparing and classifying jobs. Information here is compiled on a *job analysis record sheet* (see Figure A3.1). Identifying information (such as job title) and a brief summary of the job are listed first. Next the job's specific tasks are listed in order of importance. Then, for each task, the analyst specifies such things as the knowledge required (for example, the facts or principles the worker must be acquainted with to do his or her job), skills required (for example, the skills needed to operate machines or vehicles), and abilities required (for example, mathematical, reasoning, problem-solving, or interpersonal abilities).

Position Analysis Questionnaire

The position analysis questionnaire (PAQ) is a very structured job analysis questionnaire.[1] The PAQ is filled in by a job analyst, a person who should be acquainted with the particular job to be analyzed. The PAQ contains 194 items, each of which (such as "written materials") represents a basic element that may or may not play an important role in the job. The job analyst decides whether each item plays a role on the job and, if so, to what extent. In Figure A3.2, for example, "Written materials" might receive a rating of 4, indicating that written materials (such as books, reports, and office notes) play a considerable role in this job.

The advantage of the PAQ is that it provides a quantitative score or profile of any job in terms of how that job rates on five basic job traits such as "having decision-making/com-munications/social responsibilities." The PAQ lets you assign a single quantitative score or value to each job. You can therefore use the PAQ results to compare jobs relative to one another; this information can then be used to assign pay levels for each job.

U.S. Department of Labor Procedure

The U.S. Department of Labor (DOL) procedure also aims to provide a standardized method by which different jobs can be quantitatively rated, classified, and compared. The heart of this analysis is a rating of each job in terms of an employee's specific functions with respect to *data, people, and things*. As illustrated in Table A3.1, a set of basic activities called *worker functions* describes what a worker can do with respect to data, people, and things. With respect to *data*, for instance, the basic functions include synthesizing, coordinating, and copying. Note also that each worker function has been assigned an importance level. Thus, "coordinating" is 1, and "copying" is 5. If you were analyzing the job of a receptionist/clerk, for example, you might label the job 5, 6, 7, which would represent copying data, speaking/signaling people, and handling things.

A Practical Job Analysis Method

Without their own job analysts or (in many cases) HR managers, many small-business owners and managers face two hurdles when doing job analyses and job descriptions. First, they often need a more streamlined

FIGURE A3.1   Portion of a Completed Civil Service Job Analysis Record Sheet

JOB ANALYSIS RECORD SHEET

IDENTIFYING INFORMATION

Name of Incumbent:	A. Adler
Organization/Unit:	Welfare Services
Title:	Welfare Eligibility Examiner
Date:	11/12/02
Interviewer:	E. Jones

BRIEF SUMMARY OF JOB

Conducts interviews, completes applications, determines eligibility, provides information to community sources regarding food stamp program; refers noneligible food stamp applicants to other applicable community resource agencies.

TASKS*

1. Decide (determine) eligibility of applicant in order to complete client's application for food stamps using regulatory policies as guide.

   Knowledge Required

   —Knowledge of contents and meaning of items on standard application form
   —Knowledge of Social-Health Services food stamp regulatory policies
   —Knowledge of statutes relating to Social-Health Services food stamp program

   Skills Required
   —None

   Abilities Required

   —Ability to read and understand complex instructions such as regulatory policies
   —Ability to read and understand a variety of procedural instructions, written and oral, and convert these to proper actions
   —Ability to use simple arithmetic: addition and subtraction
   —Ability to translate requirements into language appropriate to laymen

   Physical Activities
   —Sedentary

   Environmental Conditions
   —None

   Typical Work Incidents
   —Working with people beyond giving and receiving instructions

   Interest Areas
   —Communication of data
   —Business contact with people
   —Working for the presumed good of people

2. Decides upon, describes, and explains other agencies available for client to contact in order to assist and refer client to appropriate community resource using worker's knowledge of resources available and knowledge of client's needs.

(Continued)

Knowledge Required
—Knowledge of functions of various assistance agencies
—Knowledge of community resources available and their locations
—Knowledge of referral procedures

Skills Required
—None

Abilities Required
—Ability to extract (discern) persons' needs from oral discussion
—Ability to give simple oral and written instructions to persons

Physical Activities
—Sedentary

Environmental Conditions
—None

Typical Work Incidents
—Working with people beyond giving and receiving instructions

Interest Areas
—Communication of data
—Business contact with people
—Abstract and creative problem solving
—Working for the presumed good of people

Note: This job might typically involve five or six tasks. For *each* task, list the knowledge, skill abilities, physical activities, environmental conditions, typical work incidents, and interest areas.

TABLE A3.1	Basic Department of Labor Worker Functions		
	Data	*People*	*Things*
Basic Activities	0 Synthesizing	0 Mentoring	0 Setting up
	1 Coordinating	1 Negotiating	1 Precision working
	2 Analyzing	2 Instructing	2 Operating/controlling
	3 Compiling	3 Supervising	3 Driving/operating
	4 Computing	4 Diverting	4 Manipulating
	5 Copying	5 Persuading	5 Tending
	6 Comparing	6 Speaking/signaling	6 Feeding/offbearing
		7 Serving	7 Handling
		8 Taking instructions/ helping	

Note: Determine employee's job "score" on data, people, and things by observing his or her job and determining, for each of the three categories, which of the basic functions illustrates the person's job. "0" is high; "6," "8," and "7" are lows in each column.

FIGURE A3.2   Portions of a Completed Page from the Position Analysis Questionnaire

---

**The PAQ
Answer Sheet**

The PAQ answer sheet is a two-sided computer-scorable answer sheet designed for optical scanning. The first side is for administrative use and should be filled out by the job analyst, simply coding in the information requested and providing in the upper left corner a brief job description of the job being analyzed. Refer to the PAQ *Job Analysis Manual* for explicit instructions on completing the information fields shown on side 1. The second side is reserved for item responses. Use only a No. 2 pencil for marking responses, filling in response bubbles completely and erasing carefully any changed responses and/or stray marks. Please do not fold or staple the answer sheet.

When entering responses to PAQ items, make sure to use the response scale that is clearly indicated in the outer narrow margin. After deciding which is the most appropriate response, darken the corresponding response bubble for the item on the answer sheet. Once you have responded to all of the items on the PAQ, please review the answer sheet to ensure that all information entered is complete and accurate. Refer to the PAQ *Job Analysis Manual* for specific instructions regarding the completion of the Pay or Income items found in section F10.

A. Information Input

**A1. Visual Sources
of Job Information**

Using the response scale at the left, rate each of the following items on the basis of the extent to which it is used by the worker as a source of information in performing the job.

Extent of Use

0 Does not apply
1 Nominal/very
   infrequent
2 Occasional
3 Moderate
4 Considerable
5 Very substantial

1. Written materials
   E.g., books, reports, office notes, articles,
   job instructions, or signs

2. Quantitative materials
   Materials that deal with quantities or amounts, e.g.,
   graphs, accounts, specifications, or tables of numbers

3. Pictorial materials
   Pictures or picture-like materials used as sources of information, e.g., drawings, blueprints, diagrams, maps, tracings, photographic films, x-ray films, or TV pictures

4. Patterns or related devices
   E.g., templates, stencils, or patterns used as sources of information when observed during use (Do not include materials described in item 3.)

5. Visual displays
   E.g., dials, gauges, signal lights, radarscopes, speedometers, or clocks

6. Measuring devices
   E.g., rules, calipers, tire pressure gauges, scales, thickness gauges, pipettes, thermometers, or protractors used to obtain visual information about physical measurements (Do *not* include devices described in item 5.)

7. Mechanical devices
   E.g., tools, equipment, or machinery that are sources of information when observed during use or operation

---

Source: Reprinted by permission of PAQ Services, Inc.

approach than those provided by question-naires like the one shown in Figure A3.3. Second, there is always the reasonable fear that in writing their job descriptions, they will overlook duties that subordinates should be assigned, or assign duties not usually associated with such positions. What they need is an encyclopedia listing all or most positions they might encounter, including a detailed listing of the duties nor-mally assigned to these positions.

Help is at hand: The small-business owner has at least three options. The *Dictionary of Occupational Titles,* mentioned earlier, pro-vides detailed descriptions of thousands of jobs and their human requirements. Web sites like www.jobdescription.com provide customizable descriptions by title and industry. And the Department of Labor's O*NET is a third alter-native. We'll focus on using O*NET for creat-ing job descriptions in this section.

Step 1. Decide on a Plan

Start by developing at least the broad out-line of a corporate plan. What do you expect your sales revenue to be next year, and in the next few years? What products do you intend to emphasize? What areas or depart-ments in your company do you think will have to be expanded, reduced, or consoli-dated, given where you plan to go with your firm over the next few years? What kinds of new positions do you think you'll need in order to accomplish your strategic goals?

Step 2. Develop an Organization Chart

Next, develop a company organization chart. Show who reports to the president and to each of his or her subordinates. Complete the chart by showing who reports to each of the other managers and supervisors in the firm. Start by drawing up the organization chart as it is now. Then, depending on how far in advance you're planning, produce a chart showing how you'd like your chart to look in the immediate future (say, in 2 months) and perhaps two or three other

charts showing how you'd like your organi-zation to evolve over the next 2 or 3 years.

You can use several tools here. For example, MS Word includes an organization charting function: On the Insert menu, click Object, then Create New. In the Object type box, click MS Organization Chart, and then OK. Software packages such as OrgPublisher for Intranet 3.0 from TimeVision of Irving, Texas, are another option.[2]

Step 3. Use a Job Analysis/Description Questionnaire

Next, use a job analysis questionnaire to determine what each job entails. You can use one of the more comprehensive question-naires (see Figure A3.3); however, the job description questionnaire in Figure A3.4 is a simpler and often satisfactory alternative. Fill in the required information, then ask the supervisors and/or employees to list the job's duties (on the bottom of the page), breaking them into daily duties, periodic duties, and duties performed at irregular intervals. You can distribute a sample of one of these duties (see Figure A3.5) to supervisors and/or employees to facilitate the process.

Step 4. Obtain Lists of Job Duties from O*NET

The list of job duties you uncovered in the previous step may or may not be complete. We'll therefore use O*NET to compile a more comprehensive list. (Refer to Figure A3.6 for a visual example as you read along.) Start by going to http://online.onetcenter. org (top). Here, click on Find Occupations. Assume you want to create job descriptions for retail salespeople. Type in Retail Sales for the occupational titles, and Sales and Related from the job families drop-down box. Click Find Occupations to continue, which brings you to the Find Occupations Search Result (middle). Clicking on Retail Salespersons—snapshots—produces the job summary and specific occupational duties for retail salespersons (bottom). For a small

FIGURE A3.3   Job Analysis Questionnaire for Developing Job Descriptions
Use a questionnaire like this to interview job incumbents, or have them fill it out.

Job Analysis Information Sheet

Job Title _____ **Date** _____

Job Code _____ **Dept.** _____

Superior's Title _____

Hours worked _____ AM to _____ PM

Job Analyst's Name _____

1. **What is the job's overall purpose?**
_____

2. **If the incumbent supervises others,** list them by job title; if there is more than one employee with the same title, put the number in parentheses following the title.
_____

3. **Check those activities** that are part of the incumbent's supervisory duties.

❏ Training

❏ Performance appraisal

❏ Inspecting work

❏ Budgeting

❏ Coaching and/or counseling

❏ Others (please specify) _____

4. **Describe the type and extent of supervision** received by the incumbent.
_____

5. **JOB DUTIES:** Describe briefly WHAT the incumbent does and, if possible, HOW he/she does it. Include duties in the following categories:

    a. Daily duties (those performed on a regular basis every day or almost every day)
_____

    b. Periodic duties (those performed weekly, monthly, quarterly, or at other regular intervals)
_____

    c. Duties performed at irregular intervals
_____

6. Is the incumbent performing duties he/she considers unnecessary? If so, describe.
_____

7. Is the incumbent performing duties not presently included in the job description? If so, describe.
_____

8. **EDUCATION:** Check the box that indicates the educational requirements for the job (not the educational background of the incumbent).

    ❏ No formal education   ❏ Eighth grade education

    ❏ High school diploma (or equivalent)   ❏ 2-year college degree (or equivalent)

    ❏ 4-year college degree (or equivalent) (specify)   ❏ Graduate work or advanced degree

    ❏ Professional license (specify)

(Continued)

9. **EXPERIENCE:** Check the amount of experience needed to perform the job.

☐ None   ☐ Less than one month

☐ One to six months   ☐ Six months to one year

☐ One to three years   ☐ Three to five years

☐ Five to ten years   ☐ More than ten years

10. **LOCATION:** Check location of job and, if necessary or appropriate, describe briefly.

☐ Outdoor   ☐ Indoor

☐ Underground   ☐ Pit

☐ Scaffold   ☐ Other (specify)

11. **ENVIRONMENTAL CONDITIONS:** Check any objectionable conditions found on the job and note afterward how frequently each is encountered (rarely, occasionally, constantly, etc.).

☐ Dirt   ☐ Dust

☐ Heat   ☐ Cold

☐ Noise   ☐ Fumes

☐ Odors   ☐ Wetness/humidity

☐ Vibration   ☐ Sudden temperature changes

☐ Darkness or poor lighting   ☐ Other (specify)

12. **HEALTH AND SAFETY:** Check any undesirable health and safety conditions under which the incumbent must perform and note how often they are encountered.

☐ Elevated workplace   ☐ Mechanical hazards

☐ Explosives   ☐ Electrical hazards

☐ Fire hazards   ☐ Radiation

☐ Other (specify)

13. **MACHINES, TOOLS, EQUIPMENT, AND WORK AIDS:** Describe briefly what machines, tools, equipment, or work aids the incumbent works with on a regular basis.

14. Have concrete work standards been established (errors allowed, time taken for a particular task, etc.)? If so, what are they?

15. Are there any personal attributes (special aptitudes, physical characteristics, personality traits, etc.) required by the job?

16. Are there any exceptional problems the incumbent might be expected to encounter in performing the job under normal conditions? If so, describe.

17. Describe the successful completion and/or end results of the job.

18. What is the seriousness of error on this job? Who or what is affected by errors the incumbent makes?

19. To what job would a successful incumbent expect to be promoted?

[**Note:** This form is obviously slanted toward a manufacturing environment, but it can be adapted quite easily to fit a number of different types of jobs.]

Source: Reprinted from www.hrnext.com, July 28, 2001 with permission of the publisher. Copyright © 2001 Business and Legal Reports, Inc., 141 Mill Rock Road East, Old Saybrook, CT 06475.

FIGURE A3.4   Job Description Questionnaire

Background Data
for Job Description

Job Title _____   Department _____

Job Number _____   Written By _____

Today's Date _____   Applicable Codes _____

I. Applicable job titles from O*NET:

II. Job Summary:
(List the more important or regularly performed tasks)

III. Reports To:

IV. Supervises: _____

V. Job Duties: _____
(Briefly describe, for each duty, what employee does and, if possible, how employee does it. Show in parentheses at end of each duty the approximate percentage of time devoted to duty.)

A. Daily Duties:

B. Periodic Duties:
(Indicate whether weekly, monthly, quarterly, etc.)

C. Duties Performed at Irregular Intervals:

FIGURE A3.5   Background Data for Examples

Example of Job Title: Customer Service Clerk

Example of Job Summary: Answers inquiries and gives directions to customers, authorizes cashing of customers' checks, records and returns lost charge cards, sorts and reviews new credit applications, works at customer-service desk in department store.

Example of One Job Duty: Authorizes cashing of checks: authorizes cashing of personal or payroll checks (up to a specified amount) by customers desiring to make payment by check. Requests identification, such as driver's license, from customers, and examines check to verify date, amount, signature, and endorsement. Initials check and sends customer to cashier.

FIGURE A3.6   Shown in the Three Screen Captures, O*NET Easily Allows the User to Develop Job Descriptions.

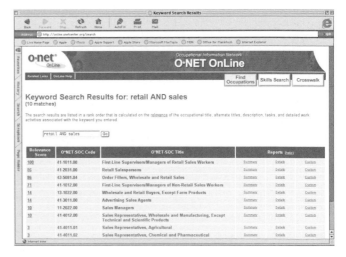

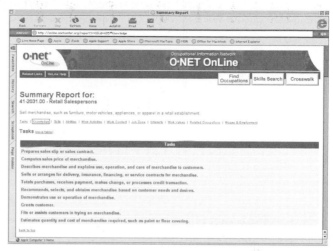

Source: Reprinted by permission of O*NET OnLine.

company or department, you might want to combine the duties of the retail salesperson with those of first-line supervisors/managers of retail salespeople.

*Step 5. Compile the Job's Specification from O*NET*
Next, return to the Snapshot for Retail Salesperson (bottom). Here, instead of choosing occupation-specific information, choose, for example, Worker Experiences, Occupational Requirements, and Worker

Characteristics. You can use this information to develop a job specification for recruiting, selecting, and training the employees.

Step 6. Complete Your Job Description
Finally, using Figure A3.4, write an appropriate job summary for the job. Then use the information obtained in Steps 4 and 5 to create a complete listing of the tasks, duties, and human requirements of each of the jobs you will need to fill.

Endnotes

1. Note that the PAQ (and other quantitative techniques) can also be used for job evaluation, which is explained in Chapter 7.

2. David Shair, "Wizardry Makes Charts Relevant," *HR Magazine* (April 2000): 127.

4

TESTING AND SELECTING EMPLOYEES

- The Basics of Testing and Selecting Employees
- Using Tests at Work
- Interviewing Prospective Employees
- Using Other Selection Techniques

When you finish studying this chapter, you should be able to:

■ Define *basic testing concepts, including validity and reliability.*

■ Discuss *at least four basic types of personnel tests.*

■ Explain *the pros and cons of background investigations, reference checks, and pre-employment information services.*

■ Explain *the factors and problems that can undermine an interview's usefulness, and techniques for eliminating them.*

INTRODUCTION

Google, Inc. recently changed its employee screening process. A few years ago, candidates went through a dozen or more in-person interviews. Then, the firm's selection team would routinely reject candidates with years of experience if they had just-average college grades. But, as Google's new head of human resources says, "Everything works if you're trying to hire 500 people a year, or 1,000." Now, Google is hiring thousands of people per year, and can't be bogged down by such a slow hiring process. They've reduced the interview load (to about five, on average) and no longer put as much weight on GPA as before. Other selection changes are in store.[1]

THE BASICS OF TESTING AND SELECTING EMPLOYEES

With a pool of completed applications, your next step is to select the best person for the job. This usually means whittling down the applicant pool by using the screening tools explained in this chapter, including tests, background and reference checks, and interviews.

Why Careful Selection Is Important

Selecting the right employees is important for several reasons. First, your own performance always depends in part on your subordinates. Employees with the right skills and attributes will do a better job for you and the company. Employees without these skills or who are abrasive or obstructionist won't perform effectively, and your own performance and the firm's will suffer.

But underperformance is not the sole problem. By some estimates, 75% of employees have stolen from their employers at least once; 33% to 75% have engaged in behaviors such as theft, vandalism, and voluntary absenteeism; almost 25% say they've had knowledge of illicit drug use among coworkers; and 7% of a sample of employees reported being victims of coworkers' physical threats.[2] The time to screen out such undesirables is before they are in the door, not after.

Effective screening is also important because it's costly to recruit and hire employees. Hiring and training even a clerk can cost $5,000 or more in fees and supervisory time. The total cost of hiring a manager could easily be 10 times as high, after search fees, interviewing time, reference checking, and travel and moving expenses are tallied.

Legal Implications and Negligent Hiring

Careful selection is also important because of the legal implications of incompetent selection. For one thing (as we saw in Chapter 2), EEO legislation and court decisions require you to make sure you're not unfairly discriminating against any protected group.

Furthermore, courts will find employers liable when employees with criminal records or other problems use their access to customers' homes or similar opportunities to commit crimes. Hiring workers with such backgrounds without proper safeguards is called *negligent hiring*. For example, after lawyers sued Wal-Mart alleging that several of its employees with criminal convictions for sexually related offenses had assaulted young girls, Wal-Mart instituted a new program of criminal background checks.[3]

Avoiding negligent hiring claims requires taking "reasonable" action to investigate the candidate's background. Among other things, employers "must make a systematic effort to gain relevant information about the applicant, verify documentation, follow up on missing records or gaps in employment, and keep a detailed log of all attempts to obtain information, including the names and dates for phone calls or other requests."[4]

Reliability

Effective screening is therefore important, and depends, to a large degree, on the basic testing concepts of validity and reliability. **Reliability** is an essential characteristic and refers to the test's consistency. It is "the consistency of scores obtained by the same person when retested with the identical tests or with an equivalent form of a test."[5] Test reliability is essential: If a person scored 90 on an intelligence test on Monday and 130 when retested on Tuesday, you probably wouldn't have much faith in the test.

There are several ways to estimate a test's consistency or reliability. You could administer the same test to the same people at two different points in time, comparing their test scores at Time 2 with their scores at Time 1; this would be a retest estimate. Or you could administer a test and then administer what experts believe to be an equivalent test at a later date; this would be an *equivalent-form estimate*. The Scholastic Aptitude Test is an example of the latter.

A test's internal consistency is another measure of its reliability. For example, assume you have 10 items on a test of vocational interest. These items are supposed to measure in various ways the person's interest in working outdoors. You administer the test and then statistically analyze the degree to which responses to these items vary together. This would provide a measure of the internal reliability of the test and is referred to as an *internal comparison estimate*. Internal consistency is one reason you often find questions that apparently are repetitive on some test questionnaires.

Validity

Any test is a sample of a person's behavior, but some tests more clearly reflect the behavior being sampled. A typing test, for instance, clearly corresponds to an on-the-job behavior—typing. At the other extreme, there may be no apparent relationship between the items on the test and the behavior. For example, in the Thematic Apperception Test illustrated in Figure 4.1, the person is asked to explain how he or she interprets the blurred picture. Is the young woman daydreaming of her affectionate mother, or hoping that a rival will grow old before her time? That interpretation is

FIGURE 4.1   Sample Picture from Thematic Apperception Test

Source: Reprinted by permission of the publishers from Henry A. Murray, THEMATIC APPERCEPTION TEST, Card 12F, Cambridge, Mass.: Harvard University Press, Copyright © 1943 by the President and Fellows of Harvard College, Copyright © 1971 by Henry A. Murray.

then used to draw conclusions about the person's personality and behavior. In such tests, it is harder to "prove" that the tests are measuring what they are purported to measure—that they are *valid*.

Test validity answers the question, Does this test measure what it's supposed to measure? Stated differently, "validity refers to the confidence one has in the meaning attached to the scores."[6] With respect to employee selection tests, the term *validity* often refers to evidence that the test is job related, in other words, that performance on the test is a *valid predictor* of subsequent performance on the job. A selection test must be valid because, without proof of its validity, there is no logical or legally permissible reason to continue using it to screen job applicants.

In employment testing, there are two main ways to demonstrate a test's validity: **criterion validity** and **content validity.** Demonstrating criterion validity means demonstrating that those who do well on the test also do well on the job, and that those who do poorly on the test do poorly on the job. In psychological measurement, a predictor is the measurement (in this case, the test score) that you are trying to relate to a criterion, such as performance on the job. In criterion validity, the two should be closely related. The term *criterion validity* comes from that terminology.

The employer demonstrates the *content validity* of a test by showing that the test constitutes a fair sample of the content of a job. A typing test used to hire a typist is an example. If the content of the typing test is a representative sample of the typist's job, then the test is probably content valid.

How to Validate a Test

What makes a test such as the Graduate Record Examination (GRE) useful for college admissions directors? What makes a mechanical comprehension test useful for managers trying to hire machinists?

The answer to both questions is usually that people's scores on these tests have been shown to be predictive of how people perform. Thus, other things equal, students who score high on the GRE also do better in graduate school. Applicants who score higher on a mechanical comprehension test perform better as machinists.

Strictly speaking, an employer should be fairly sure that scores on the tests are related in a predictable way to performance on the job before using that test to screen employees. In other words, it is important that you validate the test before using it. You generally do this by ensuring that test scores are a good predictor of some criterion such as job performance. In other words, you should demonstrate the test's criterion validity. This validation process usually requires the expertise of an industrial psychologist, and is summarized in Figure 4.2.

Ethical and Legal Questions in Testing

Equal Employment Opportunity Aspects of Testing

We've seen that various federal and state laws bar discrimination on the basis of race, color, age, religion, sex, disability, and national origin. With respect to testing, these laws boil down to two things: (1) You must be able to prove that your tests were related to success or failure on the job, and (2) you must prove that your tests don't unfairly discriminate against either minority or nonminority subgroups. If confronted by a legitimate discrimination charge, the burden of proof rests with you. Once the plaintiff

---

FIGURE 4.2   How to Validate a Test

Step 1: Analyze the Job. First, analyze the job and write job descriptions and job specifications. Specify the human traits and skills you believe are required for adequate job performance. For example, must an applicant be aggressive? Must the person be able to assemble small, detailed components? These requirements become your predictors. They are the human traits and skills you believe to be predictive of success on the job.

In this first step, you must also define what you mean by "success on the job" because it is this success for which you want predictors. The standards of success are called *criteria*. You could focus on production-related criteria (quantity, quality, and so on), personnel data (absenteeism, length of service, and so on), or judgments (of worker performance by persons such as supervisors). For an assembler's job, predictors for which to test applicants might include manual dexterity and patience. Criteria that you would hope to predict with your test might then include quantity produced per hour and number of rejects produced per hour.

Step 2: Choose the Tests. Next, choose tests that you think measure the attributes (predictors) important for job success. This choice is usually based on experience, previous research, and best guesses, and you usually won't start off with just one test. Instead, you choose several tests, combining them into a test battery aimed at measuring a variety of possible predictors, such as aggressiveness, extroversion, and numeric ability.

Step 3: Administer Tests. Administer the selected test(s) to employees. Predictive validation is the most dependable way to validate a test. The test is administered to applicants before they are hired. Then these applicants are hired using only existing selection techniques, not the results of the new test you are developing. After they have been on the job for some time, you measure their performance and compare it to their performance on the earlier test. You can then determine whether their performance on the test could have been used to predict their subsequent job performance.

Step 4: Relate Test Scores and Criteria. Next, determine whether there is a significant relationship between scores (the predictor) and performance (the criterion). The usual way to do this is to determine the statistical relationship between scores on the test and performance through correlation analysis, which shows the degree of statistical relationship.

Step 5: Cross-Validate and Revalidate. Before putting the test into use, you may want to check it by cross-validating, by again performing steps 3 and 4 on a new sample of employees. At a minimum, an expert should validate the test periodically.

---

shows that one of your selection procedures has an adverse impact on his or her protected class, you must demonstrate the validity and selection fairness of the allegedly discriminatory test or item. *Adverse impact* means there is a significant discrepancy between rates of rejection of members of the protected groups and others. For example, a federal court recently ruled that Dial Corp. discriminated against female job applicants at a meatpacking facility by requiring employees to take a preemployment strength test. The test had an adverse impact on women. Furthermore, there appeared to be no compelling need for strength on the job.[7]

You can't avoid EEO laws by not using tests, by the way. EEO guidelines and laws apply to any and all screening or selection devices, including interviews, applications, and references. In other words, the same burden of proving job relatedness falls on interviews and other techniques (including performance appraisals) that falls on tests.

Individual Rights of Test Takers and Test Security

Test takers have various privacy and information rights. Under the American Psychological Association's standard for educational and psychology tests (which guide professional psychologists but are not legally enforceable), they have the right to the confidentiality of the test results and the right to informed consent regarding the use of these results. They have the right to expect that only people qualified to interpret the scores will have access to them or that sufficient information will accompany the scores to ensure their appropriate interpretation. They have the right to expect that the test is secure; no person taking the test should have prior information concerning the questions or answers.

Using Tests as Supplements

Do not use tests as your only selection technique; instead, use them to supplement other techniques such as interviews and background checks. Tests are not infallible. Even in the best cases, the test score usually accounts for only about 25% of the variation in the measure of performance. In addition, tests are often better at telling you which candidates will fail than which will succeed.

USING TESTS AT WORK

Employers have long used tests to predict behavior and performance, and they can be effective. For example, researchers administered an aggression questionnaire to high-school hockey players prior to the season. Preseason aggressiveness as measured by the questionnaire predicted the amount of minutes they subsequently spent in the penalty box for penalties such as fighting, slashing, and tripping.[8]

Tests are widely used by employers. For example, about 41% of companies the American Management Association surveyed tested applicants for *basic skills* (defined as the ability to read instructions, write reports, and perform common workplace arithmetic tasks).[9]

Want to see what such tests are like? Try the short test in Figure 4.3 to see how prone you might be to on-the-job accidents.

How Are Tests Used at Work?

Employers use tests to measure a wide range of candidate attributes, including cognitive (mental) abilities, motor and physical abilities, personality and interests, and achievement. Many firms such as Kinko's have applicants take online or offline computerized tests—sometimes online, and sometimes by phone, using a touchtone keypad—to quickly prescreen applicants prior to more in-depth interviews and background checks.[10] And, firms don't just use tests for lower level workers. For example, Barclays Capital gives graduate and undergraduate job candidates aptitude tests instead of first-round interviews.[11]

Example

Employee testing is not just for large employers. For example, Outback Steakhouse (which now has 45,000 employees) has used preemployment testing since 1991, just 2 years after the company started. Outback is looking for employees who are highly social, meticulous, sympathetic, and adaptable. They use a special personality assessment test as part of a three-step preemployment interview process. Applicants take the test, and the company then compares the candidate's results to the profile for

FIGURE 4.3	Sample Selection Test

CHECK YES OR NO	YES	NO
1. You like a lot of excitement in your life.		
2. An employee who takes it easy at work is cheating on the employer.		
3. You are a cautious person.		
4. In the past three years you have found yourself in a shouting match at school or work.		
5. You like to drive fast just for fun.		

Analysis: According to John Kamp, an industrial psychologist, applicants who answered no, yes, yes, no, no to questions 1, 2, 3, 4, and 5 are statistically likely to be absent less often, to have fewer on-the-job injuries, and, if the job involves driving, to have fewer on-the-job driving accidents. Actual scores on the test are based on answers to 130 questions.

Source: Courtesy of *The New York Times.*

Outback Steakhouse employees. Those who score low on certain traits (like compassion) don't move to the next step. Those who do get interviewed by two managers. The latter focus on asking "behavioral" questions, such as, What would you do if a customer asked for a side dish we don't have on the menu?[12] The basic types of tests are as follows.

Tests of Cognitive Abilities

Employers often want to assess a candidate's cognitive or mental abilities. For example, you may be interested in determining whether a supervisory candidate has the intelligence to do the paperwork required of the job or a bookkeeper candidate has the required numeric aptitude.

Intelligence tests, such as IQ tests, are tests of general intellectual abilities. They measure not a single intelligence trait, but rather a range of abilities, including memory, vocabulary, verbal fluency, and numeric ability. Today, psychologists often measure intelligence with individually administered tests such as the Stanford–Binet or the Wechsler test. Employers use other IQ tests such as the Wonderlic to provide quick measures of IQ for both individuals and groups of people.

There are also measures of specific mental abilities. Tests in this category are often called *aptitude tests* because they aim to measure the applicant's aptitudes for the job in question. For example, consider the Test of Mechanical Comprehension illustrated in Figure 4.4. It tests the applicant's understanding of basic mechanical principles. It may therefore reflect a person's aptitude for jobs—such as engineer—that require mechanical comprehension.

FIGURE 4.4   Two Problems from the Test of Mechanical Comprehension

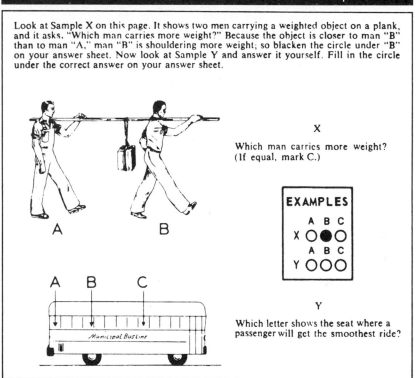

Look at Sample X on this page. It shows two men carrying a weighted object on a plank, and it asks, "Which man carries more weight?" Because the object is closer to man "B" than to man "A," man "B" is shouldering more weight; so blacken the circle under "B" on your answer sheet. Now look at Sample Y and answer it yourself. Fill in the circle under the correct answer on your answer sheet.

X

Which man carries more weight?
(If equal, mark C.)

Y

Which letter shows the seat where a passenger will get the smoothest ride?

Source: Bennett Mechanical Comprehension Test (BMCT). Copyright © 1942, 1967–1970, 1980 by Harcourt Assessment, Inc. Reproduced with permission. All rights reserved.

Tests of Motor and Physical Abilities

There are many motor or physical abilities you might want to measure, such as finger dexterity, strength, manual dexterity, and reaction time (for instance, for machine operators or police candidates). The Stromberg Dexterity Test is one example. It measures the speed and accuracy of simple judgment as well as the speed of finger, hand, and arm movements.

Measuring Personality

A person's mental and physical abilities alone seldom explain his or her job performance. Other factors, such as motivation and interpersonal skills, are important, too. Personality and interests inventories are sometimes used as predictors of such intangibles. As a consultant put it, most people are hired based on qualifications, but most are fired for nonperformance. And *nonperformance* (or *performance*) "is usually the result of personal characteristics, such as attitude, motivation, and especially, temperament."[13] Employers use personality and interests inventories to measure and predict such intangibles. In fact, some online dating services, like eHarmony.com, have prospective members take online personality tests, and reject those whom its software judges are unmatchable.

Personality tests measure basic aspects of an applicant's personality, such as introversion, stability, and motivation. Many of these tests are projective, meaning that the person taking the test must interpret or react to an ambiguous stimulus such as an inkblot or clouded picture. Because the pictures are ambiguous, the person supposedly projects into the picture his or her own emotional attitudes about life. Thus, a security-oriented person might describe the woman in Figure 4.1 as "Me worrying about my mother worrying about what I'll do if I lose my job."

Personality tests—particularly the projective type—are the most difficult to evaluate and use. An expert must analyze the test taker's interpretations and reactions and infer from them his or her personality. The usefulness of such tests for selection then assumes that you find a relationship between a measurable personality trait (such as extroversion) and success on the job. Because they are personal in nature, employers should always use personality tests with caution, particularly where the focus is on aberrant behavior. Rejected candidates may (validly) claim that the results are false, or that they violate the Americans with Disabilities Act (ADA).

Personality Test Effectiveness

The difficulties notwithstanding, studies confirm that personality tests can help companies hire more effective workers. Industrial psychologists often study the "big five" personality dimensions as they apply to personnel testing: extroversion, emotional stability, agreeableness, conscientiousness, and openness to experience.[14] One study focused on how these five personality dimensions predicted performance (for instance, in terms of job and training proficiency) for professionals, police officers, managers, sales workers, and skilled/semiskilled workers. Conscientiousness showed a consistent relationship with all job performance criteria for all the occupations. Extroversion was a valid predictor of performance for managers and sales employees—two of the occupations involving the most social interaction. Openness to experience and extroversion predicted training proficiency for all occupations.[15] See also the *Global Issues in HR* box on the next page.

A review of personality testing reached several conclusions. Employers are increasingly using personality tests. The weight of evidence is that personality measures (particularly the big five) contribute to predicting job performance. And, employers can reduce personality test faking by warning applicants that faking may reduce the chances of the person being hired.[16]

Interest Inventories

Interest inventories compare one's interests with those of people in various occupations. Thus, if a person takes the Strong–Campbell Interest Inventory, he or she receives a report comparing his or her interests to those of people already in occupations such as accounting, engineering, management, and medical technology.

Achievement Tests

An *achievement test* is basically a measure of what a person has learned. Most of the tests you take in school are achievement tests. They measure your knowledge in areas such as economics, marketing, or management. In addition to job knowledge, achievement tests can measure applicants' abilities; a typing test is one example.[17]

Computerized Testing

Computerized tests are increasingly replacing conventional paper-and-pencil and manual tests. For example, a computerized testing procedure was developed for the

WOULD YOUR COMPANY PICK YOU TO BE AN INTERNATIONAL EXECUTIVE?

With many firms going global these days, there's a high likelihood you'll be interviewed for an assignment that involves some time abroad. What do companies look for when trying to identify international executives, and do you think you might have what it takes? A study provides some insights into these questions. The behavioral scientists studied 838 lower-, middle-, and senior-level managers from 6 international firms and 21 countries, focusing particularly on the manager's personal characteristics.

Fourteen personal characteristics successfully distinguished the managers identified by their companies as high potential from those identified as not high potential in 72% of the cases. To get an initial, tentative impression of how you would rate, review the 14 characteristics (along with some sample items), which are listed in Figure 4.5. For each,

FIGURE 4.5	Traits Distinguishing Successful International Executives	
SCALE	**SAMPLE ITEM**	**SCORE**
Sensitive to Cultural Differences	When working with people from other cultures, works hard to understand their perspectives.	
Business Knowledge	Has a solid understanding of our products and services.	
Courage to Take a Stand	Is willing to take a stand on issues.	
Brings Out the Best in People	Has a special talent for dealing with people.	
Acts with Integrity	Can be depended on to tell the truth regardless of circumstances.	
Is Insightful	Is good at identifying the most important part of a complex problem or issue.	
Is Committed to Success	Clearly demonstrates commitment to seeing the organization succeed.	
Takes Risks	Takes personal as well as business risks.	
Uses Feedback	Has changed as a result of feedback.	
Is Culturally Adventurous	Enjoys the challenge of working in countries other than his/her own.	
Seeks Opportunities to Learn	Takes advantage of opportunities to do new things.	
Is Open to Criticism	Appears brittle—as if criticism might cause him/her to break.*	
Seeks Feedback	Pursues feedback even when others are reluctant to give it.	
Is Flexible	Doesn't get so invested in things that he/she cannot change when something doesn't work.	

Note: *Reverse scored.

Source: Copyright © 1997 by the American Psychological Association. Adapted with permission from "Early Identification of International Executive Potential" by Gretchen Spreitzer, Morgan McCall, Jr., and Joan Mahoney, *Journal of Applied Psychology* Vol. 82, No. 1 (Feb. 1997). No further reproduction or distribution is permitted without written permission from the American Psychological Association.

(Continued)

indicate (by placing a number in the space provided) whether you strongly agree (7), strongly disagree (1), or fall somewhere in between.[18] The average would be about 50.

Generally speaking, the higher you score on these 14 characteristics, the more likely it is that you might have been identified as a high-potential international executive in this study.

selection of clerical personnel in a large manufacturing company.[19] The consultants constructed eight test components to represent actual work performed by secretarial personnel, such as maintaining and developing databases and spreadsheets, answering the telephone and filing, and handling travel arrangements. For example, for the word-processing test, applicants got 3 minutes (monitored by the computer) to type as much of a letter as possible; the computer recorded and corrected the manuscript.[20]

Many other computerized selection tools are in use. For example, automated in-basket tests require job candidates to deal with a "virtual in-box" composed of e-mails, phone calls, and documents and folders to assess the candidates' decision-making and problem-solving skills. Candidates for architectural certification solve online architectural problems, for instance, designing building layouts to fit specified space constraints.[21]

Example

One fast-growing auto repair chain, City Garage, knew they'd never be able to implement their growth strategy without a dramatic change in how they tested and hired employees.[22] Their old hiring process consisted of a paper-and-pencil application and one interview, immediately followed by a hire/don't hire decision. While that might work for a slow-growth operation, it was unsatisfactory for a fast-growing operation like City Garage. For one thing, local shop managers didn't have the time to evaluate every applicant, so "if they had been shorthanded too long, we would hire pretty much anybody who had experience," said training director Rusty Reinoehl. Complicating the problem was that City Garage competitively differentiates itself with an "open garage" arrangement, where customers interact directly with technicians. Therefore, finding mechanics who not only tolerate but also react positively to customer inquiries is essential.

City Garage's solution was to purchase the Personality Profile Analysis (PPA) online test from Dallas-based Thomas International USA. Now, after a quick application and background check, likely candidates take the 10-minute, 24-question PPA. City Garage staff then enter the answers into the PPA Software system, and receive test results in less than 2 minutes. These show whether the applicant is high or low in four personality characteristics. It also produces follow-up questions about areas that might cause problems. For example, applicants might be asked how they've handled possible weaknesses such as lack of patience. If candidates answer those questions satisfactorily, they're asked back for extensive, all-day interviews, after which hiring decisions are made.

Management Assessment Centers

In a **management assessment center,** management candidates take tests and make decisions in simulated situations, and observers score them on their performance. The time at the assessment center is usually 2 or 3 days and involves 10 to 12 management candidates performing realistic management tasks (such as making presentations) under the observation of expert assessors. The center may be a plain conference room, but often it is a special room with a one-way mirror to facilitate unobtrusive observations. Examples of the simulated but realistic exercises included in a typical assessment center are as follows:

- *The in-basket.* In this exercise, the candidate is faced with an accumulation of reports, memos, notes of incoming phone calls, letters, and other materials collected in the in-basket of the simulated job he or she is to take over. The candidate takes appropriate action on each of these materials.
- *The leaderless group discussion.* A leaderless group is given a discussion question and told to arrive at a group decision. The raters then evaluate each group member's interpersonal skills, acceptance by the group, leadership ability, and individual influence.
- *Individual presentations.* A participant's communication skills and persuasiveness are evaluated by having the person make an oral presentation on an assigned topic.

In practice, employers use assessment centers for selection, promotion, and development. Supervisor recommendations usually play a big role in choosing center participants. Line managers usually act as assessors and typically arrive at their ratings through consensus.[23] Centers are expensive to set up, but at least one study (of 40 police candidates) found that such centers are worth the extra cost. The researchers concluded: "assessment center performance shows a unique and substantial contribution to the prediction of future police work success, justifying the usage of such method."[24]

Testing on the Web

Firms are increasingly using the Web to test and screen applicants. For example, the financial firm CapitalOne's new online system eliminates the previous time-consuming paper-and-pencil test process.[25] Applicants for call center jobs complete an online application and online math and biodata tests. They also take an online role-playing call simulation. For the latter, they put on a headset, and the program plays seven different customer situations. Applicants (playing the role of operators) answer multiple-choice questions online regarding how they would respond.

Studies suggest that proctored Web-based and paper-and-pencil tests of applicants produce similar results, for instance, on personality and judgment tests.[26] However, keep several practical things in mind when using Web-based tests. A timed test may take longer for applicants on the Web, due to downloading problems and the fact that there are fewer items presented on the viewable page. Similarly, tests takers generally find it more difficult to go back and review their results on Web-based tests. Proctoring is another problem. A proctor should at least ensure the test taker's identity and monitor against cheating. However there is "currently no way to completely prevent [online] test takers from cheating or copying items during testing" or to ensure there's not someone looking over the test taker's shoulder.[27]

Strategy and HR

In the face of the need to add thousands of new employees each year, Google's top managers decided to revamp the firm's employee selection process. Google no longer requires most of their candidates to endure multiple interviews, often spread over many months. They've streamlined the process, in part by testing all their current employees to see what makes them successful. Then Google tests candidates to see if they too have these traits.

INTERVIEWING PROSPECTIVE EMPLOYEES

Although not all companies use tests or assessment centers, it is very unusual for a manager not to interview a prospective employee; interviewing is thus an indispensable management tool. An **interview** is a procedure designed to solicit information from a person's oral responses to oral inquiries. A *selection interview,* which we'll focus on in this chapter, is "a selection procedure designed to predict future job performance on the basis of applicants' oral responses to oral inquiries."[28]

Types of Selection Interviews

As you probably know from your own experience, there are several types of selection interviews.

Structure

First, we can distinguish between *nonstructured* and *structured interviews.* In the former, you ask questions as they come to mind, and there is generally no set format to follow. In a more structured or directive interview, such as the one in Figure 4.6, the questions and perhaps even acceptable responses are specified in advance, and the responses may be rated for appropriateness of content. (Also see Figure 4.7, page 136.)

Type of Questions

We also classify interviews according to the type of questions they emphasize. In *situational interviews,* questions focus on the candidate's ability to project what his or her behavior would be in a given situation.[29] For example, you might ask a candidate for a supervisor position how he or she would respond to a subordinate coming to work late 3 days in a row. A *behavioral interview* is another type of interview. Here you ask interviewees how they behaved in the past in some situation. Thus, an interviewer might ask, "Did you ever have a situation in which a subordinate came in late? If so, how did you handle the situation?" For example, when Citizen's Banking Corporation in Flint, Michigan, found that 31 of the 50 people in its call center quit in 1 year, Cynthia Wilson, the center's head, switched to behavioral interviews. Many of those who left did so because they didn't enjoy fielding questions from occasionally irate clients. So Wilson no longer tries to predict how candidates will act based on asking them if they want to work with angry clients. Instead, she asks behavioral questions like, "Tell me about a time you were speaking with an irate person, and how you turned the situation around." Wilson says this makes it much harder to fool the interviewer, and, indeed, only four people left her center in the following year.[30]

How Administered

We can also classify interviews based on how we administer them. For example, most interviews are administered *one-on-one:* Two people meet alone and one interviews

FIGURE 4.6   Officer Programs Applicant Interview Form

Department of Homeland Security CG-5527 (04-03)	**Officer Programs Applicant Interview Form**	Date:

Name of Applicant (Last, First, MI)

DIRECTIONS: This interview form is designed to help the selection panel reach a consensus on the merits of the applicant under consideration. The form is heavily based on the Officer Evaluation Report. While it should be remembered that applicants are not yet Coast Guard Officers, they should have had opportunities to exhibit qualities that show they possess the character and potential necessary to be successful Officers. The scale for each category below is based on performance standards presented on the Officer Evaluation Report. Provide written comments in support of numeric markings for each category. Base these comments on what you observe during the interview or see in the supporting documentation in the applicant's package. Marks in the overall impression block should summarize the panel's recommendation on the applicant's suitability for service as a Coast Guard Officer.

Planning and Preparedness: Ability to determine goals, set priorities and deadlines and develop strategies.
1☐   2☐   3☐   4☐   5☐   6☐   7☐
Comments:

Using Resources: Ability to manage time, materials, information, money and people.
1☐   2☐   3☐   4☐   5☐   6☐   7☐
Comments:

Adaptability: Ability to modify work methods and priorities in response to new information, changing conditions or unexpected obstacles.
1☐   2☐   3☐   4☐   5☐   6☐   7☐
Comments:

Speaking and Listening: Ability to speak effectively and listen to understand.
1☐   2 ☐   3☐   4☐   5☐   6☐   7☐
Comments:

Looking out for Others: Ability to consider and respond to others *personal* needs and capabilities.
1☐   2 ☐   3☐   4☐   5☐   6☐   7☐
Comments:

(Continued)

Page 2 - CG-5527 (04-03)

Directing Others: Ability to influence or direct others in accomplishing tasks or goals.

1☐   2☐   3☐   4☐   5☐   6☐   7☐

Comments:

Teamwork: Ability to manage, lead and participate in teams, encourage cooperation and develop espirit de corps.

1☐   2☐   3☐   4☐   5☐   6☐   7☐

Comments:

Initiative: Ability to originate and act on new ideas and seek responsibility without guidance and supervision.

1☐   2☐   3☐   4☐   5☐   6☐   7☐

Comments:

Responsibility: Ability to act ethically, courageously, and dependably and inspire the same in others.

1☐   2☐   3☐   4☐   5☐   6☐   7☐

Comments:

Professional Presence: Ability to bring credit to the Coast Guard through one's actions, demeanor and appearance.

1☐   2☐   3☐   4☐   5☐   6☐   7☐

Comments:

Overall Impression: Compare this applicant to others you have interviewed, **blocks two through seven constitute a recommendation for selection.**

Unsatisfactory	Qualified	One of many competent applicants for this program		Exceptional	Distinguished
1☐	2☐	3☐	4☐ 5☐	6☐	7☐

Names of Panel Members	Rank	Command/Unit	Signature	Interviews Conducted

Source: Adapted from www.uscg.mil/jobs/dc/DCPrograms/OProgramForms/PDFS/DCA/Interview% 20CG-5527pdf, accessed May 9, 2007.

the other by seeking oral responses to oral inquiries. Most selection processes are also sequential. In a *sequential interview* several people interview the applicant in sequence before a selection decision is made. In a *panel interview* the candidate is interviewed simultaneously by a group (or panel) of interviewers, rather than sequentially.

Some interviews are done by *phone*. These interviews can actually be more accurate than face-to-face ones for judging an applicant's conscientiousness, intelligence, and interpersonal skills. Since neither side has to worry about things like clothing or handshakes, the telephone interviews may let both focus more on substantive answers. Or perhaps candidates—somewhat surprised by unexpected calls from recruiters—simply give more spontaneous answers.[31] In a typical study, interviewers tended to evaluate applicants more favorably in telephone versus face-to-face interviews, particularly where the interviewees were less physically attractive. The interviewers came to about the same conclusions regarding the interviewees whether the interview was face-to-face or by videoconference. Applicants themselves preferred the face-to-face interviews.[32]

How Useful Are Interviews?

While virtually all employers use interviews, the statistical evidence regarding their validity is quite mixed. Much of the early research gave selection interviews low marks for reliability and validity.[33] However, today studies confirm that the "validity of the interview is greater than previously believed."[34] The key is that the interview's usefulness depends on how you administer it. Specifically, we can make the following generalizations, based on one study of interview validity:

- With respect to predicting job performance, situational interviews yield a higher mean (average) validity than do behavioral interviews.
- Structured interviews, regardless of content, are more valid than unstructured interviews for predicting job performance. They are more valid partly because they are more reliable—for example, the same interviewer administers the interview more consistently from candidate to candidate.[35]
- Both when they are structured and when they are unstructured, individual interviews tend to be more valid than are panel interviews, in which multiple interviewers provide ratings in one setting.[36]

In summary, structured situational interviews (in which you ask the candidates what they would do in a particular situation) conducted one-on-one seem to be the most useful for predicting job performance. However, whether you are an effective interviewer depends in part on avoiding common interviewing mistakes, a subject to which we now turn.

How to Avoid Common Interviewing Mistakes

Several common interviewing mistakes can undermine an interview's usefulness. Some of these common mistakes—and suggestions for avoiding them—are described in this section.

Snap Judgments

One of the most consistent findings is that interviewers tend to jump to conclusions—make snap judgments—about candidates during the first few minutes of the interview. In fact, this often occurs even before the interview begins, based on test scores or résumé data.[37] One London-based psychologist interviewed the chief executives of 80 top companies. She came to this conclusion about snap judgments in selection interviews: "Really, to make a good impression, you don't even get time to open your mouth. . . . An interviewer's response to you will generally be preverbal—how you walk through the door, what your posture is like, whether you smile, whether you have a captivating aura, whether you have a firm, confident handshake. You've got about half a minute to make an impact and after that all you are doing is building on a good or bad first impression. . . . It's a very emotional response."[38]

For interviewees, such findings underscore why it's important to start off on the right foot with the interviewer. Interviewers usually make up their minds about you during the first few minutes of the interview, and prolonging the interview past this point usually adds little to change their decisions. From the interviewer's point of view, the findings underscore the importance of consciously delaying a decision and keeping an open mind until the interview is over.

Negative Emphasis

Jumping to conclusions is especially troublesome given the fact that interviewers also tend to have a consistent negative bias. They are generally more influenced by unfavorable than favorable information about the candidate. Furthermore, their impressions are much more likely to change from favorable to unfavorable than from unfavorable to favorable. Often, in fact, interviews are mostly searches for negative information.

What are the implications? As an interviewer, remember to keep an open mind and consciously work against being preoccupied with negative impressions. As an interviewee, remember the old saying that "You only have one chance to make a good first impression." If you start with a poor initial impression, you'll find it almost impossible to overcome that first, bad impression during the interview.

Not Knowing the Job

Interviewers who don't know precisely what the job entails and what sort of candidate is best suited for it usually make decisions based on incorrect stereotypes about what makes a good applicant. They then erroneously match interviewees against these incorrect stereotypes. Studies therefore have long shown that more job knowledge on the part of interviewers translates into better interviews.[39] Interviewers should know as much as possible about the nature of the position for which they're interviewing, and about the human requirements (e.g., interpersonal skills, job knowledge) that the job requires.

Pressure to Hire

Being under pressure to hire undermines an interview's usefulness. In one study, a group of managers were told to assume that they were behind in their recruiting quota. A second group was told that they were ahead of their quota. Those behind evaluated the same recruits much more highly than did those ahead.[40]

Candidate Order (Contrast) Error

Candidate order (or contrast) error means that the order in which you see applicants affects how you rate them. In one study, researchers asked managers to evaluate a candidate who was "just average" after first evaluating several "unfavorable" candidates. The average candidate was evaluated more favorably than he might otherwise have been, because in contrast to the unfavorable candidates the average one looked better than he actually was.[41]

Influence of Nonverbal Behavior

Not just what the candidate says but how he or she looks and behaves can influence the interviewer's ratings. For example, studies show that interviewers rate applicants who demonstrate more eye contact, head moving, smiling, and similar nonverbal behaviors higher. Such behaviors often account for over 80% of the applicant's rating.[42] In another study, vocal cues (such as the interviewee's pitch, speech rates, and pauses) and visual cues (such as physical attractiveness, smile, and body orientation) correlated with the evaluator's judgments of whether the interviewees could be liked and trusted, and were credible.[43] In one study of 99 graduating college seniors, the interviewee's apparent level of extroversion influenced whether he or she received follow-up interviews and job offers.[44] Extroverted applicants seem particularly prone to self-promotion, and self-promotion is strongly related to the interviewer's perceptions of candidate job fit.[45]

Attractiveness

An applicant's attractiveness and sex also play a role.[46] In general, studies of attractiveness find that individuals ascribe more favorable traits and more successful life outcomes to attractive people.[47] In another study, researchers asked subjects to evaluate candidates for promotability based on photographs. Men were perceived to be more suitable for hire and more likely to advance to the next executive level than were equally qualified women, and more attractive candidates, especially men, were preferred over less attractive ones.[48] These stereotypes are changing. However, women still account for only about 16% of corporate officers and 1% of CEOs at Fortune 500 companies.[49]

Race

Race also plays a role. One study examined racial differences in ratings of black and white interviewees when the interviewees appeared before three interview panels: panels in which the racial composition was primarily black (75% black, 25% white), racially balanced (50% black, 50% white), and primarily white (75% white, 25% black).[50] On the primarily black panels, black and white raters judged black and white candidates similarly. On the other hand, in the primarily white panels or in those in which black and white interviewers were equally represented, white candidates were rated higher by white interviewers, and black candidates were rated higher by black interviewers.

Ingratiation

Interviewees also boost their chances for job offers through self-promotion and ingratiation. *Ingratiation* involves, for example, agreeing with the recruiter's opinions and thus signaling that they share similar beliefs. *Self-promotion* means promoting one's own skills and abilities to create the impression of competence.[51]

Implications

Evidence like this suggests several implications. With respect to nonverbal behavior (such as eye contact), it seems apparent that otherwise inferior candidates who are trained to "act right" in interviews are often appraised more highly than are more competent applicants without the right nonverbal interviewing skills. Interviewers should thus endeavor to look beyond the behavior to who the person is and what he or she is saying. Second, demographic and physical attributes, such as attractiveness, sex, or race, may influence your decisions as an interviewer. Because such attributes are generally irrelevant to job performance, interviewers should anticipate the potential impact of such biases and guard against letting them influence their ratings.

Applicant Disability and the Employment Interview

A study by the Research and Evaluation Center at the National Center for Disability Services provides some insight into what disabled people who use "assistive technology" (such as voice recognition software) at work expect and prefer from interviewers.[52]

Researchers surveyed 40 disabled people from various occupations to arrive at their conclusions. The basic finding was that, from the disabled person's point of view, interviewers tend to avoid directly addressing the disability, and therefore make their decisions without getting all the facts. What the disabled people prefer is an open discussion, one that would allow the employer to fully clarify his or her concerns and reach a knowledgeable conclusion. Among the questions disabled persons said they would like interviewers to ask were these:

- Is there any kind of setting or special equipment that will facilitate the interview process for you? And,
- Is there any specific technology that you currently use or have used in previous jobs that assists the way you work?

Guidelines for Conducting an Interview

You can generally conduct the interview more effectively if you follow the guidelines outlined in this section.

Plan the Interview

Begin by reviewing the candidate's application and résumé, and note any areas that are vague or that may indicate strengths or weaknesses. Review the job specification and plan to start the interview with a clear picture of the traits of an ideal candidate. In one study, about 39% of the 191 applicants said interviewers were unprepared or unfocused.[53]

Structure the Interview

Few steps are as important as structuring the interview. Doing so not only assures greater consistency. It also helps ensure that you ask questions that provide real insight into how the person will perform on the job—and that, of course, is the main point of the interview. There are several ways to increase the standardization of the interview or otherwise assist the interviewer to ask more consistent and job-relevant questions.[54] They include:[55]

1. Study the job description and base questions on actual job duties.
   Minimize irrelevant questions based on inaccurate beliefs about the job's requirements.

2. Use job knowledge, situational or behavioral questions, and objective criteria to evaluate the interviewee's responses. Questions that ask for opinions and attitudes, goals and aspirations, and self-descriptions and self-evaluations encourage self-promotion and allow candidates to avoid revealing weaknesses. Examples of structured questions include: (1) situational questions like "Suppose you were giving a sales presentation and a difficult technical question arose that you could not answer. What would you do?"; (2) past behavior questions like "Can you provide an example of a specific instance where you developed a sales presentation that was highly effective?"; (3) background questions like "What work experiences, training, or other qualifications do you have for working in a teamwork environment?"; (4) job knowledge questions like "What factors should you consider when developing a TV advertising campaign?"

3. Train interviewers. For example, review EEO laws with prospective interviewers and train them to avoid irrelevant or potentially discriminatory questions. Studies show training interviewers boosts their effectiveness.[56]

4. Use the same questions with all candidates. Using the same questions with all candidates can also reduce bias by giving all the candidates the exact same opportunity.

5. Use rating scales to rate answers, if possible. For each question, provide a range of sample ideal answers, and a quantitative score for each. Then rate each candidate's answers against this scale. (See Figure 4.6, pages 129–130.)

6. Use multiple interviewers. Doing so can reduce bias by diminishing the importance of one interviewer's idiosyncratic opinions, and by bringing in more points of view.

7. If possible, use a structured interview form. Interviews based on structured guides, like the one in Figure 4.7, usually result in superior interviews.[57] At the very least, list your questions before the interview.

8. Take brief notes during the interview. Doing so may help to overcome "the recency effect" (in other words, putting too much weight on the last few minutes of the interview). It may also help the interviewer keep an open mind rather than making a snap judgment based on inadequate information early into the interview, and may also help the interviewer jog his or her memory once the interview is complete. The research suggests that the interviewer should take notes, but not copious ones, instead noting just the key points of what the interviewee says.[58]

The interview should take place in a private room where telephone calls are not accepted and you can minimize interruptions.

Establish Rapport

The main reason for the interview is to find out about the applicant. To do this, start by putting the person at ease. Greet the candidate and start the interview by asking a noncontroversial question, perhaps about the weather or the traffic conditions that day. As a rule, all applicants—even unsolicited drop-ins—should receive friendly, courteous treatment, not only on humanitarian grounds but also because your reputation is on the line.

FIGURE 4.7   Structured Interview Guide

APPLICANT INTERVIEW GUIDE

To the interviewer: This Applicant Interview Guide is intended to assist in employee selection and placement. If it is used for all applicants for a position, it will help you to compare them, and it will provide more objective information than you will obtain from unstructured interviews.

Because this is a general guide, all of the items may not apply in every instance. Skip those that are not applicable and add questions appropriate to the specific position. Space for additional questions will be found at the end of the form.

Federal law prohibits discrimination in employment on the basis of sex, race, color, national origin, religion, disability, and in most instances, age. The laws of most states also ban some or all of the above types of discrimination in employment as well as discrimination based on marital status or ancestry. Interviewers should take care to avoid any questions that suggest that an employment decision will be made on the basis of any such factors.

Job Interest

Name _____ Position applied for _____

What do you think the job (position) involves? _____

Why do you want the job (position)? _____

Why are you qualified for it? _____

What would your salary requirements be? _____

What do you know about our company? _____

Why do you want to work for us? _____

Current Work Status

Are you now employed? _____ Yes _____ No. If not, how long have you been unemployed? _____

Why are you unemployed? _____

If you are working, why are you applying for this position? _____

When would you be available to start work with us? _____

Work Experience

(Start with the applicant's current or last position and work back. All periods of time should be accounted for. Go back at least 12 years, depending upon the applicant's age. Military service should be treated as a job.)

Current or last
employer _____ Address _____

Dates of employment: from _____ to _____

Current or last job title _____

What are (were) your duties? _____

Have you held the same job throughout your employment with that company? _____ Yes _____ No. If not, describe the

various jobs you have had with that employer, how long you held each of them, and the main duties of each. _____

_____

What was your starting salary? _____ What are you earning now? _____ Comments _____

_____

Name of your last or current supervisor _____

What did you like most about that job? _____

What did you like least about it? _____

Why are you thinking of leaving? _____

Why are you leaving right now? _____

Interviewer's comments or observations _____

What did you do before you took your last job? _____

Where were you employed? _____

Location _____ Job title _____

Duties _____

Did you hold the same job throughout your employment with that company? _____ Yes _____ No. If not,

describe the jobs you held, when you held them, and the duties of each. _____

_____

What was your starting salary? _____ What was your final salary? _____

Name of your last supervisor _____

May we contact that company? _____ Yes _____ No

What did you like most about that job? _____

What did you like least about that job? _____

Why did you leave that job? _____

Would you consider working there again? _____

Interviewer: If there is any gap between the various periods of employment, the applicant should be asked about them. _____

_____

Interviewer's comments or observations _____

_____

What did you do prior to the job with that company? _____

What other jobs or experience have you had? Describe them briefly and explain the general duties of each. _____

_____

Have you been unemployed at any time in the last five years? _____ Yes _____ No. What efforts did you make to find work?

_____

What other experience or training do you have that would help qualify you for the job applied for? Explain how and where you

obtained this experience or training. _____

_____

Educational Background

What education or training do you have that would help you in the job for which you have applied? _____

_____

Describe any formal education you have had. (Interviewer may substitute technical training, if relevant.) _____

_____

Off-Job Activities

What do you do in your off-hours? _____ Part-time job _____ Athletics _____ Spectator sports _____ Clubs _____ Other

Please explain. _____

Interviewer's Specific Questions

Interviewer: Add any questions to the particular job for which you are interviewing, leaving space for brief answers.
(Be careful to avoid questions which may be viewed as discriminatory.)

_____

_____   _____

_____

Personal

Would you be willing to relocate? _____ Yes _____ No

Are you willing to travel? _____ Yes _____ No

What is the maximum amount of time you would consider traveling? _____

_____

(Continued)

Are you able to work overtime? _____

What about working on weekends? _____

Self-Assessment

What do you feel are your strong points? _____

_____

What do you feel are your weak points? _____

_____

Interviewer: Compare the applicant's responses with the information furnished on the application for employment. Clear up any

discrepancies. _____

_____

Before the applicant leaves, the interviewer should provide basic information about the organization and the job opening, if this has not already been done. The applicant should be given information on the work location, work hours, the wage or salary, type of remuneration (salary or salary plus bonus, etc.), and other factors that may affect the applicant's interest in the job.

Interviewer's Impressions

Rate each characteristic from 1 to 4, with 1 being the highest rating and 4 being the lowest.

Personal Characteristics	1	2	3	4	Comments
Personal appearance					
Poise, manner					
Speech					
Cooperation with interviewer					
Job-Related Characteristics					
Experience for this job					
Knowledge of job					
Interpersonal relationships					
Effectiveness					

Overall Rating for Job

1	2	3	4	5
_____ Superior	_____ Above average	_____ Average	_____ Marginal	_____ Unsatisfactory
	(well qualified)	(qualified)	(barely qualified)	

Comments or remarks _____

_____

_____

Interviewer _____ Date _____

Source: Adapted from The Dartnell Corporation, © 1992.

Ask Questions

Try to follow your structured interview guide or the questions you wrote out ahead of time. You'll find a menu of questions to choose from (such as "What best qualifies you for the available position?") in Figure 4.8.

One way to get more candid answers is to make it clear you're going to conduct reference checks. Ask, "If I were to ask your boss, and if the boss were very candid with

---

FIGURE 4.8   Some Interview Questions to Ask or to Expect

What salary do you expect to receive? _____

Why do you want to change jobs or why did you leave your last job? _____
_____

What do you identify as your most significant accomplishment in your last job? _____
_____

How many hours do you normally work per week? _____

What did you like and dislike about your last job? _____

How did you get along with your superiors and subordinates? _____

How would you evaluate the company you were with last? _____

What best qualifies you for the available position? _____

What interests you most about the available position? _____

How would you structure this job or organize your department? _____

What control or financial data would you want and why? _____

How would you establish your primary inside and outside lines of communication? _____
_____

What would you like to tell me about yourself? _____

Have you kept up in your field? How? _____

What do you do in your spare time? _____

What steps are you taking to help achieve your goals? _____

What did your father do? Your mother? _____

What do your brothers and sisters do? _____

Have you ever worked on a group project and, if so, what role did you play? _____

How do you spend a typical day? _____

What motivates you to work? _____

Would you rather work alone or in a team? _____

What do you look for when hiring people? _____

Will you sign a noncompete agreement or employment contract? _____

Why should we hire you? _____

DOS AND DON'TS OF INTERVIEW QUESTIONS

- **Don't** ask questions that can be answered yes or no.
- **Don't** put words in the applicant's mouth or telegraph the desired answer, for instance, by nodding or smiling when the right answer is given.
- **Don't** interrogate the applicant as if the person is a criminal, and don't be patronizing, sarcastic, or inattentive.
- **Don't** monopolize the interview by rambling, nor let the applicant dominate the interview so you can't ask all your questions.

- **Do** ask open-ended questions.
- **Do** listen to the candidate to encourage him or her to express thoughts fully.
- **Do** draw out the applicant's opinions and feelings by repeating the person's last comment as a question (e.g., "You didn't like your last job?").
- **Do** ask for examples.[59] For instance, if the candidate lists specific strengths or weaknesses, follow up with, "What are specific examples that demonstrate each of your strengths?"

me, what's your best guess as to what he or she would say are your strengths, weaker points, and overall performance?"[60]

The *HR in Practice* box above summarizes some dos and don'ts for asking questions.

Close the Interview

Toward the close of the interview, leave time to answer any questions the candidate may have and, if appropriate, to advocate your firm to the candidate.

Try to end all interviews on a positive note. Tell the applicant whether there is an interest and, if so, what the next step will be. Similarly, make rejections diplomatically (for instance, with a statement such as "Although your background is impressive, there are other candidates whose experience is closer to our requirements").

Review the Interview

After the candidate leaves, review your interview notes, fill in the structured interview guide (if this was not done during the interview), and review the interview while it's fresh in your mind.

USING OTHER SELECTION TECHNIQUES

Background Investigations and Reference Checks

About 82% of HR managers report checking applicants' backgrounds; 80% do criminal convictions searches, and 35% do credit history reports.[61] There are two key reasons for checking backgrounds. One is to verify the accuracy of factual information previously provided by the applicant; the other is to uncover damaging background information such as criminal records and suspended drivers' licenses. In Chicago, for instance, a pharmaceutical firm discovered that it had hired gang members in mail delivery and computer repair.

The gang members were stealing close to a million dollars per year in computer parts and then using the mail department to ship them to a nearby computer store they owned.[62]

What to Verify

The most commonly verified background areas are legal eligibility for employment (to comply with immigration laws), dates of prior employment, military service (including discharge status), education, and identification (including date of birth and address).[63] Other items should include county criminal records (current residence, last residence), motor vehicle record, credit, licensing verification, Social Security number, and reference checks.[64] The position determines how deeply you search. For example, a credit and education check would be more important for hiring an accountant than a groundskeeper. In any case, do not limit your background checks only to new hires. For example, also periodically check, say, the credit ratings of employees who have easy access to company assets, and the driving records of employees who routinely use company cars.

Collecting Background Information

There are several ways to collect background information. Most employers at least try to verify an applicant's current position, salary, and employment dates with his or her current employer by phone (assuming that the candidate cleared doing so). Others call the applicant's current and previous supervisors to try to discover more about the person's motivation, technical competence, and ability to work with others. As we'll see in a moment, some employers get background reports from commercial credit rating companies or employment screening services. These can provide information about an applicant's credit standing, indebtedness, reputation, character, lifestyle, and the truthfulness of the person's application data. There are also thousands of online databases and sources for obtaining background information, including sex offender registries; workers compensation histories; nurses aid registries; and sources for criminal, employment, and educational histories.[65] Top employee background providers include Kroll Background Screenings Group (www.Krollworldwide.com), ChoicePoint (www.choicepoint.com), and First Advantage (www.FADV.com).[66]

Checking Social Networking Sites

More employers are checking candidates' social networking sites' postings. One employer went to Facebook.com and found that a top candidate described his interests as smoking marijuana and shooting people. The student may have been kidding, but did not get the offer.[67] After conducting such online reviews, recruiters found that 31% of applicants had lied about their qualifications and 19% had posted information about their drinking or drug use, according to a Careerbuilder.com survey.[68]

Reference Check Effectiveness

Handled correctly, background checks are an inexpensive and straightforward way of verifying factual information (such as current and previous job titles) about applicants. However, reference checking can also backfire. For one thing, it is not easy for the reference to prove that the bad reference he or she gave an applicant was warranted. The rejected applicant thus has various legal remedies, including suing the reference for defamation of character, a fact that can understandably inhibit former employers and supervisors from giving candid references.[69] In one case, for instance, a man was awarded $56,000 after being turned down for a job because, among other things, he was called a "character" by a former employer.

It is not just the fear of legal reprisal that can lead to a useless or misleading reference. Many supervisors don't want to diminish a former employee's chances for a job. Others rather give an incompetent employee good reviews if it will get rid of him or her. Even when checking references via the phone, therefore, be careful to ask the right questions, and to judge whether the reference's answers are evasive and, if so, why.

Making Reference Checks More Productive

You can do several things to make your reference checking more productive.

First, use a structured form as in Figure 4.9. The form helps ensure that you don't overlook important questions.

Second, use the references offered by the applicant as merely a source for other references who may know of the applicant's performance. Thus, you might ask each of the applicant's references, "Could you please give me the name of another person who might be familiar with the applicant's performance?" In that way, you begin getting information from references who may be more objective because they weren't referred directly by the applicant. Perhaps contact two superiors, two peers, and two subordinates from each job previously held by the candidate to form a reliable picture of the candidate.

Third, also ask open-ended questions, such as "How much direction does the applicant need in his or her work?" in order to get the references to talk more about the candidate.

Fourth, companies fielding requests for references should ensure that only authorized managers give them. Employees have taken legal action for defamatory references. There are companies that, for a fee, will call former employers on behalf of former employees who believe they're getting bad references from their former employers. One supervisor, describing a former city employee, reportedly "used swear words, said he was incompetent and said that he almost brought the city down on its knees."[70] There are reportedly now "dozens" of reference-checking firms like Allison & Taylor Reference Checking Inc. in Jamestown, New York, doing this sort of work.[71]

There are several other things the employer can do to screen out undesirables. Always get at least two forms of identification and always require applicants to fill out a job application. Always compare the application to the résumé (people tend to be more creative on their résumés than on their application forms, where they must certify the information).[72]

Using Preemployment Information Services

Online databases have made it easier to check background information about candidates. As a result, numerous employment screening services such as HireCheck (see www.hirecheck.com) now use databases to conduct background checks for employers. They access dozens of databases, by county, to quickly compile background information for employers.

Although they are valuable, the employer should make sure the screening service does not ensnare it by taking any actions that run afoul of Equal Employment

FIGURE 4.9   Reference Checking Form

(Verify that the applicant has provided permission before conducting reference checks.)

Candidate
Name _____

Reference
Name _____

Company
Name _____

Dates of Employment
From: _____ To: _____

Position(s)
Held _____

Salary
History _____

Reason for
Leaving _____

Explain the reason for your call and verify the above information with the supervisor (including the reason for leaving)
_____
_____
_____

1. Please describe the type of work for which the candidate was responsible.
_____
_____

2. How would you describe the applicant's relationships with coworkers, subordinates (if applicable), and with superiors?
_____
_____

3. Did the candidate have a positive or negative work attitude? Please elaborate.
_____
_____

4. How would you describe the quantity and quality of output generated by the former employee?
_____
_____

5. What were his/her strengths on the job?
_____
_____

6. What were his/her weaknesses on the job?
_____
_____

7. What is your overall assessment of the candidate?
_____
_____

8. Would you recommend him/her for this position? Why or why not?
_____
_____

9. Would this individual be eligible for rehire? Why or why not?
_____
_____

Other comments?
_____
_____

Source: Society for Human Resource Management, © 2004. Reproduced with permission via Copyright Clearance Center.

Opportunity (EEO) laws. As discussed in Chapter 2, numerous equal employment laws discourage or prohibit using unfairly discriminatory information in employee hiring. For example, under the ADA, employers should avoid preemployment inquiries into the existence, nature, or severity of a disability. In choosing a screening firm to use, the employer should make sure the firm requires an applicant-signed release authorizing the background check, complies with relevant laws such as the Fair Credit Reporting Act, and uses only legal data sources. A basic criminal check might cost $25, while a comprehensive background check costs about $200.[73]

Honesty Testing

Polygraph Tests

The *polygraph* (or "*lie detector*") machine is a device that measures physiological changes such as increased perspiration. The assumption is that such changes reflect changes in the emotional stress that accompanies lying. The usual procedure is to attach the applicant or current employee to the machine with painless electronic probes. He or she is then asked a series of neutral questions by the polygraph expert. Once the person's emotional reactions to giving truthful answers to neutral questions have been ascertained, questions such as "Have you ever taken anything without paying for it?" can be asked. In theory, the expert can determine with some accuracy whether the applicant is lying.

Complaints about offensiveness as well as grave doubts about the polygraph's accuracy culminated in signing the Employee Polygraph Protection Act into law in 1988. With few exceptions, the law prohibits most employers from conducting polygraph examinations of all applicants and most employees. Even in the case of ongoing investigations of theft, the employer's right to use polygraphs is quite limited under the act.

Paper-and-Pencil Honesty Tests

The virtual elimination of the polygraph as a screening device triggered a burgeoning market for other types of honesty testing devices. Paper-and-pencil honesty tests are psychological tests designed to predict job applicants' proneness to dishonesty. Most of these tests measure attitudes regarding things such as tolerance of others who steal, acceptance of rationalizations for theft, and admission of theft-related activities.

Psychologists initially raised concerns about the proliferation of paper-and-pencil honesty tests, but studies do tend to support these tests' validity. One study focused on 111 employees hired by a major retail convenience store chain to work at convenience store or gas station outlet counters.[74] "Shrinkage" was estimated to equal 3% of sales, and internal theft was believed to account for much of this. The researchers found that scores on an honesty test successfully predicted theft, as measured by termination for theft.

In practice, detecting dishonest candidates involves not only paper-and-pencil tests but also a comprehensive screening procedure including reference checking and interviews. One expert suggests following the steps in the *HR in Practice* box.

Graphology

The use of graphology (handwriting analysis) is based on the assumption that the writer's basic personality traits will be expressed in his or her handwriting. Handwriting analysis thus has some resemblance to projective personality tests.

HOW TO DETECT DISHONESTY

Ask blunt questions. You can ask very direct questions in the face-to-face interview. For example, there is probably nothing wrong with asking the applicant, "Have you ever stolen anything from an employer?"; "Have you recently held jobs other than those listed on your application?"; and "Is any information on your application misrepresented or falsified?"

Listen, rather than talk. Allow the applicant to do the talking so you can learn as much as possible about the person.

Ask for a credit check. Include a clause in your application form that gives you the right to certain background checks on the applicant, including credit checks and motor vehicle reports.

Check all references. Rigorously pursue employment and personal references.

Consider using a paper-and-pencil test. Consider utilizing paper-and-pencil honesty tests and psychological tests as part of your honesty screening.

Test for drugs. Devise a drug testing program and give each applicant a copy of the policy.

Conduct searches. Establish a search-and-seizure policy. Give each applicant a copy of the policy and require each to return a signed copy. The policy should state that all lockers, desks, and similar property remain the property of the company and may be inspected routinely.

Use caution. Being rejected for dishonesty carries with it more stigma than does being rejected for, say, poor mechanical comprehension. Furthermore, some states, including Massachusetts and Rhode Island, limit the use of paper-and-pencil honesty tests. Therefore, ensure that you are protecting your candidates' and employees' rights to privacy and that you are adhering to the law in using honesty tests.

Although some writers estimate that more than 1,000 U.S. companies use handwriting analysis to assess applicants for certain strategic positions, the validity of handwriting analysis is questionable, to say the least. In general, the evidence suggests that graphology does not predict job performance.[75]

Physical Exams

Physical examinations are often the next step in the selection process, and there are several reasons for requiring them. Such exams can confirm that the applicant qualifies for the physical requirements of the position and can unearth any medical limitations that should be taken into account in placing the applicant. The examination can also detect communicable diseases that may be unknown to the applicant. Under the ADA, a person with a disability can't be rejected for the job if he or she is otherwise qualified and if the person could perform the essential job functions with reasonable accommodation. According to the ADA, a medical exam is permitted during the period between the job offer and the commencement of work, but only if such exams are standard practice for all applicants for that job category.[76]

Drug Screening

Employers are increasingly conducting drug tests. The most common practice is to test new applicants just before they are formally hired. Many firms also test current employees when there is reason to believe an employee has been using drugs after a work accident, or when there are obvious behavioral symptoms or chronic lateness or high absenteeism. Some firms administer drug tests on a random or periodic basis, while others do so only when transferring or promoting an employee.[77] Virtually all (96%) employers that conduct such tests use urine sampling.

Problems

Unfortunately, drug testing in general doesn't always correlate closely with actual impairment levels.[78] Although Breathalyzers and blood tests for alcohol such as those given at the roadside to inebriated drivers correlate closely with impairment levels, urine and blood tests for other drugs only indicate whether the drug residues are present. They cannot measure impairment or, for that matter, habituation or addiction.[79]

Furthermore, "there is a swarm of products that promise to help employees (both male and female) beat drug tests."[80] Drug testing therefore raises several issues. Without strong evidence linking blood or urine drug levels to impairment, some argue that drug testing violates citizens' rights to privacy and due process, and that the procedures themselves are degrading and intrusive. Others argue that workplace drug testing might identify one's use of drugs during leisure hours, but have little or no relevance to the job itself.[81] Furthermore, some employees will claim that drug tests violate their rights to privacy.

In fact, it is not clear that drug testing improves either safety or performance. At least one study, reported by a committee of the National Academy of Sciences, concluded that other than alcohol, there is no clear evidence that drugs diminish safety or job performance.[82] Another study, conducted in three hotels, concluded that preemployment drug testing seemed to have little or no effect on workplace accidents. However, a combination of preemployment and random ongoing testing was associated with a significant reduction in workplace accidents.[83]

Legal Issues

Several federal laws have direct relevance for workplace drug testing. Under the ADA, courts might well view a former drug user (one who no longer uses illegal drugs and successfully completed or is participating in a rehabilitation program) as a qualified applicant with a disability.[84] U.S. Department of Transportation workplace regulations require firms with more than 50 eligible employees in transportation industries to conduct alcohol testing on workers with sensitive or safety-related jobs. These include mass-transit workers, air traffic controllers, train crews, and school-bus drivers.[85]

Particularly where safety-sensitive jobs are concerned, courts appear to side with employers when questions arise. In one case, for instance, the U.S. Court of Appeals for the First Circuit ruled that Exxon acted properly in firing a truck driver who failed a drug test. Exxon Corporation's drug-free workplace program included random testing of employees in safety-sensitive jobs. In this case, the employee drove a tractor trailer carrying 12,000 gallons of flammable motor fuel and tested positive for cocaine. Exxon discharged him.[86]

Realistic Job Previews

Sometimes, a dose of realism makes the best screening tool. For example, Wal-Mart found that associates who quit within the first 90 days did so because of conflict in their schedules or because they preferred to work in another geographic area. The firm then began explicitly explaining and asking about work schedules and work preferences.[87] One study even found that some applicants accepted jobs with the intention to quit, a fact that more realistic interviewing might have unearthed.[88]

Complying with the Immigration Law

Under the Immigration Reform and Control Act of 1986, people must prove that they are eligible to be employed in the United States. A person does not have to be a U.S. citizen to be employed under this act. However, employers should ask a candidate who is about to be hired whether he or she is a U.S. citizen or an alien lawfully authorized to work in the United States.

How to Comply

There are two basic ways prospective employees can show their eligibility for employment. One is to show a document such as a U.S. passport or alien registration card with photograph that proves both identity and employment eligibility. However, many prospective employees do not have either of these documents. Therefore, the other way to verify employment eligibility is to see a document that proves the person's identity, along with a separate document showing the person's employment eligibility, such as a work permit.

Employers run the risk of accepting fraudulent documents, and here they can protect themselves in several ways. Systematic background checks are the most obvious. Preemployment screening should include employment verification, criminal record checks, drug screens, and reference checks. You can verify Social Security cards by calling the Social Security Administration. Employers can avoid accusations of discrimination by verifying the documents of all applicants, not just those they think may be suspicious.[89]

Employers cannot and should not use the I-9 Employment Eligibility Verification form required to document eligibility to discriminate in any way based on race or country of national origin. The requirement to verify eligibility does not provide any basis to reject an applicant just because he or she is a foreigner, or not a U.S. citizen, or an alien residing in the United States, as long as that person can prove his or her identity and employment eligibility.

Evaluating the Selection Process

More employers today wisely take the time to evaluate just how effective their recruitment and screening processes are. GE, for example, compares its various recruiting sources to the performances of the employees they produce, and in that way fine-tunes what recruiting sources it uses. Some firms use "mystery shoppers" to help evaluate their recruitment and staffing processes. Thus the consulting firm Bernard Hodes worked with one client to create phantom applicants, complete with résumés. These phantoms then applied to the client employer and reported back on the effectiveness of the employer's recruitment and selection processes.[90] Table 4.1 summarizes the validity, cost, and potential adverse impact of some popular selection methods.

TABLE 4.1 Evaluation of Assessment Methods on Four Key Criteria

Assessment Method	Validity	Adverse Impact	Costs (Develop/Administer)	Applicant Reactions
Cognitive ability tests	High	High (against minorities)	Low/low	Somewhat favorable
Job knowledge test	High	High (against minorities)	Low/low	More favorable
Personality tests	Low to moderate	Low	Low/low	Less favorable
Biographical data inventories	Moderate	Low to high for different types	High/low	Less favorable
Integrity tests	Moderate to high	Low	Low/low	Less favorable
Structured interviews	High	Low	High/high	More favorable
Physical fitness tests	Moderate to high	High (against females and older workers)	High/high	More favorable
Situational judgment tests	Moderate	Moderate (against minorities)	High/low	More favorable
Work samples	High	Low	High/high	More favorable
Assessment centers	Moderate to high	Low to moderate, depending on exercise	High/high	More favorable
Physical ability tests	Moderate to high	High (against females and older workers)	High/high	More favorable

Note: There was limited research evidence available on applicant reactions to situational judgment tests and physical ability tests. However, because these tests tend to appear very relevant to the job, it is likely that applicant reactions to them would be favorable.

Source: Elaine Pulakos. *Selection Assessment Methods.* SHRM Foundation, 2005, p. 17. Reprinted by permission of Society for Human Resource Management via Copyright Clearance Center.

Review

Summary

1. In this chapter we discuss several techniques for screening and selecting job candidates: The first is testing.

2. Test validity answers the question, What does this test measure? Criterion validity means demonstrating that those who do well on the test do well on the job. Content validity is demonstrated by showing that the test constitutes a fair sample of the content of the job.

3. As used by psychologists, the term *reliability* always means "consistency." One way to measure reliability is to administer the same (or equivalent) tests to the same people at two different points in time. Or you could focus on internal consistency, comparing the responses to roughly equivalent items on the same test.

4. There are many types of personnel tests in use, including intelligence tests, tests of physical skills, tests of achievement, aptitude tests, interest inventories, and personality tests.

5. Under equal opportunity legislation, an employer may have to prove that his or her tests are predictive of success or failure on the job. This usually requires a predictive validation study, although other means of validation are often acceptable.

6. Management assessment centers are screening devices that expose applicants to a series of real-life exercises. Performance is observed and assessed by experts, who then check their assessments by observing the participants when they are back at their jobs. Examples of such real-life exercises include a simulated business game, an in-basket exercise, and group discussions.

7. Several factors and problems can undermine the usefulness of an interview: making premature decisions, letting unfavorable information predominate, not knowing the requirements of the job, being under pressure to hire, not allowing for the candidate order effect, and nonverbal behavior.

8. The five steps in the interview include plan, establish rapport, question the candidate, close the interview, and review the data.

9. Other screening tools include reference checks, background checks, physical exams, and realistic previews.

10. Once you've selected and hired your new employees, they must be trained. We turn to training in the following chapter.

Key Terms

- reliability
- test validity
- criterion validity
- content validity
- management assessment centers
- interview

Discussion Questions and Exercises

1. Explain what is meant by *reliability* and *validity*. What is the difference between them? In what respects are they similar?

2. Write a short essay discussing some of the ethical and legal considerations in testing.

3. Working individually or in groups, contact the publisher of a standardized test such as the SAT and obtain written information regarding the test's validity and reliability. Present a short report in class discussing what the test is supposed to measure and the degree to which you think the test does what it is supposed to do, based on the reported validity and reliability scores.

4. Give some examples of how interest inventories could be used to improve employee selection. In doing so, suggest several examples of occupational interests that you believe might predict success in various occupations, including college professor, accountant, and computer programmer.
5. Why is it important to conduct preemployment background investigations? How would you go about doing so?
6. For what sorts of jobs do you think computerized interviews are most appropriate? Why?
7. Give a short presentation titled "How to Be Effective as an Interviewer."
8. Briefly discuss and give examples of at least five common interviewing mistakes. What recommendations would you give for avoiding these interviewing mistakes?

APPLICATION EXERCISES

Case Incident *The Tough Screener*

Everyone who knows Mark Rosen knows he is a very tough owner when it comes to screening applicants for jobs in his firm. His company, located in a large northeastern city, provides financial planning advice to wealthy clients and sells insurance and sets up pension plans for individuals and businesses. His firm's clients range from professionals such as doctors and lawyers to business owners, who are fairly sophisticated in financial matters and very busy people. They expect accurate advice provided in a clear and expeditious manner.

Rosen has always been described as somewhat autocratic. The need to be very selective in whom he hires has led him to be extraordinarily careful about how he screens his job applicants. Some of his methods are probably beyond reproach. For example, he requires every applicant to provide a list of names and phone numbers for at least five people he or she worked with at each previous employer to be used as references. The resulting reference check is time consuming but effective.

On the other hand, given legislation including the Civil Rights Act of 1991 and the ADA, some of his other "tough" screening methods could be problematic. For example, Rosen requires that all applicants take a purported honesty test, which he found in the catalog of an office supply store. He also believes it is extremely important to check every viable applicant's credit history and workers' compensation history in order to screen out what he refers to as "potential undesirables." Unknown to his applicants, he runs a credit check on each of them and also retains the services of a firm that checks workers' compensation and driving violation histories. ■

QUESTIONS

1. What specific legal problems do you think Rosen might run into as a result of his firm's current screening methods? What steps would you suggest he take to eliminate these problems?
2. Given what you know about Rosen's business, write a two-page proposal describing an employee testing and selection program that you would recommend for his firm. Say a few words about the sorts of tests, if any, you would recommend and the application form questions you would ask, as well as other methods, including drug screening and reference checking.

Continuing Case

LearnInMotion.com: Do You Have Sales Potential?

Of all the positions LearnInMotion had to fill, none were more pressing—or problematic—than those of the company's salespeople. The job was pressing because the clock was already ticking on the uses of the company's funds. The firm was already paying over $5,000 a month in rent and had signed obligations for a wide range of other expenses, including monthly computer payments to Dell ($2,000 a month), a phone system ($800 a month), a burglar alarm ($200 a month), advertising (required by their venture capital fund, and equal to $4,000 a month), their own salaries ($10,000 a month), high-speed DSL lines ($600 a month), phones ($400 a month), and the services of a consulting programmer ($4,000 a month). As a result, even "doing nothing" they were burning through almost $40,000 per month. They had to have a sales force.

However, hiring good salespeople was becoming increasingly difficult. Hiring people like this should have been fairly straightforward: LearnInMotion's salespeople have to sell to basically two types of customers. They have to try to get potential customers to purchase banner space or button space on LearnInMotion's various Web site pages. To make this easier, Jennifer and Mel had prepared an online media kit. It describes the Web site metrics—for instance, in terms of monthly page views, and in terms of typical user metrics such as reported age and income level. In addition to selling banner ads, salespeople also have to try to get the companies that actually produce and make available educational CD-ROMs and courses to make those courses and programs available through LearnInMotion.com. None of these are "big-ticket" sales: Because the site is new and small, they can't really charge advertisers based on the number of users who click on their ads, so they simply charge a quarterly fee of $1,500 to list courses, or place ads. Content providers also have to agree to split any sales 50–50 with LearnInMotion. The Web surfer and office manager spend part of their time scouring the Web to identify specific people as potential customers. The salespeople then contact these people, "take them through" the Web site to show its advantages and functions, and answer the potential customer's questions.

This sales job, in other words, was fairly typical, so it shouldn't have been so difficult to fill, but difficult it was. Perhaps it was because it was a dot-com, or perhaps they just weren't offering enough compensation; whatever it was, the two owners were finding it extremely difficult to hire one, let alone two, good salesperson.

Perhaps the biggest problem here was deciding which of the personable candidates who showed up actually had sales potential. Jennifer and Mel did learn a couple of interesting things about interviewing sales candidates. For example,

when they asked the first what his average monthly sales had been in the past 6 months at his former employer, he answered, "Oh, I got the award for highest sales last month." That seemed great to Mel, until later Jennifer pointed out to him that that answer really didn't answer their question. Things got even "weirder"—to use Mel's term—when five out of six of the next sales candidates gave more or less the same answer: "I was the top producer"; "I was one of the top three producers"; "They sent me to Las Vegas for being the top sales producer"; and so on. Getting applicants to actually divulge, specifically, what their average monthly sales had been in the past 6 months was, as they say, like pulling teeth. Given that fact, and the relatively few sales candidates they have had, it has become increasingly obvious to the owners that basing their hiring decision solely on the person's experience is not going to work. In other words, they have to have some way to ascertain whether the candidate has sales potential, and whether he or she has the cognitive aptitude to discuss LearnInMotion's services with what were, in fact, quite sophisticated customers. They want you, their management consultants, to help them. Here's what they want you to do for them. ■

QUESTIONS AND ASSIGNMENTS

1. What would be the advantages and disadvantages to our company of routinely administering a "sales potential" test to sales candidates? Which would you suggest?
2. Specifically, what other screening techniques should our company use to select high-potential sales candidates?
3. Tell us: What have we been doing wrong, and what should we do now?
4. Create a set of situational and behavioral questions you think we should ask candidates in our interviews with them.

EXPERIENTIAL EXERCISE

The Structured Interview

Purpose: The purposes of this exercise are:

1. To give you practice in developing a structured interview form
2. To give you practice in using this form

Required Understanding: The reader should be familiar with the interviewing problems discussed, and with the example of the structured interview guide presented in Figures 4.6 and 4.7.

How to Set Up the Exercise/Instructions:

1. Set up groups of four or five students. One student will be the interviewee, and the other students in the group will develop the structured interview form and, as a group, interview the interviewee.
2. Instructions for the interviewee: Please do not read the exercise beyond this point (you can leave the room for a few minutes).
3. Instructions for the interviewers: You are a business owner who has to interview a candidate for telesales representative in about an hour. Each of you knows it's best to use a structured interview form to guide the interview, so you're now meeting for about half an hour to develop such a form, based in part on the job description presented in Figure 3.1, pages 68–69. (*Hint:* Start by listing the most relevant abilities and then rate these in importance on a 5-point scale. Then use the high-rated abilities on your interview form.)
4. As soon as you have completed your structured interview form, call in your interviewee and explain that he or she is a candidate for the job and that you (to whom the candidate will report if hired) and perhaps one or more managers will interview him or her as a group. You may tell the interviewee what his or her job summary calls for.

Next, interview the candidate, with each interviewer separately keeping notes on his or her own copy of the group's structured interview form. Each interviewer can take turns asking questions.

After the interview, discuss the following questions in the group. Based on each interviewer's notes, how similar were your perceptions of the candidate's responses? Did you all agree on the candidate's potential for the job? Did the candidate ask good questions of his or her interviewers? Did any of the interviewers find themselves jumping to conclusions about the candidate?

Summary of Telesales Job Description: The person in this position is responsible for generating approximately $2 million in revenue, for meeting operating expense budget of approximately $4,000, and a sampling budget of approximately 10,000 units. Prior sales or publishing experience preferred. One year of company experience in a customer service or marketing function with broad knowledge of company products and services is desirable. The person in this position is responsible for selling college textbooks, software, and multimedia products to professors, via incoming and outgoing telephone calls, and to carry out selling strategies to meet sales goals in assigned territories of smaller colleges and universities. In addition, the individual in this position will be responsible for generating a designated amount of editorial leads and communicating product feedback and market trends observed in the assigned territory to the publishing groups. No supervisory responsibilities. Bachelor's degree with strong academic performance or work equivalent experience preferred. Must have strong organizational and persuasive skills. Must have excellent verbal and written communications skills and must be PC proficient.

Primary Responsibilities: Driving sales; achieve quantitative sales goal for assigned territory of smaller colleges and universities; determine sales priorities and strategies for territory and develop a plan for implementing those strategies; conduct 15–20 professor interviews per day during the academic sales year that accomplishes those priorities; conduct product presentations (including texts, software, and Web site); effectively articulate author's central vision of key titles; conduct sales interviews using the Pearson sales model; conduct "walk-through" of books and technology. ∎

Endnotes

1. Kevin Delaney, "Google Adjusts Hiring Process as Needs Grow," *Wall Street Journal* (October 23, 2006): B1, B8.

2. See Rebecca Bennett and Sandra Robinson, "Development of a Measure of Workplace Deviance," *Journal of Applied Psychology* 85, no. 3 (2000): 349.

3. "Wal-Mart to Scrutinize Job Applicants," *CNN Money*, August 12, 2004, http://money.cnn.com/2004/08/12/News/fortune500/wal-mart_jobs/index.htm, accessed August 8, 2005.

4. Fay Hansen, "Taking 'Reasonable' Action to Avoid Negligent Hiring Claims," *Workforce Management* (September 11, 2006): 31.

5. Anne Anastasi, *Psychological Patterns* (New York: Macmillan, 1968). See also Kevin Murphy and Charles David Shafer, *Psychological Testing* (Upper Saddle River, NJ: Prentice Hall, 2001), pp. 108–124.

6. Robert M. Guion, "Changing Views for Personnel Selection Research," *Personnel Psychology* 40, no. 2 (Summer 1987): 199–213.

7. "Hiring Based on Strength Test Discriminates Against Women," *BNA Bulletin to Management* (February 22, 2005): 62.

8. Brad Bushman and Gary Wells, "Trait Aggressiveness and Hockey Penalties: Predicting Hot Tempers on the Ice," *Journal of Applied Psychology* 83, no. 6 (1998): 969–974.

9. "One-third of Job Applicants Flunked Basic Literacy and Math Tests Last Year, American Management Association Survey Finds", *American Management Association*, www.amanet.org/press/amanews/bjp2001.htm, accessed January 11, 2008.

10. Scott Hayes, "Kinko's Dials into Automated Applicants Screening," *Workforce* 78, no. 11 (November 1999): 71–73; Note that the U.S. Department of Labor recently reminded federal contractors that even if they use a third party to prepare an employment test, the contractors themselves are "ultimately responsible" for ensuring the tests' job relatedness and EEO compliance. "DOL Officials Discuss Contractors' Duties on Validating Tests," BNA Bulletin to Management (September 4, 2007): 287.

11. For some other examples see William Shepherd, "Increasing Profits By Assessing Employee Work Styles", *Employment Relations Today*, 32, NO. 1 (Spring 2005): 19–23, and Eric Krell, "Personality Counts", *HR Magazine* (November 2005): 47–52.

12. Sarah Gale, "Three Companies Cut Turnover with Tests," *Workforce* (April 2002): 66–69.

13. William Wagner, "All Skill, No Finesse," *Workforce* (June 2000): 108–116. See also for example, James Diefendorff and Kajal Mehta, "The Relations of Motivational Traits with Workplace Deviance," *Journal of Applied Psychology* 92, no. 4 (2007): 967–977.

14. See, for example, Douglas Cellar et al., "Comparison of Factor Structures and Criterion-Related Validity Coefficients for Two Measures of Personality Based on the Five Factor Model," *Journal of Applied Psychology* 81, no. 6 (1996): 694–704; Joyce Hogan, et al., "Personality Measurement, Faking, and Employee Selection," *Journal of Applied Psychology* 92, no. 5 (2007): 1270–1285.

15. Murray Barrick and Michael Mount, "The Big Five Personality Dimensions and Job Performance: A Meta Analysis," *Personnel Psychology* 44, no. 1 (Spring 1991): 1–26. See also Robert Schneider, Leatta Hough, and Marvin Dunnette, "Broad-Sided by Broad Traits: How to Sink Science in Five Dimensions or Less," *Journal of Organizational Behavior* 17, no. 6 (November 1996): 639–655. See also Paula Caligiuri, "The Big Five Personality

Characteristics as Predictors of Expatriate's Desire to Terminate the Assignment and Supervisor Rated Performance," *Personnel Psychology* 53 (2000): 67–68.

16. Mitchell Rothstein and Richard Goffin, "The Use of Personality Measures in Personnel Selection: What Does Current Research Support?" *Human Resource Management Review* 16 (2006): 155–180.

17. Kathryn Tyler, "Put Applicants' Skills to the Test," *HR Magazine* (January 2000): 75–79.

18. Gretchen Spreitzner, Morgan McCall Jr., and John Mahoney, "Early Identification of International Executive Potential," *Journal of Applied Psychology* 82, no. 1 (February 1997): 6–29.

19. Neal Schmitt et al., "Computer Based Testing Applied to Selection of Secretarial Candidates," *Personnel Psychology* 46 (1991): 149–165.

20. Randall Overton et al., "The Pen-Based Computer as an Alternative Platform for Test Administration," *Personnel Psychology* 49 (1996): 455–464.

21. Brian O'Leary et al., "Selecting the Best and Brightest," *Human Resource Management* 41, no. 3 (Fall 2002): 25–34.

22. Gilbert Nicholson, "Automated Assessments," 102–107.

23. Annette Spychalski, Miguel Quinones, Barbara Gaugler, and Katja Pohley, "A Survey of Assessment Center Practices in Organizations in the United States," *Personnel Management* 50, no. 10 (Spring 1997): 71–90. See also Winfred Arthur Jr. et al., "A Meta Analysis of the Criterion Related Validity of Assessment Center Data Dimensions," *Personnel Psychology* 56 (2003): 124–154.

24. Kobi Dayan et al., "Entry-Level Police Candidate Assessment Center: An Efficient Tool or a Hammer to Kill a Fly?" *Personnel Psychology* 55 (2002): 827–848.

25. Gilbert Nicholson, "Automated Assessments," 102–107.

26. Robert Plyhart et al., "Web–Based and Paper-and-Pencil Testing of Applicants in a Proctored Setting: Are Personality, Biodata and Situational Judgment Tests Comparable?" *Personnel Psychology* 56, (2003): 733–752.

27. Denise Potosky and Philip Bob Bobko, "Selection Testing Via the Internet: Practical Considerations and Exploratory Empirical Findings," *Personnel Psychology* 57 (2004): 1025.

28. Michael McDaniel et al., "The Validity of Employment Interviews: A Comprehensive Review and Meta-Analysis," *Journal of Applied Psychology* 79, no. 4 (1994): 599. See also Richard Posthuma et al., "Beyond Employment Interview Validity: A Comprehensive Narrative Review of Recent Research and Trends over Time," *Personnel Psychology* 55 (2002): 1–81.

29. Ibid., 601. See also Allen Huffcutt et al., "Comparison of Situational and Behavior Description Interview Questions for Higher Level Positions," *Personnel Psychology* 54 (Autumn 2001): 619–644; Stephen Maurer, "A Practitioner Based Analysis of Interviewer Job Expertise and Scale Format as Contextual Factors in Situational Interviews," *Personnel Psychology* 55 (2002): 307–327.

30. Bill Stoneman, "Matching Personalities with Jobs Made Easier with Behavioral Interviews," *American Banker* 165, no. 229 (November 30, 2000): 8a.

31. "Phone Interviews Might Be the Most Telling, Study Finds," *BNA Bulletin to Management* (September 1998): 273.

32. Susan Strauss et al., "The Effects of Videoconference, Telephone, and Face-to-Face Media on Interviewer and Applicant Judgments in Employment Interviews," *Journal of Management* 27, no. 3 (2001): 363–381. If the employer records a video **interview** with the intention of sharing it with hiring managers who don't participate in the interview, it's advisable to first obtain the candidates written permission. Matt Bolch, "Lights, Camera . . . Interview!," *HR Magazine* (March 2007): 99–102.

33. See, for example, M. M. Harris, "Reconsidering the Employment Interview: A Review of Recent Literature and Suggestions for Future Research," *Personnel Psychology* 42 (1989): 691–726; Richard Posthuma et al., "Beyond Employment Interview Validity: A Comprehensive Narrative Review of Recent Research and Trends over Time," *Personnel Psychology* 55, no. 1 (Spring 2002): 1–81.

34. Timothy Judge et al., "The Employment Interview: A Review of Recent Research and Recommendations for Future Research," *Human Resource Management* 10, no. 4 (2000): 392. There is disagreement regarding the relative superiority of individual versus panel interviews. See, for example, Marlene Dixon et al., "The Panel Interview: A Review of Empirical Research and Guidelines for Practice," *Public Personnel Management* (Fall 2002): 397–328.

35. Frank Schmidt and Ryan Zimmerman, "A Counterintuitive Hypothesis about Employment Interview Validity and Some Supporting Evidence," *Journal of Applied Psychology* 89, no. 3 (2004): 553–561.

36. The validity discussion and these findings are based on McDaniel et al., "Validity of Employment Interviews," 607–610. See also Robert Dipboye et al., "The Validity of Unstructured Panel Interviews," *Journal of Business & Strategy* 16, no. 1 (Fall 2001): 35–49, and Marlene Dixon et al., "The Panel Interview: A Review of Empirical Research and Guidance," *Public Personnel Management* 3, no. 3 (Fall 2002): 397–428. See also Todd Maurer and Jerry Solamon, "The Science and Practice of a Structured Employment Interview Coaching Program," *Personnel Psychology* 59 (2006): 433–456.

37. Ibid., 608.

38. Anita Chaudhuri, "Beat the Clock: Applying for a Job? A New Study Shows that Interviewers Will Make up Their Minds about You Within a Minute," *The Guardian* (June 14, 2000): 2–6.

39. Don Langdale and Joseph Weitz, "Estimating the Influence of Job Information on Interviewer Agreement," *Journal of Applied Psychology* 57 (1973): 23–27.

40. R. E. Carlson, "Selection Interview Decisions: The Effects of Interviewer Experience, Relative Quota Situation, and Applicant Sample on Interview Decisions," *Personnel Psychology* 20 (1967): 259–280.

41. R. E. Carlson, "Effects of Applicant Sample on Ratings of Valid Information in an Employment Setting," *Journal of Applied Psychology* 54 (1970): 217–222.

42. See, for example, Scott Fleischmann, "The Messages of Body Language in Job Interviews," *Employee Relations* 18, no. 2 (Summer 1991): 161–176. See also James Westpall and Ithai Stern, "Flattery Will Get You Everywhere (Especially if You're a Male Caucasian): How Ingratiation, Board Room Behavior, and a Demographic Minority Status Affect Additional Board Appointments at U.S. Companies," *Academy of Management Journal* 50, no. 2 (2007): 267–288.

43. Tim DeGroot and Stephen Motowidlo, "Why Visual and Vocal Interview Cues Can Affect Interviewer's Judgments and Predicted Job Performance," *Journal of Applied Psychology* (December 1999): 968–984.

44. David Caldwell and Jerry Burger, "Personality Characteristics of Job Applicants and Success in Screening Interviews," *Personnel Psychology* 51 (1998): 119–136.

45. Amy Kristof-Brown et al., "Applicant Impression Management: Dispositional Influences and Consequences for Recruiter Perceptions of Fit and Similarity," *Journal of Management* 28, no. 1 (2002): 27–46. See also Linda McFarland et al., "Impression Management Use and Effectiveness Across Assessment Methods," *Journal of Management* 29, no. 5 (2003): 641–661.

46. See, for example, Cynthia Marlowe, Sondra Schneider, and Carnot Nelson, "Gender and Attractiveness Biases in Hiring Decisions: Are More Experienced Managers Less Biased?" *Journal of Applied Psychology* 81, no. 1 (1996): 11–21; see also Shari Caudron, "Why Job Applicants Hate HR," *Workforce* (June 2002): 36.

47. Marlowe et al., "Gender and Attractiveness Biases in Hiring Decisions," 11.

48. Ibid., 18.

49. Emily Duehr and Joyce Bono, "Men, Women, and Managers: Are Stereotypes Finally Changing?" *Personnel Psychology* 59 (2006): 837.

50. Amelia J. Prewett-Livingston et al., "Effects of Race on Interview Ratings in a Situational Panel Interview," *Journal of Applied Psychology* 81, no. 2 (1996): 178–186; see also Richard White Jr., "Ask Me No Questions, Tell Me No Lies: Examining the Uses and Misuses of the Polygraph," *Public Personnel Management* 30, no. 4 (Winter 2001): 483–493.

51. Chad Higgins and Timothy Judge, "The Effect of Applicant Influence Tactics on Recruiter Perceptions of Fit and Hiring Recommendations: A Field Study," *Journal of Applied Psychology* 89, no. 4 (2004): 622–632.

52. Andrea Rodriguez and Fran Prezant, "Better Interviews for People with Disabilities," *Workforce,* accessed from workforce.com. on November 14, 2003.

53. "The Tables Have Turned," *American Management Association International* (September 1998): 6.

54. Williamson et al., "Employment Interview on Trial," 901; Michael Campion, David Palmer, and James Campion, "A Review of Structure in the Selection Interview," *Personnel Psychology* 50 (1997): 655–702.

55. Unless otherwise specified, the following are based on Williamson et al., "Employment Interview on Trial," 901–902.

56. Todd Maurer and Jerry Solamon, "The Science and Practice of a Structured Employment Interview Coaching Program," *Personnel Psychology* 59 (2006): 433–456.

57. Carlson, "Selection Interview Decisions," 259–280.

58. Catherine Middendorf and Therese Macan, "Note Taking in the Employment Interview: Effects on Recall and Judgment," *Journal of Applied Psychology* 87, no. 2 (2002): 293–303.

59. "Looking to Hire the Very Best? Ask the Right Questions. Lots of Them," *Fortune* (June 21, 1999): 192–194.

60. Panel Kaul, "Interviewing Is Your Business," *Association Management* (November 1992): 29. See also Nancy Woodward, "Asking for Salary Histories," *HR Magazine* (February 2000): 109–112. Gathering information about specific interview dimensions such as social ability, responsibility, and independence (as is often done with structured interviews) can improve interview accuracy, at least for more complicated jobs. See also Andrea Poe, "Graduate Work: Behavioral Interviewing Can Tell You if an Applicant Just out of College Has Traits Needed for the Job," *HR Magazine* 48, no. 10 (October 2003): 95–96.

61. "Are Your Background Checks Balanced? Experts Identify Concerns Over Verifications," *BNA Bulletin to Management* (May 13, 2004): 153.

62. Based on Samuel Greengard, "Have Gangs Invaded Your Workplace?" *Personnel Journal* (February 1996): 47–57; Carroll Lachnit, "Protecting People and Profits with Background Checks," *Workforce* (February 2002): 52.

63. Adler, "Verifying a Job Candidate's Background," *Review of Business* 15, no. 2 (Winter 1993): 6.

64. Lachnit, "Protecting People and Profits with Background Checks," 52. See also Robert Howie and Lawrence Shapero, "Preemployment Criminal Background Checks: Why Employers Should Look Before They Leap," *Employee Relations Law Journal* (Summer 2002): 63–77.

65. Ibid., 50ff.

66. "Top Employee Background Checking and Screening Providers," *Workforce Management* (November 7, 2005) p. 14.

67. Alan Finder, "When a Risqué Online Persona Undermines a Chance for a Job," *New York Times* (June 11, 2006): 1.

68. "Vetting Via Internet Is Free, Generally Legal, but Not Necessarily Smart Hiring Strategy," *BNA Bulletin to Management* (February 20, 2007): 57–58.

69. For example, see Lawrence Dube Jr., "Employment References and the Law," *Personnel Journal* 65, no. 2 (February 1986): 87–91. See also Mickey Veich, "Uncover the Resume Ruse," *Security Management* (October 1994): 75–76; Anjali Athavaley, "Job References You Can't Control," *Wall Street Journal* (September 27, 2007): B1.

70. "Undercover Callers Tipoff Job Seekers to Former Employers' Negative References," *BNA Bulletin to Management* (May 27, 1999): 161. See also Diane Cadrain "Job Detectives Dig Deep for Defamation," *HR Magazine* 49, no. 10 (October 2004): 34 FF.

71. Kris Maher, "Reference Checking Firms Flourish, but Complaints about Some Arise," *Wall Street Journal* (March 5, 2002): B8.

72. Lachnit, "Protecting People and Profits," 54; Shari Caudron, "Who Are You Really Hiring?" *Workforce* (November 2002): 31.

73. Lachnit, "Protecting People," 52.

74. John Bernardin and Donna Cooke, "Validity of an Honesty Test in Predicting Theft Among Convenience Store Employees,"

Academy of Management Journal 36, no. 5 (1993): 1097–1108, and Commerce Clearing House, Ideas and Trends, December 29, 1998, pp. 222–223. Note that some suggest that by possibly signaling mental illness, integrity tests may conflict with the Americans with Disabilities Act, but one review concludes that such tests pose little legal risk to employers. Christopher Berry et al., "A Review of Recent Developments in Integrity Test Research," *Personnel Psychology* 60 (2007): 271–301.

75. Anthony Edwards, "An Experiment to Test the Discrimination Ability of Graphologists," *Personality and Individual Differences B,* no. 1 (January 1992): 69–74; George Langer, "Graphology in Personality Assessment: A Reliability and Validity Study," *Dissertation Abstracts International: Section B: The Sciences and Engineering* 54, no. 7-B (1994): 38–56.

76. Mick Haus, "Pre-Employment Physicals and the ADA," *Safety and Health* (February 1992): 64–65.

77. MacDonald et al., "The Limitations of Drug Screening in the Workplace," *International Labor Review* 132, no. 1 (1993): 98. See also Diane Cadrain, "Are Your Employees' Drug Tests Accurate?," *HR Magazine* (January 2003): 40–45.

78. MacDonald, op cit.

79. MacDonald, op cit.

80. Diane Cadrain, "Are Your Employees' Drug Tests Accurate?" *HR Magazine* (January 2003): 40–45.

81. MacDonald et al., "The Limitations of Drug Screening in the Workplace," 105–106.

82. Lewis Maltby, "Drug Testing: A Bad Investment," *Business Ethics* 15, no. 2 (March 2001): 7.

83. Frank Lockwood et al., "Drug Testing Programs and Their Impact on Workplace Accidents: A Time Series Analysis," *Journal of Individual Employment Rights* 8, no. 4 (2000): 295–306.

84. O'Neill, "Legal Issues Presented by Hair Follicle Testing," 411.

85. Richard Lisko, "A Manager's Guide to Drug Testing," *Security Management* 38, no. 8 (August 1994): 92.

86. *Exxon Corp.* v. *Esso Workers Union, Inc.,* CA1#96–2241, July 8, 1997; discussed in *BNA Bulletin to Management* (August 7, 1997): 249.

87. Coleman Peterson, "Employee Retention: The Secrets behind Wal-Mart's Successful Hiring Policies," *Human Resource Management* 44, no. 1, (Spring 2005): 85–88.

88. Murray Barrick and Ryan Zimmerman, "Reducing Voluntary, Avoidable Turnover through Selection," *Journal of Applied Psychology* 90, no. 1 (2005): 159–166.

89. Russell Gerbman, "License to Work," *HR Magazine* (June 2000): 151–160.

90. Diane Caudrain, "Mystery Shoppers Can Improve Recruitment," *HR Magazine* (November 2006): 26.

CHAPTER

5 | TRAINING AND DEVELOPING EMPLOYEES

- Orienting Employees
- The Training Process
- Training Techniques
- Managerial Development and Training
- Evaluating the Training and Development Effort

When you finish studying this chapter, you should be able to:

■ Describe *the basic training process.*

■ Discuss *at least two techniques used for assessing training needs.*

■ Explain *the pros and cons of at least five training techniques.*

■ Explain *what management development is and why it is important.*

■ Describe *the main development techniques.*

INTRODUCTION

With 32,000 restaurants worldwide and a strategy based on consistency, McDonald's must effectively train its employees if the company is to prosper. As McDonald's president Ralph Alvarez said, "our success is because of the training and replication systems we put in place that allowed us to change our menu and deliver operations at a higher level than before." The question is, what types of training systems to put in place?[1]

ORIENTING EMPLOYEES

After screening and selecting the new employees, management turns to the task of orienting and training them on their new jobs. **Employee orientation** provides new employees with the basic background information they need to perform their jobs satisfactorily, such as information about company rules. Orientation is one component of the employer's new-employee socialization process. Socialization is the ongoing process of instilling in all employees the attitudes, standards, values, and patterns of behavior that the organization and its departments expect.[2] For example, the Mayo Clinic recently revised its orientation program to include the clinic's history, values, and culture. It's new "heritage and culture" orientation session covers matters such as core principles, history, work atmosphere, teamwork, personal responsibility, innovation, integrity, diversity, customer service, and mutual respect.[3]

Types of Programs

Orientation programs range from brief, informal introductions to lengthy, formal programs of half a day or possibly more. In either, new employees usually receive printed or Web-based handbooks that cover matters such as working hours, performance reviews, getting on the payroll, and vacations, as well as a tour of the facilities. Other information might cover employee benefits, personnel policies, the employee's daily routine, company organization and operations, and safety measures and regulations.[4] (Because there is a possibility that courts will find that your employee handbook's contents represent a contract with the employee, disclaimers should be included. These should make it clear that statements of company policies, benefits, and regulations do not constitute the terms and conditions of an employment contract, either expressed or implied.)

Purposes

A successful orientation should accomplish four things. The new employee should feel welcome. He or she should understand the organization in a broad sense (its past, present, culture, and vision of the future), as well as key facts such as policies and procedures. The employee should be clear about what the firm expects in terms of work and behavior. And, hopefully, the person should begin the process of becoming socialized into the firm's preferred ways of acting and doing things.[5]

Technology

Technology can help improve the orientation process. For example, some firms provide incoming managers with preloaded personal digital assistants. These contain information the new managers need to better adjust to their new jobs, such as key contact information, main tasks to undertake, and even digital images of employees the new manager needs to know.[6] Some firms provide all new employees with disks containing discussions of corporate culture, videos of corporate facilities, and welcoming addresses from top managers. Others create orientation Web sites. Particularly for new managers, these include information such as the company's approaches to hiring, ethics, procurement policies, and performance management.

The HR specialist usually performs the first part of the orientation and explains such matters as working hours and vacation. The employee then meets his or her new supervisor. The latter continues the orientation by explaining the exact nature of the job, introducing the person to his or her new colleagues, and familiarizing the new employee with the workplace and the job.

THE TRAINING PROCESS

Training refers to the methods used to give new or present employees the skills they need to perform their jobs.

Training's focus is broader today than it was several years ago. Training used to focus on teaching technical skills, such as training assemblers to solder wires or training teachers to write lesson plans. Today, it might also mean remedial-education training, because quality improvement programs require employees to produce charts and graphs and analyze data. Similarly, employees today may require team-building, decision-making, and communication skills training. And, as firms become more technologically advanced, employees require training in technological and computer skills, such as computer-aided design and manufacturing.[7] Training experts today increasingly use the phrase "workplace learning and performance" in lieu of training, to underscore training's ultimate dual aims of employee learning and organizational performance.[8]

Companies spent about $826 per employee for training in one recent year and offered each about 28 hours of training.[9] Training has a fairly impressive record of influencing organizational effectiveness, scoring higher than appraisal and feedback and just below goal setting in its effect on productivity.[10]

Training plays an increasingly vital role in implementing the employer's strategic plans. As one trainer puts it: "We don't just concentrate on the traditional training objectives anymore. . . . We sit down with management and help them identify strategic goals and objectives and the skills and knowledge needed to achieve them. Then we work together to identify whether our staff has the skills and knowledge, and when they don't, that's when we discuss training needs."[11] Similarly, training today plays a key role in employers' performance management process. Basically, performance management means taking a systematic approach to training, appraising, and rewarding employees so that their efforts make sense in terms of the company's needs and goals.[12] Taking a performance management approach to training means that the training effort should explicitly make sense in terms of what the company wants each employee to contribute to achieving the company's goals. In one survey, IBM and the American Society for Training and Development (ASTD) found that "establishing a linkage between learning and organizational performance" was the number one pressing issue facing training professionals.[13]

Training Program Example

For example, after many years of public subsidies, Channel 4 in the United Kingdom had to start competing more on its own. With the UK's new broadcasting act, Channel 4 had to start selling and transmitting its own air time. And that meant quickly instituting training programs to support an expanded sales force and new high-tech control system.

Management accomplished this in part by introducing a series of interactive, intranet-based e-learning training programs. Says the managing director of the company that created the programs for Channel 4, "By working closely with the HR, business affairs and ultimate rights departments at Channel 4, we have produced a series of learning programs that are high on visual impact and fit in with the culture of the channel." Employees access the training modules through Channel 4's intranet. The training programs include animated meetings that demonstrate the different scenarios employees might face on the job.[14]

The Training and Development Process

We can visualize training and development programs as consisting of five steps, as summarized in Figure 5.1: Needs Analysis, Instructional Design, Validation, Implementation, and Evaluation.

FIGURE 5.1   The Five Steps in the Training and Development Process

1. **NEEDS ANALYSIS**
   - Identify specific skills needed to improve performance and productivity.
   - Ensure that the program will be suited to trainees' specific levels of education, experience, and skills.
   - Set training objectives.

2. **INSTRUCTIONAL DESIGN**
   - Compile training objectives, methods, media, description and sequence of content, examples, exercises, and activities. Organize them into a curriculum.
   - Make sure all materials, such as leaders' guides and trainees' workbooks, complement each other, are written clearly, and blend into a unified training program that makes sense in terms of the stated learning objectives.
   - The process typically results in a training manual. This might contain the person's job description, an outline of the training program, and a written description of what the trainee is expected to learn, as well as (possibly) several short self-tests.

3. **VALIDATION**
   - Introduce and validate the training before a representative audience. Base final revisions on pilot results to ensure program effectiveness.

4. **IMPLEMENTATION**
   - When applicable, use a train-the-trainer workshop that focuses on presentation knowledge and skills in addition to training content. Then implement training program.

5. **EVALUATION**
   - Evaluate trainees' reactions, learning, behavior, and/or results.

Sources: Adapted from *H RFocus*, April 1993. Copyright © 1993 American Management Association International. See also, P. Nick Blanchard and James Thacker, *Effective Training* (Upper Saddle River, NJ: Pearson, 2007), pp. 6–9.

Training Needs Analysis

The first step in training is to determine what training, if any, is required. Some call this the "skills gapping" process. Employers determine the skills each job requires, and the skills of the job's current or prospective employees. Training is then designed to eliminate the skills gap.[15] Assessing new employees' training needs usually involves *task analysis*—breaking the jobs into subtasks and teaching each to the new employee. Needs analysis for current employees is more complex: Is training the solution, or is performance down because the person is not motivated? Here *performance analysis* is required. We'll look at each.

Task analysis is used for determining new employees' training needs. With inexperienced personnel, your aim is to provide the new employees with the skills and knowledge required for effective performance. How do you determine what skills and knowledge are required? *Task analysis* is a detailed study of the job to determine what specific skills—such as soldering (in the case of an assembly worker) or interviewing (in the case of a supervisor)—are required. The job description and job specification will provide useful information. They list the specific duties and skills required on the job and become the basic reference point in determining the training required for performing the job. Figure 5.2 summarizes methods for uncovering a job's training requirements.

For current employees whose performance is deficient, task analysis is usually not enough. **Performance analysis** means verifying that there is a performance deficiency and determining whether that deficiency should be rectified through training or through some other means (such as transferring the employee or changing the compensation plan).

Employers identify employees' performance deficiencies and training needs in several ways. A typical list would include:

- supervisor, peer, self-, and 360-degree performance reviews
- job-related performance data (including productivity, absenteeism and tardiness, accidents, short-term sickness, grievances, waste, late deliveries, product quality, downtime, repairs, equipment utilization, and customer complaints)
- observation by supervisors or other specialists
- interviews with the employee or his or her supervisor
- tests of things like job knowledge, skills, and attendance
- attitude surveys
- individual employee daily diaries
- devised situations such as role plays and case studies and other types of tests
- assessment centers
- management-by-objective type evaluations.[16]

The first step is usually to appraise the employee's performance. Examples of specific performance deficiencies follow:

"I expect each salesperson to make 10 new contracts per week, but John averages only six."
"Other plants our size average no more than two serious accidents per month; we're averaging five."

| FIGURE 5.2 | Tools for Uncovering a Job's Training Needs |

Sources for Obtaining Job Data	*Training Need Information*
1. Job Descriptions	Outlines the job's typical duties and responsibilities but is not meant to be all-inclusive. Helps define performance discrepancies.
2. Job Specifications or Task Analysis	List specified tasks required for each job. More specific than job descriptions. Specifications may extend to judgments of knowledge and skills required of job incumbents.
3. Performance Standards	Objectives of the tasks of job, and standards by which they are judged. This may include baseline data as well.
4. Perform the Job	Most effective way of identifying a job's specific tasks, but has serious limitations in higher-level jobs because performance requirements typically have longer gaps between performance and resulting outcomes.
5. Observe Job-Work Sampling	Same as 4 above.
6. Review Literature Concerning the Job a. Research in other industries b. Professional journals c. Documents d. Government sources e. Ph.D. theses	Possibly useful, but far removed from either unique aspects of the job within any *specific* organization or specific performance requirements.
7. Ask Questions About the Job a. Of the job holder b. Of the supervisor c. Of higher management	Inputs from several viewpoints can often reveal training needs or training desires.
8. Training Committees or Conferences	Same as 7 above.
9. Analysis of Operating Problems a. Downtime reports b. Waste c. Repairs d. Late deliveries e. Quality control	Indications of task interference, environmental factors, etc.

Source: Adapted from P. Nick Blanchard and James Thacker, *Effective Training Systems Strategies and Practices* (Upper Saddle River, NJ: Prentice Hall, 1999), pp. 138–139.

Distinguishing between "can't do" and "won't do" problems is the heart of performance analysis. First, determine whether it's a "can't do" problem and, if so, its specific causes. For example, perhaps the employees don't know what to do or what your standards are, or there are obstacles in the system such as lack of tools or supplies. Perhaps job aids are needed, such as color-coded wires that show assemblers what wire goes where; or poor screening results in hiring people who haven't the skills to do the job; or training is inadequate. On the other hand, it might be a "won't do" problem here employees *could* do a good job if they wanted to. If this is the case, the manager may have to change the reward system, perhaps by implementing an incentive plan.

Competency Models

Many companies, including Sharp Electronics, develop generic competency models for jobs or closely related groups of jobs. In this context, *competency* means knowledge, skills, and behaviors that enable employees to effectively perform their jobs. Sharp's process for identifying a job's competencies begins with interviews with senior executives, to crystallize the firm's strategy and objectives. Human resource specialists then interview the job's top performers, to identify the competencies (such as "demonstrates creativity," and "focuses on the customer") that together will comprise the job's competency model. Subsequent training and development then aims, in part, to develop these competencies.[17]

Setting Training Objectives

After training needs have been uncovered, concrete, measurable training objectives should be set. Training, development, or (more generally) instructional objectives are "a description of a performance you want learners to be able to exhibit before you consider them competent."[18] For example:

> Given a tool kit and a service manual, the technical representative will be able to adjust the registration (black line along paper edges) on this Xerox duplicator within 20 minutes according to the specifications stated in the manual.[19]

Objectives specify what the trainee should be able to accomplish after successfully completing the training program. They thus provide a focus for the efforts of both the trainee and the trainer and a benchmark for evaluating the success of the training program.

A helpful tactic is also to create, for the trainee, a perceived motivational training need, such as by illustrating with a filmed example what can go wrong if the training isn't taken seriously.[20] Training is futile if the trainee lacks the ability or motivation to benefit from it.[21] The employer can take several steps to increase the trainee's motivation to learn. Providing opportunities for active practice, and letting the trainee make errors and explore alternate solutions improve motivation and learning.[22] Feedback—including periodic performance assessments and more frequent verbal critiques—is also important.[23] The employer should also make the material meaningful. For example, provide an overview of the material, and ensure that the program uses familiar examples and concepts to illustrate key points.[24]

TRAINING TECHNIQUES

After you have determined the employees' training needs, created a perceived need, and set training objectives, you can design, validate, and implement a training program. Most employers can choose training materials from packaged on-and-offline programs already available from vendors like the American Management Association.[25] We describe popular training techniques in this section.

On-the-Job Training

There are several types of **on-the-job training (OJT).** The most familiar is the coaching or understudy method. Here an experienced worker or the trainee's supervisor trains the employee, on the job. At lower levels, trainees may acquire skills for, say, running a machine by observing the supervisor. But this technique is also widely used at top-management levels. Some firms use the position of "assistant to" to train and develop the company's future top managers, for instance. Job rotation, in which an employee (usually a management trainee) moves from job to job at planned intervals, is another on-the-job technique. Special assignments similarly give lower level executives first-hand experience in working on actual problems.

The Men's Wearhouse, with 455 stores nationwide, makes extensive use of on-the-job training. It has few full-time trainers. Instead, the Men's Wearhouse has a formal process of "cascading" responsibility for training: Every manager is formally accountable for the development of his or her direct subordinates.[26]

Informal Learning

Employers should not underestimate the importance or value of informal training. Surveys from the American Society for Training and Development estimate that as much as 80% of what employees learn on the job they learn not through formal training programs but through informal means, including performing their jobs in collaboration with their colleagues.[27]

Although managers don't arrange informal learning, there's a lot they can do to ensure that it occurs. Most of the steps are simple. For example, Siemens Power Transmission and Distribution in Raleigh, North Carolina, places tools in cafeteria areas to take advantage of the work-related discussions taking place. Even simple things like installing white boards and keeping them stocked with markers can facilitate informal learning.

Apprenticeship Training

More employers are going "back to the future" by implementing apprenticeship training programs, an approach to training that began in the Middle Ages. Apprenticeship training is a structured process by which individuals become skilled workers through a combination of classroom instruction and on-the-job training, usually under the tutelage of a master craftsman. It is widely used to train individuals for many occupations, including electrician and plumber.[28] When steelmaker Dofasco discovered that many of their employees would be retiring during the next 5 to 10 years, the company decided to revive its apprenticeship training program. Applicants are pre-screened; new recruits then spend about 32 months in an internal training program that emphasizes apprenticeship training, learning various jobs under the tutelage of experienced craftspersons.[29] The Siemens Stromberg-Carlson plant in Florida has apprenticeships for adults and high school students training for jobs as electronics technicians. Here:

> Adults work on the factory floor, receive classroom instruction at Seminole Community College, and also study at the plant's hands-on apprenticeship lab. Graduates receive Associates Degrees in telecommunications and electronics engineering. High school students spend two afternoons per week at the apprenticeship lab.[30]

Vestibule Training

Vestibule training is a technique in which trainees learn on the actual or simulated equipment they will use on the job but receive their training off the job. Therefore, it aims to obtain the advantages of on-the-job training without actually putting the trainee on the job. Such training is a necessity when it is too costly or dangerous to train employees on the job. Putting new assembly-line workers right to work could slow production, for instance, and when safety is a concern—as with pilots—simulated training may be the only practical alternative.

Vestibule training may just take place in a separate room with the equipment the trainees will actually be using on the job (thus, "vestibule" training.) However, it often involves the use of equipment simulators. In pilot training, for instance, the main advantages of flight simulators are:

- *Safety*. Crews can practice flight maneuvers in a controlled environment.
- *Learning efficiency*. The absence of the conflicting air traffic chatter allows for total concentration on how to fly the craft.
- *Money*. The cost of using a flight simulator is only a fraction of the cost of flying an aircraft.

Audiovisual and Traditional Distance Learning Techniques

Audiovisual techniques such as films, closed-circuit television, audiotapes, and videotapes or disks can be very effective and are widely used. The Ford Motor Company uses videos in its dealer training sessions to simulate sample reactions to various customer complaints, for example. Firms of course also use various distance learning methods for training. Distance learning methods include the traditional correspondence courses, as well as teletraining, videoconferencing, and Internet-based classes.[31] For example, Macy's established the Macy's Satellite Network teletraining (television based training program), in part to provide training to the firm's employees around the country.

Videoconference Distance Learning

Videoconferencing is a popular way to train employees who are geographically separated from each other—or from the trainer. It is "a means of joining two or more distant groups using a combination of audio and visual equipment."[32] Videoconferencing allows people in one location to communicate live with people in another city or country or with groups in several other cities.[33] The communication often involves sending compressed audio and video signals over cable broadband lines, the Internet, or via satellite. Keypad systems allow for audience–trainer interactivity.[34] Management Recruiters International (MRI) uses the firm's PC-based ConferView system to train hundreds of employees—each in their individual offices—simultaneously.[35]

Computer-Based Training

In one Stanford University hospital training room, medical students wearing virtual reality headsets control computer screen avatars. The avatars are computerized simulations dressed in medical scrubs. Each avatar plays a different role, such as nurse and emergency room technician. The residents and medical students use their keypads to control their avatar's every move in the virtual reality trauma center. One avatar props up the patient; another rushes to clear his airway. On the screen, the patient's vital signs react appropriately to the medical students' and residents' decisions. Later, instructors replay the scenario, showing trainees what they did right and wrong.[36] Increasingly today, training is computer-based.

In **computer-based training** (CBT), the trainee uses a computer-based system to interactively increase his or her knowledge or skills. Today this often means (as at Stanford) presenting trainees with computerized simulations, and using multimedia including videodiscs to help the trainee learn how to do the job.[37] But often, the computer-based training is less complex. For example, in one training program, recruitment trainees start with a computer screen that shows the "applicant's" employment application, as well as information about the job. The trainee then begins a simulated interview by typing in questions, which are answered by a videotaped model acting as the applicant and whose responses to a multitude of questions have been programmed into the computer. At the end of the session, the computer tells the trainee where he or she went wrong (perhaps in asking discriminatory questions, for instance) and offers further instructional material to correct these mistakes.

Strategy and HR DVD-Based Training

McDonald's developed about 11 different computer-disk–based courses for its franchises' employees. The programs consist of graphics-supported lessons and require trainees to make choices to show their understanding.[38] Specialist multimedia software houses like Graphic Media of Portland, Oregon, produce much of the content for CBT programs like these. They produce both custom titles and generic programs like a $999 package for teaching workplace safety.

Simulated Learning

"Simulated learning" means different things to different people. A recent survey asked training professionals what experiences qualified as simulated learning experiences. The percentages of trainers choosing each experience were:

- Virtual reality-type games 19%
- Step-by-step animated guide 8%
- Scenarios with questions and decision trees overlaying animation 19%
- Online role-play with photos and videos 14%
- Software training including screenshots with interactive requests for responses 35%
- Other 6%[39]

As at Stanford, employers increasingly rely on computerized simulations to inject more realism into their training programs. For example, Orlando-based Environmental Tectonics Corporation created an Advanced Disaster Management simulation for emergency medical response trainees. One of the simulated scenarios involves a passenger plane crashing into an airport runway. So realistic that it's "unsettling," trainees including firefighters and airport officials respond to the simulated crash's sights and sounds via pointing devices and radios.[40]

Training via the Internet, and Learning Portals

Internet-based learning is rapidly replacing many other types of training. Many firms simply let their employees take online courses offered by online course providers such as Click2Learn.com. Others use their proprietary internal *intranets* to facilitate computer-based training. For example, Silicon Graphics transferred many of its training materials onto CD-ROMs. However, they soon replaced the CD-ROM distribution method with distribution of training materials via its intranet. "Now employees can access the programs whenever they want. Distribution costs are zero, and if the company wants to make a change to the program, it can do so at a central location."[41]

Learning Portals

Many firms use their intranets to host their business portals. Also called Enterprise Information Portals (EIPs), categories of a firm's employees—secretaries, engineers, salespeople, and so on—are able to access all the corporate applications they need, and "get the tools you need to analyze data inside and outside your company, and see the customized content you need, like industry news and competitive data."[42]

Companies increasingly convey their employee training through such portals. They often contract with so-called applications service providers such as SkillSoft (www.skillsoft.com) and, for health and safety training, puresafety (www.puresafety. com) to deliver online training courses to the firms' employees, which the employees access via their employer's portal.[43]

Learning portals put more information into employees' hands, when they want it. Instead of limiting training opportunities to teacher-led conventional classes or to periodic training sessions, training becomes available "24–7." Employees can learn at their own pace, when they want to.[44] Note, however, that while e-learning is beneficial, one study, by Michigan State University researchers, found that onsite employee education programs produced better results than online training, in terms of subsequent test results.[45]

Web based training is popular, but, in practice, it's usually not a choice for one form of training or another. The trend is toward blended learning solutions, wherein the trainee uses several delivery methods (for instance, manuals, in-class lectures, self-guided e-learning programs, and Web-based seminars or "webinars") to learn the material.[46]

Learning Management Systems

Learning management systems (LMS) play an important role in helping employers identify training needs, and to schedule, deliver, and assess and manage the online training itself. For example, General Motors uses a new LMS to help its dealers in Africa and the Middle East deliver high-quality training programs. The Internet-based LMS includes a course catalog, two-step enrollment (supervisor approved self-enrollment), facilities and training schedule management, and assessment systems (including pre-and post-course tests). Dealers, supervisors, and employees can review the list of courses on the LMS. They then choose courses based upon their needs, for instance in specific areas such as automobile transmissions and sales management. The system then automatically schedules the individual's training.[47]

MP3/iPod-Based Training

Employers are increasingly capitalizing on the widespread popularity of MP3 players, iPods, and similar mobile devices to provide employees with "corporate training and downloads on everything from how to close an important sales deal to optimizing organizational change to learning business Spanish . . . you can be on an airplane, you can be taking a walk or riding your bike" while listening to the training program.[48]

Financial services firm CapitalOne purchased 3,000 iPods for trainees who had enrolled in one of 20 instructor-led courses at its CapitalOne University. The training department then had an Internet audio book provider create an audio learning site within CapitalOne's firewall. Employees used it to download the instructor-requested books and other materials to their iPods.[49]

Instant Messaging

Some employers, including J.P. Morgan, encourage employees to use instant messaging as a quick learning device. Employers also use instant messaging to supplement classroom training, for instance by using IM for online office hours, and for coaching and group chats.

The Virtual Classroom

Conventional Web-based learning tends to be limited to the sorts of online learning with which many college students are already familiar—reading PowerPoint presentations, participating in instant message–type chat rooms, and taking online exams, for instance.

The virtual classroom takes online learning to a new level. A **virtual classroom** uses special collaboration software to enable multiple remote learners, using their PCs or laptops, to participate in live audio and visual discussions, communicate via written text, and learn via content such as PowerPoint slides.

The virtual classroom combines the best of Web-based learning offered by systems like Blackboard and WebCT, with live video and audio. For example, Elluminate Inc. makes one popular virtual classroom system, Elluminate live! It enables learners to communicate with clear, two-way audio, build communities with user profiles and live video, collaborate with chat and shared whiteboards, and learn with shared applications such as PowerPoint slides.[50]

Improving Web-Based Learning

There are some obvious and less obvious ways to improve e-based learning. From a practical point of view, one needs to keep in mind that trainees tend to be slower taking online exams than they are paper-and-pencil ones. This is because the Web page tends to have fewer questions in larger font than do paper quizzes, and because going back and reviewing one's answers tends to take longer online. It's also important to make sure that the trainee can actually make use of the extra control that Web-based learning should provide. For example, a Web-based program may give learners the opportunity to choose the content they'll focus on, and the learning's sequence and pacing.[51] Therefore, make sure to explain to the trainees the control that they have and how they can use it, such as how to change the learning sequence.

Training for Special Purposes

Training today does more than just prepare employees to perform their jobs effectively. Training for special purposes—dealing with diversity, for instance—is required too. A sampling of such special-purpose training programs follows.

Literacy Training Techniques

Functional illiteracy—the inability to handle basic reading, writing, and arithmetic—is a serious problem at work. By one estimate, about 39 million people in the U.S. have a learning disability that makes it challenging for them to read, write, or do arithmetic.[52] Yet literacy is crucial. Today's emphasis on teamwork and quality requires employees to have the ability to adequately read, write, and understand numbers.

Employers take various approaches to teaching literacy and other basic skills. The Life Skills program implemented at the Bellwood plant of Borg-Warner Automotive, Inc. is one example. Based on test scores, managers chose employee participants and placed them in three classes of 15 students each. There were two trainers from a local training company. Each session was to run a maximum of 200 hours. However, employees could leave when they reached a predetermined skill level, so that some were in the program for only 40 hours and others stayed the entire course.[53] Classes were 5 days per week, 2 hours per day, with classes scheduled so that 1 hour was during the employee's personal time and the second was on company time. In this program, employees were paired so that they could help each other (for instance, someone good with decimals was paired with someone who was not). The students then helped each other through a series of timed exercises in math and reading.

Another simple approach is to have supervisors teach basic skills by giving employees writing and speaking exercises. One way to do this is to convert materials used in the employee's job into instructional tools. For example, if an employee needs to use a manual to find out how to change a part, teach that person how to use an index to locate the relevant section. Another approach is to bring in outside professionals (such as teachers from a local high school) to teach, say, remedial reading or writing. Having employees attend adult education or high school evening classes is another option.

Diversity Training

With an increasingly diverse workforce, more firms have implemented diversity training programs. *Diversity training* refers to "techniques for creating better cross-cultural sensitivity among supervisors and nonsupervisors with the aim of creating more harmonious working relationships among a firm's employees." For example, Adams Mark Hotel & Resorts conducted a diversity training seminar for about 11,000 employees. It combined lectures, video, and employee role-playing to emphasize sensitivity to race and religion.[54]

Diversity training is no panacea, and a poorly conceived program can backfire. Potential negative outcomes include "the possibility of post-training participant discomfort, reinforcement of group stereotypes, perceived disenfranchisement or backlash by white males, and even lawsuits based on managers' exposure of stereotypical beliefs blurted out during 'awareness raising' sessions."[55]

There are a variety of training programs aimed at counteracting potential problems associated with a diverse workforce. These include programs for improving interpersonal skills, understanding/valuing cultural differences, improving technical skills, socializing into corporate culture, indoctrinating recent immigrants into the U.S. work ethic, and improving bilingual skills for English-speaking employees.

Training for Teamwork and Empowerment

Most employees must be trained to be good team members. For instance, Toyota devotes many hours to training new employees to listen to each other and to cooperate. Toyota's training process stresses dedication to teamwork. For example, the program uses short exercises to illustrate examples of good and bad teamwork, and to mold new employees' attitudes regarding good teamwork.

Some firms use outdoor training such as Outward Bound programs to build teamwork. Outdoor training usually involves taking a firm's management team out into rugged, mountainous terrain. For example, Howard Atkins, chief financial officer for Wells Fargo & Company, helped organize a retreat for 73 of his firm's financial officers and accountants. While all his participants were already top performers, Atkins' goal was something more: "they are very individualistic in their approach to their work. . . . What I have been trying to to do is get them to see the power of acting more like a team."[56]

The following *Global Issues in HR* box discusses some special training needs abroad.

SUPERVISORY TRAINING ABROAD

Sometimes, supervisory training programs address special issues when implemented abroad. For example, Gap Inc. recently signed an agreement with a World Bank affiliate to provide supervisory training for line managers in Gap's vendors' Cambodian garment factories.[57] Gap was not just aiming to improve these managers' supervisory skills. The firm's broader goal was to improve labor relations of their vendors abroad. Gap's supervisory training program therefore covers matters such as how to handle worker complaints, human resource management, personal productivity, and conflict resolution.

MANAGERIAL DEVELOPMENT AND TRAINING

Management development is any attempt to improve managerial performance by imparting knowledge, changing attitudes, or increasing skills. It thus includes in-house programs such as courses, coaching, and rotational assignments; professional programs such as American Management Association (AMA) seminars; and university programs such as executive MBA programs.

The ultimate aim of such development programs is, of course, to enhance the future performance of the organization itself. For this reason, the overall management development process consists of assessing the company's needs (for instance, to fill future executive openings, or to make the firm more responsive), appraising the managers' performance, and then developing the managers themselves.

Globalization and increased competitiveness mean it's more important today for leader development programs to be organizationally relevant and effective. The program should make sense in terms of the company's strategy and goals. This means involving the top management team in formulating the program's aims, and also specifying concrete competencies and knowledge outcomes, rather than just attitudes. There is also more emphasis on supplementing traditional development methods (such as lectures, case discussion groups, and simulations) with realistic methods like action learning projects where trainees solve actual company problems.[58] Several principles for designing leader development programs (such as "use practical, concrete content") are summarized in Figure 5.3.

Development methods (many equally useful for first-line supervisors, too) are described on the next few pages.

FIGURE 5.3   Management and Leadership Development Guidelines

1. Design the program so that it flows from and makes sense in terms of the company's strategy and goals.
2. Involve the top management team in formulating the program's aims.
3. Make sure to design the program to improve manager's deficiencies and needs that you identify ahead of time.
4. Aim for practicality rather than just theory.
5. Specify concrete competencies and skills outcomes, not just knowledge and attitude changes, and use realistic learning methods like action learning projects where trainees solve real company problems.
6. Aim for short, high-involvement, 3-4 day programs rather than longer immersion programs.

Sources: Adapted from P. Nick Blanchard and James Thacker, *Effective Training* (Upper Saddle River, NJ: Pearson, 2007), pp. 439–467; Jack Zenger, Dave Ulrich, and Norm Smallwood, "The New Leadership Development," *Training & Development* (March 2000): 22–27; W. David Patton and Connie Pratt, "Assessing the Training Needs of High Potential Managers," *Public Personnel Management* 31, no. 4 (Winter 2002): 465–474; and Ann Locke and Arlene Tarantino, "Strategic Leadership Development," *Training & Development* (December 2006): 53–55.

Managerial On-the-Job Training

On-the-job training is not just for nonsupervisory employees. It is also a popular manager development method. Important variants include **job rotation,** the **coaching/understudy method,** and **action learning.** *Job rotation* means moving management trainees from department to department to broaden their understanding of all parts of the business. The trainee—often a recent college graduate—may spend several months in each department; this helps not only broaden his or her experience but also discover the jobs he or she prefers. The person may be just an observer in each department, but more commonly becomes fully involved in its operations. The trainee thus learns the department's business by actually doing it, whether it involves sales, production, finance, or some other function. With the *coaching/understudy* method, the new manager, of course, receives ongoing advice, often from the person he or she is scheduled to replace.

Action Learning

Action learning means letting managers work full time on real projects, analyzing and solving problems, usually in departments other than their own. The trainees meet periodically within a four- or five-person project group to discuss their findings. The groups then present their recommendations to the president and executive staff of the CEO and the head of the division they've been studying.

The Case Study Method

The **case study method** presents a trainee with a written description of an organizational problem. The person analyzes the case, diagnoses the problem, and presents his or her findings and solutions in a discussion with other trainees.[59]

The case study method has several aims. It aims, first, to give trainees realistic experience in identifying and analyzing complex problems in an environment in which their trained discussion leader can subtly guide their progress. Through the class discussion of the case, trainees also learn that there are usually many ways to approach and solve complex organizational problems. And, they learn that their own needs and values often influence the solutions they suggest.

Integrated case scenarios expand the case analysis concept by creating long-term, comprehensive case situations. For example, the FBI Academy created an integrated case scenario. The scripts include themes, background stories, detailed personal histories, and role-play instructions. In the case of the FBI, the scenarios are aimed at developing specific training skills, such as interviewing witnesses and analyzing crime scenes.[60]

Management Games

In computerized **management games,** trainees split into five- or six-person companies, each of which has to compete with the others in a simulated marketplace. Each company can make several decisions. For example, the group may be allowed to decide how much to spend on advertising, how much to produce, how much inventory to maintain, and how many of which product to produce. Usually, the game compresses a 2- or 3-year period into days, weeks, or months. As in the real world, each company usually can't see what decisions the other firms have made, although these decisions do affect their own sales. For example, if a competitor decides to increase its advertising expenditures, that firm may end up increasing its sales at the expense of the others.[61]

Improvisation is a recent variant. For example, Nike Corporation asked Second City Communications, the consulting arm of the comedy improvisational group Second City, to help prepare some Nike engineers for an assignment. The engineers were to spend a month watching kids in playgrounds, so as to design new Nike shoes. Second City trainers put the engineers through an improvisational game called "word ball." In this game, trainees pass a make-believe ball to one another, each time calling out one word. (Thus, the first person might pass the ball and call out "cat," the second catches and then passes on the make-believe ball and calls out "furry," and so on). The aim was to get the Nike engineers "to instantly react without thinking, . . . to be unafraid to look foolish."[62]

Outside Seminars

Many organizations offer management development seminars and conferences. The AMA, for instance, provides thousands of courses in areas such as general management, human resources, sales and marketing, and international management. Courses cover topics such as how to sharpen business writing skills, strategic planning, and assertiveness training for managers. Other organizations offering management development services include AMR International, Inc., the Conference Board, and many universities. SHRM—the Society for Human Resource management—offers numerous courses for HR professionals.

Most of these programs offer continuing education units (CEUs) for course completion. CEUs generally can't be used to obtain degree-granting credit at most colleges or universities, but they provide a record of the fact that the trainee participated in and completed a conference or seminar.

University-Related Programs

Colleges and universities provide several types of management development activities. First, many schools provide continuing education programs in leadership, supervision, and the like. As with the AMA, these range from 1- to 4-day programs to executive development programs lasting 1 to 4 months. Many also offer individual courses in areas such as business, management, and health care administration. Managers can take these as matriculated or nonmatriculated students to fill gaps in their backgrounds. Schools of course also offer degree programs such as the master of business administration (MBA).

Joint Programs

Some companies offer selected employees in-house degree programs in cooperation with colleges and universities. Many also offer a variety of in-house lectures and seminars by university staff. For example, Technicon, a high-tech medical instruments company, had one university offer a program for its key managers.

University-based executive education is becoming more realistic, for instance relying more on active learning, business simulations, and experiential learning.[63] Employers are also becoming more sophisticated in how they select and manage university-related development programs. For example, Home Depot created a "preferred network" of university partners. Home Depot arranges for employees who take courses at an in-network university to get discount course prices.[64]

Examples

Employer–university management development partnerships can be effective. For example, when Hasbro Inc. needed to improve the creativity skills of its top executives, it turned to the Amos Tuck business school at Dartmouth University. It wanted "a custom approach to designing a program that would be built from the ground up to suit Hasbro's specific needs."[65]

Hasbro and Tuck's executive program faculty directors designed a special version of Tuck's 1-week Global Leadership Development Program, with four basic elements. First, when participants first arrive, they receive sealed envelopes containing their "360-degree" performance assessment reports, carefully secured for confidentiality. Second, managers receive both group and individual coaching from special "executive coaches." The aim here is to help Hasbro executives identify "blind spots" that may be hampering their performance and to develop plans to address these issues. Third, they participate in "MBA-type" courses, selected to be relevant for them, based on their and Hasbro's needs. Finally, the executives work in action learning project teams, under the guidance of Hasbro's in-house coaches.

Behavior Modeling

Behavior modeling involves showing trainees the right (or *model*) way of doing something, letting each person practice the right way to do it, and providing feedback regarding each trainee's performance. The basic behavior modeling procedure is as follows:

1. *Modeling.* First, trainees watch films or videotapes or disks that show model persons behaving effectively in a problem situation.
2. *Role-playing.* Next, the trainees are given roles to play in a simulated situation.
3. *Social reinforcement.* The trainer provides praise and constructive feedback based on how the trainee performs in the role-playing situation.
4. *Transfer of training.* Finally, trainees are encouraged to apply their new skills when they are back on their jobs.

Firms don't use behavior modeling just for teaching supervisory-type skills. For example, by one estimate, firms spend more of their training dollars on computer skills training than they do on sales training, supervisory training, or communication training.[66] Behavior modeling has proved particularly effective for teaching computer skills. For instance, "one consistent research finding is that the behavior modeling approach to computer skills training, in which trainees watch a model demonstrate computer skills and then the trainees reenact the model behavior, is more effective than alternative methods such as computer aided instruction."[67]

In-House Development Centers

Many firms have **in-house development centers** or "universities," which usually combine classroom learning (lectures and seminars, for instance) with other techniques such as assessment centers and online learning opportunities to help develop employees and other managers. For example, at General Electric's (GE) Leadership Institute, the courses range from entry-level programs in manufacturing and sales to a business course for English majors. Companies today try to avoid the country club atmospheres of earlier corporate universities. For example, at Boeing's Leadership Center, you won't find the golf course that sometimes marks other such universities. And the training experience is described as "intense, but . . . one of the most useful intense experiences I've ever had."[68]

Learning Portals

For many firms, their online learning portals are becoming their virtual in-house development centers. While firms such as General Electric have long had their own bricks-and-mortar corporate universities, learning portals let even smaller firms have their own corporate universities, on the Web. Bain & Company, a management consulting firm, has such a Web-based virtual university for its employees. It provides a means not only for conveniently coordinating all the company's training efforts but also for delivering Web-based modules that cover topics from strategic management to mentoring.[69]

Executive Coaches

Many firms use executive coaches to develop their top managers' effectiveness. An *executive coach* is an outside consultant who questions the executive's boss, peers, subordinates, and (sometimes) family in order to identify the executive's strengths and weaknesses, and to counsel the executive so he or she can capitalize on those strengths and weaknesses. About two thirds of executive coaches are reportedly female, and coaches come from a variety of backgrounds including teaching, counseling, and the mental health professions. Some firms, including Becton Dickinson & Co., encourage professional and management employees to coach each other.[70]

Executive coaching can be effective. Participants in one study included about 1,400 senior managers who had received "360-degree" performance feedback from bosses, peers, and subordinates. About 400 worked with an executive coach to review the feedback. Then, about a year later, these 400 managers and about 400 who did not receive coaching again received multiscore feedback. It was apparent that managers who received executive coaching were more likely to set more effective, specific goals for their subordinates, and to have received improved ratings from subordinates and supervisors.[71] Because executive coaching can cost as much as $50,000 per executive, experts recommend using formal assessments prior to coaching, to uncover strengths and weaknesses and provide more focus for the coaching.[72]

Organizational Development

Organizational development (OD) aims to change the attitudes, values, and beliefs of employees so that the employees can identify and implement changes (such as reorganizations), usually with the aid of an outside change agent, or consultant.

Action research is the foundation of most OD programs or interventions. It means gathering data about the organization and its operations and attitudes, with an eye toward solving a particular problem (for example, conflict between the sales and production departments); feeding back these data to the employees involved; and then having them team-plan solutions to the problems.

Specific examples of OD efforts (or "interventions") include survey feedback, sensitivity training, and team building. **Survey feedback** uses questionnaires to survey employees' attitudes and to provide feedback. The aim here is usually to crystallize for the managers the fact that there is a problem that must be addressed. Then the department managers can use the results to turn to the job of discussing and solving it.

Sensitivity training aims to increase participants' insights into their behavior and the behavior of others by encouraging an open expression of feelings in the trainer-guided "T-group laboratory" (the "T" is for training). Sensitivity training seeks to accomplish its aim of increasing interpersonal sensitivity by requiring frank, candid discussions in the small, off-site T-group, specifically discussions of participants' personal feelings, attitudes, and behavior. As a result, it is a controversial method surrounded by heated debate and is used much less today than in the past.

Finally, **team building** refers to a group of OD techniques aimed at improving the effectiveness of teams at work. The typical team-building program begins with the consultant interviewing each of the group members prior to the group meeting. He or she asks them what their problems are, how they think the group functions, and what obstacles are in the way of the group performing better.[73] The consultant usually categorizes the interview or attitude survey data into themes and presents the themes to the group at the beginning of the meeting. They might include, for example, "Not enough time to get my job done," or "I can't get any cooperation around here." The group then ranks the themes by importance. The most important ones form the agenda for the meeting. The group examines and discusses the issues, examines the underlying causes of the problem, and begins work on a solution to the problems.

Web-Based Tools

There are many Web-based tools one can use to facilitate organizational development programs. For example, there are Web-based surveys, including ones at surveymonkey.com, Zoomerang.com, and brainbench.com. The manager will also find OD-related self-assessment tools at Web sites such as CPP.com.[74]

Building High-Performance Learning Organizations

In a fast-changing world, the last thing a company needs is for new information—about competitors' actions, customers' preferences, or technological improvements—to be ignored or lost in a bureaucratic sinkhole. Some firms, such as Microsoft and GE, are traditionally quick on their feet; others are not.

HR's Role in Building Learning Organizations

Firms such as GE have successfully made the leap into rebuilding themselves as learning organizations. A **learning organization** "is an organization skilled at creating, acquiring, and transferring knowledge, and at modifying its behavior to reflect new knowledge and insights."[75]

Training can help develop such skills. Xerox, for instance, trains employees to analyze and display data on special simple statistical charts and to plan the actions they will take to solve the problem using special planning charts.

Providing Employees with Lifelong Learning

In today's empowered organizations, employers must depend on first-line employees—the team members building the Saturn cars, or the Microsoft programmers—to recognize new opportunities, identify problems, and react quickly with analyses and recommendations. As a result, there's a need for encouraging lifelong learning, in other words, for providing extensive continuing training from basic remedial skills to advanced decision-making techniques, throughout employees' careers.

Programs like these typically contain several elements, including training, as appropriate, in such things as English as a second language, basic literacy, arithmetic, and computer literacy; in-house college course work; and job-related training sessions.

Organizational Change

Today, intense international competition means companies have to change fast, perhaps changing their strategies to enter new businesses, or their organization charts, or their employees' attitudes and values.

Major organizational changes like these are never easy, but perhaps the hardest part of leading a change is overcoming the resistance to it. Individuals, groups, and even entire organizations may resist the change, perhaps because they are accustomed to the usual way of doing things or because of perceived threats to their power and influence, or some other reason.

Lewin's Process for Overcoming Resistance

Psychologist Kurt Lewin formulated a model of change to summarize what he believed was the basic process for implementing a change with minimal resistance. To Lewin, all behavior in organizations was a product of two kinds of forces: those striving to maintain the status quo and those pushing for change. Implementing change thus meant either reducing the forces for the status quo or building up the forces for change. Lewin's process consisted of three steps:

1. *Unfreezing,* which means reducing the forces that are striving to maintain the status quo, usually by presenting a provocative problem or event to get people to recognize the need for change and to search for new solutions.
2. *Moving,* which means developing new behaviors, values, and attitudes, sometimes through organizational structure changes and sometimes through the other management development techniques (such as team building).
3. *Refreezing,* which means building in the reinforcement to make sure the organization doesn't slide back into its former ways of doing things.

Of course, the devil is in the details, and actually finding the right techniques that will help you accomplish each of those three steps and then using them is the difficult part. A 10-step process for leading organizational change is summarized in the *HR in Practice* box.[76]

A 10-STEP PROCESS FOR LEADING ORGANIZATIONAL CHANGE

1. *Establish a sense of urgency.* For instance, create a crisis by exposing managers to major weaknesses relative to competitors.

2. *Mobilize commitment to change through joint diagnosis of business problems.* Next, create one or more task forces to diagnose the business problems. Such teams can produce a shared understanding of what can and must be improved and thereby mobilize the commitment of those who must actually implement the change.

3. *Create a guiding coalition.* No leader can accomplish any significant change alone. That's why most leaders create a guiding coalition of influential people who can be missionaries and implementers of change.

4. *Develop a shared vision.* Create a general statement of the organization's intended direction that evokes emotional feelings in organization members.

5. *Communicate the vision.* Use multiple forums, repetition, and leading by example to foster support for the new vision.

6. *Remove barriers to the change.* Empower employees. Accomplishing the change usually requires the assistance of the employees themselves, but sometimes this requires empowering them—in other words, removing barriers that stand in the way of their being able to actually assist in making the changes. For example, Sony's CEO removed his former studio executives and installed a new team when he set about fixing Sony's movie

business. AlliedSignal CEO Lawrence Bossidy put all of his 80,000 employees through quality training within 2 years.

7. *Generate short-term wins.* Maintain employees' motivation to stay involved in the change by ensuring that they have short-term goals to achieve from which they will receive positive feedback.

8. *Consolidate gains and produce more change.* As momentum builds and changes are made, the leader has to guard against renewed complacency. To do this, the leader and guiding coalition can use the increased credibility that comes from short-term wins to change all the systems, structures, and policies that don't fit well with the company's new vision.

9. *Anchor the new ways of doing things in the company's culture.* Few organizational changes survive without a corresponding change in employees' shared values. For example, if you want to emphasize more openness, camaraderie, and customer service, you as a leader must get the organization's employees to share those values. Do this by issuing a core value statement, by "walking the talk," and by using signs, symbols, rewards, and ceremonies to reinforce the values you want your employees to share.

10. *Monitor progress and adjust the vision as required.* For example, use regular surveys to monitor customer and employee attitudes.

EVALUATING THE TRAINING AND DEVELOPMENT EFFORT

There are two basic issues to address when evaluating a training program. The first is how to design the evaluation study and, in particular, whether to use controlled experimentation. The second is what training effect to measure.

Controlled experimentation is the best method to use in evaluating a training program. A controlled experiment uses both a training group and a control group (which receives no training). Data (for instance, on quantity of production or quality of soldered junctions) are obtained both before and after the training effort in the group exposed to training, and before and after a corresponding work period in the control group. In this way it is possible to determine the extent to which any change in performance in the training group resulted from the training itself rather than from some organization-wide change such as a raise in pay; we assume that the latter would have equally affected employees in both groups. This controlled approach is feasible and is sometimes used.[77] In terms of current practices, however, few firms use this approach. Most simply measure trainees' reactions to the program; some also measure the trainees' job performance before and after training.

Training Effects to Measure

Four basic categories of training outcomes can be measured:

1. *Reaction.* First, evaluate trainees' reactions to the program. Did they like the program? Did they think it worthwhile?
2. *Learning.* Second, test the trainees to determine whether they learned the principles, skills, and facts they were supposed to learn.
3. *Behavior.* Next, ask whether the trainees' behavior on the job changed because of the training program. For example, are employees in the store's complaint department more courteous toward disgruntled customers than previously?
4. *Results.* Finally, but probably most importantly, ask: What final results were achieved in terms of the training objectives previously set? Did the number of customer complaints about employees drop? Did the reject rate improve? Did scrappage cost decrease? Was turnover reduced?

Evaluation in Practice

In today's metrics-oriented industrial environment, employers increasingly demand quantified training evaluations, either of reactions, learning, behavior, results, or some combination of these. In one survey, most responding employers said they set formal response-rate goals (in terms of number of trainees responding) for end-of-training class evaluations. In general, the actual response rate depended on the method the employer used to obtain the response. The response rate of trainees was about 82% with paper-and-pencil end-of-class evaluation surveys, 59% with online surveys, and 53% with e-mail surveys. Response rates for delayed, follow-up surveys were only about 38%. Most firms collecting end-of-class evaluation data—about 90%—use paper-and-pencil surveys.[78]

Computerization is facilitating the evaluation process. For example, Bovis Lend Lease in New York City offers its 625 employees numerous courses in construction and other subjects. The firm uses special learning management software to monitor which employees are taking which courses, and the extent to which employees are improving their skills.[79]

Transfer of Training

Only about 10% to 35% of trainees are transferring what they learned to their jobs a year after training. Managers can improve this. *Prior to training*, get trainee and supervisor input in designing the program, institute a training attendance policy, and encourage employees to participate. *During training*, provide trainees with training experiences and conditions (surroundings, equipment) that resemble the actual work environment. *After training* reinforce what trainees learned, for instance, by appraising and rewarding employees for using new skills, and by ensuring they have the tools and materials they need to use their new skills.[80]

Strategy and HR

To support McDonald's strategy of consistency, its managers attend its famous Hamburger University. Employees at "seed stores" in each local area provide employees from surrounding stores with hands-on training. These seed store-trained employees then train their own stores' teams.

    McDonald's measures training effectiveness in several ways. They ask trainees to evaluate classes, and test them on what they've learned. McDonald's also speaks with the employees' supervisors about how the trainees did before and after the training, to try to determine the extent to which the trainees changed their behavior.[81]

Review

Summary

1. The training process consists of five steps: needs analysis, instructional design, validation, implementation, and evaluation.

2. Vestibule training, or simulated training, combines the advantages of on- and off-the-job training.

3. On-the-job training might take the form of the coaching/understudy method, job rotation, or special assignments and committees. Other training methods include audiovisual techniques, lectures, computer-aided instruction, apprenticeship training, simulated training, DVD/CD-ROM- and Internet-based training, learning portals, and special-purpose training.

4. Management development is aimed at preparing employees for future managerial jobs with the organization, or at solving organization-wide problems concerning, for instance, inadequate interdepartmental communication.

5. On-the-job experience is the most popular form of management development.

6. Managerial on-the-job training methods include job rotation, coaching, and action learning. Case studies, management games, outside seminars, university-related programs, behavior modeling, and in-house development centers are other methods.

7. Organizational development is an approach to instituting change in which employees themselves play a major role in the change process by providing data, by obtaining feedback on problems, and by team-planning solutions. There are several OD methods, including sensitivity training, team development, and survey feedback.

8. Overcoming employee resistance is a crucial aspect of implementing organizational change. The *HR in Practice* box summarizes the organizational change process.

Key Terms

- employee orientation
- training
- task analysis
- performance analysis
- on-the-job training (OJT)
- vestibule training
- computer-based training
- virtual classroom
- management development
- job rotation
- coaching/understudy method
- action learning
- case study method
- management games
- improvisation
- behavior modeling
- in-house development centers
- organizational development (OD)
- survey feedback
- sensitivity training
- team building
- learning organization
- controlled experimentation

Discussion Questions and Exercises

1. A well-thought-out orientation program is especially important for employees (such as recent graduates) who have had little or no work experience. Explain why you agree or disagree with this statement.
2. You're the supervisor of a group of employees whose task is to assemble devices that go into cell phones. You find that quality is not what it should be and that many of your group's devices have to be brought back and reworked; your own boss says, "You better start doing a better job of training your workers."
   a. What are some of the staffing factors that could be contributing to this problem?
   b. Explain how you would go about assessing whether it is, in fact, a training problem.
3. Explain how you would go about developing a training program for teaching this course.
4. John Santos is an undergraduate business student majoring in accounting. He has just failed the first accounting course, Accounting 101, and is understandably upset. Explain how you would use performance analysis to identify what, if any, are Santos's training needs.
5. What are some typical on-the-job training techniques? What do you think are some of the main drawbacks of relying on informal on-the-job training for helping new employees become accustomed to their jobs?
6. Experts argue that one reason for implementing special global training programs is the need to avoid lost business "due to cultural insensitivity." What sort of cultural insensitivity do you think is referred to and how might that translate into lost business? What sort of training program would you recommend to avoid such cultural insensitivity?
7. Do you think job rotation is a good method to use for management trainees? Why or why not?
8. Working individually or in groups, obtain, perhaps via the Web, copies of management development seminars from a vendor such as the American Management Association. At what levels of managers do they aim their seminar offerings? What seems to be the most popular type of development program? Why do you think that's the case?
9. Working individually or in groups, discuss whether you think the college you are currently attending is or is not a learning organization. On what do you base your conclusion?
10. By mid-2003, the U.S.-led coalition in Iraq was sending hundreds of trainers to that country to train new cadres of Iraqi workers, from teachers to police officers. Perhaps no training task was more pressing than that involved in creating the country's new police force. These were the people who were to help the coalition bring security to Iraq at that time. However, many new officers had no experience in police work. There were language barriers between trainers and trainees. And some trainees found themselves quickly under fire from insurgents when they went as trainees out into the field. Based on what you have learned about training from this chapter, list the five most important things you would tell the officer in charge of training (a former U.S. big-city police chief) to keep in mind as he designs the training program.

APPLICATION EXERCISES

Case Incident   *Reinventing the Wheel at Apex Door Company*

Jim Delaney, president of Apex Door Company, has a problem. No matter how often he tells his employees how to do their jobs, they invariably "decide to do things their way," as he puts it, and arguments ensue between Delaney, the employee, and the employee's supervisor. One example is in the door-design department. The designers are expected to work with the architects to design doors that meet the specifications. Although it's not "rocket science," as Delaney puts it, the designers often make mistakes—such as designing in too much steel—a problem that can cost Apex tens of thousands of wasted dollars, especially considering the number of doors in, say, a 30-story office tower.

The order processing department is another example. Although Jim has a specific, detailed way he wants each order written up, most of the order clerks don't understand how to use the multipage order form, and they improvise when it comes to a question such as whether to classify a customer as "industrial" or "commercial."

The current training process is as follows. None of the jobs have training manuals per se, although several have somewhat out-of-date job descriptions. The training for new employees is all on the job: Usually, the person leaving the company trains the new person during the 1- or 2-week overlap period, but if there's no overlap, the new person is trained as well as possible by other employees who have occasionally filled in on the job in the past. The training is basically the same throughout the company—for machinists, secretaries, assemblers, and accounting clerks, for example. ■

QUESTIONS

1. What do you think of Apex's training process? Could it help to explain why employees "do things their way," and if so, how?
2. What role do job descriptions play in training?
3. Explain in detail what you would do to improve the training process at Apex. Make sure to provide specific suggestions.

Continuing Case

LearnInMotion.com: The New Training Program

"I just don't understand it," said Mel. "No one here seems to follow instructions, and no matter how many times I've told them how to do things, they seem to do them their own way." At present, LearnInMotion.com has no formal orientation or training policies or procedures. Jennifer believes that is one reason why employees generally ignore the standards that she and Mel would like employees to adhere to.

Several examples illustrate this. One of the jobs of the Web designer (her name is Maureen) is to take customers' copy for banner ads and

adapt it for placement on LearnInMotion.com. She has been told several times not to tinker in any way with a customer's logo: Most companies put considerable thought and resources into logo design, and, as Mel has said, "whether or not Maureen thinks the logo is perfect, it's the customer's logo, and she's to leave it as it is." Yet just a week ago, they almost lost a big customer when Maureen, to "clarify" the customer's logo, modified its design before posting it on LearnInMotion.

That is just the tip of the iceberg. As far as Jennifer and Mel are concerned, it is the sales effort that is completely out of control. For one thing, even after several months on the job, it still seems as if the salespeople don't know what they're talking about. For example, LearnInMotion has several co-brand arrangements with Web sites like Yahoo! This means if Yahoo! users are interested in ordering educational courses or CDs, other sites' users can easily click through to LearnInMotion. Jennifer has noticed that during conversations with customers, the two salespeople often have no idea of which sites co-brand with LearnInMotion, or how to get to the LearnInMotion site from the partner Web site.

The salespeople also need to know a lot more about the products themselves. For example, one salesperson was trying to sell someone who produces programs on managing call centers on the idea of listing its products under LearnInMotion's "communications" community. In fact, the "communications" community is for courses on topics like interpersonal communications and how to be a better listener; it has nothing to do with managing the sorts of call centers that, for instance, airlines use for handling customer inquiries. As another example, the Web surfer is supposed to get a specific e-mail address with a specific person's name for the salespeople to use; instead he often just comes back with an "information@xyz"-type e-mail address off a Web site. The list goes on and on.

Jennifer feels the company has had other problems because of the lack of adequate employee training and orientation. For example, a question came up recently when employees found they weren't paid for the July 4 holiday: They assumed they'd be paid, but they were not. Similarly, when a salesperson left after barely a month on the job, there was considerable debate

about whether the person should receive severance pay and accumulated vacation pay. Other matters to cover during an orientation, says Jennifer, include company policy regarding lateness and absences, health and hospitalization benefits (there are none, other than workers' compensation), and matters like maintaining a safe and healthy workplace, personal appearance and cleanliness, personal telephone calls and e-mail, substance abuse, and eating or smoking on the job.

Jennifer believes that implementing orientation and training programs would help ensure that employees know how to do their jobs. She and Mel further believe that it is only when employees understand the right way to do their jobs that there is any hope those jobs will in fact be carried out in the way the owners want them to be. Now they want you, their management consultants, to help them. Here's what they want you to do for them. ■

QUESTIONS AND ASSIGNMENTS

1. Specifically, what should we cover in our new employee orientation program, and how should we convey this information?
2. In the HR course Jennifer took, the book suggested using task analysis to identify tasks performed by an employee. Should we use this for the salespeople? If so, what would be involved in the task analysis process if she used it (include some specific tasks)?
3. Which specific training techniques should we use to train our salespeople, Web designer, and Web surfer, and why?

EXPERIENTIAL EXERCISE

Flying the Friendlier Skies

Purpose: The purpose of this exercise is to give you practice in developing a training program for the job of airline reservation clerk for a major airline.

Required Understanding: You should be fully acquainted with the material in this chapter and should read the following description of an airline reservation clerk's duties:

Description: Customers contact our airlines reservation clerks to obtain flight schedules, prices, and itineraries. The reservation clerks look up the requested information on our airline's online flight schedule system, which are updated continuously. The reservation clerk must deal courteously and expeditiously with the customer and be able to quickly find alternative flight arrangements in order to provide the customer with the itinerary that fits his or her needs. Alternative flights and prices must be found quickly, so that the customer is not kept waiting, and so that our reservations operations group maintains its efficiency standards. It is often necessary to look under various routings, since there may be a dozen or more alternative routes between the customer's starting point and destination.

You may assume that we just hired 30 new clerks, and that you must create a 3-day training program.

How to Set Up the Exercise/Instructions: Divide the class into teams of five or six students. Airline reservation clerks obviously need numerous skills to perform their jobs. This major airline has asked you to quickly develop the outline of a training program for its new reservation clerks. You may want to start by listing the job's main duties. In any case, please produce the requested outline, making sure to be very specific about what you want to teach the new clerks, and what methods and aids you suggest using to train them. ■

Endnotes

1. Tony Bingaman and Pat Galagan, "Training: They're Lovin' It," *Training & Development* (November 2006): 30.
2. For a good discussion of socialization see, for example, George Chao et al., "Organizational Socialization: Its Content and Consequences," *Journal of Applied Psychology* 79, no. 5 (1994): 730–743; see also Talya Bauer, et al., "Newcomer Adjustment During Organizational Socialization: A Meta-Analytic Review of Antecedents, Outcomes, and Methods," *Journal of Applied Psychology* 92, no. 3 (2007): 707–721.
3. Sheila Hicks, et al., "Orientation Redesign," *Training and Development* (July 2006): 43–46.
4. John Kammeyer-Mueller and Connie Wanberg, "Unwrapping the Organizational Entry Process: Disentangling Multiple Antecedents and Their Pathways to Adjustments," *Journal of Applied Psychology* 88, no. 5 (2003): 779–794.
5. Sabrina Hicks, "Successful Orientation Programs," *Training & Development* (April 2000): 59. See also Howard Klein and Natasha Weaver, "The Effectiveness of an Organizational Level Orientation Program in the Socialization of New Hires," *Personnel*

Psychology 53 (2000): 47–66; and Laurie Friedman, "Are You Losing Potential New Hires at Hello?" *Training & Development* (November 2006): 25–27.
6. This section is based on Darin Hartley, "Technology Kicks Up Leadership Development," *Training and Development* (March 2004): 22–24.
7. Harley Frazis, Diane Herz, and Michael Horrigan, "Employer-Provided Training: Results from a New Survey," *Monthly Labor Review* (May 1995): 3–17.
8. Brenda Sugrue et al., "What in the World is WLP?" *Training and Development* (January 2005): 51–54.
9. "Companies Invested More in Training Despite Economic Setbacks, Survey Says," *BNA Bulletin to Management* (March 7, 2002): 73. American Express was first in terms of training hours per employee, see "Annual Training Hours Per Employee," *Training* 43, no. 3 (March 2006): 72(1).
10. Winfred Alfred Jr. et al., "Effectiveness of Training in Organizations: A Meta Analysis of Design and Evaluation Features," *Journal of Applied Psychology* 88, no. 2 (2003): 242.
11. Christine Ellis and Sarah Gale, "A Seat at the Table," *Training* (March 2001): 90–96.

12. Peter Glendinning, "Performance Management: Pariah or Messiah?" *Public Personnel Management* 31, no. 2 (Summer 2002): 161–178.

13. Nancy DeViney and Brenda Sugrue, "Learning Outsourcing: A Reality Check," *Training and Development* (December 2004): 41.

14. Cathy Cooper, "Connect Four," *People Management*, 7, no. 3 (February 8, 2001): 42–43.

15. Marcia Jones, "Use Your Head when Identifying Skills Gaps," *Workforce* (March 2000): 118.

16. P. Nick Blanchard and James Thacker, *Effective Training: Systems, Strategies, and Practices* (Upper Saddle River, NJ: Prentice Hall, 1999), pp. 154–156.

17. Richard Montier, et al., "Competency Models Develop Top Performance," *Training and Development* (July 2006): 47–50.

18. Richard Camp et al., *Toward a More Organizationally Effective Training Strategy and Practice* (Upper Saddle River, NJ: Prentice Hall, 1986), p. 100.

19. J. P. Cicero, "Behavioral Objectives for Technical Training Systems," *Training and Development Journal* 28 (1973): 14–17. See also Larry D. Hales, "Training: A Product of Business Planning," *Training and Development Journal* 40, no. 7 (July 1986): 87–92; Pamela Prewitt, "Army Job Standard vs. Training Standard," *Training and Development Journal* 51, no. 9 (September 1997): 52–53.

20. Erica Gordon Sorohan, "We Do; Therefore, We Learn," *Training & Development* (October 1993): 47–55; Melvin LeBlanc, "Learning Objectives Key to Quality Safety," *Occupational Hazards* (January 1994): 127–128. See also Kimberly A. Smith-Jentsch et al., "Can Pre-Training Experiences Explain Individual Differences in Learning?" *Journal of Applied Psychology* 81, no. 1 (1996): 110–116.

21. Kenneth Wexley and Gary Latham, *Development and Training Human Resources in Organizations* (Upper Saddle River, NJ: Prentice Hall, 2002), p. 107.

22. Ibid., 82.

23. Ibid., 87.

24. Ibid., 90.

25. The American Society for Training & Development (ASTD) offers thousands of packaged training programs, such as "Be a Better Manager," "Strategic Planning 101," "12 Habits of Successful Trainers," "Mentoring," and "Using Job Aids." American Society for Training & Development, Spring and Fall Line Catalog 2007; American Society for Training and Development 2007 Buyers Guide, American Society for Training & Development, 1640 King St., Box 1443, Alexandria, VA 22313.

26. Donna Goldwaser, "Me a Trainer?" *Training* (April 2001): 60–66.

27. Robert Weintraub and Jennifer Martineau, "The Just in Time Imperative," *Training and Development* (June 2002): 52.

28. Frazis et al., "Employer-Provided Training," 4.

29. Cindy Waxer, "Steelmaker Revives Apprentice Program to Address Graying Workforce, Forge Next Leaders," *Workforce Management* (January 30, 2006): 40.

30. David Finegold and Karin Wagner, "Are Apprenticeships Still Relevant in the 21st Century? The Case Study of Changing Youth Training Arrangements in German Banks," *Industrial and Labor Relations Review* (July 2002): 667–685.

31. Michael Blotzer, "Distance Learning," *Occupational Hazards* (March 2000): 53–54.

32. Michael Emery and Margaret Schubert, "A Trainer's Guide to Videoconferencing," *Training* (June 1993): 60. See also Mark Van Buren, "Learning Technologies: Can They or Can't They?" *Training & Development* (April 2000): 62.

33. Ibid., 60.

34. "Employer to Learn the Benefits of Distance Learning," *BNA Bulletin to Management* (April 25, 1996): 130.

35. Shari Caudron, "Your Learning Technology Primer," *Personnel Journal* (June 1996): 120–136. As another example, see "Larta Institute Announces Selection of Israeli Companies in US-Israel Life Sciences Bridge Program," Entrepreneurs to Receive Videoconference Training Starting April 15; Three Candidates Will Come to L.A. for One-Month Incubation Visit," *Internet Wire* (April 20, 2004).

36. David Raths, "Virtual Reality in the OR," *Training and Development* (August 2006): 36–43.

37. See for example, Kim Kleps, "Virtual Sales Training Scores a Hit," *Training & Development* (December 2006): 63–64.

38. Dina Berta, "Computer-Based Training Clicks with Both Franchisees and Their Employees," *Nation's Restaurant News* (July 9, 2001): 1, 18; see also "What Do Simulations Cost?," *Training & Development* (June 2007): 88.

39. Michael Laff, "Simulations: Slowly Proving Their Worth," *Training & Development* (June 2007): 30–34.

40. Jenni Jarventaus, "Virtual Threat, Real Sweat," *Training & Development* (May 2007): 72–78.

41. Larry Stevens, "The Intranet: Your Newest Training Tool?" *Personnel Journal* (July 1996): 27–31; see also Kenneth Brown, "Using Computers to Deliver Training: Which Employees Learn and Why?" *Personnel Psychology* 54, no. 2 (Summer 2001): 271–296; Jason Lewis and Dan Michaluk, "Four Steps to Building E-learning Success," *Workforce* (May 2002): 42. See also Elizabeth Welsch et al., "E-Learning: Emerging Uses, Empirical Results and Future Directions," *International Journal of Training and Development* 7, no. 4 (December 2003): 245–258.

42. David Kirkpatrick, "The Portal of the Future? Your Boss Will Run It," *Fortune* (August 2, 1999): 222–227. See also Cynthia Pantazis, "Maximizing E-Learning to Train the 21st Century Workforce," *Public Personnel Management* (Spring 2002): 21–26.

43. Tom Barron, "A Portrait of Learning Portals," www.learningcircuits.com/may2000/barron.html, accessed 2000. See also Paul Giguere and Jennifer Minotti, "Rethinking Web-Based E-Learning," *Training and Development* (January 2005): 15–16.

44. Eileen Garger, "Goodbye Training, Hello Learning," *Workforce* (November 1999): 35–42.

45. Brian O'Connell, "A Poor Grade for E-learning," *Workforce* 81, no. 7 (July 2002): 15.

46. "The Next Generation of Corporate Learning," *Training and Development* (June 2004): 47.

47. John Zonneveld, "GM Dealer Training Goes Global," *Training & Development* (December 2006): 47–51.

48. Elizabeth Agnvall, "Just-In-Time Training," *HR Magazine* (May 2006): 67–78.

49. Ibid. See also Jennifer Taylor Arnold, "Learning On-the-Fly," *HR Magazine* (September 2007): 137.

50. Traci Sitzmann, et al.,"The Comparative Effectiveness of Web-Based and Classroom Instruction: A Meta-Analysis," *Personnel Psychology* 59 (2006): 623–664.

51. Renee DeRouin et al., "Optimizing E-Learning: Research-Based Guidelines for Learner Controlled Training," *Human Resource Management* 43, no. 2 (Summer/Fall 2004): 147–162.

52. Paula Ketter, "The Hidden Disability," *Training and Development* (June 2006): 34–40.

53. Valerie Frazee, "Workers Learn to Walk so They Can Run," *Personnel Journal* (May 1996): 115–120. See also Kathryn Tyler, "I Say Potato, You Say Patata: As Workforce and Customer Diversity Grow, Employers Offer Foreign Language Training To Staff," *HR Magazine* 49, no. 1 (January 2004): 85–87.

54. "Adams Mark Hotel & Resorts Launches Diversity Training Program," *Hotel and Motel Management* 216, no. 6 (April 2001): 15.

55. Sara Rynes and Benson Rosen, "What Makes Diversity Programs Work?" *HR Magazine* (October 1994): 64. See also Thomas Diamante and Leo Giglio, "Managing a Diverse Workforce: Training as a Cultural Intervention Strategy," *Leadership & Organization Development Journal* 15, no. 2 (1994): 13–17.

56. Douglas Shuit, "Sound of the Retreat," *Workforce Management* (September 2003): 40.

57. "For Gap, Management Training Doesn't Stop at the Border," *BNA Bulletin to Management* (February 2005): 63.

58. Jack Zenger, Dave Ulrich, and Norm Smallwood, "The New Leadership Development," *Training & Development* (March 2000): 22–27. See also W. David Patton and Connie Pratt, "Assessing the Training Needs of High Potential Managers," *Public Personnel Management* 31, no. 4 (Winter 2002): 465–474, and Ann Locke and Arlene Tarantino, "Strategic Leadership Development," *Training & Development* (December 2006): 53–55.

59. Wexley and Latham, *Developing and Training Human Resources in Organizations,* 193.

60. Chris Whitcomb, "Scenario-Based Training at the FBI," *Training & Development* (June 1999): 42–46.

61. See, for example, Michael Laff, "Serious Gaming: The Trainer's New Best Friend," *Training & Development* (January 2007): 52–56.

62. Jean Thilmany, "Acting Out," *HR Magazine* (January 2007): 95–100.

63. Chris Musselwhite, "University Executive Education Gets Real," *Training & Development* (May 2006): 57.

64. Jeanne Meister, "Universities Put to the Test," *Workforce Management* (December 11, 2006): 27–30.

65. Ann Pomcroy, "Head of the Class," *HR Magazine* (January 2005): 57.

66. Fred Davis and Mun Yi, "Improving Computer Skill Training: Behavior, Modeling, Symbolic Mental Rehearsal, and the Role of Knowledge Structures," *Journal of Applied Psychology* 89, no. 3 (2004): 519–523.

67. Ibid., 519.

68. Carolyn Cole, "Boeing U," *Workforce* (October 2000): 63–68.

69. Russell Gerbman, "Corporate Universities 101," *HR Magazine* (February 2000): 101–106. Before creating an in-house university, the employer needs to ensure that the corporate university's vision, mission, and programs support the company's strategic goals. See also Michael Laff, "Centralized Training Leads to Nontraditional Universities," *Training & Development* (January 2007): 27–29.

70. Joseph Toto, "Untapped World of Peer Coaching," *Training and Development* (April 2006): 69–72.

71. James Smither et al., "Can Working with an Executive Coach Improve Multisource Feedback Ratings Over Time?" *Personnel Psychology* 56, no. 1 (Spring 2003): 23–44.

72. "As Corporate Coaching Goes Mainstream, Keyed Prerequisite Overlooked: Assessment," *BNA Bulletin to Management* (May 16, 2006): 153.

73. Wendell French and Cecil Bell Jr., *Organization Development* (Upper Saddle River, NJ: Prentice Hall, 1999). See also, P. Nick Blanchard and James Thacker, *Effective Training* (Upper Saddle River, NJ: Pearson, 2007) pp. 38–46.

74. Darin Hartley, "OD Wired," *Training and Development* (August 2004): 20–24.

75. David A. Garvin, "Building a Learning Organization," *Harvard Business Review* (July/August 1993): 80.

76. The 10 steps are based on Michael Beer et al., "Why Change Programs Don't Produce Change," *Harvard Business Review* (November/December 1990): 158–166; John Kotter, *Leading Change* (Boston: Harvard Business School Press, 1996). See also David Herold et al., "Beyond Change Management: A Multilevel Investigation of Contextual and Personal Influences on Employee's Commitment to Change," *Journal of Applied Psychology* 92, no. 4 (2007): 949.

77. See, for example, Charlie Morrow, M. Quintin Jarrett, and Melvin Rupinski, "An Investigation of the Effect and Economic Utility of Corporate-Wide Training," *Personnel Psychology* 50 (1997): 91–119. See also Antonio Aragon-Sanchez et al., "Effects of Training on Business Results," *International Journal of Human Resource Management* 14, no. 6, (September 2003): 956–980.

78. Jeffrey Berk, "Training Evaluations," *Training and Development* (September 2004): 39–45.

79. Todd Raphel, "What Learning Management Reports Do for You," *Workforce* 80, no. 6 (June 2001): 56–58.

80. Alan Saks and Monica Belcourt, "An Investigation of Training Activities and Transfer of Training in Organizations," *Human Resource Management* 45, no. 4 (Winter 2006): 629–648.

81. Tony Bingaman and Pat Galagan, "Training: They're Lovin' It," *Training & Development* (November 2006): 30.

6

PERFORMANCE MANAGEMENT AND APPRAISAL

- Basic Concepts in Performance Management
- An Introduction to Appraising Performance
- Basic Appraisal Methods
- The Appraisal Feedback Interview
- Toward More Effective Appraisals
- Performance and Career Management

When you finish studying this chapter, you should be able to:

■ Explain *the purpose of performance appraisal.*

■ Answer *the question, Who should do the appraising?*

■ Discuss *the pros and cons of at least eight performance appraisal methods.*

■ Explain *how to conduct an appraisal feedback interview.*

INTRODUCTION

With more than 100,000 employees in 36 countries, administering employee appraisals and managing performance is a complicated process in a company like TRW.[1] A few years ago, the firm was deeply in debt, and the company's heavy investment in the automotive business was draining its profits. TRW's top management knew that they had to take steps to make the firm more competitive and performance driven. To do that, it needed to focus employees' attention on performance, in part by instituting a new performance management and appraisal system.

BASIC CONCEPTS IN PERFORMANCE MANAGEMENT

Performance appraisal means evaluating an employee's current and/or past performance relative to his or her performance standards. Although "appraising performance" usually brings to mind specific appraisal tools such as the teaching appraisal form in Figure 6.1, the actual forms are only part of the appraisal process. Appraising performance also assumes that performance standards have been set, and also that you'll give the employee feedback and incentives to help him or her eliminate performance deficiencies or continue to perform above par.

The idea that appraisals are just one element in the process of improving employee performance is nothing new. However, managers generally take the integrated nature of that process—of setting goals, training employees, and then appraising and rewarding them—much more seriously today than they have in the past.

Performance Management

They call the whole, integrated process **performance management.** This is the process through which companies ensure that employees are working toward organizational goals, and includes practices through which the manager defines the employee's goals and work, develops the employee's skills and capabilities, continuously appraises the person's goal-directed behavior, and then rewards him or her in a fashion that hopefully makes sense in terms of both the company's needs and the person's career aspirations.[2] The idea is to ensure that these elements are internally consistent, and that they all make sense in terms of what the company wants to achieve. In comparing performance management and appraisal, "the distinction is the contrast between a year-end event—the completion of the appraisal form—and a process that starts the year with performance planning and is integral to the way people are managed throughout the year."[3]

Today's performance management approach reflects managers' attempts to more explicitly recognize the interrelated nature of the factors that influence employee performance. And, it reflects the emphasis managers place today on fostering high-performance goal-directed efforts in a globally competitive world.

Strategy and HR

TRW, with over 100,000 employees, needed a new performance management system. It needed one that would focus each employee's attention on helping the company execute its new high-performance strategy. Top management charged a special team with creating such a system. The team created an online system, one in which most TRW employees and supervisors worldwide could input and review their goals and performance data electronically. To facilitate filling in the online form's pages, the team created a wizard that leads the user from step to step. It also includes embedded prompts and pull-down menus.

The new system focuses everyone's attention on goal-oriented performance. It identifies employee development needs that are both organizationally relevant and of use to the employee. It gives managers instantaneous access to employee performance data. And, perhaps most importantly, it helps keep each employee's performance focused on achieving individual goals that support TRW's strategic goals.[4]

FIGURE 6.1   Departmental Teaching Appraisal Form

Faculty Evaluation Form

INSTRUCTIONS FOR COMPLETING STUDENT EVALUATION FORM

Today you are being asked to evaluate this course and the instructor. Please read and answer each question thoughtfully and honestly.

Evaluations are helpful to faculty in improving their teaching and their courses. They are also an important element in the College's ongoing evaluation of faculty for tenure and promotion.

Your answers are anonymous and confidential. Comments will be typed so that the instructor cannot identify your handwriting. Your answers will be returned to the instructor only after final grades for this course have been recorded.

Your written comments on the last page are especially helpful.

CRN _____   Course _____

Instructor _____   Term _____

STUDENT EVALUATION OF INSTRUCTION

Student Information: (Please circle your answers).

1. I had completed the recommended preparation (prerequisites) for this course before beginning the course. *(Select NA if the course has no prerequisites.)*

All   Most   Some   Very Few   Don't Know   NA

2. I attended classes.

All   Most   Some   Very Few   NA

3. To be adequately prepared for this class, I feel I need to spend this many hours per week outside of class, studying and preparing assignments:

15+ hours   12-14 hours   9-11 hours   7-8 hours   4-6 hours   1-3 hours

4. For this course, I expect to receive a grade of:

A   B   C   D   F

Evaluation of Instruction: *(7 = strongly agree .... 1 = strongly disagree).*

1. The learning objectives (competencies) of this course have been made clear.

7   6   5   4   3   2   1

2. The course activities are related to the learning objectives (competencies).

7   6   5   4   3   2   1

3. The instructor is well-prepared for class.

7 6 5 4 3 2 1

4. The instructor is available during posted office hours or by appointment.

7 6 5 4 3 2 1

5. Feedback on my work is timely, constructive, and clear enough to benefit my learning.

7 6 5 4 3 2 1

6. My grades accurately measure my learning in this class.

7 6 5 4 3 2 1

7. The instructor creates a learning environment in which diverse points of view are respected and can be freely expressed.

7 6 5 4 3 2 1

8. Based on what I have learned, I would recommend this course to other students.

7 6 5 4 3 2 1

COMMENTS

Your written comments are especially helpful. Comments will be typed so that the instructor cannot identify your handwriting. Your answers will be returned to the instructor only after final grades for this course have been recorded.

1. What are the most valuable aspects of this course and/or the way the course was taught?

2. Even excellent courses can be improved. Can you give some constructive suggestions for making the course better?

3. Do you wish to comment on any of your ratings in the "Evaluation of Instruction" section on the Previous page? If so, please state the item number to which your comment refers.

Defining the Employee's Goals and Work Efforts

At the heart of performance management is the idea that the employee's efforts should be goal directed.[5] On the one hand, the manager should appraise the employee based on how that person did with respect to achieving the specific standards by which he or she expected to be measured. On the other hand, the manager should make sure that the employee's goals and performance standards make sense in terms of the company's broader goals. Ideally, in any company, there is a hierarchy of goals. Top management's goals—say, to double sales—imply subordinate goals for each manager and employee down the chain of command.

Yet, clarifying what you expect from your employee is trickier than it may appear. Employers usually write job descriptions, but the descriptions rarely include specific goals. All sales managers in the firm might have the same job description, for instance. Your sales manager's job description may list duties such as "supervise sales force" and "be responsible for all phases of marketing the division's products." However, you may also expect your sales manager to personally sell at least $600,000 worth of products per year by handling the division's two largest accounts. Unfortunately, some supervisors tend to be lax when it comes to setting specific goals for their employees. They then wonder why they have problems managing those employees' performance.

You therefore have to quantify your expectations. The most straightforward way to do this (for the sales manager job, for instance) is to set measurable standards for each expectation. You might measure the "personal selling" activity in terms of how many dollars of sales the manager is to generate personally. Perhaps measure "keeping the sales force happy" in terms of turnover (on the assumption that less than 10% of the sales force will quit in any given year if morale is high). The point is that employees should always know ahead of time how and on what basis you're going to appraise them.[6] You can't expect them to manage their own performance if they don't know the standards you will use to appraise their performance.

Effective Goal Setting

Setting goals is one thing; setting effective goals is another. One way to think of this is to remember that the goals you set should be "SMART." They are *specific*, and clearly state the desired results. They are *measurable*, and answer the question, How much? They are *attainable*. They are *relevant*, and clearly derive from what the manager and company want to achieve. And, they are *timely*, and reflect deadlines and milestones.[7]

Research known as "the goal-setting studies" provides useful insights into setting motivational goals. These studies suggest four things:

1. *Assign Specific Goals.* Employees who are given specific goals usually perform better than those who are not.
2. *Assign Measurable Goals.* Put goals in quantitative terms and include target dates or deadlines. Goals set in absolute terms (such as "an average daily output of 300 units") are less confusing than goals set in relative terms (such as "improve production by 20%"). If measurable results will not be available, then "satisfactory completion"—such as "satisfactorily attended workshop" or "satisfactorily completed his or her degree"—is the next best thing. In any case, target dates or deadlines should always be set.
3. *Assign Challenging but Doable Goals.* Goals should be challenging, but not so difficult that they appear impossible or unrealistic.

4. *Encourage Participation.* Throughout your management career (and often several times a day) you'll be faced with this question: Should I just tell my employees what their goals are, or should I let them participate with me in setting their goals? The evidence suggests that participatively set goals do not consistently result in higher performance than assigned goals, nor do assigned goals consistently result in higher performance than participatively set ones. It is only when the participatively set goals are more difficult (are set higher) than the assigned ones that the participatively set goals produce higher performance. It does tend to be easier to set higher standards when your employees can participate in the process, and to that extent participation can facilitate standards setting and performance.[8]

AN INTRODUCTION TO APPRAISING PERFORMANCE

Why Appraise Performance?

There are three main reasons to appraise subordinates' performance. First, appraisals provide important input on which the supervisor can make promotion and salary raise decisions.[9] Second, the appraisal lets the boss and subordinate develop a plan for correcting any deficiencies the appraisal might have unearthed, and to reinforce the things the subordinate does correctly. Finally, appraisals can serve a useful career-planning purpose, by providing the opportunity to review the employee's career plans in light of his or her exhibited strengths and weaknesses.

Who Should Do the Appraising?

Appraisals by the immediate supervisor are still the heart of most appraisal processes. Getting a supervisor's appraisal is relatively straightforward and also makes sense. The supervisor should be—and usually is—in the best position to observe and evaluate his or her subordinate's performance. He or she is also responsible for that person's performance. Most appraisals (92% in one survey) are made by the employee's immediate supervisor. These appraisals were in turn reviewed by the supervisor's own supervisor in 74% of the respondents in this survey.[10]

Yet, although widely used, supervisors' ratings are no panacea, and relying solely on them is not always advisable. For example, an employee's supervisor may not understand or appreciate how people such as customers and colleagues who depend on the employee rate the person's performance. Furthermore, it is conceivable that an immediate supervisor may be biased for or against the employee. If so, there are several options available.

Peer Appraisals

With more firms using self-managing teams, appraisal of an employee by his or her peers—**peer appraisal**—is more popular. At Digital Equipment Corporation, for example, an employee due for an annual appraisal chooses an appraisal chairperson. The latter then selects one supervisor and three peers to evaluate the employee's work.

Research indicates that peer appraisals can be effective. One study involved undergraduates placed into self-managing work groups. The researchers found that peer appraisals had "an immediate positive impact on [improving] perception of open communication, task motivation, social loafing, group viability, cohesion, and satisfaction."[11]

Rating Committees

Some companies use rating committees. A rating committee is usually composed of the employee's immediate supervisor and three or four other supervisors.

Using multiple raters can be advantageous. It can help cancel out problems such as bias on the part of individual raters. It can also provide a way to include in the appraisal the different facets of an employee's performance observed by different appraisers.

Self-Ratings

Employees' self-ratings of performance are also sometimes used, usually in conjunction with supervisors' ratings. The basic problem with self-ratings is that employees usually rate themselves higher than their supervisors or peers would rate them.[12] One study found that, when asked to rate their own job performances, 40% of employees in jobs of all types placed themselves in the top 10%, and virtually all remaining employees rated themselves at least in the top 50%.[13]

In another study, a person's self-ratings actually correlated negatively with the person's subsequent performance in an assessment center; in contrast, an average of the person's supervisor, peer, and subordinate ratings predicted the person's assessment center performance.[14]

Appraisal by Subordinates

Some firms let subordinates evaluate their supervisors' performance, a process many call **upward feedback.**[15] Such feedback can help top managers understand their subordinates' management styles, identify potential people problems, and take corrective action with individual managers, as required. Firms such as FedEx use upward feedback to help improve supervisory performance; for example, if a supervisor scores low on the item "I feel free to tell my manager what I think," FedEx managers are trained to ask their groups questions such as "What do I do that makes you feel that I'm not interested?"

Anonymity affects the usefulness of upward feedback. Managers who get feedback from subordinates who identify themselves view the upward feedback process more positively than do managers who get anonymous feedback. However, subordinates are more comfortable giving anonymous responses, and those who must identify themselves tend to give inflated ratings.[16]

Research supports the idea that upward feedback can improve a manager's performance. One study focused on 252 managers during five annual administrations of an upward feedback program. Managers who were initially "rated poor or moderate showed significant improvements in [their] upward feedback ratings over the five-year period." Furthermore, managers who met with their subordinates to discuss their upward feedback improved more than the managers who did not.[17]

360-Degree Feedback

With 360-degree feedback, performance information is collected all around an employee, from his or her supervisors, subordinates, peers, and internal or external customers.[18] This is generally done for development rather than for pay raises. The usual process is to have the raters complete online appraisal surveys on the ratee. Computerized systems then compile all this feedback into individualized reports that go to ratees. The person may then meet with his or her supervisor to develop a self-improvement plan.

Results are mixed. Participants seem to prefer this approach, but one study concluded that multi-source feedback led to "generally small" improvements on subsequent ratings by supervisors, peers, and subordinates. Improvement was most likely to occur when the feedback the person received indicated that change was necessary, and when the recipients believed that change was necessary and had a positive view of the change process.[19] Such 360 appraisals are also more helpful when it's clear they're for developmental rather than salary or promotion decisions; subordinates tend to be more candid when they know rewards or promotions are not involved.[20]

There are several ways to make such appraisals more useful.

- Anchor the 360-degree appraisals with behavioral competencies (such as "effectively deals with conflicts"). In one study, doing so predicted retail managers' success in a subsequent assessment center.[21]
- Carefully assess the potential costs of the program, focus any feedback on specific goals, carefully train the people who are giving and receiving the feedback, and do not rely solely on 360-degree feedback for performance appraisal.[22]
- Particularly with so many appraisers involved, make sure that the feedback the person receives is productive, unbiased, and development oriented.[23]
- Reduce the administrative costs associated with collecting multi-source feedback by using a Web-based or a PC-based system such as Visual 360 from MindSolve Technologies of Gainesville, Florida. This lets the rater log in, open a screen with a rating scale, and rate the person along a series of competencies with ratings such as "top five percent."[24]

Even if you do not opt for a 360-degree approach, it still makes sense to have more than one supervisor appraise an employee. Multiple raters often do see different facets of an employee's performance. Studies often find that the ratings obtained from different sources rarely match.[25] It's therefore advisable to obtain ratings from both the supervisor, his or her boss, and perhaps another manager who is familiar with the employee's work.[26]

BASIC APPRAISAL METHODS

The manager usually conducts the appraisal using one or more of the formal methods described in this section.

Graphic Rating Scale Method

A **graphic rating scale** lists a number of traits and a range of performance for each. As in Figure 6.2, it lists traits (such as quality and reliability) and a range of performance values (in this case from unsatisfactory to outstanding) for each trait. The supervisor rates each subordinate by circling or checking the score that best describes the subordinate's performance for each trait, then totals the scores for all traits.

FIGURE 6.2　Sample Graphic Rating Form with Behavioral Examples

Sample Performance Rating Form

Employee's Name _____　　Level: Entry-level employee

Manager's Name _____

Key Work Responsibilities	Results/Goals to be Achieved
1. _____	1. _____
2. _____	2. _____
3. _____	3. _____
4. _____	4. _____

Behavioral Assessment of Competencies

Communication

1	2	3	4	5

Below Expectations	Meets Expectations	Role Model
Even with guidance, fails to prepare straightforward communications, including forms, paperwork, and records, in a timely and accurate manner; products require minimal corrections.	With guidance, prepares straightforward communications, including forms, paperwork, and records, in a timely and accurate manner; products require minimal corrections.	Independently prepares communications, such as forms, paperwork, and records, in a timely, clear, and accurate manner; products require few, if any, corrections.
Even with guidance, fails to adapt style and materials to communicate straightforward information.	With guidance, adapts style and materials to communicate straightforward information.	Independently adapts style and materials to communicate information.

Organizational Know-How

1	2	3	4	5

Below Expectations	Meets Expectations	Role Model
<performance standards appear here>	<performance standards appear here>	<performance standards appear here>

Personal Effectiveness

1	2	3	4	5

Below Expectations	Meets Expectations	Role Model
<performance standards appear here>	<performance standards appear here>	<performance standards appear here>

Teamwork

1	2	3	4	5

Below Expectations	Meets Expectations	Role Model
<performance standards appear here>	<performance standards appear here>	<performance standards appear here>

Achieving Business Results

1	2	3	4	5

Below Expectations	Meets Expectations	Role Model
<performance standards appear here>	<performance standards appear here>	<performance standards appear here>

Results Assessment

Accomplishment 1: _____

1	2	3	4	5
Low Impact		Moderate Impact		High Impact
The efficiency or effectiveness of operations remained the same or improved only minimally. The quality of products remained the same or improved only minimally.		The efficiency or effectiveness of operations improved quite a lot. The quality of products improved quite a lot.		The efficiency or effectiveness of operations improved tremendously. The quality of products improved tremendously.

Accomplishment 2: _____

1	2	3	4	5
Low Impact		Moderate Impact		High Impact
The efficiency or effectiveness of operations remained the same or improved only minimally. The quality of products remained the same or improved only minimally.		The efficiency or effectiveness of operations improved quite a lot. The quality of products improved quite a lot.		The efficiency or effectiveness of operations improved tremendously. The quality of products improved tremendously.

Narrative

_____

_____

_____

_____

_____

Areas to be Developed	Actions	Completion Date

Manager's Signature _____ Date _____

Employee's Signature _____ Date _____

The above employee signature indicates receipt of, but not necessarily concurrence with, the evaluation herein.

Source: "Sample Performance Rating Form" from Elaine D. Pulakos, *Performance Management: A Roadmap for Developing, Implementing and Evaluating Performance Management Systems* (SHRM Foundation, 2004), pp. 16–17.

Alternation Ranking Method

Ranking employees from best to worst on a trait or traits is another popular appraisal method. Because it is usually easier to distinguish between the worst and best employees than to rank them, an **alternation ranking method** is useful. With this method a form like that in Figure 6.3 is used to indicate the employee who is highest on the trait being measured and also the one who is the lowest, alternating between highest and lowest until all employees to be rated have been addressed.

Paired Comparison Method

With the **paired comparison method,** every subordinate to be rated is paired with and compared to every other subordinate on each trait.

For example, suppose there are five employees to be rated. With this method, a chart such as that in Figure 6.4 shows all possible pairs of employees for each trait. Then for each trait, the supervisor indicates (with a plus or minus) who is the better employee of the pair. Next, the number of times an employee is rated better is added up. In Figure 6.4, employee Maria ranked highest (has the most plus marks) for "quality of work," and Art ranked highest for "creativity."

FIGURE 6.3   Alternation Ranking Method

ALTERNATION RANKING SCALE

For the Trait: _____

For the trait you are measuring, list all the employees you want to rank. Put the highest-ranking employee's name on line 1. Put the lowest-ranking employee's name on line 20. Then list the next highest ranking on line 2, the next lowest ranking on line 19, and so on. Continue until all names are on the scale.

Highest-ranking employee

1. _____   11. _____

2. _____   12. _____

3. _____   13. _____

4. _____   14. _____

5. _____   15. _____

6. _____   16. _____

7. _____   17. _____

8. _____   18. _____

9. _____   19. _____

10. _____   20. _____

Lowest-ranking employee

FIGURE 6.4	Paired Comparison Method

FOR THE TRAIT "QUALITY OF WORK"							FOR THE TRAIT "CREATIVITY"					
Employee Rated:							Employee Rated:					
As Compared to:	A Art	B Maria	C Chuck	D Diane	E José		As Compared to:	A Art	B Maria	C Chuck	D Diane	E José
A Art		+	+				A Art					
B Maria	–		–	–	–		B Maria	+		–	+	+
C Chuck	–	+		+	–		C Chuck	+	+		–	+
D Diane	+	+	–		+		D Diane	+	–	+		–
E José	+	+	+	–			E José	+	–	–	+	

↑ Maria Ranks Highest Here   ↑ Art Ranks Highest Here

Note: + means "better than," – means "worse than." For each chart, add up the number of +'s in each column to get the highest ranked employee.

Forced Distribution Method

With the **forced distribution method,** the manager places predetermined percentages of subordinates in performance categories, as when a professor "grades on a curve." About a fourth of Fortune 500 companies including Sun, Microsoft, Conoco, and Intel use forced distribution. GE popularized forced ranking, but now tells managers not to adhere to its famous 20/70/10 split.[27]

At Sun Microsystems managers appraise employees in groups of about 30. There is a top 10%, a middle 70%, and a bottom 10%. The bottom 10% can either take a quick exit package or embark on a 90-day performance improvement action plan. If they're still in the bottom 10% in 90 days, they get a chance to resign and take severance pay. Some decide to stay, but "if it doesn't work out," the firm fires them without severance.[28]

While widely used, some balk at forced distribution appraisals. One survey found that 77% of responding employers were at least "somewhat satisfied" with forced ranking, while the remaining 23% were dissatisfied with it. The biggest complaints: 44% said it damages morale, and 47% said it creates interdepartmental inequities, since "high-performing teams must cut 10% of their workers while low-performing teams are still allowed to retain 90% of theirs."[29] Some writers refer unkindly to forced ranking as the "Rank and Yank" approach to appraisals.[30]

As most students know, forced distribution grading systems are more unforgiving than are most other means of appraising performance. With a forced distribution system, you're either in the top 5% or 10% (and thus get that "A"), or you're not. And, if you're in the bottom 5% or 10%, you get an "F", no questions asked. Your professor hasn't the wiggle room to give everyone As, Bs, and Cs. Some students have to fail.

Given this, employers need to be doubly careful to protect their appraisal plans from managerial abuse. Office politics and managerial bias can taint ratings. To protect against bias claims, employers should therefore take several steps.[31] Appoint a review committee to review any employee's low ranking. Train raters to be objective. And consider using 360-degree appraisals (or at least multiple raters) in conjunction with the forced distribution approach.

Critical Incident Method

The **critical incident method** entails keeping a record of uncommonly good or undesirable examples of an employee's work-related behavior and reviewing it with the employee at predetermined times.

Employers often use the critical incident method to supplement a rating or ranking method. This helps ensure that the supervisor thinks about the subordinate's appraisal all during the year, because the incidents must be accumulated; therefore, the rating does not just reflect the employee's most recent performance. Keeping a running list of critical incidents should also provide concrete examples of what specifically your subordinates can do to eliminate any performance deficiencies, and provide opportunities for mid-year corrections if required.

Behaviorally Anchored Rating Scales

A behaviorally anchored rating scale (BARS) is an appraisal method that combines the benefits of both narrative critical incidents and quantitative ratings, by anchoring a quantified scale with specific narrative examples of good and poor performance.

Figure 6.5 is an example that shows the behaviorally anchored rating scale for the trait "salesmanship skills" used for armed forces recruiters. Note how the various performance levels are anchored with specific behavioral examples such as "When a prospect states an objection to being in the Navy, the recruiter ends the conversation."

Appraisal Forms in Practice

Effective appraisal forms typically merge several approaches. For example, Figure 6.2 (pages 198–199) merges a graphic rating scale with critical examples. This form also illustrates an important fact regarding appraisals. Even if the company does not use a full-blown behaviorally anchored rating scale approach, anchoring the scale with illustrative examples, as here, usually improves the appraisal scale's reliability and validity.

The Management by Objectives Method

The **management by objectives (MBO)** method requires the manager to set specific measurable goals with each employee and then periodically discuss the latter's progress toward these goals. The term *MBO* usually refers to an organization-wide goal-setting and appraisal program that consists of six steps:

1. *Set the organization's goals.* Establish an organizationwide plan for next year and set goals.
2. *Set departmental goals.* Department heads and their superiors jointly set goals for their departments.

FIGURE 6.5	Behaviorally Anchored Rating Scale

Salesmanship Skills

Skillfully persuading prospects to join the navy; using navy benefits and opportunities effectively to sell the navy; closing skills; adapting selling techniques appropriately to different prospects; effectively overcoming objections to joining the navy.

9 ⌐ A prospect stated he wanted the nuclear power program or he would not sign up. When he did not qualify, the recruiter did not give up; instead, he talked the young man into electronics by emphasizing the technical training he would
8 ─ receive.

The recruiter treats objections to joining the navy seriously; he works hard to counter the objections with relevant, positive arguments for a navy career.

7 ─

When talking to a high school senior, the recruiter mentions names of other seniors from that school who have already enlisted.

6 ─

When an applicant qualifies for only one program, the recruiter tries to convey to the applicant that it is a desirable program.

5 ─

When a prospect is deciding on which service to enlist in, the recruiter tries to sell the navy by describing navy life at sea and adventures in port.

4 ─

During an interview, the recruiter said to the applicant, "I'll try to get you the school you want, but frankly it probably won't be open for another three months, so why don't you take your second choice and leave now."

3 ─

The recruiter insisted on showing more brochures and films even though the applicant told him he wanted to sign up right now.

2 ─

When a prospect states an objection to being in the navy, the recruiter ends the conversation because he thinks the prospect must not be interested.

1 ⌐

Source: Berk, Ronald A. *Performance Assessment: Methods and Applications*, p. 103, Figure 3.2, "Salesmanship Skills." Copyright © 1986. Reproduced with permission of The Johns Hopkins University Press.

3. *Discuss departmental goals.* Department heads discuss the department's goals with all subordinates in the department and ask them to develop their own individual goals. In other words, how can each employee contribute to the department attaining its goals?
4. *Define expected results (set individual goals).* Department heads and their subordinates set short-term performance targets.

5. *Conduct performance reviews and measure the results.* Department heads compare the actual performance of each employee with expected results.

6. *Provide feedback.* Department heads hold periodic performance review meetings with subordinates to discuss and evaluate the subordinates' progress in achieving expected results.

Computerized and Web-Based Performance Appraisals

Appraisals today are most often Web-or PC-based. For example, Employee Appraiser (Austin-Hayne Corporation, San Mateo, California) presents a menu of more than a dozen evaluation dimensions, including dependability, initiative, communication, decision making, leadership, judgment, and planning and productivity. Within each dimension are various performance factors, again presented in menu form. For example, under "Communication" are separate factors for writing, verbal communication, receptivity to feedback and criticism, listening skills, ability to focus on the desired results, keeping others informed, and openness.

When the user clicks on a performance factor, he or she is presented with a relatively sophisticated version of a graphic rating scale. However, instead of numbers, Employee Appraiser uses behaviorally anchored examples. For example, for verbal communication there are six choices, ranging from "presents ideas clearly" to "lacks structure." After the manager picks the phrase that most accurately describes the worker, Employee Appraiser generates an appraisal with sample text.

PerformancePro.net from the HRN Management Group is an Internet-based performance review system. It helps the manager and his or her subordinates develop performance objectives for the employee, and to conduct the annual review.[32]

The Web site improvenow.com lets employees fill out a 60-question assessment online with or without their supervisor's approval, and then give the supervisor the team's feedback with an overall score.[33] Other appraisal packages include PeopleSoft HR management and SAP R/3 HR.[34] About a third of employers use online performance management tools to facilitate the process for at least some employees.[35]

Figure 6.6 presents an example of an online appraisal tool.

Electronic Performance Monitoring

Electronic performance monitoring (EPM) systems use computer network technology to allow managers access to their employees' computers and telephones. They thus allow "managers to determine at any moment throughout the day the pace at which employees are working, their degree of accuracy, log-in and log-off times, and even the amount of time spent on bathroom breaks."[36]

Research indicates that EPM can improve productivity in certain circumstances. For example, for more routine, less complex jobs, highly skilled and monitored subjects keyed in more data entries than did highly skilled unmonitored participants.[37] However, EPM can also backfire. In this same study, low-skilled but highly monitored participants did more poorly than did low-skilled, unmonitored participants. Empirical studies also provide strong evidence linking EPM with increased stress.[38]

FIGURE 6.6 Sample Web-Based Performance Appraisal Tool

Source: Performance Pro by HRN Management Group. www.hrnonline.com. Accessed January, 10, 2008.

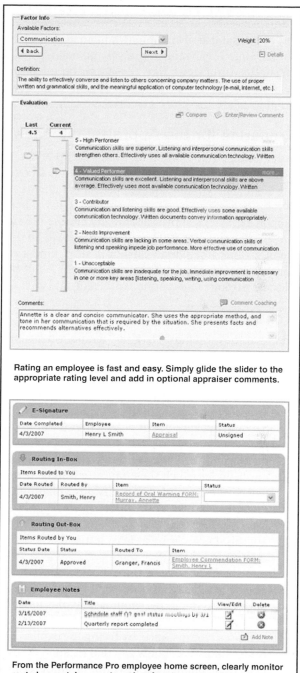

Rating an employee is fast and easy. Simply glide the slider to the appropriate rating level and add in optional appraiser comments.

From the Performance Pro employee home screen, clearly monitor routed or sent documents and performance notes. Also receive notification of documents requiring electronic signature.

THE APPRAISAL FEEDBACK INTERVIEW

An appraisal usually culminates in an **appraisal interview,** in which the supervisor and subordinate review the appraisal and make plans to remedy deficiencies and reinforce strengths. Interviews like these can be uncomfortable because few people like to receive—or give—negative feedback.[39] Adequate preparation and effective implementation are therefore essential.

Preparing for the Appraisal Interview

Adequate preparation involves three steps. First, give the subordinate at least a week's notice to review his or her work, and to read over his or her job description, analyze problems, and compile questions and comments. Next, study his or her job description, compare the employee's performance to his or her standards, and review the files of the person's previous appraisals. Finally, choose the right place for the interview and schedule enough time for it. The interview should be done in a private area where you won't be interrupted by phone calls or visitors. Find a mutually agreeable time for the interview and leave enough time—perhaps one-half-hour for lower-level personnel such as clerical workers and maintenance staff, and an hour or so for management employees.

Conducting the Interview

There are several things to keep in mind when actually conducting appraisal interviews.

- First, the interview's main aim is to reinforce satisfactory performance or to diagnose and improve unsatisfactory performance. One way to help do this is to be direct and specific. Talk in terms of objective work data, using examples such as absences, quality records, inspection reports, and tardiness.
- Second, get agreement before the subordinate leaves on how things will be improved and by when. An action plan showing steps and expected results can be useful. If a formal written warning is required, it should identify the standards under which the employee is judged, make it clear that the employee was aware of the standard, specify any violation of the standard, and show that the employee had an opportunity to correct his or her behavior.
- Third, ensure that the process is fair. Letting the employee participate in the appraisal process by at least letting his or her opinions be heard is therefore essential.[40]
- Fourth, the supervisor may have to deal with defensiveness. For example, when a person is accused of poor performance, the first reaction is usually denial. By denying the fault, the employee avoids having to question his or her own competence. Such defensiveness is normal. It is prudent not to attack the person's defenses (for instance, by trying to "explain someone to themselves" by saying things like, "You know the real reason you're using that excuse is that you can't bear to be blamed for anything"). Another tactic is to postpone action—for instance, by giving the person a 5-minute breather to cool down after being informed of unsatisfactory performance.
- Finally, remember that just as job candidates may try to influence recruiters by ingratiating themselves to them, subordinates can successfully influence their ratings by using ingratiation tactics like agreement during the appraisal interview.[41]

TOWARD MORE EFFECTIVE APPRAISALS

Recently a 60-year-old long-term NASA employee smuggled a revolver into the space center and, after speaking with his former supervisor for several minutes, said, "You're the one who's going to get me fired" and murdered him. The supervisor had apparently given the shooter a poor job review, and the person feared being fired.[42]

While such reactions are not the norm, few supervisory tasks are fraught with more peril than appraising subordinates' performance.[43] Employees in general tend to be overly optimistic about what their ratings are, and also know that their raises, career progress, and peace of mind may hinge on how they are rated. This alone should make it somewhat difficult to rate performance. Even more problematic, however, are the numerous structural problems (discussed below) that can cast doubt on just how fair the process is.[44]

Dealing with Common Appraisal Problems

Several chronic problems undermine appraisals and graphic rating scales in particular. Fortunately, as explained in this section, there are also ways to avoid or solve these problems.

Unclear Standards

The unclear standards appraisal problem means the appraisal scale is too open to interpretation. As in Figure 6.7, the rating scale may seem objective, but would probably result in unfair appraisals because the traits and degrees of merit are open to interpretation. For example, different supervisors would probably define "good" performance differently. The same is true of traits such as "quality of work." The best way to rectify this problem is to develop and include descriptive phrases that define each trait and degree of merit.

Halo Effect

The **halo effect** means that the rating of a subordinate on one trait (such as "gets along with others") influences the way you rate the person on other traits (such as "quantity of work"). Thus, an unfriendly employee might be rated unsatisfactory for all traits rather than just for the trait "gets along with others." Being aware of this problem is a major step toward avoiding it.

FIGURE 6.7	A Graphic Rating Scale with Unclear Standards			
	Excellent	Good	Fair	Poor
Quality of work				
Quantity of work				
Creativity				
Integrity				

Note: For example, what exactly is meant by "good," "quantity of work," and so forth?

Central Tendency

The **central tendency** problem refers to a tendency to rate all employees about average. For example, if the rating scale ranges from 1 to 7, a supervisor may tend to avoid the highs (6 and 7) and lows (1 and 2) and rate most of his or her employees between 3 and 5. Such restriction can distort the evaluations, making them less useful for promotion, salary, and counseling purposes. Ranking employees instead of using a graphic rating scale can eliminate this problem because all employees must be ranked and thus can't all be rated average.

Leniency or Strictness

Conversely, some supervisors tend to rate all their subordinates consistently high or low, a problem referred to as the strictness/leniency problem. Again, one solution is to insist on ranking subordinates, because that forces the supervisor to distinguish between high and low performers.

The appraisal you do may be less objective than you realize. One study focused on how personality influenced the peer evaluations students gave their peers. Raters who scored higher on "conscientiousness" tended to give their peers lower ratings; those scoring higher on "agreeableness" gave higher ratings.[45]

Bias

Indeed, appraisees' (and appraisers') personal characteristics (such as age, race, and sex) can affect their ratings, often quite apart from each ratee's actual performance. Appraisals often say more about the appraiser than about the appraised.[46] Studies suggest that "rater idiosyncratic biases account for the largest percentage of the observed variances in performance ratings."[47]

For example, one study found that raters penalized successful women for their success.[48] Earlier studies had found that raters tend to demean women's performance, particularly when they excel at what seems like male-typical tasks, and that's exactly what happened here. In this new study, the researchers told the subject-raters that they'd view information about someone who was one of 30 people who had just finished a year-long management training program. The researchers were careful to give the impression that the training program was mostly for male employees, for instance, by emphasizing that most of the trainees were men. The researchers found, "there are many things that lead an individual to be disliked, including obnoxious behavior, arrogance, stubborness, and pettiness, [but] it is only women, not men, for whom a unique propensity toward dislike is created by success in a nontraditional work situation."[49]

Table 6.1 summarizes the pros and cons of the most popular rating methods.

Legal Issues in Performance Appraisal

The performance appraisal affects raises, promotions, training opportunities, and other career-related HR actions. If the manager is inept or biased in the appraisals he or she does, how can the promotion decisions that stem from those appraisals be defended? In one case, a 36-year-old supervisor ranked a 62-year-old subordinate at the bottom of the department's rankings, and then terminated him. The U.S. Court of Appeals for the

TABLE 6.1	Important Similarities and Differences, and Advantages and Disadvantages of Appraisal Tools		
Tool	*Similarities/Differences*	*Advantages*	*Disadvantages*
Graphic rating scale	These are both absolute scales aimed at measuring an employee's *absolute* performance based on objective criteria as listed on the scales.	Simple to use; provides a quantitative rating for each employee.	Standards may be unclear; halo effect, central tendency, leniency, bias can also be problems.
BARS		Provides behavioral "anchors." BARS is very accurate.	Difficult to develop.
Alternation ranking	These are both methods for judging the *relative* performance of employees relative to each other, but still based on objective criteria.	Simple to use (but not as simple as graphic rating scales); avoids central tendency and other problems of rating scales.	Can cause disagreements among employees and may be unfair if all employees *are,* in fact, excellent.
Forced distribution method		End up with a predetermined number of people in each group.	Appraisal results depend on the adequacy of your original choice of cutoff points.
Critical incident method	These are both more subjective, narrative methods for appraising performance, generally based, however, on the employee's absolute performance.	Helps specify what is "right" and "wrong" about the employee's performance; forces supervisor to evaluate subordinates on an ongoing basis.	Difficult to rate or rank employees relative to one another.
MBO		Tied to jointly agreed-upon performance objectives.	Time consuming.

10th Circuit determined that the decision to terminate might have been influenced by the discriminatory motives of the younger boss.[50]

The employer's appraisal process must be legally defensible. You will find recommendations in the *HR in Practice* box for ensuring the legal defensibility of an employer's performance appraisal system.

MAKING SURE YOUR APPRAISALS ARE DEFENSIBLE

Steps to take to ensure your appraisals are legally defensible include:

- Develop appraisal criteria from documented job analyses. Specifically, a formal job analysis should be conducted as a prerequisite for the development of valid performance appraisal criteria.

- Communicate performance standards to employees in writing.

- Base appraisals on separate evaluations of each of the job's performance dimensions. Use of a single overall rating of performance or ranking of employees on a similar global standard is not acceptable to the courts.[51] Courts often characterize such systems as vague. Courts generally require that separate ratings along each performance dimension be combined through some formal weighting system to yield a summary score.

- Include an employee appeals process. Employees should have the opportunity to review and make comments, written or verbal, about their appraisals before they become final and should have a formal appeals process through which to appeal their ratings.

- One appraiser should never have absolute authority to determine a personnel action. This is one reason why multiple-raters procedures are becoming more popular.

- Document all information bearing on a personnel decision in writing. Three experts assert that "without exception, courts condemn informal performance evaluation practices that eschew documentation."[52]

- Train supervisors in the use of the appraisal instruments. If formal rater training is not possible, at least provide raters with written instructions for using the rating scale for evaluating personnel.[53]

PERFORMANCE AND CAREER MANAGEMENT

Once you've appraised their performance, it's often necessary to address career-related issues and to communicate these issues to the subordinates. We may define *career* as the "occupational positions a person has had over many years." **Career management** is a process for enabling employees to better understand and develop their career skills and interests, and to use these skills and interests most effectively both within the company and after they leave the firm. *Career development* is the lifelong series of activities (such as workshops) that contribute to a person's career exploration, establishment, success, and fulfillment. *Career planning* is the deliberate process through which someone becomes aware of personal skills, interests, knowledge, motivations, and other characteristics; acquires information about opportunities and choices; identifies career-related goals; and establishes action plans to attain specific goals.

Roles in Career Development

The employee, the manager, and the employer all play roles in planning, guiding, and developing the employee's career. However, the employee must always accept full responsibility for his or her own career development and career success. This is one task that no employer (or employee) should ever leave to a manager or employer. For the individual employee, the career planning process means matching individual strengths and weaknesses with occupational opportunities and threats. The person wants to pursue occupations, jobs, and a career that capitalizes on his or her interests, aptitudes, values, and skills. He or she also wants to choose occupations, jobs, and a career that makes sense in terms of projected future demand for various types of occupations.

The Employee's Role

Making decisions like these is the employee's responsibility. For example, an employee unhappy with his or her job can do several things short of changing occupations. Ask yourself what you're looking for in a job, and to what extent your current position is fulfilling your needs. Get rid of energy-draining, low-impact responsibilities. Enhance your networks, for instance, by joining a cross-functional team at work, discussing your career goals with role models, conducting informational interviews with people whose jobs interest you, or becoming a board member for a nonproft organization so you can interact with new people. If you are satisfied with your occupation and where you work, but not with your job as it is currently organized, reconfigure your job. For example, consider alternative work arrangements such as part-time work, flexible hours, or telecommuting; delegate or eliminate the job functions that you least prefer; and seek out a "stretch assignment" that will let you work on something that you find challenging.[54]

Mentoring

Studies also suggest that having a mentor—a senior person who can be a sounding board for your career questions and concerns, and can provide career-related guidance and assistance—can significantly enhance career satisfaction and success.[55] Suggestions for doing so include:

- Choose an appropriate potential mentor. The mentor should be able to remain objective to offer good career advice, so someone who doesn't have direct supervisory responsibility of you may be best.
- Make it easier for a potential mentor to agree to your request by clarifying what you expect in terms of time and advice.
- Have an agenda. Bring an agenda to your first mentoring meeting that lays out key issues and topics for discussion.
- Respect the mentor's time. Be selective about the work-related issues that you bring to the table—this person isn't there to be your personal management consultant.
  - Mandatory mentoring is OK. Studies suggest that mandatory participation is no less effective than voluntary participation in a mentoring program.[56]
  - Match mentors. On the other hand, having input into the mentor matching is important. Both the mentor and a protégé should have some impact into who the company matches them with.[57]
  - Provide training. Finally, provide participants with training aimed at enabling them to get the most out of the mentoring relationship.[58]

The accounting firm KPMG made an online mentoring program part of its "employer of choice" initiative, which also includes flexible work schedules and community volunteer opportunities with pay and benefits.[59]

The Employer's Role in Career Management

The employer's career development tasks depend on how long the employee has been with the firm.

Before hiring, *realistic job interviews* can help prospective employees more accurately gauge whether the job is indeed for them, and particularly whether a job's demands are a good fit with a candidate's skills and interests.

Especially for recent college graduates, the first job can be crucial for building confidence and a more realistic picture of what he or she can and cannot do: Providing *challenging first jobs* (rather than relegating new employees to "jobs where they can't do any harm") and having an experienced mentor who can help the person learn the ropes are important. Some refer to this as preventing reality shock, a phenomenon that occurs when a new employee's high expectations and enthusiasm confront the reality of a boring, unchallenging job.

After the person has been on the job for a while, an employer can take steps to contribute in a positive way to the employee's career. *Career-oriented appraisals*—in which the manager is trained not just to appraise the employee but also to match the person's strengths and weaknesses with a feasible career path and required development work—is one important step. Similarly, providing periodic *job rotation* can help the person develop a more realistic picture of what he or she is (and is not) good at, and thus the sort of future career moves that might be best. Firms can also provide mentoring opportunities.

Innovative Corporate Career Development Initiatives

Employers' corporate career development initiatives may also include innovative programs like these:[60]

1. *Provide each employee with an individual career development budget.* He or she can use this budget for learning about career options and personal development.[61]
2. *Offer on-site or online career centers.* These might include an on- or offline library of career development materials, career workshops, workshops on related topics (such as time management), and also provide individual career coaches for career guidance.
3. *Encourage role reversal.* Have employees temporarily work in different positions in order to develop a better appreciation of their occupational strengths and weaknesses.
4. *Establish a "corporate campus."* Make career and development courses and programs available, perhaps through partnerships with local colleges and consultants.
5. *Help organize "career success teams."* These are small groups of employees from the same or different departments who meet periodically to network and support one another in achieving their goals.
6. *Provide career coaches.* For example, Allmerica Financial Corp. hired 20 career development coaches to assist its 850-person information technology staff. This coaching program was part of a broader organizational change program to centralize information technology teams. The coaches help individual IT employees identify their development needs and obtain the training, professional development, and networking opportunities that they need to satisfy those needs.[62]
7. *Provide career planning workshops.* A *career planning workshop* is a "planned learning event in which participants are expected to be actively involved,

completing career planning exercises and inventories and participating in career skills practice sessions.[63]

8. *Computerized on- and offline programs are available for improving the organizational career planning process.* For example, WorkforceVision from Criterion, Inc., in Irving, Texas, helps the company analyze an employee's training needs. Clicking on the employee's name launches his or her work history, competencies, career path, and other information. For each competency (such as leadership and customer focus), a bar chart graphically shows a "gap analysis" highlighting the person's strengths and weaknesses. The firm can then organize development activities around the person's needs.[64]

9. *First USA Bank has what it calls the Opportunity Knocks program.* Its purpose is to help employees crystallize their career goals and achieve them within the company. In addition to career training and follow-up support, First USA Bank has also outfitted special career development facilities at its worksites that employees can use on company time. These contain materials such as career assessment and planning tools.[65]

10. *Provide Web support.* For example, Alyeska, the company that manages the trans-Alaska pipeline, has a user-friendly portal that lets employees "see their full training history, development plans, and upcoming deadlines; register for courses; or do career planning—usually without having to ask for help.[66] At the same time, "managers can get a quick picture of the training needs for a particular group or see all the employees who have a specific qualification."[67]

Gender Issues in Career Development

Women and men face different challenges as they advance through their careers. In one study, promoted women had to receive higher performance ratings than promoted men to get promoted, "suggesting that women were held to stricter standards for promotion."[68] Women report greater barriers (such as being excluded from informal networks) than do men, and more difficulty getting developmental assignments and geographic mobility opportunities. Women have to be more proactive to get such assignments. Because developmental experiences like these are so important, "organizations that are interested in helping female managers advance should focus on breaking down barriers that interfere with women's access to developmental experiences."[69]

Minority Women

In these matters, minority women may be particularly at risk. Women of color hold only a small percentage of professional and managerial private-sector positions. The minority women in one survey reported that the main barriers to advancement included not having an influential mentor (47%), lack of informal networking with influential colleagues (40%), lack of company role models for members of the same racial or ethnic group (29%), and a lack of high-visibility assignments (28%).[70]

Adding to the problem is the fact that some corporate career development programs may actually be inconsistent with the needs of minority and nonminority women. For example, many programs assume that the workplace plays a central role in people's lives, but family needs may well play the major role in many women's (and men's) lives. Similarly, such programs may assume that career paths are orderly, sequential, and continuous; yet the need to stop working for a time to attend to family needs may well punctuate the career paths of many people of color and women (and perhaps men).[71] And, in any case, one study concluded that three organizational career development activities—fast-track programs, individual career counseling, and career planning workshops—were less available to women than to men.[72] Many refer to this combination of subtle and not-so-subtle barriers to women's career progress as the *glass ceiling.*

Managing Promotions and Transfers

Promotions are, of course, one of the more significant HR decisions to result from the performance appraisal. In developing promotion policies, employers need to address several issues.

One issue concerns seniority versus competence. Competence is normally the basis for promotions, although in many organizations civil service or union requirements and similar constraints still give an edge to more senior applicants.

Furthermore, if competence is to be the basis for promotion, how should we measure it? Defining past performance is usually straightforward. Managers use performance appraisals for this. However, sizing up how even a high-performing employee will do in a new, more challenging job is not so easy. Innumerable great salespeople turn out to be awful managers, for instance. Many employers therefore use formal selection devices like tests and assessment centers to supplement the performance appraisals.

With firms downsizing and flattening their organizations, "promotions" today often mean lateral moves or transfers. In such situations, the promotional aspect is not so much a higher level job or more pay, but the opportunity to assume new, same-level responsibilities (such as a salesperson moving into HR) or increased, enriched decision-making responsibilities within the same job.

A *transfer* is a move from one job to another, usually with no change in salary or grade. Employees may seek transfers not just for advancement but also for noncareer reasons, such as better hours, location of work, and so on.

Retirement

For many employees, years of appraisals and career development end with retirement.

Retirement planning is now a significant issue for employers. In the United States, the number of 25- to 34-year-olds is growing relatively slowly, and the number of 35- to 44-year-olds is declining. With many older employees moving towards traditional retirement age, employers face a labor shortage. Many have wisely chosen to fill their staffing needs in part with current or soon-to-be retirees: "in the past few years, companies have been so focused on downsizing to contain costs that they largely neglected a looming threat to their competitiveness. . . . A severe shortage of talented workers."[73]

Therefore, "retirement planning" is no longer just for helping current employees slip into retirement.[74] It should also enable the employer to retain, in some capacity, the skills and brain power of those who would normally retire and leave the firm. Fortuitously, 78% of employees in one survey said they expect to continue working in some capacity after normal retirement age (64% said they want to do so part-time). Only about a third said they plan to continue work for financial reasons; about 43% said they just wanted to remain active.[75]

Recruiting and/or retaining retirees requires several things. In general, human resource policies tend to discourage older workers' employment. Suggestions include:

- **Create a culture that honors experience.** At some employers, the work environment and human resource practices are biased against older workers. Changing this culture, and making the workplace more attractive to those of retirement age, requires concrete actions. For example, knowing that traditional recruiting channels such as want ads and help-wanted signs might not attract older workers, the CVS pharmacy chain works through the National Council on Aging, city agencies, and community organizations to find new employees. They've also made it clear to retirees with their policies that they welcome older workers: "I'm too young to retire. [CVS] is willing to hire older people. They don't look at your age but your experience" said one dedicated older worker.[76]

- **Modify selection procedures.** Other employers modify testing procedures. For example, one British bank stopped using psychometric tests, replacing them with role-playing exercises to gauge how candidates deal with customers.

- **Offer flexible work.** Companies, "need to design jobs such that staying on is more attractive than leaving." One of the simplest ways to do this is through flexible work, specifically, making where one works (as with telecommuting) and when the work is performed flexible.[77]

- **Phased retirement.** Many employers are implementing phased retirement programs. These combine reduced work hours, job change, reduced responsibilities, and sometimes transitioning to independent contractor status, so as to extend the employee's participation in the company beyond what would normally be his or her retirement age.

Employers are well advised to conduct the necessary numerical analyses for dealing with the prospect of retirements. This assessment should include a demographic analysis (including a census of the company's employees), a determination of the average retirement age for the company's employees, and a review of how retirement is going to impact the employer's health care and pension benefits. The employer can then determine the extent of the "retirement problem," and take fact-based steps to address it.[78]

Technology and Career Planning

Employers can use various software programs for improving the career planning process. For example, Workforce Vision from Criterion, Inc., in Irving, Texas, helps the company analyze an employee's training needs. The supervisor and employee can use it to organize developmental activities around the person's needs.[79]

Many people use the Web to help analyze and advance their careers. Well-known Web-based career assessment tools include www.self-directed-search.com, www.review.com/birkman, www.keirsey.com, and www.careerdiscovery.com. Some firms have created their own internal career development Web sites. For example, Unisys's Web-based career center helps its employees identify their strengths and improve their career understanding and progress.[80]

A Final Word

In a sense, *performance management* starts at the end and works backward. Top management asks, What is our strategy and what do we want to achieve? Each manager in the chain of command then asks, What does this mean for the goals we set for our employees, and for how we train, appraise, promote, and reward them? The performance appraisal is just one link in that process. Poor performance does not always reflect low motivation. It may suggest inadequate training or ineffective goals, for instance. This is why managing performance requires looking beyond just the appraisal. It requires taking an integrated, performance management approach to improving performance. It means continuously ensuring that employees are working toward organizational goals, and involves defining those goals, developing the employee's skills, appraising the person's goal-directed behavior, and then rewarding him or her.

Improving Productivity through HRIS

Basically, performance management merges the best of traditional management by objectives programs, plus appraisals, plus personal development. Employees get personal goals that make sense in terms of their units' and employer's goals. Then they are appraised based on achieving those goals. Then they prepare and pursue personal development plans that make sense in terms of their appraised strengths and weaknesses.

Doing this, particularly for larger companies, usually requires Web-based performance management systems. For example, Seagate Technology uses "Enterprise Suite" for managing the performance of its 39,000 employees.[81] Early in Seagate's first fiscal quarter, employees enter the system and set goals and development plans for themselves that make sense in terms of Seagate's corporate objectives. Employees update their plans quarterly, and then do self-evaluations at the end of the year, with follow-up reviews by their supervisors.

A Web-based system like this has several advantages over less automated systems. For one, it helps each employee see where his or her goals fit in the overall view of what the company is trying to accomplish. Specifically, it enables individual employees to set their goals based on a "cascading goals" system: With Enterprise Suite, they can easily see the company's goals, their unit's goals, and their supervisor's goals. This makes it easier for employees to set goals that make sense in terms of Seagate's goals. And, of course, a system like this makes it easier for Seagate's widely disbursed employees to fill in and update their goals, plans, and appraisals whenever and wherever they need to.

Review

Summary

1. Performance appraisal means evaluating an employee's current or past performance relative to his or her performance standards. Performance management is the process through which companies ensure that employees are working toward organizational goals, and includes defining goals, developing skills, appraising performance, and rewarding the employee.

2. Managers appraise their subordinates' performance to obtain input on which promotion and salary raise decisions can be made, to develop plans for correcting performance deficiencies, and for career planning purposes. Supervisory ratings are still at the heart of most appraisal processes.

3. The appraisal is generally conducted using one or more popular appraisal methods or

tools. These include graphic rating scales, alternation ranking, paired comparison, forced distribution, critical incidents, behaviorally anchored rating scales, MBO, computerized performance appraisals, and electronic performance monitoring.

4. An appraisal typically culminates in an appraisal interview. Adequate preparation, including giving the subordinate notice, reviewing his or her job description and past performance, choosing the right place for the interview, and leaving enough time for it are essential. In conducting the interview, the aim is to reinforce satisfactory performance or to diagnose and improve unsatisfactory performance. A concrete analysis of objective work data and development of an action plan are therefore advisable. Employee defensiveness is normal and needs to be dealt with.

5. The appraisal process can be improved, first, by eliminating chronic problems that often undermine appraisals and graphic rating scales in particular. These common problems include unclear standards, halo effect, central tendency, leniency or strictness, and bias.

6. Care should also be taken to ensure that the performance appraisal is legally defensible. For example, appraisal criteria should be based on documented job analyses, employees should receive performance standards in writing, and multiple performance dimensions should be rated.

7. Career management is the process for enabling employees to better understand and develop their career skills and interests, and to use these most effectively, both within the company and after they leave the firm.

Key Terms

- performance appraisal
- performance management
- peer appraisal
- upward feedback
- graphic rating scale
- alternation ranking method
- paired comparison method
- forced distribution method
- critical incident method
- management by objectives (MBO)
- appraisal interview
- halo effect
- central tendency
- career management

Discussion Questions and Exercises

1. Discuss the pros and cons of at least four performance appraisal tools.
2. Working individually or in groups, develop a graphic rating scale for the following jobs: secretary, engineer, and directory assistance operator.
3. Working individually or in groups, evaluate the rating scale in Figure 6.1. Discuss ways to improve it.
4. Explain how you would use the alternation ranking method, the paired comparison method, and the forced distribution method.
5. Working individually or in groups, develop a set of critical incidents covering the classroom performance of one of your instructors.
6. Explain the problems to be avoided in appraising performance.
7. Discuss the pros and cons of using various potential raters to appraise an employee's performance.
8. Explain how to conduct an appraisal interview.

APPLICATION EXERCISES

Case Incident   *Back with a Vengeance*

Conducting an effective appraisal is always important. However, an appraisal can have life-and-death implications when you're dealing with unstable employees, particularly those who must be dismissed. An employee of a U.S. Postal Service station was terminated. The employee came back and shot and killed several managers who had been instrumental in the former employee's dismissal. It turned out this person had a history as a troublemaker and that many clues regarding his unstable nature over many years had been ignored. ∎

QUESTIONS

1. Could a company with an effective appraisal process have missed so many signals of instability over several years? Why? Why not?
2. What safeguards would you build into your appraisal process to avoid missing such potentially tragic signs of instability and danger?
3. What would you do if confronted during an appraisal interview by someone who began making threats regarding the use of firearms?

Continuing Case

LearnInMotion.com: The Performance Appraisal

Jennifer and Mel disagree over the importance of having performance appraisals. Mel says it's quite clear whether any particular LearnInMotion employee is doing his or her job. It's obvious, for instance, if the salespeople are selling, if the Web designer is designing, if the Web surfer is surfing, and if the content management people are managing to get the customers' content up on the Web site in a timely fashion. Mel's position, like that of many small-business managers, is that "we have 1,000 higher-priority things to attend to" such as boosting sales and creating the calendar. And in any case, he says, the employees already get plenty of day-to-day feedback from him or Jennifer regarding what they're doing right and what they're doing wrong.

This informal feedback notwithstanding, Jennifer believes that a more formal appraisal approach is required. For one thing, they're approaching the end of the 90-day introductory period for many of these employees, and the owners need to make decisions about whether

they should go or stay. And from a practical point of view, Jennifer believes that sitting down and providing formal, written feedback is more likely to reinforce what employees are doing right, and to get them to modify what they may be doing wrong. "Maybe this is one reason we're not getting enough sales," she says. They've been debating this for about an hour. Now, they want you, their management consultants, to advise them on what to do. Here's what they want you to do for them. ∎

QUESTIONS AND ASSIGNMENTS

1. Is Jennifer right about the need to evaluate the workers formally? Why or why not? If you think she's right, how do you counter Mel's arguments?
2. Develop a performance appraisal method for the salespeople, or Web designer, or Web surfer. Please make sure to include any form you want the owners to use.

EXPERIENTIAL EXERCISE

Appraising an Instructor

Purpose: The purpose of this exercise is to give you practice in developing and using a performance appraisal form.

Required Understanding: You are going to develop a performance appraisal form for an instructor and should therefore be thoroughly familiar with the discussion of performance appraisals in this chapter.

How to Set Up the Exercise/Instructions: Divide the class into groups of four or five students.

1. First, based on what you now know about performance appraisals, do you think Figure 6.1 is an effective scale for appraising instructors? Why or why not?

2. Next, your group should develop its own tool for appraising the performance of an instructor. Decide which of the appraisal tools (graphic rating scales, alternation ranking, and so on) you are going to use, and then design the instrument itself.

3. Next, have a spokesperson from each group put his or her group's appraisal tool on the board. How similar are the tools? Do they all measure about the same factors? Which factor appears most often? Which do you think is the most effective tool on the board? Can you think of any way of combining the best points of several of the tools into a new performance appraisal tool? ∎

Endnotes

1. D. Bradford Neary, "Creating a Company-Wide, Online, Performance Management System: A Case Study at TRW Inc.," *Human Resource Management* 41, no. 4 (Winter 2002): 495.

2. Peter Glendinning, "Performance Management: Pariah or Messiah," *Public Personnel Management* 31, no. 2 (Summer 2002): 161–178. See also Herman Aguinis, *Performance Management* (Upper Saddle River, NJ 2007): 2.

3. Howard Risher, "Getting Serious about Performance Management," *Compensation and Benefits Review* (November/December 2003): 19.

4. D. Bradford Neary, op. cit., 495.

5. Vesa Suutari and Marja Tahbanainen, "The Antecedents of Performance Management among Finnish Expatriates," *Journal of Human Resource Management* 13, no. 1 (February 2002): 53–75.

6. See, for example, Doug Cederblom and Dan Pemerl, "From Performance Appraisal to Performance Management: One Agency's Experience," *Personnel Management* 31, no. 2 (Summer 2002): 131–140.

7. "Get SMART About Setting Goals," *Asia Africa Intelligence Wire* (May 22, 2005).

8. See, for example, Robert Renn, "Further Examination of the Measurement of Properties of Leifer & McGannon's 1996 Goal Acceptance and Goal Commitment Scales," *Journal of Occupational and Organizational Psychology* (March 1999): 107–114.

9. Experts debate the pros and cons of tying appraisals to pay decisions. One side argues that doing so distorts the appraisals. A recent study concludes the opposite. Based on an analysis of surveys from over 24,000 employees in more than 6,000 workplaces in Canada, the researchers concluded: (1) linking the employees' pay to their performance appraisals contributed to improved pay satisfaction; (2) even when appraisals are not directly linked to pay, they apparently contributed to pay satisfaction, "probably through mechanisms related to perceived organizational justice"; and (3) whether or

not the employees received performance pay, "individuals who do not receive performance appraisals are significantly less satisfied with their pay." Mary Jo Ducharme et al., "Exploring the Links between Performance Appraisals and Pay Satisfaction," *Compensation and Benefits Review* (September/October 2005): 46–52. See also Robert Morgan, "Making the Most of Performance Management Systems," *Compensation and Benefits Review* (September/October 2006): 22–27.

10. Allan Locher and Kenneth Teel, "Appraisal Trends," *Personnel Journal* (September 1988): 139–145. The survey included 324 responding companies. See also Gail Dutton, "Making Reviews More Efficient and Fair," *Workforce* (April 2001): 76–80; Carla Joinson, "Making Sure Employees Measure Up," *HR Magazine* (March 2001): 36–41.

11. Vanessa Druskat and Steven Wolf, "Effects and Timing of Developmental Peer Appraisals in Self-Managing Work-Groups," *Journal of Applied Psychology* 84, no. 1 (1999): 58–74.

12. Such findings may be culturally related. One study compared self and supervisor ratings in "other-oriented" cultures (as in Asia, where values tend to emphasize teams). It found that self and supervisor ratings were related. M. Audrey Korsgaard et al., "The Effect of Other Orientation on Self: Supervisor Rating Agreement," *Journal of Organizational Behavior* 25, no. 7 (November 2004): 873–891.

13. Forest Jourden and Chip Heath, "The Evaluation Gap in Performance Perceptions: Illusory Perceptions of Groups and Individuals," *Journal of Applied Psychology* 81, no. 4 (August 1996): 369–379. See also, Sheri Ostroff, "Understanding Self-Other Agreement: A Look at Rater and Ratee Characteristics, Context, and Outcomes," *Personnel Psychology* 57, no. 2 (Summer 2004): 333–375.

14. Paul Atkins and Robert Wood, "Self versus Others Ratings as Predictors of Assessment Center Ratings: Validation Evidence for 360 Degree Feedback Programs," *Personnel Psychology* 55, no. 4 (Winter 2002): 871–904.

15. Manuel London and Arthur Wohlers, "Agreement Between Subordinate and Self-Ratings in Upward Feedback," *Personnel Psychology* 44 (1991): 375–390; See also Todd Maurer et al., "Peer and Subordinate Performance Appraisal Measurement Equivalents," *Journal of Applied Psychology* 83, no. 5 (1998): 693–702, and Herman Aguinis, *Performance Management* (Upper Saddle River, NJ: Pearson, 2007): 130.

16. David Antonioni, "The Effects of Feedback Accountability on Upward Appraisal Ratings," *Personnel Psychology* 47 (1994): 349–355.

17. Alan Walker and James Smither, "A Five-Year Study of Upward Feedback: What Managers Do with Their Results Matters," *Personnel Psychology* 52 (1999): 393–423.

18. Kenneth Nowack, "360-Degree Feedback: The Whole Story," *Training and Development* (January 1993): 69; Matthew Budman, "The Rating Game," *Across the Board* 31, no. 2 (February 1994): 35–38. See also "360-Degree Feedback on the Rise Survey Finds," *BNA Bulletin to Management* (January 23, 1997): 31. See also Leanne Atwater, et al., "Multisource Feedback: Lessons Learned and Implications for Practice," *Human Resource Management* 46, no. 2 (Summer 2007): 285.

19. James Smither et al., "Does Performance Improve Following Multi-Score Feedback? A Theoretical Model, Meta Analysis, and Review of Empirical Findings," *Personnel Psychology* 58, (2005): 33–36. See also Fred Luthans and Suzanne Peterson, "360 Degree Feedback with Systematic Coaching: Empirical Analysis Suggests a Winning Combination," *Human Resource Management* 42, no. 3 (Fall 2003): 243–255.

20. Herman Aguinis, *Performance Management* (Upper Saddle River, NJ: Pearson, 2007): 179.

21. Christine Hagan et al., "Predicting Assessment Center Performance with 360 Degree, Top-Down, and Customer-Based Competency Assessments," *Human Resource Management* 45, no. 3 (Fall 2006): 357–390.

22. Bruce Pfau, "Does a 360-Degree Feedback Negatively Affect the Company Performance?" *HR Magazine* (June 2002): 55–59.

23. Jim Meade, "Visual 360: A Performance Appraisal System That's 'Fun,'" *HR Magazine* (July 1999): 118–119.

24. Scott Winer, "The Dark Side of 360-Degree Feedback," *Training and Development* (September 2002): 37–42.

25. Jeffrey Facteau and S. Bartholomew Craig, "Performance Appraisal Ratings from Different Rating Scores," *Journal of Applied Psychology* 86, no. 2 (2001): 215–227.

26. See also Kevin Murphy et al., "Raters Who Pursue Different Goals Give Different Ratings," *Journal of Applied Psychology* 89, no. 1 (2004): 158–164.

27. Steven Scullen et al., "Forced Distribution Rating Systems and the Improvement of Workforce Potential: A Baseline Simulation," *Personnel Psychology* 58 (2005): 1, and Jena McGregor, "The Struggle to Measure Performance," *BusinessWeek* (January 9, 2006): 26.

28. Del Jones, "More Firms Cut Workers Ranked at Bottom to Make Way for Talent," *USA Today* (May 30, 2001): B1; "Straight Talk about Grading on a Curve," *BNA Bulletin to Management* (November 1, 2001): 351; Steve Bates, "Forced Ranking," *HR Magazine* (June 2003): 63–68.

29. "Survey Says Problems with Forced Ranking Include Lower Morale and Costly Turnover," *BNA Bulletin to Management* (September 16, 2004): 297.

30. Steve Bates, "Forced Ranking: Why Grading Employees on a Scale Relative to Each Other Forces a Hard Look at Finding Keepers, Losers May Become Weepers," *HR Magazine* 48, no. 6 (June 2003): 62.

31. "Straight Talk about Grading Employees on a Curve," *BNA Bulletin to Management* (November 1, 2001): 351.

32. Gary Meyer, "Performance Reviews Made Easy, Paperless," *HR Magazine* (October 2000): 181–184. See also www.employeeappraiser.com/index.php, accessed January 10, 2008.

33. Ann Harrington, "Workers of the World, Rate Your Boss!" *Fortune* 16 (2000): 340–342.

34. "Appraisal Puts 15 Leading HRIS's to the Test," *BNA Bulletin to Management* (October 25, 2000): 340.

35. "Software Simplifies Performance Reviews, but Is It Affecting Employee Development," *BNA Bulletin to Management* (March 27, 2003): 97.

36. John Aiello and Kathryn Kolb, "Electronic Performance Monitoring and Social Context: Impact on Productivity and Stress," *Journal of Applied Psychology* 80, no. 3 (1995): 339. See also Stoney Alder and Maureen Ambrose, "Towards Understanding Fairness Judgments Associated with Computer Performance Monitoring: An Integration of the Feedback, Justice, and Monitoring Research," *Human Resource Management Review* 15, no. 1 (March 2005): 43–67.

37. Aiello and Kolb, "Electronic Performance Monitoring and Social Context," 339–353.

38. See, for example, John Aiello and Y. Shao, "Computerized Performance Monitoring," paper presented at the Seventh Conference of the Society for Industrial and Organizational Psychology, Montreal, Quebec, Canada, May 1992.

39. Donald Fedor and Charles Parsons, "What Is Effective Performance Feedback?" in Gerald Ferris and M. Ronald Buckley, *Human Resources Management,* 3rd ed. (Upper Saddle River, NJ: Prentice Hall, 1996), pp. 265–270. See also Herman Aguinis, *Performance Management* (Upper Saddle River, NJ: Pearson 2007): 196–219.

40. Brian Cawley et al., "Participation in the Performance Appraisal Process and Employee Reactions: A Meta-Analytic Review of Field Investigations," *Journal of Applied Psychology* 83, no. 4 (1998): 615–633.

41. Lynne McFarland et al., "Impression Management's Use and Effectiveness Across Assessment Methods," *Journal of Management* 29, no. 5 (2003): 641–661.

42. Rasha Madkour, "NASA Shooting Suspect Received Poor Job Review and Feared Being Fired, Police Say," Associated Press news, April 21, 2007.

43. See, for example, "Communicating Beyond the Ratings Can Be Difficult," *Workforce, Workforce Management* (April 24, 2006): 35.

44. See, for example, Manuel London, Edward Mone and John C. Scott, "The Contributions of Psychological Research to HRM: Performance Management and Assessment—Methods for Improved Rater Accuracy and Employee Goal Setting," *Human Resource Management* 43, no. 4 (Winter 2004): 319–336.

45. H. John Bernardin et al., "Conscientious-ness and Agreeableness as Predictors of Rating Leniency," *Journal of Applied Psychology* 85, no. 2 (2000): 232–234.

46. Clinton Wingrove, "Developing a New Blend of Process and Technology in the New Era of Performance Management," *Compensation and Benefits Review* (January/February 2003): 25–30.

47. Gary Gregures et al., "A Field Study of the Effects of Rating Purpose on the Quality of Multiscore Ratings," *Personnel Psychology* 56 (2003): 1–21.

48. Madeleine Heilman et al., "Penalties for Success: Reactions to Women Who Succeed at Male Gender Type Tasks," *Journal of Applied Psychology* 89, no. 3 (2004): 416–427.

49. Ibid., 426. Another study found that successful female managers didn't usually suffer such a fate when those rating them saw them as supportive, caring, and sensitive to their needs. Madeleine Heilmann and Tyler Okimoto, "Why Are Women Penalized for Success at Male Tasks?: The Implied Communality Deficit," *Journal of Applied Psychology*, 92, no. 1 (2007): 81–92.

50. "Flawed Ranking System Revives Workers Bias Claim," *BNA Bulletin to Management* (June 28, 2005): 206.

51. James Austin, Peter Villanova, and Hugh Hindman, "Legal Requirements and Technical Guidelines Involved in Implementing Performance Appraisal Systems," in Gerald Ferris and M. Ronald Buckley, *Human Resources Management,* 3rd ed. (Upper Saddle River, NJ: Prentice Hall, 1996), pp. 271–288.

52. Ibid., 282.

53. But beware: one problem with training raters to avoid rating errors is that, sometimes, what appears to be an error—such as leniency—isn't an error at all, as when all subordinates really are superior performers. Manuel London, Edward Mone, and John Scott, "Performance Management and Assessment: Methods for Improved Rater Accuracy and Employee Goal Setting," *Human Resource Management* 43, no. 4 (Winter 2004): 319–336.

54. Deb Koen, "Revitalize Your Career," *Training and Development* (January 2003): 59–60.

55. Michael Doody, "A Mentor Is a Key to Career Success," *Health-Care Financial Management* 57, no. 2 (February 2003): 92–94.

56. Tammy Allen et al., "The Relationship between Formal Mentoring Program Characteristics and Perceived Program Effectiveness," *Personnel Psychology* 59 (2006) 125–153.

57. Tammy Allen et al., "The Relationship between Formal Mentoring Program Characteristics and Perceived Program Effectiveness," *Personnel Psychology* 59 (2006) 125–153.

58. Ibid.

59. Donna Owens, "Virtual Mentoring," *HR Magazine* (March 2006): 15–17.

60. See also Yehuda Baruch, "Career Development in Organizations and Beyond: Balancing Traditional and Contemporary Viewpoints," *Human Resource Management Review* 16 (2006): 131.

61. Barbara Greene and Liana Knudsen, "Competitive Employers Make Career Development Programs a Priority," *San Antonio Business Journal* 15, no. 6 (July 20, 2001): 27.

62. Julekha Dash, "Coaching to Aid IT Careers, Retention," *Computerworld* (March 20, 2000): 52.

63. Fred Otte and Peggy Hutcheson, *Helping Employees Manage Careers* (Upper Saddle River, NJ: Prentice Hall, 1992): 143.

64. Jim Meade, "Boost Careers and Succession Planning," *HR Magazine* (October 2000): 175–178.

65. Patrick Kiger, "First USA Bank, Promotions and Job Satisfaction," *Workforce* (March 2001): 54–56.

66. Tim Harvey, "Enterprise Training System is Trans Alaska Pipelines's Latest Safety Innovation," *Pipeline and Gas Journal* 229, no. 12 (December 2002): 28–32.

67. Ibid.

68. Karen Lyness and Madeline Heilman, "When Fit Is Fundamental: Performance Evaluations and Promotions of Upper-Level Female and Male Managers," *Journal of Applied Psychology* 91, no. 4 (2006): 777–775.

69. Karen Lyness and Donna Thompson, "Climbing the Corporate Ladder: Do Female and Male Executives Follow the Same Route?" *Journal of Applied Psychology* 85, no. 1 (2000): 86–101.

70. "Minority Women Surveyed on Career Growth Factors," *Community Banker* 9, no. 3 (March 2000): 44.

71. In Ellen Cook et al., "Career Development of Women of Color and White Women: Assumptions, Conceptualization, and Interventions from an Ecological Perspective," *Career Development Quarterly* 50, no. 4 (June 2002): 291–306.

72. Jan Selmer and Alicia Leung, "Are Corporate Career Development Activities Less Available to Female than to Male Expatriates?" *Journal of Business Ethics* (March 2003): 125–137.

73. Ken Dychtwald et al., "It's Time to Retire Retirement," *Harvard Business Review* (March 2004): 49.

74. See for example, Matt Bolch, "Bidding Adieu," *HR Magazine* (June 2006): 123–127.

75. "Employees Plan to Work Past Retirement, but not Necessarily for Financial Reasons," *BNA Bulletin to Management* (February 19, 2004): 57–58. See also Mo Wang, "Profiling Retirees in the Retirement Transition and Adjustment Process: Examining the Longitudinal Change Patterns of Retirees' Psychological Well-Being," *Journal of Applied Psychology* 92, no. 2 (2007): 455–474.

76. Dychtwald et al., op. cit., 52.

77. Dychtwald et al., op. cit., 52.

78. Luis Flcites and Lou Valentino, "The Case for Phased Retirement," *Compensation & Benefits Review* (March and/April 2007): 42–46.

79. Jim Meade, "Boost Careers and Succession Planning," *HR Magazine* (October 2000): 175–178.

80. Gina Imperato, "Get Your Career in Sight," *Fast Company* (March 2000): 318–334.

81. Drew Robb, "Building a Better Workforce," *HR Magazine* (October 2004): 87–94.

7 COMPENSATING EMPLOYEES

- What Determines How Much You Pay?
- How Employers Establish Pay Rates
- Current Trends in Compensation
- Incentive Plans
- Employee Benefits

When you finish studying this chapter, you should be able to:

■ Explain *each of the five basic steps in establishing pay rates.*

■ Discuss *four basic factors determining pay rates.*

■ Compare *and* contrast *piecework and team or group incentive plans.*

■ List *and* describe *each of the basic benefits most employers might be expected to offer.*

INTRODUCTION

The retail grocery business traditionally has low profit margins and is highly competitive. So when Wal-Mart moves into a grocery's area, the knee-jerk reaction is usually to cut costs, particularly wage rates and benefits. For example, several years ago, Safeway Stores cut employee health-care benefits, precipitating a strike by its California employees. As Wegman's Food Markets Inc. adds more stores and increasingly confronts competition from Wal-Mart, its management similarly needs to decide what to do about pay. Should they cut pay-related expenses to better compete based on cost, or pursue a different compensation policy?[1]

Employee compensation refers to all forms of pay or rewards going to employees and arising from their employment. It has two main components: *direct* *financial payments* (in the form of wages, salaries, incentives, commissions, and bonuses) and *indirect payments* (in the form of financial benefits like employer-paid insurance and vacations). We'll discuss both in this chapter.

WHAT DETERMINES HOW MUCH YOU PAY?

Four basic factors determine what people are paid: legal, union, policy, and equity factors. We'll look at each, starting with legal considerations.

Some Important Compensation Laws

Numerous laws stipulate what employers can or must pay in terms of minimum wages, overtime rates, and benefits. For example:[2]

1938 Fair Labor Standards Act

The **Fair Labor Standards Act,** passed in 1938 and since amended many times, contains minimum wage, maximum hours, overtime pay, equal pay, record-keeping, and child labor provisions covering most U.S. workers—virtually anyone engaged in producing or selling goods for interstate and foreign commerce.

One well-known provision governs overtime pay. It states that employers must pay overtime at a rate of at least one and a half times normal pay for any hours worked over 40 in a workweek.

The act also sets a minimum wage, which sets a floor for employees covered by the act (and usually bumps up wages for practically all workers when Congress raises the minimum). The minimum wage will rise in steps from $5.85 per hour in 2007 for the majority of those covered by the act to $6.55 in July 2008, to $7.25 per hour in July 2009.[3] (Several states and about 80 municipalities have their own, higher, minimum wages.)

The act also contains child labor provisions. These prohibit employing minors between 16 and 18 years of age in hazardous occupations such as mining, and also carefully restrict employment of those under 16.

Exempt/Non-Exempt

Specific categories of employees are *exempt* from the act or certain provisions of the act, and particularly from the act's overtime provisions—they are "exempt employees." A person's exemption depends on his or her responsibilities, duties, and salary. Bona fide executive, administrative (like office managers), and professional employees (like architects) are generally exempt from the minimum wage and overtime requirements of the act.[4] A white collar worker earning more than $100,000 and performing any one exempt administrative, executive, or professional duty is automatically ineligible for overtime pay. Other employees can generally earn up to $23,660 per year and still automatically get overtime pay (so most employees earning less than $455 per week are non-exempt and earn overtime).[5]

If an employee is exempt from the FLSA's minimum wage provisions, then he or she is also exempt from its overtime pay provisions. However, certain employees are always exempt from overtime pay provisions. They include, among others: agricultural employees, live-in household employees, taxicab drivers, outside sales employees, and motion picture theater employees.[6]

As noted, some jobs—for example, top managers and lawyers—are clearly exempt, while others—such as office workers earning less than $23,660 per year—are non-exempt. Unfortunately, beyond the obvious categorizations, it's generally advisable to do some analyses before classifying a job as exempt or non-exempt. Figure 7.1

FIGURE 7.1   Who Is Exempt? Who Is Not Exempt?

*Three step procedure for estimating if position is exempt.** *

1. Does employee earn at least $455 per week ($23,660 per year)? If not, employee is Non exempt. If yes, go to question 2.

2. Does position involve typical duties of one of following: executive, administrative (non-manual office work), professional/ creative, computer professional, outside sales? If not, employee is Non exempt. If yes, go to question 3.

3. Finally, conduct careful job analysis to ascertain if *both* the pay and duties of the job qualify it as exempt.

*Sample Exempt/Non Exempt Positions** *

Exempt Professionals
 Attorneys
 Engineers
 Teachers
 Certified public accountants
 Computer systems analysts

Non Exempt
 Paralegals
 Non-licensed accountants
 Working supervisor
 Management trainees
 Secretaries

Exempt Administrators
 Executive assistant to the president
 Personnel directors
 Credit managers
 Purchasing agents

Exempt Executives
 Corporate officers
 Department heads
 Individual in sole charge of store

*****Note:** Exceptions exist. Discuss specifics with attorney.

presents a procedure for making this decision. Note that in all but the clearest situations, it's advisable to carefully review the person's job description to make sure, for instance, that the job currently does in fact require that the person perform, say, a supervisory duty.[7]

Violating this act's provisions can be problematic. Even giant firms make FLSA errors. Wal-Mart voluntarily told the Department of Labor that Wal-Mart had failed to pay some management trainees overtime pay, and had not included incentive pay in some employees' overtime pay calculations. Wal-Mart settled with the Department of Labor for $33 million.[8] Other firms try to evade the law by claiming that employees who are doing, say, computer programming are not employees but "independent contractors" (who are more like consultants than employees); this tactic rarely works, when challenged.

1963 Equal Pay Act

The **Equal Pay Act,** an amendment to the Fair Labor Standards Act, states that employees of one sex may not be paid wages at a rate lower than that paid to employees of the opposite sex for doing roughly equivalent work. Specifically, if the work requires equal skills, effort, and responsibility and is performed under similar working conditions, employees of both sexes must receive equal pay unless the differences in pay are based on a seniority system, a merit system, the quantity or quality of production, or any factor other than sex.

1964 Civil Rights Act

Title VII of the **Civil Rights Act** makes it an unlawful practice for an employer to discriminate against any individual with respect to hiring, compensation, terms, conditions, or privileges of employment because of race, color, religion, sex, or national origin.

Other Discrimination Laws

Various other discrimination laws influence compensation decisions. For example, the Age Discrimination in Employment Act prohibits age discrimination against employees who are 40 years of age and older in all aspects of employment, including compensation. The Americans with Disabilities Act similarly prohibits discrimination against qualified persons with disabilities in all aspects of employment, including compensation. The Family and Medical Leave Act entitles eligible employees, both men and women, to take up to 12 weeks of unpaid, job-protected leave for the birth of a child or for the care of a child, spouse, or parent. Employers that are federal government contractors or subcontractors are required by various executive orders not to discriminate and to take affirmative action in various areas of employment, including compensation.

How Unions Influence Compensation Decisions

For unionized companies, union-related issues of course also influence pay plan design. The National Labor Relations Act (NLRA) of 1935 granted employees the right to organize, to bargain collectively, and to engage in concerted activities for the purpose of collective bargaining or other mutual aid or protection. Historically, the wage rate has been the main issue in collective bargaining. However, other pay-related issues including time off with pay, income security (for those in industries with periodic layoffs), cost-of-living adjustments, and various benefits such as health care are also important.[9]

Compensation Policies

As at Wegman's, an employer's strategy and compensation policies significantly impact the wages and benefits it pays. For example, a hospital might have a policy of starting nurses at a wage at least 20% above the prevailing market wage. Other important policies include the basis for salary increases, foreign pay differentials, and overtime pay policy. Locality also plays a role. For example, the average base pay recently for an executive secretary would have ranged from $37,300 in Albuquerque, New Mexico to $41,900 (Tampa, Florida), $59,800 (New York, New York), and $60,100 (San Francisco, California).[10]

Distinguishing between high and low performers is another important pay policy. For example, for many years Payless ShoeSource hardly distinguished in pay among high and low performers. However, after seeing its market share drop over several years, management decided to embark on a turnaround plan. The plan included revising its compensation policies to differentiate more aggressively between top performers and others.[11]

Equity and Its Impact on Pay Rates

Equity, specifically the need for external equity and internal equity, is a key factor in determining pay rates. Externally, pay must compare favorably with rates in other companies, or an employer will find it hard to attract and retain qualified employees. Pay must also be equitable internally: Each employee should view his or her pay as equitable given other employees' pay in the organization. For example, in one study turnover of retail buyers was significantly lower when the buyers perceived fair treatment in the amount or rewards and in the methods employers used to allocate rewards.[12]

Salary inequities can trigger disappointment and conflict. Some firms therefore maintain secrecy over pay matters. However, online pay forums on sites like Salary.com, Wageweb.com, and Futurestep.com make it relatively easy today for employees to judge if they're being paid equitably externally.[13]

HOW EMPLOYERS ESTABLISH PAY RATES

In practice, setting pay rates while ensuring external and internal equity usually entails five steps:

1. Conduct a salary survey of what other employers are paying for comparable jobs (to price benchmark jobs and help ensure external equity).
2. Employee committee determines the worth of each job in your organization through job evaluation (to help ensure internal equity).
3. Group similarly paid jobs into pay grades.
4. Price each pay grade by using wage curves.
5. Develop rate ranges.

We explain each of these steps in this section, starting with salary surveys.

Step 1: Conduct the Salary Survey

Salary (or compensation) surveys—formal or informal surveys of what other employers are paying for similar jobs—play a central role in pricing jobs. Most employers therefore conduct such surveys for pricing one or more jobs.

Employers use salary surveys in three ways. First, they use them to price *benchmark jobs.* These anchor the employer's pay scale. The manager slots other jobs around them, based on their relative worth to the firm. (*Job evaluation,* explained next, is the technique used to determine the relative worth of each job.) Second, employers usually price 20% or more of their positions directly in the marketplace (rather than relative to the firm's benchmark jobs), based on a formal or informal survey of what comparable firms are paying for comparable jobs. Finally, surveys also collect data on benefits such as insurance, sick leave, and vacation time.

Finding salary data and negotiating raises are not as mysterious as they used to be, thanks to the Internet. Figure 7.2 summarizes some popular salary Web sites. The Bureau of Labor Statistics organized its various pay surveys into a new National

FIGURE 7.2   Some Pay Data Web Sites

Sponsor	Internet Address	What It Provides	Downside
Salary.com	Salary.com	Salary by job and zip code, plus job and description, for hundreds of jobs	Adapts national averages by applying local cost-of-living differences
Wageweb	www.wageweb.com	Average salaries for more than 150 clerical, professional, and managerial jobs	Charges $169 for breakdowns by industry, location, etc.
U.S. Office of Personnel Management	www.opm.gov/oca/07tables/	Salaries and wages for U.S. government jobs, by location	Limited to U.S. government jobs
Job Smart	http://jobstar.org/tools/salary/sal-prof.php	Profession-specific salary surveys	Necessary to review numerous salary surveys for each profession
moving.com	moving.com	Median salaries for thousands of jobs, by city	Doesn't consider factors like company size or benefits
cnnmoney.com	cnnmoney.com	Input your current salary and city, and this gives you comparable salary in destination city	Based on national averages adapted to cost of living differences

Note: All sites accessed May 2007.

Compensation Survey, and publishes this information on the Web. The Internet site is *http://stats.bls.gov*.[14]

Step 2: Determine the Worth of Each Job: Job Evaluation

Purpose of Job Evaluation

Job evaluation is a formal and systematic comparison of jobs to determine the worth of one job relative to another. The basic job evaluation procedure is to compare the content of jobs in relation to one another, for example, in terms of their effort, responsibility, and skills. Suppose you know (based on your salary survey and compensation policies) how to price key benchmark jobs, and can use job evaluation to determine the relative worth of all the other jobs in your firm relative to these key jobs. Then you are well on your way to being able to equitably price all the jobs in your organization.

Compensable Factors

There are two basic approaches to comparing the worth of several jobs. First, you could take an intuitive approach. You might decide that one job is more important than another and not dig any deeper into why in terms of specific job-related factors.

As an alternative, you could compare the jobs based on certain basic factors they have in common. In compensation management, these basic factors are called **compensable factors.** They are the factors that determine your definition of job content. And, they establish how the jobs compare to each other, and set the compensation paid for each job. For example, the Equal Pay Act focuses on four compensable factors: skills, effort, responsibility, and working conditions. Several years ago, Wal-Mart instituted a new wage structure based on knowledge, problem-solving skills, and accountability requirements.

Job Evaluation Methods

The simplest job evaluation method ranks each job relative to all other jobs, usually based on some overall compensable factor such as job difficulty. There are several steps in this *job ranking* method, as the *HR in Practice* box summarizes. *Job classification* is another simple, widely used method. Here the manager categorizes jobs into groups based on their similarity in terms of compensable factors such as skills and responsibility. The groups are called *classes* if they contain similar jobs, or *grades* if they contain jobs that are similar in difficulty but otherwise different. Thus, in the federal government's pay grade system, a press secretary and a fire chief might both be graded GS-10 (GS stands for General Schedule). The *point method* is a quantitative job evaluation technique. It involves identifying several compensable factors, each having several degrees, and then assigning points based on the number of degrees so as to come up with a total number of points for each job.

Step 3: Group Similar Jobs into Pay Grades

Once a job evaluation method has been used to determine the relative worth of each job, the evaluation committee can start assigning pay rates to each job; it usually first

STEPS IN RANKING METHOD OF JOB EVALUATION

1. *Obtain job information.* Job analysis is the first step in the **ranking method.** This method involves ordering jobs from high to low, usually based on some overall measure such as job difficulty. Job descriptions for each job are prepared, and these are usually the basis on which the rankings are made. (Sometimes job specifications also are prepared, but the job ranking method usually ranks jobs according to the whole job rather than a number of compensable factors. Therefore, job specifications—which provide an indication of the demands of the job in terms of problem solving, decision making, and skills, for instance—are not as necessary with this method as they are for other job evaluation methods.)

2. *Select raters and jobs to be rated.* It is often not practical to make a single ranking of all jobs in an organization. The more usual procedure is to rank jobs by department or in clusters (such as factory workers and clerical workers). This eliminates the need for having to compare directly, say, factory jobs and clerical jobs.

3. *Select compensable factors.* In the ranking method, it is common to use just one factor (such as job difficulty) and to rank jobs on the basis of the whole job. Regardless of the number of factors you choose, it's advisable to explain the definition of the factor(s) to the evaluators carefully so that they evaluate the jobs consistently.

4. *Rank jobs.* Next the jobs are ranked. The simplest way is to give each rater a set of index cards, each of which contains a brief description of a job. These cards are then ranked from lowest to highest. Some managers use an alternation ranking method for making the procedure more accurate; they use the cards to first choose the highest and the lowest, and then the next highest and next lowest, and so forth until all the cards have been ranked. Because it is usually easier to choose extremes, this approach facilitates the ranking procedure. Table 7.1 illustrates a job ranking. Jobs in this small health facility are ranked from maid up to office manager. The corresponding pay scales are shown on the right.

5. *Combine ratings.* Usually several raters rank the jobs independently. Then the rating committee (or employer) can average the rankings.

TABLE 7.1	Job Ranking by Olympia Health Care
Ranking Order	***Annual Pay Scale***
1. Office manager	$48,000
2. Chief nurse	47,500
3. Bookkeeper	39,000
4. Nurse	37,500
5. Cook	36,000
6. Nurse's aide	33,500
7. Maid	30,500

Note: After ranking, it becomes possible to slot additional jobs between those already ranked and to assign each an appropriate wage rate.

groups jobs into pay grades. A *pay grade* comprises jobs of approximately equal difficulty or importance as determined by job evaluation. If the point method were used, the pay grade would consist of jobs falling within a range of points. If the ranking plan were used, the grade would consist of all jobs that fall within two or three ranks. If the classification system were used, then the jobs are already categorized into classes or grades. Ten to 16 grades per job cluster (or logical grouping such as factory jobs, clerical jobs, etc.) are common.

Step 4: Price Each Pay Grade: Wage Curves

The next step is to assign average pay rates to each of the pay grades. (Of course, if you choose not to slot jobs into pay grades, an individual pay rate has to be assigned to each individual job.) Assigning pay rates to each pay grade (or to each job) is usually accomplished with the help of a **wage curve,** which shows the average pay rates currently being paid for jobs in each pay grade, relative to the points or rankings assigned to each job or grade by the job evaluation. Figure 7.3 illustrates a wage curve. The purpose of a wage curve is to show the relationship between (1) the value of the job as determined by one of the job evaluation methods and (2) the current average pay rates for the grades. The wage line then becomes the target for wages or salary rates for the jobs in each pay grade.

Step 5: Develop Rate Ranges

Finally, most employers do not just pay one rate for all jobs in a particular pay grade. Instead, they develop rate ranges for each grade. So, there might be 10 levels or steps and 10 corresponding pay rates within each pay grade. The employer may then fine-tune pay rates to account for any unique circumstances.

Pricing Managerial and Professional Jobs

For managerial and professional jobs, job evaluation provides only a partial answer to the question of how to pay these employees. Managerial and professional jobs

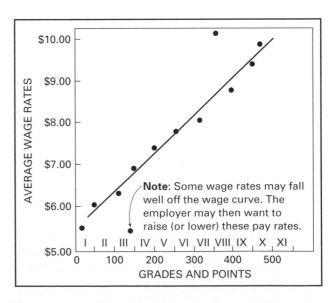

FIGURE 7.3   Plotting a Wage Curve

Note: The average pay rates for jobs in each grade (Grade I, Grade II, Grade III, etc.) are plotted, and the wage curve is fitted to the resulting points.

Note: Some wage rates may fall well off the wage curve. The employer may then want to raise (or lower) these pay rates.

tend to emphasize nonquantifiable factors like judgment and problem solving more than do production and clerical jobs. There is also more of a tendency to pay managers and professionals based on their performance, on what competitors are paying, or on what they can do, rather than on intrinsic job demands such as working conditions. One study concluded that three main factors, *job complexity* (span of control, the number of functional divisions over which the executive has direct responsibility, and management level), the employer's *ability to pay* (total profit and rate of return), and the executive's *human capital* (educational level, field of study, work experience) accounted for about two thirds of executive compensation variance.[15]

Elements

For a company's top executives, the compensation plan generally consists of four main components; base salary, short-term incentives, long-term incentives, and executive benefits and perks.[16] *Base salary* includes the obvious fixed compensation paid regularly as well as, often, guaranteed bonuses such as "10% of pay at the end of the fourth fiscal quarter, regardless of whether the company makes a profit." *Short-term incentives* are usually paid in cash or stock for achieving short-term goals, such as year-to-year increases in sales revenue. Incentives equal 31% or more of a typical executive's base pay in many countries, including the United States, United Kingdom, France, and Germany.[17] *Long-term incentives* include such things as stock options, which generally give the executive the right to purchase stock at a specific price for a specific period of time and are aimed at encouraging the executive to take actions that will drive up the price of the company's stock. Finally, special *executive benefits and perks* might include supplemental executive retirement plans, supplemental life insurance, and health insurance without a deductible or coinsurance. Supplemental retirement plans generally head the list of executive perks. Other popular executive perks include leased automobiles, automobile allowance, and free medical examinations.

Strategy and Executive Pay

As with any pay plans, those for professionals should make sense strategically. To accomplish this:

- Identify the company's strategic direction, and translate this into specific business goals.
- List the skills and competencies your professional employees should have and the behaviors they should exhibit to accomplish these goals.
- Evaluate the extent to which the existing pay plan produces these skills competencies, and behaviors. (For example, ask: Do you now provide competitive pay and rewards for those who demonstrate the required competencies and skills? Does the pay plan motivate employees to acquire these skills? Does it motivate employees to achieve their goals?)[18]
- Finally, design and implement the new pay plan. Make sure it "communicates to employees what's important about performance and what is not important."[19]

CURRENT TRENDS IN COMPENSATION

How employers pay employees has been evolving.[20] Overall, there is less emphasis on basing pay on seniority, and more on the employee's contribution, performance, and value to the business; less emphasis on the job's duties, and more on the person's skills and competencies and on how his or her contribution fits with the firm's overall strategic needs; finally, there's less emphasis on narrowly defined pay ranges and jobs, and more on broader jobs and pay ranges. This section looks at three important trends: competency-based pay, broadbanding, and board oversight of executive pay.[21]

Competency- and Skill-Based Pay

Some question whether job evaluation's tendency to slot jobs into narrow cubbyholes might not actually be counterproductive in today's high-performance work systems. Systems like these depend on flexible, multiskilled job assignments and on high-involvement techniques like teamwork and participative decision making. There's thus no place for employees who say, "That's not my job." Competency-based pay (and broadbanding, explained later) aim to avoid this problem.[22]

With competency- or skill-based pay, you pay the employee for the skills and knowledge he or she is capable of using rather than for the responsibilities of the job currently held.[23] *Competencies* are demonstrable personal characteristics such as knowledge, skills, and behaviors.

Why pay employees based on the skill levels they achieve, rather than based on the jobs they're assigned to? The answer is, to encourage the person to become more multiskilled. With more companies organizing around project teams, employers expect employees to be able to rotate among jobs. Doing so requires having more skills.

Elements

Skill-based pay programs generally contain five main elements. The employer *defines* specific skills, and chooses a *method* for tying the person's pay to his or her skill competencies. A *training* system lets employees seek and acquire skills. There is a formal competency *testing* system. And, the work is *designed* in such a way that employees can easily move among jobs of varying skill levels.

In practice, competency-based pay usually comes down to pay for knowledge or skill-based pay.[24] Pay-for-knowledge plans reward employees for learning organizationally relevant knowledge—for instance, you might pay a new waiter more once he or she memorizes the menu. With skill-based pay, the employee earns more after developing organizationally relevant skills—Microsoft pays programmers more as they master the skill of writing new programs.

Broadbanding

Most firms end up with pay plans that slot jobs into classes or grades, each with its own vertical pay rate range. For example, the U.S. government's pay plan consists of 18 main grades (GS-1 to GS-18), each with its own pay range. For an employee whose job falls in one of these grades, the pay range for that grade dictates his or her minimum and maximum salary.

The question is, How wide should the salary grades be, in terms of the number of job evaluation points they include? There is a downside to having narrow grades. For instance, if you want someone whose job is in grade 2 to fill in for a time in a job that happens to be in grade 1, it's difficult to reassign that person without lowering his or her salary. Similarly, if you want the person to learn about a job that happens to be in grade 3, the employee might object to the reassignment without a corresponding raise to grade 3 pay. Traditional grade pay plans thus breed inflexibility.

That is why some firms are broadbanding their pay plans. Broadbanding means collapsing salary grades and ranges into just a few wide ranges, or bands, each of which contains a relatively wide range of jobs and salary levels. Figure 7.4 illustrates this. In Figure 7.4, the company's previous six pay grades are consolidated into two broadbands.

FIGURE 7.4 Broadbanded Structure and How It Relates to Traditional Pay Grades and Ranges

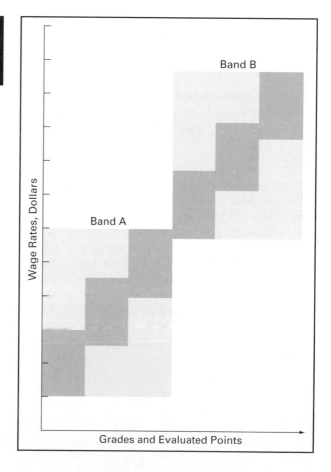

What to Broadband

A company may create broadbands for all its jobs, or for specific groups such as managers or professionals. The pay rate range of each broadband is relatively large, since it ranges from the minimum pay of the lowest grade the firm merged into the broadband up to the maximum pay of the highest merged grade. Thus, for example, instead of having 10 salary grades, each of which contains a salary range of $15,000, the firm might collapse the 10 grades into three broadbands, each with a set of jobs such that the difference between the lowest and highest paid jobs might be $40,000 or more. For the jobs that fall in each broadband, there is therefore a much wider range of pay rates. You can move employees from job to job within the broadband more easily, without worrying about the employees moving outside the relatively narrow rate range associated with a traditional narrow pay grade. Broadbanding therefore breeds flexibility. The *Global Issues* box explains some issues in paying expatriate employees.

Board Oversight of Executive Pay

For 15 years, the Board of Directors of UnitedHealth Group Inc. supported its CEO with almost $2 billion in compensation. Recently, the board ousted him, allegedly because, as the *Wall Street Journal* put it, "his explanation for a pattern of unusually well-timed stock option grants didn't add up."[25]

GLOBAL ISSUES IN HR

COMPENSATING EXPATRIATE EMPLOYEES

With dramatically different costs of living among countries, compensating managers who are sent to work abroad is never easy. Most North American companies use what experts call the *balance sheet method* to compute the expatriate manager's pay. The aim here is to make sure the person's compensation remains consistent with what it would have been if he or she had stayed home. The person's base salary reflects the salaries in his or her home country. Then, the employer layers on additional payments to cover things like housing costs, tax differences, and other living expenses (such as private schools for the person's children).[26] At the other extreme, some employers pay the manager based on what people are earning in the host country. This is known as the "host-country-based" or "going-rate" approach.

Each approach has pros and cons. The balance sheet approach makes it easier to repatriate employees, and generally elicits less resistance from the employees themselves (who might object to having their salaries slashed just because they're moving from high-cost New York to low-cost Bangalore). On the other hand, paying the expatriate more can lead to tensions between the manager and his or her host-country peers. The country-based approach has the advantage of integrating the expatriate better, since he or she is earning what his or her host country peers are earning. But it can mean slashing an employee's salary, hardly a practical option.

There are various reasons why boards like United Healthcare's are clamping down on executive pay. The Financial Accounting Standards Board now requires that most public companies recognize as an expense the fair value of the stock options they grant.[27] The Securities and Exchange Commission (SEC) now requires filing more compensation related information. The Sarbanes-Oxley Act makes executives personally liable, under certain conditions, for corporate financial oversight lapses.[28] The net result is that lawyers specializing in executive pay suggest that boards of directors ask themselves these questions:

- Has our compensation committee thoroughly identified its duties and processes?
- Is our compensation committee being appropriately advised? (Government regulators and commentators strongly encourage this.)
- Are there particular executive compensation issues that our committee should address?
- Do our procedures demonstrate diligence and independence? (This demands careful deliberations and records).
- Is our committee appropriately communicating its decisions? How will shareholders react?[29]

INCENTIVE PLANS

Many—perhaps most—employees don't just earn a salary or hourly wage. They also earn some type of incentive. This section addresses some popular **incentive plans.** *Individual incentive programs* give performance-based pay to individual employees. *Variable pay* refers to group pay plans that tie payments to productivity or to some other measure of the firm's profitability.[30]

Traditionally, all incentive plans are pay-for-performance plans. They pay all employees based on the employee's performance. Several incentive plan examples follow.

Piecework Plans

Piecework is the oldest incentive plan and still the most commonly used. Pay is tied directly to what the worker produces: The person is paid a "piece rate" for each unit he or she produces. Thus, if Tom Smith gets $0.40 apiece for finding addresses on the Web, then he would make $40 for finding 100 a day and $80 for 200.

Team or Group Incentive Plans

Companies often want to pay groups (rather than individuals) on an incentive basis, such as when they want to encourage teamwork. There are several ways to do so. One company, for instance, set up a pool of money such that if the company reached 100% of its overall goal, the employees would share in about 5% of this. That 5% pool was then divided by the number of employees to arrive at the value of a share. Each work team then received two goals. If the team achieved both of its goals, each employee would earn one share (in addition to his or her base pay). Employees on teams that reached only one goal would earn a half-share. Those on teams reaching neither goal earned no shares.[31]

A group incentive plan's main disadvantage is that each worker's rewards are not based just on his or her own efforts. If the person does not see his or her effort translating directly into proportional rewards, a group plan may be less effective than an individual plan.

Incentives for Managers and Executives

Managers play a central role in influencing divisional and corporate profitability, and most firms therefore put considerable thought into how to reward them. Most managers get short-term bonuses and long-term incentives in addition to salary.[32] For firms offering short-term incentive plans, virtually all—96%—provide those incentives in cash. For those offering long-term incentive plans, about 48% offer stock options, which are intended to motivate and reward management for long-term corporate growth, prosperity, and shareholder value. For mature companies, executives' base salary, short-term incentives, long-term incentives, and benefits might be 60%, 15%, 15%, and 10%, respectively. For growth companies, the corresponding figures might be 40%, 45%, 25%, and 10%.[33] The size of the bonus (in terms of percentage of salary) is usually greater for top-level executives.

Stock Options

The stock option is one incentive companies use for managerial (and other) employees. A **stock option** is the right to purchase a specific number of shares of company stock at a specific price during a period of time. The executive hopes to profit by exercising his or her option to buy the shares in the future, but at today's price. The firm's profitability and growth affect its stock price, and because the executive can affect these factors, the stock option can be an incentive.

The chronic problem with stock options is that firms traditionally used them to reward managers for even lackluster performance. There is therefore a trend toward using new types of options, tied more explicitly to performance goals. For example, with *premium priced options*, the exercise price is higher than the stock's closing price on the date of the grant, so the executive can't profit from the options until the stock makes significant gains.[34]

Firms have begun de-emphasizing stock option plans for several reasons. Many blame stock options for contributing to the numerous corporate scandals recently, in which some executives allegedly manipulated the dates they received their options to maximize their returns. Furthermore, until recently, most companies did not treat stock options as an expense. This could distort a company's reported financial performance by making expenses look less than they really were. More companies are trying to emphasize accuracy and transparency in financial statements, so more are now expensing stock options. But, as one compensation consultant puts it, "The fact that this is now 'costing' them something will mean that they will have to do more of the cost/benefit analysis to see which design will give them the best return for their dollar."[35]

Sarbanes-Oxley

The Sarbanes-Oxley Act of 2002 affects how employers formulate their executive incentive programs. Congress passed Sarbanes-Oxley to inject a higher level of responsibility into executives' and board members' decisions. It makes them personally liable for violating their fiduciary responsibilities to their shareholders. The act also requires that CEOs and CFOs of a public company repay any bonuses, incentives, or equity-based compensation received from the company during the 12-month period following the issuance of a financial statement that the company must restate due to material noncompliance with a financial reporting requirement as a result of misconduct.[36]

Incentives for Salespeople

Most companies pay their salespeople a combination of salary and commissions, usually with a sizable salary component. Typical is a 70% base salary/30% incentive mix. This cushions both the downside risk from the salesperson's point of view and limits the risk that the rewards would be too great from the firm's point of view.

Setting effective quotas is an art. Questions to ask include: Are quotas communicated to the sales force within 1 month of the start of the period? Does the sales force know how their quotas are set? Do you combine bottom-up information (like account forecasts) with top-down requirements (like the company business plan)? Are quotas stable through the performance period? Are returns and debookings reasonably low? And, has your firm generally avoided compensation-related lawsuits?[37] One expert suggests the following as a rule of thumb as to whether the sales incentive plan is effective: 75% or more of the sales force achieving quota or better; 10% of the sales force achieving higher performance level (than previously); 5% to 10% of the sales force achieving below-quota performance and receiving performance development coaching.[38]

Some salespeople respond more positively to fixed salary plans while others prefer incentives. As a result, human resource and sales managers need to carefully select salespeople at least partly based on whether the job is commission or salary-based.[39]

An Example: Auto Dealers

Commission rates vary by industry, but a look at how auto dealers set their salesperson's commission rates provides some interesting insights. Compensation for car salespeople ranges from a high of 100% commission to a small base salary with commission accounting for most of the total compensation. Commission is generally based on the net profit on the car when it's delivered to the buyer. This promotes precisely the sorts of behaviors the car dealers want to encourage. For example, it encourages the salesperson to hold firm on the retail price, and to push "after-sale products" like floor mats, side moldings, undercoating, car alarms, and trunk-mounted CDs. Car dealers also use short-term incentives. For helping sell slow moving vehicles, the salesperson may be offered a "spiff"—a car dealer term for an extra incentive bonus over commission.[40]

Non-Tangible and Recognition-Based Awards

Studies show that recognition has a positive impact on performance, either alone or in conjunction with financial rewards.[41] It's therefore not surprising that in one survey, 78% of CEOs and 58% of HR vice presidents said their firms were using performance recognition programs.[42] At American Skandia, which provides insurance and financial planning products and services, customer service reps who exceed standards receive a plaque, a $500 check, their photo and story on the firm's internal Web site, and a dinner for them and their teams.[43] One survey of 235 managers found that the most-used rewards to motivate employees (from most used to least) were:[44]

- Employee recognition
- Gift certificates
- Special events
- Cash rewards
- Merchandise incentives
- E-mail/print communications
- Training programs
- Work/life benefits
- Variable pay
- Group travel
- Individual travel
- Sweepstakes

Online Award Programs

If there's a downside to recognition programs, it's that they're expensive to administer. Many firms—including Levi Strauss & Co., Barnes and Noble, Citibank, and Wal-Mart—now therefore partner with online incentive firms to expedite the whole process. Management consultant Hewitt Associates uses *www.bravanta.com* to help its managers more easily recognize exceptional employee service with special awards. Internet incentive/recognition sites include bravanta.com, premierchoiceaward.com, giveanything. com, incentivecity.com, netcentives.com, salesdriver.com, and kudoz.com.

Merit Pay as an Incentive

Merit pay, or a **merit raise,** is any salary increase awarded to an employee based on his or her individual performance. It is different from a bonus in that it usually becomes part of the employee's base salary, whereas a bonus is a one-time payment. Although the term *merit pay* can apply to the incentive raises given to any employee—exempt or nonexempt, office or factory—the term is more often used with respect to white-collar employees and particularly professional, office, and clerical employees.

Merit pay has both advocates and detractors. Advocates argue that only rewards like these that are tied directly to performance can motivate improved performance. Detractors say it can undermine teamwork, and that, since the merit pay typically depends on the performance appraisal, unfair appraisals will lead employees to perceive the pay as unfair, too.

Profit-Sharing Plans

In a **profit-sharing plan,** most employees receive a share of the company's annual profits. Research on the effectiveness of such plans is sketchy. One study concludes that there is "ample" evidence that profit-sharing plans boost productivity, but that their effect on profits is insignificant, once you factor in the costs of the plans' payouts.[45] Although there are many such plans, cash plans are the most popular. Here, employees receive a percentage of profits (usually 15% to 20%) as profit shares at regular intervals.

Employee Stock Ownership Plan

Employee stock ownership plans (ESOPs) are company-wide plans in which a corporation contributes shares of its own stock—or cash to be used to purchase such stock—to a trust established to purchase shares of the firm's stock for employees. The firm generally makes these contributions annually in proportion to total employee compensation, with a limit of 15% of compensation. The trust holds the stock in individual employee accounts. It then distributes it to employees upon retirement (or other separation from service), assuming the person has worked long enough to earn ownership of the stock. (Traditional stock options, as discussed elsewhere in this chapter, go directly to the employees individually to use as they see fit, rather than into a retirement trust.) One study compared performance of 229 "new economy" firms offering broad-based stock options to that of their non-stock-option counterparts. Those offering stock options had higher shareholder returns than those not offering the options.[46]

ESOPs have several advantages. The corporation receives a tax deduction equal to the fair market value of the shares that it transfers to the trustee. It can also claim an income tax deduction for dividends paid on stock the ESOP owns. Employees are not taxed until they receive a distribution from the trust, usually at retirement when they usually have a reduced tax rate. And the **Employee Retirement Income Security Act (ERISA)** allows a firm to borrow against employee stock held in trust. The employer can then repay the loan in pretax rather than in after-tax dollars, which is another ESOP tax incentive. ESOPs may also encourage employees to develop a sense of ownership in and commitment to the firm.[47]

Broad-Based Stock Options

For many years, employers have awarded stock options to all or most employees (not just executives) as part of the employers' profit sharing incentive plans. Recently, a number of large companies including Time Warner, Microsoft, Aetna, and Charles Schwab announced they were discontinuing distributing stock options to most employees. Some of them, including Microsoft, are instead awarding stock. With companies now having to show the options as an expense when awarded, firms like Microsoft apparently feel awarding stock instead of stock options is a more direct and immediate way of linking pay to performance.[48]

Scanlon/Gainsharing Plans

The **Scanlon plan** is an incentive plan developed in 1937 by Joseph Scanlon, a United Steel Workers Union official,[49] and is remarkably progressive considering that it was developed long ago. It is one of many **gain-sharing plans,** the aim of which is to encourage improved employee productivity by sharing resulting financial gains with employees. Other popular types of gain-sharing plans include the Rucker and Improshare plans.

Features

Scanlon plans today have five basic features.[50] The first is the *philosophy of cooperation* on which it is based. This philosophy assumes that managers and workers should rid themselves of the "us" and "them" attitudes that normally inhibit employees from developing a sense of ownership in the company. It substitutes instead a climate in which everyone cooperates because he or she understands that economic rewards are contingent on honest cooperation.

A second feature of a Scanlon plan is *identity*. This means that to focus employee efforts, the company's mission or purpose must be clearly articulated, and employees must understand how the business operates in terms of customers, prices, and costs, for instance. *Competence* is a third basic feature. The plan, say three experts, "explicitly recognizes that a Scanlon plan demands a high level of competence from employees at all levels."[51]

The fourth feature is the *involvement system*.[52] This takes the form of two levels of committees—the departmental level and the executive level. Employees present productivity-improving suggestions to the appropriate departmental-level committees, which transmit the valuable ones to the executive-level committee. The latter then decides whether to implement the suggestions.

The fifth feature of the plan is the *sharing of benefits formula*. The Scanlon plan assumes that employees should share directly in any extra profits resulting from their cost-cutting suggestions. For example, if a suggestion is implemented and successful, all employees might share in 75% of the savings.

Earnings-at-Risk Pay Plans

The basic characteristic of an earnings-at-risk pay plan is that some portion of the employee's base salary is at risk. For example, suppose in one department, the employees' at-risk pay is 6%. This means that each employee's base pay will be 94% of his or her counterpart's salary in other (not-at-risk) departments. If the department achieves its goals, the employees get their full pay; if it exceeds its goals, they may receive a bonus exceeding the 6%.

Three researchers concluded that the employees they studied were dissatisfied with their lower base salary, but that this dissatisfaction seemed to motivate them to work harder to earn the incentive and thereby raise their total pay.[53]

An Example: Incentives at Nucor Corporation

We've seen that in today's performance-oriented environment, employers increasingly pay all or most employees an incentive. For example, Nucor Corp. is the largest steel producer in the United States; it also has the highest productivity, highest wages, and lowest labor cost per ton in the American steel industry.[54]

Nucor employees earn bonuses of 100% or more of base salary. All participate in one of four performance-based incentive plans. With the *production incentive plan*, plant operating and maintenance employees and supervisors get weekly bonuses based on their workgroup's productivity. The *department manager incentive plan* pays department managers annual incentive bonuses based mostly on the ratio of net income to dollars of assets employed for their division. With the *professional and clerical bonus plan*, employees who are not in one of the two previous plans get bonuses based on their division's net income return on assets. Finally, under the *senior officers incentive plan*, Nucor senior managers (whose base salaries are lower than those of executives in comparable firms) get bonuses based on Nucor's annual overall percentage of net income to stockholder's equity.[55]

HRIS and Productivity

Incentives are becoming ever more complicated. For one thing, as we've seen, more employees—not just salespeople—now get incentives. Furthermore, the range of behaviors for which employers pay incentives is now quite broad, from better service to cutting costs to answering more calls per hour.[56]

Tracking performance of dozens or hundreds of measures like these and then computing individual employees' incentives can be very time consuming. Several companies such as Incentives Systems Inc. therefore provide software known as Enterprise Incentive Management (EIM) systems to automate the planning and management of plans like these. As one expert says, "EIM software automates the planning, calculation, modeling, and management of incentive compensation plans, enabling companies to align their employees with corporate strategy and goals."[57]

For a large business with thousands of sales reps, employee incentive management (EIM) systems can cost between $1 million and $10 million to install. But when you consider that it costs an average of $1,500 a year per employee to manage a manual system, an EIM system can pay for itself in the first year or two. According to the Gartner Inc. consulting group, the market for EIM systems now probably exceeds a billion dollars.[58]

Employers also increasingly use the Web to support their sales and other incentive programs. For example, SalesDriver, in Maynard, Massachusetts, runs Web-based sales-performance–based incentive programs. Firms like these create online sales incentive programs. SalesDriver can help a company launch a campaign Web template in a day or less. Using the template, the sales manager can select from a catalog of 1,500 reward items, and award these to sales and marketing reps for meeting quotas for things like lead generation and total sales.[59]

EMPLOYEE BENEFITS

Benefits represent an important part of just about every employee's pay. They are defined as indirect monetary and nonmonetary payments an employee receives for continuing to work for the company. Benefits include such things as time off with pay, health and life insurance, and child-care facilities.

Most full-time employees in the United States receive benefits. Virtually all employers—99%—offer some health insurance coverage.[60]

Benefits are a major expense for most employers. Employee benefits account for about one third of wages and salaries (or about 28% of total payrolls), with legally required benefits, followed by health insurance, the most expensive single benefit cost Consultants Towers Perrin estimate that the recent cost of medical coverage alone was about $888 per month for family coverage.[61]

There are many benefits and various ways to classify them. In the remainder of this section we classify benefits as pay for time not worked, insurance benefits, retirement benefits, and employee services benefits.

Pay for Time Not Worked

Supplemental pay benefits, or pay for time not worked, are typically one of an employer's most expensive benefits because of all the time off that employees receive. Common time-off-with-pay benefits include holidays, vacations, jury duty, bereavement leave, military duty, sick leave, sabbatical leave, maternity leave, and unemployment insurance payments for laid-off or terminated employees.

Unemployment Insurance

All states have unemployment insurance or compensation acts, which provide for weekly benefits if a person is unable to work through some fault other than his or her own. The benefits derive from an unemployment tax on employers that can range from 0.1% to 5% of taxable payroll in most states. States each have their own unemployment laws, which follow federal guidelines. An organization's unemployment tax reflects its experience with personnel terminations.

Unemployment benefits are not meant for all dismissed employees, only for those terminated through no fault of their own. Thus, strictly speaking, a worker fired for chronic lateness has no legitimate claim to benefits. But in practice, many managers take a lackadaisical attitude toward protecting their employers against unwarranted claims. Therefore, employers spend thousands of dollars more per year on unemployment taxes than would be necessary if they protected themselves—for instance, by keeping careful records of lateness and absences, and by warning employees whose performance is inadequate.[62]

Vacations and Holidays

On average, American workers get about 9 days of leave after one year's employment. Days off rises to about 11 after 3 years, 14 after 5 years, and 16 after 10 years. The average number of annual vacation days varies around the world. For example, vacation allowances vary from 6 days in Mexico to 10 days in Japan, 25 in Sweden, and 25 in France. In the United States, the number of paid holidays similarly varies considerably from employer to employer, from a minimum of about 5 to 13 or more.

Sick Leave

Sick leave provides pay to employees when they are out of work because of illness. Most sick leave policies grant full pay for a specified number of permissible sick days, usually up to about 12 per year. The sick days often accumulate at the rate of approximately 1 day per month of service.

Sick leave pay causes consternation for many employers. The problem is that although many employees use their sick days only when they are legitimately sick, others (in the eyes of some employers) take advantage of sick leave by using it as if it's extra vacation time, whether they are sick or not. One survey found that the average cost of absenteeism per employee per year was about $789, with personal illness accounting for about a third of the absences.[63]

Employers utilize several tactics to eliminate or reduce this problem:

- Many use *pooled paid leave* plans. These plans—which lump together sick leave, vacation, and holidays into a single leave pool—have grown from 21% of firms surveyed 5 years ago to 66% recently.[64]
- Other firms buy back unused sick leave at the end of the year by paying their employees a daily equivalent pay for each sick leave day not used. The drawback is that the policy can encourage legitimately sick employees to come to work despite their illness.

- Others hold monthly lotteries in which only employees with perfect attendance are able to participate; those who participate are eligible to win a cash prize.
- Still others aggressively investigate all unplanned absences, for instance, by calling the absent employees at their homes when they are taking sick days.

FMLA

Sick leave policy depends to some extent on the Family and Medical Leave Act of 1993 (FMLA). Among its provisions, the law stipulates that:

1. Private employers of 50 or more employees must provide eligible employees up to 12 weeks of unpaid leave for their own serious illness, the birth or adoption of a child, or the care of a seriously ill child, spouse, or parent.
2. Employers may require employees to take any unused paid sick leave or annual leave as part of the 12-week leave provided in the law.
3. Employees taking leave are entitled to receive health benefits while they are on unpaid leave under the same terms and conditions as when they were on the job.
4. Employers must guarantee most employees the right to return to their previous or equivalent position with no loss of benefits at the end of the leave.

Severance Pay

Many employers provide **severance pay**—a one-time separation payment—when terminating an employee. Other firms provide "bridge" severance pay by keeping employees (especially managers) on the payroll for several months, until they have found new jobs. About half of employers surveyed give white-collar and exempt employees one week of severance pay per year of service, and about one third do the same for blue-collar workers. It is most common to award severance pay as part of a reduction in workforce. It is somewhat less common to award it when dismissing someone for poor performance. It is uncommon to pay severance when employees quit or are fired for cause.[65]

Severance payments make sense on several grounds. It is a humanitarian gesture as well as good public relations. In addition, most managers expect employees to give them at least 1 or 2 weeks' notice if they plan to quit; it is therefore appropriate (and in some states mandatory) to provide at least one pay period's severance pay if an employee is terminated. Such payments can also reduce the possibility that a terminated employee will litigate.

Things to keep in mind when crafting the severance plan include,

- List the situations for which the firm will pay severance, such as layoffs resulting from internal reorganizations. Indicate that action regarding other situations will be determined by management as necessary.
- Require signing of a waiver/general release prior to remittance of any severance pay, absolving the employer from employment-related liability. To be an effective release, the signing of the release must be knowing and voluntary, and there are additional legal requirements.

- Reserve the right to terminate or alter the policy.
- Remember that as with all personnel actions, the employer must make severance payments, if any, equitably.[66]

Plant closings and downsizings have put thousands of employees out of work, often with little or no notice or severance pay. *The Worker Adjustment and Retraining ("plant closing") Act* of 1989 requires covered employers to give employees 60 days' written notice of plant closures or mass layoffs.

Insurance Benefits

Workers' Compensation

Workers' compensation laws are aimed at providing sure, prompt income and medical benefits to work-related accident victims or their dependents, regardless of fault. Every state has its own workers' compensation law, and some states offer their own insurance programs. However, most require employers to purchase workers' compensation insurance through private state-approved insurance companies, for instance in terms of increased benefits for disability and death.

Workers' compensation benefits can be either monetary or medical. In the event of a worker's death or disablement, the person or his or her beneficiary is paid a cash benefit based on prior earnings—usually one half to two thirds of the worker's average weekly wage, per week of employment. In most states there is a set time limit—such as 500 weeks—for which an employee can receive benefits. If the injury causes a specific loss (such as loss of an arm), the employee may receive additional benefits based on a statutory list of losses, even though he or she may return to work. In addition to these cash benefits, employers must furnish medical, surgical, and hospital services needed by the employee.

For an injury or illness to be covered by workers' compensation, the employee need only prove that it arose while he or she was on the job. It does not matter that the employee may have been at fault or disregarded instructions. If he or she was on the job when the injury occurred, he or she is entitled to workers' compensation.

Many, or most, workers' compensation claims are legitimate, but some are not. Supervisors should be aware of typical red flags of fraudulent claims, including vague accident details, minor accidents resulting in major injuries, lack of witnesses, injuries occurring late Friday or very early Monday, and late reporting.[67]

Hospitalization, Medical, and Disability Insurance

Health care benefits top employees' desired benefits. Seventy-five percent of respondents in one recent survey said they considered health care benefits their most important benefits.[68]

Most employers therefore offer their employees some type of hospitalization, medical, and disability insurance (see Table 7.2). Many offer membership in a health maintenance organization (HMO) as a hospital/medical option. The HMO is a medical organization consisting of numerous specialists (surgeons, psychiatrists, etc.) operating out of a community-based health care center. Preferred provider organizations (PPOs) let employees select providers (such as participating physicians) who agree to provide price discounts and submit to certain utilization controls, such as on the number of diagnostic tests that can be ordered.

TABLE 7.2	Percentage of Employers Offering Various Health Benefits			
		Yes%	*No%*	*Plan to%*
Prescription drug program coverage		95	5	
Dental insurance		94	5	1
Mail order prescription program		87	12	1
PPO (preferred provider organization)		87	12	1
Mental health insurance		73	27	
Vision insurance		79	20	1
Employee assistance program		73	25	2
Vaccinations onsite (example: flu shots)		62	37	1
Chiropractic insurance		80	20	
Wellness program, resources, and information		68	26	6
CPR training/first aid		55	42	3
HMO (health maintenance organization)		48	51	1

Source: Adapted from SHRM/SHRM Foundation 2007 Benefits Survey.

The Pregnancy Discrimination Act

The Pregnancy Discrimination Act (PDA) is aimed at prohibiting sex discrimination based on "pregnancy, childbirth, or related medical conditions." Before enactment of this law in 1978, employers generally paid temporary disability benefits for pregnancies in the form of either sick leave or disability insurance, if at all. However, although most employers provide temporary disability income to their employees for up to 26 weeks for most illnesses, those that provided benefits for pregnancy usually limited benefits to only 6 weeks for normal pregnancies. Many believed that the shorter duration of pregnancy benefits constituted discrimination based on sex.

The act requires employers to treat women affected by pregnancy, childbirth, or related medical conditions the same as any employee not able to work, with respect to all benefits, including sick leave and disability benefits, and health and medical insurance. For example, if an employer provides up to 26 weeks of temporary disability income to employees for all illnesses, it is also required to provide up to 26 weeks for pregnancy and childbirth or related medical conditions.

COBRA Requirements

The ominously titled COBRA—Consolidated Omnibus Budget Reconciliation Act—requires most private employers to make available to terminated or retired employees and their families continued health benefits for a period of time, generally 18 months. If the former employee chooses to continue these benefits, he or she must pay for them, as well as a small fee for administrative costs.

Take care in administering COBRA, especially with respect to informing employees of their COBRA rights. For example, you don't want a separated employee to be injured and come back and claim she didn't know her insurance coverage could have been continued. Therefore, when a new employee first becomes eligible for your company's insurance plan, the employee should receive and acknowledge having received an explanation of COBRA rights. More important, all employees separated from the company should sign a form acknowledging that they have received and understand their COBRA rights.

Cost Control

With health care costs spiraling, containing those costs is a huge employer concern. Strategies include the following:

Cost Containment Specialists   Many are using cost-containment specialists— companies that specialize in helping employers reduce their health care costs. For example, health care containment companies can use their network of contacts with PPOs to help employers obtain the best PPO coverage for their needs.

Online Administration   Other big savings come from automating health care plan administration, for instance, by making online enrollment by employees mandatory.[69]

Defined Benefits   Other employers are moving toward defined contribution health care plans. Under defined contribution health care plans, each employee has a medical allotment that he or she can use for co-payments or discretionary medical costs, rather than a health care benefits package with open-ended costs.

Deductibles   Other firms are moving toward offering plans with high deductibles—more than $1,000—for individual coverage.[70]

Outsourcing   Outsourcing is another option. For example, 84% of firms in one survey said they were outsourcing employee assistance and counseling, and 53% were outsourcing health care benefits administration.[71]

Wellness Programs   Medical experts believe that many illnesses are preventable, and studies show that controlling health risks can reduce illnesses and health-care costs.[72] Almost all large employers (and perhaps 80% of small ones) therefore offer some form of preventive services as benefits. *Clinical prevention* programs include things like mammograms, immunizations, and routine checkups. *Health promotion and disease prevention* programs include things like seminars and incentives aimed at improving health by changing unhealthy behaviors or modifying lifestyles.[73]

Claims Audits   Many employers pay out thousands or millions of dollars in erroneous health claims. The industry standard for percentage of claims dollars actually paid in error is 1%; in two recent years the *actual* percentage of claims dollars paid in error were 3.5% and 3.3%. Setting standards for errors, and then aggressively auditing the claims being paid, may be the most direct way to reduce employer health care expenses.[74]

Medical Tourism   *"Medical tourism"* is another option. Here employers encourage employees to have some non-urgent medical procedures done overseas. Hospitals in Brazil or Malaysia may charge half what a U.S. hospital would for shoulder surgery, for instance. The key question is quality of care, but (while many people have successfully used this option) it's still not entirely clear how to assess overseas medical quality.[75]

Long-Term Care

Today, there are many types of long-term care—care to support older persons in their old age—for which employers can provide insurance benefits for their employees. For example, adult day-care facilities offer social and recreational activities. Assisted-living facilities offer shared housing and supervision for those who cannot function independently. Home care is care received at home from a nurse, an aide, or another specialist.

Retirement Benefits

Social Security

There are three types of Social Security benefits. First are the familiar *retirement benefits*, which provide an income if the employee retires at age 62 or thereafter and is insured under the Social Security Act. Second, survivor's or *death benefits* provide monthly payments to dependents regardless of the employee's age at death, again assuming the employee was insured under the Social Security Act. Finally, *disability payments* provide monthly payments to an employee and his or her dependents if the employee becomes totally disabled for work and meets specified work requirements. The Social Security system also administers the Medicare program, which provides a wide range of health services to people 65 and over.

"Full retirement age" traditionally was 65—the usual age for retirement. However, full retirement age to collect Social Security rose gradually, and is now 67 for those born in 1960 or later. In 2007, the maximum earnings subject to Social Security tax was $97,500.

Pension Plans

Pensions provide income to individuals in their retirement, and just over half of full-time workers participate in some type of pension plan at work.

We can classify pension plans in three basic ways: contributory versus noncontributory plans; qualified versus nonqualified plans; and defined contribution versus defined benefit plans.[76] The employee contributes to the contributory pension plan, while the employer makes all contributions to the noncontributory pension plan. Employers derive certain tax benefits from contributing to qualified pension plans, such as tax deductions for contributions; nonqualified pension plans get less favorable tax treatment for employees and employers.

With **defined benefit plans,** the employee knows ahead of time the pension benefits he or she will receive. The defined pension benefit itself is usually set by a formula that ties the person's retirement pension to an amount equal to a percentage of the person's preretirement pay (for instance, to an average of his or her last 5 years of employment), multiplied by the number of years he or she worked for the company.

Defined contribution plans specify what contribution the employee and employer will make to the employee's retirement or savings fund. Here, the contribution is defined, not the pension. With a defined benefit plan, the employee knows what his or her retirement benefits will be upon retirement. With a defined contribution plan, the person's pension will depend on the amounts contributed to the fund and on the retirement fund's investment earnings. Defined contribution plans are increasingly popular among employers today, because of their relative ease of administration, favorable tax treatment, and other factors. **Portability**—making it easier for employees who leave the firm prior to retirement to take their accumulated pension funds with them—is enhanced by switching from defined benefit to defined contribution plans.

401(k) Plans

The 401(k) plan is one defined contribution plan. Under the 401(k) plan (based on Section 401[k] of the Internal Revenue Code), employees have the employer place a portion of their compensation, which would otherwise be paid in cash, into a company profit-sharing or stock bonus plan. This results in a pretax reduction in salary, so the employee isn't taxed on those set-aside dollars until after he or she retires (or removes the money from the pension fund). Some employers also match a portion of what the employee contributes to the 401(k) plan. One attraction of 401(k) is that employees may have a range of investment options for the 401(k) funds, including mutual stock funds and bond funds.

Cash Balance Pension Plans

In a defined benefit plan, to get the maximum benefit, the person generally must "put in" his or her full 30 or so years with the firm. This approach tends to favor older employees (whose income is often higher and who have been with the firm for a number of years). Younger employees and/or those who want the option of moving on with their vested pension benefits) after say 7 or 8 years might prefer defined contribution plans. Here the employee gets the full vested value to that point of his or her pension.

Cash balance plans are a hybrid; they are defined benefit plans for federal tax purposes, but they have the portability advantages of defined contribution plans. They provide the portability of defined contribution plans with the more predictable benefits of defined benefit plans.[77]

ERISA

The Employee Retirement Income Security Act (ERISA) aims to protect the pensions of workers and to stimulate pension plan growth. Before enactment of ERISA, pension plans often failed to deliver expected benefits to employees. Any number of reasons, such as business failure and inadequate funding, could result in employees losing their expected pensions and facing the prospect of being unable to retire.

Vesting

Under ERISA, pension rights had to be **vested**—guaranteed to the employee—under one of three formulas. Today (the rules changed in 2002) employers can choose one of two minimum vesting schedules (employers can allow funds to vest faster if they wish). With *cliff vesting*, the time period for acquiring a nonforfeitable right in employer matching contributions (if any) is 3 years. So, the employee must have nonforfeitable rights to these funds by the end of three years. With the second option (*graded vesting*) participants in pension plans must receive nonforfeitable rights to the matching contributions as follows: 20% after 2 years, and then 20% for each succeeding year, with a 100% nonforfeitable right by the end of 6 years.

Among other things, the Pension Benefits Guarantee Corporation (PBGC) was established under ERISA to ensure that pensions meet their obligations; PBGC also insures pensions should a plan terminate without sufficient funds to meet its vested obligations.[78] However, the PBGC guarantees only defined benefit, not defined contribution plans. Furthermore, it will only pay someone a pension of up to about $49,000 per year (for someone 65 years of age) with a plan terminating in 2007. So, high income workers may still end up with reduced pensions if a plan fails.

Employee Services and Family-Friendly Benefits

Although an employer's time off, insurance, and retirement benefits account for the main part of its benefits costs, many employers also provide a range of services, including personal services (such as legal and personal counseling), job-related services (such as subsidized child-care facilities), educational subsidies, and executive perquisites (such as company cars and planes for its executives).

For example, **Employee Assistance Programs (EAPs)** provide counseling and advisory services, which might include, for instance, personal legal and financial services, child- and elder-care referrals, adoption assistance, mental health counseling, and life event planning.[79] EAPs are increasingly popular, with more than 60% of larger firms offering such programs. Some employers offer employees full or partial *college tuition* reimbursement. These may help employers attract recruits, retain employees who might otherwise leave, and provide promotable employees with the educations they need to move up. However, that same enhanced mobility makes it easier for employees to leave. Two researchers studied the U.S. Navy's tuition assistance program. Tuition assistance usage significantly decreased the probability of staying in the Navy.[80]

Family-Friendly Benefits

Companies today also offer "*family-friendly*" workplace benefits. For example, software giant SAS Institute offers preschool child-care centers, a gym, a full-time in-house elder-care consultant, 3 weeks' paid vacation, a flexible ("flextime") work schedule, and a standard 35-hour workweek.

Several such benefits are increasingly popular. One survey found that about half the 2,586 workers surveyed felt they were working too much and putting too little time into "other things in life that really matter." In response, employers such as Hartford Financial Services Group and Nationwide Mutual Insurance are handing out *time off* as a performance reward; tracking employees' time off to avert burnout; giving new hires more vacation; and offering employees more long weekends on holidays.[81]

What to do when your child is sick and you need to get to work? More employers are offering *emergency child care benefits*, for instance, for when a young child's regular babysitter is a no-show. For example, Canadian financial services company CIBC is expanding its on-site child care center to handle last-minute emergencies.[82] Similarly, with more older workers, about 120 million Americans are now or have in the past cared for an adult relative or friend. Employers therefore increasingly offer *adult-care support*, including counseling and adult day care centers.[83] Some employers enrich their *parental leave plans* to make it more attractive for mothers to return from maternity leave, for instance, offering meaningful jobs with reduced travel and hours.[84]

Why Family-Friendly Benefits?

For the employer, programs like these produce advantages, not just costs. For example, sick family members and health problems such as depression account for many of the sick-leave days employees take. Employers can reduce these absences with programs that provide advice on issues like elder-care referrals and personal counseling.[85]

Family-friendly benefits may improve a firm's bottom line in some less obvious ways. One study found that when employees experienced work-family conflict, the employees were more likely to exhibit guilt and hostility at work and at home. "Therefore, when work family conflict causes employees to feel guilty and angry, it is likely that the service [customers] encounter will be affected negatively."[86]

Flexible Benefits

Employees tend to differ in what benefits they want and need. About 70% of employees in one survey chose flexible health care options.[87]

Flexible benefits plans were initially called cafeteria plans because employees could spend their benefits allowances on a choice of benefits options. Either way, the idea is to let the employee put together his or her own benefit package, subject to two constraints. First, the employer must carefully limit total cost for each benefit package. Second, each benefit plan must include certain nonoptional items, including, for example, Social Security, workers' compensation, and unemployment insurance.

Benefits and Employee Leasing

Employee leasing firms arrange to have all the employer's employees transferred to the employee leasing firm's payroll. *Employee leasing* means the employee leasing firm becomes the legal employer and handles all the employer's employee-related paperwork. This usually includes recruiting, hiring, paying tax liabilities (Social Security payments, unemployment insurance, etc.), and handling day-to-day details such as performance appraisals (with the assistance of the onsite supervisor). However, it is with respect to benefits management that employee leasing is often most advantageous.

Getting insurance is often the most serious personnel problem smaller employers face. Even group rates for life or health insurance can be high when only 20 or 30 employees are involved. This is where employee leasing comes in. Remember that the leasing firm is the legal employer of the other company's employees. Therefore, the employees are absorbed into a much larger insurable group (along with other employers' former employees). The employee leasing company can therefore often offer benefits smaller companies can't obtain at such a low cost.

Employee leasing may sound too good to be true, and it sometimes is. Many employers are uncomfortable letting a third party become the legal employer of their employees (who are actually terminated by the employer and rehired by the leasing firm). Some employee leasing firms have gone out of business after apparently growing successfully for several years. Such a business failure means that the original employer has to hire back all its employees and find new insurance carriers to insure these "new" employees.

Benefits Web Sites

To reduce the costs of administering benefits, many employers enable employees to manage much of their own benefits changes (dependants, 401[k], health plan, and so on) themselves, via the employer's (or an outside vendor's) Web site.

Employers are adding new services to their benefits Web sites. In addition to offering things like self-enrollment, the insurance company USAA's Web site helps employees achieve better work–life balance. For example, click on the "today, I'm feeling . . ." menu. Here employees can respond to a list of words (such as "stressed"), and from there see suggestions for dealing with (in this case) stress. Go to, "my child is behaving badly," and the employee gets access to resources like, "guide to addressing child behavior problems."[88]

Strategy and HR

Employers today want to ensure that their compensation plans (1) add value in terms of (2) promoting the employee performance that is required for (3) achieving the firm's strategic goals. Therefore, employers should ask, "does our total pay plan (in terms of base pay, short- and long-term incentives, and benefits) make sense in terms of our strategic goals?" Answering this requires asking two further questions: What skills and performance does achieving our strategic goals require? And, do our compensation plans make sense in terms of the specific performances we expect from our employers?

It may seem counterintuitive, but cutting pay rates does not always translate into higher profits, since one must also take productivity and quality into account. Wegman's Food Market's compensation policies illustrate this. With competition from Wal-Mart and other chains, Wegman's chose to pay above average wages and provide all its employees with free health coverage. Management's assumption, as their human resources head put it, is that "if we take care of our employees, they will take care of our customers."[89] Wegman's pay strategy seems to be working. Their larger stores each average about $950,000 a week in sales, compared to the national average of about $361,564 for grocery stores. Similarly, Wegman's employee retention figures are well above national averages for retail stores. Wegman's management decided that its competitive strategy was to compete with other grocery chains (including Wal-Mart's) based on productivity and quality of service. Its compensation strategy effectively supports that competitive strategy.

Review

Summary

1. Establishing pay rates involves five steps: conduct salary survey, evaluate jobs, develop pay grades, use wage curves, and develop pay ranges.
2. Job evaluation is aimed at determining the relative worth of a job. It compares jobs to one another based on their content, which is usually defined in terms of compensable factors such as skills, effort, responsibility, and working conditions.
3. Most managers group similar jobs into wage or pay grades for pay purposes. These grades are composed of jobs of approximately equal difficulty or importance as determined by job evaluation.
4. Developing a compensation plan for executive, managerial, and professional personnel is complicated by the fact that factors such as performance and creativity must take precedence over static factors such as working conditions. Market rates, performance, and incentives and benefits thus play a much greater role than does job evaluation for these employees.
5. Broadbanding means collapsing salary grades and ranges into just a few wide levels or bands, each of which then contains a relatively wide range of jobs and salary levels.
6. Piecework is the oldest type of incentive plan; a worker is paid a piece rate for each unit he or she produces. With a straight piecework plan, workers are paid on the basis of the number of units produced. With

a guaranteed piecework plan, each worker receives his or her base rate (such as the minimum wage) regardless of how many units he or she produces.

7. Profit sharing and the Scanlon plan are examples of organization-wide incentive plans. The problem with such plans is that the link between a person's efforts and rewards is sometimes unclear. Merit plans are other popular incentive plans.
8. Supplemental pay benefits provide pay for time not worked. They include unemployment insurance, vacation and holiday pay, severance pay, and supplemental unemployment benefits.
9. Insurance benefits are another type of employee benefit. Workers' compensation, for example, is aimed at ensuring prompt income and medical benefits to work accident victims or their dependents, regardless of fault. Most employers also provide group life insurance and group hospitalization, accident, and disability insurance.
10. Two types of retirement benefits are Social Security and pensions. Social Security covers not only retirement benefits but also survivors and disability benefits. One of the critical issues in pension planning is vesting the money that employer and employee have placed in the latter's pension fund, which cannot be forfeited for any reason. ERISA ensures that pension rights become vested and protected after a reasonable amount of time.

Key Terms

- employee compensation
- Fair Labor Standards Act
- Equal Pay Act
- Civil Rights Act
- salary (or compensation) surveys
- job evaluation
- compensable factors
- ranking method
- wage curve
- incentive plan

- piecework
- stock option
- merit pay (merit raise)
- profit-sharing plan
- employee stock ownership plan (ESOP)
- Employee Retirement Income Security Act (ERISA)
- Scanlon plan
- gain-sharing plan

- benefits
- severance pay
- workers' compensation
- defined benefit plan
- defined contribution plan
- portability
- vested
- Employee Assistance Program (EAP)
- flexible benefits plan

Discussion Questions and Exercises

1. What is the difference between exempt and nonexempt jobs?
2. What is the relationship between compensable factors and job specifications?
3. Working individually or in groups, conduct salary surveys for the following positions: entry-level accountant and entry-level chemical engineer. What sources did you use, and what conclusions did you reach? If you were the HR manager for a local engineering firm, what would you recommend that you pay for each job?
4. Working individually or in groups, use published (Internet or other) wage surveys to determine local area earnings for the following positions: file clerk I, accounting clerk II, and secretary V. How do the published figures compare with comparable jobs listed in your Sunday newspaper? What do you think accounts for any discrepancy?
5. Working individually or in groups, use the ranking method to evaluate the relative worth of the jobs listed in question 4. (You may use the Department of Labor's O*NET as an aid.) To what extent do the local area earnings for these jobs correspond to your evaluations of the jobs?
6. Working individually or in groups, develop an incentive plan for the following positions: chemical engineer, plant manager, and used-car salesperson. What factors did you have to consider in reaching your conclusions?
7. A state university system in the Southeast instituted a Teacher Incentive Program for its faculty. Faculty committees within each of the university's colleges were told to award $5,000 raises (not bonuses) to about 40% of their faculty members based on how good a job they did teaching undergraduates and how many they taught per year. What are the potential advantages and pitfalls of such an incentive program? How well do you think it was accepted by the faculty? Do you think it had the desired effect?
8. What is merit pay? Do you think it's a good idea to award employees merit raises? Why or why not?
9. Working individually or in groups, research and compile a list of the perks available to the following individuals: the head of your local airport, the president of your college or university, and the president of a large company in your area. Do they all have certain perks in common? What do you think accounts for any differences?
10. You are the HR consultant to a small business with about 40 employees. At the present time the business offers 5 days of vacation, five paid holidays, and legally mandated benefits such as unemployment insurance payments. Develop a list of other benefits you believe the firm should offer, along with your reasons for suggesting them.
11. It was recently reported in the news that the average pay for most university presidents was around $250,000 per year, but that a few earned much more. For example, the new president of Vanderbilt received $852,000 in one recent year. Discuss why you would (or would not) pay university presidents as much or more than you would pay many corporate CEOs.

APPLICATION EXERCISES

Case Incident   *Salary Inequities at Acme Manufacturing*

Joe Black was trying to figure out what to do about a problem salary situation he had in his plant. Black recently took over as president of Acme Manufacturing. The founder, Bill George, had been president for 35 years. The company was family owned and located in a small eastern Arkansas town. It had approximately 250 employees and was the largest employer in the community. Black was a member of the family that owned Acme, but he had never worked for the company prior to becoming president. He had an MBA and a law degree, plus 15 years of management experience with a large manufacturing organization, where he was senior vice president for human resources when he made his move to Acme.

A short time after joining Acme, Black started to notice that there was considerable inequity in the pay structure for salaried employees. A discussion with the human resources director led him to believe that salaried employees' pay was very much a matter of individual bargaining with the past president. Hourly paid factory employees were not part of the problem because they were unionized and their wages were set by collective bargaining. An examination of the salaried payroll showed that there were 25 employees, ranging in pay from that of the president to that of the receptionist. A closer examination showed that 14 of the salaried employees were female. Three of these were front-line factory supervisors and one was the HR director. The other 10 were nonmanagement.

This examination also showed that the human resources director appeared to be underpaid, and that the three female supervisors were paid somewhat less than were any of the male supervisors. However, there were no similar supervisory jobs in which there were both male and female job incumbents. When asked, the HR director said she thought the female supervisors may have been paid at a lower rate mainly because they were women, and perhaps Bill George did not think that women needed as much money because they had working husbands. However, she added that they may have been paid less because they supervised less-skilled

employees than did male supervisors. Black was not sure that this was true.

The company from which Black had moved had a good job evaluation system. Although he was thoroughly familiar and capable with this compensation tool, Black did not have time to make a job evaluation study at Acme. Therefore, he decided to hire a compensation consultant from a nearby university to help him. Together they decided that all 25 salaried jobs should be in the job evaluation cluster, that a ranking method of job evaluation should be used, and that the job descriptions recently completed by the HR director were current, accurate, and usable in the study.

The job evaluation showed that there was no evidence of serious inequities or discrimination in the nonmanagement jobs, but that the HR director and the three female supervisors were being underpaid relative to comparable male salaried employees.

Black was not sure what to do. He knew that if the underpaid female supervisors took the case to the local EEOC office, the company could be found guilty of sex discrimination and then have to pay considerable back wages. He was afraid that if he gave these women an immediate salary increase large enough to bring them up to where they should be, the male supervisors would be upset and the female supervisors might comprehend the total situation and want back pay. The HR director told Black that the female supervisors had never complained about pay differences, and they probably did not know the law to any extent.

The HR director agreed to take a sizable salary increase with no back pay, so this part of the problem was solved. Black believed he had four choices relative to the female supervisors:

1. To do nothing
2. To gradually increase the female supervisors' salaries
3. To increase their salaries immediately
4. To call the three supervisors into his office, discuss the situation with them, and jointly decide what to do ■

QUESTIONS

Source: This case was prepared by Professor James C. Hodgetts of the Fogelman College of Business and Economics of the University of Memphis. All names are disguised. Used with permission.

1. What would you do if you were Black? Why?
2. How do you think the company got into a situation like this in the first place?
3. Why would you suggest Black pursue the alternative you suggested?

Continuing Case

LearnInMotion.com: The Incentive Plan

Of all its HR programs, those relating to pay for performance and incentives are LearnInMotion.com's most fully developed. For one thing, the venture capital firm that funded it was very explicit about reserving at least 10% of the company's stock for employee incentives.

The agreement with the venture capital firm also included very explicit terms and conditions regarding LearnInMotion's stock option plan. The venture fund agreement included among its 500 or so pages a specific written agreement that LearnInMotion.com would have to send to each of its employees, laying out the details of the company's stock option plan. While there was some flexibility, the stock option plan details came down, in a nutshell, to this: (1) Employees would get stock options (the right to buy shares of LearnInMotion.com stock) at a price equal to 15% less than the venture capital fund paid for those shares when it funded LearnInMotion.com; (2) the shares will have a vesting schedule of 36 months, with one third of the shares vesting once the employee has completed 12 full months of employment with the company, and one third vesting upon successful completion of each of the following two full 12 months of employment; (3) if an employee leaves the company for any reason prior to his or her first full 12 months with the firm, the person is eligible for no stock options; (4) if the person has stock options and leaves the firm for any reason, he or she must exercise the options within 90 days of the date of leaving the firm, or lose the right to exercise them.

The actual number of options an employee gets depends on the person's bargaining power and on how much Jennifer and Mel think the person brings to the company: The options granted generally range from options to buy 10,000 shares for some employees up to 50,000 shares for other employees, but this has not raised any questions to date. When a new employee signs on, he or she receives a letter of offer. This provides minimal details regarding the option plan; after the person has completed the 90-day introductory period, he or she receives the five-page document describing the stock option plan, which Jennifer or Mel, as well as the employee, signs.

Beyond that, the only company incentive plan is the one for the two salespeople. In addition to their respective salaries, both salespeople receive about 20% of any sales they bring in, whether those sales are from advertising banners or course listing fees. It's not clear to Jennifer and Mel whether this incentive is effective. Each salesperson gets a base salary regardless of what he or she sells (one gets about $50,000; the other, about $35,000). However, sales have simply not come up to the levels anticipated. Jennifer and Mel are not sure why. It could be that Internet advertising dried up after March 2000. It could be that their own business model is no good, and there's not enough demand for their company's services. They may be charging too much or too little. It could be that the salespeople can't do the job due to inadequate skills or inadequate training. Or, of course, it could be the incentive plan. ("Or it could be all of the above," as Mel somewhat dejectedly said late one Friday evening.) They want to try to figure out what the problem is. They want you, their management consultants, to help them figure out what to do. Here's what they want you to do for them. ∎

QUESTIONS AND ASSIGNMENTS

1. Up to this point we've awarded only a tiny fraction of the total stock options available for distribution. Should we give anyone or everyone additional options? Why or why not?

2. Should we put other employees on a pay-for-performance plan that somehow links their monthly or yearly pay to company sales? Why or why not? If so, how should we do it?

3. Is there another incentive plan you think would work better for the salespeople? What is it?

4. On the whole, what do you think the sales problem is?

EXPERIENTIAL EXERCISE

Job Evaluation at the University

Purpose: The purpose of this exercise is to give you experience in performing a job evaluation using the ranking method.

  Required Understanding: You should be thoroughly familiar with the ranking method of job evaluation and obtain (or write) job descriptions for your college's dean, department chairperson, and your professor.

  How to Set Up the Exercise/Instructions: Divide the class into groups of four or five students. The groups will perform a job evaluation of the positions of dean, department chairperson, and professor using the ranking method.

1. Perform a job evaluation by ranking the jobs. You may use one or more compensable factors.

2. If time permits, a spokesperson from each group can put his or her group's ratings on the board. Did the groups end up with about the same results? How did they differ? Why do you think they differed?

Endnotes

1. Elayne Robertson Demby, "Two Stores Refused to Join the Race to the Bottom for Benefits and Wages," *Workforce Management* (February 2004): 57–59.

2. Richard Henderson, *Compensation Management* (Reston, VA: Reston 1980), Joseph Martocchio, *Strategic Compensation* (Upper Saddle River, NJ: Prentice Hall, 2004), pp. 44–60.

3. "Senate Passes Minimum Wage Increase that Includes Small-Business Tax Provisions," *BNA Bulletin to Management* (February 6, 2007): 41;

www.dol.gov/esa/whd/flsa/, accessed August 12, 2007.

4. For a description of exemption requirements see Jeffrey Friedman, "The Fair Labor Standards Act Today: A Primer," *Compensation* (January/February 2002): 51–54.

5. "Employer Ordered to Pay $2 Million in Overtime," *BNA Bulletin to Management* (September 26, 1996): 308–309. See also "Restaurant Managers Awarded $2.9 Million in Overtime Wages for Nonmanagement

Work," *BNA Bulletin to Management* (August 30, 2001): 275.

6. Because the overtime and minimum wage rules only changed in 2004, exactly how to apply these rules is still in a state of flux. If there's doubt about exemption eligibility, it's probably best to check with the local Department of Labor Wage and Hour office. See, for example, "Attorneys Say FLSA Draws a Fine Line between Exempt/Nonexempt Employees," *BNA Bulletin to Management* (July 5, 2005): 219; "DOL Releases Letters on Administrative Exemption, Overtime," *BNA Bulletin to Management* (October 18, 2005): 335.

7. See, for example, Jeffrey Friedman, "The Fair Labor Standards Act Today: A Primer," *Compensation* (January/February 2002): 53; Andre Honoree, "The New Fair Labor Standards Act Regulations and the Sales Force: Who Is Entitled to Overtime Pay?" *Compensation & Benefits Review* (January/February 2006): 31; www.shrm.org/issues/FLSA, accessed August 12, 2007; www.dol.gov/esa/whd/flsa/, accessed August 12, 2007.

8. *BNA Bulletin to Management*, "Wal-Mart to Pay More than $33 Million in Settlement with the DOL Involving Overtime" (January 30, 2007): 33.

9. Henderson, *Compensation Management*, pp. 101–127.

10. "Salaries for Similar Jobs Vary Significantly across the United States," *Compensation & Benefits Review* (January/February 2006): 9.

11. Jessica Marquez, "Raising the Performance Bar," *Workforce Management* (April 24, 2006): 31–32.

12. James DeConick and Dane Bachmann, "An Analysis of Turnover among Retail Buyers," *Journal of Business Research* 58, no. 7 (July 2005): 874–882.

13. See, for example, "Who Needs Midpoints? On-Line Pay Forums Are Convincing Workers of Their Net Worth," *BNA Bulletin to Management* (March 9, 2000): 73; and David Terpstra and Andre Honoree, "The Relative Importance of External, Internal, Individual, and Procedural Equity to Pay Satisfaction," *Compensation and Benefits Review* (November/December 2003): 67–74.

14. Allison Wellner, "Salaries in Site," *HR Magazine* (May 2001): 89–96. See also "Web Access Transforms Compensation Surveys," *Workforce Management* (April 24, 2006): 34.

15. Syed Tahir Hijazi, "Determinants of Executive Compensation and Its Impact on Organizational Performance", *Compensation & Benefits Review* (March/April 2007): 58–59.

16. Mark Meltzer and Howard Goldsmith, "Executive Compensation for Growth Companies," *Compensation and Benefits Review* (November/December 1997): 41–50. See also Bruce Ellig, "Executive Pay: A Primer," *Compensation and Benefits Review* (January/February 2003): 44–50.

17. "Executive Pay," *Wall Street Journal* (April 11, 1996): R16, R170; and Fay Hansen, "Current Trends in Compensation and Benefits," *Compensation and Benefits Review* 36, no. 2 (March/April 2004): 7–8.

18. Patricia Zingheim and Jay Schuster, "Designing Pay and Rewards in Professional Services Companies," *Compensation & Benefits Review* (January/February 2007): 55–62.

19. Ibid., p. 60.

20. See, for example, Patricia Zingheim and Jay Schuster, "The Next Decade for Pay and Rewards," *Compensation and Benefits Review* (January/February 2005): 29; and Patricia Zingheim and Jay Schuster, "What Are Key Pay Issues Right Now?" *Compensation & Benefits Review* (May/June 2007): 51–55.

21. Another dubious trend is that U.S. wage disparities are rising. Those with high salaries have seen their pay rise much faster in the past 20 or so years than have those at the bottom. Increased demand for the skills that come through education (for instance, for more skilled workers as manufacturing facilities became computerized) explains much of this. The wage gap has not grown as much in Europe, in part because "unions in Europe were and are still more powerful and able to keep up [workers'] wages." Thomas Atchison, "Salary Trends in the United States and Europe," *Compensation & Benefits Review* (January/February 2007): 36.

22. See for example, Hai-Ming Chen, et al., "Key Trends of the Total Reward System in the 21st Century," *Compensation & Benefits Review* (November/December 2006): 64–70.

23. See, for example, Robert Henneman and Peter LeBlanc, "Development of an Approach for Valuing Knowledge Work," *Compensation and Benefits Review* (July/August 2002): 47.

24. Martocchio, *Strategic Compensation*, p. 168.

25. Jamison Bandler and Charles Forelle, "How a Giant Insurer Decided to Oust Hugely Successful CEO," *Wall Street Journal* (December 7, 2006): A1.

26. Bobby Watson Jr. and Gangaram Singh, "Global Pay Systems: Compensation in Support of Multinational Strategy," *Compensation and Benefits Review* (January/ February 2005): 33–36.

27. Mark Poerio and Eric Keller, "Executive Compensation 2005: Many Forces, One Direction," *Compensation & Benefits Review* (May/June 2005): 34–40.

28. The federal government also recently introduced new compensation disclosure rules, and these are affecting executive compensation. For example, corporations must now list a single dollar figure to represent an executive's total pay, including salary, bonus, perquisites, long-term incentives, and retirement benefits. They must also be more diligent in listing all executive perquisites. The net effect of this greater transparency will probably be to pressure employers to increasingly link their executives' pay with the company's performance. See Brent Longnecker and James Krueger, "The Next Wave of Compensation Disclosure," *Compensation & Benefits Review* (January/ February 2007): 50–54.

29. Ibid.

30. Note that the employer needs to beware of instituting so many incentive plans (cash bonuses, stock options, recognition programs, and so on) tied to so many different behaviors that employees don't have a clear picture of the employer's priorities. Stephen Rubenfeld and Jennifer David, "Multiple Employee Incentive Plans. Too Much of a Good Thing?" *Compensation & Benefits Review* (March/April 2006): 35–43.

31. Richard Seaman, "Rejuvenating an Organization with Team Pay," *Compensation and Benefits Review* (September/October 1997): 25–30.

32. Mark Meltzer and Howard Goldsmith, "Executive Compensation for Growth Companies," *Compensation and Benefits Review* (November/December 1997): 41–50; and Barbara Kiviat, "Everyone into the Bonus Pool," *Time* (December 15, 2003): A5.

33. Ibid. See also Eric Krell, "Getting a Grip on Executive Pay," *Workforce* (February 2003): 30–32, and "Realities of Executive Compensation—2006/2007 Report on Executive Pay and Stock Options," www.watsonwyatt.com/research/resrender.asp?id=2006-US-0085&page=1, accessed May 20, 2007.

34. Meltzer and Goldsmith, "Executive Compensation," 47–48. See also, Steven Balsam and Setiyono Miharjo, "The Effect of Equity Compensation on Voluntary Executive Turnover," *The Journal of Accounting and Economics* 43, no. 1 (March 2007): 95.

35. Elaine Denby, "Weighing Your Options," *HR Magazine* (November 2002): 46.

36. "Impact of Sarbanes-Oxley on Executive Compensation," downloaded December 11, 2003, from www.thelenreid.com, Thelen, Reid, and Priest, L.L.P. See also, Brent Cougnecker and James Krueger, "The Next Wave of Compensation Disclosure," *Compensation & Benefits Review* (January/February 2007): 50–54.

37. S. Scott Sands, "Ineffective Quotas: The Hidden Threat to Sales Compensation Plans," *Compensation and Benefits Review* (March/April 2000): 35–42. "Driving Profitable Sales Growth: 2006/2007 Report on Sales Effectiveness," www.watsonwyatt.com/research/resrender.asp?id=2006-US-0060&page=1, accessed May 20, 2007.

38. Peter Gundy, "Sales Compensation Programs: Built to Last," *Compensation and Benefits Review* (September/October 2002): 21–28.

39. James M. Pappas and Karen E. Flaherty, "The Moderating Role of Individual-Difference Variables in Compensation Research," *Journal of Managerial Psychology* 21, no. 1 (January 2006): 19–35.

40. Peter Glendinning, "Kicking the Tires of Automotive Sales Compensation," *Compensation and Benefits Review* (September/October 2000): 47–53; and Michele Marchetti, "Why Sales Contests Don't Work," *Sales and Marketing Management* 156 (January 2004): 19.

41. See, for example, Suzanne Peterson and Fred Luthans, "The Impact of Financial and

Nonfinancial Incentives on Business Unit Outcomes over Time," *The Journal of Applied Psychology* 91, no. 1 (2006): 156–165.

42. Leslie Yerkes, "Motivating Workers in Tough Times," *Incentives* 75, no. 10 (October 2001): 120. See also, "Incentives, Motivation and Workplace Performance," *Incentive Research Foundation,* www.incentivescentral.org/employees/whitepapers, accessed May 19, 2007.

43. Ibid. See also Chris Taylor, "On-the-Spot Incentives," *HR Magazine* (May 2004): 80–85.

44. Charlotte Huff, "Recognition that Resonates," *Workforce Management* (September 11, 2006): 25–29. See also Scott Jeffrey and Victoria Schaffer, "The Motivational Properties of Tangible Incentives," *Compensation & Benefits Review* (May/June 2007): 44–50.

45. Seongsu Kim, "Does Profit Sharing Increase Firms' Profits?" *Journal of Labor Research* (Spring 1998): 351–371. See also Jacqueline Coyle-Shapiro et al., "Using Profit-Sharing to Enhance Employee Attitudes: A Longitudinal Examination of the Effects on Trust and Commitment," *Human Resource Management* 41, no. 4 (Winter 2002): 423–449.

46. James Sesil et al., "Broad-Based Employee Stock Options in U.S. New Economy Firms," *British Journal of Industrial Relations* 40, no. 2 (June 2002): 273–294.

47. John Gamble, "ESOPs: Financial Performance and Federal Tax Incentives," *Journal of Labor Research* 9, no. 3 (Summer 1998): 529–542.

48. "Time Warner Stops Granting Stock Options to Most of Staff," *New York Times* (February 19, 2005): page na.

49. Brian Moore and Timothy Ross, *The Scanlon Way to Improved Productivity: A Practical Guide* (New York: Wiley, 1978), p. 2. See also Woodruff Imberman, "Is Gainsharing the Wave of the Future?" *Management Accounting* (November 1995): 35–38.

50. Based in part on Steven Markham, K. Dow Scott, and Walter Cox Jr., "The Evolutionary Development of a Scanlon Plan," *Compensation and Benefits Review* (March/April 1992): 50–56.

51. Ibid., 51.

52. Moore and Ross, *Scanlon Way to Improved Productivity,* pp. 1–2.

53. Robert Renn et al., "Earnings and Risk Incentive Plans: A Performance, Satisfaction and Turnover Dilemma," *Compensation and Benefits Review* (July/August 2001): 68–72.

54. Janet Wiscombe, "Can Pay for Performance Really Work?" *Workforce* (August 2001): 30.

55. Susan Marks, "Incentives that Really Reward and Motivate," *Workforce* (June 2001): 108–114.

56. William Bulkeley, "Incentives System Fine-Tunes Pay/Bonus Plans," *Wall Street Journal* (August 16, 2001): B4.

57. Nina McIntyre, "EIM Technology to Successfully Motivate Employees," *Compensation and Benefits Review* (July/August 2001): 57–60.

58. Jeremy Wuittner, "Plenty of Incentives to Use E.I.M. Software Systems," *American Banker* 168, no. 129 (July 8, 2003): 680.

59. Kathleen Cholewka, "Tech Tools," *Sales and Marketing Management* 153, no. 7 (July 2001): 24. See also Andrew Perlmutter, "Taking Motivation and Recognition Online," *Compensation and Benefits Review* (March–April 2002): 70–74.

60. "Survey Finds 99 Percent of Employers Providing Health-Care Benefits," *Compensation and Benefits Review* (September/October 2002): 11. See also National Compensation Survey: Employee Benefits in Private Industry in the United States, March 2006, U.S. Department of Labor, U.S. Bureau of Labor Statistics, August 2006.

61. "Employers Face Fifth Successive Year of Major Heath Cost Increases, Survey Finds," *BNA Human Resources Report* (October 6, 2003): 1050; and National Compensation Survey: Employee Benefits in Private Industry in the United States, March 2006, U.S. Department of Labor, U.S. Bureau of Labor Statistics, August 2006.

62. See, for example, Laurie Nacht, "Make an Appealing Case: How to Prepare for and Present an Unemployment Insurance Appeal," *Society for Human Resource Management Legal Report* (March/April 2004): 1–8.

63. Unscheduled Employee Absences Cost Companies More than Ever," *Compensation and Benefits Review* (March/April 2003): 19.

64. "SHRM Benefits Survey Finds Growth in Employer Use of Paid Leave Pools," *BNA Bulletin to Management* (March 21, 2002): 89.

65. Terry Baglieri, "Severance Pay," www.SHRM.org, accessed December 23, 2006.

66. Terry Baglieri, "Severance Pay," www.SHRM. org, accessed December 23, 2006.

67. "Workers Comp Claims Rise with Layoffs, but Employers Can Identify, Prevent Fraud," *BNA Bulletin to Management* (October 4, 2001): 313.

68. "Healthcare Tops List of Value Benefits," *BNA Bulletin to Management* (April 24, 2007): 132.

69. "As Workers Feel the Effect of Cost Hikes, Employers Turn to Health Remedies," *BNA Bulletin to Management* (April 18, 2002): 121.

70. "High Deductible Plans Might Catch On," *BNA Human Resource Report* (September 15, 2003): 967.

71. "HR Outsourcing: Managing Costs and Maximizing Provider Relations," *BNA, Inc.* 21, no. 11 (Washington, DC: November 2003): 10.

72. Ron Finch, "Preventive Services: Improving the Bottom Line for Employers and Employees," *Compensation & Benefits Review* (March/April 2005): 18.

73. Ibid. See also Josh Cable, "The Road to Wellness," *Occupational Hazards* (April 2007): 23–27.

74. Vanessa Fuhrmanns, "Oops! As Health Plans Become More Complicated, They're Also Subject to a Lot More Costly Mistakes," *Wall Street Journal* (January 24, 2005): r4.

75. Betty Liddick, "Going the Distance for Health Savings," *HR Magazine* (March 2007): 51–55.

76. Martocchio, *Strategic Compensation,* pp. 245–248; and Lin Grensing-Pophal, "A Pension Formula that Pays Off," *HR Magazine* (February 2003): 58–62.

77. "New Pension Law Plus a Recent Court Ruling Doom Age-Related Suits, Practitioners Say," *BNA Bulletin to Management* 57, no. 36 (September 5, 2006): 281–282.

78. James Benson and Barbara Suzaki, "After Tax Reform, Part III: Planning Executive Benefits," *Compensation and Benefits Review* 20, no. 2 (March/April 1988): 45–57; "Post-Retirement Benefits Impact of FASB New Accounting Rule" (February 23, 1989): 57.

79. Joseph O'Connell, "Using Employee Assistance Programs to Avoid Crises," *Long Island Business News* (April 19, 2002): 10.

80. Richard Buddin and Kanika Kapur, "The Effect of Employer-Sponsored Education on Job Mobility: Evidence from the U.S. Navy," *Industrial Relations* 44, no. 2 (April 2005): 341–363; see also Michael Laff, "US Employers Tighten Reins on Tuition Reimbursement," *Training and Development* (July 2006): 18.

81. Sue Shellenbarger, "Companies Retool Time Off Policies to Prevent Burnout, Reward Performance," *Wall Street Journal* (January 5, 2006): D1.

82. Brian O'Connell, "No Baby Sitter? Emergency Child Care to the Rescue" (May 2005) www.SHRM.org/rewards/library, accessed December 23, 2006; Kathy Gurchiek, "Give Us Your Sick," *HR Magazine* (January 2007): 91–93.

83. "Employers Gain from Elder Care Programs by Boosting Workers Morale, Productivity," *BNA Bulletin to Management* 57, no. 10 (March 7, 2006): 73–74.

84. Sue Shellenbarger, "The Mommy Drain: Employers Beef Up Perks to Lure New Mothers Back to Work," *Wall Street Journal* (September 28, 2006): D1.

85. "Making Up for Lost Time: How Employers Can Curb Excessive Unscheduled Absences," *BNA Human Resources Report* (October 20, 2003): 1097.

86. Timothy Judge et al., "Work Family Conflict and Emotions: Effects at Work and at Home," *Personnel Psychology* 50 no. 9 (2006): 779–814. (Op. cit., page 807.)

87. "Couples Want Flexible Benefits," *BNA Bulletin to Management* (February 19, 1998): 53; *2003 Benefits Survey,* SHRM/SHRM Foundation, p. 2.

88. Scott Harper, "Online Resources System Boosts Worker Awareness," *BNA Bulletin to Management* (April 10, 2007): 119.

89. Elayne Robertson Demby, "Two Stores Refused to Join the Race to the Bottom for Benefits and Wages," *Workforce Management* (February 2004): 57.

8

ETHICS AND FAIR TREATMENT IN HUMAN RESOURCE MANAGEMENT

- Ethics and Fair Treatment at Work
- What Shapes Ethical Behavior at Work?
- Ethics, Fair Treatment, and the Role of HR Management
- Employee Discipline and Privacy
- Managing Dismissals

When you finish studying this chapter, you should be able to:

- Explain *what is meant by ethical behavior.*

- Discuss *important factors that shape ethical behavior at work.*

- Discuss *at least four specific ways in which HR management can influence ethical behavior at work.*

- Exercise *fair disciplinary practices.*

- Discuss *at least four important factors in managing dismissals effectively.*

INTRODUCTION

Wal-Mart recently instituted a new employee scheduling system, to improve how the firm utilizes its personnel. Formerly, employees had predictable work shifts, for instance Tuesday–Friday, noon–5. With the new system, employees must list, on "availability forms," what hours during the day and night they are ready and willing to work. Then, as the store's customer traffic rises and falls, supervisors will call in to work or send home employees to meet demand. This is good for the stores' staffing needs. However, many Wal-Mart critics felt that by forcing employees to work relatively unpredictable hours, the new system would rip apart many employees' family lives, and so was unethical and unfair.

ETHICS AND FAIR TREATMENT AT WORK

People face ethical choices every day. For example, is it wrong to use company e-mail for personal reasons? Is a $50 gift to a boss unacceptable? Compare your answers to those of other Americans by answering the quiz in Figure 8.1.

FIGURE 8.1   *The Wall Street Journal* Workplace—Ethics Quiz

The spread of technology into the workshop has raised a variety of new ethical questions, and many old ones still linger. Compare your answers with those of other Americans surveyed, on page 291.

Office Technology

1. Is it wrong to use company e-mail for personal reasons?
   ☐ Yes   ☐ No

2. Is it wrong to use office equipment to help your children or spouse do schoolwork?
   ☐ Yes   ☐ No

3. Is it wrong to play computer games on office equipment during the workday?
   ☐ Yes   ☐ No

4. Is it wrong to use office equipment to do Internet shopping?
   ☐ Yes   ☐ No

5. Is it unethical to blame an error you made on a technological glitch?
   ☐ Yes   ☐ No

6. Is it unethical to visit pornographic Web sites using office equipment?
   ☐ Yes   ☐ No

Gifts and Entertainment

7. What's the value at which a gift from a supplier or client becomes troubling?
   ☐ $25   ☐ $50   ☐ $100

8. Is a $50 gift to a boss unacceptable?
   ☐ Yes   ☐ No

9. Is a $50 gift *from* the boss unacceptable?
   ☐ Yes   ☐ No

10. Of gifts from suppliers: Is it OK to take a $200 pair of football tickets?
    ☐ Yes   ☐ No

11. Is it OK to take a $120 pair of theater tickets?
    ☐ Yes   ☐ No

12. Is it OK to take a $100 holiday food basket?
    ☐ Yes   ☐ No

13. Is it OK to take a $25 gift certificate?
    ☐ Yes   ☐ No

14. Can you accept a $75 prize won at a raffle at a supplier's conference?
    ☐ Yes   ☐ No

Truth and Lies

15. Due to on-the-job pressure, have you ever abused or lied about sick days?
    ☐ Yes   ☐ No

16. Due to on-the-job pressure, have you ever taken credit for someone else's work or idea?
    ☐ Yes   ☐ No

Source: Wall Street Journal (21 Oct 1999): B1–B4. Ethics Offer Association Belmont, MA: Ethics Leadership Group.

While headlines tend to focus on top management WorldCom-type financial misdeeds, many ethical blunders actually stem from HR-related tasks such as disciplinary fairness, sexual harassment, and performance reviews.[1] One survey found that 6 of the 10 most serious ethical issues—workplace safety, security of employee records, employee theft, affirmative action, comparable work, and employee privacy rights—were HR related.[2]

Of course, human resource activities need not just be a potential hotbed of ethical misdeeds. Instead, HR activities can drive positive ethical change, and can play a central role in the company's ethics efforts. We focus on how in this and the following sections. Let's look first at what *ethics* means.

The Meaning of Ethics

Ethics refers to "the principles of conduct governing an individual or a group,"[3] and specifically to the standards you use to decide what your conduct should be. Ethical decisions are always characterized by two things. First, ethical decisions always involve normative judgments.[4] A *normative judgment* implies that "something is good or bad, right or wrong, better or worse."[5] "You are wearing a skirt and blouse" is a nonnormative statement; "That's a great outfit!" is a normative one.

Ethical decisions—principles of conduct—are also always rooted in *morality*, which is society's accepted standards of behavior. Moral standards differ from other standards in several ways.[6] They address matters of serious consequence to society's well-being, such as murder, lying, and slander. They cannot be established or changed by decisions of authoritative bodies like legislatures,[7] and they should override self-interest. Many people believe that moral judgments are never situational. They would argue that something that is morally right (or wrong) in one situation is right (or wrong) in another. Violating moral standards may make you feel ashamed or remorseful.[8]

Ethics and the Law

Perhaps surprisingly, the law is not the best guide about what is ethical, because something may be legal but not right, and something may be right but not legal. Firing a 38-year-old employee with 20 years' tenure without notice may be unethical, but still legal, for instance. Sometimes behavior is illegal and unethical. For example, one huge meat processor had to respond to a federal indictment charging it with smuggling illegal immigrants from Mexico to cut factory costs.[9] Patrick Gnazzo, vice president for business practices at United Technologies Corp. (and a former trial lawyer) put it this way: "Don't lie, don't cheat, don't steal. We were all raised with essentially the same values. *Ethics* means making decisions that represent what you stand for, not just what the laws are."[10]

Ethics, Fair Treatment, and Justice

Companies where fairness and justice prevail also tend to be ethical companies. One study concluded that, "to the extent that survey respondents believed that employees were treated fairly . . . [they] reported less unethical behavior in their organizations. They also reported that employees and their organizations were more aware of ethical issues [and] more likely to ask for ethical advice."[11] Similarly, "[H]iring, performance evaluation, discipline, and terminations can be ethical issues because they all involve

FIGURE 8.2	Perceptions of Fair Interpersonal Treatment Scale

What is your organization like most of the time? Circle YES if the item describes your organization, NO if it does not describe your organization, and ? if you cannot decide.

IN THIS ORGANIZATION . . .

1. Employees are praised for good work	Yes	?	No
2. Supervisors yell at employees (R)	Yes	?	No
3. Supervisors play favorites (R)	Yes	?	No
4. Employees are trusted	Yes	?	No
5. Employees' complaints are dealt with effectively	Yes	?	No
6. Employees are treated like children (R)	Yes	?	No
7. Employees are treated with respect	Yes	?	No
8. Employees' questions and problems are responded to quickly	Yes	?	No
9. Employees are lied to (R)	Yes	?	No
10. Employees' suggestions are ignored (R)	Yes	?	No
11. Supervisors swear at employees (R)	Yes	?	No
12. Employees' hard work is appreciated	Yes	?	No
13. Supervisors threaten to fire or lay off employees (R)	Yes	?	No
14. Employees are treated fairly	Yes	?	No
15. Co-workers help each other out	Yes	?	No
16. Co-workers argue with each other (R)	Yes	?	No
17. Co-workers put each other down (R)	Yes	?	No
18. Co-workers treat each other with respect	Yes	?	No

Note: R = the item is reverse scored.

Source: Michelle A. Donovan et al., "The Perceptions of Their Interpersonal Treatment Scale: Development and Validation of a Measure of Interpersonal Treatment in the Workplace," *Journal of Applied Psychology* 83, no. 5 (1998): 692. Copyright © 1997 by Michelle A. Donovan, Fritz Drasgow, and Liberty J. Munson at the University of Illinois at Urbana-Champaign. All rights reserved.

honesty, fairness, and the dignity of the individual."[12] In practice, fair treatment reflects concrete actions such as "employees are trusted," "employees are treated with respect," and "employees are treated fairly" (see Figure 8.2).[13]

Workplace Unfairness

Workplace unfairness can be blatant. For example, some supervisors are workplace bullies, yelling at or ridiculing subordinates, humiliating them, and sometimes even making threats. Not surprisingly, employees of abusive supervisors are more likely to quit their jobs, and to report lower job and life satisfaction and higher stress if they remain in those jobs.[14]

The employer should of course always prohibit such behavior, and many firms do have antiharassment policies. The policy at the Oregon Department of Transportation is that "it is the policy of the department that all employees, customers, contractors and visitors to the work site are entitled to a positive, respectful and productive work environment, free from behavior, actions, [and] language constituting workplace harassment."[15]

Why Treat Employees Fairly?

There are many reasons that managers should be fair and just, and some are more obvious than others. The golden rule is one obvious reason: As management guru Peter Drucker has said, "[t]hey're not employees, they're people," and the manager should treat people with dignity and respect. An increasingly litigious workforce is another reason. The manager wants to be sure to institute disciplinary and discharge procedures that will survive the scrutiny of arbitrators and the courts.

What may not be quite so obvious is that employees' perceptions of fairness also have important organizational ramifications. For example, perceptions of fairness relate to enhanced employee commitment; enhanced satisfaction with the organization, jobs, and leaders; and enhanced organizational citizenship behaviors.[16]

Example

A study provides a vivid illustration. College instructors completed surveys regarding the extent to which they saw their colleges as treating them with *procedural* and *distributive justice*. (Researchers generally distinguish between procedural justice and distributive justice. The former refers to fair processes, while the latter refers to fair outcomes.) The procedural justice questions included, for example, "In general, the department/college's procedures allow for requests for clarification for additional information about a decision." The distributive justice questions included, "I am fairly rewarded considering the responsibilities I have." These instructors also completed organizational commitment questionnaires. These included questions such as "I am proud to tell others that I am part of this department/college." Their students then completed surveys. These contained items such as "the instructor put a lot of effort into planning the content of this course," "the instructor was sympathetic to my needs," and "the instructor treated me fairly."

The results were telling. Instructors who perceived high distributive and procedural justice reported higher organizational commitment. Furthermore, their students reported higher levels of instructor effort, prosocial behaviors, and fairness, as well as more positive reactions to their instructors. "Overall," as the researcher says, "the results imply that fair treatment of employees has important organizational consequences...."[17]

WHAT SHAPES ETHICAL BEHAVIOR AT WORK?

Whether a person acts ethically at work is usually not a result of any one thing. Let's look first at the factors that shape ethical behavior, and then, in the following section, turn to the steps the manager can take to help ensure that ethics prevails.

Individual Factors

Because people bring to their jobs their own ideas of what is morally right and wrong, the individual must shoulder much of the credit (or blame) for the ethical choices he or she makes. Researchers conducted a survey of CEOs to explain the CEOs' intentions to engage (or to not engage) in two questionable business practices: soliciting a competitor's technological secrets and making payments to foreign government officials. The researchers concluded that the CEOs' personal predispositions more strongly affected their decisions than did environmental pressures or organizational characteristics.[18]

Traits

In terms of traits, it's hard to generalize about the characteristics of ethical or unethical people, but age is a factor. One study surveyed 421 employees to measure the degree to which age, gender, marital status, education, dependent children, region of the country, and years in business influenced responses to ethical decisions. (Decisions included "doing personal business on company time," and "calling in sick to take a day off for personal use.") Older workers in general had stricter interpretations of ethical standards and made more ethical decisions than did younger employees.

In any case, honesty testing (as discussed in Chapter 4) shows that some people are more inclined toward making the wrong ethical choice. How would you rate your own ethics? Figure 8.3 presents a short self-assessment survey for helping you answer that question.

Organizational Factors

If people did unethical things at work solely for personal gain, it perhaps would be understandable (though inexcusable). The scary thing about unethical behavior at work is that it's often not driven by personal interests. Table 8.1 on page 269 summarizes the results of one survey of the principal causes of ethical compromises, as reported by six levels of employees and managers.

As you can see, being under the gun to meet scheduling pressures was the number-one factor in causing ethical lapses. For most of these employees, "meeting overly aggressive financial or business objectives" and "helping the company survive" were the two other top causes. "Advancing my own career or financial interests" ranked toward the bottom of the list of principal reported causes of ethical compromises. Thus (at least in this case), most ethical lapses occurred because employees were under the gun to do what they thought was best to help their companies.

Examples

Several years ago, a judge sentenced WorldCom's former CFO to 5 years in jail, allegedly for helping the firm's former chairman, Bernard Ebbers, mask WorldCom's deteriorating financial situation. Among other things, the government accused him of instructing underlings to fraudulently book accounting entries, and of filing false statements with the SEC. Why, as a star CFO and someone trained to protect the interest of his shareholders, would the CFO do such a thing? "I took these actions, knowing they were wrong, in a misguided attempt to preserve the company to allow it to withstand what I believed were temporary financial difficulties."[19]

Having rules on the books forbidding this sort of thing does not, by itself, seem to work. For example, several years ago, New York's attorney general filed charges against Merrill Lynch, alleging that several of its analysts had issued optimistic ratings on stocks, while privately expressing concerns about those same stocks. The allegation was that they did so to aid and support Merrill Lynch's investment banking relationships with these companies. In making his case, the attorney general released numerous e-mails and other documents written by Merrill analysts. One, for instance, reportedly read:

> Some of the communication with the goto people and the bankers prior to the initiation may have been a technical violation of the firm's written policies and procedures (which, I have now learned, say the company's bankers should not be told what the proposed rating is or will be, even if the company isn't currently under coverage), so my guess is the lawyers will want to offer this in detail. From what they've told me, however, even if there was a violation, this is not a big deal.[20]

FIGURE 8.3   How Do My Ethics Rate?

Instrument

Indicate your level of agreement with these 15 statements using the following scale:

    1 = Strongly disagree
    2 = Disagree
    3 = Neither agree nor disagree
    4 = Agree
    5 = Strongly agree

	1	2	3	4	5
1. The only moral of business is making money.	1	2	3	4	5
2. A person who is doing well in business does not have to worry about moral problems.	1	2	3	4	5
3. Act according to the law, and you can't go wrong morally.	1	2	3	4	5
4. Ethics in business is basically an adjustment between expectations and the ways people behave.	1	2	3	4	5
5. Business decisions involve a realistic economic attitude and not a moral philosophy.	1	2	3	4	5
6. "Business ethics" is a concept for public relations only.	1	2	3	4	5
7. Competitiveness and profitability are important values.	1	2	3	4	5
8. Conditions of a free economy will best serve the needs of society. Limiting competition can only hurt society and actually violates basic natural laws.	1	2	3	4	5
9. As a consumer, when making an auto insurance claim, I try to get as much as possible regardless of the extent of the damage.	1	2	3	4	5
10. While shopping at the supermarket, it is appropriate to switch price tags on packages.	1	2	3	4	5
11. As an employee, I can take home office supplies; it doesn't hurt anyone.	1	2	3	4	5
12. I view sick days as vacation days that I deserve.	1	2	3	4	5
13. Employees' wages should be determined according to the laws of supply and demand.	1	2	3	4	5
14. The business world has its own rules.	1	2	3	4	5
15. A good businessperson is a successful businessperson.	1	2	3	4	5

ANALYSIS AND INTERPRETATION

Rather than specify "right" answers, this instrument works best when you compare your answer to those of others. With that in mind, here are mean responses from a group of 243 management students. How did your responses compare?

1. 3.09	6. 2.88	11. 1.58
2. 1.88	7. 3.62	12. 2.31
3. 2.54	8. 3.79	13. 3.36
4. 3.41	9. 3.44	14. 3.79
5. 3.88	10. 1.33	15. 3.38

Source: Adapted from A. Reichel and Y. Neumann, *Journal of Instructional Psychology* (March 1988): 25–53. With permission of the authors.

TABLE 8.1	Principal Causes of Ethical Compromises					
	Senior Mgmt.	*Middle Mgmt.*	*Front Line Supv.*	*Prof. Non-Mgmt.*	*Admin. Salaried*	*Hourly*
Meeting schedule pressure	1	1	1	1	1	1
Meeting overly aggressive financial or business objectives	3	2	2	2	2	2
Helping the company survive	2	3	4	4	3	4
Advancing the career interests of my boss	5	4	3	3	4	5
Feeling peer pressure	7	7	5	6	5	3
Resisting competitive threats	4	5	6	5	6	7
Saving jobs	9	6	7	7	7	6
Advancing my own career or financial interests	8	9	9	8	9	8
Other	6	8	8	9	8	9

Note: 1 is high; 9 is low.

Source: O. C. Ferrell and John Fraedrich, *Business Ethics,* 3d ed. (New York: Houghton Mifflin, 1997), p. 28. Adapted from Rebecca Goodell, *Ethics in American Business: Policies, Programs, and Perceptions* (1994), p. 54. Permission provided courtesy of the Ethics Resource Center, 1120 6th Street, NW, Washington, DC, 20005.

The Boss's Influence

Another essential element seems to be the extent to which employees can model their ethical behavior on the ethical behavior of their supervisors. According to one report, for instance, "the level of misconduct at work dropped dramatically when employees said their supervisors exhibited ethical behavior." Only 25% of employees who agreed that their supervisors "set a good example of ethical business behavior" said they had observed misconduct in the last year, compared with 72% of those who did not feel that their supervisors set good ethical examples.[21] Yet, in another poll, only about 27% of employees strongly agreed that their organizations' leadership is ethical.[22]

Examples of how supervisors knowingly (or unknowingly) lead subordinates astray ethically include:

- Tell staffers to do whatever is necessary to achieve results.
- Overload top performers to ensure that work gets done.
- Look the other way when wrongdoing occurs.
- Take credit for others' work or shift blame.[23]

Ethics Policies and Codes

An ethics policy and code is one way to signal that the firm is serious about ethics. For example, IBM's code of ethics has this to say about tips, gifts, and entertainment:

> No IBM employee, or any member of his or her immediate family, can accept gratuities or gifts of money from a supplier, customer, or anyone in a business relationship. Nor can they accept a gift or consideration that could be perceived as having been offered because of the business relationship. "Perceived" simply means this: if you read about it in the local newspaper, would you wonder whether the gift just might have had something to do with a business relationship? No IBM employee can give money or a gift of significant value to a customer, supplier, or any one if it could reasonably be viewed as being done to gain a business advantage.[24]

Sometimes ethics codes work, and sometimes they don't. Enron's ethical principles were widely available on the company's Web site. (Several years ago Enron was the target of various ethics and legal accusations.) They stated, among other things that, "as a partner in the communities in which we operate, Enron believes it has a responsibility to conduct itself according to certain basic principles." Those include, "respect, integrity, communication and excellence."[25]

Quick Test

Some firms urge employees to apply a quick "ethics test" to evaluate whether what they're about to do fits the company's code of conduct. For example, the Raytheon Co. asks employees who are faced with ethical dilemmas to ask:

Is the action legal?
Is it right?
Who will be affected?
Does it fit Raytheon's values?
How will it "feel" afterwards?
How will it look in the newspaper?
Will it reflect poorly on the company?[26]

Enforcement

However, don't underestimate the importance of enforcement. As one study of ethics concludes, "strong statements by managers may reduce the risk of legal and ethical violations by their work forces, but enforcement of standards has the greatest impact."[27] An increasing number of firms, such as Lockheed Martin Corp., appoint chief ethics officers—in Lockheed's case, Nancy Higgins, executive vice president of ethics and business conduct.[28]

The Organization's Culture

Ethics codes cannot themselves head off unethical behavior. About three fourths of U.S. firms have formal ethics codes, and most offer ethics training. Yet about 4 of every 10 employees in the United States say they witnessed serious legal or ethical problems where they work. Over 50% of all workers in the financial services and insurance industries said they felt under pressure to act illegally or unethically. Just under half reported participating in such activities.[29] What accounts for these anomalies?

One, as noted above, is that it's usually not just one or two things that create the environment in which unethical behavior can flourish; several things—the individual, the boss, the ethics code, and the degree of competition, for instance—interact. Another is that when it comes to ethical behavior, the manager sets values and creates a culture through what he or she says and does. Employees then take their signals from that behavior and culture, and it influences what they do. It's therefore important that the firm's culture send clear signals about what is and isn't acceptable behavior.

What Is Organizational Culture?

By *organizational culture* we mean the characteristic values, traditions, and behaviors a company's employees share. A *value* is a basic belief about what is right or wrong, or about what you should or shouldn't do. ("Honesty is the best policy" would be a value.) Values are important because they guide behavior. Managing people and shaping their ethical (and other) behavior therefore depends on influencing the values they use as behavioral guides.

To an outside observer, a company's culture would reflect itself in several ways. You could sense it from the employees' *patterns of behavior*, such as ceremonial events and written and spoken comments. For example, managers and employees may engage in behaviors such as hiding information, politicking, or expressing honest concern when a colleague requires assistance. You could also sense it from *physical manifestations* or symbols of the company's behavior, such as written rules, office layouts, organizational structure, and dress codes.[30]

These cultural symbols and behaviors tend to reflect the firm's shared values, such as "the customer is always right" or "don't be bureaucratic." If management and employees really believe "honesty is the best policy," the written rules they follow and the things they do should reflect this value. To encourage ethical behavior, the manager therefore has to ask, How can I send the signal that we believe in ethical values?

Culture and the Manager

They do so in the following ways:

Clarify Expectations   First, make it clear what your expectations are with respect to the values you want subordinates to follow. Publishing a corporate ethics code is one way to do this. For example, Johnson & Johnson's ethical code says, "We believe our first responsibility is to the doctors, nurses and patients, to mothers and fathers and all others who use our products and services." (Even in ethical companies, allegations of unethical behavior still arise. For example, two former Johnson & Johnson salesman recently sued J&J, alleging, amongst other things, that the firm unduly pressured salespeople to encourage sales of a new drug.)[31]

Use Signs and Symbols   "Walk the talk." *Symbolism*—what the manager actually does and thus the signals he or she sends—ultimately does the most to create and sustain the company's culture. For example, Southwest Airlines is known for its fun work attitude.[32] However, the company doesn't just talk about fun or humor in its mission statement. Instead, it sets the tone by what it does from the first day a person is hired. For example, new employees "are welcomed with balloons, games, toys, and gifts. New hires, even pilots, learn company songs or cheers during orientation."[33]

Provide Physical Support   The physical manifestations of the manager's values—the firm's incentive plan, appraisal system, and disciplinary procedures, for instance—send strong signals regarding what employees should and should not do. Does the firm reward ethical behavior or penalize it?

Use Stories   Managers use stories to illustrate important company values. For example, IBM has stories, such as how IBM salespeople took dramatic steps (like driving all night through storms) to get parts to customers.

Organize Rites and Ceremonies   For example, at JC Penney, new management employees are inducted at ritualistic conferences into the "Penney Partnership." Here they commit to the firm's ideology as embodied in its statement of core values. Each inductee solemnly swears allegiance to these values and then receives his or her "HCSC lapel pin." These letters symbolize JC Penney's core values of honor, confidence, service, and cooperation.

ETHICS, FAIR TREATMENT, AND THE ROLE OF HR MANAGEMENT

We've seen that there's no single cause of unethical behavior at work, so it is not surprising that there's no one "silver bullet" to prevent it. Creating a culture that encourages employees to do the right thing is one element. But, in addition, managers must take several steps to ensure ethical behavior by their employees. Many of these actions are clearly within the realm of HR. Let's consider specific examples.

Staffing and Selection

One writer says, "the simplest way to tune up an organization, ethically speaking, is to hire more ethical people."[34]

Dissuading ethically undesirable applicants can start before the applicant even applies. For example, the human resource department can create recruitment materials containing explicit references to the company's stress on integrity and ethics. Employers can then use tools such as honesty tests and meticulous background checks (discussed in Chapter 4) to screen out those who may not fit their ethical standards.[35]

The selection process also sends signals about what the company's values really are. For example, "if prospective employees perceive that the hiring process does not treat people fairly, they may assume that ethical behavior is not important in the company, and that 'official' pronouncements about the importance of ethics can be discounted."[36]

Managers don't necessarily need paper-and-pencil honesty tests to screen out ethically undesirable applicants. Comprehensive background checks—reference checks—are essential. And, having trained interviewers ask behavioral questions such as "Have you ever observed someone stretching the rules at work? What did you do about it?" and, "Have you ever had to go against company guidelines or procedures in order to get something done?" are useful. Make sure that everyone involved in interviewing the candidate reviews and shares all the information.[37]

Training

For all practical purposes, ethics training is basically mandatory today. Since 1991, federal sentencing guidelines have prescribed reduced penalties for employers accused of misconduct who implement codes of conduct and ethics training.[38] And the Sarbanes-Oxley Act of 2002 (see the Improving Productivity through HRIS Feature) makes ethics training even more important.

Ethics training usually includes showing employees how to recognize ethical dilemmas, how to use ethical frameworks (such as codes of conduct) to resolve problems, and how to use HR functions (such as interviews and disciplinary practices) in ethical ways.[39] However, emphasizing the mechanics of ethics compliance is not enough. Instead, the training should also emphasize the moral underpinnings of the ethical choice and the company's deep commitment to integrity and ethics, and include the participation of top managers to underscore that commitment. Some ethics training may simply be futile. For example, honest employees may be more amenable to ethics training than dishonest ones.[40]

Improving Productivity through HRIS: Web-Based Training for Sarbanes-Oxley

Particularly in very large companies, designing and managing ethics programs isn't easy or cheap. Doing so requires the almost continuous attention of the company's top managers, as well as a considerable investment in setting up and monitoring ethics codes and training employees.

Passage of the Sarbanes-Oxley Act of 2002 made ethics compliance even more expensive. Among other things, the act requires that the CEO and the CFO of publicly traded companies personally attest to the accuracy of their companies' financial statements, and also to the fact that its internal controls are adequate.[41] As one lawyer put it, "Sarbanes-Oxley has added a wide range of new issues to the traditional compliance function."[42]

With their personal credibility on the line, the new law has focused top management's attention on ensuring that all the firm's employees take ethics very seriously. This means big, publicly traded firms are becoming much more serious about providing ethics-related education and training and about making sure they can prove that their employees actually got trained.

The problem is, training and following up programs like this can be very expensive. Larger firms need a cost-effective way of making such training available. That's why when DTE Energy, with 14,000 employees, needed an ethics training system, it turned to a Web-based program from Integrity Interactive Corp. of Waltham, Massachusetts. Now, all the company's employees have easy access to a standardized ethics training program through their PCs, and DTE can easily track who has taken the training and who has not. The employees can take the training when they want to, and the company can monitor their progress. As one officer at Integrity Interactive puts it:

> It would have been easy in the 1990s for companies to say, "We have 30,000 employees and 40% turnover. There's no way to train all these people in our code of conduct and ethical compliance. . . . The Internet has taken that excuse away. It is now physically possible to reach anyone, anywhere on the globe—and what's more, to prove that you're doing it."[43]

FIGURE 8.4   The Role of Training in Ethics

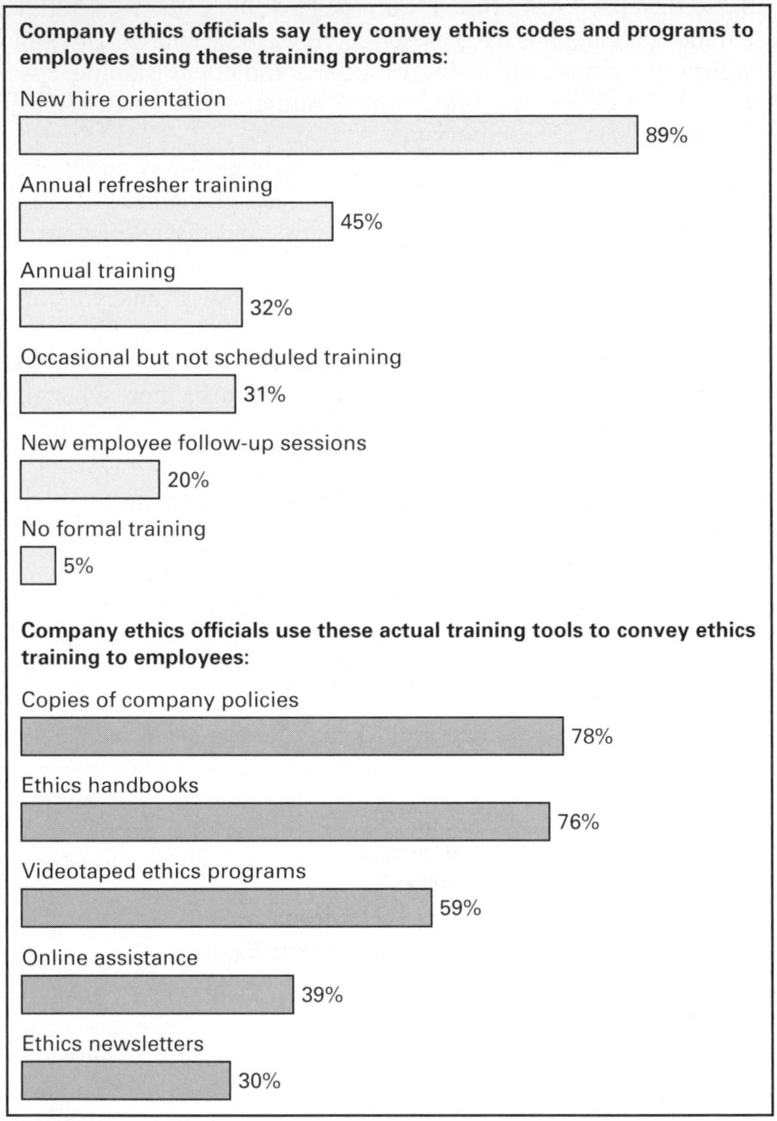

Company ethics officials say they convey ethics codes and programs to employees using these training programs:

New hire orientation
89%

Annual refresher training
45%

Annual training
32%

Occasional but not scheduled training
31%

New employee follow-up sessions
20%

No formal training
5%

Company ethics officials use these actual training tools to convey ethics training to employees:

Copies of company policies
78%

Ethics handbooks
76%

Videotaped ethics programs
59%

Online assistance
39%

Ethics newsletters
30%

Source: Susan Wells, "Turn Employees into Saints," *HR Magazine* (December 1999): p. 52. Copyright © 1999 by Society for Human Resource Management (SHRM). Reproduced with permission of Society for Human Resource Management (SHRM) in the format Textbook via Copyright Clearance Center.

Figure 8.4 shows how other employers use training in their ethics programs. Other online training tools to help employers promote ethics at work include Business Ethics, an online course from skillsoft.com; and two online courses, Ethical Decision-Making and Managerial Business Ethics, both from netG.com.[44]

Performance Appraisal

Studies confirm that, in practice, some managers ignore accuracy and honesty in performance appraisals and instead use the process for political purposes (such as encouraging employees with whom they don't get along to leave the firm).[45] To send the signal that fairness and ethics are supreme, the employees' standards should be clear, employees should understand the basis on which they're going to be appraised, and the appraisals themselves should be performed objectively and fairly.[46]

Reward and Disciplinary Systems

To the extent that behavior is a function of its consequences, the company (and HR) must ensure that the firm rewards ethical behavior and penalizes unethical behavior. In fact, "research suggests that employees expect the organization to dole out relatively harsh punishment for unethical conduct."[47] Where the company does not do so, it's often the ethical employees (not the unethical ones) who feel punished. Particularly in light of the top executives' ethics problems in the headlines recently, it's also important for the company to send the right signals by also disciplining executives who misbehave.[48]

Workplace Aggression and Violence

We will see in Chapter 10 that workplace aggression and violence are increasingly serious problems, as well as problems that often stem from real or perceived inequities. Thus, employees who see themselves as unfairly underpaid may take negative actions ranging from employee theft to destruction of company property.

Similarly, many human resource actions including layoffs, being passed over for promotion, terminations, and discipline can prompt perceptions of unfair treatment that translate into dysfunctional behavior.[49] For one thing, mistreatment at work makes it more likely the employee will resign, and also that the person will show higher levels of "work withdrawal," in other words show up for work, but not do his or her best.[50]

Building Two-Way Communication

The opportunity for two-way communication affects our perceptions of how fairly we're being treated. Studies support this commonsense observation. One study concluded that three actions contributed to perceived fairness in business settings. These included *engagement* (involving individuals in the decisions that affect them by asking for their input and allowing them to refute the merits of one another's ideas and assumptions), *explanation* (ensuring that everyone involved and affected should understand why final decisions are made as they are and of the thinking that underlies the decisions), and *expectation clarity* (making sure everyone knows up front by what standards they will be judged and the penalties for failure).[51]

Steps to Take

Many employers therefore take steps to facilitate two-way communication. For example, at Toyota Motor Manufacturing in Lexington, Kentucky, a *hotline* gives employees an anonymous way to bring questions or problems to management's attention. The hotline is available 24 hours per day. Employees can pick up any phone, dial the hotline extension (the number is posted on the plant bulletin boards), and deliver their messages to the recorder. The HR manager reviews and answers all messages. Other firms administer periodic **opinion surveys.** For example, the FedEx Survey Feedback Action (SFA) program includes an anonymous survey. This lets employees express feelings about the company and their managers, and to some extent about service, pay, and benefits. Each manager then has an opportunity to discuss the anonymous department results with his or her subordinates, and create an action plan for improving work group commitment. Sample questions include:

> "I can tell my manager what I think."
> "My manager tells me what is expected."
> "My manager listens to my concerns."
> "My manager keeps me informed."

Other Illustrative HR Ethics Activities

Human resource management supports the employer's ethics programs in other ways. For example, it is usually either HR or the firm's legal department that heads up its ethical compliance efforts. One study of Fortune 500 companies concluded that a human resources officer was responsible for the program in 28% of responding firms. Another 28% gave the firm's legal officers responsibility, and 16% established separate ethics or compliance departments. The rest of the firms spread the responsibility among auditing departments, or positions such as public affairs and corporate communications.[52] Every 2 years Lockheed Martin surveys its employees regarding their adherence to the Lockheed's ethics code. It then institutes new ethics training programs based on the feedback it receives.[53]

Strategy and HR

Many people accused Wal-Mart of unfairness after it instituted its new policy requiring employees to basically stand ready to come to work at a moment's notice, depending on their stores' last-minute needs. From Wal-Mart's point of view, the change made strategic sense. Their competitive advantage is low costs (and thus "low prices—every day"). The new employee scheduling policy enabled Wal-Mart to minimize labor costs when stores were slow. Would you consider Wal-Mart's new store staffing policy to be unethical? Why or why not? If it is, how do you think that might affect Wal-Mart's performance going forward?

EMPLOYEE DISCIPLINE AND PRIVACY

The purpose of **discipline** is to encourage employees to behave sensibly at work (where *sensible* is defined as adhering to rules and regulations). In an organization, rules and regulations serve about the same purpose that laws do in society; discipline is called for when one of these rules or regulations is violated.[54] A fair and just discipline process is based on three pillars: rules and regulations, a system of progressive penalties, and an appeals process.

Three Pillars

Rules

A set of clear rules and regulations is the first pillar. These rules address issues such as theft, destruction of company property, drinking on the job, and insubordination. Examples of rules include:

> *Poor performance is not acceptable.* Each employee is expected to perform his or her work properly and efficiently and to meet established standards of quality.
>
> *Alcohol and drugs do not mix with work.* The use of either during working hours and reporting for work under the influence of either are both strictly prohibited.
>
> *The vending of anything in the plant without authorization is not allowed; nor is gambling in any form permitted.*

The purpose of these rules is to inform employees ahead of time what is and is not acceptable behavior. Employees must be told, preferably in writing, what is not permitted. This usually occurs during the employee's orientation. The employee orientation handbook usually contains the rules and regulations.

Penalties

A system of progressive penalties is a second pillar of effective discipline. Penalties may range from oral warnings to written warnings to suspension from the job to discharge. The severity of the penalty is usually a function of the type of offense and the number of times the offense has occurred. For example, most companies issue warnings for the first unexcused lateness. However, for a fourth offense, discharge is the usual disciplinary action.

Appeals Process

Finally, an appeals process should be part of the disciplinary process; this helps to ensure that supervisors mete out discipline fairly and equitably.

Consider FedEx's **guaranteed fair treatment** multistep program. In *step 1, management review,* the complainant submits a written complaint to a member of management (manager, senior manager, or managing director). Then the manager, senior manager, and managing director of the employee's group review all relevant information; hold a telephone conference and/or meeting with the complainant; make a decision to either uphold, modify, or overturn management's action; and communicate their decision in writing to the complainant and the department's personnel representative.

If not satisfied, then in *step 2, officer complaint,* the complainant submits a written appeal to the vice president or senior vice president of the division within 7 calendar days of the step 1 decision.

Finally, in *step 3, executive appeals review,* the complainant may submit a written complaint within 7 calendar days of the step 2 decision to the employee relations department. This department then investigates and prepares a case file for the executive review appeals board. The appeals board—the CEO, the COO, the chief HR officer, and three senior vice presidents—then reviews all relevant information and makes a decision to uphold, overturn, or initiate a board of review or to take other appropriate action. The *HR in Practice* box summarizes discipline guidelines.

FAIR DISCIPLINE GUIDELINES

- *Make sure the evidence supports the charge of employee wrongdoing.* In one study, "the employer's evidence did not support the charge of employee wrongdoing" was the most frequent reason arbitrators gave for reinstating discharged employees or for reducing disciplinary suspensions.[55]

- *Ensure that the employees' due process rights are protected.* Arbitrators normally reverse discharges and suspensions that are imposed in a manner that violates basic notions of fairness or employee due process procedures.[56] For example, follow established progressive discipline procedures, and don't deny the employee an opportunity to tell his or her side of the story.[57]

- *The discipline should be in line with the way management usually responds to similar incidents.*[58]

- *Adequately warn the employee of the disciplinary consequences of his or her alleged misconduct.*

- *The rule that allegedly was violated should be "reasonably related" to the efficient and safe operation of the particular work environment.*

- *Management must fairly and adequately investigate the matter before administering discipline.*

- *The investigation should produce substantial evidence of misconduct.*

- *Applicable rules, orders, or penalties should be applied evenhandedly and without discrimination.*

- *The penalty should be reasonably related to the misconduct and to the employee's past work history.*

- *Maintain the employee's right to counsel.* For example, all union employees generally have the right to bring help when they are called in for an interview that they reasonably believe might lead to disciplinary action.

- *Don't rob your subordinate of his or her dignity.* For example, discipline your subordinate in private.

- *Remember that the burden of proof is on you.* In U.S. society, a person is always considered innocent until proven guilty.

- *Get the facts.* Don't base your decision on hearsay evidence or on your general impression.

- *Don't act while angry.* Very few people can be objective and sensible when they are angry.

- *Use ombudsmen.* Some companies establish independent ombudsmen, neutral counselors outside the normal chain of command to whom employees who believe they were treated unfairly can turn for confidential advice.[59]

Discipline Without Punishment

Traditional discipline has two potential flaws. It often leaves a residue of ill will. And, forcing your rules on employees may gain their short-term compliance, but not their cooperation when you're not around to enforce the rules.

Discipline without punishment (or nonpunitive discipline) aims to avoid these disciplinary problems. It does this by gaining the employees' acceptance of your rules and by reducing the punitive nature of the discipline itself. Typical steps include:

1. *Issue an oral reminder.* Here, your goal is to get the employee to agree to solve the disciplinary problem.

2. *Should another incident arise within 6 weeks, issue the employee a formal written reminder, a copy of which is placed in the personnel file.* In addition, privately hold a second discussion with the employee, again without any threats.

3. *Give a paid 1-day "decision-making leave."* If another incident occurs after the written warning in the next 6 weeks or so, the employee is told to take a 1-day leave with pay to stay home and consider whether the job is right for him or her and whether he or she wants to abide by the company's rules. When the employee returns to work, he or she meets with you and gives you a decision regarding whether he or she will follow the rules.

4. *If no further incidents occur in the next year or so, the 1-day paid suspension is purged from the person's file.* If the behavior is repeated, dismissal (see later discussion) is required.[60]

The process would not apply to exceptional circumstances. Criminal behavior or in-plant fighting might be grounds for immediate **dismissal,** for instance. And if several incidents occurred at very close intervals, the supervisor might skip step 2—the written warning.

Electronic Employee Privacy

A New Jersey court recently found an employer there liable when one of its employees used his company computer at work to distribute child pornography. (Someone had previously alerted the employer to the suspicious activity and the employer had not taken action.[61])

Managing and monitoring company e-mail is an urgent problem. About one-third of U.S. companies recently investigated suspected leaks, via e-mail, of confidential or proprietary information. One hospital found that, to facilitate working at home, many medical staff were e-mailing patients' confidential health care records to themselves, in violation of federal privacy statutes. Other employers must routinely produce employee e-mail as part of litigation, as when one employee accuses another of sexual harassment. It's therefore not surprising that in one recent survey, over half of employers said they were monitoring their employees' incoming and outgoing e-mail; 27% monitor internal e-mail as well.[62] Such monitoring raises privacy issues.

Types of Privacy Violations

The four main types of employee privacy violations upheld by courts are intrusion (locker room and bathroom surveillance), publication of private matters, disclosure of medical records, and appropriation of an employee's name or likeness for commercial purposes.[63] Background checks, monitoring off-duty conduct and lifestyle, drug testing, workplace searches, and monitoring of workplace activities trigger most privacy violations.

Extent

Employee monitoring and surveillance are widespread. For example, as noted above, over half of employers report monitoring employees' e-mail. Employers ranging from United Parcel Service to the City of Oakland, California, use GPS units to monitor their truckers', delivery people's, and street sweepers' whereabouts.[64] And, many more employers, like Bronx Lebanon Hospital in New York, use biometric scanners, for instance, to ensure that the employee that clocks in is really who he or she says they are.[65]

Software can "secretly record everything your spouse, children and employees do online" on a particular computer.[66] When Turner Broadcasting System Inc. noticed that employees at its CNN London business bureau were piling up overtime claims, they installed new software to monitor every Web page every worker used. Now, "If we see people were surfing the Web all day, then they don't have to be paid for that overtime."[67]

Legal Issues

Electronic eavesdropping is legal—up to a point. For example, federal law and most states' laws allow employers to monitor their employees' phone calls "in the ordinary course of business," says one legal expert. However, they must stop listening once they see the conversation is personal, not business related.[68] E-mail service may also be intercepted under federal law when it is to protect the property rights of the provider.[69]

However, to be safe, more employers today are issuing e-mail and online services usage policies to, for instance, forewarn employees that those systems are intended to be used for business purposes only. They are having employees sign e-mail monitoring and telephone monitoring acknowledgment statements. One reason for explicit policy statements is the risk that employers may be held liable for illegal acts committed by their employees via e-mail. For example, messages sent by supervisors that contain sexual innuendo could mean problems for the employer if the employer hasn't taken steps to prohibit such e-mail misuse.

Videotaping in the workplace seems to call for more legal caution. In one case, one U.S. Court of Appeals ruled that an employer's continuous video surveillance of employees in an office setting did not constitute an unconstitutional invasion of privacy.[70] Yet, a Boston employer had to pay over $200,000 to five workers it secretly videotaped in an employee locker room, after they sued in state court.[71]

MANAGING DISMISSALS

Because dismissal is the most drastic disciplinary step, the manager should ensure that the dismissal is fair, warranted, and just. On those occasions that require immediate dismissal, the manager still needs to ensure that the action is humane.

The best way to "handle" a dismissal is to avoid it in the first place, when possible. Many dismissals start with bad hiring decisions. Using sound selection practices including assessment tests, reference and background checks, drug testing, and clearly defined jobs can reduce the need for dismissals.[72]

Termination at Will

For more than 100 years, the prevailing rule in the United States has been that without an employment contract, either the employer or the employee can **terminate at will** the employment relationship. In other words, the employee could resign for any reason, at will, and the employer could similarly dismiss an employee for any reason, at will. Today, however, dismissed employees are increasingly taking their cases to court, and in many cases employers are finding that they no longer have a blanket right to fire.

Termination at Will Exceptions

Three main protections against wrongful discharge have eroded the termination-at-will doctrine—statutory exceptions, common law exceptions, and public policy exceptions.

First, in terms of *statutory exceptions*, federal and state equal employment and workplace laws prohibit specific types of dismissals. For example, Title VII of the Civil Rights Act of 1964 prohibits discharging employees based on race, color, religion, sex, or national origin.[73]

Second, numerous *common law exceptions* exist. For example, a court may decide that an employee handbook promising termination only "for just cause" may create an exception to the at-will rule.[74]

Finally, under the *public policy exception*, courts have held a discharge to be wrongful when it was against an explicit, well-established public policy (for instance, the employer fired the employee for refusing to break the law).

Grounds for Dismissal

There are four bases for dismissal: unsatisfactory performance, misconduct, lack of qualifications for the job, and changed requirements of (or elimination of) the job. *Unsatisfactory performance* may be defined as a persistent failure to perform assigned duties or to meet prescribed standards on the job.[75] Specific reasons include excessive absenteeism; tardiness; a persistent failure to meet normal job requirements; or an adverse attitude toward the company, supervisor, or fellow employees. *Misconduct* is deliberate and willful violation of the employer's rules and may include stealing, rowdy behavior, and insubordination. *Lack of qualifications for the job* is an employee's inability to do the assigned work, although he or she is diligent. Because in this case the employee may be trying to do the job, it is reasonable for the employer to do what's possible to salvage him or her—perhaps by assigning the employee to another job, or retraining the person. *Changed requirements of the job* involve an employee's incapability of doing the work assigned, after the nature of the job has been changed. Similarly, you may have to dismiss an employee when his or her job is eliminated. Again, the employee may be industrious, so it is reasonable to retrain or transfer this person, if possible.

Insubordination, a form of misconduct, is sometimes the grounds for dismissal. Stealing, chronic tardiness, and poor-quality work are concrete grounds for dismissal, but insubordination is sometimes harder to translate into words. Some acts should be deemed insubordinate whenever and wherever they occur. These include, for instance, direct disregard of the boss's authority, and disobedience of, or refusal to obey, the boss's orders—particularly in front of others.

Dismissing employees is never easy, but at least the employer can try to ensure the employee views the process as fair and just. Communication is important. One study found that "individuals who reported that they were given full explanations of why and how termination decisions were made were more likely to (1) perceive their layoff as fair, (2) endorse the terminating organization, and (3) indicate that they did not wish to take the past employer to court."[76]

Avoiding Wrongful Discharge Suits

In what it recently referred to as a "fear of the firing," *Business Week* magazine described several examples of how some employers—even when faced with employee theft—were reluctant to terminate disruptive employees, for fear of lawsuits. In practice, plaintiffs only win a tiny fraction of such suits. However, the cost of defending the suits is still huge.[77]

Wrongful discharge occurs when an employee's dismissal does not comply with the law or with the contractual arrangement stated or implied by the firm via its employment application forms, employee manuals, or other promises. (In a *constructive discharge* claim, the plaintiff argues that he or she quit, but had no choice because the employer made the situation so intolerable at work.[78]) The time to protect against such suits is before the manager has erred and suits are filed.

If humanitarianism and wrongful discharge suits aren't enough to encourage you to be fair in dismissing, consider this. Managers run double their usual risk of suffering a heart attack during the week after they fire an employee.[79] During one 5-year period, physicians interviewed 791 working people who had just undergone heart attacks to find out what might have triggered them. The researchers concluded that the stress associated with firing someone doubled the usual risk of a heart attack for the person doing the firing, during the week following the dismissal.

Procedural Steps

Avoiding wrongful discharge suits requires a two-prong strategy. First is to lay the groundwork—starting with the employment application—that will help avoid such suits before they get started. Steps to take include the following:

- Have applicants sign the employment application. Make sure it contains a statement that employment is for no fixed term and that the employer can terminate at any time.
- Review your employee manual to look for and delete statements that could prejudice your defense in a wrongful discharge case. For example, delete any reference to the fact that "employees can be terminated only for just cause."
- Have written rules listing infractions that may require discipline and discharge, and then make sure to follow the rules.
- If a rule is broken, get the worker's side of the story in front of witnesses, and preferably get it signed. Then make sure to check out the story.
- Be sure that employees get a written appraisal at least annually. If an employee shows evidence of incompetence, give that person a warning and provide an opportunity to improve.
- Keep careful confidential records of all actions such as employee appraisals, warnings or notices, and so on.
- Ask: Is the employee covered by any type of written agreement, including a collective bargaining agreement? Is a defamation claim likely? Is there a possible discrimination allegation? Is there any workers' compensation involvement? Have reasonable rules and regulations been communicated and enforced? Has employee been given an opportunity to explain any rule violations or to correct poor performance? Have all monies been paid within 24 hours after separation? Has employee been advised of his or her rights under COBRA?[80]

Fairness Safeguards

Second, use practices (such as those in this chapter) that help ensure the fairness of the decision.[81] People who are fired and who walk away with the feeling that they've been

FIGURE 8.5	Median Weeks of Severance Pay by Job Level		
Severance Calculation Method	Median Weeks of Severance		
	Executives	Managers	Professionals
Fixed	26	6	4
Variable Amount by Employment Tenure			
1 year	4	2	2
3 years	7	5	5
5 years	10	7	7
10 years	20	12	10
15 years	26	16	15
Maximum	39	26	24

Source: Culpepper eBulletin, July 2007. Complimentary subscriptions at: www.culpepper.com/eBulletin.

embarrassed, stripped of their dignity, or treated unfairly financially (for instance, in terms of severance pay) are more likely to seek retribution in the courts. To some extent, employers can use severance pay to blunt a dismissal's sting. Figure 8.5 summarizes typical severance policies in manufacturing and service industries. You can't make a termination pleasant, but at least handle it with fairness and justice.

Personal Supervisory Liability

Courts sometimes hold managers personally liable for their supervisory actions, particularly with respect to actions covered by the Fair Labor Standards Act and the Family and Medical Leave Act.[82] The Fair Labor Standards Act defines *employer* to include "any person acting directly or indirectly in the interest of an employer in relation to any employee . . . ," and this can mean the individual supervisor.

Steps to Take

There are several ways to avoid creating situations in which personal liability becomes an issue.

- *Follow company policies and procedures,* because an employee may initiate a claim against a supervisor who he or she alleges did not follow company policies and procedures.
- Administer the discipline in a manner that does not add to the *emotional hardship* on the employee (as would dismissing them in public, and making them publicly collect their belongings and leave the office). Most employees will try to present "their side of the story," and allowing them to do so can provide some measure of satisfaction to the employee that you treated the person fairly.
- *Do not act in anger,* since doing so personalizes the situation and undermines any appearance of objectivity.
- Finally, *utilize the HR department* for advice regarding how to handle difficult disciplinary matters.

The Termination Interview

Dismissing an employee is one of the most difficult tasks you can face at work.[83] The dismissed employee, even if warned many times in the past, may still react with disbelief or even violence. Guidelines for the **termination interview** itself are as follows:

1. *Plan the interview carefully.* According to experts at Hay Associates, this includes:
   - Make sure the employee keeps the appointment time.
   - Never inform an employee over the phone.
   - Allow 10 minutes as sufficient time for the interview.
   - Use a neutral site, not your own office.
   - Have employee agreements, the human resource file, and a release announcement (internal and external) prepared in advance.
   - Be available at a time after the interview in case questions or problems arise.
   - Have phone numbers ready for medical or security emergencies.

2. *Get to the point.* As soon as the employee enters your office, give the person a moment to get comfortable and then inform him or her of your decision.

3. *Describe the situation.* Briefly, in three or four sentences, explain why the person is being let go. For instance, "Production in your area is down 4%, and we are continuing to have quality problems. We have talked about these problems several times in the past 3 months, and the solutions are not being followed through. We have to make a change."[84] Describe the situation rather than attack the employee personally by saying things like, "Your production is just not up to par." Also emphasize that the decision is final and irrevocable.

4. *Listen.* Continue the interview until the person appears to be talking freely and reasonably calmly about the reasons for his or her termination and the support package (including severance pay).

5. *Review the severance package.* Describe severance payments, benefits, access to office support people, and the way references will be handled. However, under no conditions should any promises or benefits beyond those already in the support package be implied.

6. *Identify the next step.* The terminated employee may be disoriented and unsure what to do next. Explain where the employee should go next, upon leaving the interview.

Outplacement Counseling

With **outplacement counseling** the employer arranges to provide terminated employees with career planning and job search skills. Outplacement firms such as Right Associates, Inc. usually provide the actual outplacement services. Managers who are let go typically have office space and secretarial services they can use at local offices of such firms, in addition to the counseling services. The outplacement counseling is part of the terminated employee's support or severance package.

Exit Interviews

Many employers conduct final **exit interviews** with employees who are leaving the firm. The HR department usually conducts the interview. The aim is to elicit information that might give the employer a better insight into what is right—or wrong—about the company. Exit interview questions to ask include: How were you recruited? Why did you join the company? Was the job presented correctly and honestly? Were your expectations met? What was the workplace environment like? What was your supervisor's management style like? What did you like most/least about the company? Were there any special problems areas? Why did you decide to leave, and how was the departure handled?[85]

The assumption, of course, is that because the employee is leaving, he or she will be candid. Based on one older survey, though, this is doubtful. The researchers found that at the time of separation, 38% of those leaving blamed salary and benefits, and only 4% blamed supervision. Followed up 18 months later, 24% blamed supervision and only 12% blamed salary and benefits.[86]

Layoffs and the Plant Closing Law

Nondisciplinary separations are a fact of life, and may be initiated by either employer or employee. For the *employer*, reduced sales or profits or the desire for more productivity may require layoffs. In one recent year, U.S. employers implemented about 1,200 mass layoffs, involving a total of almost 144,000 workers.[87] *Employees* may leave to retire or to seek better jobs. The Worker Adjustment and Retraining Notification Act (WARN Act, or the plant closing law) requires employers of 100 or more employees to give 60 days' notice before closing a facility or starting a layoff of 50 or more people.

A **layoff,** in which the employer sends workers home for a time for lack of work, is usually not a permanent dismissal (although it may turn out to be), but rather a temporary one, which the employer expects will be short term. However, some employers use the term *layoff* as a euphemism for discharge or termination. Layoffs are often subject to additional constraints abroad, as the *Global Issues* box illustrates.

The Layoff Process

A study illustrates one firm's layoff process. In this company, senior management first met to make strategic decisions about the size and timing of the layoffs. These managers also debated the relative importance of the skill sets they thought the firm needed going forward. Front-line supervisors assessed their subordinates, rating their nonunion employees either A, B, or C (union employees were covered by a union agreement making layoffs dependant on seniority). The front-line supervisors then informed each of their subordinates about his or her A, B, or C rating, and told each that those employees with C grades were designated "surplus" and most likely to be laid off.[88]

Layoff's Effects

Layoffs "tend to result in deleterious psychological and physical health outcomes for employees who lose their jobs" as well as for the survivors who, witnessing the layoffs of their coworkers and friends, face uncertainty and discomfort.[89]

Furthermore, it is not just the "victims" and "survivors" who suffer negative effects. In one study, the researchers "found that the more managers were personally responsible for handing out WARN notices to employees, regardless of their age,

EMPLOYMENT CONTRACTS

Businesses expanding abroad soon discover that hiring, disciplining, and discharging employees in Europe require much more stringent communication than they do in the United States. For example, the European Union (EU) has a directive (law) that requires employers to provide employees with very explicit contracts of employment, usually within 2 months of their starting work.

How employers must comply with this law varies by country. In the United Kingdom, the employee must be given a written contract specifying, among other things, name of employer, grievance procedure, job title, rate of pay, disciplinary rules, pension plan, hours of work, vacation and sick-leave policies, pay periods, and date when employment began. In Germany, the contracts need not be in writing, although they customarily are, given the amount of detail they must cover, including minimum notice prior to layoff, wages, vacations, maternity/paternity rights, equal pay, invention rights, noncompetition clause, and sickness pay. The contract need not be in writing in Italy, but again, it usually is. Items covered include start date, probationary period, working hours, job description, place of work, basic salary, and a noncompetition clause. In France, the contract must be in writing, and specify information such as the identity of the parties, place of work, type of job or job descriptions, notice period, dates of payment, and work hours.

gender, and marital status, the more likely they were to report physical health problems, to seek treatment for these problems, and to complain of disturbed sleep . . ."[90]

Adjusting to Downsizings and Mergers

Downsizing—reducing, usually dramatically, the number of people employed by a firm—is being done by more and more employers.[91] The basic idea is to cut costs and raise profitability.

Downsizings require careful consideration of several matters. One is *compliance with all applicable laws*, including WARN. Second is ensuring that the employer executes the dismissals in a manner that is *just and fair*. Third is the practical consideration of *security,* for instance, with respect to retrieving keys and ensuring that those leaving do not take any prohibited items with them.

Fourth is to take additional steps to reduce the remaining *employees' uncertainty* and to address their concerns. This typically involves a postdownsizing announcement and an activities program, including meetings at which senior managers field questions from the remaining employees. It is usually also advisable for supervisors to meet with their employees informally to encourage an open discussion of any concerns. However, it's neither wise nor fair to make any assertions about "no more layoffs" unless they are true.

Downsizings aren't pleasant but need not be unfair. Information sharing (in terms of providing advanced notice regarding the layoff) and interpersonal sensitivity (in terms of the manager's demeanor during layoffs) can both help cushion the otherwise negative effects.[92]

Review

Summary

1. Ethics refers to the principles of conduct governing an individual or a group, and specifically to the standards you used to decide what your conduct should be.

2. Ethical decisions are always characterized by two things. First, ethical decisions always involve normative judgments. Second, ethical decisions also always involve morality, which is society's accepted standards of behavior.

3. Numerous factors shape ethical behavior at work. These include individual factors, organizational factors, the boss's influence, ethics policies and codes, and the organization's culture.

4. HR management can influence ethics and fair treatment at work in numerous ways. For example, having a fair and open selection process that emphasizes the company's stress on integrity and ethics, establishing special ethics training programs, measuring employees' adherence to high ethical standards during performance appraisals, and rewarding (or disciplining) ethical (or unethical) work-related behavior are some examples.

5. Firms give employees avenues through which to express opinions and concerns. For example, Toyota's hotline provides employees with an anonymous channel through which they can express concerns to top management. Firms such as FedEx engage in periodic anonymous opinion surveys.

6. Guaranteed fair treatment programs, such as the one at FedEx, help to ensure that grievances are handled fairly and openly. Steps include management review, officer complaint, and executive appeals review.

7. A fair and just discipline process is based on three prerequisites: rules and regulations, a system of progressive penalties, and an appeals process. A number of discipline guidelines are important, including that discipline should be in line with the way management usually responds to similar incidents; that management must adequately investigate the matter before administering discipline; and that managers should not rob a subordinate of his or her dignity.

8. The basic aim of discipline without punishment is to gain an employee's acceptance of the rules by reducing the punitive nature of the discipline itself. In particular, an employee is given a paid day off to consider his or her infraction before more punitive disciplinary steps are taken.

9. Managing dismissals is an important part of any supervisor's job. Among the reasons for dismissal are unsatisfactory performance, misconduct, lack of qualifications, changed job requirements, and insubordination. In dismissing one or more employees, however, remember that termination at will as a policy has been weakened by exceptions in many states. Furthermore, great care should be taken to avoid wrongful discharge suits.

10. Dismissing an employee is always difficult, and the termination interview should be handled properly. Specifically, plan the interview carefully (for instance, early in the week), get to the point, describe the situation, and then listen until the person has expressed his or her feelings. Then discuss the severance package and identify the next step.

11. Nondisciplinary separations such as layoffs and retirement occur all the time. The plant closing law (the Worker Adjustment and Retraining Notification Act) outlines requirements to be followed with regard to official notice before operations with 50 or more people are to be closed down.

12. Disciplinary actions are a big source of grievances. Discipline should be based on rules and adhere to a system of progressive penalties, and it should permit an appeals process.

Key Terms

- ethics
- opinion surveys
- discipline
- guaranteed fair treatment
- dismissal
- terminate at will
- insubordination
- wrongful discharge
- termination interview
- outplacement counseling
- exit interviews
- layoff
- downsizing

Discussion Questions and Exercises

1. Describe the similarities and differences between a program such as FedEx's guaranteed fair treatment program and your college or university's student grievance process.

2. Explain how you would ensure fairness in disciplining, discussing particularly the prerequisites to disciplining, disciplining guidelines, and the discipline without punishment approach.

3. Why is it important to manage dismissals properly?

4. What techniques would you use as alternatives to traditional discipline? What do such alternatives have to do with "organizational justice"? Why do you think alternatives like these are important, given industry's current need for highly committed employees?

5. Working individually or in groups, interview managers or administrators at your employer or college in order to determine the extent to which the employer or college builds two-way communication, and the specific types of programs that are used. Do the managers think they are effective? What do the employees (or faculty members) think of the programs if they are in use at the employer or college?

6. Working individually or in groups, obtain copies of the student handbook for your college and determine to what extent there is a formal process through which students can air grievances. Do you think the process should be an effective one? Based on your contacts with other students, has it been an effective grievance process?

7. Working individually or in groups, determine the nature of the academic discipline process in your college. Do you think it is an effective one? Based on what you read in this chapter, would you recommend any modification of the student discipline process?

APPLICATION EXERCISES

Case Incident　　　　*Allstate's Disappearing Agents*

Like many companies, Allstate faces pressure both to be cost competitive and to provide new services to its customers. It also faces pressure for continuous improvement in its financial performance from its shareholders. Assuming that for Allstate to survive and prosper it needs to respond to both customers and shareholders, what ethical responsibilities does it have toward another important group of stakeholders, its employees?

Here's the situation. Several years ago, the Allstate Corporation announced a series of strategic initiatives to (1) expand its selling service capabilities, (2) buy back company shares to raise its stock price, and (3) cut expenses by reducing the workforce. As part of its restructuring, Allstate would transfer its existing agents to an exclusive independent contractor program, whereby Allstate agents would become basically self-employed "independent contractors." This would markedly reduce the need for Allstate to provide agency support staff. In its press release on this initiative, Allstate management also announced it would soon eliminate 4,000 nonagent positions, or approximately 10% of the company's nonagents workforce.

Said Allstate's CEO, "Now, many of our customers and potential customers are telling us they want our products to be easier to buy, easier to service, and more competitively priced. We will combine the power of our agency distribution system with the growth potential of direct selling and electronic commerce."

Proponents of restructurings like these might argue that Allstate is simply taking the steps needed to be competitive. They might even say that if Allstate did not cut jobs to create the cash flow required to fund new competitive initiatives, it might ultimately fail as a business, putting all 54,000 of its employees at risk.

Yet Allstate's program raises concerns. One analyst noted that by encouraging customers to purchase insurance products directly via the Internet, they threaten the commissions of its more than 15,000 agents. The announcement of cost cutting came 1 day after Allstate announced it would meet its regular quarterly dividend of 15 cents per share. The company has raised its dividend annually since the mid-1990s. ■

DISCUSSION QUESTIONS

1. Is reducing the number of employees in a company in and of itself unethical? Why or why not?
2. If you decided it was generally ethical, what would the company have to do to make the employee dismissals unethical?
3. What responsibilities does a company like Allstate have toward its employees?
4. Is there a moral dimension to the question of marketing Allstate insurance via the Internet? If so, what is it?

Continuing Case

LearnInMotion.com: Are Our Ethics Out of Control?

It's probably safe to say that in creating Learn InMotion.com, Jennifer and Mel gave absolutely no thought to ethical behavior in their company. They did of course put endless hours into developing their business plan, raising money, installing computers and broadband lines, and

trying to generate sales. But as far as taking specific concrete steps toward ensuring that everything that they and their employees did was aboveboard and ethical, they were batting zero, not because they were unethical people, but simply because the matter simply never entered their minds.

However, several ethics-related issues have recently come up, and they're causing concern for both Jennifer and Mel. Yesterday they received word from one of the main Internet service providers that someone in their company was using spamming techniques to send unsolicited LearnInMotion.com advertising information to tens of thousands of its subscribers, and threatening legal action if the spamming did not cease. A customer called last week to complain that they'd recently learned that LearnInMotion.com was not reaching even half the number of potential users that LearnInMotion's sales brochures said it did, and the customer therefore wanted a rebate. The CEO of LearnInMotion's largest competitor called Mel to say that their own internal tracking systems had noticed that someone at LearnInMotion.com had been methodically downloading its customers' names and files, and that if the electronic monitoring did not cease, his company would file a lawsuit. All this, and more, led Jennifer and Mel to believe that they have to do something to ratchet up the ethical level in their company. Now, they want you, their management consultants, to help them actually do it. Here's what they want you to do for them. ■

QUESTIONS AND ASSIGNMENTS

1. Are the sorts of issues raised in the case ethical ones? Why or why not?

2. Tell us: What are the sorts of factors that shape ethical behavior in a company like LearnInMotion.com?

3. In terms of human resource management, list at least six concrete staffing and selection, training, performance appraisal, and reward/disciplinary actions we can take right now to institute a greater appreciation for the high ethical standards we think our company should have.

EXPERIENTIAL EXERCISE

To Discipline or Not?

Purpose: The purpose of this exercise is to provide you with some experience in analyzing and handling an actual disciplinary action.

Required Understanding: Students should be thoroughly familiar with the following case, titled "Botched Batch." However, *do not read the "Award" or "Discussion" sections until after the groups have completed their deliberations.*

How to Set Up the Exercise/Instructions: Divide the class into groups of four or five students. Each group should take the arbitrator's point of view and assume that they are to analyze the case and make the arbitrator's decision. Review the case again at this point, but please do not read the award and discussion.

Each group should answer the following questions:

1. What would your decision be if you were the arbitrator? Why?

2. Do you think that following their experience in this arbitration the parties will be more or less inclined to settle grievances by themselves without resorting to arbitration?

Botched Batch

Facts: A computer department employee made an entry error that botched an entire run of computer reports. Efforts to rectify the situation produced a second set of improperly run reports. As a result of the series of errors, the employer incurred extra costs of $2,400, plus a weekend of overtime work by other computer department staffers. Management suspended the employee for 3 days for negligence, and also revoked a promotion for which the employee had previously been approved.

Protesting the discipline, the employee stressed that she had attempted to correct her error in the early stages of the run by notifying the manager of computer operations of her mistake. Maintaining that the resulting string of errors could have been avoided if the manager had followed up on her report and stopped the initial run, the employee argued that she had been treated unfairly because the manager had not been disciplined even though he compounded the problem, whereas she was severely punished. Moreover, citing her "impeccable" work record and management's acknowledgment that she had always been a "model employee," the employee insisted that the denial of her previously approved promotion was "unconscionable."

(Please do not read beyond this point until after you have completed the Experiential Exercise.)

Award: The arbitrator upholds the 3-day suspension, but decides that the promotion should be restored.

Discussion: "There is no question," the arbitrator notes, that the employee's negligent act "set in motion the train of events that resulted in running two complete sets of reports reflecting improper information." Stressing that the employer incurred substantial cost because of the error, the arbitrator cites "unchallenged"

testimony that management had commonly issued 3-day suspensions for similar infractions in the past. Thus, the arbitrator decides, the employer acted with just cause in meting out an "evenhanded" punishment for the negligence.

Turning to the denial of the already approved promotion, the arbitrator says that this action should be viewed "in the same light as a demotion for disciplinary reasons." In such cases, the arbitrator notes, management's decision normally is based on a pattern of unsatisfactory behavior, an employee's inability to perform, or similar grounds. Observing that management had never before reversed a promotion as part of a disciplinary action, the arbitrator says that by tacking on the denial of the promotion in this case, the employer substantially varied its disciplinary policy from its past practice. Because this action on management's part was not "evenhanded," the arbitrator rules, the promotion should be restored.[93] ∎

ETHICS QUIZ ANSWERS

Quiz is Figure 8.1 on page 263.

1. 34% said personal e-mail on company computers is wrong.
2. 37% said using office equipment for schoolwork is wrong.
3. 49% said playing computer games at work is wrong.
4. 54% said Internet shopping at work is wrong.
5. 61% said it's unethical to blame your error on technology.
6. 87% said it's unethical to visit pornographic sites at work.
7. 33% said $25 is the amount at which a gift from a supplier or client becomes troubling, while 33% said $50, and 33% said $100.
8. 35% said a $50 gift to the boss is unacceptable.

9. 12% said a $50 gift *from* the boss is unacceptable.
10. 70% said it's unacceptable to take the $200 football tickets.
11. 70% said it's unacceptable to take the $120 theater tickets.
12. 35% said it's unacceptable to take the $100 food basket.
13. 45% said it's unacceptable to take the $25 gift certificate.
14. 40% said it's unacceptable to take the $75 raffle prize.
15. 11% reported they lie about sick days.
16. 4% reported they take credit for the work or ideas of others.

Endnotes

1. "What Role Should HR Play in Corporate Ethics?" *HR Focus* 81, no. 1 (January 2004): 3.
2. Kevin Wooten, "Ethical Dilemmas in Human Resource Management: An Application of a Multidimensional Framework, A Unifying

Taxonomy, and Applicable Codes," *Human Resource Management Review* 11 (2001): 161.
3. Manuel Velasquez, *Business Ethics: Concepts and Cases* (Upper Saddle River, NJ: Prentice Hall, 1992), p. 9. See also Joel Lefkowitz, "The

Constancy of Ethics amidst the Changing World of Work," *Human Resource Management Review* 16 (2006): 245–268.

4. The following discussion, except as noted, is based on Manuel Velasquez, *Business Ethics,* 9–12. See also O. C. Ferrell, John Fraedrich, and Linog Ferrell, *Business Ethics* (Boston: Houghton Mifflin, 2008).

5. Ibid., 9.

6. This discussion is based on ibid., 12–14.

7. Ibid., 12. For further discussion, see Kurt Baier, *Moral Points of View,* abbr. ed. (New York: Random House, 1965), p. 88. See also Milton Bordwin, "The 3 R's of Ethics," *Management Review* (June 1998): 59–61.

8. For further discussion of ethics and morality, see Tom Beauchamp and Norman Bowie, *Ethical Theory and Business* (Upper Saddle River, NJ: Prentice Hall, 2001), pp. 1–19.

9. Carroll Lachnit, "Recruiting Trouble for Tyson," *Workforce, HR Trends and Tools for Business Results* 81, no. 2 (February 2002): 22.

10. Richard Osborne, "A Matter of Ethics," *Industry Week* 49, no. 14 (September 4, 2000): 41–42.

11. Gary Weaver and Linda Trevino, "The Role of Human Resources in Ethics/Compliance Management: A Fairness Perspective," *Human Resource Management Review* 11 (2001): 115.

12. Linda Trevino and Katherine Nelson, *Managing Business Ethics* (New York: John Wiley, 1999) p. 134.

13. Michelle Donovan et al., "The Perceptions of Fair Interpersonal Treatment Scale: Development and Validation of a Measure of Interpersonal Treatment in the Workplace," *Journal of Applied Psychology* 83, no. 5 (1998): 683–692.

14. Bennett Tepper, "Consequences of Abusive Supervision," *Academy of Management Journal* 43, no. 2 (2000): 178–190. See also Samuel Aryee et al., "Antecedents and Outcomes of Abusive Supervision: A Test of a Trickle-Down Model," *Journal of Applied Psychology* 92, no. 1 (2007): 191–201.

15. Rudy Yandrick, "Lurking in the Shadows," *HR Magazine* (October 1999): 61–68.

16. Weaver and Trevino, "Role of Human Resources," 117.

17. Suzanne Masterson, "A Trickle-Down Model of Organizational Justice: Relating Employees' and Customers' Perceptions of and Reactions to Fairness," *Journal of Applied Psychology* 86, no. 4 (2001): 594–601.

18. Sara Morris et al., "A Test of Environmental, Situational, and Personal Influences on the Ethical Intentions of CEOs," *Business and Society* (August 1995): 119–147. See also Dennis Moberg, "Ethics Blind Spots in Organizations: How Systematic Errors in Person's Perception Undermine Moral Agency," *Organization Studies* 27, no. 3 (2006): 413–428.

19. "Former CEO Joins WorldCom's Indicted," *Miami Herald* (March 3, 2004): 4C.

20. Gretchen Morgenson, "Requiem for an Honorable Profession," *New York Times* (May 5, 2002): Business 1.

21. "Ethics Policies Are Big with Employers, but Workers See Small Impact on the Workplace," *BNA Bulletin to Management* (June 29, 2000): 201.

22. Jennifer Schramm, "Perceptions on Ethics," *HR Magazine* (November 2004): 176.

23. From Guy Brumback, "Managing Above the Bottom Line of Ethics," *Supervisory Management* (December 1993): 12.

24. Quoted in Beauchamp and Bowie, *Ethical Theory and Business,* 109.

25. James Kunen, "Enron Division (and Values) Thing," *New York Times* (January 19, 2002): A19. For another example, see Heather Tesoriero and Avery Johnson, "Suit Details How J&J Pushed Sales of Procrit," *The Wall Street Journal* (April 10, 2007).

26. Dayton Fandray, "The Ethical Company," *Workforce* 79, no. 12 (December 2000): 74–77.

27. Richard Beatty et al., "HR's Role in Corporate Governance: Present and Prospective," *Human Resource Management* 42, no. 3 (Fall 2003): 268.

28. Dale Buss, "Corporate Compasses," *HR Magazine* (June 2004): 127–132.

29. S. Greengard, "50 Percent of Your Employees are Lying, Cheating, and Stealing," *Workforce* 76 (October 1997): 44–53; Deborah Wells and Marshall Schminke, "Ethical Development and Human Resources Training: An Integrator Framework," *Human Resource Management Review* 11 (2001): 135–138.

30. James G. Hunt, *Leadership* (Newbury Park, CA: Sage Publications, 1991), pp. 220–224. One writer describes organizational culture as a sort of "organizational DNA," since "it's the stuff, mostly intangible, that determines the basic character of a business." See James Moore, "How Companies Have Sex," *Fast Company* (October–November 1997): 66–68.

31. Heather Won Tesoriero and Avery Johnson, "Suit Details How J&J Pushed Sales of Procrit," *Wall Street Journal* (April 10, 2007): B1(1).

32. "Promoting Workplace Fun Draws Serious Attention," *BNA Bulletin to Management* (August 8, 1999): 215.

33. Ibid.

34. J. Krohe Jr., "The Big Business of Business Ethics," *Across the Board* 34 (May 1997): 23–29, in Deborah Wells and Marshall Schminke, "Ethical Development and Human Resources Training," 135–58. For an interesting explanation of how the United States Military Academy uses its student admission and socialization processes to promote character development, see Evan Offstein and Ronald Dufresne, "Building Strong Ethics and Promoting Positive Character Development: The Influence of HRM at the United States Military Academy at West Point," *Human Resource Management* 46, no. 1 (Spring 2007): 95–114.

35. Editorial: "Ethical Issues in the Management of Human Resources," *Human Resource Management Review* 11 (2001): 6.

36. Weaver and Trevino, "Role of Human Resources," 123.

37. William Byham, "Can You Interview for Integrity?" *Across-The-Board* 41, no. 2 (March/April 2004): 34–38.

38. Kathryn Tyler, "Do the Right Thing: Ethics Training Programs Help Employees Deal with Ethical Dilemmas," *HR Magazine* (February 2005): 99–102.

39. Editorial: "Ethical Issues in the Management of Human Resources," 6.

40. Weaver and Trevino, "Role of Human Resources," 123.

41. Michael Burr, "Corporate Governance: Embracing Sarbanes-Oxley," *Public Utilities Fortnightly* (October 15, 2003): 20–22.

42. Ibid.

43. W. Chan Kim and Rene Mauborgne, "Fair Process: Managing in the Knowledge Economy," *Harvard Business Review* (July/August 1997): 65–75.

44. Tom Asacker, "Ethics in the Workplace," *Training and Development* (August 2004): 44.

45. M. Ronald Buckley et al., "Ethical Issues in Human Resources Systems," *Human Resource Management Review* 11 (2001): 11, 29. See also Ann Pomeroy, "The Ethics Squeeze," *HR Magazine* (March 2006): 48–55.

46. Weaver and Trevino, "Role of Human Resources," 113–34.

47. Ibid., 125.

48. Robert Grossman, "Executive Discipline," *HR Magazine* 50, no. 8 (August 2005): 46–51.

49. Buckley et al., "Ethical Issues in Human Resources Systems," 11, 29. See also Helge Hoel and David Beale, "Workplace Bullying, Psychological Perspectives and Industrial Relations: Towards a Contextualized and Interdisciplinary Approach," *British Journal of Industrial Relations* 44, no. 2 (June 2006): 239–262.

50. Wendy Boswell and Julie Olson-Buchanan, "Experiencing Mistreatment at Work: The Role of Grievance Filing, Nature of Mistreatment, and Employee Withdrawal," *Academy of Management Journal* 47, no. 1 (2004): 129–139. See also, Samuel Aryee, et al., "Antecedents and Outcomes of Abusive Supervision: A Test of a Trickle-Down Model," *Journal of Applied Psychology* (2007): 191–201.

51. Kim and Mauborgne, "Fair Process: Managing in the Knowledge Economy," 65–75.

52. Weaver and Trevino, "Role of Human Resources," 114.

53. "Corporations' Drive to Embrace Ethics Gives HR Leaders Chance to Take Reins," *BNA Bulletin to Management* (November 7, 2002): 353.

54. Lester Bittel, *What Every Supervisor Should Know* (New York: McGraw-Hill, 1974), p. 308; see also Paul Falcone, "The Fundamentals of Progressive Discipline," *HR Magazine* (February 1997): 90–92.

55. For an example of a peer review appeals process see, for example, Dawn Anfuso, "Coors Taps Employee Judgement," *Personnel Journal* (February 1994): 50–59.

56. George Bohlander, "Why Arbitrators Overturn Managers in Employee Suspension and Discharge Cases," *Journal of Collective Negotiations* 23, no. 1 (1994): 76–77.

57. Ibid., 82.

58. Ibid. See also Ahman Karim, "Arbitration Considerations in Modifying Discharge Decisions in the Public Sector," *Journal of Collective Negotiations* 22, no. 3 (1993): 245–251; Joseph Martocchio and Timothy Judge, "When We Don't See Eye to Eye: Discrepancies Between Supervisors and Subordinates in Absence Disciplinary Decisions," *Journal of Management* 21, no. 2 (1995): 251–278.

59. "Employers Turn to Corporate Ombuds to Defuse Internal Ticking Time Bombs," *BNA Bulletin to Management* (August 9, 2005): 249.

60. Nonpunitive discipline discussions based on David Campbell et al., "Discipline Without Punishment—At Last," *Harvard Business Review* (July/August 1995): 162–178; "Positive Discipline Replaces Punishment," *BNA Bulletin to Management* (April 27, 1995): 136.

61. "After Employer Found Liable for Worker's Child Porn, Policies May Need to Be Revisited," *BNA Bulletin to Management* (March 21, 2006): 89.

62. Rita Zeidner, "Keeping E-Mail in Check," *HR Magazine* (June 2007): 70–74.

63. Morris Attaway, "Privacy in the Workplace on the Web," *Internal Auditor* 58, no. 1 (February 2001): 30; and Declan Leonard and Angela France, "Workplace Monitoring: Balancing Business Interests with Employee Privacy Rights," *Society for Human Resource Management Legal Report* (May/June 2003): 3–6.

64. "Do You Know Where Your Workers Are? GPS Units Aid Efficiency, Raise Privacy Issues," *BNA Bulletin to Management* (July 22, 2004): 233.

65. "Time Clocks Go High Touch, High Tech to Keep Workers from Gaining the System," *BNA Bulletin to Management* (March 25, 2004): 97.

66. Cynthia Kemper, "Big Brother," *Communication World* 18, no. 1 (December 2000/January 2001): 8–12.

67. Michael McCarthy, "Now the Boss Knows Where You're Clicking," *Wall Street Journal* (October 21, 1999): B1.

68. "Surveillance of Employees," *BNA Bulletin to Management* (April 25, 1996): p. 136.

69. "Telephone and Electronic Monitoring: A Special Report on the Issues and the Law," *BNA Bulletin to Management* (April 3, 1997): 2.

70. *Vega-Rodriguez* v. *Puerto Rico Telephone Company,* CAL 962061, 4/8/97; discussed in "Video Surveillance Withstands Privacy Challenge," *BNA Bulletin to Management* (April 17, 1998): 121.

71. "Secret Videotaping Leads to $200,000 Settlement," *BNA Bulletin to Management* (January 22, 1998): 17.

72. Andrea Poe, "Make Foresight 20/20," *HR Magazine* (February 20, 2000): 74–80. See also Nancy Hatch Woodward, "Smoother Separations," *HR Magazine* (June 2007): 94–97.

73. Robert Lanza and Morton Warren, "United States: Employment at Will Prevails Despite Exceptions to the Rule," *Society for Human Resource Management Legal Report* (October–November 2005): 1–8.

74. Ibid.

75. Joseph Famularo, *Handbook of Modern Personnel Administration,* (New York, McGraw Hill, 1982): 63–65. See also, Carolyn Hirschman, "Off Duty, Out of Work," *HR Magazine,* www.shrm.org/hrmagazine/articles/0203/0203hirschman.asp, accessed January 1, 2008.

76. Connie Wanderg et al., "Perceived Fairness of Layoffs among Individuals Who Have Been Laid Off: A Longitudinal Study," *Personnel Psychology* 52 (1999): 59–84. See also Nancy Hatch Woodward, "Smoother Separations," *HR Magazine* (June 2007): 94–97.

77. Michael Orey, "Fear of Firing," *Business Week* (April 23, 2007): 52–54.

78. Paul Falcon, "Give Employees the (Gentle) Hook," *HR Magazine* (April 2001): 121–128.

79. "One More Heart Risk: Firing Employees," *The Miami Herald* (March 20, 1998): C1, C7.

80. Kenneth Sovereign, *Personnel Law* (Upper Saddle River, NJ: Prentice Hall, 1999), p. 185.

81. "Fairness to Employees Can Stave Off Litigation," *BNA Bulletin to Management* (November 27, 1997): 377.

82. Edward Isler et al., "Personal Liability and Employee Discipline," *Society for*

Human Resource Management Legal Report (September–October 2000): 1–4.

83. Based on James Coil III and Charles Rice, "Three Steps to Creating Effective Employee Releases," *Employment Relations Today* (Spring 1994): 91–94. See also Martha Frase-Blunt, "Making Exit Interviews Work," *HR Magazine* (August 2004): 9–11.

84. William J. Morin and Lyle York, *Outplacement Techniques* (New York: AMACOM, 1982), pp. 101–131; F. Leigh Branham, "How to Evaluate Executive Outplacement Services," *Personnel Journal* 62 (April 1983): 323–326; Sylvia Milne, "The Termination Interview," *Canadian Manager* (Spring 1994): 15–16. There is debate regarding what is the "best day of the week" on which to terminate an employee. Some say Friday to give the employee a few days to "cool off"; others suggest midweek, in order to allow employees "who remain in the department or in the immediate work group some time to process the change and to talk with each other to sort it out." See Jeffrey Connor, "Disarming Terminated Employees," *HR Magazine* (January 2000): 113–114.

85. Paul Brada, "Before You Go . . . ," *HR Magazine* (December 1998): 89–102.

86. Joseph Zarandona and Michael Camuso, "A Study of Exit Interviews: Does the Last Word Count?" *Personnel* 62, no. 3 (March 1981): 47–48.

87. "Workers Hit by Mass Layoffs Rose to 143,977 in February," *BNA Bulletin to Management* (April 3, 2007), 109.

88. Leon Grunberg, Sarah Moore, and Edward Greenberg, "Managers' Reactions to Implementing Layoffs: Relationship to Health Problems and Withdrawal Behaviors," *Human Resource Management* 45, no. 2 (Summer 2006): 159–178.

89. Ibid.

90. Ibid.

91. See, for example, "Cushioning the Blow of Layoffs," *BNA Bulletin to Management* (July 3, 1997): 216; "Levi Strauss Cushions Blow of Plant Closings," *BNA Bulletin to Management* (November 20, 1997): 370.

92. "Communication Can Reduce Problems, Litigation after Layoffs, Attorneys Say," *BNA Bulletin to Management* (April 14, 2003): 129.

93. Facts adapted from Bureau of National Affairs, *Bulletin to Management* (September 13, 1985): 3.

CHAPTER

9

MANAGING LABOR RELATIONS AND COLLECTIVE BARGAINING

- The Labor Movement
- Unions and the Law
- The Union Drive and Election
- The Collective Bargaining Process
- What's Next for Unions?

When you finish studying this chapter, you should be able to:

■ Discuss *the nature of the major federal labor relations laws.*

■ Describe *the process of a union drive and election.*

■ Discuss *the main steps in the collective bargaining process.*

INTRODUCTION

The U.S. Department of Labor's National Labor Relations Board (NLRB) recently accused Starbucks of breaking the law in trying to prevent workers in some of its New York coffee shops from unionizing. Among other things, the NLRB accused Starbucks managers in those stores of retaliating against workers who wanted to unionize, by firing two of them, threatening to terminate several others, and illegally interrogating employees about their union inclinations. A spokesperson for Starbucks said the company believes the allegations are baseless and that the firm would vigorously defend itself.[1]

THE LABOR MOVEMENT

Just over 15 million U.S. workers belong to unions—around 12% of the total number of men and women working in this country.[2] Many are still blue-collar workers, but unions increasingly appeal to white-collar workers, too. For instance, federal, state, and local governments employ almost 7 million union members, or about 37% of total government employees.

However, such figures mask the dramatic changes taking place in unions today: U.S. union membership peaked at about 34% in 1955. It has consistently fallen since then due to factors such as the shift from manufacturing to service jobs, and new legislation (such as occupational safety laws) that provide the sorts of protections that workers could once only obtain from their unions. Indeed, hundreds of local, state, and federal laws and regulations now address the sorts of concerns that helped drive the early union movement.[3]

Even with such declines, however, we can't write off unions. In the United States, for instance, a growing number of government and white-collar employees are turning to unions. In some industries (such as transportation and public utilities), it's still not easy to get a job without joining a union. Union membership also ranges widely, from over 20% in Michigan, Hawaii, and New York, down to just over 4% in North Carolina.[4] And, although union membership around the world is also declining, union membership is still high in most countries—about 33% in Germany and the United Kingdom, for instance.

Furthermore, do not assume, as a knee-jerk reaction, that unions only negatively impact employers. For example, perhaps by professionalizing the staff and/or systematizing company practices, unionization may also improve performance. Thus in one study, researchers concluded that heart attack mortality among patients in hospitals with unionized registered nurses was 5%–9% lower than in nonunion hospitals.[5] Another study found a significant, negative relationship between union membership and employees' intent to leave their jobs.[6]

Why Do Workers Organize?

People have spent much time analyzing why workers unionize, and they've proposed many theories. Yet, there is no simple answer, partly because each worker probably joins for his or her own reasons.

It's clear that workers don't unionize just to get more pay, although the pay issue is important. In fact, union members' weekly earnings are higher than nonunion workers'. For example, recent median weekly wages for union workers was $781, while that for nonunion workers was $612.[7]

But, pay is not always the issue. Often, the urge to unionize seems to boil down to the workers' belief that it is only through unity that they can protect themselves from arbitrary managerial whims. For example, a butcher hired by Wal-Mart said he was told he would be able to start management training and possibly move up to supervisor. He started work and bought a new car for the commute. However, he said his supervisor never mentioned the promotion again after the employee hurt his back at work and was out for 5 weeks. Faced with high car payments and feeling cheated, the butcher went to the Grocery Workers Union, which sent an organizer to speak with the employee. The store's meat cutters eventually voted to unionize. A week later Wal-Mart announced it would switch to completely prepackaged meat. Henceforth, the meat suppliers would do all the cutting at their factories, and the stores' meat cutters would no longer be required.[8]

Research Findings

Studies suggest that two things—employer unfairness, and the availability of a union that the employees believed had clout—explain why employees unionize.

In one study, of an Australia-based international banking firm, researchers found that employer unfairness played a big role: "Individuals who believe that the company rules or policies were administered unfairly or to their detriment were more likely to turn to unions as a source of assistance."[9]

However, unfairness itself was not enough to prompt a vote to unionize; the union also needed clout. Employees were more likely to join in those situations where they "perceived that the union was effective in the area of wages and benefits and protection against unfair dismissals."[10] One labor relations lawyer put it this way, "the one major thing unions offer is making you a "for cause" instead of an "at will" employee, which guarantees a hearing and arbitration if you're fired."[11]

When Kaiser Permanente's San Francisco Medical Center cut back on vacation and sick leave for its pharmacists and other workers, the pharmacists' union won back the lost vacation days. Said one staff pharmacist, "Kaiser is a pretty benevolent employer, but there's always the pressure to squeeze a little."[12]

What Do Unions Want? What Are Their Aims?

We can generalize by saying that unions have two sets of aims, one for union security and one for improved wages, hours, working conditions, and benefits for their members.

Union Security

First and probably foremost, unions seek to establish security for themselves. They fight hard for the right to represent a firm's workers and to be the *exclusive* bargaining agent for all employees in the unit. (As such, they negotiate contracts for all employees, including those who are not members of the union.) Five types of union security are possible:

1. *Closed shop.*[13] The company can hire only union members. This was outlawed in 1947 but still exists in some industries (such as printing).
2. *Union shop.* The company can hire nonunion people, but they must join the union after a prescribed period of time and pay dues. (If not, they can be fired.)
3. *Agency shop.* Employees who do not belong to the union still must pay union dues on the assumption that the union's efforts benefit *all* the workers.
4. *Preferential shop.* Union members get preference in hiring, but the employer can still hire union members.
5. *Maintenance of membership arrangement*. Employees do not have to belong to the union. However, union members employed by the firm must maintain membership in the union for the contract period.

Not all states give unions the right to require union membership as a condition of employment. **Right-to-work** "is a term used to describe state statutory or constitutional provisions banning the requirement of union membership as a condition of employment."[14] Section 14(b) of the Taft-Hartley Act (an early labor relations act that we'll discuss later in more detail) permits states to forbid the negotiation of compulsory union membership provisions, not just for firms engaged in intrastate commerce but also for those in interstate commerce. Right-to-work laws don't outlaw unions. They do outlaw (within those states) any of the forms of union security. This understandably inhibits union formation in those states. In 2001, Oklahoma became the 22nd state to pass Right-to-Work legislation. Some believe that this—combined with a loss of manufacturing jobs—explains why Oklahoma's union membership dropped dramatically in the next 3 years.[15] There were 23 right to work states in 2008.

Improved Wages, Hours, Working Conditions, and Benefits for Members

Once their security is assured, unions fight to better the lot of their members—to improve their wages, hours, and working conditions, for example. The typical labor agreement also gives the union a role in other HR activities, including recruiting, selecting, compensating, promoting, training, and discharging employees.

The AFL-CIO

The American Federation of Labor and Congress of Industrial Organizations (**AFL-CIO**) is a voluntary federation of about 100 national and international labor unions in the United States. It resulted from the merger of the AFL and CIO in 1955, with the AFL's George Meany as its first president. For many people, it has become synonymous with the word *union* in the United States.

However, over 7.0 million workers belong to unions that are not affiliated with the AFL-CIO. Four big unions—the Service Employees' International Union (SEIU), the International Brotherhood of Teamsters, the United Food and Commercial Workers, and UNITE—announced in 2001 they were leaving the AFL-CIO and establishing their own Federation, called the Change to Win Coalition. Among other things, Change to Win plans to be much more aggressive about organizing workers than they say the AFL-CIO was.[16]

UNIONS AND THE LAW

Until about 1930, there were no special labor laws. Employers didn't have to engage in collective bargaining with employees and were virtually unrestrained in their behavior toward unions. The use of spies, blacklists, and the firing of agitators was widespread. "Yellow dog" contracts, whereby management could require nonunion membership as a condition for employment, were widely enforced. Most union weapons—even strikes—were illegal.

This one-sided situation lasted in the United States from the Revolution to the Great Depression (around 1930). Since then, in response to changing public attitudes, values, and economic conditions, labor law has gone through three clear changes: from "strong encouragement" of unions, to "modified encouragement coupled with regulation," to "detailed regulation of internal union affairs."[17]

Period of Strong Encouragement: The Norris-LaGuardia Act (1932) and the National Labor Relations Act (1935)

The **Norris-LaGuardia Act** set the stage for an era in which government encouraged union activity. The act guaranteed to each employee the right to bargain collectively "free from interference, restraint, or coercion." It declared yellow dog contracts unenforceable. It limited the courts' abilities to issue injunctions for activities such as peaceful picketing and payment of strike benefits.[18]

Yet this act did little to restrain employers from fighting labor organizations by whatever means they could muster. Therefore, the National Labor Relations Act (or **Wagner Act**) was passed in 1935 to add teeth to the Norris-LaGuardia Act. It did this by banning certain unfair labor practices, providing for secret-ballot elections and majority rule for determining whether a firm's employees were to unionize, and creating the **National Labor Relations Board (NLRB)** for enforcing these two provisions.

In addition to activities like overseeing union elections, the NLRB periodically issues interpretive rulings. For example, about 6 million employees fall under the "contingent" or "alternative" employee umbrella today. The NLRB therefore recently ruled that temporary employees could join the unions of permanent employees in the companies where their employment agencies assign them to work.[19]

Unfair Employer Labor Practices

The Wagner Act deemed as "statutory wrongs" (but not crimes) five unfair labor practices used by employers:

1. It is unfair for employers to "interfere with, restrain, or coerce employees" in exercising their legally sanctioned right of self-organization.
2. It is an unfair practice for company representatives to dominate or interfere with either the formation or the administration of labor unions. Among other management actions found to be unfair under practices 1 and 2 are bribing employees, using company spy systems, moving a business to avoid unionization, and blacklisting union sympathizers.
3. Employers are prohibited from discriminating in any way against employees for their legal union activities.
4. Employers are forbidden to discharge or discriminate against employees simply because the latter file unfair practice charges against the company.
5. Finally, it is an unfair labor practice for employers to refuse to bargain collectively with their employees' duly chosen representatives.

An unfair labor practice charge may be filed (see Figure 9.1) with the NLRB. The board then investigates the charge and determines whether it should take formal action. Possible actions include dismissal of the complaint, request for an injunction against the employer, and an order that the employer cease and desist.

From 1935 to 1947

Union membership increased quickly after passage of the Wagner Act in 1935. Other factors such as an improving economy and aggressive union leadership contributed to this as well. But by the mid-1940s, the tide had begun to turn. Largely because of a series of

FIGURE 9.1   NLRB Form 501: Filing an Unfair Labor Practice Charge

FORM NLRB 501
(2 81)

FORM EXEMPT UNDER
44 U.S.C. 3512

UNITED STATES OF AMERICA
NATIONAL LABOR RELATIONS BOARD
CHARGE AGAINST EMPLOYER

INSTRUCTIONS: File an original and 4 copies of this charge with NLRB Regional Director for the region in which the alleged unfair labor practice occurred or is occurring.	DO NOT WRITE IN THIS SPACE	
	CASE NO.	DATE FILED

1. EMPLOYER AGAINST WHOM CHARGE IS BROUGHT

a. NAME OF EMPLOYER	b. NUMBER OF WORKERS EMPLOYED	
c. ADDRESS OF ESTABLISHMENT *(street and number, city, State, and ZIP code)*	d. EMPLOYER REPRESENTATIVE TO CONTACT	e. PHONE NO.
f. TYPE OF ESTABLISHMENT *(factory, mine, wholesaler, etc.)*	g. IDENTIFY PRINCIPAL PRODUCT OR SERVICE	

h. THE ABOVE-NAMED EMPLOYER HAS ENGAGED IN AND IS ENGAGING IN UNFAIR LABOR PRACTICES WITHIN THE MEANING OF SECTION 8(a), SUBSECTIONS (1) AND _____ OF THE NATIONAL
(list subsections)
LABOR RELATIONS ACT, AND THESE UNFAIR LABOR PRACTICES ARE UNFAIR LABOR PRACTICES AFFECTING COMMERCE WITHIN THE MEANING OF THE ACT.

2. BASIS OF THE CHARGE *(be specific as to facts, names, addresses, plants involved, dates, places, etc.)*

BY THE ABOVE AND OTHER ACTS, THE ABOVE-NAMED EMPLOYER HAS INTERFERED WITH, RESTRAINED, AND COERCED EMPLOYEES IN THE EXERCISE OF THE RIGHTS GUARANTEED IN SECTION 7 OF THE ACT.

3. FULL NAME OF PARTY FILING CHARGE   *(if labor organization, give full name, including local name and number)*

4a. ADDRESS *(street and number, city, State, and ZIP code)*	4b. TELEPHONE NO.

5. FULL NAME OF NATIONAL OR INTERNATIONAL LABOR ORGANIZATION OF WHICH IT IS AN AFFILIATE OR CONSTITUENT UNIT *(to be filled in when charge is filed by a labor organization)*

6. DECLARATION

I declare that I have read the above charge and that the statements therein are true to the best of my knowledge and belief.

By _____   _____
    (signature of representative or person filling charge)   (title, if any)

Address _____   _____   _____
                                        (telephone number)   (date)

WILLFULLY FALSE STATEMENTS ON THIS CHARGE CAN BE PUNISHED BY FINE AND IMPRISONMENT
(U.S. CODE, TITLE 18, SECTION 1001)

massive postwar strikes, public policy began to shift against what many viewed as the union excesses of the times. The stage was set for passage of the Taft-Hartley Act of 1947.

Period of Modified Encouragement Coupled with Regulation: The Taft-Hartley Act (1947)

The **Taft-Hartley** (or Labor Management Relations) **Act** reflected the public's less enthusiastic attitudes toward unions. It amended the Wagner Act with provisions aimed at limiting unions in four ways: by prohibiting unfair union labor practices; by enumerating the rights of employees as union members; by enumerating the rights of employers; and by allowing the president of the United States to temporarily bar national emergency strikes.

Unfair Union Labor Practices

The Taft-Hartley Act enumerated several labor practices that unions were prohibited from engaging in:

1. Unions were banned from restraining or coercing employees from exercising their guaranteed bargaining rights.
2. It is an unfair labor practice for a union to cause an employer to discriminate in any way against an employee in order to encourage or discourage his or her membership in a union.
3. It is an unfair labor practice for a union to refuse to bargain in good faith with the employer about wages, hours, and other employment conditions.

Rights of Employees

The Taft-Hartley Act also protected the rights of employees against their unions. For example, many people felt that compulsory unionism violated the basic U.S. right of freedom of association. The new *right-to-work laws* sprang up in 19 states (mainly in the South and Southwest); as noted, these outlawed labor contracts that made union membership a condition for keeping one's job.

In general, the National Labor Relations Act does not restrain unions from unfair labor practices to the extent that it does employers. Unions may not restrain or coerce employees. However, "violent or otherwise threatening behavior or clearly coercive or intimidating union activities are necessary before the NLRB will find an unfair labor practice."[20] Examples here would include physical assaults or threats of violence, economic reprisals, and mass picketing that restrains the lawful entry or leaving of a work site. In one typical case, *Pattern Makers* v. *National Labor Relations Board*, the U.S. Supreme Court found the union guilty of an unfair labor practice when it tried to fine some members for resigning from the union and returning to work during a strike.[21]

Rights of Employers

The Taft-Hartley Act also explicitly gave employers certain rights. For example, it gave them full freedom to express their views concerning union organization. Thus, a manager can tell his or her employees that in his or her opinion unions are worthless, dangerous to the economy, and immoral. A manager can even, generally speaking, hint that unionization and subsequent high-wage demands might result in the permanent closing of the plant (but not in its relocation). Employers can set forth the union's record in regard to violence and corruption, if appropriate, and can play on the racial prejudices of workers by describing the union's philosophy toward integration. In fact, the only major restraint is that there can be no threat of reprisal or force or promise of benefit.[22]

The employer also cannot meet with employees on company time within 24 hours of an election or suggest to employees that they vote against the union while they are at home or in the employer's office, although he or she can do so while in their work area or where they normally gather.

National Emergency Strikes

The Taft-Hartley Act also allows the U.S. president to intervene in **national emergency strikes,** which are strikes (for example, on the part of steel firm employees) that might imperil national health and safety. The president may appoint a board of inquiry and, based on its report, apply for an injunction restraining the strike for 60 days. If no settlement is reached during that time, the injunction can be extended for another 20 days. During this period, employees are polled in a secret ballot to ascertain their willingness to accept the employer's last offer.

Period of Detailed Regulation of Internal Union Affairs: The Landrum-Griffin Act (1959)

In the 1950s, senate investigations revealed unsavory practices on the part of some unions, and the result was the **Landrum-Griffin Act** (officially, the Labor Management Reporting and Disclosure Act). An overriding aim of this act was to protect union members from possible wrongdoing on the part of their unions. It was also an amendment to the Wagner Act.

The Landrum-Griffin Act contains a bill of rights for union members. Among other things, this provides for certain rights in the nomination of candidates for union office. It also affirms a member's right to sue his or her union and ensures that no member can be fined or suspended without due process. The latter includes a list of specific charges, time to prepare a defense, and a fair hearing.

The act also laid out rules regarding union elections. For example, national and international unions must elect officers at least once every 5 years, using some type of secret-ballot mechanism.

The senate investigators also discovered flagrant examples of employer wrongdoing. The Landrum-Griffin Act therefore also greatly expanded the list of unlawful employer actions. For example, companies can no longer pay their own employees to entice them not to join the union.

THE UNION DRIVE AND ELECTION

It is through the union drive and election that a union tries to be recognized to represent employees. This process has five basic steps: initial contact, authorization cards, hearing, campaign, and the election.

Step 1: Initial Contact

During the initial contact stage, the union determines the employees' interest in organizing, and establishes an organizing committee.

The initiative for the first contact between the employees and the union may come from the employees, from a union already representing other employees of the firm, or from a union representing workers elsewhere. Sometimes, a union effort starts with a disgruntled employee's contacting the local union to learn how to organize his or her place of work (as at Wal-Mart). Sometimes, though, the campaign starts when a union decides it wants to expand to representing other employees in the firm or when the company looks like an easy one to organize. (For instance, the Teamsters Union— already firmly in place at UPS—began an intensive organizing campaign at FedEx.) In any case, there is an initial contact between a union representative and a few employees.

The Union Rep

When an employer becomes a target, a union official usually assigns a representative to assess employee interest. The representative visits the firm to determine whether enough employees are interested to make a union campaign worthwhile. He or she also identifies employees who would make good leaders in the organizing campaign and calls them together to create an organizing committee. The objective is to "educate the committee about the benefits of forming a union, the law and procedures involved in forming a local union, and the issues management is likely to raise during a campaign."[23]

Contact Guidelines

The union must follow certain guidelines when it starts contacting employees. The law allows union organizers to solicit employees for membership as long as it doesn't endanger the performance or safety of the employees. Therefore, much of the contact takes place off the job, perhaps at home or at eating places near work. Organizers can also safely contact employees on company grounds during off hours (such as lunch or break time). Under some conditions, union representatives may solicit employees at their workstations, but this is rare. In practice, there will be much informal organizing going on at the workplace as employees debate the merits of organizing. In any case, this initial contact stage may be deceptively quiet. In some instances the first inkling management has of a union campaign is the distribution or posting of a handbill soliciting union membership.

Labor Relations Consultants

Labor relations consultants are increasingly influencing the unionization process, with both management and unions using outside advisors. The use by management of consultants (who are often referred to disparagingly by unions as *union busters*) has grown considerably. One study found management consultants involved in 75% of the elections they surveyed.[24]

One expert says an employer's main goal shouldn't be to win representation elections, but to avoid them altogether. He says doing so means taking fast action when the first signs of union activity appear. His advice in a nutshell: Don't just ignore the union's efforts while it spreads pro-union rumors, such as "If we had a union, we wouldn't have to work so much overtime." Retain an attorney and react at once.[25]

Union Salting

Unions are also not without creative ways to win elections, one of which is called union salting. **Union salting** refers to a union organizing tactic by which workers who are employed full time by a union as undercover union organizers are hired by unwitting employers. The National Labor Relations Board defines "salting" as "placing of union members on nonunion job sites for the purpose of organizing."[26] A U.S. Supreme Court decision, *NLRB* v. *Town and Country Electric,* held the tactic to be legal.

The Web

The Web is a potent union contact tool. Unions can mass email announcements to collective bargaining unit members, and use mass email to reach supporters and government officials for their corporate campaigns. For example, the group trying to organize Starbucks workers (the Starbucks Workers Union) set up their own Web site (www.starbucksunion.org). It includes notes like, "Starbucks managers monitored internet chatrooms and eavesdropped on party conversations in a covert campaign to identify employees agitating for union representation at the coffee chain, internal emails reveal."[27]

Step 2: Authorization Cards

For the union to petition the NLRB for the right to hold an election, it must show that a sizable number of employees may be interested in being organized. The next step is thus for union organizers to try to get the employees to sign **authorization cards** (see Figure 9.2). Before an election can be petitioned, 30% of the eligible employees in an appropriate bargaining unit must sign.

During this stage, both union and management typically use various forms of propaganda. The union claims it can improve working conditions, raise wages, increase benefits, and generally get the workers better deals. Management need not be silent; it can attack the union on ethical and moral grounds and cite the cost of union membership, for example. Management can also explain its record, express facts and opinions, and explain to its employees the law applicable to organizing campaigns and the meaning of the duty to bargain in good faith (if the union should win the election). However, neither side can threaten, bribe, or coerce employees. Further, an employer may not make promises of benefit to employees or make unilateral changes in terms and conditions of employment that were not planned to be implemented prior to the onset of union organizing activity. Managers also should not look through signed authorization cards if confronted with them by union representatives. Doing so could be construed as an unfair labor practice by the NLRB, which could view it as spying on those who signed.

During this stage, unions can picket the company, subject to three constraints: The union must file a petition for an election within 30 days after the start of picketing, the firm cannot already be lawfully recognizing another union, and there cannot already have been a valid NLRB election during the past 12 months.

Step 3: The Hearing

After the authorization cards have been collected, one of three things can occur. The employer may choose not to contest union recognition, in which case no hearing is needed and a *consent election* is held immediately. The employer may choose not to

FIGURE 9.2	Sample Authorization Card

AFL-CIO
Service Employees International Union
SEIU Local 100

Authorization For Representation

Fill out form, print and send to your local 100 chapter. click here for addresses.

I hearby authorize Local 100 SEIU, AFL-CIO, to represent me for the purpose of collective bargaining with my employer, and to negotiate and conclude all agreements respecting wages, house and conditions of employment. I understand that this information may be used by the union to obtain recognition from my employer without an election.

Name:

Address 1:

Address 2:

City, State, Zip

Phone:

Employed at:

Shift:

Hourly Wage: $

Authorization to Deduct Dues

Name:
[last, first, middle]

Social Security Number

To:
[Employer]

Effective _____, I hereby request and authorize you to deduct from my earnings each payroll period, an amount sufficient to provide for the regular payment of the current rate of monthly union dues and inititation fee (if owing) established by Local 100, Service International Union, AFL-CIO, or an equivilent amount. The amount shall be in accordance with the provisions of the constitution of Local 100 and shall be applicable of my membership status in the Union. The amount deducted shall be irrrevocable for the period of one (1) year from the date thereof, and shall be automatically recieved and irrevocable for successive similar periods unless revoked by written notice to the employer and to the Treasurer of Local 100 within the period of fifteen (15) days prior to the anniversary of my checkoff.

Signature:_____

Source: http://seiu100.org/OLDSITE/membershipapp.htm. Accessed August 9, 2007.

contest the union's *right to an election* (and/or the scope of the bargaining unit, or which employees are eligible to vote in the election), in which case no hearing is needed and the parties can stipulate an election. Or, the employer may contest the union's right, in which case it can insist on a *hearing* to determine those issues. An employer's decision about whether to insist on a hearing is a strategic one based on the facts of each case and whether it feels it needs additional time to develop a campaign to try to persuade a majority of its employees not to elect a union to represent them.

Most companies contest the union's right to represent their employees, and thus decline to voluntarily recognize the union: They claim that a significant number of their employees do not really want the union. It is at this point that the U.S. Labor Department's NLRB gets involved. The NLRB is usually contacted by the union, which requests a hearing. Based on this, the regional director of the NLRB sends a hearing officer to investigate. (For example, did 30% or more of the employees in an appropriate bargaining unit sign the authorization cards?) The examiner sends both management and the union a notice of representation hearing that states the time and place of the hearing.

The **bargaining unit** is one decision to come out of the hearing; it is the group of employees that the union will be authorized to represent and bargain for collectively.

Finally, if the results of the hearing are favorable for the union, the NLRB directs that an election be held. It issues a Decision and Direction of Election notice to that effect and sends NLRB Form 666 (see Figure 9.3) to the employer to post.

Step 4: The Campaign

During the campaign that precedes the election, the union and employer appeal to employees for their votes. The union emphasizes that it will prevent unfairness, set up a grievance/seniority system, and improve unsatisfactory wages. Union strength, they'll say, will give employees a voice in determining wages and working conditions. Management emphasizes that improvements such as those the union promises don't require unionization, and that wages are equal to or better than they would be with a union contract. Management also emphasizes the financial cost of union dues; the fact that the union is an "outsider"; and that if the union wins, a strike may follow.[28] It can even attack the union on ethical and moral grounds, while insisting that employees will not be as well off and may lose freedom. But neither side can threaten, bribe, or coerce employees.

The Supervisor's Role

Supervisors must be knowledgeable about what they can and can't do to legally hamper organizing activities, lest they commit unfair labor practices. Such practices could cause a new election to be held after the company has won a previous election or cause the company to forfeit the second election and go directly to contract negotiation. In one case, a plant superintendent reacted to a union's initial organizing attempt by prohibiting distribution of union literature in the plant's lunchroom. Because solicitation of off-duty workers in nonwork areas is generally legal, the company subsequently allowed the union to post union literature on the company's bulletin board and to distribute union literature in nonworking areas inside the plant. However, the NLRB still ruled that the initial act of prohibiting distribution of the literature was an unfair labor practice, one that was not "made right" by the company's subsequent efforts. The NLRB used the superintendent's action as one reason for invalidating an election that the company won.[29]

Strategy and HR

Starbucks bases its strategy in part on owning all its stores. Given the difficulties in monitoring what employees are doing in its far-flung stores, Starbucks managers can't just rely on traditional control tools like budgets to monitor what's happening in each store. The company therefore works hard to encourage employees to control themselves—by making them "partners," and by providing excellent benefits and stock option plans. As a company that provides excellent benefits and working conditions, Starbucks executives were surprised that some employees may have expressed a desire to unionize. Be that as it may, the allegations that some local managers may have tried

FIGURE 9.3   NLRB Form 666: Notice to Employees

Form NLRB 666
(7–72)

★ NOTICE TO EMPLOYEES

FROM THE

National Labor Relations Board

A PETITION has been filed with this Federal agency seeking an election to determine whether certain employees want to be represented by a union.

The case is being investigated and NO DETERMINATION HAS BEEN MADE AT THIS TIME by the National Labor Relations Board.   IF an election is held Notices of Election will be posted giving complete details for voting.

It was suggested that your employer post this notice so the National Labor Relations Board could inform you of your basic rights under the National Labor Relations Act.

YOU HAVE THE RIGHT under Federal Law

- To self-organization
- To form, join, or assist labor organizations
- To bargain collectively through representatives of your own choosing
- To act together for the purposes of collective bargaining or other mutual aid or protection
- To refuse to do any or all of these things unless the union and employer, in a state where such agreements are permitted, enter into a lawful union security clause requiring employees to join the union.

It is possible that some of you will be voting in an employee representation election as a result of the request for an election having been filed.   While NO DETERMINATION HAS BEEN MADE AT THIS TIME, in the event an election is held, the NATIONAL LABOR RELATIONS BOARD wants all eligible voters to be familiar with their rights under the law IF it holds an election.

The Board applies rules which are intended to keep its elections fair and honest and which result in a free choice. If agents of either Unions or Employers act in such a way as to interfere with your right to a free election, the election can be set aside by the Board.   Where appropriate the Board provides other remedies, such as reinstatement for employees fired for exercising their rights, including backpay from the party responsible for their discharge.

NOTE:

The following are examples of conduct which interfere with the rights of employees and may result in the setting aside of the election.

- Threatening loss of jobs or benefits by an Employer or a Union
- Misstating important facts by a Union or an Employer where the other party does not have a fair chance to reply
- Promising or granting promotions, pay raises, or other benefits, to influence an employee's vote by a party capable of carrying out such promises
- An Employer firing employees to discourage or encourage union activity or a Union causing them to be fired to encourage union activity
- Making campaign speeches to assembled groups of employees on company time within the 24-hour period before the election
- Incitement by either an Employer or a Union of racial or religious prejudice by inflammatory appeals
- Threatening physical force or violence to employees by a Union or an Employer to influence their votes

Please be assured that IF AN ELECTION IS HELD every effort will be made to protect your right to a free choice under the law. Improper conduct will not be permitted. All parties are expected to cooperate fully with this agency in maintaining basic principles of a fair election as required by law. The National Labor Relations Board as an agency of the United States Government does not endorse any choice in the election.

NATIONAL LABOR RELATIONS BOARD
an agency of the
UNITED STATES GOVERNMENT

THIS IS AN OFFICIAL GOVERNMENT NOTICE AND MUST NOT BE DEFACED BY ANYONE

to retaliate against employees who favored the union underscore why all employers must carefully train supervisors in how to react when the union comes to call.

To avoid such problems, employers should have rules governing distribution of literature and solicitation of workers and train supervisors in how to apply them.

Rules Regarding Literature and Solicitation

An employer can take a number of steps to legally restrict union organizing activity.[30] For example:

- Nonemployees can always be barred from soliciting employees during their work time—that is, when the employee is on duty and not on a break.
- Employers can usually stop employees from soliciting other employees for any purpose if one or both employees are on paid-duty time and not on a break.
- Most employers (not including retail stores, shopping centers, and certain other employers) can bar nonemployees from the building's interiors and work areas as a

right of private property owners. In certain cases, nonemployees can also be barred from exterior private property such as parking lots—if there is a business reason (such as safety) and the reason is not just to interfere with union organizers.

Such restrictions are valid only if the employer does not impose them in a discriminatory manner. For example, if employees are permitted by company policy to collect money for a wedding shower and baby gifts, to sell Avon-type products or to engage in other solicitation during their working time, the employer will not be able to lawfully prohibit them from union soliciting during work time.

Finally, remember that there are many more ways to commit unfair labor practices than just keeping union organizers off your private property. For example, one employer decided to have a cookout and paid day off 2 days before a union representation election. The NLRB held that this was too much of a coincidence and represented coercive conduct. The union had lost the first vote but won the second vote as a result.[31]

Improving Productivity through HRIS

As noted, the Internet is rendering some of these employer tactics moot. As one expert recently asked, "If faster and more powerful ways of communicating enable companies to compete in a quickly changing and challenging environment, shouldn't they also make unions stronger and more efficient as organizations and workplace representatives?"[32]

In fact, employers need to know that the Internet is revolutionizing union activity, much as it revolutionized how firms do business. E-mail and the Internet means unions can mass e-mail announcements to collective bargaining unit members, and use mass e-mail to reach supporters and government officials for their corporate campaigns.

Union-based Web sites are becoming integral parts of many such unionization campaigns: Alliance@IBM provides one example. Managed by the Communications Workers of America, Alliance@IBM seeks to encourage IBM employees to join the Communications Workers of America. It does so by providing information on a range of issues, such as why IBM employees need a union, questions and concerns about unions, and how employees can join the union and get involved. For example, one page addresses the issue "Why We Need Alliance@IBM."

Step 5: The Election

Finally, the election can be held within 30 to 60 days after the NLRB issues its Decision and Direction of Election. The election is by secret ballot. The NLRB provides the ballots (see Figure 9.4), as well as the voting booth and ballot box. It also counts the votes and certifies the results of the election. Historically, the more workers that vote, the less likely a union victory. This is probably because more workers who are not strong union supporters end up voting. The union is important, too: The Teamsters union is less likely than other unions to win a representation election.[33]

The union becomes the employees' representative if it wins the election, and winning means getting a majority of the votes cast, not a majority of the workers in the bargaining unit. (It is also important to keep in mind that when an employer commits an unfair labor practice, a "no union" election may be reversed. As representatives of their employer, supervisors must therefore be very careful not to commit such unfair practices.) The union typically wins just over half of such elections.

| FIGURE 9.4 | Sample NLRB Ballot |

UNITED STATES OF AMERICA

National Labor Relations Board

OFFICIAL SECRET BALLOT

FOR CERTAIN EMPLOYEES OF

Do you wish to be represented for purposes of collective bargaining by —

MARK AN "S" IN THE SQUARE OF YOUR CHOICE

YES   NO

☐   ☐

DO NOT SIGN THIS BALLOT. Fold and drop in ballot box.
If you spoil this ballot return it to the Board Agent for a new one.

Decertification Elections: When Employees Want to Oust Their Union

Winning an election and signing an agreement do not necessarily mean that the union is in the company to stay—quite the opposite. The same law that grants employees the right to unionize also gives them a way to legally terminate the union's right to represent them. The process is *decertification*. There are around 450 to 500 decertification elections each year, of which unions usually win around 30%.[34] That's actually a more favorable rate for management than the rate for the original, representation elections.

Decertification campaigns don't differ much from certification campaigns.[35] The union organizes membership meetings and house-to-house visits, mails literature to homes, and uses phone calls, NLRB appeals, and (sometimes) threats and harassment to win the election. Managers use meetings—including one-on-one meetings, small-group meetings, and meetings with entire units—as well as legal or expert assistance, letters, improved working conditions, and subtle or not-so-subtle threats in its attempts to win a decertification vote. Employers are also increasingly using consultants.

THE COLLECTIVE BARGAINING PROCESS

What Is Collective Bargaining?

When and if the union is recognized as a company's employees' representative, a day is set for meeting at the bargaining table. Representatives of management and the union meet to negotiate a labor contract that contains agreements on specific provisions covering wages, hours, and working conditions.

What exactly is **collective bargaining?** According to the National Labor Relations Act:

> For the purpose of (this act) to bargain collectively is the performance of the mutual obligation of the employer and the representative of the employees to meet at reasonable times and confer in good faith with respect to wages, hours, and terms and conditions of employment, or the negotiation of an agreement, or any question arising thereunder, and the execution of a written contract incorporating any agreement reached if requested by either party, but such obligation does not compel either party to agree to a proposal or require the making of a concession.

In plain language, this means that both management and labor are required by law to negotiate wages, hours, and terms and conditions of employment "in good faith." In a moment we will see that the specific terms that are negotiable (because wages, hours, and conditions of employment are too broad to be useful in practice) have been clarified by a series of court decisions.

What Is Good-Faith Bargaining?

Good-faith bargaining means that proposals are matched with counterproposals and that both parties make every reasonable effort to arrive at an agreement. It does not mean that either party is compelled to agree to a proposal. Nor does it require that either party make any specific concessions (although as a practical matter, some may be necessary).

When Is Bargaining Not in Good Faith?

In assessing whether the party has violated its good-faith obligations, it is the totality of conduct by each of the parties that is of prime importance to the NLRB and the courts.[36] However, as interpreted by the NLRB and the courts, examples of a violation of the requirements for good-faith bargaining may include:

1. *Surface bargaining.* This involves going through the motions of bargaining without any real intention of completing a formal agreement.
2. *Proposals and demands.* The NLRB considers the advancement of proposals as a positive factor in determining overall good faith.
3. *Withholding information.* The NLRB and courts expect management to furnish information on matters such as wages, hours, and other terms of employment that union negotiators request and legitimately require. Failing to provide such information in a timely manner and usable form may reflect bad-faith bargaining.[37]

4. *Dilatory tactics.* The law requires that the parties meet and "confer at reasonable times and intervals." It does not require management to meet at the time and place dictated just by the union. It may not be unusual for employers to try to delay the meeting so as to "disrupt a union's bargaining momentum."[38] However, inordinately delaying the meeting or refusing to meet with the other party may reflect bad-faith bargaining.
5. *Concessions.* The law does not require either party to make concessions, in other words, to give in to the other party's demand. However, being willing to compromise during negotiations is a crucial ingredient of good-faith bargaining.
6. *Unilateral changes in conditions.* This is viewed as a strong indication that the employer is not bargaining with the required intent of reaching an agreement.
7. *Bypassing the representative.* An employer violates its duty to bargain when it refuses to negotiate with the union representative.

The Negotiating Team

Both union and management send a negotiating team to the bargaining table, and both teams usually go into the bargaining sessions having done their research. Union representatives have sounded out union members on their desires and conferred with union representatives of related unions.

Similarly, management uses several techniques to prepare for bargaining. For example, it compiles pay and benefit data, including comparisons to local pay rates and rates paid for similar jobs in the industry. Management also carefully "costs" the current labor contract and determines the increased cost—total, per employee, and per hour—of the union's demands. It also tries to identify probable union demands and to size up which are more important to the union. It uses information from grievances and feedback from supervisors to determine ahead of time what the union's demands might be and thus prepare counteroffers and arguments ahead of time.

One collective bargaining expert says, "The mistake I see most often is [HR professionals who] enter the negotiations without understanding the financial impact of things they put on the table. The thing you give up can make or break your employer . . . For example, the union wants 3 extra vacation days. That doesn't sound like a lot, except that in some states, if an employee leaves, you have to pay them for unused vacation time. Now [therefore] your employer has to carry that liability on their books at all times."[39]

Bargaining Items

Labor law sets out categories of items that are subject to bargaining: These are *mandatory, voluntary,* and *illegal items.*

Voluntary (or permissible) **bargaining items** are neither mandatory nor illegal; they become a part of negotiations only through the joint agreement of both management and union. Neither party can be compelled against its wishes to negotiate over voluntary items. An employee cannot hold up signing a contract because the other party refuses to bargain on a voluntary item.

Illegal bargaining items are forbidden by law. The clause agreeing to hire "union members exclusively" would be illegal in a right-to-work state, for example.

FIGURE 9.5	Bargaining Items	

MANDATORY	PERMISSIBLE	ILLEGAL
Rates of pay	Indemnity bonds	Closed shop
Wages	Management rights as	Separation of employees
Hours of employment	to union affairs	based on race
Overtime pay	Pension benefits of	Discriminatory
Shift differentials	retired employees	treatment
Holidays	Scope of the bargaining unit	
Vacations	Including supervisors	
Severance pay	in the contract	
Pensions	Additional parties to	
Insurance benefits	the contract such as	
Profit-sharing plans	the international	
Christmas bonuses	union	
Company housing,	Use of union label	
meals, and discounts	Settlement of unfair	
Employee security	labor charges	
Job performance	Prices in cafeteria	
Union security	Continuance of past	
Management–union	contract	
relationship	Membership of bargaining	
Drug testing	team	
of employees	Employment of strikebreakers	

Source: Carrell, Michael R.; Heavrin, Christina, *Labor Relations and Collective Bargaining: Cases, Practice, and Law,* 4th, © 1995. Electronically reproduced by permission of Pearson Education, Inc., Upper Saddle River, New Jersey.

About 70 **mandatory bargaining items** exist, some of which are in Figure 9.5. They include wages, hours, rest periods, layoffs, transfers, benefits, and severance pay. Others are added as the law evolves. For instance, drug testing evolved into a mandatory item as a result of NLRB decisions.

Bargaining Stages[40]

Bargaining typically goes through several stages.[41] First, each side presents its demands. At this stage, both parties are usually quite far apart on some issues. Indeed, labor negotiators use the term *blue-skying* to refer to demands (such as swimming pools and 17 paid holidays, including Valentine's Day) that some negotiators have been known to bring to the table. Second, there is a reduction of demands. At this stage, each side trades off some of its demands to gain others, a process called *trading points.* Third come the subcommittee studies: The parties form joint subcommittees or study groups to try to work out reasonable alternatives. Fourth, the parties reach an informal settlement, and each group goes back to its sponsor. Union representatives check informally with their superiors and the union members; management representatives

NEGOTIATING GUIDELINES

1. *Set clear objectives* for every bargaining item and understand on what grounds the objectives are established.

2. *Do not hurry.*

3. When in doubt, *caucus* with your associates.

4. Be *well prepared* with firm data supporting your position.

5. Always strive to keep some *flexibility* in your position. Don't get yourself out on a limb.

6. Don't just concern yourself with what the other party says and does; *find out why.* Remember that economic motivation is not the only explanation for the other party's actions.

7. Respect the importance of *face saving* for the other party.

8. Constantly be alert to the *real intentions* of the other party with respect not only to goals but also to priorities.

9. Be a good *listener.*

10. Build a reputation for *being fair but firm.*

11. Learn to *control your emotions;* don't panic. Use emotions as a tool, not as an obstacle.

12. Be sure as you make each bargaining move that you know its *relationship* to all other moves.

13. Measure each move against your *objectives.*

14. Pay close attention to the *wording* of every clause renegotiated; words and phrases are often sources of grievances.

15. Remember that collective bargaining negotiations are, by nature, part of a *compromise* process. There is no such thing as having all the pie.

16. Consider the impact of present negotiations on those in *future years.*

check with top management. Finally, when everything is in order, the parties fine-tune, proofread, and sign a formal agreement. The *HR in Practice* box summarizes negotiating guidelines.

Impasses, Mediation, and Strikes

Impasses Signing the agreement assumes everything is in order, and that there are no insurmountable disagreements. If there are, the parties may declare an impasse. For example, a few years ago, the National Hockey League informed the NLRB that it had reached an impasse in its negotiations with the National Hockey League Players Association.[42] The parties must get past the impasse for the contract to be signed.

An impasse usually occurs because one party demands more than the other offers. Sometimes an impasse can be resolved through a third party, a disinterested person such as a mediator or arbitrator. If the impasse is not resolved in this way, a work stoppage, or *strike,* may be called by the union to pressure management.

Third-Party Involvement

Three types of third-party interventions are used to overcome an impasse: mediation, fact-finding, and arbitration. With **mediation,** a neutral third party tries to assist the principals in reaching agreement. The mediator usually holds meetings with each party to determine where each stands regarding its position. He or she then uses this information to find common ground for further bargaining. For example, Southwest Airlines and its mechanics union requested federal mediation to help the parties overcome a deadlock over pay.[43] The mediator is always a go-between. As such, he or she communicates assessments of the likelihood of a strike, the possible settlement packages available, and the like. The mediator does not have the authority to insist on a position or make a concession. However, he or she may—and probably will—provide leadership by making his or her position on some issue crystal clear.

In certain situations (as in a national emergency dispute in which the president of the United States determines that it would be a national emergency for a strike to occur), a fact-finder may be appointed. A **fact-finder** is a neutral party. He or she studies the issues and makes a public recommendation of what a reasonable settlement ought to be. For example, presidential emergency fact-finding boards have successfully resolved impasses in certain critical transportation disputes.

Arbitration is the most definitive type of third-party intervention because the arbitrator may have the power to decide and dictate settlement terms. Unlike mediation and fact-finding, arbitration can guarantee a solution to an impasse. With *binding arbitration,* both parties are committed to accepting the arbitrator's award. With *nonbinding arbitration,* they are not. Arbitration may also be voluntary or compulsory (in other words, imposed by a government agency). In the United States, voluntary binding arbitration is the most prevalent.

Arbitration may not always be as impartial as it's thought to be. Researchers studied 391 arbitrated cases in baseball over about 20 recent years. They expected decisions to be about evenly split between players and teams. In fact, arbitrator awards favored teams 61% of the time. They concluded that (at least in baseball) "self-interested behavior by arbitrators" may lead to bias against players, and particularly against players of African-American and Latin ancestry.[44]

Sources of Third-Party Assistance

Various public and professional agencies make arbitrators and mediators available. For example, the American Arbitration Association (AAA) represents and provides the services of thousands of arbitrators and mediators to employers and unions requesting their services. The U.S. government's Office of Arbitration Services maintains a roster of arbitrators qualified to hear and decide disputes over the interpretation or application of collective-bargaining agreements, and provides the parties involved with lists and panels of arbitrators. During fiscal year 2006, the Office processed about 17,000 requests for arbitration panels and decided about 2,400 cases. In addition, most states provide arbitrator and mediation services.

Strikes

A strike is a withdrawal of labor. There are four main types of strikes. An **economic strike** results from a failure to agree on the terms of a contract—from an impasse, in other words. **Unfair labor practice strikes** protest illegal conduct by the employer.

A **wildcat strike** is an unauthorized strike occurring during the term of a contract. A **sympathy strike** occurs when one union strikes in support of the strike of another.

Strikes needn't be an inevitable result of the bargaining process. Instead, studies show that they are often avoidable, but occur as a result of mistakes made during the bargaining process. Mistakes include discrepancies between union leaders' and rank-and-file members' expectations, and misperceptions regarding each side's bargaining goals.[45]

*Picketing i*s one of the first activities occurring during a strike. The purpose of picketing is to inform the public about the existence of the labor dispute and often to encourage others to refrain from doing business with the employer against whom the employees are striking.

Dealing with a Strike

Employers can make several responses when they become the object of a strike. One is to shut down the affected area and thus halt their operations until the strike is over. A second alternative is to contract out work during the duration of the strike in order to blunt the effects of the strike on the employer. A third alternative is for the employer to continue operations, perhaps using supervisors and other nonstriking workers to fill in for the striking workers. A fourth alternative is the hiring of replacements for the strikers. In an economic strike, such replacements can be deemed permanent and would not have to be let go to make room for strikers who decided to return to work. If the strike were an unfair labor practice strike, the strikers would be entitled to return to their jobs if the employer makes an unconditional offer for them to do so.

When Northwest Airlines began giving permanent jobs to 1,500 substitute workers it hired to replace striking mechanics, the strike by the Aircraft Mechanics Fraternal Association basically fell apart.[46]

Other Responses

Management and labor both use other methods to try to break an impasse and achieve their aims. The union, for example, may resort to a *corporate campaign.* This is an organized effort by the union that exerts pressure on the corporation by pressuring the company's other unions, shareholders, directors, customers, creditors, and government agencies, often directly. Thus, individual members of the board of directors might be shocked by picketing of their homes, and the company's banks might become targets of a union member **boycott,** a removal of patronage.[47]

Unions continue to use corporate campaigns to good effect. Sometimes also called *advocacy* or *comprehensive campaigns,* they recently helped unions organize several health care firms, including Sutter Health in California.[48]

Inside games are union efforts to convince employees to impede or to disrupt production. They might do this, for example, by slowing the work pace, refusing to work overtime, filing mass charges with governmental agencies, or refusing to do work without receiving detailed instructions from supervisors (even though such instruction has not previously been required). Other inside games include scolding management and holding sickouts.[49] Inside games can thus be viewed as essentially de facto strikes, albeit "strikes" in which the employees are being supported by the company, which continues to pay them. In one inside game at Caterpillar's Aurora, Illinois, plant, United Auto Workers' grievances in the final stage before arbitration rose from 22 to 336. The effect, of course, was to clog the grievance procedure and tie up workers and management.[50]

Lockouts

Employers can try to break an impasse with lockouts. A **lockout** is a refusal by the employer to provide opportunities to work. The company (often literally) locks out employees and prohibits them from doing their jobs (and thus from getting paid).

The NLRB does not generally view a lockout as an unfair labor practice. For example, if your product is a perishable one (such as vegetables), then a lockout may be a legitimate tactic to neutralize or decrease union power. A lockout is viewed as an unfair labor practice by the NLRB only when the employer acts for a prohibited purpose. It is not a prohibited purpose to try to bring about a settlement of negotiations on terms favorable to the employer. Lockouts are not widely used today, though. Employers are usually reluctant to cease operations when employees are willing to continue working (even though there may be an impasse at the bargaining table).[51]

Injunctions

During the impasse, both employers and unions can seek injunctive relief if they believe the other side is taking actions that could irreparably harm the other party. To obtain such relief, the NLRB must show the district court that an unfair labor practice—such as interfering with the union organizing campaign—if left unremedied, will irreparably harm the other party's statutory rights. (For example, if the employer is unfairly interfering with the union's organization campaign, or if the union is retaliating against employees for trying to gain access to the NLRB, the other side might press the NLRB for 10[j] injunctive relief.) Such relief is requested after the NLRB issues an unfair labor practices complaint. The *injunctive relief* is a court order compelling a party or parties either to resume or to desist a certain action.[52]

The Contract Agreement

The contract agreement itself may be 20 or 30 pages long or longer. It may contain just general declarations of policy or a detailed specification of rules and procedures. However, the tendency today is toward the longer, more detailed contract. This is largely because of the increased number of items the agreements cover. The main sections of a typical contract cover subjects such as:

1. Management rights
2. Union security and automatic payroll dues deduction
3. Grievance procedures
4. Arbitration of grievances
5. Disciplinary procedures
6. Compensation rates
7. Hours of work and overtime

8. Benefits such as vacation, holidays, insurance, and pension
9. Health and safety provisions
10. Employee security seniority provisions
11. Contract expiration date

Handling Grievances

Signing the labor agreement is not the end of the process, because questions will always arise about what various clauses really mean. The *grievance process* addresses these issues. It is the process or steps that the employer and union have agreed to follow to ascertain whether some action violated the agreement. The grievance process is not supposed to renegotiate contract points. Instead, the aim is to clarify what those points really mean, in the context of addressing grievances regarding things like time off, disciplinary action, and pay.

The potential for grievances and discontent is always present at work. Employees will use just about any issue involving wages, hours, or conditions of employment as the basis of a grievance. Discipline cases and seniority problems (including promotions, transfers, and layoffs) would probably top the list. Others would include grievances growing out of job evaluations and work assignments, overtime, vacations, incentive plans, and holidays.

Sometimes the grievance process gets out of hand. For example, members of American Postal Workers Union, Local 482, filed 1,800 grievances at the Postal Service's Roanoke, Virginia, mail processing facility (the usual rate is about 800 grievances per year). The employees apparently were responding to job changes, including transfers triggered by the Postal Service's efforts to further automate its processes.[53]

Whatever the source of the grievances, many firms today (and virtually all unionized ones) do (or should) give employees some means through which to air and settle their grievances. Grievance procedures are invariably a part of the labor agreement. But, even in nonunion firms, such procedures can help ensure that labor–management peace prevails.

Contract Administration

In unionized companies, grievance handling is often called *contract administration*, since no labor contract can ever be so complete that it covers all contingencies and answers all questions. For example, suppose the contract says you can discharge an employee only for "just cause." You subsequently discharge someone for speaking back to you in harsh terms. Was it within your rights to discharge this person? Was speaking back to you harshly "just cause"? The grievance procedure would handle and settle disagreements like these. It involves interpretation only, and generally would not involve renegotiating all or parts of the agreement.

The Grievance Procedure

Grievance procedures are typically multistep processes. For example, step one might require the grievant to try to work out an agreement with his or her supervisor, perhaps with a union officer or colleague present. Appeals may then be taken successively to the supervisor's boss, then that person's boss, and perhaps finally to a special arbitrator.

Guidelines for Handling Grievances

It is generally best, but not always possible, to develop a work environment in which grievances don't occur in the first place. Doing so depends on being able to recognize, diagnose, and correct the causes of potential employee dissatisfaction before they become formal grievances. Typical causes include unfair appraisals, inequitable wages, or poor communications. Yet, in practice, grievances can possibly be minimized, but never eradicated. There will probably always be a need to interpret what some clause or clauses in the agreement means. The *HR in Practice* box presents some guidelines for handling a grievance should one occur.

HR IN PRACTICE

HOW TO HANDLE A GRIEVANCE[54]

DO

- Investigate and handle each and every case as though it may eventually result in an arbitration hearing.
- Talk with the employee about his or her grievance; give the person a good and full hearing.
- Require the union to identify specific contractual provisions allegedly violated.
- Comply with the contractual time limits of the company for handling the grievance.
- Visit the work area of the grievance.
- Determine whether there were any witnesses.
- Examine the grievant's personnel record.
- Fully examine prior grievance records.
- Treat the union representative as your equal.
- Hold your grievance discussion privately.
- Fully inform your own supervisor of grievance matters.

DON'T

- Discuss the case with the union steward alone—the grievant should definitely be there.
- Make arrangements with individual employees that are inconsistent with the labor agreement.
- Hold back the remedy if the company is wrong.
- Admit to the binding effect of a past practice.
- Relinquish to the union your rights as a manager.
- Settle grievances on the basis of what is "fair." Instead, stick to the labor agreement, which should be your only standard.
- Bargain over items not covered by the contract.
- Treat as subject to arbitration claims demanding the discipline or discharge of managers.
- Give long, written grievance answers.
- Trade a grievance settlement for a grievance withdrawal (or try to make up for a bad decision in one grievance by bending over backward in another).
- Deny grievances on the premise that your "hands have been tied by management."
- Agree to informal amendments in the contract.

WHAT'S NEXT FOR UNIONS?

For years, Jerry Sullivan, the head of Ford's United Auto Workers union, fought hard for increased benefits for his union members. But recently, he's been urging his union colleagues to accept productivity enhancing plans, such as outsourcing Ford's factory jobs to lower paid workers. "Ford is in a desperate situation," he says, and "if this company goes down, I want to be able to look in the mirror and say I did everything I could."[55]

Why the Union Decline?

Several factors contributed to the decline in union membership over the past 40 or so years. Unions traditionally appealed mostly to blue-collar workers, and the proportion of blue-collar jobs has been decreasing as service-sector and white-collar service jobs have increased. Furthermore, several economic factors, including intense international competition, have put unions under further pressure. Globalization increases competition, and competition increases pressures on employers to cut costs and boost productivity. This in turn puts unions in a squeeze, as at Ford. Other factors pressuring employers and unions include the deregulation of trucking, airlines, and communications, outdated equipment and factories, mismanagement, new technology, and government regulations (such as Title VII). The effect of all this has been the permanent layoff of hundreds of thousands of union members, the permanent closing of company plants, the relocation of companies to nonunion settings (either in the United States or overseas), and mergers and acquisitions that have eliminated union jobs and affected collective bargaining agreements.

How Unions Are Changing

Of course, unions are not sitting idly by and just watching their numbers dwindle.[56] The priorities of the Change to Win Coalition (whose members broke off from the AFL-CIO) illustrate what may be the new union strategies. They,

> Make it our first priority to help millions more workers form unions so we can build a strong movement for rewarding work in America [and] unite the strength of everyone who works in the same industry so we can negotiate with today's huge global corporations for everyone's benefit . . .[57]

Change to Win

In practice, this means several things. Change to Win will be very aggressive about trying to organize workers, will focus on organizing women and minority workers, will focus more on organizing temporary or contingent workers, and will target specific multinational companies for international campaigns.[58]

Employee Free Choice Act

Unions are pushing Congress to pass the Employee Free Choice Act. This would, among other things, make it more difficult for employers to inhibit workers from trying to form a union. Unions are also pushing for a new means of obtaining union recognition. Instead of secret-ballot elections, unions are pushing for a "*card check*" system. Here the union would win recognition when a majority of workers signed authorization cards saying they want to unionize. Several large companies, including Cingular Wireless, agreed to the card check process.[59]

Class Action Lawsuits

Unions are also using class action lawsuits to support employees in non-unionized companies, so as to pressure employers. For example, unions recently used class action lawsuits to support workers' claims under the Fair Labor Standards Act, and the Equal Pay Act.[60]

Coordination

Unions are becoming more proactive in terms of coordinating their efforts.[61] For example, the Union of Needle Trades, Industrial and Textile Employees used their "Voice at Work" Campaign to coordinate 800 workers at one employer's distribution center with others at the employer's New York City headquarters and with local activists and international unions throughout Europe. This forced the employer's parent company, a French conglomerate, to cease resisting the union's organizing efforts. In its "Union Cities" campaigns, AFL-CIO planners work with local labor councils and individual unions to gain the support of a target city's elected officials. In Los Angeles, this helped the service workers' union organize janitors in that city.

Example

The steps that UNITE took against Cintas Corp. illustrate some of unions' new aggressive tactics. In their organizing effort against Cintas, UNITE did not petition for an NLRB election. Instead, UNITE proposed using the "card check" process. They filed a $100 million class action suit against the company in support of its sales representatives. Then Cintas workers in California filed a lawsuit claiming that the company was violating a nearby municipality's "living wage" law. UNITE then joined forces with the Teamsters union, which in turn began targeting Cintas' delivery people.[62]

Cooperative Arrangements

Another, somewhat more risky (for the unions) approach is to agree to enter into more cooperative pacts with employers—for instance, working with them in developing team-based employee participation programs. About half of all collective bargaining agreements encourage cooperative labor–management relationships. *Cooperative clauses* cover things like joint committees to review drug problems, health care, and safety issues.[63]

Global Campaigns

Unions are also forcefully extending their reach overseas, as the *Global Issues* feature explains.

UNIONS GO GLOBAL

Any company that thinks it can avoid unions by sending manufacturing and jobs abroad is sorely mistaken. Today, as we've seen, most businesses are "going global," and regional trade treaties like the North American Free Trade Agreement (NAFTA) are further boosting the business done by firms abroad. This fact is not lost on unions, some of which are already expanding their influence abroad.

The global union campaigns reflect the belief, as the Service Employees' International Union puts it, that "huge global service sector companies routinely cross national borders and industry lines as they search for places where they can shift operations to exploit workers with the lowest possible pay and benefits ..." SEIU is therefore strengthening its alliances with unions in other nations, with the goal of uniting workers in particular multinational companies and industries, around the globe.[64] For example, the head of the United States' Service Employees International Union recently worked with China's All China Federation of Trade Unions (ACFTU) to help the latter organize China's Wal-Mart stores.[65] Similarly, U.S. unions are helping Mexican unions to organize, especially in U.S.-owned factories. Thus, the United Electrical Workers is subsidizing organizers at Mexican plants of the General Electric Company.

U.S. unions gain several things by forming alliances with unions abroad. By helping workers in other countries unionize, they help raise the wage and living standards of local workers. That may in turn discourage corporate flight from the United States in search of low wages. Unions also help their own positions in the United States with the added leverage they get from having unions abroad that can help them fight their corporate campaigns back in the U.S.

Review

Summary

1. In addition to improved wages and working conditions, unions seek security when organizing. There are five possible arrangements, including the closed shop, the union shop, the agency shop, the open shop, and maintenance of membership.

2. The AFL-CIO is a national federation comprising about 100 national and international unions. It can exercise only the power it is allowed to exercise by its constituent national unions.

3. During the period of strong encouragement of unions, the Norris-LaGuardia Act and the NLRA were passed; these marked a shift in labor law from repression to strong encouragement of union activity. They did this by banning certain types of unfair labor practices, by providing for secret-ballot elections, and by creating the NLRB.

4. The Taft-Hartley Act reflected the period of modified encouragement coupled with regulation. It enumerated the rights of employees with respect to their unions, enumerated the rights of employers, and allowed the U.S. president to temporarily bar national emergency strikes. Among other things, it also enumerated certain union unfair labor practices. For example, it banned unions from restraining or coercing employees from exercising their guaranteed bargaining rights. And employers were explicitly given the right to express their views concerning union organization.

5. The Landrum-Griffin Act reflected the period of detailed regulation of internal union affairs. It grew out of discoveries of wrongdoing on the part of both management and union leadership and contained a bill of rights for union members. (For example, it affirms a member's right to sue his or her union.)

6. There are five steps in a union drive and election: the initial contact, obtaining authorization cards, holding a hearing with the NLRB, the campaign, and the election itself. Remember that the union need only win a majority of the votes cast, *not* a majority of the workers in the bargaining unit.

7. Bargaining collectively in good faith is the next step if and when the union wins the election. Good faith means that both parties communicate and negotiate, and that proposals are matched with counterproposals. Some hints on bargaining include do not hurry, be prepared, find out why, and be a good listener.

8. An impasse occurs when the parties aren't able to move further toward settlement. Third-party involvement—namely, arbitration, fact-finding, or mediation—is one alternative. Sometimes, though, a strike occurs. Responding to the strike involves such steps as shutting the facility, contracting out work, or possibly replacing the workers. Boycotts and lockouts are two other anti-impasse weapons sometimes used by labor and management.

Key Terms

- closed shop
- union shop
- agency shop
- open shop
- right-to-work
- AFL-CIO
- Norris-LaGuardia Act
- Wagner Act
- National Labor Relations Board (NLRB)
- Taft-Hartley Act
- national emergency strikes
- Landrum-Griffin Act
- union salting
- authorization cards
- bargaining unit
- collective bargaining
- good-faith bargaining
- voluntary bargaining items
- illegal bargaining items
- mandatory bargaining items
- mediation
- fact-finder
- arbitration
- economic strike
- unfair labor practice strike
- wildcat strike
- sympathy strike
- boycott
- lockout

Discussion Questions and Exercises

1. Discuss the steps in an NLRB election.
2. Describe important tactics you would expect the union to use during the union drive and election.
3. Briefly explain why labor law has gone through a cycle of repression and encouragement.
4. What is good-faith bargaining? When is bargaining not in good faith?
5. Define *impasse, mediation,* and *strike,* and explain the techniques that are used to overcome an impasse.
6. In teams of five to six students, choose an organization (such as this university, or a company in which one student works), and list the areas in which the union has had an impact.
7. Several years ago 8,000 Amtrak workers agreed not to disrupt service by walking out, at least not until a court hearing was held. Amtrak had asked the courts for a temporary restraining order, and the Transport Workers Union of America was actually pleased to postpone the walkout. The workers were apparently not upset at Amtrak, but at Congress, for failing to provide enough funding to Amtrak. What if anything can an employer do when employees threaten to go on strike, not because of what the employer did, but what a third party—in this case, Congress—has done or not done? What laws would prevent the union from going on strike in this case?

APPLICATION EXERCISES

Case Incident   *Disciplinary Action*

The employee, a union shop steward, was on her regularly scheduled day off at home. She was called by her supervisor and told to talk to three union members and instruct them to attend a work function called a "Quest for Quality Interaction Committee" meeting. The Quest for Quality program was a high priority with the employer for improving patient care at the hospital facility and was part of a corporate program. The union had objected to the implementation of the Quest for Quality program and had taken the position that employees could attend the program if their jobs were threatened, but they should do so under protest and then file a grievance afterward.

On the day in question, the union shop steward, in a conference call with the three employees, said she would not order them to attend the Quest for Quality meeting, although her supervisor had asked her to. The supervisor who had called the union shop steward had herself refused to order the employees to attend the meeting, but relied on the union shop steward to issue the order to the employees. When the shop steward failed to order the employees to attend the meeting, the employer suspended her for 2 weeks. She grieved the 2-week suspension.

The union position was that the company had no authority to discipline the union shop steward on her day off for failure to give what it termed "a management direction to perform the specific job function of attending a mandatory corporate meeting." The union pointed out that it was unfair that the employer refused to order the employees directly to attend the meeting but then expected the union shop steward to do so. The union argued that while it is not unusual to call a union shop steward for assistance in problem solving, the company had no right to demand that he or she replace supervisors or management in giving orders and then discipline the union official for refusing to do so.

The company position was that the opposition of the union to the Quest for Quality meetings put the employees in a position of being unable to attend the meetings without direction from the union shop steward; that the union shop steward was given a job assignment of directing the employees to attend the meeting; and that failure to follow that job assignment was insubordination and just cause for her suspension.

Nonetheless, the union contended that the arbitrator must examine the nature of the order when deciding whether the insubordination was grounds for discipline. As to the nature of the order in this case, the employer had to demonstrate that the order was directly related to the job classification and work assignment of the employee disciplined. The refusal to obey such an order must be shown to pose a real challenge to supervisory authority. The employee did not dispute the fact that she failed to follow the orders given to her by her supervisor, but pointed out that she was not on duty at the time and that the task being given to her was not because of her job with the company but because of her status as a union shop steward. ■

QUESTIONS

1. If the union's opposition to the Quest for Quality program did encourage the employees not to participate, why shouldn't the union also be held responsible for directing the employees to attend?

2. As the arbitrator, do you think the employer had just cause to discipline the employee? Why or why not?

Source: Adapted from Cheltenham Nursing Rehabilitation Center 89 LA 361 (1987); discussion in Michael Carrell and Christina Heavrin, *Labor Relations and Collective Bargaining* (Upper Saddle River, NJ: Prentice Hall, 1995), pp. 100–101.

Continuing Case

LearnInMotion.com: Keeping a Watchful Eye Out for the Union

The employees at firms like LearnInMotion.com are young, well paid, and technologically sophisticated, and they're doing interesting, creative work with flexible hours. They are, in other words, exactly the sort of employees you might assume would have no interest in joining a union.

Jennifer, however, was surprised to find that unions are actively attempting to organize several dot-coms. For example, one article she happened to come across read, "Union activity at U.S. Internet companies is on the increase and is illustrated by the Washington alliance of technology workers attempting to unionize Amazon. com. [The union] claims to be receiving inquiries on a daily basis regarding union membership, as workers at Amazon complain of low pay and long hours."[66] "That's all we'd need is to have some disgruntled current or former employee call a union in on us," said Mel.

The fact that LearnInMotion.com is in New York (which has a relatively high proportion of union workers) and that several employees have left under less-than-pleasant circumstances suggest to Jennifer that perhaps she should be vigilant, and take steps now to prevent a problem later. The question is, what should she and Mel do? Now, they want you, their management consultants, to help them decide what to do. Here's what they want you to do for them. ■

QUESTIONS AND ASSIGNMENTS

1. Use the Internet to determine if the union mentioned (or any other union) organized or tried to organize a dot-com in the New York area in the past 2 years.
2. Produce a one-page position paper for us explaining concrete steps we can take today to avoid being unionized tomorrow.
3. How can we tell we're in the first, early stages of an organizing campaign? How can we find out for sure?

EXPERIENTIAL EXERCISE

The Organizing Campaign

Purpose: The purpose of this exercise is to give you practice in dealing with some of the elements of a union organizing campaign.

Required Understanding: You should be familiar with the material covered in this chapter, as well as the following incident, "An Organizing Question on Campus."

How to Set Up the Exercise/Instructions: Divide the class into groups of four or five students. Assume that you are labor relations consultants retained by the college to identify the problems and issues involved and to advise Art Tipton about what to do next. Each group will spend about 45 minutes discussing the issues and outlining those issues as well as an action plan for Tipton. What should he do now?

If time permits, a spokesperson from each group should list on the board the issues involved and the group's recommendations.

An Organizing Question on Campus[67]

Art Tipton is a human resources director of Pierce University, a private university located in a large urban city. Ruth Ann Zimmer, a supervisor in the maintenance and housekeeping services division of the university, has just come into his office to discuss her situation. Zimmer's division of the university is responsible for maintaining and cleaning physical facilities of the university. Zimmer is one of the department supervisors who supervises employees who maintain and clean on-campus dormitories.

In the next several minutes, Zimmer proceeds to express her concerns about a union organizing campaign that has begun among her employees. According to Zimmer, a representative of the Service Workers Union has met with a number of the employees, urging them to sign union authorization cards. She has observed several of her employees "cornering" other employees to talk to them about joining the union and urge them to sign union authorization (or representation) cards. Zimmer even observed this during the working hours as employees were going about their normal duties in the dormitories. Zimmer reports that a number of her employees have come to her asking for her opinions about the union. They reported to her that several other supervisors in the department had told their employees not to sign any union authorization cards and not to talk about the union at any time while they were on campus. Zimmer also reports that one of her fellow supervisors told his employees in a meeting that anyone who was caught talking about the union or signing a union authorization card would be disciplined and perhaps terminated.

Zimmer says that the employees are very dissatisfied with their wages and many of the conditions that they have endured from students, supervisors, and other staff people. She says that several employees told her that they had signed union cards because they believed that the only way university administration would pay attention to their concerns was if the employees had a union to represent them. Zimmer says that she made a list of employees whom she felt had joined or were interested in the union, and she could share these with Tipton if he wanted to deal with them personally. Zimmer closes her presentation with the comment that she and other department supervisors need to know what they should do in order to stomp out the threat of unionization in their department. ■

Endnotes

1. Steven Greenhouse, "Board Accuses Starbucks of Trying to Block Union," *New York Times* (April 3, 2007): B2.
2. "Union Members Summary," www.bls.gov/news.release/unions.toc.htm, accessed May 25, 2007.
3. James Bennett and Jason Taylor, "Labor Unions: Victims of Their Political Success?" *Journal of Labor Research* 22, no. 2 (Spring 2001): 261–273. See also Robert Flanagan, "What Do Unions Do? A 25 Year Perspective: Has Management Strangled US Unions?," *Journal of Labor Research* 26, no. 1, Winter 2005: 33–63.
4. "Union Membership by State," *Monthly Labor Review* 122, no. 6 (June 1999): 39.
5. Michael Ash and Jean Seago, "The Effect of Registered Nurses' Unions on Heart Attack Mortality," *Industrial and Labor Relations Review* 57, no. 3 (April 2004): 422–442.
6. Steven Abraham et al., "The Impact of Union Membership on Intent to Leave," *Employee Responsibilities and Rights* 17, no. 4, (2005): 21–23.
7. Paul Monies, "Unions Hit Hard by Job Losses, Right to Work," *Daily Oklahoman* (via Knight Ridder/Tribune Business News) (February 1, 2005), downloaded May 25, 2005.
8. Ann Zimmerman, "Pro-Union Butchers at Wal-Mart Win a Union Battle but Lose War," *Wall Street Journal* (April 11, 2000): A14. See also Steven Greenhouse, "Report Assails Wal-Mart over Unions," *New York Times* (May 1, 2007): C3.
9. Donna Buttigieg et al., "An Event History Analysis of Union Joining and Leaving," *Journal of Applied Psychology* 92, no. 3 (2007): 829–839.
10. Ibid., page 836; see also, Lois Tetrick, et al., "A Model of Union Participation: The Impact of Perceived Union Support, Union Instrumentality, and Union Loyalty." *Journal of Applied Psychology* 92, no. 3 (2007): 820–828.

11. Robert Grossman, "Unions Follow Suit." *HR Magazine* (May 2005): 49.

12. Kris Maher, "The New Union Worker." *Wall Street Journal* (September 27, 2005): B1, B11.

13. Benjamin Taylor and Fred Witney, *Labor Relations Law* (Upper Saddle River, NJ: Prentice Hall, 1992): 157–184. See also Arthur Sloane and Fred Whitney, *Labor Relations* (Upper Saddle River, NJ: Prentice Hall 2007): 335–336.

14. Taylor and Witney, *Labor Relations Law,* 170–171.

15. "Unions Hit Hard by Job Losses, Right to Work," *Daily Oklahoman* (via Knight Ridder/ Tribune Business News) (February 1, 2005), downloaded May 25, 2005; and www. dol. gov/esa/programs/whd/state/righttowork. htm, accessed January 13, 2008.

16. Steven Greenhouse, "Fourth Union Quits AFL-CIO in a Dispute Over Organizing," *New York Times* (September 15, 2005): A14.

17. The following material is based on Arthur Sloane and Fred Witney, *Labor Relations* (Upper Saddle River, NJ: Prentice Hall, 2001), pp. 63–120. See also www.NLRB.gov/NRLB/, "The National Labor Relations Board and You: Unfair Labor Practices."

18. Ibid., 106.

19. Karen Robinson, "Temp Workers Gain Union Access," *HR News, Society for Human Resource Management* 19, no. 10 (October 2000): 1.

20. Michael Carrell and Christina Heavrin, *Labor Relations and Collective Bargaining* (Upper Saddle River, NJ: Pearson, 2004): p. 180.

21. Ibid., 179.

22. Sloane and Witney, *Labor Relations,* 102–106.

23. William Fulmer, "Step by Step Through a Union Election," *Harvard Business Review* 60 (July/August 1981): 94–102. For an interesting description of contract negotiations, see Peter Cramton and Joseph Tracy, "The Determinants of U.S. Labor Disputes," *Journal of Labor Economics* 12, no. 2 (April 1994): 180–209.

24. Sloane and Witney, *Labor Relations,* p. 29.

25. Jonathan Segal, "Expose the Union's Underbelly," *HR Magazine* (June 1999): 166–176.

26. "Some Say Salting Leaves Bitter Taste for Employers," *BNA Bulletin to Management* (March 4, 2004): 79. For a management lawyer's perspective, see www.fklaborlaw.com/ union_salt-objectives.html, accessed May 25, 2007.

27. For more information on the Starbucks Workers Union go to www.starbucksunion.org, accessed January 14, 2008.

28. Fulmer, "Step by Step through a Union Election," 94.

29. Frederick Sullivan, "Limiting Union Organizing Activity Through Supervisors," *Personnel* 55 (July/August 1978): 55–65. Richard Peterson, Thomas Lee, and Barbara Finnegan, "Strategies and Tactics in Union Organizing Campaigns," *Industrial Relations* 31, no. 2 (Spring 1992): 370–381. See also Edward Young and William Levy, "Responding to a Union-Organizing Campaign: Do You and Your Supervisors Know the Legal Boundaries in a Union Campaign?," *Franchising World* 39, no. 3 (March 2007): 45–49.

30. Sullivan, op. cit.

31. B&D Plastics, Inc. 302 NLRB No. 33, 1971, 137 LRRM 1039; discussed in "No Such Thing as a Free Lunch," *BNA Bulletin to Management* (May 23, 1991): 153–154.

32. Gary Chaison, "Information Technology: The Threat to Unions," *Journal of Labor Research* 23, no. 2 (Spring 2002): 249–260.

33. Edwin Arnold et al., "Determinants of Certification Election Outcomes in the Service Sector," *Labor Studies Journal* 25, no. 3 (Fall 2000): 51.

34. "Union Decertifications Up in First Half of 1998," *BNA Bulletin to Management* (December 24, 1998): 406. See also www. nlrb.gov/nlrb/shared_files/brochures/rpt_ september2002.pdf, accessed January 14, 2008.

35. Carrell and Heavrin, *Labor Relations and Collective Bargaining,* 120–121.

36. Terry Leap, *Collective Bargaining and Labor Relations* (Upper Saddle River, NJ: Prentice Hall, 1995). See also www.nlrb.gov/nlrb/ shared_files/brochures/basicguide.pdf, accessed January 14, 2008.

37. Leap, *Collective Bargaining and Labor Relations,* 307–309.

38. Leap, *Collective Bargaining and Labor Relations,* 308.

39. Kathryn Tyler, "Good-Faith Bargaining," *HR Magazine* (January 2005): 52.

40. Bargaining items based on Reed Richardson, *Collective Bargaining by Objectives* (Upper Saddle River, NJ: Prentice Hall, 1997), pp. 113–15; see also Sloane and Witney, *Labor Relations,* 180–217.

41. Sloane and Witney, *Labor Relations,* 192–220.

42. "The Road to Impasse," *CBS Sports Online,* March 4, 2005, www.CDC.com/sports/.

43. Monica Roman, "Southwest Air's Family Feud," *Business Week* (July 15, 2002): 48,

44. John Burger and Steven Walters, "Arbitrator Bias and Self-Interest: Lessons from the Baseball Labor Market." *Journal of Labor Research* 26, no. 2 (Spring 2005): 267–280.

45. Jonathan Kramer and Thomas Hyclak, "Why Strikes Occur: Evidence from the Capital Markets," *Industrial Relations* 41, no. 1 (January 2002): 80–93.

46. Micheline Maynard and Jeremey Peters, "Northwest Airlines Threatens to Replace Strikers Permanently," *New York Times* (August 26, 2005): C3.

47. For a discussion, see Herbert Northrup, "Union Corporate Campaigns and Inside Games as a Strike Form," *Employee Relations Law Journal* 19, no. 4 (Spring 1994): 507–549.

48. Melanie Evans, "Labor Pains: As Membership Slides, Unions Have Turned to Provocative Corporate Campaigns," *Modern Health Care* 34, no. 26 (December 6, 2004): 26.

49. Northrup, op.cit.

50. Ibid., 518.

51. The NLRB held in 1986 in Charter Equipment, Inc. 280 NLRB No. 71, that an employer could lawfully hire temporary replacements during the course of a lockout, in the absence of proof of specific antiunion motivation, in order to bring economic pressure to bear upon a union to support a legitimate bargaining position.

52. Clifford Koen Jr., Sondra Hartmen, and Dinah Payne, "The NLRB Wields a Rejuvenated Weapon," *Personnel Journal* (December 1996): 85–87; and Sloane and Whitney (2007): 84.

53. Duncan Adams, "Worker Grievances Consume Roanoke, VA, Mail Distribution Center," Knight-Ridder/Tribune Business News (March 27, 2001), item 1086009.

54. Walter Baer, *Grievance Handling: 101 Guides for Supervisors* (New York: American Management Association, 1970).

55. Jeffrey McCracken, "Desperate to Cut Costs, Ford Gets Union's Help," *Wall Street Journal* (March 2, 2007): A1, A9.

56. See, for example, Jo Blandon et al., "Have Unions Turned the Corner? New Evidence on Recent Trends in Union Recognition in UK Firms," *British Journal of Industrial Relations* 44, no 2 (June 2006): 169–190.

57. Jennifer Schramm, "The Future of Unions," *Society of Human Resource Management Society for Human Resource Management, Workplace Visions,* no. 4, (2005): 1–8.

58. Ibid.

59. "The Limits of Solidarity," *Economist* (September 23, 2006): 34.

60. "Unions Using Class Actions to Pressure Nonunion Companies," *BNA Bulletin to Management* (August 22, 2006): 271.

61. Dean Scott, "Unions Still a Potent Force," *Kiplinger Business Forecasts* (March 26, 2003).

62. Andy Meisler "Who Will Fold First?" *Workforce Management* (January 2004): 28–38.

63. "Contracts Call for Greater Labor Management Teamwork," *BNA Bulletin to Management* (April 29, 1999): 133.

64. Schramm, op.cit., 6.

65. Mei Fong and Kris Maher, "US Labor Chief Moves into China," *Wall Street Journal Asia* (June 22–24 , 2007): 1.

66. "U.S.: Rise in Union Activity at Dot.Com Firms," *Guardian* (December 13, 2000): 18.

67. Raymond L. Hilgert and Cyril C Ting, *Cases and Experiential Exercises in Human Resource Management* (Upper Saddle River, NJ: Prentice Hall, 1996), pp. 291–292.

10 PROTECTING SAFETY AND HEALTH

- Employee Safety and Health: An Introduction
- What Causes Accidents?
- How to Prevent Accidents
- Employee Health: Problems and Remedies

When you finish studying this chapter, you should be able to:

■ Discuss *OSHA and how it operates.*

■ Describe *the supervisor's role in safety.*

■ Explain *in detail three basic causes of accidents.*

■ Explain *how to prevent accidents at work.*

■ Discuss *major health problems at work and how to remedy them.*

INTRODUCTION

Con Edison delivers electric, gas, and steam to more than 3 million New York homes and businesses, and reliability has always been its top priority. It's therefore not surprising that for over 180 years, its basic mission was to "Get the lights back on fast." Con Ed's employees had a "can do" attitude. Unfortunately, they sometimes ignored safety for the sake of getting outages fixed fast.

All that changed recently. An explosion near New York City's Grand Central Station in July 2007 killed one person and injured several others. Some feared the explosion may have contaminated surrounding areas with asbestos. Con Ed accepted the blame, and reemphasized its new safety strategy, "Get the lights back on fast—but, first do it safely." Now it had to implement that new safety-conscious strategy throughout the firm.

EMPLOYEE SAFETY AND HEALTH: AN INTRODUCTION

Why Employee Safety and Health Are Important

Providing a safe work environment is important for several reasons, one of which is the staggering number of work-related accidents. For example, in one recent year, 5,559 U.S. workers died in workplace incidents. There were also over 3.8 million occupational injuries and illnesses resulting from accidents at work—roughly 4.4 cases per 100 full-time workers in the United States per year.[1] However, the Bureau of Labor Statistics may actually underestimate the real number of injuries and illnesses by two or three times.[2]

The individual accidents are prohibitively expensive. For example, the direct injury costs of a forklift accident might be $4,500, but the indirect costs for things like forklift damage, lost production time, maintenance time, and emergency supplies could raise the bill to $18,000 or more.[3]

Dangerous workplaces aren't limited to manufacturing plants. For example, busy commercial kitchens are filled with potential dangers like knives, hot surfaces, congestion, and slippery floors. In restaurants, slips and falls account for about a third of all worker injury cases. Employers could eliminate most of these falls by requiring slip resistant shoes.[4]

A Manager's Briefing on Occupational Law

Congress passed the **Occupational Safety and Health Act**[5] in 1970 "to assure so far as possible every working man and woman in the nation safe and healthful working conditions and to preserve our human resources." The main employers not covered by the act are self-employed persons, farms in which only immediate members of the employer's family are employed, and certain workplaces that are already protected by other federal agencies or under other statutes. Federal agencies are covered by the act, although provisions of the act usually don't apply to state and local governments in their role as employers.

The act created the **Occupational Safety and Health Administration (OSHA)** within the Department of Labor. OSHA's basic purpose is to administer the act and to set and enforce the safety and health standards that apply to almost all workers in the United States. OSHA has inspectors working out of branch offices throughout the country to ensure compliance.

OSHA Standards

OSHA operates under the "general duty clause," that each employer:

> shall furnish to each of his [or her] employees employment and a place of employment which are free from recognized hazards that are causing or are likely to cause death or serious physical harm to his [or her] employees.

To carry out this basic mission, OSHA is responsible for promulgating legally enforceable standards. The standards are very complete and cover just about every conceivable hazard, in detail. Figure 10.1 shows a small part of the standard governing handrails for scaffolds.

| FIGURE 10.1   OSHA Standards Examples |

Guardrails not less than 2" × 4" or the equivalent and not less than 36" or more than 42" high, with a midrail, when required, of a 1" × 4" lumber or equivalent, and toeboards, shall be installed at all open sides on all scaffolds more than 10 feet above the ground or floor. Toeboards shall be a minimum of 4" in height. Wire mesh shall be installed in accordance with paragraph [a] (17) of this section.

Source: www.osha.gov/pls/oshaweb/owadisp.show_document?p_id=9720&p_table=STANDARDS, accessed May 25, 2007.

OSHA Record-Keeping Procedures

Under OSHA, employers with 11 or more employees must maintain a record of, and report, occupational injuries and occupational illnesses. An *occupational illness* is any abnormal condition or disorder caused by exposure to environmental factors associated with employment. This includes acute and chronic illnesses caused by inhalation, absorption, ingestion, or direct contact with toxic substances or harmful agents.

As summarized in Figure 10.2, employers must report all occupational illnesses.[6] They must also report most occupational injuries, specifically those that result in medical treatment (other than first aid), loss of consciousness, restriction of work (1 or more lost workdays), restriction of motion, or transfer to another job.[7]

If an on-the-job accident results in the death of an employee or in the hospitalization of five or more employees, all employers, regardless of size, must report the accident in detail to the nearest OSHA office. OSHA's latest record-keeping rules streamline the job of reporting occupational injuries or illnesses.[8] The rules continue to presume that an injury or work illness that resulted from an event in or exposure to the work environment is work related. However, it allows the employer to conclude that the event was not job related (and needn't be reported) if the fact so warrants—such as if a worker breaks his leg on his car's bumper when parked on the company lot.

Inspections and Citations

OSHA standards are enforced through inspections and (if necessary) citations. However, OSHA may not conduct warrantless inspections without an employer's consent.

Voluntary Consultation

Like many government agencies, OSHA has wide-ranging compliance responsibilities but limited funds. As a result, OSHA has tried to encourage cooperative safety programs rather than rely only on inspections and citations. For example, OSHA provides free on-site safety and health services for small businesses. This service uses safety experts from state governments, and provides consultations, usually at the employer's workplace. According to OSHA, this consultation program is separate from the OSHA inspection effort, and no citations are issued or penalties proposed.

The employer triggers this process by requesting a voluntary consultation. When Jan Anderson, president of her own steel installation company in Colorado, realized her workers' compensation costs were higher than her payroll, Anderson joined with

FIGURE 10.2   What Accidents Must Be Reported Under the Occupational Safety and Health Act

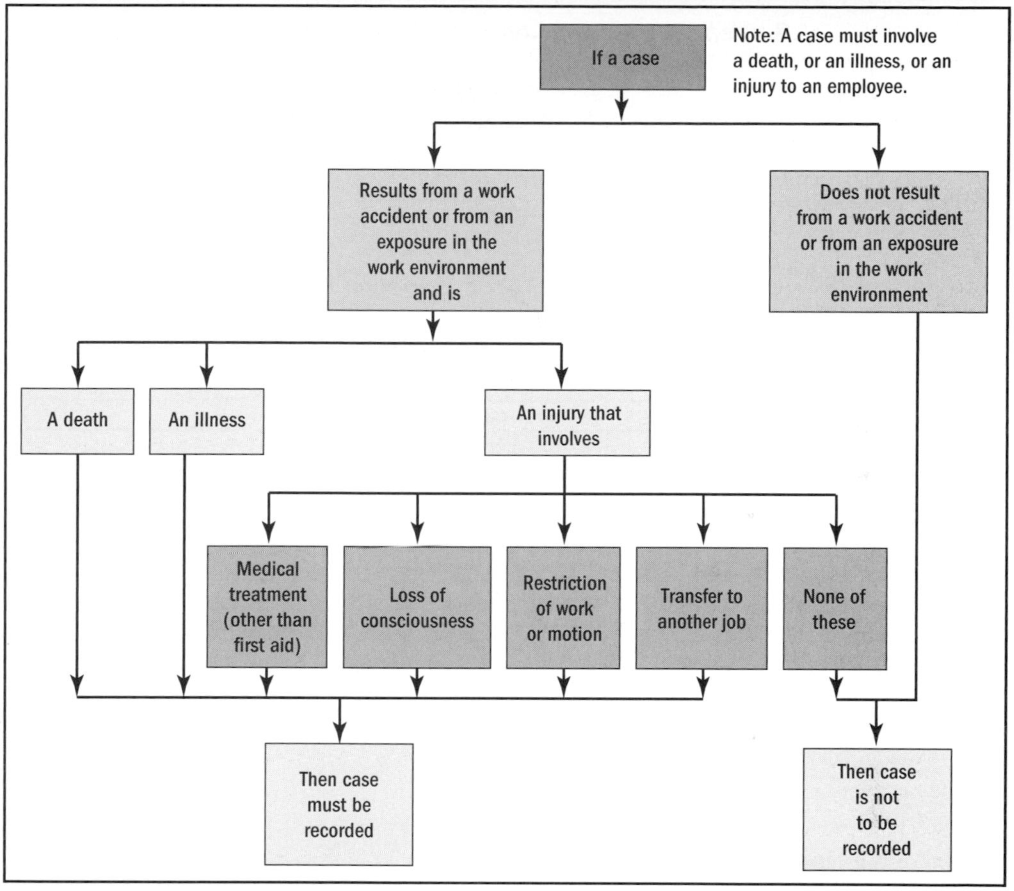

similar Colorado firms for help. At the group's request, OSHA helped draft new safety systems, created educational materials, and provided inspections that were more cooperative than adversarial. As a result, says Anderson, "Our workers' compensation costs have decreased significantly, we have had no accidents, and there is an awareness that we take safety seriously."[9]

Inspection Priorities

Such efforts notwithstanding, OSHA does of course still make extensive use of inspections. OSHA takes a "worst-first" approach in setting inspection priorities. Priorities include, from highest to lowest, catastrophes and fatal accidents; employee complaints; specific high-hazard industries; and follow-up inspections.[10] In one recent year, OSHA conducted just over 39,000 inspections. Of these, 9,176 were prompted by complaints or accidents, 21,576 were high-hazard targeted, and 8,415 were prompted by follow-ups and referrals.[11]

FIGURE 10.3	Ten Safety Standards OSHA Cited for Penalties Most Frequently, 2005–2006.

U.S. Department of Labor
Occupational Safety & Health Administration

www.osha.gov | MyOSHA | Search | GO Advanced Search | A-Z Index

Standards Cited for SIC ALL; All sizes; Federal

ALL *SIC Codes*

Listed below are the standards which were cited by **Federal OSHA** for the specified SIC during the period October 2005 through September 2006. Penalties shown reflect current rather than initial amounts. For more information, see definitions.

Standard	#Cited	#Insp	$Penalty	Description
Total	111529	28183	89370521	
19260451	9774	3756	10369193	Scaffolds—General requirements.
19101200	7124	3627	1546760	Hazard Communication.
19260501	6886	6134	8346946	Duty to have fall protection.
19100134	4654	1922	1393672	Respiratory Protection.
19100147	3976	2115	3763302	The control of hazardous energy (lockout/tagout).
19100178	3183	2130	2050999	Powered industrial trucks.
19100305	3028	1863	1433020	Wiring methods, components, and equipment for general use.
19100212	2866	2310	4031408	General requirements for all machines.
19261053	2541	1910	1329484	Ladders.
19100303	2267	1692	1181507	Electrical equipment installation—General requirements.

Source: www.osha.gov/pls/imis/citedstandard.sic?p_esize=&p_state=FEFederal&p_sic=all, accessed May 26, 2007.

The Inspection

OSHA inspectors look for violations of all types, but some potential problem areas—such as scaffolding and fall protection—seem to grab more of their attention. Figure 10.3 summarizes the 10 most frequent OSHA inspection violation areas.[12]

After the inspector submits the report to the local OSHA office, the area director determines what citations, if any, to issue. The **citations** inform the employer and employees of the regulations and standards that have been violated and of the time set for rectifying the problem.

Penalties

OSHA can also impose penalties. In general, OSHA calculates these based on the gravity of the violation and usually takes into consideration such factors as the size of the business, the firm's compliance history, and the employer's good faith. Penalties generally range from $5,000 to up to $70,000 for willful or repeat serious violations, although in practice the penalties can be far higher. Many cases are settled with OSHA before litigation in what attorneys call *precitation settlements.* The citation and agreed-on penalties are issued simultaneously, after the employers initiate negotiation settlements with OSHA.[13]

In practice, OSHA must have a final order from the independent Occupational Safety and Health Review Commission (OSHRC) to enforce a penalty. Although that appeals process is quicker now than in the past, an employer who files a notice of contest can still drag out an appeal for years.

Inspectors and their superiors don't look just for specific hazards but also for evidence of a comprehensive safety approach. For example, factors contributing to a firm's OSHA liability include lack of a systematic safety approach; sporadic or irregular safety meetings; a lack of responsiveness to safety audit recommendations; not following up on employee safety complaints; and failure to regularly inspect the workplace, for instance, through employer walk-throughs and self-inspections.[14]

While some employers understandably view OSHA inspections with some trepidation, the inspection checklist in Figure 10.4 can help the manager prepare and reduce problems ahead of time. It includes questions to ask prior to the inspection such as, "Are all work areas clean, sanitary, and orderly?"[15]

Responsibilities and Rights of Employers and Employees

Both employers and employees have responsibilities and rights under the Occupational Safety and Health Act. For example, employers are responsible for providing "a workplace free from recognized hazards," for being familiar with mandatory OSHA standards, and for examining workplace conditions to make sure they conform with applicable standards.

Employees also have rights and responsibilities but OSHA can't cite them for violations of their responsibilities. They are responsible, for example, for complying with all applicable OSHA standards, for following all employer safety and health rules and regulations, and for reporting hazardous conditions to the supervisor. Employees have a right to demand safety and health on the job without fear of punishment. Employers are forbidden to punish or discriminate against workers who complain to OSHA about job safety and health hazards. However, the Occupational Safety and Health Review Commission that reviews OSHA decisions says employers must make "a diligent effort to discourage, by discipline if necessary, violations of safety rules by employees."[16]

WHAT CAUSES ACCIDENTS?

Following an accident in which four workers lost their lives, management at the Golden Eagle refinery east of San Francisco Bay knew they had to ensure that no such tragedy occurred again. They shut down the facility for four months, retrained all employees in safety methods, and created six new safety management positions. Then they turned their attention to other steps they could take.[17]

Accidents occur for three main reasons: chance occurrences, unsafe working conditions, and unsafe acts by employees. Chance occurrences (such as walking past a window just as someone throws a rock through it) contribute to accidents but are more or less beyond management's control; we will therefore focus on unsafe conditions and unsafe acts.

FIGURE 10.4   Supervisor's Safety Checklist

FORM **CD-574**
(2/03)

U.S. Department of Commerce
Office Safety Inspection Checklist for
Supervisors and Program Managers

Name:	Division:
Location:	Date:
Signature:	

This checklist is intended as a guide to assist supervisors and program managers in conducting safety and health inspections of their work areas. It includes questions relating to general office safety, ergonomics, fire prevention, and electrical safety. Questions which receive a "NO" answer require corrective action. If you have questions or need assistance with resolving any problems, please contact your safety office. More information on office safety is available through the Department of Commerce Safety Office website at **http://ohrm.doc.gov/safetyprogram/safety.htm**.

Work Environment

Yes	No	N/A	
O	O	O	Are all work areas clean, sanitary, and orderly?
O	O	O	Is there adequate lighting?
O	O	O	Is the noise level within an acceptable range?
O	O	O	Is ventilation adequate?

Walking / Working Surfaces

Yes	No	N/A	
O	O	O	Are aisles and passages free of stored material that may present trip hazards?
O	O	O	Are tile floors in places like kitchens and bathrooms free of water and slippery substances?
O	O	O	Are carpet and throw rugs free of tears or trip hazards?
O	O	O	Are hand rails provided on all fixed stairways?
O	O	O	Are treads provided with anti-slip surfaces?
O	O	O	Are step ladders provided for reaching overhead storage areas and are materials stored safely?
O	O	O	Are file drawers kept closed when not in use?
O	O	O	Are passenger and freight elevators inspected annually and are the inspection certificates available for review on-site?
O	O	O	Are pits and floor openings covered or otherwise guarded?
O	O	O	Are standard guardrails provided wherever aisle or walkway surfaces are elevated more than 48 inches above any adjacent floor or the ground?
O	O	O	Is furniture free of any unsafe defects?
O	O	O	Are heating and air conditioning vents clear of obstructions?

Ergonomics

Yes	No	N/A	
O	O	O	Are employees advised of proper lifting techniques?
O	O	O	Are workstations configured to prevent common ergonomic problems? (Chair height allows employees' feet to rest flat on the ground with thighs parallel to the floor, top of computer screen is at or slightly below eye level, keyboard is at elbow height. Additional information on proper configuration of workstations is available through the Commerce Safety website at http://ohrm.doc.gov/safetyprogram/safety.htm)
O	O	O	Are mechanical aids and equipment, such as; lifting devices, carts, or dollies provided where needed?
O	O	O	Are employees surveyed annually on their ergonomic concerns?

Emergency Information (Postings)

Yes	No	N/A	
O	O	O	Are established emergency phone numbers posted where they can be readily found in case of an emergency?
O	O	O	Are employees trained on emergency procedures?
O	O	O	Are fire evacuation procedures/diagrams posted?
O	O	O	Is emergency information posted in every area where you store hazardous waste?
O	O	O	Is established facility emergency information posted near a telephone?
O	O	O	Are the OSHA poster, and other required posters displayed conspicuously?
O	O	O	Are adequate first aid supplies available and properly maintained?
O	O	O	Are an adequate number of first aid trained personnel available to respond to injuries and illnesses until medical assistance arrives?
O	O	O	Is a copy of the facility fire prevention and emergency action plan available on site?
O	O	O	Are safety hazard warning signs/caution signs provided to warn employees of pertinent hazards?

FORM **CD-574**
(2/03)

Fire Prevention

Yes	No	N/A	
O	O	O	Are flammable liquids, such as gasoline, kept in approved safety cans and stored in flammable cabinets?
O	O	O	Are portable fire extinguishers distributed properly (less than 75 feet travel distance for combustibles and 50 feet for flammables)?
O	O	O	Are employees trained on the use of portable fire extinguishers?
O	O	O	Are portable fire extinguishers visually inspected monthly and serviced annually?
O	O	O	Are areas around portable fire extinguishers free of obstructions and properly labeled ?
O	O	O	Is heat-producing equipment used in a well ventilated area?
O	O	O	Are fire alarm pull stations clearly marked and unobstructed?
O	O	O	Are proper clearances maintained below sprinkler heads (i.e., 18″ clear)?

Emergency Exits

Yes	No	N/A	
O	O	O	Are doors, passageways or stairways that are neither exits nor access to exits and which could be mistaken for exits, appropriately marked "NOT AN EXIT," "TO BASEMENT," "STOREROOM," etc.?
O	O	O	Are a sufficient number of exits provided?
O	O	O	Are exits kept free of obstructions or locking devices which could impede immediate escape?
O	O	O	Are exits properly marked and illuminated?
O	O	O	Are the directions to exits, when not immediately apparent, marked with visible signs?
O	O	O	Can emergency exit doors be opened from the direction of exit travel without the use of a key or other significant effort when the building is occupied?
O	O	O	Are exits arranged such that it is not possible to travel toward a fire hazard when exiting the facility?

Electrical Systems

(Please have your facility maintenance person or electrician accompany you during this part of the inspection)

Yes	No	N/A	
O	O	O	Are all cord and cable connections intact and secure?
O	O	O	Are electrical outlets free of overloads?
O	O	O	Is fixed wiring used instead of flexible/extension cords?
O	O	O	Is the area around electrical panels and breakers free of obstructions?
O	O	O	Are high-voltage electrical service rooms kept locked?
O	O	O	Are electrical cords routed such that they are free of sharp objects and clearly visible?
O	O	O	Are all electrical cords grounded?
O	O	O	Are electrical cords in good condition (free of splices, frays, etc.)?
O	O	O	Are electrical appliances approved (Underwriters Laboratory, Inc. (UL), etc)?
O	O	O	Are electric fans provided with guards of not over one-half inch, preventing finger exposures?
O	O	O	Are space heaters UL listed and equipped with shutoffs that activate if the heater tips over?
O	O	O	Are space heaters located away from combustibles and properly ventilated?
O	O	O	In your electrical rooms are all electrical raceways and enclosures securely fastened in place?
O	O	O	Are clamps or other securing means provided on flexible cords or cables at plugs, receptacles, tools, equipment, etc., and is the cord jacket securely held in place?
O	O	O	Is sufficient access and working space provided and maintained about all electrical equipment to permit ready and safe operations and maintenance? (This space is 3 feet for less than 600 volts, 4 feet for more than 600 volts)

Material Storage

Yes	No	N/A	
O	O	O	Are storage racks and shelves capable of supporting the intended load and materials stored safely?
O	O	O	Are storage racks secured from falling?
O	O	O	Are office equipment stored in a stable manner, not capable of falling?

Source: www.sefsc.noaa.gov/PDFdocs/CD-574OfficeInspectionChecklistSupervisors.pdf, accessed May 26, 2007.

Unsafe Conditions

Unsafe conditions are one main cause of accidents. These include such obvious factors as:

- Improperly guarded equipment
- Defective equipment
- Unsafe storage, such as congestion or overloading
- Improper illumination, such as glare or insufficient light
- Improper ventilation, such as insufficient air change or impure air source[18]

The basic remedy here is to eliminate or minimize the unsafe conditions. OSHA standards address the mechanical and physical working conditions that cause accidents. The manager can use a checklist of unsafe conditions for spotting problems as in Figure 10.4, another checklist is in checklist is in the *HR in Practice* box. The *Occupational Hazards* magazine Web site (occupationalhazards.com) is a good source for safety, health, and industrial hygiene information.

CHECKLIST OF MECHANICAL OR PHYSICAL ACCIDENT-CAUSING CONDITIONS

I. GENERAL HOUSEKEEPING

Adequate and wide aisles—no materials protruding into aisles

Parts and tools stored safely after use—not left in hazardous positions that could cause them to fall

Even and solid flooring—no defective floors or ramps that could cause falling or tripping accidents

Waste and trash cans—safely located and not overfilled

Material piled in safe manner—not too high or too close to sprinkler heads

All work areas clean and dry

All exit doors and aisles clean of obstructions

Aisles kept clear and properly marked; no air lines or electric cords across aisles

II. MATERIAL HANDLING EQUIPMENT AND CONVEYANCES

On all conveyances, electric or hand, check to see that the following items are all in sound working condition:

Brakes—properly adjusted

Not too much play in steering wheel

Warning device—in place and working

Wheels—securely in place; properly inflated

Fuel and oil—enough and right kind

No loose parts

Cables, hooks, or chains—not worn or otherwise defective

Suspended chains or hooks

Safely loaded

Properly stored

III. LADDERS, SCAFFOLD, BENCHES, STAIRWAYS, ETC.

The following items of major interest to be checked:

Safety feet on straight ladders

Guardrails or handrails

Treads, not slippery

No splintered, cracked, or rickety stairs

Ladders properly stored

Extension ladder ropes in good condition

Toeboards

IV. POWER TOOLS (STATIONARY)

Point of operation guarded

Guards in proper adjustment

Gears, belts, shafting, counterweights guarded

Foot pedals guarded

Brushes provided for cleaning machines

Adequate lighting

Properly grounded

Tool or material rests properly adjusted

Adequate work space around machines

Control switch easily accessible

Safety glasses worn

Gloves worn by persons handling rough or sharp materials

No gloves or loose clothing worn by persons operating machines

V. HAND TOOLS AND MISCELLANEOUS

In good condition—not cracked, worn, or otherwise defective
Properly stored
Correct for job

Goggles, respirators, and other personal protective equipment worn where necessary

VI. SPRAY PAINTING

Explosion-proof electrical equipment
Proper storage of paints and thinners in approved metal cabinets

Fire extinguishers adequate and suitable; readily accessible
Minimum storage in work area

VII. FIRE EXTINGUISHERS

Properly serviced and tagged
Readily accessible

Adequate and suitable for operations involved

Source: Courtesy of the Insurance Services Office, Inc., from "A Safety Committee Man's Guide" (1977): 1–64. Includes copyrighted material of ISO Properties, Inc. with its permission.

Although accidents can occur anywhere, there are some high-danger zones. About one third of industrial accidents occur around forklift trucks, wheelbarrows, and other handling and lifting areas. The most serious accidents usually occur near metal and woodworking machines and saws, or around transmission machinery such as gears, pulleys, and flywheels.[19]

Other Working–Condition-Related Causes of Accidents

Some working–condition-related causes of accidents are less obvious because they involve the psychology or "safety climate" of the workplace. For example, one early study focused on the official hearings of fatal accidents suffered by offshore British oil workers in the North Sea.[20] A strong pressure to complete the work as quickly as possible, employees who are under stress, and a poor safety climate—for instance, supervisors who never mention safety—are some of the not-so-obvious working conditions that set the stage for accidents.

Example

The subjects of one safety climate study were 1,127 nurses working in 42 large acute-care hospitals in the United States. The researchers measured safety climate using items like, "job duties on this unit often prevent nurses from acting as safely as they would like," "the best nurses on this unit care about safety," and "the nurse manager on this unit emphasizes safety."

Safety climate influenced safety: "the results revealed that safety climate predicted medication errors, nurse back injuries, urinary tract infections, [and] patient satisfaction."[21]

Work schedules and fatigue also affect accident rates. Accident rates usually don't increase too noticeably during the first 5 or 6 hours of the workday, but after 6 hours, the accident rate accelerates. This is due partly to fatigue and partly to the fact that accidents occur more often during night shifts.

Accidents also occur more frequently in plants with a high seasonal layoff rate and where there is hostility among employees, garnished wages, and blighted living conditions. Temporary stress factors such as high workplace temperature, poor illumination, and a congested workplace are also related to accident rates.

Unsafe Acts

In practice, it's impossible to eliminate accidents just by reducing unsafe conditions. People cause accidents, and no one has found a surefire way to eliminate **unsafe acts** such as:

- Throwing materials
- Operating or working at unsafe speeds—either too fast or too slow
- Making safety devices inoperative by removing, adjusting, or disconnecting them
- Lifting improperly[22]

There is no one explanation for why an employee may behave in an unsafe manner. Sometimes (as noted above) the working conditions may set the stage for unsafe acts. For instance, employees who are under stress may behave in an unsafe manner even if they know better. Sometimes, employees aren't adequately trained in safe work methods; some companies don't provide employees with the correct safe procedures to use, and employees may simply develop their own (often bad) work habits. However, it's often the employee's attitudes, personality, or skills that account for the bad behavior.

What Traits Characterize "Accident-Prone" People?

Unsafe acts can undo even the best attempts to reduce unsafe conditions. The problem is that there are no easy answers to the question of what causes people to act recklessly.

It may seem intuitively obvious that some people are simply accident prone, but the research isn't all that clear.[23] On closer inspection it turns out that some "accident repeaters" were just unlucky, or may have been more meticulous about reporting their accidents.[24] However, there is growing evidence that people with specific traits may indeed be accident prone. For example, people who are impulsive, sensation seeking, extremely extroverted, and less conscientious (in terms of being less fastidious and dependable) are more likely to have accidents.[25]

Furthermore, the person who is accident prone on one job may not be so on a different job. Driving is one familiar example. Personality traits that correlate with filing vehicular insurance claims include *entitlement* ("bad drivers think there's no reason they should not speed or run lights"), *impatience* ("drivers with high claim frequency were 'always in a hurry'"), *aggressiveness* ("always the first to want to move when the red light turns green"), and *distractability* ("easily and frequently distracted by cell phones, eating, drinking, and so on"). A study in Thailand similarly found that drivers who are naturally competitive and prone to anger are particularly risky drivers.[26]

HOW TO PREVENT ACCIDENTS

The thing to remember about preventing accidents is that it's not always the employees who are causing them: "Although it is clear that individual behavior influences accidents, starting and ending one's investigation at this level ignores the broader contextual influence on behavior in organizations."[27] Certainly, screening out or firing impulsive employees may reduce the incidence of unsafe behaviors. However, so will mopping up oil spills and placing guardrails around machines; psychological factors such as reducing stress and pressure are important, too. In practice, accident causes tend to be multifaceted, so the manager has to take a multifaceted approach to preventing them.[28]

Reduce Unsafe Conditions

Imagine that you decide to repair a lamp that you think is unplugged and then discover, with a shock, that it is plugged in. At work, lockout/tagout aims to avoid such situations. *Lockout/tagout* is a procedure to disable equipment to avoid an unexpected release of electrical or other energy. It means affixing a lockout/tagout tag to the equipment, to show it's disabled.[29]

Reducing unsafe conditions is an employer's first line of safety defense. Sometimes (as with the lamp) the solution is obvious. For example, slips and falls are often caused by debris or a slippery floor.[30] Employers work with safety engineers to "engineer out" potentially hazardous conditions, for instance, by placing guardrails around moving machines.

Once this is done, management can make available personal protective equipment. For example, the organization Prevent Blindness America estimates that each year, more than 700,000 Americans injure their eyes at work, and that employers could avoid 90% of these injuries with safety eyewear.[31]

Reducing Unsafe Acts

While guardrails and personal protective equipment (PPE) are advisable, human misbehavior can short circuit even the best laid safety efforts. For one thing, people-based safety problems needn't be intentional. Often, people just don't pay attention. For example, distractions—whether from cell phones or glancing back to check on a child—contribute to at least half of all car accidents. At work, not noticing moving or stationary objects or that a floor is wet are frequent accident causers.[32] Furthermore, (and ironically) "making a job safer with machine guards or PPE lowers people's risk perceptions and thus can lead to an increase in at-risk behavior."[33]

Unfortunately, just telling employees to "pay attention" is usually not enough. Instead, it requires a process. First identify and try to eliminate potential risks, such as unguarded equipment or slippery floors. Next reduce potential distractions, such as noise, heat, and stress. Then, carefully screen and train employees, as we explain next.

Use Screening to Reduce Unsafe Acts

Accidents are similar to other types of poor performance, and psychologists have had success in screening out individuals who might be accident prone for some specific job. The basic technique is to identify the human trait (such as visual skill) that might relate to accidents on the specific job. Then determine whether scores on this trait predict accidents on the job.

As explained above, driving is a familiar example. For example, screening prospective delivery drivers for traits like impatience and aggressiveness might be sensible.[34]

Use Posters and Other Propaganda

Propaganda such as safety posters can also help reduce unsafe acts. In one study, their use apparently increased safe behavior by more than 20%.[35] However, posters need to be combined with other techniques such as screening and training to reduce unsafe conditions and acts.

Provide Safety Training

Safety training can also reduce accidents. Such training is especially appropriate with new employees. It is important to instruct them in safe practices and procedures, warn them of potential hazards, and work on developing their predisposition toward safety. Delta Airlines encourages supervisors to use personal anecdotes to motivate and train employees to wear hearing protection. For example, "a lot of the old-timers have terrible stories and terrible hearing, because whatever they did in their past jobs—whether they worked here or somewhere else—they didn't wear hearing protection."[36]

Use Incentives and Positive Reinforcement

Some firms award incentives (such as cash bonuses) if particular safety goals are met. However, some contend that programs like these are misguided. OSHA has argued, for instance, that such plans don't actually cut down on injuries or illnesses but only on injury and illness *reporting.* One option is to emphasize nontraditional reinforcement, for instance, by giving employees recognition awards for attending safety meetings, for identifying hazards, or for demonstrating their safety and health proficiency.[37]

Safety incentives needn't be complicated. One organization uses a suggestion box. Employees make suggestions for improvements regarding unsafe acts or conditions. The employer follows up on all suggestions, the best of which result in gift certificates for their authors.[38] Management at the Golden Eagle refinery in California instituted one safety incentive plan. Employees earn "WINGS" points for engaging in one or more of 28 safety activities, such as conducting safety meetings, and taking emergency response training. Employees can earn up to $20 per month per person by accumulating points.[39]

Three Caveats

With respect to safety incentives, keep three things in mind. First, such programs are not substitutes for comprehensive safety programs: "For an incentives program to be successful, all other pieces/parts of a comprehensive safety program need to be in place," says one expert.[40]

Second, take care that your incentives program does not simply produce false accident reporting, by encouraging workers to underreport their accidents as a way of obtaining rewards.[41]

Third, such programs can have unforeseen consequences. Their basic aim is to produce, through reinforcement, habitually safe behavior. However, safety experts warn against relying on habitual behavior. Habitual behavior takes place without thinking, and when it comes to safety it's usually better to have employees thinking about what they're doing, lest they be lulled into not paying attention.[42]

Emphasize Top-Management Commitment

Safety programs require a strong and obvious management commitment to safety. Here's an example:

> One of the best examples I know of in setting the highest possible priority for safety takes place at a DuPont Plant in Germany. Each morning at the DuPont Polyester and Nylon Plant the director and his assistants meet at 8:45

to review the past 24 hours. The first matter they discuss is not production, but safety. Only after they have examined reports of accidents and near misses and satisfied themselves that corrective action has been taken do they move on to look at output, quality, and cost matters.[43]

In another show of top-management commitment to safety, Weyerhaeuser recently discharged the plant manager and safety manager at its West Virginia facility, allegedly because they failed to report 38 injuries and illnesses at the plant.[44]

Foster a Culture of Safety

When it comes to creating a safety-oriented workplace, what the supervisor does is as, or more, important than what he or she says. In other words, it's crucial to show by word and deed that safety is very important. One study assessed safety culture in terms of items such as "my supervisor says a good word whenever he sees the job done according to the safety rules," and "my supervisor approaches workers during work to discuss safety issues." The study found that (1) employees did develop consistent perceptions concerning supervisory safety practices, and (2) these safety culture perceptions predicted safety records in the months following the survey.[45]

According to one safety expert, five characteristics of a culture of safety are:

1. Teamwork, in the form of management commitment to and employee involvement in safety;
2. Safety communication and collaboration are highly visible and interactive;
3. A shared vision of safety excellence (in particular, an overriding attitude that all accidents and injuries are preventable);
4. Assignment of critical safety functions to specific individuals or teams; and,
5. Continuous efforts toward quality improvement. In particular, a consistent and ongoing process of identifying and correcting problems and hazards in the workplace.[46]

Establish a Safety Policy

A safety policy should emphasize that the firm will do everything practical to eliminate or reduce accidents and injuries. It should also emphasize the fact that accident and injury prevention is not just important but of the utmost importance at your firm.

Set Specific Loss Control Goals

Analyze the number of accidents and safety incidents, then set specific safety goals to be achieved; for example, set safety goals in terms of frequency of lost-time injuries per number of full-time employees.

Conduct Safety and Health Inspections Regularly

Routinely inspect all premises for possible safety and health problems using checklists such as those in the *HR in Practice* box (on p. 338–339) as aids. Similarly, investigate all accidents and "near misses" and have a system in place for letting employees notify management about hazardous conditions.[47] *Safety audits* measure several things, such as injury and illnesses statistics, workers' compensation costs, and vehicle accident statistics.[48]

FIGURE 10.5   Steps to Take to Reduce Workplace Accidents
• Reduce unsafe conditions.
• Reduce unsafe acts.
• Use posters and other propaganda.
• Provide safety training.
• Use positive reinforcement.
• Emphasize top-management commitment.
• Emphasize safety.
• Establish a safety policy.
• Set specific loss control goals.
• Conduct safety and health inspections regularly.
• Monitor work overload and stress.

Similarly, employee safety committees can improve workplace safety. Typical committee activities include evaluating safety adequacy, monitoring safety audit findings, and suggesting strategies for improving health and safety performance.[49] Figure 10.5 summarizes these and other safety steps.

Strategy and HR

Safety is particularly a problem in a large, complex utility like Con Ed, many of whose facilities go back 60 years or more. Back then, people didn't understand the risks of using products like asbestos, so today Con Ed employees find themselves working with hazardous materials on a daily basis. The Grand Central explosion forced management to reconsider Con Ed's strategy. Today, "get the lights back on fast—but, first do it safely" sums up the firm's basic corporate approach, and that new approach has triggered big changes in how the company does things.

Injecting a "safety first" mentality into all the firm's operations involved many HR activities. For example, Con Ed recruited and trained new people for its environmental health and safety staff. Con Ed also created thousands of pages of new policies and procedures that translate federal, state, and local environmental regulations into operating procedures its employees can actually use. Con Ed's experience shows how top management can use its specific human resources strategies and practices to support its strategy.

Protecting Vulnerable Workers

In designing safe and healthy environments, employers need to pay special attention to vulnerable workers, those who are "unprepared to deal with hazards in the workplace," either due to lack of education, ill-fitting personal protective equipment, physical limitations, or cultural reasons. Among others, these may include young workers, immigrant workers, aging workers, and women workers.[50]

For example, although about half of all workers today are women, most machinery and personal protective equipment (like gloves) are designed for men. Women may thus have to use makeshift platforms or stools to reach machinery controls, or safety goggles that don't really fit. The solution is to make sure the equipment and machines women use are appropriate for their size.[51]

Similarly, with more workers postponing retirement, older workers are doing a rising percentage of manufacturing jobs. They can do these jobs effectively. However,

CRIME AND PUNISHMENT ABROAD

Particularly when traveling in areas where medical facilities may not meet developed-country standards, dramatic events—sudden illnesses or serious accidents, for instance—can be very serious abroad. Language difficulties, cultural misunderstandings, lack of normal support and infrastructure systems (such as telephones) can all combine to make an accident or illness that may be manageable in one country a disaster in another.

Cultural differences can cause surprises. In one hospital abroad, for instance, the doctor would not perform a heart surgery until receiving $40,000 in cash. As a result, many multinationals brief their business travelers and expatriates about what to expect and how to react when confronted with a health or safety problem abroad. Many employers therefore contract with international security firms. For example, International SOS has over 1,300 medical professionals staffing its regional centers and clinics.[52]

there are numerous physical changes associated with aging, including loss of strength, loss of muscular flexibility, reduced grip strength, and reduced blood flow. This means that employers may have to make some special provisions, for instance, providing mechanical assists and providing older workers with additional insulation, if they work for long periods in the cold.[53]

The *Global Issues in HR* box provides a global perspective.

EMPLOYEE HEALTH: PROBLEMS AND REMEDIES

Most workplace health hazards aren't obvious ones like unguarded equipment or slippery floors. Many are unseen hazards (like mold) that the company inadvertently produces as part of its production processes. Other problems, like drug abuse, the employees may create for themselves. In either case, these health hazards are often as much or more dangerous to workers' health and safety than are obvious hazards like slippery floors. Typical workplace hazards may include:

1. Alcoholism and substance abuse.
2. Chemicals and other hazardous materials.
3. Excessive noise and vibrations.
4. Temperature extremes.
5. Biohazards including those that are normally occurring (such as mold) and man-made (such as anthrax).
6. Ergonomic hazards (such as poorly designed computer equipment that forces workers to do their jobs while contorted into unnatural positions).
7. And, the many familiar safety-related hazards such as slippery floors and blocked passageways we discussed above.[54]

Alcoholism and Substance Abuse

Workplace substance abuse is a serious problem at work. Of the 16.7 million illicit drug users age 16 or older in one recent year, 12.4 million, or about 74%, are employed full- or part-time.[55] A recent study concluded that about 15% of the U.S. workforce (just over 19 million workers) "has either been hung over at work, been drinking shortly before showing up for work, or been drinking or impaired while on the job at least once during the previous year."[56]

Recognizing the alcoholic on the job isn't easy. Early symptoms such as tardiness can be similar to those of other problems and thus difficult to classify. The supervisor is not a psychiatrist, and without specialized training, identifying and dealing with the alcoholic is difficult. For many employers, dealing with alcohol and substance abuse begins with substance abuse testing. For example, more than one third of businesses report testing applicants and/or employees for alcohol.[57]

Tools

Several tools are available to screen for alcohol or drug abuse. The most widely used self-reporting screening instruments for alcoholism are the 4-item CAGE and the 25-item Michigan Alcoholism Screening Test (MAST). The former asks the following: Have you ever (1) attempted to cut back on alcohol, (2) been annoyed by comments about your drinking, (3) felt guilty about drinking, (4) had an eye-opener first thing in the morning to steady your nerves.[58]

Table 10.1 shows observable behavior patterns that indicate alcohol-related problems. As you can see, alcohol-related problems range from tardiness in the earliest stages of alcohol abuse to prolonged, unpredictable absences in its later stages.[59]

Drug tests may not have the desired effect on reducing workplace accidents. One study, conducted in three hotels, concluded that pre-employment drug testing seemed to have little or no effect on workplace accidents. However, a combination of pre-employment and random ongoing testing was associated with a significant reduction in workplace accidents.[60]

Dealing with Substance Abuse

Ideally, a drug-free workplace program includes five components: a drug-free workplace policy, supervisor training, employee education, employee assistance, and drug testing. The policy should state, at a minimum, "the use, possession, transfer or sale of illegal drugs by employees is prohibited." And, it should lay out the employer's rationale for the policy, and an explanation of the consequences for violating it (including discipline up to and including termination). Supervisors should be trained to monitor employees' performance, and to stay alert to drug-related performance problems.

As explained earlier in this book, most firms test applicants and (often) current employees for drugs. Such testing is generally effective. Pre-employment drug testing discourages those on drugs from applying for work or coming to work for employers who do testing. One study found that over 30% of regular drug users employed full-time said they were less likely to work for a company that conducted pre-employment screening.[61] Some applicants or employees may try to evade the test, for instance, by purchasing "clean" specimens to use. Several states, including New Jersey, North

Stage	Absenteeism	General Behavior	Job Performance Action
TABLE 10.1 Observable Alcohol-Related Behavior Patterns			
I Early	Tardiness Quits early Absence from work situations	Complaints from fellow employees for not doing his or her share Overreaction Complaints of not "feeling well"	Misses deadlines Commits errors (frequently) Lower job efficiency
II Middle	("I drink to relieve tension") Frequent days off for vague or implausible reasons ("I feel guilty about sneaking drinks"; "I have tremors")	Makes untrue statements Marked changes Undependable statements Avoids fellow employees Borrows money from fellow employees Exaggerates work accomplishments Frequent hospitalization Minor injuries on the job (repeatedly)	Criticism from the boss General deterioration Cannot concentrate Occasional lapse of memory Warning from boss
III Late Middle	Frequent days off; several days at a time Does not return from lunch ("I don't feel like eating"; "I don't want to talk about it"; "I like to drink alone")	Aggressive and belligerent behavior Domestic problems interfere with work Financial difficulties (garnishments, etc.) More frequent hospitalization Resignation: does not want to discuss problems Problems with the laws in the community	Far below expectation Punitive disciplinary action
IV Approaching Terminal Stage	Prolonged unpredictable absences ("My job interferes with my drinking")	Drinking on the job (probably) Completely undependable Repeated hospitalization Serious financial problems Serious family problems: divorce	Uneven Generally incompetent Faces termination or hospitalization

Note: Based on content analysis of files of recovering alcoholics in five organizations. From *Managing and Employing the Handicapped: The Untapped Potential,* by Gopal C. Pati and John I. Adkins Jr., with Glenn Morrison (Lake Forest, IL: Brace-Park, Human Resource Press, 1981). Recent evidence supports these earlier studies. See, for example, http://pubs.niaaa.nih.gov/publications/aa44.htm, www.nmsu.edu/~personel/dahandbook/albob.html, and www.usda.gov/da/pdsd/Security%20Guide/Eap/Alcohol.htm#Warning%20Signs, all accessed May 26, 2007.

Source: "Gopal C. Pati and John I. Adkins, Jr., "The Employer's Role in Alcoholism Assistance," *Personnel Journal* 62, no. 7 (July 1983), p. 570.

Carolina, Virginia, Oregon, South Carolina, Pennsylvania, Louisiana, Texas, and Nebraska have laws making drug-test fraud a crime. An oral fluid test is more reliable.[62]

The Problems of Job Stress and Burnout

Problems such as alcoholism and drug abuse sometimes stem from stress, especially *job stress.* Eighty-eight percent of managers in one survey reported elevated stress levels, with most reporting feeling under more stress than they could ever remember.[63] Northwestern National Mutual Life found that one fourth of all employees surveyed viewed their jobs as the number one stressor in their lives.[64]

A variety of external factors can trigger stress. These include work schedule, pace of work, job security, route to and from work, workplace noise, and the number and nature of customers or clients.[65] However, no two people react the same because personal factors also influence stress. For example, those with Type A personalities—people who are **workaholics** and who feel driven to always be on time and meet deadlines—normally place themselves under greater stress than do others.

Consequences

Job stress has serious consequences for both the employee and the organization. The human consequences of job stress include anxiety, depression, anger, and various physical consequences, such as cardiovascular disease, headaches, and accidents. Stress also has serious consequences for the organization. These include diminished performance, and increased absenteeism, turnover, grievances, and health care costs.[66] A study of 46,000 employees concluded that health care costs of the high-stress workers were 46% higher than those of their less-stressed coworkers.[67] Yet stress is not necessarily dysfunctional. Some people, for example, find that they are more productive as a deadline approaches.

Reducing Your Own Job Stress

A person can do several things to alleviate stress. These include commonsense remedies like getting more sleep and eating better. Finding a more suitable job, getting counseling, and planning each day's activities are other sensible responses. In his book, *Stress and the Manager,* Dr. Karl Albrecht suggests the following to reduce job stress:[68]

- Build rewarding, pleasant, cooperative relationships with as many of your colleagues and employees as you can.
- Don't bite off more than you can chew.
- Build an especially effective and supportive relationship with your boss.
- Understand the boss's problems and help him or her to understand yours.
- Negotiate with your boss for realistic deadlines on important projects. Be prepared to propose deadlines yourself, instead of having them imposed on you.
- Find time every day for detachment and relaxation.
- Get away from your office from time to time for a change of scene and a change of mind.
- Don't put off dealing with distasteful problems.
- Make a constructive "worry list." Write down the problems that concern you, and beside each write down what you're going to do about it.

Meditation is another possible solution. Choose a quiet place with soft light, sit comfortably, and then meditate by focusing your thoughts, for instance, by counting breaths, or by visualizing a calming location such as a beach. When your mind wanders, just bring it back to focusing on your breathing, or the beach.[69] Several years ago, World Bank employees were apparently experiencing high stress levels. Several times a week trainers from a Washington, DC-based Buddhist meditation instruction company ran meditation classes at the bank. Employees generally felt the classes were useful in reducing stress.[70]

What the Employer Can Do

The employer and its human resource specialists and supervisors can also help identify and reduce job stress. One British firm follows a three-tiered approach to managing workplace stress.[71] First is *primary prevention*, which focuses on ensuring that things like job designs and workflows are correct. Second involves *intervention*, including individual employee assessment, attitude surveys to find sources of stress at work, personal conflicts on the job, and supervisory intervention. Third is *rehabilitation* through employee assistance programs and counseling.[72]

Burnout

Burnout is a phenomenon closely associated with job stress. Experts define *burnout* as the total depletion of physical and mental resources caused by excessive striving to reach an unrealistic work-related goal. Burnout doesn't just spontaneously appear. Instead, it builds gradually, manifesting itself in symptoms such as irritability, discouragement, entrapment, and resentment.[73]

What can a burnout candidate do? Here are some suggestions:

- *Break your patterns.* First, survey how you spend your time. Are you doing a variety of things or the same one repeatedly? The more well rounded your life is, the better protected you are against burnout.
- *Get away from it all periodically.* Schedule occasional periods of introspection during which you can get away from your usual routine, perhaps alone, to seek a perspective on where you are and where you are going.
- *Reassess your goals in terms of their intrinsic worth.* Are the goals you've set for yourself attainable? Are they really worth the sacrifices you'll have to make?
- *Think about your work.* Could you do as good a job without being so intense or also by pursuing outside interests?

Depression

Stress and burnout aren't the only psychological health problems at work. For example, one *Journal of the American Medical Association* study calculated that depressed workers cost their employers $44 billion per year, either in absenteeism or in reduced performance while at work.[74] Employers apparently need to work harder to ensure that depressed employees utilize support services. One survey found that while about two thirds of large firms offered employee assistance programs covering depression, only about 14% of employees with depression said they ever used one.[75] Training managers to recognize signs of depression—persistent sad moods, sleeping too little, reduced appetite, difficulty in concentrating, and loss of interest in activities once enjoyed, for instance—and then making assistance more readily available can help.

Asbestos Exposure at Work

There are four major sources of occupational respiratory diseases: asbestos, silica, lead, and carbon dioxide. Of these, asbestos has become a major concern, in part because of publicity surrounding numerous huge lawsuits alleging asbestos-related diseases.

OSHA standards require several actions with respect to asbestos. They require that companies monitor the air whenever an employer expects the level of asbestos to rise to one-half the allowable limit (0.1 fibers per cubic centimeters). Engineering controls—walls, special filters, and so forth—are required to maintain an asbestos level that complies with OSHA standards. Respirators can only be used if additional efforts are then still required to achieve compliance.

Computer Monitor Health Problems and How to Avoid Them

Even with advances in computer screen technology (such as flat-panel screens and color) there's still a risk of monitor-related health problems at work. Problems include short-term eye burning, itching, and tearing, as well as eyestrain and eye soreness. Backaches and neckaches are also widespread. These often occur because employees try to compensate for monitor problems (such as glare) by maneuvering into awkward body positions. There may also be a tendency for computer users to suffer from cumulative motion disorders, such as carpal tunnel syndrome, caused by repetitive use of the hands and arms at uncomfortable angles.[76] OSHA has no specific standards that apply to computer workstations. It does have general standards that might apply, regarding, for instance, radiation, noise, and electrical hazards.[77]

The National Institute of Occupational Health (NIOSH) provides general recommendations regarding computer monitors. These include:[78]

1. *Give employees rest breaks.* NIOSH recommends a 15-minute rest break after 2 hours of continuous work for operators under moderate workloads and 15-minute breaks every hour for those with heavy workloads.
2. *Design the maximum flexibility into the workstation so that it can be adapted to the individual operator.* For example, use movable keyboards, adjustable chairs with midback supports, and a video display in which screen height and position are independently adjustable.
3. *Reduce glare with devices such as shades over windows, terminal screen hoods properly positioned, antiglare screen filters, and recessed or indirect lighting.* Special "personal glare screen" eyeglasses can also lower the effect of glare.
4. *Give workers a complete preplacement vision exam to ensure properly corrected vision for reduced visual strain.*
   Other suggestions include:
5. The height of the table or chair should allow wrists to be positioned at the same level as the elbow.
6. The wrists should be able to rest lightly on a pad for support.
7. The feet should be flat on the floor, or on a footrest.

Workplace Smoking

To some extent, the problem of workplace smoking is becoming moot. For example, a series of states including Delaware, Connecticut, California, and New York have barred smoking in most workplaces.[79] Yet, smoking continues to be a serious problem for employees and employers. Costs derive from higher health and fire insurance, as well as increased absenteeism and reduced productivity (which occurs when, for instance, a smoker takes a 10-minute break to smoke a cigarette down the hall).

What You Can and Cannot Do

In general, you can deny a job to a smoker. The EEOC says that a policy of not hiring smokers is legal as long as the rules apply to all applicants and employees.[80] A "no-smokers hired" policy does not, according to one expert, violate the ADA. Smoking is not considered a disability, and, in general, "employers' adoption of a 'no-smokers-hired' policy is not illegal under federal law."[81] Therefore, you can probably institute a policy against hiring people who smoke.

Some firms take an extraordinarily hard-line approach. For example, WEYCO Inc., a benefits services company in Michigan, first gave employees 15 months warning and offered smoking cessation assistance. Then they began firing or forcing out all its workers who smoke, including those who do so in the privacy of their homes.[82]

Dealing with Violence at Work

A disgruntled long-term employee walked into DaimlerChrysler's Ohio Jeep assembly plant and fatally shot one worker, after reportedly being involved in an argument with a supervisor.[83]

Violence against employees is a huge problem at work. By one estimate, workplace violence costs employers about $4 billion a year.[84] One report called bullying the "silent epidemic" of the workplace, "where abusive behavior, threats, and intimidation often go unreported."[85] And, workplace violence isn't always aimed just at people. It can also manifest itself in sabotaging the firm's property, software, or information databases.[86]

Reducing Workplace Violence

Most workplace violence incidents are predictable and avoidable. *Risk Management Magazine* estimates that about 86% of past workplace violence incidents were anticipated by coworkers, who had brought them to management's attention prior to the incidents actually occurring. Yet, in most cases, management did little or nothing.[87] HR managers can take several steps to reduce the incidence of workplace violence. They include the following.

Heighten Security Measures

Heightened security measures are an employer's first line of defense against workplace violence, whether that violence derives from coworkers, customers, or outsiders. According to OSHA, these measures include[88] improve external lighting; use drop safes to minimize cash on hand and post signs noting that only a limited amount of cash is on hand; install silent alarms and surveillance cameras; increase the number of staff on duty; provide staff training in conflict resolution and nonviolent response; close establishments during high-risk hours late at night and early in the morning; and issue a weapons policy that states, for instance, that regardless of their legality, firearms or other dangerous or deadly weapons cannot be brought onto the facility either openly or concealed.

Improve Employee Screening

With about 30% of workplace attacks committed by coworkers, screening out potentially explosive internal and external applicants is the employer's next line of defense.

Personal and situational factors do influence workplace aggression. In general, men and individuals scoring higher on "trait anger" (the predisposition to respond to situations with hostility) are more likely to exhibit workplace aggression. In terms of the situation, interpersonal injustice and poor leadership predict aggression against supervisors.[89]

Steps to Take

Obtain a detailed employment application and solicit an applicant's employment history, educational background, and references.[90] Sample interview questions to ask might include, for instance, "What frustrates you?" and "Who was your worst supervisor and why?"[91] Certain background circumstances, such as the following, may provide a red flag indicating the need for a more in-depth background investigation of the applicant:[92]

- An unexplained gap in employment
- Incomplete or false information on the résumé or application
- A negative, unfavorable, or false reference
- Prior insubordinate or violent behavior on the job
- A criminal history involving harassing or violent behavior
- A prior termination for cause with a suspicious (or no) explanation
- History of drug or alcohol abuse
- Strong indications of instability in the individual's work or personal life as indicated, for example, by frequent job changes or geographic moves
- Lost licenses or accreditations[93]

Use Workplace Violence Training

Supervisors can be trained to identify the clues that typify potentially violent employees. Common clues include:[94]

- An act of violence on or off the job
- Erratic behavior evidencing a loss of perception or awareness of actions
- Overly confrontational or antisocial behavior
- Sexually aggressive behavior
- Isolationist or loner tendencies
- Insubordinate behavior with a threat of violence
- Tendency to overreact to criticism
- Exaggerated interest in war, guns, violence, mass murders, catastrophes, and so on
- Commission of a serious breach of security
- Possession of weapons, guns, knives, or like items in the workplace
- Violation of privacy rights of others, such as searching desks or stalking
- Chronic complaining and the raising of frequent, unreasonable grievances
- A retributory or get-even attitude

The U.S. Postal Service took steps to reduce workplace threats and assaults. The steps include more background checks, drug testing, a 90-day probationary period for new hires, more stringent security (including a hotline that allows employees to

FIRING A HIGH-RISK EMPLOYEE

When firing a high-risk employee, plan all aspects of the meeting, including its time, location, the people to be present, and agenda; involve security enforcement personnel; advise the employee that he or she is no longer permitted onto the employer's property; conduct the meeting in a room with a door leading to the outside of the building; keep the termination brief and to the point; make sure he or she returns all company-owned property at the meeting; don't let the person return to his or her workstation; conduct the meeting early in the week and early in the morning so he or she has time to meet with employment counselors or support groups; offer as generous a severance package as possible; and protect the employee's dignity by not advertising the event.[95]

report threatening situations), a zero-tolerance policy for reporting and recording potentially violent incidents, and training managers to create a healthier workplace culture.[96]

The *HR in Practice* box presents some other suggestions.

Violence Toward Women at Work

While men have more fatal occupational injuries than do women, the proportion of women who are victims of assault is much higher. The Gender-Motivated Violence Act, part of the comprehensive Violence Against Women Act passed by Congress in 1994 (and expanded by Congress in 2006), imposes significant liabilities on employers whose women employees become violence victims.[97]

Fatal workplace violence against women has several sources. Of all females murdered at work, more than three fourths are victims of random criminal violence carried out by an assailant unknown to the victim, as might occur during a robbery. The remaining criminal acts are carried out by coworkers, family members, or previous friends or acquaintances. Tangible security improvements including better lighting, cash-drop boxes, and similar steps are especially pertinent in reducing such violent acts against women.

Terrorism

The employer can take several steps to protect its employees and physical assets from terrorist attack. Steps to take include institute policies to check mail carefully; identify ahead of time a lean "crisis organization" that can run the company on an interim basis after a terrorist threat; identify in advance under what conditions you will close the company down, as well as what the shutdown process will be and who can order it; institute a process to put the crisis management team together; prepare evacuation plans and make sure exits are well marked and unblocked; designate an employee who will communicate with families and off-site employees; identify an upwind, uphill off-site location near your facility to use as a staging area for all evacuated personnel; and designate in advance several employees who will do headcounts at the evacuation staging area.[98]

Employers are increasingly using text messaging to quickly communicate hazardous conditions. Several years ago, as an ice storm approached, University of Texas/Austin administrators text-messaged their 70,000 students, and faculty and staff, telling them to stay home.[99]

Setting Up a Basic Security Program

In simplest terms, instituting a basic security program[100] requires analyzing the current level of risk, and then installing mechanical, natural, and organizational security systems.

Security programs often start with an analysis of the facility's current level of risk. The employer, preferably with the aid of security experts, should assess the company's exposure. Here, it is logical to start with the obvious. For example, what is the neighborhood like? Is your facility close to major highways or railroad tracks (where, for instance, toxic fumes from the trains could present a problem)?

Having assessed the potential current level of risk, the employer then turns its attention to assessing and improving three basic sources of facility security: natural security, mechanical security, and organizational security.[101]

Natural security means taking advantage of the facility's natural or architectural features to minimize security problems. For example, do stacks of boxes in front of your windows prevent police officers from observing what's happening in front of your facility at night? Are there unlit spots in your parking lot?

Mechanical security is the utilization of security systems such as locks, intrusion alarms, access control systems, and surveillance systems in a cost-effective manner that will reduce the need for continuous human surveillance.[102] Here, technological advances are making it easier for employers. Thus, for access security, biometric scanners that read thumb or palm prints or retina or vocal patterns make it easier to enforce plant security.[103]

Finally, *organizational security* means using good management to improve security. For example, it means properly training and motivating security staff and lobby attendants. As another example, it means making sure that security staff have written orders that clearly define their duties, especially in situations such as fire, elevator entrapment, or suspicious packages.[104]

Review

Summary

1. The area of safety and accident prevention is of concern to managers partly because of the staggering number of deaths and accidents occurring at work.

2. The purpose of OSHA is to ensure every working person a safe and healthful workplace. OSHA standards are complete and detailed, and are enforced through a system of workplace inspections. OSHA inspectors can issue citations and recommend penalties to their area directors.

3. There are three basic causes of accidents: chance occurrences, unsafe conditions, and unsafe acts on the part of employees. In addition, three other work-related factors—the job itself, the work schedule, and the psychological climate—also contribute to accidents.

4. Unsafe acts on the part of employees are a main cause of accidents. Such acts are to some extent the result of certain behavior tendencies on the part of employees, and

these tendencies are possibly the result of certain personal characteristics.

5. Experts differ on whether there are accident-prone people who have accidents regardless of the job. The consensus seems to be that the person who is accident prone in one job may not be on a different job. For example, vision is related to accident frequency for drivers and machine operators, but might not be for other workers, such as accountants.

6. There are several approaches to preventing accidents. One is to reduce unsafe conditions. The other approach is to reduce unsafe acts—for example, through selection and placement, training, positive reinforcement, propaganda, and top-management commitment.

7. Alcoholism, drug addiction, stress, and emotional illness are four important and growing health problems among employees.

Alcoholism is a particularly serious problem that can drastically lower the effectiveness of your organization. Techniques including disciplining, discharge, in-house counseling, and referrals to an outside agency are used to deal with these problems.

8. Stress and burnout are other potential health problems at work. An employee can reduce job stress by getting away from work for a while each day, delegating, and developing a worry list.

9. Violence against employees is an enormous problem at work. Steps that can reduce workplace violence include improved security arrangements, better employee screening, and violence-reduction training.

10. Basic facility security relies on natural security, mechanical security, and organizational security.

Key Terms

- Occupational Safety and Health Act
- Occupational Safety and Health Administration (OSHA)
- citations
- unsafe conditions
- unsafe acts
- workaholic
- burnout

Discussion Questions and Exercises

1. How would you go about providing a safer work environment for your employees?
2. Discuss how you would go about minimizing the occurrence of unsafe acts on the part of your employees.
3. Discuss the basic facts about OSHA—its purpose, standards, inspection, and rights and responsibilities.
4. Explain the supervisor's role in safety.
5. Explain what causes unsafe acts.
6. Answer the question, Is there such a thing as an accident-prone person?
7. Describe at least five techniques for reducing accidents.
8. Explain how an employee could reduce stress at work.
9. In groups of 3 or 4 students, spend 15 minutes walking around the building in which your class is held or where you are now, listing possible natural, mechanical, and organizational security measures you'd suggest to the building's owner.

APPLICATION EXERCISES

Case Incident   *The New Safety Program*

Employees' safety and health are very important matters in the laundry and cleaning business. Each dry-cleaning store is a small production plant in which machines, powered by high-pressure steam and compressed air, work at high temperatures washing, cleaning, and pressing garments often under very hot, slippery conditions. Chemical vapors are continually produced, and caustic chemicals are used in the cleaning process. High-temperature stills are almost continually "cooking down" cleaning solvents in order to remove impurities so that the solvents can be reused. If a mistake is made in this process—such as injecting too much steam into the still—a boilover occurs, in which boiling chemical solvent erupts out of the still, onto the floor, and onto anyone who happens to be standing in its way.

As a result of these hazards and the fact that chemically hazardous waste is continually produced in these stores, several government agencies (including OSHA and the Environmental Protection Agency) have strict guidelines regarding the management of these plants. For example, posters have to be placed in each store notifying employees of their right to be told what hazardous chemicals they are dealing with and what is the proper method for handling each chemical. Special waste-management firms must be used to pick up and properly dispose of the hazardous waste.

A chronic problem the owners have is the unwillingness on the part of the cleaning-spotting workers to wear safety goggles. Not all the chemicals they use require safety goggles, but some—like the hydrofluorous acid used to remove rust stains from garments—are very dangerous. The latter is kept in special plastic containers because it dissolves glass. Some of the employees feel that wearing safety goggles can be troublesome; they are somewhat uncomfortable, and they also become smudged easily and thus cut down on visibility. As a result, it is sometimes almost impossible to get employees to wear their goggles. ■

QUESTIONS

1. How should a dry cleaner go about identifying hazardous conditions that should be rectified? Name four probable hazardous conditions or areas in such a store, based on dry cleaning stores that you have seen.
2. Would it be advisable for such a firm to set up a procedure for screening out accident-prone individuals?
3. How would you suggest that owners get all employees to behave more safely at work? Also, how would you advise them to get those who should be wearing goggles to do so?

Continuing Case

LearnInMotion.com: The New Safety and Health Program

At first glance, a dot-com is one of the last places you'd expect to find potential safety and health hazards—or so Jennifer and Mel thought. There's no danger of moving machinery, no high-pressure lines, no cutting or heavy lifting, and certainly no forklift trucks. However, there are safety and health problems.

In terms of accident-causing conditions, for instance, the one thing dot-com companies have is lots of cables and wires. There are cables connecting the computers to each other and to the servers, and in many cases separate cables running from some computers to separate printers. There are 10 telephones in the office, all on 15-foot phone lines that always seem to be snaking around chairs and tables. There is, in fact, an astonishing amount of cable considering this is an office with less than 10 employees.

When the installation specialists wired the office (for electricity, high-speed DSL, phone lines, burglar alarms, and computers), they estimated they used well over 5 miles of cables of one sort or another. Most of these are hidden in the walls or ceilings, but many of them snake their way from desk to desk, and under and over doorways. Several employees have tried to reduce the nuisance of having to trip over wires whenever they get up by putting their plastic chair pads over the wires closest to them. However, that still leaves many wires unprotected. In other cases, they brought in their own packing tape, and tried to tape down the wires in those spaces where they're particularly troublesome, such as across doorways.

The cables and wires are only one of the more obvious potential accident-causing conditions. The firm's programmer, before he left the firm, had tried to repair the main server while the unit was still electrically alive. To this day, they're not sure exactly where he stuck the screwdriver, but the result was that he was "blown across the room," as Mel puts it. He was all right, but it was still a scare. And while they haven't yet received any claims, every employee spends hours at his or her computer, so carpal tunnel syndrome is a risk, as are a variety of other problems such as eyestrain and strained backs.

One recent accident particularly scared them. The firm uses independent contractors to deliver the firm's book– and CD-ROM/ DVD–based courses in New York and two other cities. A delivery person was riding his bike at the intersection of Second Avenue and East 64th Street in New York when he was struck by a car. Luckily he was not hurt, but the bike's front wheel was wrecked, and the close call got Mel and Jennifer thinking about their lack of a safety program.

It's not just the physical conditions that concern the company's two owners. They also have some concerns about potential health problems such as job stress and burnout. While the business may be (relatively) safe with respect to physical conditions, it is also relatively stressful in terms of the demands it makes in hours and deadlines. It is not at all unusual for employees to get to work by 7:30 or 8:00 in the morning and to work through until 11:00 or 12:00 at night, at least 5 and sometimes 6 or 7 days per week. Just getting the company's new calendar fine-tuned and operational required 70-hour workweeks for 3 weeks of five of LearnInMotion.com's employees.

The bottom line is that both Jennifer and Mel feel quite strongly that they need to do something about implementing a health and safety plan. Now, they want you, their management consultants, to help them actually do it. Here's what they want you to do for them. ■

QUESTIONS AND ASSIGNMENTS

1. Based on your knowledge of health and safety matters and your actual observations of operations that are similar to ours, make a list of the potential hazardous conditions employees and others face at LearnInMotion.com. What should we do to reduce the potential severity of the top five hazards?
2. Would it be advisable for us to set up a procedure for screening out stress-prone or accident-prone individuals? Why or why not? If so, how should we screen them?
3. Write a short position paper on what we should do to get all our employees to behave more safely at work.
4. Based on what you know and on what other dot-coms are doing, write a short position paper on what we can do to reduce the potential problems of stress and burnout in our company.

EXPERIENTIAL EXERCISE

Checking for Unsafe Conditions

Purpose: The purpose of this exercise is to give you practice in identifying unsafe conditions.

Required Understanding: You should be familiar with material covered in this chapter, particularly that on unsafe conditions and the checklist in the *HR in Practice* box (pages 338–339), and Figure 10.4.

How to Set Up the Exercise/Instructions: Divide the class into groups of four or five students.

Assume that you are a safety committee retained by your school to identify and report on any possible unsafe conditions in and around the school building.

Each group will spend about 45 minutes in and around the building you are now in for the purpose of identifying and listing possible unsafe conditions. (*Hint:* Make use of the *HR in Practice* checklist.)

Return to the class in about 45 minutes, and a spokesperson for each group should list on the board the unsafe conditions you think you have identified. How many were there? Do you think these also violate OSHA standards? How would you go about checking? ■

Endnotes

1. All data refers to 2006. See www.bls.gov/iif/oshwc/osh/os/ostb1757.txt, accessed January 19, 2008.
2. "BLS Likely Underestimating Injury and Illness Estimates," *Occupational Hazards* (May 2006): 16
3. David Ayers, "Mapping Support for an E. H. S. Management System," *Occupational Hazards* (June 2006): 53–54
4. Katherine Torres, "Stepping into the Kitchen: Food Protection for Food Workers," *Occupational Hazards* (January 2007): 29–30
5. Based on *All About OSHA*, rev. ed. (Washington, DC: U.S. Department of Labor, 1980). www.OSHA.gov, accessed January 19, 2008.
6. "OSHA Hazard Communication Standard Enforcement," *BNA Bulletin to Management* (February 23, 1980): 13. See also William Kincaid, "OSHA vs. Excellence in Safety Management," *Occupational Hazards* (December 2002): 34–36.
7. "What Every Employer Needs to Know about OSHA Record Keeping," U.S. Department of Labor, Bureau of Labor Statistics (Washington, DC), report 412–3, p. 3.
8. Arthur Sapper and Robert Gombar, "Nagging Problems Under OSHA's New Record-Keeping Rules," *Occupational Hazards* (March 2002): 58.
9. Lisa Finnegan, "Industry Partners with OSHA," *Occupational Hazards* (February 1999): 43–45.
10. Steven Hollingsworth, "How to Survive an OSHA Inspection: Knowing What Is Likely to Trigger an OSHA Inspection and How to Prepare for One Can Make This Process Much Less Painful," *Occupational Hazards* 66, no. 3 (March 2004): 31–35. See also www.osha.gov/Publications/osha2098.pdf+OSHA+inspection+priorities&hl=en&ct=clnk&cd=1&gl=us, accessed January 19, 2008.
11. www.OSHA.gov, accessed May 28, 2005; and www.osha.gov/pls/oshaweb/owadisp.show_document?p_table=NEWS_RELEASES&p_id=14883, accessed January 19, 2008.
12. William Atkinson, "When OSHA Comes Knocking," *HR Magazine* (October 1999): 35–38.

13. "Settling Safety Violations Has Benefits," *BNA Bulletin to Management* (July 31, 1997): 248.

14. Jim Lastowka, "Ten Keys to Avoiding OSHA Liability," *Occupational Hazards* (October 1999): 163–170; and www.osha.gov/Publications/osha2098.pdf+OSHA+inspection+priorities&hl=en&ct=clnk&cd=1&gl=us, accessed January 19, 2008.

15. Robert Grossman, "Handling Inspections: Tips from Insiders," *HR Magazine* (October 1999): 41–50.

16. Arthur Sapper, "The Oft-Missed Step: Documentation of Safety Discipline," *Occupational Hazards* (January 2006): 59.

17. Don Williamson and Jon Kauffman, "From Tragedy to Triumph: Safety Grows Wings at Golden Eagle." *Occupational Hazards* (February 2006): 17–25.

18. "A Safety Committee Man's Guide," *Aetna Life and Casualty Insurance Company,* Catalog 872684. See also Todd Nighswonger, "Get a Grip on Slips," *Occupational Hazards* (September 2000): 47–50.

19. "A Safety Committee Man's Guide," op cit. see also "Workplace Fatalities," *BNA Bulletin to Management* (August 28, 1997): 276–277.

20. For a discussion of this, see David Hofmann and Adam Stetzer, "A Cross-Level Investigation of Factors Influencing Unsafe Behaviors and Accidents," *Personnel Psychology* 49 (1996): 307–308.

21. David Hofman and Barbara Mark, "An Investigation of the Relationship between Safety Climate and Medication Errors as Well as Other Nurse and Patient Outcomes," *Personnel Psychology* 50 no. 9, (2006): 847–869

22. List of unsafe acts from "A Safety Committee Man's Guide," *Aetna Life and Casualty Insurance Company.*

23. Dunne Schultz and Sydney Schultz, *Psychology and Work Today* (Upper Saddle River, NJ: Prentice Hall, 1998), p. 351.

24. Robert Pater and Robert Russel, "Drop That Accident Prone Tag: Look for Causes Beyond Personal Issues," *Industrial Safety and Hygiene News* 38, no. 1 (January 2004): 50.

25. Discussed in Douglas Haaland, "Who Is the Safest Bet for the Job? Find Out Why the Guy in the Next Cubicle May Be the Next Accident Waiting to Happen," *Security Management* 49, no. 2, (February 2005): 51–57.

26. "Thai Research Points to Role of Personality in Road Accidents," *Asia and Africa Intelligence Wire* (February 23, 2005); Donald Bashline et al., "Bad Behavior: Personality Tests Can Help Underwriters Identify High-Risk Drivers," *Best's Review* 105, no. 12 (April 2005): 63–64.

27. R. House, D. M. Rousseau, and M. Thomas-Hunt, "The Meso Paradigm: A Framework for the Integration of Micro and Macro Organizational Behavior," in L. L. Cummings and B. M. Staw (eds.), *Research in Organizational Behavior* 17 (Greenwich, CT: JAI Press, 1995), pp. 71–114.

28. Michael Frone, "Predictors of Work Injuries among Employed Adolescents," *Journal of Applied Psychology* 83, no. 4 (1998): 565–576.

29. Benjamin Mangan, "Lockout/Tagout Prevents Workplace Injuries and Saves Lives," *Occupational Hazards* (March 2007): 59–60.

30. Susanna Figura, "Don't Slip Up on Safety," *Occupational Hazards* 58, no. 11 (November 1996): 29–31. See also Russ Wood, "Defining the Boundaries of Safety," *Occupational Hazards* (January 2001): 41–43.

31. James Nash, "Beware the Hidden Eye Hazards," *Occupational Hazards* (February 2005): 48–51.

32. Robert Pater and Ron Bowles, "Directing Attention to Boost Safety Performance," *Occupational Hazards* (March 2007): 46–48.

33. E. Scott Geller, "The Thinking and Seeing Components of People-Based Safety," *Occupational Hazards* (December 2006): 38–40.

34. "Thai Research Points to Role of Personality in Road Accidents," *Asia and Africa iIntelligence Wire* (February 23, 2005), accessed May 28, 2005; Donald Bashline et al., "Bad Behavior: Personality Tests Can Help Underwriters Identify High-Risk Drivers," *Best's Review* 105, no. 12 (April 2005): 63–64.

35. S. Laner and R. J. Sell, "An Experiment on the Effect of Specially Designed Safety Posters," *Occupational Psychology* 34 (1960): 153–169; Ernest McCormick and

Joseph Tiffin, *Industrial Psychology* (Upper Saddle River, NJ: Prentice Hall, 1974), p. 536.

36. See also Josh Cable, "Erring on the Side of Caution," *Occupational Hazards* (February 2007): 21–22; and Shel Siegel, "Incentives: Small Investments Equal Big Rewards," *Occupational Hazards* (August 2007): 42–44.

37. James Nash, "Rewarding the Safety Process," *Occupational Hazards* (March 2000): 29–34.

38. J. Nigel Ellis and Susan Warner, "Using Safety Awards to Promote Fall Prevention," *Occupational Hazards* (June 1999): 59–62. See also William Atkinson, "Safety Incentive Programs: What Works?" *Occupational Hazards* (August 2004): 35–39.

39. Don Williamson and Jon Kauffman, "From Tragedy to Triumph: Safety Grows Wings at Golden Eagle," *Occupational Hazards* (February 2006): 17–25.

40. Quoted in Josh Cable, "Seven Suggestions for a Successful Safety Incentives Program," *Occupational Hazards* 67, no. 3 (March 2005): 39–43.

41. John Dominic, "Improve Safety Performance and Avoid False Reporting," *HR Magazine* 49, no. 9 (September 2004): 110–119; see also Josh Cable, "Safety Incentives Strategies," *Occupational Hazards* 67, no. 4 (April 2005): 37.

42. See also Kelly Rowe, "OSHA and Small Businesses: A Winning Combination," *Occupational Hazards* (March 2007): 33–38.

43. Willie Hammer, *Occupational Safety Management and Engineering* (Upper Saddle River, NJ: Prentice Hall, 1985), pp. 62–63. See also "DuPont's 'STOP' Helps Prevent Workplace Injuries and Incidents," *Asia Africa Intelligence Wire* (May 17, 2004).

44. James Nash, "Weyerhaeuser Fires Plant, Safety Managers for Record-Keeping Abuses," *Occupational Hazards* (November 2004): 27–28.

45. Dov Zohar, "A Group Level Model of Safety Climate: Testing the Effect of a Group Climate on Students in Manufacturing Jobs," *Journal of Applied Psychology* 85, no. 4 (2000): 587–596. See also Steven Yule, Rhona Flin, Andy Murdy, "The Role of Management and Safety Climate in Preventing Risk-Taking at Work," *International Journal of Risk Assessment and Management* 7 no. 2 (December 20, 2006): 137.

46. Quoted from Sandy Smith, "Breakthrough Safety Management," *Occupational Hazards* (June 2004): 43. For a discussion of developing a safety climate survey see, Sara Singer; Mark Meterko; Laurence Baker; David Gaba; Alyson Falwell; and Amy Rosen "Workforce Perceptions of Hospital Safety Culture: Development and Validation of the Patient Safety Climate in Healthcare Organizations Survey," *Health Services Research* 42 no. 5 (October 2007): 1999.

47. "Workplace Safety: Improving Management Practices," *BNA Bulletin to Management* (February 9, 1989): 42, 47. See also Linda Johnson, "Preventing Injuries: The Big Payoff," *Personnel Journal* (April 1994): 61–64; David Webb, "The Bathtub Effect: Why Safety Programs Fail," *Management Review* (February 1994): 51–54.

48. Howard Street, "Getting Full Value from Auditing and Metrics," *Occupational Hazards* (August 2000): 33–36.

49. Lisa Cullen, "Safety Committees: A Smart Business Decision," *Occupational Hazards* (May 1999): 99–104.

50. Sandy Smith, "Protecting Vulnerable Workers," *Occupational Hazards* (April 2004): 25–28.

51. Linda Tapp, "We Can Do It: Protecting Women," *Occupational Hazards* (October 2003): 26–28.

52. Cynthia Ross, "How to Protect the Aging Workforce," *Occupational Hazards* (January 2005): 38–42; and Cynthia Ross, "How to Protect the Aging Workforce," *Occupational Hazards* (February 2005): 52–54.

53. Ann Pomeroy, "Protecting Employees in Harm's Way," *HR Magazine* (June 2007): 113–122.

54. This is based on Paul Puncochar, "The Science and Art to Identifying Workplace Hazards," *Occupational Hazards* (September 2003): 50–54.

55. Figures for 2003, see www.OSHA.gov, accessed May 28, 2005. See also "15% of Workers Drinking, Drunk, or Hung Over while at Work, According to New University Study," *BNA Bulletin to Management* (January 24, 2006): 27.

56. "15% of Workers Drinking, Drunk, or Hung Over While at Work, According to New University Study," *BNA Bulletin to Management* (January 24, 2006): 27

57. "Employee Alcohol Testing on the Rise," *BNA Bulletin to Management* (August 20, 1998): 261. See also Sandy Smith, "What Every Employer Should Know about Drug Testing in the Workplace," *Occupational Hazards* (August 2004): 45–47.

58. www.DOL.gov/ASP/programs/drugs/workingpartners, accessed May 28, 2005.

59. *Managing and Employing the Handicapped: The Untapped Potential,* by Gopal C. Pati and John I. Adkins Jr., with Glenn Morrison (Lake Forest, IL: Brace-Park) *Human Resource Press,* 1981; See also Commerce Clearing House, "How Should Employers Respond to Indications an Employee May Have an Alcohol or Drug Problem?" *Ideas and Trends* (April 6, 1989): 53–57; and "Employer's Role," 568–572. "The Employer's Role in Alcoholism Assistance," *Personnel Journal* 62, no. 7 (July 1983): 568–572.

60. Frank Lockwood et al., "Drug Testing Programs and Their Impact on Workplace Accidents: A Time Series Analysis," *Journal of Individual Employment Rights* 8, no. 4 (2000): 295–306.

61. William Corinth, "Pre-Employment Drug Testing," *Occupational Hazards* (July 2002): 56.

62. Diane Cadrain, "Are Your Employees' Drug Tests Accurate?" *HR Magazine* (January 2003): 41–45; and Sally Roberts, "Random Drug Testing Can Help Reduce Accidents for Construction Companies; Drug Abuse Blamed for Heightened Risk in the Workplace," *Business Insurance* 40 (October 23, 2006): 6.

63. Marice Cavanaugh et al., "An Empirical Examination of Self Reported Work Stress among U.S. Managers," *Journal of Applied Psychology* 85, no. 1 (2000): 65–74.

64. www.OSHA.gov, accessed May 28, 2005.

65. Eric Sundstrom et al., "Office Noise, Satisfaction, and Performance," *Environment and Behavior*, no. 2 (March 1994): 195–222; and javascript:bkmUrl('/purl=rc1_GBFM_0_A153706318&dyn=38!xrn_35_0_A153706 318'), "Stress: How to Cope with Life's Challenges," *American Family Physician* 74 no. 8 (October 15, 2006).

66. Michael Manning, Conrad Jackson, and Marcelline Fusilier, "Occupational Stress, Social Support, and the Costs of Health Care," *Academy of Management Journal* 39, no. 3 (1996): 738–750; "Failing to Tackle Stress Could Cost You Dearly," *Personnel Today* (September 12, 2006); and "Research Brief: Stress May Accelerate Alzheimer's," *GP* (September 8, 2006): 02.

67. "Stress, Depression Cost Employers," *Occupational Hazards* (December 1998): 24. See also Patricia B. Gray, "Hidden Costs of Stress," *Money* 36, no. 12 (December 2007): 44.

68. Karl Albrecht, *Stress and the Manager* (Upper Saddle River, NJ: Prentice Hall, 1979), pp. 253–255. Reprinted by permission. See also "Stress: How to Cope with Life's Challenges," *American Family Physician* 74, no. 8 (October 15, 2006).

69. Catalina Dolar, "Meditation Gives Your Mind Permanent Working Holiday; Relaxation Can Improve Your Business Decisions and Your Overall Health," *Investors Business Daily* (March 24, 2004): 89.

70. "Meditation Helps Employees Focus, Relieve Stress," *BNA Bulletin to Management* (February 20, 2007): 63.

71. "Going Head to Head With Stress," *Personnel Today* (April 26, 2005): 1.

72. Ibid.

73. Madan Mohan Tripathy, "Burnout Stress Syndrome in Managers," *Management and Labor Studies* 27, no. 2 (April 2002): 89–111 See also Jonathon R.B. Halbesleben and Cheryl Rathert, "Linking Physician Burnout and Patient Outcomes: Exploring the Dyadic Relationship Between Physicians and Patients," *Health Care Management Review* 33, no. 1 (January–March 2008): 29.

74. Andy Meisler, "Mind Field," *Workforce Management* (September 2003): 58.

75. "Employers Must Move from Awareness to Action in Dealing with Worker Depression," *BNA Bulletin to Management* (April 29, 2004): 137.

76. J. A. Savage, "Are Computer Terminals Zapping Workers' Health?" *Business and Society Review* (1993) p. 41–43.

77. www.OSHA.gov, accessed May 28, 2005, See also www.cdc.gov/od/ohs/Ergonomics/compergo.htm, accessed May 26, 2007.

78. Anne Chambers, "Computervision Syndrome: Relief Is in Sight," *Occupational Hazards* (October 1999): 179–184, and www. OSHA.gov/ETOOLS/computerwork stations/index.html, accessed May 28, 2005.

79. Diane Cadrain, "Smoking and Workplace Laws Ensnaring HR," *HR Magazine* 49, no. 6 (June 2004): 38–39.

80. Daniel Warner, "We Do Not Hire Smokers: May Employers Discriminate Against Smokers?" *Employee Responsibilities and Rights,* no. 2 (June 1994): 129–140.

81. Ibid., 138.

82. Stephen Bates, "Where There Is Smoke, There Are Terminations: Smokers Fired to Save Health Costs," *HR Magazine* 50, no. 3 (March 2005): 28–29.

83. "Worker Opens Fire at Ohio Jeep Plant," *Occupational Hazards* (March 2005): 16.

84. "Violence in Workplace Soaring, New Study Says," *Baltimore Business Journal* 18, no. 34 (January 5, 2001): 24.

85. "Bullies Trigger 'Silent Epidemic' at Work, but Legal Cures Remain Hard to Come By," *BNA Bulletin to Management* (February 24, 2000): 57.

86. Jennifer Laabs, "Employees Sabotage," *Workforce* (July 1999): 33–42.

87. Paul Viollis and Doug Kane, "At Risk Terminations: Protecting Employees, Preventing Disaster," *Risk Management Magazine* 52, no. 5 (May 2005): 28–53.

88. See also "Creating a Safer Workplace: Simple Steps Bring Results," *Safety Now* (September 2002): 1–2; see also J. W. Elphonestone, "Better Safe Than Sorry: Hotels, Malls Balance Security Measures with Public Accessibility," *Commercial Property News* 19, no. 10 (May 16, 2005): 30.

89. M. Sandy Hershcovis et al., "Predicting Workplace Aggression: A Meta-Analysis,"

Journal of Applied Psychology 92, no. 1 (2007): 228–238.

90. Alfred Feliu, "Workplace Violence and the Duty of Care: The Scope of an Employer's Obligation to Protect against the Violent Employee," *Employee Relations Law Journal* 20, no. 3 (winter 1994/95): 395.

91. Dawn Anfuso, "Workplace Violence," *Personnel Journal* (October 1994): 66–77.

92. Feliu, "Workplace Violence and the Duty of Care," 395.

93. Quoted from ibid.

94. Felin, "Workplace Violence and the Duty of Care," 401–402.

95. "Employers Battling Workplace Violence Might Consider Postal Service Plan," *BNA Bulletin to Management* (August 5, 1999): 241.

96. Paul Viollis and Doug Kane, "At Risk Terminations: Protecting Employees, Preventing Disaster," *Risk Management* 52, no. 15 (May 2005): 28–33.

97. Kenneth Diamond, "The Gender-Motivated Violence Act: What Employers Should Know," *Employee Relations Law Journal* 25, no. 4 (Spring 2000): 29–41; and "Bush Signs 'Violence Against Women Act'; Funding Badly Needed Initiatives to Prevent Domestic & Sexual Violence, Help Victims," The *America's Intelligence Wire* (January 5, 2006).

98. Lloyd Newman, "Terrorism: Is Your Company Prepared?" *Business and Economic Review* 48, no. 2 (February 2002): 7–10.

99. Li Yuan et al., "Texting When There's Trouble," *Wall Street Journal* (April 18, 2007): B1.

100. Unless otherwise noted, the following is based on Richard Maurer, "Keeping Your Security Program Active," *Occupational Hazards* (March 2003): 49–52.

101. Ibid., 50.

102. Ibid.

103. Della Roberts, "Are You Ready for Biometrics?" *HR Magazine* (March 2003): 95–99.

104. Maurer, "Keeping Your Security Program Alive," 52.

A | MANAGING HR GLOBALLY

- HR and the Internationalization of Business
- How to Implement a Global HR System
- Improving International Assignments Through Selection
- Training and Maintaining International Employees

HR AND THE INTERNATIONALIZATION OF BUSINESS

Wal-Mart, famously resistant to unions in America, recently had a surprise. Opening stores in China at a fast clip, it tried to dissuade local unions there from organizing Wal-Mart's China employees. However, the All China Federation of Trade Unions (ACFTU), with strong government backing, quickly organized several stores, and it now seems likely that they'll unionize many Wal-Mart China workers.

Companies are increasingly doing business abroad. Firms like IBM and Sony have long done business abroad, of course. But with the opening of Eastern Europe and the rapid growth of demand in Asia and other parts of the world, even small firms' success depends on being able to market and manage overseas.

This confronts firms (like Wal-Mart) with some interesting management challenges. For one thing, managers now need to formulate and execute their market, product, and production plans on a worldwide basis. And, of course, the employer must also be able to address international human resource management issues. For example, "Should we staff the local offices with local or U.S. managers?" "How should we appraise and pay our local employees?" "How should we deal with the unions in our offices abroad?".

In fact, employers are finding that even employees who never leave the home office need (to some extent) to be "internationalized." As one article recently put it, "cultural diversity isn't just for expatriates or frequent flying executives. Cube dwellers increasingly need to work, often virtually, across borders with people whose first language is not English, who don't have the same cultural touch points as US employees do, and who don't approach business in the same way that Americans do."[1] We'll address these topics in this module.

The Human Resource Challenges of International Business

When researchers asked senior international HR managers in eight large companies, "What are the key global pressures affecting human resource management practices in your firm currently and for the projected future?" the three that emerged were:[2]

- Deployment. Easily getting the right skills to where we need them, regardless of geographic location.
- Knowledge and innovation dissemination. Spreading state-of-the-art knowledge and practices throughout the organization regardless of where they originate.
- Identifying and developing talent on a global basis. Identifying who can function effectively in a global organization and developing his or her abilities.[3]

Dealing with global staffing pressures like these is quite complex. The employer faces a variety of political, social, legal, and cultural differences among countries abroad. In the face of these differences, the employer needs to create—for each local facility and for the company as a whole—effective methods for candidate selection, cultural and language orientation and training, compensation administration and payroll processing, tax administration, career planning and development, and handling of spouse and dependent matters.[4]

At firms like Ford Motor Company, having a global HR perspective "requires understanding different cultures, what motivates people from different societies, and how that's reflected in the structure of international assignments."[5] In China, for instance, special insurance should cover emergency evacuations for serious health problems; and medical facilities in Russia may not meet international standards.[6] So the challenge of conducting human resources activities abroad comes not just from the vast distances involved (though this is important) but also from the cultural, political, legal, and economic differences among countries and their peoples. Let's look at this.

How Intercountry Differences Affect Human Resource Management

Companies operating only within the borders of the United States generally have the luxury of dealing with a relatively limited set of economic, cultural, and legal variables. The United States is a capitalist, competitive society. And while the U.S. workforce reflects a multitude of cultural and ethnic backgrounds, shared values (such as an appreciation for democracy) help to blur potentially sharp cultural differences. Although the different states and municipalities certainly have their own laws affecting HR, a basic federal framework helps produce a fairly predictable set of legal guidelines regarding matters such as employment discrimination, labor relations, and safety and health.

A company operating multiple units abroad isn't blessed with such homogeneity. For example, even with the European Union's increasing standardization, minimum legally mandated holidays range from none in the United Kingdom to 5 weeks per year in Luxembourg. And while Italy has no formal requirements for employee representatives on boards of directors, they're required in Denmark for companies with more than 30 employees. The point is that the need to adapt personnel policies and procedures to the differences among countries complicates HR management in multinational companies. For example, consider the following.

Cultural Factors

Countries differ widely in their cultures—in other words, in the basic values their citizens adhere to, and in the ways these values manifest themselves in the nation's arts, social programs, politics, and ways of doing things.

Cultural differences from country to country necessitate corresponding differences in management practices among a company's subsidiaries. For example, in a study of about 330 managers from Hong Kong, the People's Republic of China, and the United States, the U.S. managers tended to be most concerned with getting the job done. Chinese managers were most concerned with maintaining a harmonious environment, and Hong Kong managers fell between these extremes.[7]

Cultural differences influence human resource policies and practices in very real ways. For example, some argue that American's emphasis on individuality and "standing on one's own feet" helps to explain why there are fewer constraints on American HR managers.[8] For example, European HR managers are much more constrained than American ones with respect to the notice they must give workers before firing them, the amount of severance pay the employees get, and the complexity of the legal process involved in laying off workers. Similarly, both union membership (at about 30%–80%, depending on the European country) and union influences are much higher in Europe than in the United States.[9]

Economic Systems

Differences in economic systems also translate into differences in HR practices. For one thing, some countries are more wedded to the ideals of free enterprise than are others. For instance, France—though a capitalist society—imposed tight restrictions on employers' rights to discharge workers, and limited the number of hours an employee could legally work each week.

Differences in labor costs are also substantial. Hourly compensation costs in U.S. dollars for production workers range from $2.75 in Mexico to $6.43 in Taiwan, $27.10 in the United Kingdom, $23.82 in the United States, and $34.21 in Germany, for instance.[10]

There are other labor costs to consider. For example, compared to the usual 2 or 3 weeks of U.S. vacation, workers in France can expect 2½ days of paid holiday per full month of service per year, Italians usually get between 4 and 6 weeks off per year, and Germans get 18 working days per year after 6 months of service.

Legal and Industrial Relations Factors Abroad: The European Union

Over the past two decades, the separate countries of the former European Community (EC) were unified into a common market for goods, services, capital, and even labor called the European Union (EU). Tariffs for goods moving across borders from one EU country to another generally disappeared, and employees (with some exceptions) now find it easy to move freely between jobs in the EU countries. The introduction of a single currency—the Euro—further blurred many of these differences.

In a process that illustrates the challenges of managing multinationally companies doing business in Europe must adjust their human resource policies and practices to both European Union (EU) directives and to country-specific employment laws. The directives are basically EU laws, the objectives of which are binding on all member countries (although each member country can implement the directives as they so choose). For example, the EU directive on confirmation of employment requires employers to provide employees with written terms and conditions of their employment, but these terms vary from country to country.[11] In England, a detailed written statement is required, including things like rate of pay, date employment began, and hours of work. Germany doesn't require a written contract, but it's still customary to have one specifying most particulars about the job and conditions of work.

The interplay of directives and country laws means that human resource practices must vary from country to country. For example:[12]

- Minimum EU wages.   Most EU countries have minimum wage systems in place. Some set national limits. Others allow employers and unions to work out their own minimum wages.
- Working hours.   The EU sets the workweek at 48 hours, but most countries set it at 40 hours a week, and some, like France, implemented a 35-hour workweek.
- Employee representation.   Europe has many levels of employee representation. In France, for instance, employers with 50 or more employees must consult with their employees' representatives on matters including working conditions, training, and profit-sharing plans and layoffs. In Italy, all employers with 15 or more employees must consult with their works councils on internal work rules and the working environment. As of 2008, most companies—including all those with 50 or more employees in the EU—must "inform and consult" employees about employee-related actions, even if the firms don't operate outside their own countries' borders. And the consultation is now "ongoing" rather than just for major, strategic decisions.[13]
- Unions.   In many European countries, **works councils** replace the informal or union-based worker-to-management mediations typical in U.S. firms. Works councils are formal, employee-elected groups of worker representatives that meet monthly with managers to discuss topics ranging from no-smoking policies to layoffs.[14] Co-determination is the rule in Germany and several other countries. **Co-determination** means employees have the legal right to a voice in setting company policies. Workers elect their own representatives to the supervisory board of the employer, and there is a vice president for labor at the top-management level.[15] In the United States, HR policies on matters such as wages and benefits are set by the employer, or by the employer in negotiations with its labor unions. The co-determination laws, including the Works Constitution Act, largely determine the nature of HR policies in many German firms.
- Termination of employment.   The U.S. practice of employment at will does not exist in Europe, where firing and laying off workers is usually time consuming and expensive. There are a wide range of required notice periods when dismissing employees in Europe. They range from none in Spain to 2 months in Italy.

HOW TO IMPLEMENT A GLOBAL HR SYSTEM

Given cross-cultural differences like these, one could reasonably ask, "Is it realistic for a company to try to institute a standardized HR system in all or most of its facilities around the world?" A recent study suggests that the answer is yes.

In this study, the researchers interviewed HR personnel from six global companies— Agilent, Dow, IBM, Motorola, Procter & Gamble, and Shell Oil Co.—as well as international HR consultants.[16] Their overall conclusion was that employers who successfully implement global HR systems apply several international HR best practices in doing so.

Making the Global HR System More *Acceptable*

First, employers engage in best practices so that the global HR systems they eventually develop will be acceptable to their local managers around the world.

1. *Remember that global systems are more accepted in truly global organizations.* These companies and all their managers think of themselves as global in scope and perspective, and all or most functions and business units operate on a truly global basis. As one Shell manager put it, "If you're truly global, then you are hiring here [the United States] people who are going to immediately go and work in the Hague, and vice versa."[17]
2. *Investigate pressures to differentiate and determine their legitimacy.* HR managers seeking to standardize selection, training, appraisal, compensation, or other HR practices worldwide will always meet resistance from local managers who insist, "You can't do that here, because we are different culturally and in other ways." Based on their research, these investigators found that these "differences" are usually not persuasive. However, this does not mean ramming through a change. Instead, ascertain whether there may in fact be some reason for using a more locally appropriate system.

Developing a More Effective Global HR System

Similarly, researchers found that these companies engaged in best practices in actually developing effective worldwide HR systems.

1. *Form global HR networks.* The firm's HR managers around the world should feel that they're not merely local HR managers, but are part of a greater whole, namely, the firm's global HR network. These six firms did this in various ways. For instance, some formed global HR development teams, and involved them in developing the new HR systems.[18] Treat the local HR managers as equal partners, not just implementers.
2. *Remember that it's more important to standardize ends and competencies than specific methods.* For example, IBM uses a more or less standardized recruitment and selection process worldwide, but "details such as who conducts the interview (hiring manager vs. recruiter) or whether the prescreen is by phone or in person, differ by country."[19]

Implementing the Global HR System

Finally, in actually implementing the global HR systems, several best practices can help ensure a more effective implementation.

1. *Remember, "You can't communicate enough."* For example, "there's a need for constant contact with the decision makers in each country, as well as the people who will be implementing and using the system."[20]
2. *Dedicate adequate resources for the global HR effort.* For example, do not expect local HR offices to suddenly start implementing the new job analysis procedures unless the head office provides adequate resources for these additional activities.

IMPROVING INTERNATIONAL ASSIGNMENTS THROUGH SELECTION

Because international assignments are the heart of international HR, it's disconcerting to see how often such assignments fail. In one survey, employers reported a 21% attrition rate for expatriate employees, compared with an average of 10% for their general employee populations.[21] However, some expatriates may fail less conspicuously, quietly running up the hidden costs of reduced productivity and poisoned customer and staff relations.[22] There is some evidence that the rate of early departures, at least, is declining. This appears to be because more employers are taking steps to reduce expats' problems abroad, for example, by selecting expats more carefully, helping spouses to get jobs abroad, and providing more ongoing support to the expat and his or her family.[23]

Why International Assignments Fail

Discovering why such assignments fail is therefore an important research task, and experts have made considerable progress.

Personality

Personality is one factor. For example, in a study of 143 expatriate employees, extroverted, agreeable, and emotionally stable individuals were less likely to want to leave early.[24] And, the person's intentions are important: For example, people who want expatriate careers try harder to adjust to such a life.[25] Similarly, person–job match is important, insofar as expatriates who are more satisfied with their jobs are more likely to adapt to the foreign assignment.[26] Studies also suggest that it's not how different culturally the host country is from the person's home country, it's the person's ability to adapt that's important. Some do fine transferred anywhere; others will fail anywhere.[27]

Family Pressures

Nonwork factors like family pressures usually loom large in expatriate failures. In one early study, U.S. managers listed, in descending order of importance for leaving early: inability of spouse to adjust, managers' inability to adjust, other family problems, managers' personal or emotional immaturity, and inability to cope with larger overseas responsibility.[28] Managers of European firms emphasized only the inability of the manager's spouse to adjust as an explanation for the expatriate's failed assignment. Other studies similarly emphasize dissatisfied spouses' effects on the international assignment.[29]

The Problem

These findings underscore a truism regarding international assignee selection: It's usually not technical incompetence, but family and personal problems that undermine the international assignee. Yet, employers still tend to select expatriates based on technical competence rather than interpersonal skills or domestic situations.[30] As one expert puts it:

> The selection process is fundamentally flawed. . . . Expatriate assignments rarely fail because the person cannot accommodate to the technical demands of the job. . . . They fail because of family and personal issues and lack of cultural skills that haven't been part of the process.[31]

Some Solutions

Yet, while nonwork aspects of foreign assignments (like living conditions in general, housing conditions, health care, and the adjustment of the spouse or significant other) can prompt assignees to leave early, that result certainly isn't inevitable. Providing realistic previews of what to expect, careful screening, improved orientation, and improved benefits packages are some obvious solutions. One way to reduce assignment problems is simply to *shorten the length* of the assignment, something employers are doing. One survey reports that 23% of the employers' overseas assignments lasted over 3 years, down from 32% about 10 years ago.[32] Some companies form "*global buddy*" programs. Here local managers assist new expatriates with advice on such matters as office politics, norms of behavior, and where to receive emergency medical assistance.[33] Many employers use more *flexible expatriate assignments*. Some dub these "short-term," "commuter," or "frequent-flier" assignments. They basically involve much travel but no formal relocation.[34] Other firms use Internet-based *video technologies* and group decision-making software to enable global virtual teams to do business without either travel or relocation.[35]

Many employers have created what are essentially international commuters, "employees who work in a foreign country but return home with some frequency."[36] This can be effective, particularly where the commutes are relatively short and inexpensive, as between Europe and the U.S. However, having the spouse back at home for only several days a month can cause family stress, and commuters may discover that they're subject to taxation in two countries.

International Staffing: Home or Local?

Multinational companies (MNCs) employ several types of international managers. **Locals** are citizens of the countries where they are working. **Expatriates** are noncitizens of the countries in which they are working.[37] **Home-country nationals** are citizens of the country in which the multinational company has its headquarters.[38] **Third-country nationals** are citizens of a country other than the parent or the host country—for example, a British executive working in the Tokyo branch of a U.S. multinational bank.[39]

Expatriates still represent a minority of multinationals' managers. Thus, "most managerial positions are filled by locals rather than expatriates in both headquarters or foreign subsidiary operations."[40]

Why Local?

There are several reasons to rely on local managers to fill your foreign subsidiary's management ranks. Many people don't want to work in a foreign country, and the cost of using expatriates is usually far greater than the cost of using local workers.[41] Locals may view the multinational as a "better citizen" if it uses local management talent, and some governments even press for the "nativization" of local management.[42] There may also be a fear that expatriates, knowing they're posted to the foreign subsidiary for only a few years, may overemphasize short-term projects rather than more necessary long-term tasks.[43]

In the United States, it's not easy bringing workers in from abroad, so using U.S. "locals" may be a necessity. Under new rules that went into effect in 2005, U.S. employers must now try to recruit U.S. workers before filing foreign labor certification requests with the Department of Labor. In particular, employers must now first post open positions in the Department of Labor's job bank, and run two Sunday newspaper advertisements before filling such requests.[44]

Some companies don't realize what it actually costs to send an expatriate abroad. Agilent Technologies routinely estimated that it cost about three times the expatriate's annual salary to keep the person abroad for 1 year. When Agilent outsourced its expatriate program, it discovered that the costs were much higher. The firm then dramatically reduced the number of expats it sent abroad, from about 1,000 to 300 per year.[45]

Why Expats?

Yet there are also reasons for using expatriates—either home-country or third-county nationals—for staffing subsidiaries. The major reason is technical competence: In other words, employers often can't find local candidates with the required technical qualifications.[46] Multinationals also view a successful stint abroad as a required step in developing top managers. (For instance, after a term abroad, the head of General Electric's Asia-Pacific region was transferred back to a top executive position as vice chairman at GE.) Control is another important reason to use expatriates. The assumption is that home-office managers are already steeped in the firm's policies and culture, and thus more likely to implement headquarters' instructions and ways of doing things.

A Hybrid Solution

Today, the choice is not just between expatriate versus local employees; there's a hybrid solution. One survey found that about 78% of employers had some form of "localization" policy. This means a policy of transferring (say) an American employee to a foreign subsidiary (say, in France) as a "permanent transferee." The assumption here is that the employee would not be an expatriate but instead would be treated as French local hire.[47]

This person, for practical purposes, became "French." The employer bought out his U.S. pension and provided temporary (not permanent) relocation assistance, and a France-based salary. The employee made contributions to the French Social Security system and local pension plan. As is usually the case with permanent transferees, the person's short-term and long-term compensation and benefits reflected what the host peers were getting (not what the firm pays its home-office employees).

Offshoring

Offshoring—having local employees abroad do jobs that the firm's domestic employees previously did in-house—is growing rapidly. Forrester Research estimated that about 588,000 U.S. jobs moved offshore between 2000 and 2005, and that that total will grow to over 3 million jobs by 2015.[48]

Offshoring (or "outsourcing") jobs is controversial. In the 1990s, it was mostly manufacturing jobs that employers shipped overseas. Between 2000 and 2015, the U.S. Labor Department and Forrester Research estimate that about 288,000 management jobs will go offshore, 472,000 computer jobs, 184,000 architecture jobs, and almost 75,000 legal jobs and about 1.7 million office jobs. Offshoring's opponents naturally worry that this job drain will mean millions fewer white-collar jobs for American workers. Proponents contend that employers must offshore jobs to remain globally competitive, and that the money employers thereby save boosts research and development and, eventually, creates even more domestic jobs for U.S. workers.

Values and International Staffing Policy

Experts sometimes classify people's values as **ethnocentric, polycentric,** or **geocentric,** and these values translate into corresponding corporate behaviors and policies.[49] In a firm whose top managers tend to be *ethnocentric,* "the prevailing attitude is that home country attitudes, management style, knowledge, evaluation criteria, and managers are superior to anything the host country might have to offer."[50] In the *polycentric* corporation, "there is a conscious belief that only host country managers can ever really understand the culture and behavior of the host country market; therefore, the foreign subsidiary should be managed by local people."[51] *Geocentric* executives believe they must scour the firm's whole management staff on a global basis, on the assumption that the best manager of a specific position anywhere may be in any of the countries in which the firm operates.

Staffing Policies

These values translate into three broad international staffing policies. With an *ethnocentric* staffing policy, the firm fills key management jobs with parent-country nationals.[52] At Royal Dutch Shell, for instance, most financial officers around the world are Dutch nationals. Reasons given for ethnocentric staffing policies include lack of qualified host-country senior-management talent, a desire to maintain a unified corporate culture and tighter control, and the desire to transfer the parent firm's core competencies (for instance, a specialized manufacturing skill) to a foreign subsidiary more expeditiously.[53]

A *polycentric*-oriented firm would staff its foreign subsidiaries with host-country nationals, and its home office with parent-country nationals. This may reduce the local cultural misunderstandings that might occur if it used expatriate managers. It will also almost undoubtedly be less expensive.

A *geocentric* staffing policy "seeks the best people for key jobs throughout the organization, regardless of nationality"—similar to what Ford Motor Company does. This may let the global firm use its human resources more efficiently by transferring the best person to the open job, wherever he or she may be. It can also help build a stronger and more consistent culture and set of values among the entire global management team.

Ethics and Codes of Conduct

With operations in several countries, employers also need to ensure that their employees abroad are adhering to their firm's ethics codes.

Doing so is not an easy matter. Exporting a firm's ethics rules requires more than having employees abroad use versions of it's U.S.-based employee handbook. Except for a few countries such as Australia and Canada, employers abroad tend to rely on codes of conduct rather than handbooks. Relying on such handbooks can cause problems. For one thing, few countries adhere to "employment at will" as does the U.S., so even handbooks with at-will disclaimers "can become binding contracts."[54] Similarly, employees in many countries have extensive rights to consultation on working conditions under their labor laws, so U.S.-style handbooks may "breach an employer's information, consultation, participation duty."[55]

One international employment lawyer recommends instituting, instead, a global code of conduct. Sometimes, the main concern may be establishing global standards for adhering to U.S. laws that have cross-border impacts. These employers should set broad policies on things like discrimination, harassment, bribery, and Sarbanes-Oxley. For other firms, such as some apparel manufacturers, the main concern may be with codes of conduct for avoiding sweatshop conditions.

In any event, dealing with a variety of cultures complicates the matter. For example, local cultural norms can undermine employers' attempts to institute uniform codes of conduct. Thus in countries with a history of fascist rule, employees often had to divulge information about their coworkers. Here, whistleblowing rules, popular in America, are frowned upon.[56]

Selecting International Managers

Selecting managers for domestic and foreign operations obviously have many similarities. Both candidates need the technical knowledge and skills to do the job, and the required intelligence and people skills.

However, we've seen that foreign assignments are different. There is the need to cope with colleagues whose culture may be drastically different from one's own, and the stress that being alone in a foreign land can put on the manager and his or her family.

Testing

Selecting managers for expat assignments therefore sometimes means testing them for traits that predict success in adapting to new environments. One study asked 338 international assignees from various countries and organizations to specify which traits were important for the success of managers on foreign assignment. The researchers identified five factors that contribute to success in such assignments: job knowledge and motivation, relational skills, flexibility/adaptability, extracultural openness, and family situation (spouse's positive opinion, willingness of spouse to live abroad, and so on; Figure M.1 shows some of the specific items that make up each of the five factors).[57] "Family situation was generally found to be the most important factor, a finding consistent with other research on international assignments and transfers."[58] Many firms also use paper-and-pencil tests such as the Overseas Assignment Inventory.

Realistic Previews

Realistic previews about the problems to expect in the new job (such as mandatory private schooling for the children) as well as about the cultural benefits, problems, and

FIGURE M.1	Five Factors and Specific Items Important to International Assignees' Success

I) Job Knowledge and Motivation

Managerial ability
Organizational ability
Imagination
Creativity
Administrative skills
Alertness
Responsibility
Industriousness
Initiative and energy
High motivation
Frankness
Belief in mission and job
Perseverance

II) Relational Skills

Respect
Courtesy and tact
Display of respect
Kindness
Empathy
Nonjudgmentalness
Integrity
Confidence

III) Flexibility/Adaptability

Resourcefulness
Ability to deal with stress
Flexibility
Emotional stability
Willingness to change
Tolerance for ambiguity
Adaptability
Independence
Dependability
Political sensitivity
Positive self-image

IV) Extracultural Openness

Variety of outside interests
Interest in foreign cultures
Openness
Knowledge of local language(s)
Outgoingness and extroversion
Overseas experience

V) Family Situation

Adaptability of spouse and family
Spouse's positive opinion
Willingness of spouse to live abroad
Stable marriage

Source: Adapted from Arthur Winfred Jr. and Winston Bennett Jr., "The International Assignee: The Relative Importance of Factors Perceived to Contribute to Success," *Personnel Psychology* 48 (1995): 106–107.

idiosyncrasies of the country are another important part of the screening process. The rule, say some experts, should always be to "spell it all out" ahead of time, as many multinationals do for their international transferees.[59]

Adaptability Screening

With flexibility and adaptability often appearing high in studies of what makes expats succeed, *adaptability screening* should be part of the expat screening process. Often conducted by a psychologist or psychiatrist, adaptability screening aims to assess the assignee's (and spouse's) probable success in handling the foreign transfer, and to alert them to issues (such as the impact on children) the move may involve.[60]

Here, experience is often the best predictor of future success. Companies look for overseas candidates whose work and nonwork experience, education, and language skills already demonstrate a commitment to and facility for living and working with different cultures. Even several successful summers spent traveling overseas or participating in foreign student programs might provide some basis to believe the potential transferee can adjust when he or she arrives overseas.

Unfortunately theory doesn't always translate into practice. The importance of adaptability screening notwithstanding, one study found that selection for positions abroad is so informal that the researchers called it "the coffee machine system": Two colleagues meet at the office coffee machine, strike up a conversation about the possibility of a position abroad, and based on that and little more a selection decision is made.[61] Perhaps this helps explain the high failure rate of foreign assignees.

Sending Women Managers Abroad

Women are underrepresented as managerial expatriates. Line managers make most of these assignments, and many of these managers suffer from misconceptions that inhibit them from recommending women to work abroad.[62] Many managers assume that women don't want to work abroad, or are reluctant to move their families abroad, or can't get their spouses to move because the husband is the main breadwinner. In fact, one survey found, women do want international assignments, they are not less inclined than male managers to move their families abroad, and their male spouses are not necessarily the families' main breadwinners.

Safety is another misperceived issue. Employers tend to assume that women posted abroad are more likely to become crime victims. However, most of the surveyed women expats said that safety was no more an issue with women than it was with men. As one said, "it doesn't matter if you're a man or a woman. If it's a dangerous city, it's dangerous for whomever."[63]

Steps

There are several steps the employer can take to short-circuit misperceptions like these, and to identify more women to assign abroad. For example, formalize a process for identifying employees who are willing to take assignments abroad. (At Gillette, for instance, supervisors use the performance review interview to identify the subordinate's career interests, including the possibility of assigning the person abroad.) Train managers to understand how employees really feel about going abroad, and what the real safety and cultural issues are. Let successful female expats recruit prospective female expats, and discuss with them the pros and cons of assignments abroad. Provide the expat's spouse with employment assistance.[64]

TRAINING AND MAINTAINING INTERNATIONAL EMPLOYEES

Careful screening is just the first step in ensuring the foreign assignee's success. The employee may then require special training. The firm will also need special international HR policies for compensating the firm's overseas employees and for maintaining healthy labor relations.

Orienting and Training Employees on International Assignment

When it comes to providing the orientation and training required for success overseas, the practices of most U.S. firms reflect more form than substance. Despite many companies' claims, there is relatively little systematic selection and training for assignments overseas.

What Training?

What sort of special training do overseas candidates need? One firm specializing in such programs prescribes a four-step approach.[65]

- Level 1 training focuses on the impact of cultural differences, and on raising trainees' awareness of such differences and their impact on business outcomes.
- Level 2 aims at getting participants to understand how attitudes (both negative and positive) are formed and how they influence behavior. (For example, unfavorable stereotypes may subconsciously influence how a new manager responds to and treats his or her new foreign subordinates.)
- Level 3 training provides factual knowledge about the target country, while
- Level 4 provides skill building in areas like language and adjustment and adaptation skills.

Beyond these special training needs, managers abroad continue to need traditional training and development. At IBM, for instance, such development includes rotating assignments that permit overseas managers to grow professionally. IBM and other firms also have management development centers around the world where executives can hone their skills. And classroom programs (such as those at the London Business School, or at INSEAD in France) provide overseas executives the sorts of educational opportunities (to acquire MBAs, for instance) that similar stateside programs do for their U.S.-based colleagues.

Trends

There are several trends in expatriate training and development. First, rather than providing only predeparture cross-cultural training, more firms are providing continuing, in-country cross-cultural training during the early stages of an overseas assignment. Second, employers are using returning managers as resources to cultivate the "global mindsets" of their home-office staff. For example, auto-motive equipment producer Bosch holds regular seminars in which newly arrived returnees pass on their knowledge and experience to relocating managers and their families.

There's also increased use of software and the Internet for cross-cultural training. For example, *Bridging Cultures* is a self-training multimedia package for people who will be traveling and/or living overseas. It uses short video clips to introduce case study intercultural problems, and then guides users to selecting the strategy to best handle the situation. Cross-cultural training firms' Web sites include www.bennettinc.com/indexie.htm, www.livingabroad.com, www.worldwise-inc. com, and www.globaldynamics.com.[66]

International Compensation

The whole area of international compensation presents some tricky problems. On the one hand, there is logic in maintaining companywide pay scales and policies so that, for instance, divisional marketing directors throughout the world are paid within the same narrow range. This reduces the risk of perceived inequities. On the other hand, how then to account for large differences in cost of living among countries?

The Balance Sheet Approach

The most common approach to formulating expatriate pay is to equalize purchasing power across countries, a technique known as the *balance sheet* approach.[67]

The basic idea is that each expatriate should enjoy the same standard of living he or she would have had at home. With the balance sheet approach, four main home-country groups of expenses—*income taxes, housing, goods and services, and discretionary expenses* (child support, car payments, and the like)—are the focus of attention. The employer estimates what each of these four expenses is in the expatriate's home country, and what each will be in the host country. The employer then pays any differences—such as additional income taxes or housing expenses.

In practice, this usually boils down to building the expatriate's total compensation around five or six separate components. For example, base salary will normally be in the same range as the manager's home-country salary. In addition, however, there might be an overseas or foreign service premium. The executive receives this as a percentage of his or her base salary, in part to compensate for the cultural and physical adjustments he or she will have to make.[68] There may also be several allowances, including a housing allowance and an education allowance for the expatriate's children. Income taxes represent another area of concern. A U.S. manager posted abroad must often pay not just U.S. taxes but also income taxes in the host country.

Table M.1 illustrates the balance sheet approach. In this case, the manager's annual earnings are $80,000, and she faces a U.S. income tax rate of 28% and a Belgium income tax rate of 70%. The other costs are based on the index of living costs abroad published in the "U.S. Department of State Indexes of Living Costs Abroad, Quarters Allowances, and Hardship Differentials," available at www.state.gov.

Incentives

While the situation is changing, performance-based incentives still tend to be less prevalent abroad. In Europe, firms still tend to emphasize a guaranteed annual salary and companywide bonus. European compensation directors do want to see more performance-based pay. However, they first have to overcome several

TABLE M.1	The Balance Sheet Approach (Assumes Base Salary of $80,000)		
Annual Expense	*Chicago, USA*	*Brussels, Belgium (U.S.$ Equivalent)*	*Required Allowance*
Housing & utilities	$35,000	$ 67,600	$32,600
Goods & services	6,000	9,500	3,500
Taxes	22,400	56,000	33,600
Discretionary income	10,000	10,000	0
Total	$73,400	$143,100	$69,700

Source: Martocchio, Joseph J., *Strategic Compensation: A Human Resource Management Approach*, 2nd Edition, © 2001. Electronically reproduced by permission of Pearson Education, Inc., Upper Saddle River, NJ.

problems—including the public relations aspects of such a move (such as selling the idea of more emphasis on performance-based pay). Indeed, the salary gap between top managers and workers in Europe is still considerably less than in the U.S.

What U.S. companies do offer are various incentives to get expatriates to accept and stay on international assignment. Foreign service premiums are financial payments over and above regular base pay, and typically range between 10% and 30% of base pay. Hardship allowances compensate expatriates for exceptionally hard living and working conditions at certain foreign locations. Mobility premiums are typically lump-sum payments to reward employees for moving from one assignment to another.

Establishing a Global Pay System

Experts say balancing global consistency in compensation with local considerations starts with establishing a single, company-wide global rewards program. This means providing "a global rewards philosophy supported by guidelines, tools, and technological support to enable compensation management and decision-making on a global basis."[69] Doing so involves a 5-phase, multi-year program:[70]

- **Phase I: Global philosophy framework**. First, the employer (1) defines its global rewards philosophy (in terms of how its rewards will help the employer achieve its strategic goals), (2) reviews and inventories its current rewards programs around the world, (3) assesses the "gap" or differences existing between these current programs and the firm's rewards philosophy, and (5) creates a preliminary compensation plan for each location.
- **Phase II: Job structure framework**. Next, systematize job descriptions and performance expectations around the world. For example, create more consistent performance assessment practices, establish consistent job requirements and performance expectations for similar worldwide jobs, and start planning personnel requirements and recruitment worldwide.
- **Phase III: Rewards framework**. The main aim of this phase is to formulate specific pay policies that are both globally consistent and locally competitive. Among other things, the employer will have to conduct surveys to assess local pay practices. It will then devise specific pay policies for each location that make sense in terms of the firm's global compensation philosophy.
- **Phase IV: Talent management framework**. Next, institute career development practices, in recognition of the fact that promotional opportunities and career progress are necessary supplements to the company's compensation programs.
- **Phase V: Ongoing program assessment**. Here, the employer periodically reevaluates its global pay policies, given the fact that its own strategic needs and its competitors' pay practices may change.

Performance Appraisal of International Managers

Several things complicate the task of appraising an expatriate's performance. Obviously, local management must have some input, but cultural differences here may distort the appraisals. Thus, host-country bosses might evaluate a U.S. expatriate manager in Peru somewhat negatively if they find his or her use of participative decision making culturally inappropriate. On the other hand, home-office managers may be so out of touch that they can't provide valid appraisals, since they're not fully aware of the situation the manager faces locally.

In fact, when it comes to appraising expatriates abroad, managers don't always do what they know they should. In one study, several years ago, the surveyed managers recognized that having a balanced set of appraisers from both the host and home countries, and more frequent appraisals, produced the best appraisals. But, in practice, most of these firms did not do this. Instead, they conducted appraisals less frequently, and had raters from the host or the home country, but not both, do the appraisals.[71]

Suggestions for improving the expatriate appraisal process include:

1. Stipulate the assignment's difficulty level, and adapt the performance criteria to the situation.
2. Weigh the evaluation more toward the onsite manager's appraisal than toward the home-site manager's.
3. If the home-office manager does the actual written appraisal, have him or her use a former expatriate from the same overseas location for advice.

International Labor Relations

As explained earlier, firms opening subsidiaries abroad will find substantial differences in labor relations practices among the world's countries and regions. For one thing, unions tend to be stronger abroad than in the U.S.: union membership is two or three times higher in most EU countries than in the U.S. for instance. Furthermore, as explained above, *works councils* and *co-determination* are pivotal labor relations mechanisms in Europe. In the United States, HR policies on matters such as wages and benefits are set by the employer, or by the employer in negotiations with its labor unions. The co-determination laws, including the Works Constitution Act, largely determine the nature of HR policies in many German firms.

Safety and Fair Treatment Abroad

Making provisions to ensure employee safety and fair treatment doesn't stop at a country's borders. While the United States has often taken the lead with respect to matters such as occupational safety, other countries are also quickly adopting such laws. In any event, it's hard to make a legitimate case for being less safety conscious or fair with workers abroad than you are with those at home. High-profile companies including Nike, Inc., have received bad publicity for—and taken steps to improve—the working conditions, long hours, and low pay rates for factory workers in countries such as Indonesia.

The increased threat of terrorism is affecting human resource activities both domestically and abroad. Domestically, for instance, federal antiterrorism laws and procedures are affecting employers' ability to import and export workers.[72] For example, the prospective employee must have an interview at his or her local U.S. Embassy, and scheduling these is a relatively time-consuming process.

Employers are also facing more safety-related resistance from prospective expats. More are reluctant to accept foreign postings and take their families abroad, and those that do are demanding more compensation.[73] And for their employees and facilities abroad, employers have had to institute more comprehensive safety plans, including, for instance, evacuation plans to get employees to safety, if that becomes necessary. Even before the 9/11 attacks several years ago, the threats facing expat employees were on the rise. For example, the number of overseas kidnappings more than doubled from 830 to 1,728 during the mid-to-late 1990s.[74] Developments like these had already prompted employers to take steps to better protect their expat employees.

Keeping business travelers out of crime and terror's way is a specialty all its own, but suggestions here include:[75]

- Provide expatriates with training about traveling, living abroad, and the place they're going to, so they're more oriented when they get there.
- Tell them not to draw attention to the fact they're Americans—by wearing flag emblems or T-shirts with American names, for instance.
- Have travelers arrive at airports as close to departure time as possible and wait in areas away from the main flow of traffic.
- Equip the expatriate's car and home with adequate security systems.
- Tell employees to vary their departure and arrival times and take different routes.
- Keep employees current on crime and other problems by regularly checking, for example, the State Department's travel advisory service and consular information sheets (http://travel.state.gov/travelwarnings.html).
- Advise employees to remain confident at all times: Body language can attract perpetrators, and those who look like victims often become victimized.[76]

Repatriation: Problems and Solutions

One of the most confounding facts about sending employees abroad is that 40% to 60% of them will probably quit within 3 years of returning home. One study suggests that a 3-year assignment abroad for one employee with a base salary of about $100,000 costs the employer $1 million, once extra living costs, transportation, and family benefits are included.[77] Given the investment the employer makes in training and sending these often high-potential people abroad, it obviously makes sense to do everything possible to make sure they stay with the firm.

For this, formal repatriation programs can be quite useful. For instance, one study found that about 5% of returning employees resigned if their firms had formal repatriation programs, while about 22% of those left if their firms had no such programs.[78]

Steps in Repatriation

The heart and guiding principle of any repatriation program is this: Make sure that the expatriate and his or her family don't feel that the company has left them adrift. For example, one firm has a three-part repatriation program, one that actually starts before the employee leaves for the assignment abroad.[79]

First, the firm matches the expat and his or her family with a psychologist trained in repatriation issues. The psychologist meets with the family before they go abroad. The psychologist discusses the challenges they will face abroad, assesses with them how well he or she thinks they will adapt to their new culture, and stays in touch with them throughout their assignment.

Second, the program makes sure that the employee always feels that he or she is still "in the loop" with what's happening back at the home office. For example, the expat gets a mentor, and travels back to the home office periodically for meetings and to socialize with his or her colleagues.

Third, once it's time for the expat employee and his or her family to return home, there's a formal repatriation service. About 6 months before the overseas assignment ends, the psychologist and an HR representative meet with the expat and the family to start preparing them for return. For example, they help plan the employee's next career move, help the person update his or her résumé, and begin putting the person in contact with supervisors back home.[80]

Review

Summary

1. International business is important to almost every business today, and so firms must increasingly be managed globally. This confronts managers with many new challenges, including coordinating production, sales, and financial operations on a worldwide basis. As a result, companies today have pressing international HR needs with respect to selecting, training, paying, and repatriating global employees.

2. Intercountry differences affect a company's HR management processes. Cultural factors such as individualism versus collectivism suggest differences in values, attitudes, and therefore behaviors and reactions of people from country to country. Economic and labor cost factors help determine whether HR's emphasis should be on efficiency, commitment building, or some other approach. Industrial relations and specifically the relationship among the worker, the union, and the employer influence the nature of a company's specific HR policies from country to country.

3. A large percentage of expatriate assignments fail, but the batting average can be improved through careful selection. There are various sources HR can use to staff domestic and foreign subsidiaries. Often managerial positions are filled by locals rather than by expatriates, but this is not always the case.

4. Selecting managers for expatriate assignments means screening them for traits that predict success in adapting to dramatically new environments. Such traits include adaptability and flexibility, cultural toughness, self-orientation, job knowledge and motivation, relational skills, extracultural openness, and family situation. Adaptability screening focusing on the family's probable success in handling the foreign assignment can be an especially important step in the selection process.

5. Training for overseas managers typically focuses on cultural differences, on how attitudes influence behavior, and on factual knowledge about the target country. The most common approach to formulating expatriate pay is to equalize purchasing power across countries, a technique known as the balance sheet approach. The employer estimates expenses for income taxes, housing, goods and services, and discretionary costs, and pays supplements to the expatriate in such a way as to maintain the same standard of living he or she would have had at home.

6. The expatriate appraisal process can be complicated by the need to have both local and home-office supervisors provide input into the performance review. Suggestions for improving the process include stipulating difficulty level, weighing the on-site manager's

appraisal more heavily, and having the home-site manager get background advice from managers familiar with the location abroad before completing the expatriate's appraisal.

7. Repatriation problems are common, but you can minimize them. They include the often well-founded fear that the expatriate is "out of sight, out of mind" and difficulties in reassimilating the expatriate's family back into the home-country culture. Suggestions for avoiding these problems include using repatriation agreements, assigning a sponsor, offering career counseling, and keeping the expatriate plugged in to home-office business.

Key Terms

- works councils
- co-determination
- locals
- expatriates
- home-country nationals
- third-country nationals
- ethnocentric
- polycentric
- geocentric

Discussion Questions and Exercises

1. What intercountry differences affect HR managers? Give several examples of how each may specifically affect an HR manager.
2. You are the HR manager of a firm that is about to send its first employees overseas to staff a new subsidiary. Your boss, the president, asks you why such assignments often fail, and what you plan to do to avoid such failures. How do you respond?
3. What special training do overseas candidates need? In what ways is such training similar to and different from traditional diversity training?
4. How does appraising an expatriate's performance differ from appraising that of a home-office manager? How would you avoid some of the unique problems of appraising the expatriate's performance?
5. Working individually or in groups, write an expatriation and repatriation plan for your professor, who your school is sending to Bulgaria to teach HR for the next 3 years.
6. Give three specific examples of multinational corporations in your area. Check in the library or Internet or with each firm to determine in what countries these firms have operations, and explain the nature of some of their operations, and whatever you can find out about their international HR policies.
7. Choose three traits useful for selecting international assignees, and create a straightforward test to screen candidates for these traits.
8. Use a library or Internet source to determine the relative cost of living in five countries as of this year, and explain the implications of such differences for drafting a pay plan for managers being sent to each country.

APPLICATION EXERCISES

Case Incident   **"Boss, I Think We Have a Problem"**

Central Steel Door Corporation has been in business for about 20 years, successfully selling a line of steel industrial-grade doors, as well as the hardware and fittings required for them. Focusing mostly in the United States and Canada, the company had gradually increased its presence from the New York City area, first into New England and then down the Atlantic Coast, then through the Midwest and West, and finally into Canada. The company's basic expansion strategy was always the same: Choose an area, open a distribution center, hire a regional sales manager, then let that regional sales manager help staff the distribution center and hire local sales reps.

Unfortunately, the company's traditional success in finding sales help has not extended to its overseas operations. With the introduction of the new European currency, Mel Fisher, president of Central Steel Door, decided to expand his company abroad, into Europe. However, the expansion has not gone smoothly at all. He tried for 3 weeks to find a sales manager by advertising in the *International Herald Tribune*, which is read by businesspeople in Europe and by American expatriates living and working in Europe. Although the ads placed in the *Tribune* also run for about a month in the *Tribune's* Internet Web site, Mr. Fisher so far has received only five applications. One came from a possibly viable candidate, whereas four came from candidates whom Mr. Fisher refers to as "lost souls"—people who seem to have spent most of their time traveling restlessly from country to country sipping espresso in sidewalk cafés. When asked what he had done for the last 3 years, one told Mr. Fisher he'd been on a "walkabout."

Other aspects of his international HR activities have been equally problematic. Fisher alienated two of his U.S. sales managers by sending them to Europe to temporarily run the European operations, but neglecting to work out a compensation package that would cover their relatively high living expenses in Germany and Belgium. One ended up staying the better part of the year, and Mr. Fisher was rudely surprised to be informed by the Belgian government that his sales manager owed thousands of dollars in local taxes. The managers had hired about 10 local people to staff each of the two distribution centers. However, without full-time local European sales managers, the level of sales was disappointing, so Fisher decided to fire about half the distribution center employees. That's when he got an emergency phone call from his temporary sales manager in Germany: "I've just been told that all these employees should have had written employment agreements and that in any case we can't fire anyone without at least 1 year's notice, and the local authorities here are really up in arms. Boss, I think we have a problem." ■

Questions

1. Based on the chapter and the case incident, compile a list of 10 international HR mistakes Mr. Fisher has made so far.
2. How would you have gone about hiring a European sales manager? Why?
3. What would you do now if you were Mr. Fisher?

Endnotes

1. Martha Frase, "Show All Employees a Wider World," *HR Magazine* (June 2007): 99–102.
2. Karen Roberts, Ellen Kossek, and Cynthia Ozeki, "Managing the Global Workforce: Challenges and Strategies," *Academy of Management Executive* 12, no. 4 (1998): 93–106.
3. Ibid., 94.
4. Nancy Wong, "Mark Your Calendar! Important Task for International HR," *Workforce* (April 2000): 72–74.
5. Charlene Solomon, "Today's Global Mobility," *Global Workforce* (July 1998): 16.

6. "Fifteen Top Emerging Markets," *Global Workforce* (January 1998): 18–21. The living conditions in China's big cities are improving. See for example, Kate Sarsfield, "Medical Assistance; Business Jet Prescription Peps up China Medevac; Increase in Corporate and Tourist Traffic Leads to Market Opening with Converted Hawker," *"Flight International* (February 11, 2003): 24; and Justin Fox, "The New China Syndrome" *Time* 170, no. 7 (August 13, 2007): 52.

7. David Ralston, Priscilla Elsass, David Gustafson, Fannie Cheung, and Robert Terpstra, "Eastern Values: A Comparison of Managers in the United States, Hong Kong, and the People's Republic of China," *Journal of Applied Psychology* 71, no. 5 (1992): 664–671. See also P. Christopher Early and Elayne Mosakowski, "Cultural Intelligence," *Harvard Business Review* (October 2004): 139–146.

8. Chris Brewster, "European Perspectives on Human Resource Management," *Human Resource Management Review* 14 (2004): 365–382.

9. Ibid.

10. 2006 figures, www.bls.gov/news.release/ichcc.nr0.htm, accessed January 25, 2008.

11. Frances Taft and Cliff Powell, "The European Pensions and Benefits Environment: A Complex Ecology," *Compensation & Benefits Review* (January/February 2005): 37–50.

12. Ibid.

13. "Inform, Consult, Impose: Workers' Rights in the EU," *Economist* (June 16, 2001): 3.

14. Carolyn Hirschman, "When Operating Abroad, Companies Must Adopt European Style HR Plan," *HR News* 20, no. 3 (March 2001): 1, 6.

15. This is discussed in Eduard Gaugler, "HR Management. An International Comparison," *Personnel* (August 1998): 28. See also Carlos Castillo, "Collective Labor Rights in Latin America and Mexico," *Relations Industrielles/Industrial Relations* 55, no. 1 (Winter 2000): 59.

16. Ann Marie Ryan et al., "Designing and Implementing Global Staffing Systems: Part 2 Best Practices," *Human Resource Management* 42, no. 1 (Spring 2003): 85–94.

17. Ibid., 86.

18. Ibid., 89.

19. Ibid., 90.

20. Ibid., 92.

21. "Survey Says Expatriates Twice as Likely to Leave Employer as Home-Based Workers," *BNA Bulletin to Management* (May 9, 2006): 147

22. Margaret Shaffer and David Harrison, "Expatriates' Psychological Withdrawal from International Assignments: Work, Nonwork, and Family Influences," *Personnel Psychology* 51 (1998): 88. See also Jan Selmer, "Psychological Barriers to Adjustment of Western Business Expatriates in China: Newcomers vs. Long Stayers," *International Journal of Human Resource Management* 15, no. 4–5 (June–August 2004): 794-815.

23. Gary Insch and John Daniels, "Causes and Consequences of Declining Early Departures from Foreign Assignments," *Business Horizons* 46, no. 6 (November–December 2002): 39–48.

24. Paula Caliguri, "The Big Five Personality Characteristics as Predictors of Expatriates' Desire to Terminate the Assignment and Supervisor-Rated Performance," *Personnel Psychology* 53, no. 1 (Spring 2000): 67–88.

25. Jan Selmer, "Expatriation: Corporate Policy, Personal Intentions and International Adjustment," *International Journal of Human Resource Management* 9, no. 6 (December 1998): 997–1007. See also Barbara Myers and Judith K. Pringle, "Self-Initiated Foreign Experience as Accelerated Development: Influences of Gender," *Journal of World Business* 40, no. 4 (November 2005): 421.

26. Hung-Wen Lee and Ching Hsing, "Determinants of the Adjustment of Expatriate Managers to Foreign Countries: An Empirical Study," *International Journal of Management* 23, no. 2 (2006): 302–311.

27. Sunkyu Jun and James Gentry, "An Exploratory Investigation of the Relative Importance of Cultural Similarity and Personal Fit in the Selection and Performance of Expatriates," *Journal of World Business* 40, no. 1 (February 2005): 1–8. See also Jan Selmer, "Cultural Novelty and Adjustment: Western Business Expatriates in China," *International Journal of Human Resource Management* 17, no. 7 (2006): 1211–1222.

28. Discussed in Charles Hill, *International Business* (Burr Ridge, IL: Irwin, 1994), pp. 511–515. See also Julia Richardson,

"Self-Directed Expatriation: Family Matters," *Personnel Review* 35, no. 4 (July 2006): 469–486.

29. Charlene Solomon, "One Assignment, Two Lives," *Personnel Journal* (May 1996): 36–47; Michael Harvey, "Dual-Career Couples During International Relocation: The Trailing Spouse," *International Journal of Human Resource Management* 9, no. 2 (April 1998): 309–330.

30. Barbara Anderson, "Expatriate Selection: Good Management or Good Luck?," *International Journal of Human Resource Management* 16, no. 4 (April 2005): 567–583.

31. Michael Schell, quoted in Charlene Marmer Solomon, "Success Abroad Depends on More than Job Skills," p. 52.

32. Carla Joinson, "Cutting Down the Days," *HR Magazine* (April 2000): 90–97; "Employers Shortened Assignments of Workers Abroad," *BNA Bulletin to Management* (January 4, 2001): 7.

33. Eric Krell, "Budding Relationships," *HR Magazine* 50, no. 6 (June 2005): 114–118.

34. Helene Mayerhofer, et al., "Flexpatriate Assignments: A Neglected Issue in Global Staffing," *International Journal of Human Resource Management* 15, no. 8 (December 2004): 1371–1389.

35. Michael Harvey et al., "Global Virtual Teams: A Human Resource Capital Architecture," *International Journal of Human Resource Management* 16, no. 9 (September 2005): 1583–1599.

36. Martha Frase, "International Commuters," *HR Magazine* (March 2007): 91–96.

37. John Daniels and Lee Radebaugh, *International Business*, p. 767. See also Carlos Castillo, "Collective Labor Rights in Latin America and Mexico," *Relations Industrielles/Industrial Relations* 55, no. 1 (Winter 2000): 59.

38. Arvind Phatak, *International Dimensions of Management* (Boston: PWS Kent, 1989), pp. 106–107.

39. Ibid., 106.

40. Daniels and Radebaugh, *International Business*, 767.

41. Ibid., 769; Phatak, *International Dimensions of Management*, 106.

42. Phatak, *International Dimensions of Management*, 108.

43. Daniels and Radebaugh, *International Business*, 769.

44. "DOL Releases Final Rule Amending Filing, Processing of Foreign Labor Certifications," *BNA Bulletin to Management* (January 11, 2005): 11.

45. Leslie Klass, "Fed Up with High Costs, Companies Winnow the Ranks of Career Expats," *Workforce Management* (October 2004): 84–88.

46. Ibid., 769; Phatak, *International Dimensions of Management*, 106.

47. Timothy Dwyer, "Localization's Hidden Costs," *HR Magazine* (June 2004): 135–144.

48. Based on Pamela Babcock, "America's Newest Export: White Collar Jobs," *HR Magazine* (April 2004): 50–57.

49. Howard Perlmutter, "The Tortuous Evolution of the Multinational Corporation," *Columbia Journal of World Business* 3, no. 1 (January–February 1969): 11–14, discussed in Phatak, *International Dimensions of Management*, 129. See also Helen Deresky, *International Management* (Upper Saddle River NJ: Pearson, 2008): 343.

50. Phatak, *International Dimensions of Management*, 129.

51. Ibid.

52. Hill, *International Business*, 507.

53. Ibid., 507–510.

54. Donald Dowling Jr., "Export Codes of Conduct, Not Employee Handbooks," *The Society for Human Resource Management Legal Report* (January/February 2007): 1–4.

55. Ibid.

56. "SOX Compliance, Corporate Codes of Conduct Can Create Challenges for U.S. Multinationals," *BNA Bulletin to Management* (March 28, 2006): 97.

57. Winfred Arthur Jr. and Winston Bennett Jr., "The International Assignee: The Relative Importance of Factors Perceived to Contribute to Success," *Personnel Psychology* 48 (1995): 99–114; table on 106–107. See also Raymond Edward Branton, "A Multifaceted Assessment Protocol for Successful International Assignees," *Dissertation Abstracts International: Section B: The Sciences and Engineering* 64, no. 8B (2004): 4024.

58. Arthur and Bennett, "The International Assignee," 110; Gretchen Spreitzer, Morgan

McCall Jr., and Joan Mahoney, "Early Identification of International Executive Potential," *Journal of Applied Psychology* 82, no. 1 (1997): 6–29.

59. P. Blocklyn, "Developing the International Executive," *Personnel* 66 (March 1989): 44–47. See also Paula M. Caligiuri and Jean M. Phillips, "An Application of Self-Assessment Realistic Job Previews to Expatriate Assignments," *International Journal of Human Resource Management* 14, no. 7 (November 2003): 1102–1115.

60. Phatak, *International Dimensions of Management* 119.

61. Hilary Harris and Chris Brewster, "The Coffee Machine System: How International Selection Really Works," *International Journal of Human Resource Management* 10, no. 3 (June 1999): 488–500.

62. Kathryn Tyler, "Don't Fence Her In," *HR Magazine* 46, no. 3 (March 2001): 69–77.

63. Ibid.

64. Ibid.

65. Valerie Frazee, "Expats Are Expected to Dive Tight In," *Personnel Journal* (December, 1996): 31. See also Rita Bennett et al., "Cross-Cultural Training: A Critical Step in Ensuring the Success of National Assignments," *Human Resource Management* 39, no. 2–3 (Summer–Fall 2000): 239–250.

66. Mark Mendenhall and Gunther Stahl, "Expatriate Training and Development: Where Do We Go from Here?" *Human Resource management* 39, no. 2–3 (Summer–Fall 2000): 251–265.

67. Hill, *International Business*, pp. 519–20; Valerie Frazee, "Is the Balance Sheet Right for Your Expats?" *Global Workforce* (September 1998): 19–26; Stephanie Overman, "Focus on International HR," *HR Magazine* (March

2000): 87–92. See also Sheila Burns, "Flexible International Assignee Compensation Plans," *Compensation and Benefits Review* (May/June 2003): 35–44.

68. Joseph J. Martocchio, *Strategic Compensation: A Human Resource Management Approach*, 2nd Edition (Upper Saddle River, NJ: Pearson, 2006): 280–294. See also "China to Levy Income Tax on Expatriates," *Asia Africa Intelligence Wire* (August 3, 2004).

69. Robin White, "A Strategic Approach to Building a Consistent Global Rewards Program," *Compensation & Benefits Review* (July/August 2005): 25.

70. Ibid., 23–40.

71. Hal Gregersen et al., "Expatriate Performance Appraisal in U.S. Multinational Firms," *Journal of International Business Studies* 27, no. 4 (Winter 1996): 711–739. See also, Anne Francesco and Barry Gold, *International Organizational Behavior*, (Upper Saddle River NJ: Pearson, 2005), P 152–153

72. "Terrorism Impacts Ability to Import, Export Workers," *BNA Bulletin to Management* (April 3, 2002): 111.

73. Ibid.

74. Frank Jossi, "Buying Protection from Terrorism," *HR Magazine* (June 2001): 155–160.

75. These are based on or quoted from Samuel Greengard, "Mission Possible: Protecting Employees Abroad," *Workforce* (August 1997): 30–32.

76. Ibid., 32

77. Carla Joinson, "Save Thousands Per Expatriate," *HR Magazine* (July 2002): 77.

78. Quoted in Leslie Klaff, "The Right Way to Bring Expats Home," *Workforce* (July 2002): 43.

79. Ibid., 43.

80. Ibid., 43.

COMPREHENSIVE CASES

Bandag Automotive*

Jim Bandag took over his family's auto supply business in 2005, after helping his father, who founded the business, run it for about 10 years. Based in Illinois, Bandag employs about 300 people, and distributes auto supplies (replacement mufflers, bulbs, engine parts, and so on) through two divisions, one that supplies service stations and repair shops, and a second that sells retail auto supplies through five "Bandag Automotive" auto supply stores.

Jim's father, and now Jim, have always endeavored to keep Bandag's organization chart as simple as possible. The company has a full-time controller, managers for each of the five stores, a manager that oversees the distribution division, and Jim Bandag's executive assistant. Jim (and his father, working part-time) handles marketing and sales.

Jim's executive assistant administers the firm's day-to-day human resource management tasks, but they outsource most HR activities to others, including an employment agency that does their recruiting and screening, a benefits firm that administers their 401(k) plan, and a payroll service that handles their paychecks. Bandag's human resource management systems consist almost entirely of standardized HR forms they purchase from an HR supplies company. It supplies HR tools including forms such as application forms, performance appraisal forms, and an "honesty" test Bandag uses to screen the staff that works in the five stores. The company performs informal salary surveys to see what other companies in the area are paying for similar positions, and uses

these results for awarding annual merit increases (which in fact are more accurately cost-of-living adjustments).

Jim's father took a fairly paternal approach to the business. He often walked around speaking with his employees, finding out what their problems were, and even helping them out with an occasional loan—for instance when he discovered that one of their children were sick, or for part of a new home down payment. Jim, on the other hand, tends to be more abrupt, and does not enjoy the same warm relationship with the employees as did his father. Jim is not unfair or dictatorial. He's just very focused on improving Bandag's financial performance, and so all his decisions, including his HR-related decisions, generally come down to cutting costs. For example, his knee-jerk reaction is usually to offer fewer days off rather than more, fewer benefits rather than more, and to be less flexible when an employee needs, for instance, a few extra days off because a child is sick.

It's therefore perhaps not surprising that over the past few years Bandag's sales and profits have increased markedly, but that the firm has found itself increasingly enmeshed in HR/equal employment type issues. Indeed, Jim now finds himself spending a day or two a week addressing HR problems. For example, Henry Jaques, an employee of one of their stores, came to Jim's executive assistant and told her he was "irate" about his recent firing and was probably going to sue. On Henry's last performance appraisal, his store manager had said Henry did the technical aspects of his job

*© Gary Dessler, Ph.D.

well, but that he had "serious problems interacting with his coworkers." He was continually arguing with them, and complaining to the store manager about working conditions. The store manager had told Jim that he had to fire Henry because he was making "the whole place poisonous," and that (although he felt sorry because he'd heard rumors that Henry suffered from some mental illness) he felt he had to go. Jim approved the dismissal.

Gavin was another problem. Gavin worked for Bandag for 10 years, the last 2 as manager of one of the company's five stores. Right after Jim Bandag took over, Gavin told him he had to take a Family and Medical Leave Act medical leave to have hip surgery, and Jim approved the leave. So far so good, but when Gavin returned from leave, Jim told him that his position had been eliminated. They had decided to close his store and open a new, larger store across from a shopping center about a mile away, and appointed a new manager in Gavin's absence. However, the company did give Gavin a (non-managerial) position in the new store as a counter salesperson, at the same salary and with the same benefits as he had before. Even so, "this job is not similar to my old one" Gavin insisted, "it doesn't have nearly as much prestige." His contention is that FMLA requires that the company bring him back in the same or equivalent position, and that this means a supervisory position, similar to what he had before he went on leave. Jim said no, and they seem to be heading toward litigation.

In another sign of the times at Bandag, the company's controller, Miriam, who had been with the company for about 6 years, went on pregnancy leave for 12 weeks in 2005 (also under the FMLA), and then received an additional 3 weeks' leave under Bandag's extended illness days program. Four weeks after she came back, she asked Jim Bandag if she could arrange to work fewer hours per week, and spend about a

day per week working out of her home. He refused, and about two months later fired her. Jim Bandag said, "I'm sorry, it's not anything to do with your pregnancy-related requests, but we've got ample reasons to discharge you—your monthly budgets have been several days late, and we've got proof you may have forged documents." She replied, "I don't care what you say your reasons are, you're really firing me because of my pregnancy, and that's illegal."

Jim felt he was on safe ground as far as defending the company for these actions, although he didn't look forward to spending the time and money that he knew it would take to fight each. However, what he learned over lunch from a colleague undermined his confidence about another case that Jim had been sure would be a "slam dunk" for his company. Jim was explaining to his friend that one of Bandag's truck maintenance service people had applied for a job driving one of Bandag's distribution department trucks, and that Jim had turned him down because the worker was deaf. Jim, (whose wife has occasionally said of him, "No one has ever accused Jim of being politically correct.") was mentioning to his friend the apparent absurdity of a deaf person asking to be a truck delivery person. His friend, who happens to work for UPS, pointed out that the U.S. Court of Appeals for the Ninth Circuit had recently decided that UPS violated the Americans with Disabilities Act by refusing to consider deaf workers for jobs driving the company's smaller vehicles.

Although Jim's father is semi retired, the sudden uptick in the frequency of such EEO-type issues troubled him, particularly after so many years of labor peace. However, he's not sure what to do about it. Having handed over the reins of the company to his son Jim, he was loath to inject himself back into the company's operational decision-making. On the other hand, he was afraid that in the short run, these issues were going to drain a great deal of Jim's time and resources, and that in the long run they might be a sign of things to come, with problems like these eventually overwhelming Bandag Auto. He comes to you, who he knows consults in human resource management, and asks you the following questions.

QUESTIONS

1. Given Bandag Auto's size, and anything else you know about it, should we reorganize the human resource management function, and if so why and how?
2. What, if anything, would you do to change and/or improve upon the current HR systems, forms, and practices that we now use?
3. Do you think that the employee that Jim fired for creating what the manager called a poisonous relationship has a legitimate claim against us, and if so why and what should we do about it?
4. Is it true that we really had to put Gavin back into an equivalent position, or was it adequate to just bring him back into a job at the same salary, bonuses, and benefits as he had before his leave?
5. Miriam, the controller, is basically claiming that the company is retaliating against her for being pregnant, and that the fact that we raised performance issues was just a smokescreen. Do you think the EEOC and/or courts would agree with her, and, in any case, what should we do now?
6. An employee who is deaf has asked us to be one of our delivery people and we turned him down. He's now threatening to sue. What should we do, and why?
7. In the previous 10 years we only had one equal employment complaint, and now in the last few years we had four or five. What should I do about it? Why?

Based generally on actual facts, but Bandag is a fictitious company. Bandag source notes: "The Problem Employee: Discipline or Accommodation?" *Monday Business Briefing,* March 8, 2005, p. n/a; "Employee Says Change in Duties after Leave Violates FMLA," *BNA Bulletin to Management,* January 16, 2007, p. 24; "Manager Fired Days after Announcing Pregnancy," *BNA Bulletin to Management,* January 2, 2007, p. 8; "Ninth Circuit Rules UPS Violated ADA by Barring Deaf Workers from Driving Jobs," *BNA Bulletin to Management,* October 17, 2006, p. 329 .

Angelo's Pizza[*]

Angelo Camero was brought up in the Bronx, New York, and basically always wanted to be in the pizza store business. As a youngster, he would sometimes spend hours at the local pizza store, watching the owner knead the pizza dough, flatten it into a large circular crust, fling it up, and then spread on tomato sauce in larger and larger loops. After graduating from college as a marketing major, he made a beeline back to the Bronx, where he opened his first Angelo's Pizza store, emphasizing its clean, bright interior, its crisp green, red, and white sign, and his all-natural, fresh ingredients. Within five years, Angelo's store was a success, and he had opened three other stores and was considering franchising his concept.

Anxious as he was to expand, his four years in business school had taught him the difference between being an entrepreneur and being a manager. As an entrepreneur/ small-business owner, he knew he had the distinct advantage of being able to personally run the whole operation himself. With just one store and a handful of employees,

---

*© Gary Dessler, Ph.D.

he could make every decision and watch the cash register, check in the new supplies, oversee the takeout, and personally supervise the service.

When he expanded to three stores, things started getting challenging. He hired managers for the two new stores (both of whom had worked for him at his first store for several years) and gave them only minimal "how to run a store"-type training, on the assumption that, having worked with him for several years, they already knew pretty much everything they needed to know about running a store. However, he was already experiencing human resource management problems, and he knew there was no way he could expand the number of stores he owned, or (certainly) contemplate franchising his idea, unless he had a system in place that he could clone in each new store, to provide the manager (or the franchisee) with the necessary management knowledge and expertise to run their stores. Angelo had no training program in place for teaching his store managers how to run their stores. He simply (erroneously, as it turned out) assumed that by working with him they would learn how to do things on the job. Since Angelo really had no system in place, the new managers were, in a way, starting off below zero when it came to how to manage a store.

There are several issues that particularly concern Angelo. Finding and hiring good employees was number one. He'd read the new National Small Business Poll from the National Federation of Independent Business Education Foundation. It found that 71% of small-business owners believed that finding qualified employees was "hard." Furthermore, "the search for qualified employees will grow more difficult as demographic and education factors" continue to make it more difficult to find employees. Similarly, reading the Kiplinger Letter one day, he noticed that just about every type of business couldn't find enough

good employees to hire. Small firms were particularly in jeopardy; the Letter said: Giant firms can outsource many (particularly entry-level) jobs abroad, and larger companies can also afford to pay better benefits and to train their employees. Small firms rarely have the resources or the economies of scale to allow outsourcing or to install the big training programs that would enable them to take untrained new employees and turn them into skilled ones.

While finding enough employees was his biggest problem, finding enough honest ones scared him even more. Angelo recalled from one of his business school courses that companies in the United States are losing a total of well over $400 billion a year in employee theft annually. As a rough approximation, that works out to about $9 per employee per day and about $12,000 a year lost annually for a typical company. Furthermore, it was small companies like Angelo's that were particularly in the cross hairs, because companies with fewer than 100 employees are particularly prone to employee theft. Why are small firms particularly vulnerable? Perhaps they lack experience dealing with the problem. More importantly: Small firms are more likely to have a single person doing several jobs, such as ordering supplies and paying the delivery person. This undercuts the checks and balances managers often strive for to control theft. Furthermore, the risk of stealing goes up dramatically when the business is largely based on cash. In a pizza store, many people come in and just buy one or two slices and a cola for lunch, and almost all pay with cash, not credit cards.

And, Angelo was not just worried about someone stealing cash. They can steal your whole business idea, something he learned from painful experience. He had been planning to open a store in what he thought would be a particularly good location, and was thinking of having one of his current employees manage the store. Instead, it turned out that this employee was, in a matter of speaking, stealing Angelo's brain—what Angelo knew about customers, suppliers, where to buy pizza dough, where to buy tomato sauce, how much everything should cost, how to furnish the store, where to buy ovens, store layout—everything. This employee soon quit and opened up his own pizza store, not far from where Angelo had planned to open his new store.

That he was having trouble hiring good employees, there was no doubt. The restaurant business is particularly brutal when it comes to turnover. Many restaurants turn over their employees at a rate of 200% to 300% per year—so every year, each position might have a series of two to three employees filling it. As Angelo said, "I was losing two to three employees a month." As he said, "We're a high-volume store, and while we should have [to fill all the hours in a week] about six employees per store, we were down to only three or four, so my managers and I were really under the gun."

The problem was bad at the hourly employee level: "We were churning a lot at the hourly level," said Angelo. "Applicants would come in, my managers or I would hire them and not spend much time training them, and the good ones would leave in frustration after a few weeks, while often it was the bad ones who'd stay behind." But in the last two years, Angelo's three company-owned stores also went through a total of three store managers—"They were just blowing through the door" as Angelo put it, in part because, without good employees, their workday was brutal. As a rule, when a small-business owner or manager can't find enough employees (or an employee doesn't show up for work), about 80% of the time the owner or manager does the job him or herself. So, these managers often ended up working 7 days a week, 10 to 12 hours a day, and many just

burned out in the end. One night, working three jobs himself with customers leaving in anger, Angelo decided he'd never just hire someone because he was desperate again, but would start doing his hiring more rationally.

Angelo knew he should have a more formal screening process. As he said, "If there's been a lesson learned, it's much better to spend time up-front screening out candidates that don't fit than to hire them and have to put up with their ineffectiveness." He also knew that he could identify many of the traits that his employees needed. For example, he knew that not everyone has the temperament to be a waiter a waitress (he has a small pizza/Italian restaurant in the back of his main store). As Angelo said, "I've seen personalities that were off the charts in assertiveness or overly introverted, traits that obviously don't make a good fit for a waiter a waitress."

As a local business, Angelo recruits by placing help-wanted ads in two local newspapers, and he's been "shocked" at some of the responses and experiences he's had in response to his help-wanted ads. Many of the applicants left voice mail messages (Angelo or the other workers in the store were too busy to answer) and some applicants Angelo "just axed" on the assumption that people without good telephone manners wouldn't have very good manners in the store either. He also quickly learned that he had to throw out a very wide net, even if only hiring one or two people. Many people, as noted, he just deleted because of the messages they left, and about half the people he scheduled to come in for interviews didn't show up. He'd taken courses in human resource management, so (as he said) "I should know better," but he hired people based almost exclusively on a single interview (he occasionally made a feeble attempt to check references). In total, his HR approach was obviously not working. It wasn't producing enough good recruits, and the people he did hire were often problematical.

What was he looking for? Service-oriented courteous people, for one. For example, he'd hired one employee who used profanity several times, including once in front of a customer. On that employee's third day, Angelo had to tell her, "I think Angelo's isn't the right place for you," and he fired her. As Angelo said, "I felt bad," but also knew that everything I have is on the line for this business, so I wasn't going to let anyone run this business down." Angelo wants reliable people (who'll show up on time), honest people, and people who are flexible about switching jobs and hours as required.

Angelo's Pizza business has only the most rudimentary human resource management system. Angelo bought several application forms at a local Office Depot, and rarely uses other forms of any sort. He uses his personal accountant for reviewing the company's books, and Angelo himself computes each employee's paycheck at the end of the week and writes the checks. Training is entirely on-the-job. Angelo personally trained each of his employees. For those employees who go on to be store managers, he assumes that they are training their own employees the way that Angelo trained them (for better or worse, as it turns out). Angelo pays "a bit above" prevailing wage rates (judging by other help-wanted ads) but probably not enough to make a significant difference in the quality of employees that he attracts. If you asked Angelo what his reputation is as an employer, Angelo, being a candid and forthright person, would probably tell you that he is a supportive but hard-nosed employer who treats people fairly, but whose business reputation may suffer from disorganization stemming from inadequate organization and training. He approaches you to ask you several questions.

QUESTIONS

1. My strategy is to (hopefully) expand the number of stores and eventually franchise, while focusing on serving only high-quality fresh ingredients. What are three specific human resource management implications of my strategy (including specific policies and practices).

2. Identify and briefly discuss five specific human resource management errors that I'm currently making

3. Develop a structured interview form that we can use for hiring (1) store managers, (2) waiters and waitresses, and (3) counter people/pizza makers.

4. Based on what you know about Angelo's, and what you know from having visited pizza restaurants, write a one-page outline showing specifically how you think Angelo's should go about selecting employees.

Based generally on actual facts, but Angelo's Pizza is a fictitious company. Angelo's Pizza source notes: Dino Berta, "People Problems: Keep Hiring from Becoming a Crying Game," *Nation's Business News*, May 20, 2002, vol. 36, issue 20, pp. 72–74; Ellen Lyon, "Hiring, Personnel Problems Can Challenge Entrepreneurs," *Patriot-News*, October 12, 2004, p. n/a; Rose Robin Pedone, "Businesses' $400 Billion Theft Problem," *Long Island Business News*, July 6, 1998, no. 27, pp. 1B–2B; "Survey Shows Small-Business Problems with Hiring, Internet," *Providence Business News*, September 10, 2001, vol. 16, pp. 1B; "Finding Good Workers Is Posing a Big Problem as Hiring Picks Up," *Kiplinger Letter*, February 13, 2004, vol. 81, p. n/a.

Google[*]

Fortune magazine recently named Google the best of the 100 best companies to work for, and there is little doubt why. Among the benefits they offer are free shuttles equipped with Wi-Fi to pick up and drop-off employees from San Francisco Bay area locations, unlimited sick days, annual all-expense-paid ski trips, free gourmet meals, five on-site free doctors, $2000 bonuses for referring a new hire, free flu shots, a giant lap pool, on-site oil changes, on-site car washes, volleyball courts, TGIF parties, free on-site washers and dryers (with free detergent), Ping-Pong and foosball tables, and free famous people lectures. For many people, it's the gourmet meals and snacks that make Google stand out. For example, human resources director Stacey Sullivan loves the Irish oatmeal with fresh berries at the company's Plymouth Rock Cafe, near Google's "people operations" group. "I sometimes dream about it," she says. Engineer Jan Fitzpatrick loves the raw bar at Google's Tapis restaurant, down the road on the Google campus. Then, of course there are the stock options—each new employee gets about 1200 options to buy Google shares (recently worth about $480 per share). In fact, dozens of early Google employees ("Googlers") are already multimillionaires thanks to Google stock.

For their part, Googlers share certain traits. They tend to be brilliant, team oriented (teamwork is the norm, especially for big projects), and driven. *Fortune* describes them as people who "almost universally" see themselves as the most interesting people on the planet, and who are happy-go-lucky on the outside, but type A—highly intense and goal directed—on the inside. They're also super-hardworking (which makes sense, since it's not unusual for engineers to be in the hallways at 3 A.M. debating some new

mathematical solution to a Google search problem). They're so team oriented that when working on projects, it's not unusual for a Google team to give up its larger, more spacious offices and to crowd into a small conference room, where they can "get things done." Historically, Googlers generally graduate with great grades from the best universities, including Stanford, Harvard, and MIT. For many years, Google wouldn't even consider hiring someone with less than a 3.7 average—while also probing deeply into the why behind any B grades. Google also doesn't hire lone wolves, but wants people who work together and people who also have diverse interests (narrow interests or skills are a turnoff at Google). Google also wants people with growth potential. The company is expanding so fast that they need to hire people who are capable of being promoted five or six times—it's only, they say, by hiring such overqualified people that they can be sure that the employees will be able to keep up as Google and their own departments expand.

The starting salaries are highly competitive. Experienced engineers start at about $130,000 a year (plus about 1200 shares of stock options, as noted), and new MBAs can expect between $80,000 and $120,000 per year (with smaller option grants). Most recently, Google had about 10,000 staff members, up from its start a few years ago with just three employees in a rented garage.

Of course, in a company that's grown from three employees to 10,000 and from zero value to hundreds of billions of dollars in about five years, it may be quibbling to talk about "problems," but there's no doubt that such rapid growth does confront Google's management, and particularly its "people operations" group, with some big challenges. Let's look at these.

---

[*] © Gary Dessler, Ph.D.

For one, Google, as noted above, is a 24-hour operation, and with engineers and others frequently pulling all-nighters to complete their projects, the company needs to provide a package of services and financial benefits that supports that kind of lifestyle, and that helps its employees maintain an acceptable work–life balance.

As another challenge, Google's enormous financial success is a two-edged sword. While Google usually wins the recruitment race when it comes to competing for new employees against competitors like Microsoft or Yahoo, Google does need some way to stem a rising tide of retirements. Most Googlers are still in their late twenties and early thirties, but many have become so wealthy from their Google stock options that they can afford to retire. One 27-year-old engineer received a million-dollar founder's award for her work on the program for searching desktop computers, and wouldn't think of leaving "except to start her own company." Similarly a former engineering vice president retired (with his Google stock profits) to pursue his love of astronomy. The engineer who dreamed up Gmail recently retired (at the age of 30).

Another challenge is that the work not only involves long hours but can also be very tense. Google is a very numbers-oriented environment. For example, consider a typical weekly Google user interface design meeting. Marisa Meyer, the company's vice president of search products and user experience runs the meeting, where her employees work out the look and feel of Google's products. Seated around a conference table are about a dozen Googlers, tapping on laptops. During the 2 hour meeting, Meyer needs to evaluate various design proposals, ranging from minor tweaks to a new product's entire layout. She's previously given each presentation an allotted amount of time, and a large digital clock on the wall ticks off the seconds. The presenters must quickly present their ideas, but also handle questions such as "what users do if the tab is moved from the side of the page to the top?" Furthermore, it's all about the numbers—no one at Google would ever say, for instance "the tab looks better in red"—you need to prove your point. Presenters must come armed with usability experiment results, showing, for instance, that a certain percent preferred red or some other color. While the presenters are answering these questions as quickly as possible, the digital clock is ticking, and when it hits the allotted time, the presentation must end, and the next team steps up to present. It is a tough and tense environment, and Googlers must have done their homework.

Growth can also undermine the "outlaw band that's changing the world" culture that fostered the services that made Google famous. Even cofounder Sergi Brin agrees that Google risks becoming less "zany" as it grows. To paraphrase one of its top managers, the hard part of any business is keeping that original innovative, small-business feel even as the company grows.

Creating the right culture is especially challenging now that Google is truly global. For example, Google works hard to provide the same financial and service benefits every place it does business around the world, but it can't exactly match its benefits in every country because of international laws and international taxation issues. Offering the same benefits everywhere is more important than it might initially appear. All those benefits make life easier for Google staff, and help them achieve a work–life balance. Achieving the right work life balance is the centerpiece of Google's culture, but also becomes more challenging as the company grows. On the one hand, Google does expect all of its employees to work super hard; on the other hand, it realizes that it needs to help them maintain some sort of balance. As one manager says, Google acknowledges "that we work hard but that work is not everything."

Recruitment is another challenge. While Google certainly doesn't lack applicants, attracting the right applicants is crucial if Google is to continue to grow successfully. Working at Google requires a special set of traits, and screening employees is easier if they recruit the right people to begin with. For instance, they need to attract people who are super-bright, love to work, have fun, can handle the stress, and who also have outside interests and flexibility.

As the company grows internationally, it also faces the considerable challenge of recruiting and building staff overseas. For example, Google now is introducing a new vertical market-based structure across Europe, to attract more business advertisers to its search engine. (By vertical market-based structure, Google means focusing on key vertical industry sectors such as travel, retail, automotive, and technology). To build these industry groupings abroad from scratch, Google promoted its former head of its U.S. financial services group to be the vertical markets director for Europe; he moved there recently. Google is thus looking for heads for each of its vertical industry groups for all of its key European territories. Each of these vertical market heads will have to educate their market sectors (retailing, travel, and so on) so Google can attract new advertisers. Most recently, Google already had about 12 offices across Europe, and its London office had tripled in size to 100 staff in just two years.

However, probably the biggest challenge Google faces is gearing up its employee selection system, now that the company must hire thousands of people per year. When Google started in business, job candidates typically suffered through a dozen or more in-person interviews, and the standards were so high that even applicants with years of great work experience often got turned down if they had just average college grades. But recently, even Google's cofounders have acknowledged to security analysts that setting such an extraordinarily high bar for

hiring was holding back Google's expansion. For Google's first few years, one of the company's cofounder's interviewed nearly every job candidate before he or she was hired, and even today one of them still reviews the qualifications of everyone before he or she gets a final offer.

The experience of one candidate illustrates what Google is up against. They interviewed a 24-year-old for a corporate communications job at Google. Google first made contact with the candidate in May, and then, after two phone interviews, invited him to headquarters. There he had separate interviews with about six people and was treated to lunch in a Google cafeteria. They also had him turn in several "homework" assignments, including a personal statement and a marketing plan. In August, Google invited the candidate back for a second round, which they said would involve another four or five interviews. In the meantime, he decided he'd rather work at a start-up, and accepted another job at a new Web-based instant messaging provider.

Google's new head of human resources, a former GE executive, says that Google is trying to strike the right balance between letting Google and the candidate get to know each other while also moving quickly. To that end, Google recently administered a survey to all Google's current employees, in an effort to identify the traits that correlate with success at Google. In the survey, employees had to respond to questions relating to about 300 variables, including their performance on standardized tests, how old they were when they first used a computer, and how many foreign languages they speak. The Google survey team that went back and compared the answers against the 30 or 40 job performance factors they keep for each employee. They thereby identified clusters of traits that Google might better focus on during the hiring process. Google is also trying to move from the free-form interviews they've had in the past to a more structured process.

QUESTIONS

1. What do you think of the idea of Google correlating personal traits from the employee's answers on the survey to their performance, and then using that as the basis for screening job candidates? In other words, is it or is it not a good idea and please explain your answer.

2. The benefits that Google pays obviously represent an enormous expense. Based on what you know about Google and on what you read in this book, how would you defend all these benefits if you're making a presentation to the security analysts who were analyzing Google's performance?

3. If you wanted to hire the brightest people around, how would you go about recruiting and selecting them?

4. To support its growth and expansion strategy, Google wants (among other traits) people who are super-bright, and who work hard, often round-the-clock and who are flexible and maintain a decent work–life balance. List five specific HR policies or practices that you think Google has implemented or should implement to support its strategy, and explain your answer.

5. What sorts of factors do you think Google will have to take into consideration as it tries transferring its culture and reward systems and way of doing business to its operations abroad?

6. Given the sorts of values and culture Google cherishes, briefly describe four specific activities you suggest they pursue during new-employee orientation.

Source notes for Google: "Google Brings Vertical Structure to Europe," *New Media Age*, August 4, 2005, p. 2; Debbie Lovewell, "Employer Profile—Google: Searching for Talent," *Employee Benefits*, October 10, 2005, p. 66; "Google Looking for Gourmet Chefs," *Internet Week*, August 4, 2005, p. n/a; Douglas Merrill, "Google's 'Googley' Culture Kept Alive by Tech," *eWeek*, April 11, 2006, p. n/a; Robert Hof, "Google Gives Employees Another Option," *BusinessWeek Online*, December 13, 2005, p. n/a; Kevin Delaney, "Google Adjusts Hiring Process as Needs Grow," *Wall Street Journal*, October 23, 2006, pp. B1, B8; Adam Lishinsky, "Search and Enjoy," *Fortune*, January 22, 2007, pp. 70–82.

Muffler Magic*

Muffler Magic is a fast-growing chain of 25 automobile service centers in Nevada. Originally started 20 years ago as a muffler repair shop by Ronald Brown, the chain expanded rapidly to new locations, and as it did so Muffler Magic also expanded the services it provided, from muffler replacement to oil changes, brake jobs, and engine repair. Today, one can bring an automobile to a Muffler Magic shop for basically any type of service, from tires to mufflers to engine repair.

Auto service is a tough business. The shop owner is basically dependent upon the quality of the service people he or she hires and retains, and the most qualified mechanics find it easy to pick up and leave for a job paying a bit more at a competitor down the road. It's also a business in which productivity is very important. The single largest expense is usually the cost of labor. Auto service dealers generally don't just make up the prices that they charge customers for various repairs. Instead, they charge based on standardized industry rates for jobs like changing spark plugs, or repairing a leaky radiator. Therefore, if, for instance, someone brings a car in for a new alternator, and the standard number of hours for changing the alternator is an hour, but it takes the mechanic two hours, the service center's owner may end up making less profit on the transaction.

Quality is a persistent problem as well. For example, "rework" has recently been a problem at Muffler Magic. A customer recently brought her car to a Muffler Magic to have the car's brake pads replaced, which the store did for her. Unfortunately, when she drove off, she only got about two blocks before she discovered that she had no brake power at all. It was simply fortuitous that she was going so slowly she was able to stop her car by slowly rolling up against a parking bumper. It subsequently turned out that the mechanic who replaced the brake pads had failed to properly tighten a fitting on the hydraulic brake tubes, and the brake fluid had run out, leaving the car with no braking power. In a similar problem the month before that, a (different) mechanic replaced a fan belt, but forgot to refill the radiator with fluid; that customer's car overheated before he got four blocks away, and Muffler Magic had to replace the whole engine. Of course problems like these not only diminish the profitability of the company's profits, but, repeated many times over, have the potential for ruining Muffler Magic's word-of-mouth reputation.

Organizationally, Muffler Magic employs about 300 people total, and Ron runs his company with eight managers, including Mr. Brown as president, a controller, a purchasing director, a marketing director, and the human resource manager. He also has three regional managers to whom the eight or nine service center managers in each area of Nevada report. Over the past two years, as the company has opened new service centers, companywide profits have actually diminished, rather than gone up. In part, these diminishing profits probably reflect the fact that Ron Brown has found it increasingly difficult to manage his growing operation ("Your reach is exceeding your grasp" is how Ron's wife puts it).

The company has only the most basic HR systems in place. They use an application form that the human resource manager modified from one that she downloaded from the Web, and they use standard employee status change request forms, sign-on forms, I-9 forms, and so on that they purchased from a human resource management supply house. Training is entirely on-the-job. They expect the experienced technicians that they hire to come to the job fully trained; as noted, to that end, the service center managers generally ask candidates for these jobs basic behavioral questions that hopefully provide a window into these applicants' skills. However most of the other technicians they hire to do jobs like rotating tires, fixing brake pads, and replacing mufflers are untrained and inexperienced. They are to be trained by either the service center manager or by more experienced technicians, on-the-job.

Ron Brown faces several HR-type problems. One, as he says, is that he faces the "tyranny of the immediate" when it comes to hiring employees. While it's fine to say that he should be carefully screening each employee and checking their references and work ethic, from a practical point of view, with 25 centers to run, the centers' managers usually just hire anyone who seems to be breathing, as long as they can answer some basic interview questions about auto repair, such as, "What do you think the problem is if a 2001 Camry is overheating, and what would you do about it?"

Employee safety is also a problem. An automobile service center may not be the most dangerous type of workplace, but it is potentially dangerous. Employees are dealing with sharp tools, greasy floors, greasy tools, extremely hot temperatures (for instance on mufflers and engines), and fast-moving engine parts including fan blades. There are some basic things that a service manager can do to ensure more safety, such as insisting that all oil spills be cleaned up immediately. However, from a practical point of view, there are a few ways to get around many of the problems—such as when the technician must check out an engine while it is running.

With Muffler Magic's profits going down instead of up, Brown's human resource manager has taken the position that the main problem is financial. As he says, "You get what you pay for" when it comes to employees, and if you compensate technicians better then your competitors do, then you get better technicians, ones who do their jobs better and stay longer with the company—and then profits will rise. So, the HR manager scheduled a meeting between himself, Ron Brown, and a professor of business who teaches compensation management at a local university. The HR manager has asked this professor to spend about a week looking at each of the service centers, analyzing the situation, and coming up with a compensation plan that will address Muffler Magic's quality and productivity problems. At this meeting, the professor makes three basic recommendations for changing the company's compensation policies.

Number one, she says that she has found that Muffler Magic suffers from what she calls "presenteeism," in other words employees drag themselves into work even when they're sick, because the company does not pay them at all if they are out—there are no sick days. In just a few days the professor couldn't properly quantify how much Muffler Magic is losing to presenteeism. However, from what she could see at each shop, there are typically one or two technicians working with various maladies like the cold or flu, and it seemed to her that each of these people were probably really only working about half of the time (although they were getting paid for the whole day). So, for 25 service centers per week, Muffler Magic could well be losing

125 or 130 personnel days per week of work. The professor suggests that Muffler Magic start allowing everyone to take three paid sick days per year, a reasonable suggestion. However, as Ron Brown points out, "Right now, we're only losing about half a day's pay for each employee who comes in and who works unproductively; with your suggestion, won't we lose the whole day?" The professor says she'll ponder that one.

Second, the professor also recommends putting the technicians on a skill-for-pay plan. Basically, here's what she suggests. Give each technician a letter grade (A through E) based upon that technician's particular skill level and abilities. An "A" technician is a team leader and needs to show that he or she has excellent diagnostic troubleshooting skills, and the ability to supervise and direct other technicians. At the other extreme, an "E" technician would typically be a new apprentice with little technical training. The other technicians fall in between those two levels, based on their individual skills and abilities.

In the professor's system, the "A" technician or team leader would assign and supervise all work done within his or her area but generally not do any mechanical repairs him or herself. The team leader does the diagnostic troubleshooting, supervises and trains the other technicians, and test drives the car before it goes back to the customer. Under this plan, every technician receives a guaranteed hourly wage within a certain range, for instance:

A tech = $25–$30 an hour
B tech = $20–$25 an hour
C tech = $15–$20 an hour
D tech = $10–$15 an hour
E tech = $8–$10 an hour

Third, to directly address the productivity issue, the professor recommends that at the end of each day, each service manager calculate each technician-team's productivity for the day and then at the end of each week. She suggests posting the running productivity total conspicuously for daily viewing. Then, the technicians as a group get weekly cash bonuses based upon their productivity. To calculate productivity, the professor recommends dividing the total labor hours billed by the total labor hours paid to technicians, in other words: Total labor hours billed, *divided by* total hours paid to technicians.

Having done some homework, the professor says that the national average for labor productivity is currently about 60%, and that only the best-run service centers achieve 85% or greater. By her rough calculations, Muffler Magic was attaining about industry average (about 60% — in other words, they were billing for (as an example) only about 60 hours for each 100 hours that they actually had to pay technicians to do the jobs. (Of course, this was not entirely the technicians' fault. Technicians get time off for breaks, and for lunch, and if a particular service center simply didn't have enough business on a particular day or during a particular week, then several technicians may well sit around idly waiting for the next car to come in.) The professor recommends setting a labor efficiency goal of 80% and posting each team's daily productivity results in the workplace to

provide them with additional feedback. She recommends that if at the end of a week the team is able to boost its productivity ratio from the current 60% to 80%, then that team would get an additional 10% weekly pay bonus. After that, for every 5% boost of increased productivity above 80%, technicians would receive an additional 5% weekly bonus. (So, if a technician's normal weekly pay is $400, that employee got an extra $40 at the end of the week when his team moved from 60% productivity to 80% productivity.)

After the meeting, Ron Brown thanked the professor for her recommendations and told her he would think about it and get back to her. After the meeting, on the drive home, Ron was pondering what to do. He had to decide whether to institute the professor's sick leave policy, and whether to implement the professor's incentive and compensation plan. Before implementing anything, however, he wanted to make sure he understood the context in which he was making his decision. For example, did Muffler Magic really have an incentive pay problem, or were the problems more broad? Furthermore, how, if at all, would the professor's incentive plan impact the quality of the work that the teams were doing? And should they really start paying for sick days? Ron Brown had a lot to think about.

QUESTIONS

1. Write out a one-page summary outline listing three or four recommendations you would make with respect to each HR function (recruiting, selection, training, and so on) that you think Ron Brown should be addressing with his HR manager now.

2. Develop a 10-question structured interview form Ron Brown's service center managers can use to interview experienced technicians.

3. If you were Ron Brown, would you implement the professor's recommendation addressing the presenteeism problem, in other words start paying for sick days? Why or why not?

4. If you were advising Ron Brown, would you recommend that he implement the professor's skill-base pay and incentive pay plans as is? Why? Would you implement it with modifications? If you would modify it, please be specific about what

you think those modifications should be, and why.

Based generally on actual facts, but Muffler Magic is a fictitious company. This case is based largely on information in Drew Paras' "The Pay Factor: Technicians' Salaries Can Be the Largest Expense in a Server Shop, as well as the Biggest Headache. Here's How One Shop Owner Tackled the Problem," *Motor Age*, November 2003, pp. 76–79; see also Jennifer Pellet, "Health Care Crisis," *Chief Executive*, June 2004, pp. 56–61; "Firms Press to Quantify, Control Presenteeism," *Employee Benefits*, December 1, 2002, p. n/a.

BP Texas City*

In March 2005, an explosion and fire at British Petroleum's (BP) Texas City, Texas refinery killed 15 people and injured 500 people in the worst U.S. industrial accident in more than 10 years. The disaster triggered three investigations, one internal investigation by BP, one by the U.S. Chemical Safety Board, and another, independent investigation chaired by former U.S. Secretary of State James Baker and an 11 member panel, and organized at BP's request.

To put the results of these three investigations into context, it's useful to understand that under its current management, BP has pursued, for the past 10 or so years, a strategy emphasizing cost-cutting and profitability. The basic conclusion of the investigations was that cost-cutting helped compromise safety at the Texas City refinery. It's useful to consider each investigation's findings.

The Chemical Safety Board's (CSB) investigation, according to Carol Merritt, the board's chairwoman, showed that "BP's global management was aware of problems with maintenance, spending, and infrastructure well before March 2005." Apparently, faced with numerous earlier accidents, BP did make some safety improvements. However, it focused primarily on emphasizing personal employee safety behaviors and procedural compliance, and on thereby reducing safety accident rates. The problem (according to the CSB) was that "catastrophic safety risks remained." For example, according to the CSB, "unsafe and antiquated equipment designs were left in place, and unacceptable deficiencies in preventive maintenance were tolerated." Basically, the CSB found that BP's budget cuts led to a progressive deterioration of safety at the Texas City refinery. Said Ms. Merritt, "In an aging facility like Texas City, it is not responsible to cut budgets related to safety and maintenance without thoroughly examining the impact on the risk of of a catastrophic accident."

Looking at specifics, the CSB said that a 2004 internal audit of 35 BP business units, including Texas City (BP's largest refinery), found significant safety gaps they all had in common, including, for instance, a lack of leadership competence, and "systemic underlying issues" such as a widespread tolerance of noncompliance with basic safety rules and poor monitoring of safety management systems and processes. Ironically, the CSB found that BP's accident prevention effort at Texas City had achieved a 70% reduction in worker injuries in the year before the explosion. Unfortunately, this simply meant that individual employees were having fewer accidents. The larger, more fundamental problem was that the potentially explosive situation inherent in the depreciating machinery remained.

The CSB found that the Texas City explosion followed a pattern of years of major accidents at the facility. In fact, there had apparently been an average of one employee death every 16 months at the

*© Gary Dessler, Ph.D.

plant for the last 30 years. The CSB found that the equipment directly involved in the most recent explosion was an obsolete design already phased out in most refineries and chemical plants, and that key pieces of its instrumentation were not working. There had also been previous instances where flammable vapors were released from the same unit in the 10 years prior to the explosion. In 2003, an external audit had referred to the Texas City refinery's infrastructure and assets as "poor" and found what it referred to as a "checkbook mentality," one in which budgets were not sufficient to manage all the risks. In particular, the CSB found that BP had implemented a 25% cut on fixed costs between 1998 and 2000 and that this adversely impacted maintenance expenditures and net expenditures, and refinery infrastructure. Going on, the CSB found that in 2004, there were three major accidents at the refinery that killed three workers.

BP's own internal report concluded that the problems at Texas City were not of recent origin, and instead were years in the making. It said BP was taking steps to address them. Its investigation found "no evidence of anyone consciously or intentionally taking actions or making decisions that put others at risk." Said BP's report, "The underlying reasons for the behaviors and actions displayed during the incident are complex, and the team has spent much time trying to understand them—it is evident that they were many years in the making and will require concerted and committed actions to address." BP's report concluded that there were five underlying causes for the massive explosion:

- A working environment that had eroded to one characterized by resistance to change, and a lack of trust
- Safety, performance, and risk reduction priorities had not been set and consistently reinforced by management

- Changes in the "complex organization" led to a lack of clear accountabilities and poor communication
- A poor level of hazard awareness and understanding of safety resulted in workers accepting levels of risk that were considerably higher then at comparable installations
- A lack of adequate early warning systems for problems, and no independent means of understanding the deteriorating standards at the plant.

The report from the BP-initiated but independent 11 person panel chaired by former U.S. Secretary of State James Baker contained specific conclusions and recommendations. The Baker panel looked at BP's corporate safety oversight, the corporate safety culture, and the process safety management systems at BP at the Texas City plant as well at BP's other refineries.

Basically, the Baker panel concluded that BP had not provided effective safety process leadership and had not established safety as a core value at the five refineries it looked at (including Texas City).

Like the CSB, the Baker panel found that BP had emphasized personal safety in recent years and had in fact improved personal safety performance, but had not emphasized the overall safety process, thereby mistakenly interpreting "improving personal injury rates as an indication of acceptable process safety performance at its U.S. refineries." In fact, the Baker panel went on, by focusing on these somewhat misleading improving personal injury rates, BP created a false sense of confidence that it was properly addressing process safety risks. It also found that the safety culture at Texas City did not have the positive, trusting, open environment that a proper safety culture required. The Baker panel's other findings included:

- BP did not always ensure that adequate resources were effectively allocated to support or sustain a high level of process safety performance

- BP's refinery personnel are "overloaded" by corporate initiatives
- Operators and maintenance personnel work high rates of overtime
- BP tended to have a short-term focus and its decentralized management system and entrepreneurial culture delegated substantial discretion to refinery plant managers "without clearly defining process safety expectations, responsibilities, or accountabilities"
- There was no common, unifying process safety culture among the five refineries
- The company's corporate safety management system did not make sure there was timely compliance with internal process safety standards and programs
- BP's executive management either did not receive refinery specific information that showed that process safety deficiencies existed at some of the plants, or did not effectively respond to any information it did receive[1]

The Baker panel made several safety recommendations for BP, including these:

1. The company's corporate management must provide leadership on process safety.
2. The company should establish a process safety management system that identifies, reduces, and manages the process safety risks of the refineries.
3. The company should make sure its employees have an appropriate level of process safety knowledge and expertise.

4. The company should involve "relevant stakeholders" in developing a positive, trusting, and open process safety culture at each refinery.
5. BP should clearly define expectations and strengthen accountability for process safety performance.
6. BP should better coordinate its process safety support for the refining line organization.
7. BP should develop an integrated set of leading and lagging performance indicators for effectively monitoring process safety performance.
8. BP should establish and implement an effective system to audit process safety performance.
9. The company's board should monitor the implementation of the panel's recommendations and the ongoing process safety performance of the refineries.
10. BP should transform into a recognized industry leader in process safety management.

In making its recommendations, the panel singled out the company's chief executive at the time, Lord Browne, by saying, "In hindsight, the panel believes if Browne had demonstrated comparable leadership on and commitment to process safety [as he did for responding to climate change] that would have resulted in a higher level of safety at refineries."

Overall, the Baker panel found that BP's top management had not provided "effective leadership" on safety. It found that the failings went to the very top of the organization, to the company's chief executive, and to several of his top lieutenants. The Baker panel emphasized the importance of top management commitment, saying, for

---

[1]These findings and the following suggestions are based on "BP Safety Report Finds Company's Process Safety Culture Ineffective," *Global Refining & Fuels Report*, January 17, 2007, p. n/a.

instance, that "it is imperative that BP leadership set the process safety tone at the top of the organization and establish appropriate expectations regarding process safety performance." It also said BP "has not provided effective leadership in making certain its management and U.S. refining workforce understand what is expected of them regarding process safety performance."

Lord Browne, the chief executive, stepped down about a year after the explosion. About the same time, some BP shareholders were calling for the company's executives and board directors to have their bonuses more closely tied to the company's safety and environmental performance in the wake of Texas City.

QUESTIONS

1. The textbook defines ethics as "the principles of conduct governing an individual or a group," and specifically as the standards one uses to decide what their conduct should be. To what extent do you believe that what happened at BP is as much a breakdown in the company's ethical systems as it is in its safety systems, and how would you defend your conclusion?

2. Are the Occupational Safety and Health Administration's standards, policies, and rules aimed at addressing problems like the ones that apparently existed at the Texas City plant? If so, how would you explain the fact that problems like these could have continued for so many years?

3. Since there were apparently at least three deaths in the year prior to the major explosion, and an average of about one employee death per 16 months for the previous 10 years, how would you account for the fact that mandatory OSHA inspections missed these glaring sources of potential catastrophic events?

4. The textbook lists numerous suggestions for "how to prevent accidents." Based on what you know about the Texas City explosion, what do you say

Texas City tells you about the most important three steps an employer can take to prevent accidents?

5. Based on what you learned in this chapter, would you make any additional recommendations to BP over and above those recommendations made by the Baker panel and the CSB? If so, what would those recommendations be?

6. Explain specifically how strategic human resource management at BP seems to have supported the company's broader strategic aims. What does this say about the advisability of always linking human resource strategy to a company's strategic aims?

Source notes for BP Texas City: Sheila McNulty, "BP Knew of Safety Problems, Says Report," *Financial Times*, October 31, 2006, p. 1; "CBS: Documents Show BP Was Aware of Texas City Safety Problems," *World Refining & Fuels Today*, October 30, 2006, p. n/a; "BP Safety Report Finds Company's Process Safety Culture Ineffective," *Global Refining & Fuels Report*, January 17, 2007, p. n/a; "BP Safety Record under Attack," *Europe Intelligence Wire*, January 17, 2007, p. n/a; Mark Hofmann, "BP Slammed for Poor Leadership on Safety, Oil Firm Agrees to Act on Review Panel's Recommendations," *Business Intelligence*, January 22, 2007, p. 3; "Call for Bonuses to Include Link with Safety Performance," *The Guardian*, January 18, 2007, p. 24.

Glossary

action learning A training technique by which management trainees are allowed to work full time analyzing and solving problems in other departments.

adverse impact The overall impact of employer practices that result in significantly higher percentages of members of minorities and other protected groups being rejected for employment, placement, or promotion.

affirmative action Steps that are taken for the purpose of eliminating the present effects of past discrimination.

AFL-CIO A voluntary federation in the United States of about 100 national and international (i.e., with branches in Canada) unions.

Age Discrimination in Employment Act of 1967 The act prohibiting age discrimination and specifically protecting individuals over 40 years old.

agency shop A form of union security in which employees who do not belong to the union must still pay union dues on the assumption that union efforts benefit all workers.

Albemarle Paper Company v. *Moody* Supreme Court case in which it was ruled that the validity of job tests must be documented and that employee performance standards must be job related.

alternation ranking method An appraisal process in which the employee who is highest on a trait being measured and also the one who is lowest is identified, alternating between highest and lowest until all employees to be rated have been addressed.

Americans with Disabilities Act (ADA) The act requiring employers to make reasonable accommodations for disabled employees; it prohibits discrimination against disabled persons.

application form The form that provides information on education, prior work record, and skills.

appraisal interview The culmination of an appraisal, in which the supervisor and subordinate review the appraisal and make plans to remedy deficiencies and reinforce strengths.

arbitration The most definitive type of third-party intervention, in which the arbitrator often has the power to determine and dictate the settlement terms.

authority The right to make decisions, direct others' work, and give orders.

authorization cards In order to petition for a union election, the union must show that at least 30% of employees may be interested in being unionized. Employees indicate this interest by signing authorization cards.

bargaining unit The group of employees the union will be authorized to represent.

behavior modeling A training technique in which trainees are first shown good management techniques in a film, are then asked to play roles in a simulated situation, and are then given feedback and praise by their supervisor.

benefits Indirect financial payments given to employees. They may include health and life insurance, vacation, pension, education plans, and discounts on company products, for instance.

bona fide occupational qualification (BFOQ) Requirement that an employee be of a certain religion, sex, or national origin where that is reasonably necessary to the organization's normal operation. Specified by the 1964 Civil Rights Act.

boycott The combined refusal by employees and other interested parties to buy or use the employer's products.

burnout The total depletion of physical and mental resources caused by excessive striving to reach an unrealistic work-related goal.

business necessity Justification for an otherwise discriminatory employment practice, provided there is an overriding legitimate business purpose.

career management A process for enabling the employees to better understand and develop their career skills and interests, and to use the skills and interests most effectively both within the company and, if necessary, after they leave the firm.

case study method A development method in which the manager is presented with a written description of an organizational problem to diagnose and solve.

central tendency The tendency to rate all employees about average.

citations Summons informing employers and employees of the regulations and standards that have been violated in the workplace.

Civil Rights Act of 1964, Title VII Law that makes it unlawful practice for an employer to discriminate against any individual with respect to hiring, compensation, terms, conditions, or privileges of employment because of race, color, religion, sex, or nation.

Civil Rights Act of 1991 (CRA 1991) This act places burden of proof back on employers and permits compensatory and punitive damages.

closed shop A form of union security in which the company can hire only union members. This was outlawed in 1947 but still exists in some industries (such as printing).

co-determination The right to a voice in setting company policies; workers generally elect representatives to the superadvisory board.

collective bargaining The process through which representatives of management and the union meet to negotiate a labor agreement.

compensable factors Fundamental, compensable elements of a job, such as skills, effort, responsibility, and working conditions.

competitive advantage The basis for differentiation over competitors and thus for hoping to claim certain customers.

content validity A test that is *content valid* is one in which the test contains a fair sample of the tasks and skills actually needed for the job in question.

controlled experimentation Formal methods for testing the effectiveness of a training program, preferably with before-and-after tests and a control group.

criterion validity A type of validity based on showing that scores on the test (*predictors*) are related to job performance (*criterion*).

critical incident method Keeping a record of uncommonly good or undesirable examples of an employee's work-related behavior and reviewing it with the employee at predetermined times.

defined benefit plan A plan that contains a formula for specifying retirement benefits.

defined contribution plan A plan in which the employer's contribution to employees' retirement or savings funds is specified.

discipline A procedure that corrects or punishes a subordinate for violating a rule or procedure.

dismissal Involuntary termination of an employee's employment with the firm.

disparate impact An unintentional disparity between the proportion of a protected group applying for a position and the proportion getting the job.

disparate treatment An intentional disparity between the proportion of a protected group and the proportion getting the job.

downsizing Refers to the process of reducing, usually dramatically, the number of people employed by the firm.

employee orientation A procedure for providing new employees with basic background information about the firm.

Employee Retirement Income Security Act (ERISA) Signed into law by President Ford in 1974 to require that pension rights be vested, and protected by a government agency, Pension Benefits Guarantee Corporation.

employee stock ownership plan (ESOP) A corporation contributes shares of its own stock to a trust to purchase company stock for employees. The trust distributes the stock to employees upon retirement or separation from service.

Equal Employment Opportunity Commission (EEOC) The commission, created by Title VII, empowered to investigate job discrimination complaints and sue on behalf of complainants.

Equal Pay Act of 1963   An amendment to the Fair Labor Standards Act designed to require equal pay for women doing the same work as men.

ethics   The study of standards of conduct and moral judgment; also the standards of right conduct.

ethnocentric   A management philosophy that leads to the creation of home market-oriented staffing decisions.

exit interviews   Interviews conducted by the employer immediately prior to the employee leaving the firm with the aim of better understanding what the employee thinks about the company.

expatriates   Non-citizens of the country in which they are working.

fact finder   In labor relations, a neutral party who studies the issues in a dispute and makes a public recommendation for a reasonable settlement.

Fair Labor Standards Act   Congress passed this act in 1936 to provide for minimum wages, maximum hours, overtime pay, and child labor protection. The law has been amended many times and covers most employees.

federal agency guidelines   Guidelines issued by federal agencies explaining recommended employer equal employment federal legislation procedures in detail.

flexible benefits plan   Individualized plans allowed by employers to accommodate employee preferences for benefits.

forced distribution method   An appraisal method by which the manager places predetermined percentages of subordinates in performance categories.

gain-sharing plan   An incentive plan that engages employees in a common effort to achieve productivity objectives and share the gains.

geocentric   A staffing policy that seeks the best people for key jobs throughout the organization, regardless of nationality.

good-faith bargaining   A term that means both parties are communicating and negotiating and that proposals are being matched with counterproposals, with both parties making every reasonable effort to arrive at agreements. It does not mean that either party is compelled to agree to a proposal.

graphic rating scale   A scale that lists a number of traits and a range of performance for each.

The employee is then rated by identifying the score that best describes his or her level of performance for each trait.

Griggs v. Duke Power Company Case   Supreme Court case in which the plaintiff argued that his employer's requirement that coal handlers be high-school graduates was unfairly discriminatory. In finding for the plaintiff, the Court ruled that discrimination need not be overt to be illegal, that employment practices must be related to job performance, and that the burden of proof is on the employer to show that hiring standards are job related.

guaranteed fair treatment   Employer programs aimed at ensuring that all employees are treated fairly, generally by providing formalized, well-documented, and highly publicized vehicles through which employees can appeal any eligible issues.

halo effect   A common appraisal problem in which the rating of a subordinate on one trait influences the way the person is rated on other traits.

home-country nationals   Citizens of the country in which the multinational company has its headquarters.

human resource management   The policies and practices one needs to carry out the "people" or human resource aspects of a management position, including recruiting, screening, training, rewarding, and appraising.

illegal bargaining items   Items in collective bargaining that are forbidden by law; for example, the clause agreeing to hire "union members exclusively" would be illegal in a right-to-work state.

incentive plan   A compensation plan that ties pay to performance.

in-house development centers   A company-based facility for exposing current or prospective managers to exercises to develop improved management skills.

insubordination   Willful disregard or disobedience of the boss's authority or legitimate orders.

interview   A procedure designed to solicit information from a person's oral responses to oral inquiries.

job analysis   The procedure for determining the duties and skill requirements of a job and the kind of person who should be hired for it.

job description   A list of a job's duties, responsibilities, reporting relationships, working conditions, and supervisory responsibilities—one product of a job analysis.

job evaluation   A formal and systematic comparison of jobs to determine the worth of one job relative to another.

job posting   Posting notices of job openings on company bulletin boards as a recruiting method.

job rotation   A management training technique that involves moving a trainee from department to department to broaden his or her experience and identify strengths and weaknesses.

job specification   A list of a job's "human requirements," that is, the requisite education, skills, personality, and so on—a product of a job analysis.

Landrum-Griffin Act   A law aimed at protecting union members from possible wrongdoing on the part of their unions.

layoff   A situation in which employees are told there is no work for them but that management intends to recall them when work is again available.

learning organization   An organization "skilled at creating, acquiring, and transferring knowledge and at modifying its behavior to reflect new knowledge and insights."

line manager   A manager who is authorized to direct the work of subordinates and responsible for accomplishing the organization's goals.

lockout   A refusal by the employer to provide opportunities to work.

management assessment centers   A facility in which management candidates are asked to make decisions in hypothetical situations and are scored on their performance.

management by objectives (MBO)   A performance management method through which the manager sets organizationally relevant goals with each employee and then periodically discusses progress toward these goals, in an organization-wide effort.

management development   Any attempt to improve current or future management performance by imparting knowledge, changing attitudes, or increasing skills.

mandatory bargaining items   Items in collective bargaining that a party must bargain over if they are introduced by the other party—for example, pay.

mediation   Labor relations intervention in which a neutral third party tries to assist the principals in reaching agreement.

merit pay (merit raise)   Any salary increase awarded to an employee based on his or her individual performance.

national emergency strikes   Strikes that might "imperil the national health and safety."

National Labor Relations Board (NLRB)   The agency created by the Wagner Act to investigate unfair labor practice charges and to provide for secret-ballot elections and majority rule in determining whether or not a firm's employees want a union.

Norris-LaGuardia Act   This law marked the beginning of the era of strong encouragement of unions and guaranteed to each employee the right to bargain collectively "free from interference, restraint, or coercion."

Occupational Safety and Health Act   The law passed by Congress in 1970 "to assure so far as possible every working man and woman in the nation safe and healthful working conditions and to preserve our human resources."

Occupational Safety and Health Administration (OSHA)   The agency created within the Department of Labor to set safety and health standards for almost all workers in the United States.

Office of Federal Contract Compliance Programs (OFCCP)   The office responsible for implementing executive orders and ensuring compliance of federal contractors.

on-the-job training (OJT)   Training a person to learn a job while working at it.

open shop   Type of union security in which the workers decide whether or not to join the union, and those who join must pay dues.

opinion surveys   Questionnaires that regularly ask employees their opinions about the company, management, and work life.

organizational development (OD)   A development method aimed at changing the attitudes, values, and beliefs of employees so that employees can improve the organization.

outplacement counseling   A systematic process by which a terminated person is trained and counseled in the techniques of self-appraisal and securing a new position.

paired comparison method   An appraisal method in which every subordinate to be rated is paired with and compared to every other subordinate on each trait.

peer appraisal Appraisal of an employee by his or her peers.

performance analysis Verifying that there is a performance deficiency and determining whether that deficiency should be rectified through training or through some other means (such as transferring the employee).

performance management The process through which companies ensure that employees are working toward organizational goals. It includes practices through which the manager defines the employees's goals and work, develops the employee's skills and capabilities, evaluates the person's goal directed behavior, and then rewards him or her in a fashion consistent with the company's and the person's needs.

personnel replacement charts Company records showing present performance and pro-motability of inside candidates for the firm's most important positions.

piecework A system of incentive pay tying pay to the number of items processed by each individual worker.

polycentric A management philosophy oriented toward staffing positions with local talent.

Pregnancy Discrimination Act (PDA) An amendment to Title VII of the Civil Rights Act that prohibits sex discrimination based on "pregnancy, childbirth, or related medical conditions."

preretirement counseling Employer-sponsored counseling aimed at providing information to ease the passage of employees into retirement.

profit-sharing plan A plan whereby most employees share in the company's profits.

protected class Persons such as older workers and women protected by equal opportunity laws including Title VII.

qualifications inventories Manual or computerized records listing employees' education, career and development interests, languages, special skills, and so on to be used in identifying inside candidates for promotion.

ranking method The simplest method of job evaluation that involves ranking each job relative to all other jobs, usually based on a job's overall difficulty.

ratio analysis A forecasting technique that involves analyzing and extrapolating the ratio of a dependent variable, such as sales persons required, with an independent variable, such as sales.

reliability The characteristic that refers to the consistency of scores obtained by the same person when retested with the identical or equivalent tests.

right to work The public policy in a number of states that prohibits union security of any kind.

salary (or compensation) survey A survey aimed at determining prevailing pay rates. Provides specific wage rates for specific jobs.

Scanlon plan An incentive plan developed in 1937 by Joseph Scanlon and designed to encourage cooperation, involvement, and sharing of benefits.

sensitivity training A method for increasing employees' insights into their own behavior through candid discussions in groups led by special trainers.

severance pay A one-time payment employers provide when terminating an employee.

sexual harassment Harassment on the basis of sex that has the purpose or effect of substantially interfering with a person's work performance or creating an intimidating, hostile, or offensive work environment.

staff manager A manager who assists and advises line managers.

stock option The right to purchase a stated number of shares of company stock at a set price at some time in the future.

strategic human resource management Linking HRM policies and practices with strategic goals and objectives in order to improve business performance.

survey feedback A method that involves surveying employees' attitudes and providing feedback to facilitate problems being solved by the managers and employees.

sympathy strike A strike that takes place when one union strikes in support of another's strike.

Taft-Hartley Act (Labor Management Relations Act) A law prohibiting union unfair labor practices and enumerating the rights of employees as union members. It also enumerates the rights of employers.

task analysis   A detailed study of a job to identify the skills required so that an appropriate training program may be instituted.

team building   Improving the effectiveness of teams through the use of consultants and team-building meetings.

terminate at will   The idea, based in law, that the employment relationship can be terminated at will by either the employer or the employee for any reason.

termination interview   The interview in which an employee is informed of the fact that he or she has been dismissed.

test validity   The degree to which a test, interview, and so on measures what it purports to measure or fulfills the function it was designed to fill.

third-country nationals   Citizens of a country other than the parent or host country.

Title VII of the 1964 Civil Rights Act   The section of the act that says an employer cannot discriminate on the basis of race, color, religion, sex, or national origin with respect to employment.

training   The process of teaching new employees the basic skills they need to perform their jobs.

trend analysis   Study of a firm's past employment needs over a period of years to predict future needs.

union salting   A union organizing tactic by which workers who are employed by a union as undercover union organizers are hired by unwitting employers.

union shop   A form of union security in which the company can hire nonunion people but they must join the union after a prescribed period of time and pay dues. (If they do not, they can be fired.)

unsafe acts   Behaviors that potentially cause accidents.

unsafe conditions   The mechanical and physical conditions that cause accidents.

upward feedback   Having subordinates evaluate their supervisors' performance.

vestibule/simulated training   A method in which trainees learn on the actual or on simulated equipment they would use on the job, but are actually trained off the job.

Vietnam Era Veterans' Readjustment Act of 1974   An act requiring that employers with government contracts take affirmative action to hire disabled veterans.

Vocational Rehabilitation Act of 1973   The act requiring certain federal contractors to take affirmative action for disabled persons.

voluntary bargaining items   Items in collective bargaining for which bargaining is neither illegal nor mandatory—neither party can be compelled to negotiate over those items.

wage curve   Shows the relationship between the relative value of the job and the average wage paid for this job.

Wagner Act   A law that banned certain types of unfair labor practices and provided for secret-ballot elections and majority rule for determining whether or not a firm's employees want to unionize.

Wards Cove v. *Atonio*   U.S. Supreme Court decision that made it difficult to prove a case of unlawful discrimination against an employer.

wildcat strike   An unauthorized strike occurring during the term of a contract.

workers' compensation   Provides income and medical benefits to work-related accident victims or their dependents regardless of fault.

works councils   Formal, employee-elected groups of worker representatives that meet with managers to discuss topics ranging, for instance, from no-smoking policies to layoffs.

wrongful discharge   An employee dismissal that does not comply with the law or does not comply with the contractual arrangement stated or implied by the firm via its employment application forms, employee manuals, or other promises.

Name Index

Subject Index

M